INSIDE IBM

Inside
IBM

THINK

Lessons of a Corporate

Culture in Action

James W. Cortada

Columbia Business School
Publishing

Columbia University Press
Publishers Since 1893
New York   Chichester, West Sussex
cup.columbia.edu

Library of Congress Cataloging-in-Publication Data
Names: Cortada, James W., author.
Title: Inside IBM : lessons of a corporate culture in action / James W. Cortada.
Description: New York : Columbia University Press, 2023. | Includes index. |
    Identifiers: LCCN 2023014399 | ISBN 9780231213004 (hardback) |
    ISBN 9780231559676 (ebook)
Subjects: LCSH: International Business Machines Corporation. |
    Corporate culture. | Social responsibility of business.
Classification: LCC HD58.7 .C646 2023 | DDC 302.3/5—dc23/eng/20230509
LC record available at https://lccn.loc.gov/2023014399

Cover design: Noah Arlow
Cover image: Sign: private collection; Background: Shutterstock

Dedicated with gratitude to the more than one million employees who created IBM's culture. ❧

CONTENTS

PREFACE

On August 19, 2019, the Business Roundtable, which represents the views of its corporate members, released a statement signed by 181 CEOs, announcing that they would lead their companies for the benefit of customers, employees, suppliers, communities, and shareholders. Specifically, they said, "We commit to delivering value to our customers," "investing in our employees," "dealing fairly and ethically with our suppliers," "supporting the communities in which we work," and "generating long-term value for shareholders." In addition, "Each of our stakeholders is essential." This new statement on "the purpose of a corporation" surprised, even shocked, some business media. Nevertheless, the declaration resulted in many social media posts, speeches, and other commentaries as if corporate America had embraced a radically new ethos.

It was a revelation to corporate employees and their management who were less than twenty-five years into their careers because, during their time, shareholder values concerned only a narrow constituency dominating the priorities of senior corporate executives. At the slight risk of being too harsh, these stakeholders were stockholders, banks funding corporations, and executives with stock options. If you read annual reports from the 1990s and 2000s, you will not find as many mentions of customers and employees as in earlier decades. Instead, financial reengineering, gamesmanship, stock values, and compensation plans spoke more about shareholders than other stakeholders. Yet business historians knew that once upon a time, the most successful, respected corporations recognized their obligations to the welfare of other stakeholders besides stockholders.

Did CEOs wake up one morning in 2019 and convert to a new commercial religion? Or had their customers and society finally pressured them to take this stand? The debate has begun, and watchful eyes are on corporations to see if they change their ways. Would fewer employees be laid off or poorly paid if they do? Would these corporations support communities with a significant presence of employees and their families with funds and other resources? There are many questions, and because so few senior executives know what that world looks like, where can they learn how best to proceed? Before the 1980s and certainly no later than the 1950s, American corporations—many members of the Business Roundtable—had functioned profitably, operating with a wider variety of stakeholders in mind. Today's corporations can learn how they did this by examining their histories and those of other firms.

A central purpose of this book is to provide a series of explorations into how one firm functioned successfully for many decades living up to the newly announced Business Roundtable principles—IBM. But, like other long-lived organizations, as successful as this company was in serving multiple stakeholders, it could not sustain that way of managing and so, like so many others, faltered, tempted into the world of financial acrobatics and interested only in privileging the interests of stockholders. I have discussed its failures in *IBM: The Rise and Fall and Reinvention of a Global Icon*, published the same year as the Business Roundtable made its grand proclamation. So, it is time to revisit IBM's experience because it has much to teach today's executive management. But, I too wish to serve a broader community of stakeholders because a more expansive set of members of a company's ecosystem benefits these institutions by arming scholars, industry watchers, and business media with more informed observations on how to navigate in this new world.

When historians and journalists write about a company, one learns about grand strategies, the role of the senior executives, battles against competitors, and disputes with regulators, yet never enough about customers. Although a great deal is available about a firm's products, almost nothing exists about employees' families or about workers. Without the latter, you do not have a corporation; at best, one might have the fiction of one, called a supply or value chain variously, holding company, or some stock manipulation scheme. That is not a corporation such as members of the Business Roundtable. Its members are a unity of buildings, people producing physical objects called products or providing services, images, and bank accounts. Historians have studied physical—material—corporations for a century and thus are equipped to help executives. But they—I—need to explore new issues relevant to the immediate needs of CEOs and evolving interests of scholars.

When I published *IBM*, I thought the book should have been enough, but I noticed two things. First, retired IBM employees bought more copies of the book than anyone of us would have thought, discussed it, and wrote to me, adding details. Second, on their websites, one with over 12,000 members, they talked frequently about historical matters concerning IBM, most of which were different than what a traditional history covers regarding a corporation. They looked at IBM's history from the bottom up, and I, and other business historians, from the top down. The two perspectives were not incompatible or contradictory, just different. What these employees reflected was working in a firm that catered to the needs of multiple stakeholders but that then deserted them in favor of the stockholder. They were the canaries in the mines warning us that prioritizing stockholders above all others was cancer eating away at a company's profitability, the productivity of its employees, and their contributions to an economy and society at large. Before the public criticized Facebook for allowing falsehoods to spread through American society, before Europeans complained that Apple, Google, and Amazon intruded too far into their private lives or constrained competition, employees pointed out problems. Some of these IBM employees were describing complaints, such as the seemingly capricious rounds of layoffs, declining salaries, or take-backs of benefits. Others reflected nostalgically on the "good old days" of better working conditions and family events, and the pride of working for a company that supported communities, the military in war, and education. The view from street level represented the experience of hundreds of thousands of employees, while the top-down version represented the actions of perhaps one-tenth the number. We were missing a big slice of the story of IBM, one that now becomes even more important to address.

The purpose of this book is to begin filling that gap to provide today's management with lessons and suggestions on how to proceed while also providing business historians suggestions on how they can enhance their investigations of the internal operations of large multinational corporations. To do so requires that we wade into two ill-defined areas of business management and history. The first area concerns what constitutes corporate culture. This includes discussing theories and frameworks that identify its features, such as the role of values and rituals, and specific cases of what that looks like on the ground where employees worked. In IBM's case, going from the general to the specific is a problem that needs to be fixed. This book examines examples of the corporate culture at work in one company.

The second gap, which many historians, cultural anthropologists, and others are now addressing, is called material culture. Their argument is the same as that of archeologists: objects have much to teach us about how an ancient society thrived or declined. Their research techniques work to explain what goes on in modern society. Unfortunately, few scholars have applied these techniques to studying individual contemporary institutions, notably businesses. Some studies, for example, investigate the role of postcards in the tourism industry, such as in Hawaii and Africa. Yet material culture has much to inform us about the values, rituals, and behaviors of corporations, IBM's too. We look at IBM coffee mugs, lapel pins, pens and pencils, the cartoons spewed out of the company's photocopiers, and even such mundane items as postcards and what might seem to many readers as very technical manuals about the workings of machines and software. But do not panic, we focus on corporate culture and ever so lightly on technology.

Along this journey, many discoveries opened new areas of potential historical research about corporations and other businesses and insights for today's management. The ones that seemed most intriguing became subjects of case studies, the bulk of the chapters in this book. They were picked based on what employees and retirees discuss the most when chattering about IBM's history and roles. For decades, historians of IBM's history have known that while a unique firm, it also behaved like many of its peers. My research on the company's history and my nearly four decades of experience as an employee resoundingly affirm that conclusion.

Moreover, a bottom-up history suggests that similar activities existed in other firms. The roles of unions, insurance, and pension benefits and of corporations in their communities are issues corporations must address. Even rituals were similar, such as the mythical gold watch we are told everyone in many companies received on the occasion of their retirement or earlier membership in an employee Quarter Century Club. The list of potential chapter topics could have easily been a dozen more, but we must start somewhere, learn what we can, and then take further steps. Those included here are meant to make a point of wide application and identify some prominent topics for further research. Meanwhile, management can seize upon current findings and lessons to apply right now.

More important, while a company does not have to publish postcards, how it treats employees and communities is essential to get right, and that might require the return of long-term employment commitments and even community events. As corporations become meaningful and powerful institutions within society, they also become guardians of its welfare, not simply extractors of profits from it. That realization unfolded as this book was written and helped explain the significance of the Business Roundtable's tagline, "An Economy That Serves All Americans." Even this group, however, did not respond fully to the impact of what is now racing at them at a terrifying speed, namely, that it is not about just serving Americans. It is about how they will work with entire societies worldwide, with varying values, regulatory environments, and diverse economies. You will see why these are old issues with long histories, and track records of how corporations responded to these are now today's "new" considerations that management must consider.

I have been researching the history of IBM and its industry for decades. My book, *IBM: The Rise and Fall and Reinvention of a Global Icon* (MIT Press,

2019) was a traditional corporate history, focusing on significant events, markets, customers, products, technologies, competitors, organizations, and biographies of key executives. This book is far different than the earlier one. Not focused on markets, sales, and competition, this one does not deal with such traditional business issues. Instead, it focuses on the corporate culture, which made it possible for IBM to be highly successful. It is an example of how other large multinational corporations and national companies leveraged their internal operations and their employees in support of corporate strategies. Business schools and consultants discuss these at length, but without benefit of historical case studies. The IBM case reflects what its retirees have long considered critical issues in understanding how IBM and large enterprises (who they knew as their customers) functioned, particularly concerning how employees were recruited, trained, retained for decades, and performed.

I consider this new volume to be broader in scope even than the 2019 study. It is also addressed to a wider audience than the earlier one that spoke to business historians, employees, and the large retiree community. This book continues to offer content for those earlier audiences (IBM has employed some one million people since 1911), the broad community of business school professors and students, and the international business community at large.

It is important to note that I am both a professionally trained historian experienced in writing business history *and* simultaneously an employee who worked at IBM for nearly thirty-nine years—during one-third of the company's history—at multiple levels in a successful career in sales, consulting, management, and executive ranks both with a U.S. and later international focus. So, to be blunt about it, I knew what issues to explore, where the skeletons were hidden, and what evidence I needed to present to make my points. My experience, like that of so many employees, gave me deep insights into the behavior and issues of other corporations, because you needed to be embedded in them to sell and service our costly systems. It was not uncommon, for example, for any of us to spend three to five (or more) years camped out in customer facilities and become experts in other industries. Gathering the highly illusive ephemera (evidence) for this volume was shaped by my IBM experience, which clarified what we needed, evidence that did not occur to other historians of this and other companies, let alone to them about how to obtain such materials. It meant hunting for years either to obtain the documentation needed or to gain the trust of participants to interview them. Additionally, I depended on retirees and current employees to help me gather material for this book (e.g., for the chapter on IBM's publishing strategy). I am unaware of any other professional historian or business practitioner writing such a book. I, therefore, consider this one unique, innovative, and revelatory about how companies work, using IBM as a case study. What others have published on the history of corporate cultures are numerous company case studies as articles and chapters, many of which informed me about issues to discuss, too.

As my chapters make clear, two realities cannot be ignored. First, the mass of employees did not create IBM's culture as a spontaneous response to the realities of their work lives. The history of IBM's culture largely accounts for how management took the initiative to create an ecosystem that made the company economically successful. More than other historians, I draw a direct line from senior management to the lowest levels of activity in the firm. This is a story of successful tactical implementation of actions on behalf of the firm. Second, to thrive in that world created by management, employees—and by extension, their families—all had to embrace that culture and behave in conformance to management's objectives to enjoy its benefits for life. There was little tolerance for alternative views and behaviors, but because of the attractiveness of the cultural ecosystem, there was little need to intensely enforce its ethos or unstated rules. Management also created mechanisms for dealing with employee concerns and changing issues.

In general, workers agreed to the Grand Bargain almost enthusiastically. It is an important reason why, for example, forty years of unionizing activities in the American branch of the company achieved so little. As the company's culture and performance began to fracture in the 1980s, one could see changes, such as layoffs by the decade's end and then rebellion and hostility toward the old culture in the 1990s. While events of that latter period are less documented in this book than other issues, they warrant comment. Specifically, why did IBM's successful implementation of a multistakeholder culture deteriorate or, as some say, evaporate? We cannot escape out the back of this book without extracting lessons from IBM's broad experiences. While this is a history book and thus has a start and end period (1910s–1990s), we will want to know something about what changed in the subsequent decades, even though those issues can be considered to lie outside the scope of this book. To that end, I include an introduction that is chapter-length. It delves into further details, for example, of the problems that financialization and stock buybacks created from the 1990s to the present.

Scholars who have studied organizational cultures and leadership opened my eyes to what was possible, indeed necessary, to describe IBM's experiences. Without their perspectives, coffee mugs, ritual events with families, and even homilies about corporate values would not have taken on the sense of seriousness they deserved, let alone how they linked together. The case studies in this book have three features. First, they were apparent topics that connected people to institutions. Second, they were subjects for which I had access to evidence to explain them. Third, they show ways today's businesses can improve their productivity and financial performance by doing what one retiree told me was "real work, making stuff and doing good." Did I cover everything needed to have a complete and thorough cultural history of the firm? No. Do these chapters provide a comprehensive case study of how to reinvent today's corporations? No, but management can draw a great deal from here. We begin with what we have, and it is a great deal. That is why I organized this book around case studies. In the last chapter, I describe gaps in this book's evidence that warrant further investigations.

This book includes all the usual academic ornaments of endnotes, citing documents and other publications, and nodding to their issues. In addition, it is graced with illustrations demonstrating IBM's culture at work: coffee mugs, postcards, cartoons, photographs of large dinner parties, and publications. Even historians highly knowledgeable about IBM have probably not seen these, or many of today's employees, but they will bring back memories to the long-retired ones.

The book was built mainly on my personal collection of IBM ephemera put together over the past forty-five years. That is essential to know about and use because relying solely on university archival collections or those of a corporation would not have worked; their collections are too limited. Academic archives do not like to collect coffee mugs. Corporate archives do not retain such things as a job application from 1938, an employee identification card from 1944, or a menu of a company dinner from 1988, let alone class notes from an IBM seminar from the 1930s or the 1960s. Companies do not preserve enough of their history, let alone learn from it. But I collected such materials, so future historians of corporate and material culture can learn what kinds they and others must preserve for these sources to become important in the context of a bottom-up history. Coffee mugs became footnotes. Archivists will have to rethink their collection strategies, but they do not have to become museums to provide the materials historians of corporate or material culture require. My coffee cup collection only takes up two banker boxes, so not so much to store. Management teams will want to consider their historical records' role in shaping their actions and strategies.

I owe a debt of gratitude to historian Thomas Misa for encouraging my research about IBM, while Phillip Scranton sharpened my explication of the intent and scope of this book. IBM's corporate archivist, Jamie Martin, assisted with illustrations and offered up her thinking. As always, Walter Friedman, of the Harvard Business School, kept me grounded in the concerns of today's managers. I was additionally helped by people not normally involved in book writing who should be thanked for their behavior, as their thoughts could assist historians writing other cultural histories. These are IBM employees and retirees who were able to answer specific questions and provided documentation needed to fill gaps in this book. For example, for the chapter on unionization, I wanted to confirm in legally credible standards what IBM did. I reached out to union organizers and, within days, had documentary evidence critical to the story. For the chapter on benefits, I needed documentation from the 1980s and 1990s, and networking through a retiree Facebook site, several sent me materials. When I wanted examples of the role of coffee in work and social settings at IBM, over a hundred offered personal experiences, often with explicit details: time, place, and names. Two non-IBMers who make their living cleaning out homes of the elderly, hoarders, and estates provided me with several hundred pages of documents they came across during their work in Georgia and California, rushing these to me knowing I was working on this book. One box of these included training materials used with IBM's managers in the 1950s through the 1970s—the smoking guns of chapter 4 that more than any other evidence demonstrated how a corporate culture was purposefully implemented. So, to all those people, I owe a debt of gratitude. To historians of corporate culture, do not overlook such individuals as sources of ephemera and oral history.

My editor at Columbia University Press, Myles C. Thompson, did a stellar job in helping me shape this book and having the press support it too. So thank you Myles; there is nothing better than working with a highly experienced editor! I want to thank the production and editorial staff at the press for turning my manuscript into a book because writing and producing a book is a team sport. In particular, our copyeditor, Caroline Define, cleaned up rough text and reminded me by her good work how important it is to learn grammar and style. I thank Jamie Martin, IBM's archivist, and her staff for finding many of the illustrations that so made this book possible and for IBM's permission to introduce them to readers in this book. Finally, I am grateful to the publishers of the IEEE *Annals for the History of Computing* for permitting me to use an article it originally published as the basis of chapter 8, "From Lapel Pins to Coffee Mugs."

The opinions expressed in this book are not necessarily those of IBM Corporation, University of Minnesota, or Columbia University Press. Failures in judgment and errors in facts are, I regret to say, my fault. Since this book reflects a new form of historical research, I would welcome discussion about it. I can be reached at jcortada@umn.edu. I am still collecting IBM ephemera, so am eager to receive any that the reader wants to dispose of; none is too trivial, and all of it has much to teach us. All of it will end up at an archive for future historians to study once my labors have ended.

James W. Cortada

INSIDE IBM

INTRODUCTION

We can't control events, but we can control how we behave. We can deserve success.

President John Adams

To be successful, you have to have your heart in your business and your business in your heart.

Thomas J. Watson, Sr.

IBM's corporate culture is relevant to readers outside of the fraternity of business historians because of the growing interest in society regarding the role of big companies, notably multinational corporations and high-tech firms. Concerns about the influence of their practices increased in the 2010s with Apple, Facebook, Google, Amazon, and most recently Twitter, among others, turned on a variety of issues, but boiled down to how companies went about their work. It has been a discussion about their corporate cultures, not just their managerial practices or business ethics and competencies. In the preface, I called attention to the Business Roundtable representing 181 corporations declaring in 2019 that they were all signing up for a new era of supporting a wider circle of stakeholders than before, as if that was new. It might have been for some, but for others, it was a return to behaviors such as those that had been practiced by IBM for over a century. Others of the 181 corporations may, like IBM, have walked away for a time from some of those older cultural norms described in this book but had them in prior times, including such manufacturing firms as Ford, GM, GE, and H-P. Since 2019, there has been much discussion, hubris, and chest beating about the subject of corporate cultures changing, but much has yet to be done.

As I was finishing writing this book, the news media was roiling over the behavior of a number of high-profile companies. Amazon had used a heavy hand to crush union activities, Starbucks similarly if more gently. Elon Musk fired half his Twitter employees in the first two weeks after acquiring the firm. Mark Zuckerberg's Facebook (now Meta) lost half its stock value and announced it would be laying off many employees in 2023. Google's algorithms were being challenged by charges of bias, while other search engines wanted to take business away from that firm. Meanwhile, the creator of the World Wide Web in 1989, Sir Tim Berners-Lee, called for people to be able to control who has access to information about themselves to address a bad behavior of many companies: "the public has been concerned about privacy—the fact that these platforms have a huge amount of data, and they abuse it."[1] Talk about data privacy had not moved to sufficient action.

This book about IBM's culture could not be more different from Musk's approach to business or Jeff Bezos's harsh personnel practices. IBM's experience is an antidote to the "bossism" that seems to be the fashion in Silicon Valley and elsewhere, where Musk's erratic behavior is making him a hero.[2] IBM was at its core from the beginning a company run by adults. They were not eccentric, they were not ignorant of the gritty ways of the world, they respected the freedom of expression and actions possible from motivated employees, they kept the good ones, they hired the best they could, they respected their customers, and they remained obligated to their communities and families. Did they make mistakes? Of course. No company that thrives and survives for well over a century is perfect, just as are none of us. As a manager at IBM for over thirty years, I did a lot of things right, but I am also remorseful about a few of my actions. There were days when I felt like a genius, and others when the potted plant in my office seemed more intelligent. But the company survived and thrived through wars, depressions, recessions, revolutions, inflation, and technological upheavals. Will Musk and Twitter? We shall see. Meanwhile, as this book explains, IBM's corporate culture was a crucial factor in its long-term survival.

Roz Brewer, CEO of Walgreens Boots Alliance, opined at the end of 2022 the same about other companies, pointing out that "every truly exceptional organization understands that culture needs to be at the center of its success." She felt compelled to remind her peers that although "company culture was viewed as the light and fluffy stuff, . . . the facts and data show that a healthy company culture delivers results, and this has never been clearer to me than right now."[3] Corporations should be managed to last forever. So much for throat-clearing. Corporations have work to do.

The IBM example has much to teach these firms. IBM's experience over the course of some 140 years demonstrates that Brewer is right—corporate culture is central to the performance of a company. Get that right and everything else management and their employees do will work, despite business bumps in the road, world wars, and economic crises. Get that wrong, and a firm becomes a TWA, Kodak, Westinghouse, Lehman Brothers, or Enron—gone. IBM's example teaches us, too, that if a firm stays in business long enough its corporate culture will not continuously protect it. In IBM's case, it entered a period of severe crisis in the 1980s and early 1990s, recovered, then drifted back into problems in 2012, and did not begin to crawl out of that circumstance until about 2022. Today, it continues to reinvent itself and its financial performance is attractive and sober. Its renewal is occurring at the same pace, as had earlier recoveries. More important, IBM's culture had the capacity to change—if always reluctantly—as it does today. Nothing is more comforting to a company's stakeholders than boring, but positive, earnings reports. Those coming out of IBM in 2023, for instance, were reassuring and unexciting—no high drama with its balance sheet.

Here I review features of IBM's culture as it evolved over the past three decades and what it has to teach today's corporate leaders. During the American Revolution of the 1770s, one of the leaders of the rebellion against Great Britain and later the second president of the United States following George Washington, John Adams, wrote frequently to his wife, Abigail, fretting over the perilous and uncertain prospects of winning the war against the mightiest military force on the planet. The epigraph at the start of this chapter captures both the uncertainty of his generation's initiative for independence and the aspiration for its success. These are no different today for a CEO building a new company or pushing it successfully into a new era. Today, it seems that every automotive CEO, for example, is in Adams's circumstance: the world wants to replace gas internal combustion cars with electrical versions, which means that essentially every supplier has to fundamentally change most of what they know about the development, manufacturing, and sale of vehicles of all types. They also have to replace or train their entire workforces in a very short period. Their customers need to learn how to buy and drive these new vehicles. Other business practices outside the industry and even traffic laws and taxing strategies need to change. That sounds much like what the Revolutionary generation faced, and they met the challenge successfully. They became the United States.

IBM had to transform from a small vendor of punch-card equipment into the world's largest provider of digital computers, and then again into the software and services firm that it is today. IBM's management of the mid-1950s would understand, for example, what General Motors CEO, Mary Barra, is going through today as she is traveling down the same path they did. The challenges IBM faced in the 1980s and 1990s as it began its slow transition out of depending overwhelmingly on sales of hardware to software and services feel very much like what Microsoft, Apple to a certain extent, and more certainly Google and social media platforms are experiencing now because, in each case, the fundamental issue is what to offer and how to create the necessary business infrastructure required to do so. We learned at IBM that a great deal had to change; in fact, more than was estimated at the start of that journey. The good news, however, was that core values and many cultural mores helped facilitate the transition. But, as the second epigraph from the long-time president of IBM, Thomas J. Watson, Sr., hinted at, it was hard work for all, as it is today across the automotive industry.

I say we discuss *briefly* similar experiences as they evolved at IBM in recent decades before moving to the main body of the history of IBM's corporate culture because the evidence historians would want to examine to do that is not yet available. Such evidence is worth mentioning because if the reader is a CEO trying to transform their company's culture, this is evidence that indicates progress (or not). Employee opinion surveys about what they believe should be and are the values of the firm are crucial because, as IBM taught historians, every new generation of employees thinks a bit differently than their predecessors. Customer surveys, of course, also provide insight, provided that what they are asked to opine on includes a discussion of corporate behavior and values since they change all the time. Consultants' analyses of economic, regulatory, legislative, and national values, aspirations, and purchasing behaviors continue to be fruitful sources. Human resource (HR) activities, while crucial, are today insufficient; those employees are not line management.

Yet IBM's case teaches us that everyone has to be involved in creating, deploying, and transforming corporate cultures from the CEO down to the newest hire. HR can monitor traffic, report results, educate everyone on the issue, and bring in academic and consulting experts to advise. There is no reason for not knowing how to implement and nurture effective corporate cultures. There is no excuse for not linking one's behavior to that of what their societies and markets increasingly are articulating as essential to continue prospering. Historical case studies inform, so these should be examined both for one's own company and industry and for others around the world. We know enough about IBM to rely on its experience as a learning tool.

We have much to do here to summarize recent developments at IBM that might be of greater interest to today's business leaders and observers of current economic trends. We proceed with a summary of IBM's business performance since the 1980s and how its culture evolved in the same period.

Because of the enormous interest in employee diversity inside multinational corporations and companies in general in the same period, I discuss how the issue plays out within the halls of such enterprises. Increasingly, executives and business observers have come to realize how corrosive financialization practices have been, so we next discuss these, as IBM was an aggressive practitioner of these. I end this introduction with seven lessons drawn from IBM's long history with recommendations aimed at today's management. The rest of the book is a historical monograph on IBM's experience since its origin in the nineteenth century.

IBM's Business Performance from the 1980s to the Present

In another book, I explored IBM's performance through 2018, devoting a third of that large book to an analysis of the company's strategies, business decisions, products, competitors, and other issues one traditionally studies when writing a corporate biography.[4] As reviewers, IBMers, and employees in other firms told me afterward, I was able to leverage my nearly four decades at IBM to decide what issues to address and my skills as a historian to flush out the data in support of my analysis. So, my comments here will be brief; one can always go to the earlier volume for the usual details.

From the early twentieth century to roughly 1960, IBM dominated the market for complex high-end data processing equipment, products used by most large enterprises and government agencies in the industrialized world. Market share hovered between 80 and 90 percent, depending on what country we are talking about. The products included tabulating equipment and punch cards. IBM developed multigenerational relationships with its customers, while its employees enjoyed economic security. A similar experience emerged when, beginning in the 1950s, IBM chose to exit the old tabulating platform, leveraged its technical knowledge of that product set, added skills in electronics, and moved aggressively into computing in the 1950s. By the end of the 1970s, it "owned" 60 to 80 percent of the digital computer market, again depending on which country one looked at. At the height of its tabulating sales, say in 1955, IBM turned in a gross income of $696 million and employed 56,300 people. At the height of its computer sales, say in 1990, gross income came in at nearly $69 billion, with just over 373,000 employees. More telling, here, is that IBM reached its high watermark of employment in 1985, when it employed 405,535 people, and then reduced this population to under 250,000 in the mid-1990s.[5]

Several other observations should be added that I explain more fully in the earlier IBM history book. First, the culture and practices inside IBM were not always ones that generated innovations; some were buried in labs for years, with some "escaping" out to the world, to use CEO Lou Gerstner's descriptor.

Some of that behavior was purposeful, to let early developers establish a market that IBM could then exploit using its corporate-wide capabilities. That strategy normally worked, until it did not due to rapid technological and market changes beginning in the 1980s. Second, the bigger the firm became, the more risk averse its managers and everyone else became; bureaucracy and rules probably caused that, so it was a cultural weakness. Third, the "finance and planning" community—keepers of the budget—constituted a fraternity that did not like risking expenditures on uncertain projects, let alone someone increasing expenses because they thought it was a good idea. They had more power to influence decisions than even the lawyers. Fourth, the company was very process oriented, a trait Watson and some of his cohorts brought over from the more mature NCR when they took over the operationally nearly out of control C-T-R. These four cultural traits collectively encouraged a reluctance to change, especially after the 1960s, after the exhausting and perilous development of the modern computer in that decade. Their hesitancy came despite being as terrific as it was for the economic well-being of the firm.

Finally, as IBM grew in size, it was difficult to see across the entire enterprise, so collaboration tended to remain insulated within a division, such as in sales, manufacturing, or research, thereby creating a silo-centric world of people living in their corner of the blue fish tank. One could spend their entire career inside of IBM and never interact with a customer or government regulator—it was that big, that isolating for thousands of employees. That would not have been the case when it was smaller in earlier decades.

Its products were intended for use in centralized big data centers for nearly a century. Yet beginning in the 1970s with minicomputers and more massively in the 1980s with the availability of personal computers (desktop computing), data processing became more dispersed and networked, rather than centralized; more competitors than in any prior era challenged IBM, resulting in its market share for mainframe large computers declining, beginning in the late 1970s and extending right into the new century. But in the 1970s and through the 1980s, senior management, raised in the old Watsonian world of the global dominance of mainframe computers, continued to believe that the demand for large systems would increase. They considered minis and personal computers (PCs) as minor players. Customers, however, wanted more computing—so IBM management was correct on that point—but in all three forms: big "glass house" data centers with big mainframe computers, minis scattered around as in engineering departments, and PCs on the desks of everyone. By the end of the 1980s, it also seemed that this same "everyone" wanted all three classes of technology to "talk" to all other computer systems in and outside their organizations. Meanwhile, assuming demand for mainframes would accelerate, IBM expanded in the 1970s and early 1980s by hiring people, expanding factories, and building new factories around the world. By the mid-1980s, even the most pro-mainframe executives could see that they had overestimated the demand for mainframes and so had to reduce costs, repurpose research, and explore increasing sales of software. Meanwhile, despite owning 50 percent of the PC market by 1985, by the end of the decade, IBM's share had shrunk roughly in half with well-working clones selling for less, all using Microsoft's operating system that had been licensed by IBM for its machines; in the process, Bill Gates became a wealthy man.

Lower costs required management to quickly reduce the number of employees. They began slowly, and then incrementally reduced the workforce faster throughout the 1990s, tossing people out because there were too many or because their salaries were too high in comparison to what was available in the market. They replaced these workers (or not) with workers with the new skills needed to sustain the firm. Between 1987 and 1995, for example, half of the employees on the payroll in the earlier year were gone, while roughly 30,000 new ones had come into the company. IBM had not seen this much churn in its workforce since the 1960s, but in that earlier period, it was caused by growth, while in this new situation, it was the result of shrinking. A new CEO came to IBM in 1993 and was quickly able to revive the business, selling mainframes, minis, software, and services. Incrementally, the business recovered its revenue stream and profits, while behind the scenes, IBM changed its business model to reflect new realities. As a consequence, its corporate culture and business practices evolved, some of which are discussed below.

The trajectory of IBM's forced new business endeavors of the 1990s continued essentially in a straight line to the late 2010s. This statement will probably grate on senior executives who ran the firm in that period, but if the reader takes time to look at my earlier book, the details confirm this observation. Across the entire period from the 1950s to the present, changes in information technologies also forced IBM and all its competitors and everyone's customers to react. Software, database tools, the surge in the use of the internet after 1995, the arrival of smartphones in 2007, and finally advances in artificial intelligence in the 2000s continued to press on everyone. At IBM, this meant hiring employees with new skills, developing new products in hardware and software, and pushing out the door employees with skills deemed no longer relevant and with no time or funding to retrain them. IBM's leadership had to develop strategies that bet on where technology and customers were headed since such bets often committed a long-surviving firm to a decade or more of a certain trajectory.

During the period from 2012 to 2020, when today's technological innovations were emerging, such as cloud computing and concerns about software security requiring protective tools, management thrashed, it was not quite clear how best to proceed. The infusion of 30,000 management consultants from PwC, while they had the positive effect of causing IBM to become more specific in its industry offerings—a request made by customers over the previous several decades—brought to the firm less understanding of changing technologies. At the same time, the research and development (R&D) side of IBM, which was very familiar with what was happening with information technologies, did not have the sufficient internal political influence to fundamentally affect the evolution of IBM's direction to the extent that was needed. The next CEO, Arvind Krishna (chairman since 2020), however, had spent his career at IBM in research, had a PhD in computer science, and persuaded the firm to go deep into hybrid computing, security services, and artificial intelligence. He will be remembered for recommending that IBM acquire Red Hat Software, an open-source supplier operating in the cloud market. It came into IBM in 2019 with some 19,000 employees and a book of business of $3.4 billion in revenues and a net income of $434 million. So, just as IBM had acquired 30,000 consultants from PwC in 2002, IBM quickly acquired another set of new skills.

IBM's financial situation changed. From 2012 to 2020, its business performance was, to be blunt, terrible. Revenues fell by 28 percent, from $107 billion (2011) to $77 billion (2019), while net income fell by 41 percent, from $16 billion to $9 billion. Revenue per employee declined, and the value of IBM stock did, too.[6] IBM was headed for a disaster when its CEO, Virginia (Ginni) Rometty, "retired."[7] In 2021, IBM spun off much of its legacy computer (infrastructure) services business into an independent firm called Kyndryl. Today, it offers hybrid cloud consulting services, too. When separated from IBM, it took with it a quarter of IBM's employees (90,000), along with $19 billion in revenue. So, a major part of the "old" IBM was now gone, freeing up the rest of the firm to pursue new lines of business. As I was writing this book, it appeared that the new strategy was working; revenues and profits were growing, and the company's offerings were quite different than what IBM offered twenty years earlier.

How IBM's Culture Evolved in That Period

A central argument made in this book is that IBM's corporate culture aligned effectively with its business objectives for most of its history—a similar message I had in my earlier book about the company's history. Harvard business professor Daniel Quinn Mills and collaborator G. Bruce Friesen argued in 1996 that IBM's business decline in the 1980s and early 1990s stemmed from senior management's failure to honor its commitments to employees and customers.[8] The biggest sin regarding employees committed by senior management was breaking the half-century commitment to never lay off IBMers. Both the empirical evidence and my observations inside IBM confirmed that this single fracture in the management of the firm did more damage than any other action. Once done in the late 1980s and continuing to the present, the company was unable to reverse. It became so routine to lay off employees that, in the past thirty years, few can remember a different time. Employment became precarious, subject to termination at a moment's notice.

During the period when Virginia (Ginni) Rometty ran the firm (2012–2020), the number of layoffs increased over those of the 1980s and 1990s. These were in addition to departures caused during the previous administration when IBM sold off portions of its business, and of course, there are the 90,000 IBMers who were moved to Kyndryl by her successor. Not all employees were pleased with that last development. Meanwhile, a new generation of employees came into the firm with no experience with the prior culture and, hence, were less devoted as loyal employees when compared to the intense loyalty exhibited by workers who knew they would probably spend the rest of their working lives at IBM. Longer-serving employees found it shocking how bluntly and fast they were told of being dismissed, certainly in the years after 2010. They felt that any sense of the old corporate belief "Respect for the Individual" was long gone.

In addition to the ongoing incremental layoffs, which left so many employees nervous about whether they would be next, benefits were also being reduced. These, again, incremental iterative "take backs" involved pensions, medical insurance, access to IBM country clubs (which were closed one after another), and termination of support for Quarter Century Clubs, holiday parties, and even community donations. It took a while for employees to push back, although a legal suit regarding age discrimination in the U.S. pension plan changes in the 1990s went against IBM in court. Yet even as late as 2001, employee opinion surveys still demonstrated satisfaction with the firm, an approval that kept declining in subsequent years concerning the company's business strategy but not regarding working conditions. These included long working hours, greater pressures to produce results, inadequate compensation, and forcing managers to lay off employees. So many new managers had come into IBM in the 1990s and early 2000s that it decreased their historic role of being defenders of the company's culture, which the new arrivals did not understand.

In the 2010s, appraisals by managers were ordered to be skewed to provide a range of rankings from outstanding to marginal that could be used as evidence for picking who to lay off next. That change in the appraisal process almost instantly discredited it; in fact, it was so badly discredited that it had to be replaced in the mid-2010s. With chat rooms and other social media outlets available inside and outside IBM in the 2000s, employees did the unthinkable: they complained in public about conditions, even naming specific individuals whom they criticized, using blunt and sometimes inappropriate language, for example, "If anyone at the highest level of IBM had half a brain . . ." (November 2014). A challenge today is for IBM's leaders to figure out how to bridge the gap between the values cherished by employees and the execution of management's professed mantras.

That is the negative trajectory of what happened to IBM's corporate culture. However, there is a positive side to the story worthy of keeping in mind. Simultaneously with all these problems, employees hung on to two of the three beliefs from the 1980s until the oldest left in the 2010s: a commitment to the old Basic Beliefs so central to corporate life in prior decades, measuring any managerial activity against this secular theology. When Lou Gerstner came to IBM in 1993, after understanding what was happening in the firm, he was impressed (a) with the values employees held, if critical of their execution, of their rigidity that made changes to business practices too slow, such as an insufficient focus on serving customers (part of the Basic Beliefs), and (b) that he was able to turn the business around so quickly. That turnaround would have been impossible to achieve so quickly if the culture did not lend itself to doing that. When he came to IBM, employees were looking for leadership and direction from the top of the house, which they believed they were not getting from his predecessor. Once he pointed to what hill to charge, like Teddy Roosevelt's Rough Riders in the Spanish-American War, up they went successfully. The culture still retained features derived from all three Basic Beliefs: respect for the individual, commitment to serving customers, and doing outstanding work. When he left, out came old THINK signs, while for years, complaints centered on violations of the Basic Beliefs and the central problem of layoffs. The lesson here is that old beliefs take time to die; they are, to use a trendy term, "sticky."

That they remained sticky influenced the judgment of employees who, for example, believed layoffs would end soon or that surely they would not be laid off since their performance ratings were good to great. They did not realize that their appraisals were irrelevant and that what organization they worked in was more influential. There were employees at Kyndryl, for example, who had outstanding appraisals but found themselves outside of IBM looking in by the end of 2019. All the reorganizations of the 1990s and beyond characterized so much of what happened at IBM; they broke personal networks and confused employees about the relevance of their part of the business, such that when a portion of it was closed and they happened to be in it, so many were caught off guard.

An ugly, yet new problem surfaced at IBM that is counter to anything discussed in this book: the issue of age discrimination. During Rometty's tenure, senior management concluded that it had too many aging employees who either cost too much or did not have the skills and image the company wanted. The number of layoffs of older workers increased, particularly in the United States, although employees were complaining about this practice a few years earlier. That led to lawsuits and publicly stated complaints. It was a further sin against the old social contract, the Grand Bargain, in which devotion to IBM was rewarded with lifetime employment, benefits, and pension. In 2022, internal emails surfaced about IBM's strategy to dismiss older employees, calling them in one message "Dinobabies." Earlier in 2020, the U.S. Equal Employment

Opportunity Commission determined that there was "top-down messaging from IBM's highest ranks directing managers to engage in an aggressive approach to significantly reduce the headcount of older workers to make room for Early Professional Hires."[9] Separately, investors outside of IBM sued the company for securities fraud. To dampen image problems and to avoid being caught guilty, at least, of age discrimination charges, the company settled cases out of court, thus avoiding disclosure of potentially incriminating emails. But thirty-four other employees had filed similar suits that were not yet settled.[10] Such behaviors would have been inconceivable during the Watsonian era or even as late as the early 1990s. The issue was widely publicized. As early as 2018, *ProPublica*, a highly respected news outlet, copublished with *Mother Jones* an extensive report on IBM's discrimination resulting in "cutting off old heads" to "correct seniority mix." It reported that some 20,000 employees over the age of forty (roughly 60 percent of all layoffs in the United States) had been dismissed in recent years.[11] The story was widely covered by American media.

So, we can conclude that the company's relations with employees have been anything but smooth in recent years. We have only IBM's financial reporting at this time to even hint at how customers view the firm. What is clear is that IBM does face numerous competitors in the hybrid cloud space from larger rivals, such as Amazon and Microsoft, but because demand for such services is substantial, its Red Hat acquisition has done well in this market. The challenge for management is to keep up with that demand, introduce viable artificial intelligence products (hardware and software), and figure out how to assuage its employees. On a personal note, I would not bet against a company that has managed to trot and trip its way through multiple eras of changes for over a century. A major reason for cautious optimism resides in the DNA of its culture.

That management recognizes these various realities is borne out by the fact that it has a senior vice president for "transformation and culture," a position of recent creation. IBM describes that role as focusing "on creating a growth & inclusive culture and enabling +250,000 IBMers to be the catalyst that makes the world work better," which translates into concentrating on "Leadership, Learning, Diversity & Inclusion, Talent Acquisition, Talent Management, Employee Experience and Transformation for IBM."[12]

Employee Diversity at IBM

Multinational corporations share common issues concerning the composition of their staffs. The previous discussion is an example of some of the embarrassing and difficult ones, but all affect different genders, age groups, and ethnicities. The issue of diversity extends to the cultures of multiple countries. At IBM, for decades that collection of realities ranged across twelve to seventy countries and, after World War II, crept up to 175 nations. Every topic discussed in this book also involves how these are handled in each country, too. The central challenge for all multinational companies is just as much one of diversity of countries and their local cultures as it is what academics and media normally want to discuss: diversity of people. Every country has its laws and regulations, which are surprisingly diverse in themselves; think about the United States versus, say, China, or going back in time, the USSR versus the West. This leads to another issue: as time passes, personnel practices change at different rates in different countries. Civil rights was a hot topic in the United States in the 1960s and 1970s, not so in Japan or China for businesses, but yes in South Africa, only radically different than as expressed in the United States. Historically, these personnel practices and perspectives varied too. Think of how Nazi Germany treated Jews in the 1930s versus, say, how this cohort was treated in the United States.[13] IBM in New York smuggled Jews out of Central Europe in the 1930s and found jobs for exiled Cuban employees who had to leave their homeland during the early years of the Castro regime of the 1960s.

Across the life of a company, it encounters circumstances that affect any discussion about whom it employs. For example, if two nations are at war and both have IBM employees, what do you do, such as about German and American employees during World War II? The company might exit one nation, such as IBM did after Russia invaded Ukraine in 2022. IBMers during World War II sometimes interacted with "enemies" of their country. Should an American IBMer turned pilot bomb a German IBM factory? What does that poor fellow do? German IBMers on the ground also faced the issue of who to be loyal to, either their nation now at war or IBM's corporate support of the Allies. So, the issue of diversity extends into the bowels of a company; IBM was no exception. After World War II as part of the American government's strategy to rebuild Germany and Japan as part of its broader Cold War activities, IBMers from the United States worked well with their ex-enemy IBMers in both nations. Why? They were all IBMers, sharing a common corporate culture and familiar with proven methods of running their organizations within the context of the greater IBM.

All of those realities exist as a company's ecosystem before one can even discuss personnel policies and practices, or aspirations to admit (or not) different genders and races, or even people who do or do not have certain levels of education. For example, to be a systems engineer coming into the company in the 1960s or a researcher at an IBM laboratory two decades earlier, one usually had to have a college (or advanced) degree, preferably in a STEM (science, technology, engineering, and mathematics) field. Today, IBM will hire people without a degree if they have relevant technical skills. I have a grandson age fourteen who might qualify as a Java programmer, except IBM will not hire fourteen-year-olds because it is against the law in most parts of the United States, but not in some countries.

So, IBM was—and is—similar to many of the tens of thousands of multinational corporations operating around the world. Management at ExxonMobile, Phillips, Siemens, Subaru, Toyota, and IBM engage with the same issues. What they all do, and did, boils down to several actions. First, each was born in a nation—the United States in the case of IBM—and so the initial shaping of their corporate culture was a by-product of their national culture. Regardless of how well their corporate culture formed, it became the underlying basis worldwide of the firm's mode of operating and expression of its values. The "IBM Way" was born in the United States, so, too, its Basic Beliefs and myriad personnel practices, such as standard training for managers and employees worldwide. The first generation of senior managers was usually homogenous because they came from the same nation and social class. It continues today. Mark Zuckerberg's earliest colleagues were students at his university. Two decades on, and one can complain that this is still too much the case at Meta, where too many Silicon Valley Americans are driving to work on Hacker Way. Phillips favored its Dutch managers, and Siemens their German ones.

The roots of how IBM treated its employees around the world were American, as described in this book, and they were applied to the extent possible in all other countries. While languages varied—although officially everyone had to be able to speak English—local culture dictated variations in policy, which is why one could drink wine in an IBM cafeteria in Paris but not in the one at Endicott, New York. If one were to study IBM's history of its personnel practices, it would have to begin with American practices. The subject is both broad and not well studied by historians. Although there are good models for how to do so, such as the research done by Melissa S. Fisher on women working on Wall Street in the securities industry, the evidence acknowledges that practices originated with the founders of a firm, lasting deep into the future.[14] There are other studies, too, but that one might be the first I would recommend someone read if interested in the issue either as a historian or a personnel manager.

Briefly, here is what happened at IBM. In the early decades, women held roles that were traditional in American society, such as clerks, secretaries, and low-level employees in factories, and left the firm when they married. Today, an estimated third of the total workforce are women; in the United States, just over 50 percent are white men and women, nearly 7 percent African Americans, and some 17 percent Asian, as of 2021. Roughly 70 percent of management in the United States is white, 17 percent Asian, another nearly 7 percent African American, and 6 percent Hispanic (similar to the total Hispanic employee population). In 2021, worldwide just over 40 percent of new hires were women, 15 percent African/African American, and 10 percent Hispanic.[15] How many African Americans and Hispanics worked at IBM before the end of World

War II has yet to be established. From its earliest days, senior management, led by Thomas Watson, Sr., welcomed women, in particular, into manufacturing, by the end of the 1930s into customer service roles, and with so many men in uniform during World War II, a few women into sales. In 1943, he promoted Ruth Leach Amonette to vice president, making her the first female executive at IBM.[16] In 2012, Virginia (Ginni) Rometty became the first female CEO.

Since the 1940s, women and African Americans increased their presence in manufacturing, systems engineering, research, product development, sales, and field engineering. In the 1970s and 1980s, the American civil rights movement and regulatory and legislative pressures resulted in a surge in diversity hiring that spread around the world. By the end of the 1970s, women began moving up the managerial ladder. In the 1980s, one could discern that dominant all-male behavior in the firm was moderating as women and minorities increased their presence, introducing their social practices into the workplace. Each minority group in the United States, but less so in other countries, formed informal support groups to help each other advance their careers. By the 1990s, women and other minorities were ubiquitous all over IBM and at all levels, not just in the United States. In short, the company had a record of bringing in diverse workers for over a century. This included hiring Catholics and Jews (i.e., regardless of one's religion). Hiring diversified in another way: by having varying ethnic, racial, and educational levels, the company brought in a diversity of experiences and ideas, considered a strength at IBM since the 1930s.

Several actions occurred over the course of at least one century. First, as societies welcomed diversity (think the diversity of people) into corporations, IBM did too. Second, as talent competition increased over the arc of the past seventy-five years, IBM's managers sought qualified employees wherever they could find them. With some 50 percent of the human race comprising women, IBM could not ignore that pool of potential workers.[17] Today, more women graduate from colleges and universities in the United States, so one can expect even more to come into the firm; female graduates have also increased in other modern economies. Third, as Watson Sr. coached his managers for decades, IBMers hired people who come from the same socioeconomic classes as their customers. So, as women and other minorities became customers, his admonition continued to be sound advice.

What occurred at IBM also unfolded in other multinational firms to be sure, although historians will debate if one firm was faster or more aggressive in hiring and promoting one group versus another. Let the academics do their diligence; what today's management understands is (a) that diverse workforces are an economic and cognitive benefit to them and (b) that, as the world—or at least the United States—becomes more ethnically diverse, its pool of future workers will too. Like other multinationals, IBM's experience with developing a diverse workforce has not all been smooth sailing. For example, African

Americans faced racial barriers in parts of the United States.[18] I am of Hispanic heritage and so witnessed a few minor bumps in the road by others, mostly in the 1980s.[19] Gay employees did, too, right into the next new century, although they were in every part of the business worldwide and increasingly in senior ranks, too. Nor was it smooth sailing for other multinational corporations; however, because these companies all needed employees worldwide, who had to collaborate and work within the context of a multinational corporate culture, they welcomed diversity more than might otherwise be so essential in companies that operated solely within the confines of one country or a few nearby countries.

All these multinational companies realized that they had to proactively force the issue of adding diversity to their workforces, less so before World War II but certainly by the early 1960s. Personnel departments categorized each employee by ethnic and racial types, asking workers to self-identify. In addition, they tabulated statistics on hiring and promotion trends, where in the organization people worked, and appraisal equities, and compared their salaries and appraisals to those of white and other groups. In the United States, much of that reporting was required by U.S. law, but when no longer—or less so—later, IBM, like the other multinationals in the United States, continued to quietly track trends. These were routinely reported to all levels of management since the 1970s. Management was trained and, for the rest of their careers, reminded to recruit and develop diverse workforces. Pressure on middle management, in particular, to ensure their organizations had a mix of such employees was pervasive in the United States and never more so than in the 1970s and 1980s when the company was increasing the size of its workforce. Afterward, it seemed less intense since IBM was either laying off employees or was forced to accept whoever walked in the door as a result of acquiring a company. One could point out, too, that by the end of the century there was less need to focus hiring and promotion campaigns on minorities since so many were in the company.

But there is a dark side to this story, too, to acknowledge. As Asian societies increased their investment in the education of their citizens, particularly in STEM topics, the number of workers that companies like IBM could hire for less than they paid their American and Western European employees proved too tempting to resist. Much work that was done at IBM in the 1990s was later moved to India and China, making it possible to lay off older, more expensive employees in the United States. Data on IBM exist for 1996–2008.[20] The proportion of African American employees declined from 9.9 percent of the total U.S. IBM workforce to 7.5 percent or 3,439 fewer in 2008 than in 1996. Asians increased in net numbers by 5,281 in an overall American IBM workforce that had gone from 125,618 IBMers in 1996 to 120,227. Hispanics accounted for 4.0 percent of the workforce in 1996, rising only to 4.2 percent in 2008. One economic report concluded that "the main reason for the decline in black employment at IBM was the reduction of employment of the types of jobs that blacks had occupied in 1996 when over 43 percent of blacks were clustered in the operative and office/clerical categories." Divesting and offshoring resulted in only seventy-eight African Americans working in the "operative category" in the United States and 885 in "office/clerical work," as compared to 1,905 holding those jobs in 1996. On the sales side, jobs proved more plentiful, with 1,248 in 1996, but then 2,853 in 2008, but with the "proportion of all marketing employees who were black declin[ing], from 7.9 percent in 1996 to 7.2 percent in 2008."[21] This is less a story about racial profiling than the observation made earlier that where an employee sat in the organization said more about the odds of being laid off than their appraisals would indicate, a point not always appreciated by those IBMers.

The Corrosive Influence of Financialization Practices

In my 2019 history of IBM, I argued that its senior management's obsession with profits and stock values was a principal cause of the firm's poor economic behavior and consequent erosion of what had been for the most part an excellent corporate culture, one that benefited employees, customers, stockholders, and society worldwide. I called their obsession a "cancer" in the firm. That cancer went from stage 1 in the 1980s to almost stage 4 during the 2000s with remission manifesting itself beginning in 2021–2022. IBM behaved as many American multinationals did, behavior that continues to this day, and in non-American firms as well. One saw it when, for example, BP announced in 2022 that it would "invest" over $2 billion in stock buybacks. We saw it when we read in the financial press about the enormous compensation packages for CEOs and stockbrokers. Something did not smell right, and thanks to the work of economists and others, we know what that cancer looks like. IBM has had a bad case of it for so long that we need to understand it. Beginning in the 1980s, executives were told largely by business school professors that they should maximize the returns on investment of shareholders above all other stakeholders in a company's ecosystem. They went too far, with IBM always in the top five in any ranking you choose. Such behavior resulted in instability in workforce employment (e.g., layoffs), produced significant income inequalities (e.g., high CEO salaries and no or few salary increases for the masses), resulted in slow or declining productivity, and skewed internal performance measurements tied tightly to quarter-to-quarter short-term financial decisions (i.e., accounting engineering).

Economists came to distinguish between two classes of potential sustainable activities in American and other national economies: value creation and value extraction. How boards of directors and senior managers balanced the two proved to be a bad show, as it led to imbalances favoring extraction over creation. Two economists looking at the situation concluded in 2020 that "the imbalance has become so extreme in the United States that *predatory value extraction* has become a central economic activity, to the point at which the U.S. economy as a whole can be aptly described as a *value-extracting economy*."[22] That is a harsh, blunt conclusion, but one we can think of as a cancer. Value creation is about what IBM did before the 1980s in investing in the development and sale of products customers were willing to pay for, resulting in the growth of productivity that made the firm profitable and able to continue thriving into the future. It is what the Watsons and their immediate successors did, even when they made such investments too aggressively, as happened in the 1970s and 1980s when management thought mainframes would dominate deep into the future. At the other extreme is value extraction, which calls for a company to take out of the firm its already created value, such as by paying dividends or investing insufficiently in developing future products and technologies. That behavior resulted in laying off employees, pulling back on benefits, killing off old rituals, and even for a while not allowing someone to fly to a conference, all to save money. In sum, executives at IBM, like peers in many other companies, focused more on immediate value extraction than on value creation, helping to almost put the company out of business in 1990–1993 and veering in that dangerous direction after 2012.

Successful companies that placed bets on value creation grew post–World War II worldwide; lifetime employment in high-tech companies made perfect sense, expanded benefits did too, and overall corporate productivity grew. This was the implementation and consequence of implementing a retain-and-reinvest strategy; it went far to explain why IBM's values, corporate culture, and business performance became so much of the positive story told in our book. Communities, too, benefitted. Company towns like Endicott and Poughkeepsie profited; children went to good schools, and people lived in comfortable homes, had job security, and were assured pensions in their old age. In contrast, when IBM and others emphasized implementing a downsize-and-distribute strategy, starting tentatively in the l980s, but subsequently as a permanent way of running the company, the opposite occurred. The IBM country clubs in those two company towns are gone, with Endicott's being torn down as I wrote this paragraph at the end of 2022. Property values dropped, and many laid off employees lacked pensions and were confused about their medical insurance programs. Savings from such practices funded cash dividends and stock buybacks. Those funds could have been used to reinvest back into the business and communities. The asset extraction strategy goes far to explain why IBM and others sold off or closed factories and entire divisions and dismissed so many workers in just a few years.

With academics advocating, then regulators permitting, the imbalance to occur between value creation and value extraction, beginning in the 1980s and continuing to the present, senior executives changed their behavior; it was too tempting to resist making vast fortunes, often running into the hundreds of millions of dollars while in the roles of presidents and CEOs. Stock-based compensation packages motivated their behavior, as I explained in more detail in my earlier book, so no need to repeat this here.[23] Economists asked the embarrassing question: "Does executive compensation reflect the success of the company in value creation, or the power of senior executives to engage in value extraction?"[24] At IBM, compensations increased beyond financial performance, most sharply in the 2000s. It became so bad at both IBM and many of its peer multinational, American-originated companies that they even went into debt to fund stock buybacks and dividends. Earnings were the first to go; then came increased use of debt and brutish cost-cutting measures.

In information technology industries, IBM led the way with such practices, practicing what is now known as financialization and what in earlier years was called "accounting reengineering." Regardless of the name, we now know this practice was far more broadly a strategy that resulted in IBM transforming away from the older practice of creating value to one that is focused on extraction. At IBM, net income between 1978 and 1987 hovered at $46 million; between 1988 and 1997, it crashed to $18.5 million; it was back up to $77.3 million between 1998 and 2007 and rose to $132.4 million between 2008 and 2017. Buybacks tell a different story: $4.7 million (1978–1987), $21.3 million (1988–1997), $76.5 million (1998–2007), and then $100.7 million (2008–2017). Put another way, between 1995 and 2019, IBM spent $208 billion in buybacks. IBM bought twice as many between 2012 and 2019 than between 2002 and 2011. Even more tragic, those purchases did not boost the value of IBM stock in the twenty-first century. One could cite other statistics for dividend payouts to reinforce the evident pattern.[25] IBM and other firms referred to their stock buyback initiatives as "investment" activities. Retained earnings, which Watson Sr. valued so much as his seed corn for future crops and that helped fund IBM's corporate culture, were consumed in recent decades. IBM laid out the details almost shamelessly in its annual reports, while CEO letters in these publications barely mentioned customers, let alone employees.

Two economists observed that "since the early 1980s major U.S. business corporations have been doing stock buybacks on top of, not instead of, making dividend payments to shareholders," even to the extent of exceeding 100 percent of net earnings by selling off their seed corn (cash reserves), disposing of factories and divisions, acquiring debt, and laying off employees. Payment ratios of buybacks and dividends for the largest twenty-five stock repurchasers just in the period 2008–2017 place IBM at number four, behind Apple (#1), ExxonMobile (#2), and Microsoft (#3). Each company spent over $100 billion on such activities, instead of spending that money on nurturing the business.[26] While IBM sought some balance between value creation and extraction in the

1980s and 1990s, that balance subsequently tipped clearly toward what economists call "predatory" value extraction practices. IBM's reduction of its labor force from 374,00 in 1990 to 220,000 in 1994—just in four years—became a poster child of no longer supporting lifetime careers, replacing that strategy with one in which needed talent was lured away from other firms, kept as long as needed, and then discarded, and their work frequently outsourced. In 2021, IBM's board of directors and its new CEO reversed course, pulling back on stock buybacks, and returned to a much older practice of acquiring small technology companies that had patents, products, and employees with relevant skills that all complimented the company's current business and technology strategies.

But let us return to the more debilitating behavior of recent decades. What surprised me at the time was how a company that was supposedly so international, with more than half its employees located outside the United States, could behave this way, given that in many countries such practices were either highly regulated or socially unacceptable, such as by senior Japanese executives who made far less than their American counterparts. But it helps explain why Asian firms, in collaboration with their national governments, in the same period chose to invest in developing innovative cost-effective products and services.[27]

In addition to nearly mortally wounding IBM, but not necessarily other companies (e.g., ExxonMobil, Apple, and Microsoft), was the broader issue of the cost to a nation's society. Let legal historian William Magnuson explain: "the blind belief that the pursuit of profit will always rebound to the benefit of society as a whole is both flawed and dangerous."[28] Flawed can mean, for example, Facebook making its offerings so addictive that fake news could proliferate, threatening political stability, democracy if you will, and convincing people not to be vaccinated against COVID-19. Magnuson went further in explaining the dangerous feature for society: "it leads executives and managers into . . . thinking that valorizes numbers over ideas. Focusing on profits to the exclusion of all else can blind us to the harm that we are doing. It can crowd out mental space that we might otherwise devote to broader questions about the role our corporations should play in improving our societies."[29] In other words, the problem is the negative consequences of too much "greed" (his term). Employees see how much their executives make and become dispirited, questioning the legitimacy of their employers, and thus slow their productivity, their "give it all to the betterment of Mother IBM."[30] Others come at the same consequence as a result of corporations conducting "value skimming," with management enriching themselves too much.[31]

Such behavior could largely be disguised from the public and employees either due to the complexity of understanding what was going on or because of some realities that have been explained as follows. With revenues coming in either tens or hundreds of billions of dollars, a CEO's compensation of, say, $100 million or more "will barely register on the shareholder radar as long as stock prices are going up." Such annual compensation "would only account for 2.5 percent of net profit at a firm."[32] The average citizen and few individual investors or regulators sit around and read executive compensation explanations detailed in American government 8-K and 10-K reports.

Seven Lessons to Take Away

Some things, perhaps many, are changing in the world's economic circumstances. COVID-19 disturbed any sense of economic equilibrium that existed before, and nowhere more so than in China, thanks to its draconian lockdown practices that so disrupted global supply chains and caused an almost immediate pivot by multinational companies to move work back to more secure geographies. A new generation of young workers wants to work remotely if they can; wants their employers and vendors to align corporate values with their own, such as concern for improving the world's environment; and is perfectly prepared to move from one firm to another. Lifelong employment seems to be in decline, particularly in Western companies. Authoritarian politics is on the rise, and defenders of democracy are in partial retreat. CEOs are becoming more political and impatient with "coddling" employees. China eyes Taiwan, and Russia decided simply to execute an old-fashion war of imperial conquest in Ukraine. Consumers are flush with money and are willing to spend it as this book was written (2023), despite unfamiliar inflationary pressures making whole economies and their citizens nervous. IBMers today would find the chapters of our book on corporate culture to be about a company with which they have almost no familiarity, or possibly even no desire to embrace. So, much is adrift.

However, much is also not unfamiliar, at least to historians and economists. Multinational corporations are not going away. There are between 60,000 and 70,000 of them, depending on whose list one uses. Just the 60,000 control 500,000 subsidiaries. As a group, the 2,000 largest multinationals are huge, with revenues each running into the tens and hundreds of billions of dollars. With their subsidiaries, they are, well, everywhere.[33] The largest 2,000 such firms, of which IBM is one, collectively generated $47.6 trillion in revenues and $5 trillion in profits and were squarely rooted in fifty-eight countries. Five hundred ninety of these are American-based firms, followed by 351 originating in China or Hong Kong.[34] To put things in some perspective, the world's economy (gross domestic product [GDP]) crossed over the $100 trillion mark in 2022. The United States still has the largest national economy, hovering at $25 trillion, with China at number two with nearly $20 trillion.[35] American firms employ approximately 44 million workers in various countries.[36] So, they are not going away, even though societies, regulators, legislators, employees, and other affected stakeholders want them to behave differently.

I offer seven observations and attendant steps such firms should consider useful for the long haul, based on historical insights from IBM. I am assuming that all multinationals wish to remain in business for decades and to be financially successful and that, today, they recognize that all stakeholders outnumber them and thus can impose collective sanctions and rules on them and also through the bites of a thousand nationally independent rules and laws. Today, for example, it is less expensive and more expedient for multinationals to adhere to the European Union's regulations regarding privacy worldwide, rather than parse out various practices country by country. That behavior is a new form of globalization that we would not have discussed a decade ago, but there it is.

The observations and recommendations below are not in priority because they should all be considered in tandem with each other. That, in itself, is a finding from the study of IBM's history and its corporate culture.

* * *

First, take the time, even if years, to craft a corporate-wide set of basic beliefs that will motivate employees at all levels to a higher purpose consistent with the business practices of the firm.

While national cultures seem quite different from one nation to another, people are less so. Employees and their families share many similar ethics and aspirations in the world. People value their families and being good and respected members of their communities, are generally proud of their nations, practice variations of the Golden Rule, and require trust and truth. Basic beliefs motivate and empower employees to do well for all the stakeholders of a multinational. IBM's experience demonstrates people in 175 countries can share and live by a set of values. Just take the time to plant it in an enterprise; it takes time or, to use the term business guru W. Edwards Deming urged, a "constancy of purpose." A good source of models for such beliefs is the military forces, such as the U.S. Marine Corps and the British Army. Their beliefs survive for centuries, not just years, even exaggerated stories, serving as practical functional mythologies. Beliefs give employees confidence in their employer, rationalizing the persistent extensive efforts they are frequently called to exert.

* * *

Second, make the use of practices and beliefs simultaneously the most important responsibility and the task of all employees, not just a personnel department or senior executives.

IBM's experience suggests that the front-line shock troops to carry this out are all levels of management and other leaders in all parts of the corporate empire. Ingrain in them the beliefs and equip them with processes and incentives to make it their primary mission at work to make practices consistent with the beliefs; the beliefs should be the primary guiding principle for all that is done, all that is decided. Make it so they are part of one's DNA, a core set of behaviors that even if they leave your corporation, as many will, they take these beliefs and practices to their next job. At their next position, they might be your customer, so would it not be convenient to have them trust you because of shared values? IBM's salesmen routinely thought the answer was yes.

* * *

Third, nurture an ecosystem that simultaneously engages all of your stakeholders with a shared body of information, beliefs, and understanding of the higher purposes of your enterprise.

For over seventy-five years, IBM "owned" the bulk of how the world viewed data processing, tabulating, and then computers, and even after its technical authority was challenged by personal computer (PC) rivals, many members of its ecosystem did not embrace desktop computing until IBM said, "It's okay to do so." Create an "IBM Way" style of doing things and viewing issues that makes sense to all your stakeholders, is relevant to them, and fits your company's style, not specifically someone else's (e.g., IBM's, H-P's, Facebook's, or Twitter's). If one's society wants the firm to focus less on a brutish collection of profits, then take some of those earnings and invest them in charitable and educational initiatives in countries you serve. That will require the allocation of staff, management energy, and time of employees to create, engage, and nurture myriad initiatives. Stay the course, and avoid what some African farmers argue, "Oh, here comes an NGO; it won't stay long, so we should not depend on it." Trust requires creating confidence that the firm will remain a good corporate citizen far into the future. Manage the ecosystem like one means it.

* * *

Fourth, develop objectives, strategies, and tactics for cultivating all your stakeholders. Take a very broad view of who constitutes your ecosystem of stakeholders.

It is remarkable how often multinationals fail to define broadly enough who the stakeholders are in their ecosystem. Social media experience has taught that ignored groups can quickly gain massive exposure, and hence social power, in support of or against a large corporation. Secrecy or ignoring relevant communities no longer works. Even China, run by an authoritarian government, had to change course in 2022 when small groups of citizens complained about

COVID-19 lockdowns, which then grew into large crowds protesting in public all over the country, as women did in Iran over what started as objecting to the treatment (ultimately murder) of one woman by the Morality Police. History is littered with examples of companies losing business because of word-of-mouth bad press. Take the time to continuously maintain an understanding of who your constituencies are, as IBM did, for instance, when it cultivated employees' children and spouses from one generation to another. Inspections and participation by all senior leaders of the firm are required worldwide to make such behavior ubiquitous.

* * *

Fifth, governments have the power to take apart or constrain the behavior of a multinational corporation.

Beyond the legal, regulatory, and policing capabilities of a nation's government, which are pretty impressive if one remembers they have rifles, armies, and jails, too, there is transnational collaboration. Today, governments and entire regions can coordinate disciplinary action against a firm that does not behave the way a particular society or its mores demand. During the Ukrainian war, Russian multinationals were sanctioned; their managers had their bank accounts, properties, and boats seized and sold; and the money collected was controlled by governments for possible use to rebuild Ukraine. China has kicked out of its landmass multinationals, and the Americans are outlawing the use of the social media platform TikTok on government computers out of concerns that Chinese authorities could extract information about individuals and organizations in the United States. That will probably cause individual users to do the same since the public increasingly wants the privacy of their information preserved by multinational firms. Public officials will follow the will of their citizens at some point, regardless of the kind of government in place.

* * *

Sixth, multinationals are so big that they no longer can just be selfishly focused on seeking profits for senior executives and investors because they have become pillars of societies. So they must act much like parents in a family, nurturing and protecting the communities and nations in which they operate.

History—and not just IBM's—demonstrates that corporations of any size can organize people to produce and make institutions productive. Ford developed the mass production process, IBM how to use information effectively, Exxon to find oil, myriad pharmaceutical firms cures for medical problems, and Facebook connecting billions of people in conversation. Use your organizing capability to do good for humanity. That means avoiding taking political sides in any nation, staying above the fray, and taking the long view in helping society. Watson Sr. spoke frequently of IBM having a future extending far into the future: it was noble, exhilarating, and motivating for members of all parts of the company's ecosystem. Mayors declared certain dates "IBM Day," while IBM built a monument to honor IBMers killed in the war. The single most important objective is not just to make a profit, not if the firm is a pillar of society. Profit will be an outcome, a by-product of a broader view. When IBM twice ignored that lesson, it suffered financially. In short, align with national interests, as successful corporations have done since their invention many centuries ago. When reporting quarterly business results, don't just talk about the numbers and toss in a few positive customer stories, as IBM and so many other corporations still do, add in measureable comments about what the firm has accomplished with and for its other stakeholders. Such reporting signals to employees, customers, regulators, and communities that the firm accepts its vitally important responsibility to support entire societies and the Earth as well.

* * *

Seventh, a company does not consist of buildings, money, or inventory; it is made up of its employees. Without them, the firm does not exist, so treat them as the precious commodity that they are.

This admonition stands in sharp contrast to union-busting, strike-averse business leaders who want to coddle or pay less to their employees. It is an old aspiration that has proven to be a false path to economic and social success. NCR, then IBM and Burroughs, rejected that approach well over a century ago; so, too, did other firms. Hire the best, pay them well, and give them a reason to solve society's problems with the company's products and services. IBMers often were said to "bleed blue," to shed tears at their retirements when reminding audiences that it was all about their colleagues. IBM's experience as described in this book took Basic Beliefs and its treatment of its employees and customers as the opening and closing narrative of its endurance for nearly 140 years. Embrace diversity of genders, races, social classes, and ideas. Put effort and purpose into it, even though more of the new hires will probably move to other organizations than might have decades ago. Be open and honest with them about progress and problems because they can help solve these; hold everyone accountable for progress; and finally, make the work so relevant that nobody wants to leave the company.

I like most of what historian William Magnuson recommends to all corporations, not just multinationals or IBM; these are lessons worth adding to the list of recommendations. Some overlap with the suggestions above. Briefly, here they are: "Don't overthrow the republic," "Think long term," "Share with shareholders," "Compete, but fairly," "Treat your workers right," "Don't destroy the planet," "Don't take all the pie for yourself," and "Don't move too fast or break too many things."[37] Give Thomas J. Watson, Sr., the last word, spoken in 1925 to a room full of salesmen: IBM "is not a temporary organization, but a most enduring one." Further, "it is an institution that will go on forever."[38] Such faith takes work and sense of purpose. A century later, we can continue to learn as we implement corporate cultures in some of the most complex organizations ever created by people. Now read the rest of the book to see how that was done inside a corporation.

CHAPTER 1

FROM THEORIES OF CORPORATE CULTURES TO THE REALITIES OF LIFE INSIDE A GLOBAL ENTERPRISE

I came to see, in my time at IBM, that culture isn't just one aspect of the game—it is the game. In the end, an organization is nothing more than the collective capacity of its people to create value.

Louis V. Gerstner, Jr., 2002[1]

If you have worked in a company—any company of any size—even for a short while, you have probably concluded that it is like a community, a neighborhood existing within a larger one called an industry. Historians, sociologists, and business school professors would applaud you for understanding correctly that companies, governments, and universities are all communities. They would remind you of the obvious, too, that each shares common values and behaviors. In the West, firms and employees subscribe to notions of capitalism and markets; in France, one negotiates in French, and in the United States, in English. If you work for a large enterprise, you are paid in local currency, but the amount of your salary is probably comparable to what peers are paid in many countries. You live by common rules and unstated ones, too.

People have met their future spouses in these companies, and colleagues have become lifelong friends (or enemies); all share the bond of common experiences. The world holds a common opinion of these companies and their employees, although each also has their own unique personality. Don't we all have an opinion about what is a typical Trump supporter, an Apple "Genius" helping us sort out an iPhone problem, a banker, a lawyer, an automobile sales-man, a cleric? For decades, IBMers—as IBM's employees were known inside and outside the company—had an image shared widely around the world. It turned out that was usually a good circumstance for them, because it was a positive one.

Try to find senior executives in any large organization that think an insti-tutional culture does not exist, or is not important, in their firm and you will probably not find many. Since corporate culture became an open subject of discussion by academics and business consultants in the 1970s and 1980s, shaping—managing—one's business culture became a high priority for senior executives. One will find a debate underway today among experts, managers, and most employees about what constitutes their respective corporate cultures, what is working (or not), what is good or bad about their culture and that of others, and what needs to change. Most people have an opinion, and if they work in an organization for even a short period, each is knowledgeable about it, indeed probably believing they are experts on the topic. Why? They spend eight or more hours a day immersed within it, normally for five or six days a week, often for years or decades.[2] So, corporate culture is an important topic of interest to many people.

While there is wide acceptance of the importance of corporate culture, there are significant gaps in our knowledge about how one is created and shaped, its effects, and even what questions and issues to explore.[3] For example, suppose a sales culture develops at a firm—as happened at IBM—what does that mean? Is everyone a salesperson? No, because some employees will have to be accoun-tants, receptionists at the company's headquarters, or an assistant to the CEO. But to sustain a sales culture, if that is what senior management desires, means that management has to think through what motivational meetings, compen-sation plans, and rituals they need across the entire enterprise involving all employees. They will also need to ensure their customers accept the activities normally associated with a sales culture as beneficial to them. Careful consid-eration would have to be given to identifying critical stakeholders and ensuring that each is satisfied in that relationship as part of what we today know to be more than just a corporation. Today, executives think increasingly in terms of ecosystems involving all stakeholders in a symbiotic codependent relationship. In short, corporate culture is not hubris or some idealized sociological inven-tion; rather, it is serious, real, and complicated to manage.

Experienced managers understand that reality; it is why someone like IBM's CEO in the 1990s, Louis Gerstner, not known for spouting trivial ideas, made the statement opening this chapter. One of the twentieth century's most respected observers of business behavior, Peter Drucker, was frequently quoted as bark-ing out that "culture eats strategy for breakfast." Gerstner would have nodded his head in concurrence. In other words, the role of culture is extraordinarily important in shaping the destiny of a firm. That is why a book about IBM's culture contributes to our understanding of how this firm, its customers, and its large peer enterprises behaved. This message cannot be repeated too often.

A second challenge faced by management is how to change a culture when it needs a makeover, often referred to by such terms as "transformation" or "innovation." IBM faced that quandary in the 1990s. It is still addressing that issue in the 2020s, because sociologists and business management scholars indicate that this process is a time-consuming and quite complicated exercise. Even shock therapies such as wars, pandemics, economic recessions, and rapid technological transformations can only slightly speed up cultural transitions. That is one of the lessons one can derive from the study of how a successful corporation evolved over the course of nearly a century. Stakeholders change over time, people's attitudes evolve slowly, ugly and positive economic realities flip back and forth faster than one's views of the world, and it takes time for the impact of technological innovations to settle in. Yet people expect changes to come quickly. At IBM, for example, it took nearly a decade to understand how the arrival of distributed processing and the PC fundamentally changed market conditions. As the company abandoned its full employment practices that it had cherished for over a half century, that abandonment took years to be fully exercised, and even three decades later, employees resisted it.[4] The company is still learning what consequences such a fundamental shift in its culture are having on its effectiveness.[5]

Corporate cultures are difficult to change because they resist change. Business consultants and academics have opined frequently on this point. With respect to IBM, one long-serving executive in the firm, Nick Donofrio, observed that "IBM's values have remained more or less the same for over 100 years. The ability to change and to respond to change are [sic] built into the values. Certainly, they have evolved over time to reflect a more global and inclusive mindset, but their essence remains in place. Some things do remain the same."[6] The evidence presented in this book generally supports his observation. One can attribute that inflexibility to the company's highly successful more than half-century initiative to create a shared culture or, to put it into sociological and anthropological language, "cultural homogenization." In other words, a body of values, behaviors, and symbols emerged at IBM embraced by hundreds of thousands of employees. These were conveniently codified by executives, most notably by the Watson executives at IBM, who reigned from 1914 to 1971, and their mentees for a subsequent two decades. Generations of executives thus participated in the "canonization of texts" crucial to understanding the "IBM Way" of going about one's work.[7]

But that rising interest in transforming an organization's culture and understanding the consequences of such an action created a problem over the past half century: lack of sufficient understanding of what constitutes a corporate culture. In contrast to the "hard sciences" of economics, corporate accounting and finance, engineering, advertising, product design, and many other business practices, corporate culture lacks the precise knowledge regarding its components that is evident in these other fields. One group of experts on the subject argued that management's understanding and analysis of cultural factors were "profoundly unsatisfactory," complaining in particular that multinational companies had "not adopted analytical tools" to enable "them to address the problems they frequently face."[8] Yet codification of what corporate culture is about and how to apply such insights to the governance of an organization is increasing.[9] So scholars and consultants trod on, looking for that familiar level of specific knowledge of what it is and how to use it. They have been busy, joined by leaders, executives, managers, and interested others. But we remain with an uncertain, even scattershot collection of insights.

While historians have been busy, too, they have almost "everything" yet to do in defining corporate culture as part of the history of business and government. Memoirs, which normally devote considerable attention to the subject, are uneven and possibly misleading. This is because they concern facets of a larger community but only focus on the variant familiar to the author. If I write a memoir of my years at IBM, I might focus by necessity on sales and managerial issues because I never worked in an IBM factory, for example, where tens of thousands of employees spent their careers.

Business consultants work based on their personal or practice's methodologies and so, too, are constrained, even more so since they live in the present with insufficient insights about the past. Again, because I spent a decade as a consultant, when engaged with a client, I focused largely on what we could discern were contemporary issues and problems—the reasons for bringing in consultants—applying formal methodologies of consulting practices to address client concerns.

As discussed in this book, there exists a dichotomy between what one understands is corporate culture from the academic and consulting perspectives and what those who live within the culture see. For example, when a business historian writes a biography of a corporation, they discuss leadership, strategy, product introductions, revenues, competition, salesmanship, government regulations, the influence of wars and national economic upturns and downturns, and so forth. Your author has done that, writing largely about IBM's experience over the course of more than a century.[10] But read the memoirs of an employee or, more broadly, the thousands of comments posted in open and closed Facebook forums of employees and retirees, and they, too, use the term "corporate culture" when discussing events and working conditions in their corner of IBM. One can read a bit about the topics scholars, consultants, and senior leaders favor but also about an equally diverse list of other issues: work practices, benefits, role of enlightened and abusive managers, social contacts, gender and racial prejudices, shared training and customer experiences, and questions about how to navigate myriad issues in the bureaucracy of their firm.

"Their" is not just a proper grammatical use of a pronoun; it is a finding unfolded in this book: people who work in or with a large company assume ownership for the culture they work in, because it is part of their own persona, their own identity. IBM's culture is not the CEO's culture to do with as they please; it belongs to all IBMers. A general does not own and maintain the military's values and cultures; they can support and encourage innovations of it, but it lives only if their troops make it their own. The epigraph for this chapter offers up two useful insights. First, it displays the confidence needed by a senior leader willing to change a corporate culture he found in need of repair, and second, it shows that this manager did not own the culture. Gerstner had to persuade and assuage hundreds of thousands of people who also owned it to change their ways. Those he had to persuade included many of IBM's customers in over 150 countries, many populated with ex-IBMers in positions important to IBM's own welfare, such as those who made decisions about acquiring the company's goods and services.

The purpose of this book is to broaden our understanding of how large international corporations in particular link to those issues seen by the mass of employees as part of their corporate culture. To increase our understanding of what constitutes a company's culture and how it works, we must first connect grand histories and accepted managerial practices to what was going on in an organization lower down the corporate ladder, providing historical perspectives on paths less traveled by scholars. I focus on one international corporation because, like so many of its peers, it employed hundreds of thousands of people and interacted with millions of individuals working for tens of thousands of customer enterprises and public agencies. It provides a window into and way to understand further how corporate culture is formed and shaped. Although later I will discuss further why IBM was chosen for this exercise, the short answer is that formal top-down histories exist, including much material about how employees worked, that can be culled for insights applicable to other multinational corporations. Additionally, there is much evidence that can be added by looking at it from the bottom-up, combining the two sets of evidence to provide a rich case study of a large corporation. We are interested in understanding how to build a culture, change it, and link it to the evolving missions of corporations. An urgent need today, for example, is to learn how to shift from the shareholder priority of such corporations to one more broadly endorsed by the members of the Business Roundtable. Platitudes and pontifications are nice to read, but the hard work of making those profitable realities means working with corporate cultures. IBM's experience offers insights shaped by the fires of realities. It has long been common to look at IBM's experience to inform the practices of other firms in the information technology arena and large enterprises in all industries.[11] For scholars in many disciplines and especially for executives of corporations, we use the tools of the historian to enlighten managerial practices.

The discussion begins with a review of studies about the state of corporate cultures because these influence the language and concepts explored in the rest of the book and because the value of typologies, models, and frameworks, to quote Schein, "is that they simplify thinking and provide useful categories for sorting out the complexities of corporate layers."[12] The same is done with respect to material cultures as I link together corporate and material cultures as an important intersection in this volume. I then make the case for why one should look at IBM as opposed to a different firm and conclude by explaining how we travel through the rest of the chapters.

The State of Corporate Cultures

When scholars want to understand corporate cultures, they generally turn first to the work of Edgar H. Schein, and for good reason. Trained as a social psychologist at Harvard University, then serving as a professor at MIT's business school, he developed clearly articulated ideas concerning the definition and features of corporate culture, effectively sweeping aside earlier models and interpretations. In the 1980s, Schein became the starting point for exploring corporate cultures, and his thinking remains relevant. Our book is influenced by his work. Schein defined organizational culture as "a learned product of group experience [that] is, therefore, to be found only where there is a definable group with a significant history."[13] This business management professor argued in sociological terms that corporate culture consists of "basic assumptions and beliefs that are shared by members of an organization, that operate unconsciously, and that define in a basic 'taken-for-granted' fashion an organization's view of itself and its environment."[14] A company's culture is developed and learned in response to the organization's need to survive and thrive. For his formal overarching definition, he connected these concepts together to provide a working concept of culture: "a pattern of basic assumptions—intended, discovered, or developed by a given group as it learns to cope with its problems of external adaptation and internal integration—that has worked well enough to be considered valid and, therefore, to be taught to new members as the correct way to perceive, think, and feel in relations to those problems."[15] Schein viewed values and behaviors as "observed manifestations of the cultural essence."[16] He continued to refine and enhance his descriptions of corporate culture deep into the next century.[17]

An ex-IBM employee and student of corporate culture, Geert Hofstede, working at the same time as Edgar Schein, called corporate culture "software of the mind."[18] He focused considerable attention on cultural values and how nationality affected employee views and ways of behaving. Like Schein, Hofstede influenced academics, business managers, and managerial consultants.[19] This book affirms that his colleagues at IBM behaved as he described.

Schein declared there were three levels of culture that interacted with each other through the behavior of an organization's employees. Those two ideas move us from his high-level definition to a more tangible engagement with the subject. He thought of "artifacts and creations," such as technology, art, and audible behavioral patterns, which are visible but not always decipherable, as being on the first level. On the second level were "values," which he saw as providing the greatest awareness and included beliefs regarding what works. On the third level were what he called "basic assumptions," which were accumulated basic beliefs about the enterprise by members of a firm and its stakeholders that were often taken for granted as invisible preconscious notions.[20]

It is easy to jump in to complain that so many other students of corporate culture have studied and written about the topic that Schein's ideas are perhaps a bit tired. Any examination of "post-Schein" models would demonstrate that his fundamental notion has only been "tuned," not replaced. Hofstede's ideas, too, have endured, despite discomfort on the part of some scholars about his generalizations about how entire societies behave.[21] Others have essentially built on Schein's ideas, adding, for example, diagnostic tools to define a company's culture and its issues, often using quantitative measuring methods. A frequently cited successor to him, Daniel R. Denison, draws similar conclusions: "an organization's culture may be seen as a code, a logic, and a system of structured behaviors and meaning that have stood the test of time and serve as a collective guide to future adaptation and survival."[22] Such characteristics help to explain why the concept of corporate culture is abstract, even fuzzy, although we know it when we see it.

Since the late 1950s and extending deep into the 1990s, management experts in academia and consulting often turned for inspiration to Edith Penrose, who added to the complexity of the issue by pointing out that corporate boundaries are not precise either: "the administrative boundaries in each of the linked firms may become increasingly amorphous and the effective extent to which any individual firm exercises control is often not at all clear."[23] Rooted in any definition of a corporate culture, then, is the understanding of what a culture is. In her words, "a firm is essentially a pool of resources the utilization of which is organized in an administrative framework."[24] The bigger the firm, the more "coordination" (her term) that is required to get things done. That is why so much of our book focuses on the role of management in doing just that, and their tool of choice and necessity is the use of corporate culture and its methods and tools. These methods and tools are derived from "internally generated knowledge within firms that is required" to get the work done.[25] But as a wise senior historian, Peter Burke, points out to his students, "'Culture' is a concept with an embarrassing variety of definitions."[26]

I have no quarrel with these definitions, or with Schein's cultural framework or Denison's discussions about "culture climate," because they are valid.[27] However, it will be demonstrated that none of these ideas appeared serendipitously. Senior management can purposefully create, encourage, enforce, and reward behaviors that support their worldview. Schein repeatedly made the same point over the years: "culture is fertilized in any work group by how that group is managed, by the daily behavior of leaders, by the incentive systems they create, by what they pay attention to and measure."[28] Our book illustrates much of this behavior. To the degree that management can align these activities and values with a successful strategy for running an organization, they conform to Schein's formal definition. Their values and behaviors become the property of the entire community of employees.[29] For example, artifacts are diverse, from dress codes and office humor to rituals, all of which everyone in an organization will recognize as part of their work world, a component of their culture, and tangible evidence of its existence. Employees create many of the physical artifacts in an impromptu manner, while management purposefully deploys most rituals and values. The two are entwined into visible elements.

Espoused values are expressed in writing, speeches, and conversations and through an organization's rules of behavior. In our case study, I show that IBM's management spent considerable energy implementing values. Again, as with artifacts, values have to align with successful strategies, and when they do not, they deteriorate, or at a minimum become the subject of internal debates. I demonstrate that this is, in fact, what happens, using IBM as our teaching case. Regarding shared basic assumptions, I illustrate how these are not assumed but articulated and "sold" to employees and that these need to be embedded, as Schein argues. Historians have almost universally agreed that in IBM's case values and behaviors were not just taken for granted but were constantly and overtly reinforced by multiple generations of management.[30] Thus, although surveys and measures of corporate culture are fashionable, the fuzziness of the topic lends itself to a more qualitative discussion of its role in companies, and so that is the fundamental approach I have taken in this book.

For example, since the start of Schein's research in the 1970s, others have suggested that effective corporate cultures required a highly engaged community involving all employees. They spent the 1980s and 1990s documenting cases, emphasizing management's role in fostering such behavior.[31] Our study validates that observation by describing specific examples. One lesson to be drawn from these cases is how comprehensive and widespread such activity had to be to make IBM's culture successful and later, as Gerstner suggested, to become a major inhibitor to further success.[32]

In addition to Schein, we draw on the work of John P. Kotter and James L. Heskett on the links between corporate culture and performance.[33] This may sound like an intramural sporting event since Schein taught at the Alfred P. Sloan School of Management at MIT and the other two taught nearby at the Harvard Business School. Each reflected cultural attributes of their environments—MIT the more academic style, Harvard the more managerial—so this provides a good blend for our project and, as a sideline, a slight example of varying academic cultures. Collectively, the three scholars remind us that when exploring business history one should understand purpose for actions, because motives for these lie barely disguised, often stated openly by management. Theory is useful for perspective, but theories must yield to effective execution, as we do in this book when each chapter explains an aspect of corporate culture and then moves quickly to how it was implemented or manifested.[34] Explaining why such events occurred returns us to theory and why Schein proved convenient to keep in mind as an intellectual navigational tool. From such an exercise, one can draw lessons to assist in addressing today's challenges.

Kotter and Heskett agree with Schein and others that circumstances and problems to be solved help shape a corporate culture. They add, however, the obvious reminder that while corporate cultures can be stable for considerable periods of time—a finding demonstrated in this book—they do not remain static, and "sufficient crisis" can wreak havoc on them. In addition, the lack of "perpetuating mechanisms" can cause the decline of organizational culture. In our study, we find the latter not to have been so much the case at IBM. In fact, the opposite was so, as the culture endured despite changing externalities crashing against corporate strategies no longer effective in the face of changing market realities. Kotter and Heskett drew four conclusions to keep in mind in studying corporate cultures. They are worth listing:

1. Corporate culture can have a significant impact on a firm's long-term economic performance.
2. Corporate culture will probably be an even more important factor in determining the success or failure of firms in the next decade. [They published this comment in 1992.]
3. Corporate cultures that inhibit strong long-term financial performance are not rare; they develop easily, even in firms that are full of reasonable and intelligent people.
4. Although tough to change, corporate cultures can be made to be more performance enhancing.[35]

My findings reaffirm their first and second observations, especially for the period from 1914 through the 1980s; the third warrants further research; and the fourth was partially affirmed through IBM's experience beginning in the 1990s. I say "partially" because although the company lived in crisis in the early 1990s, this specific crisis was short-lived, and IBM did not experience a longer-term one until 2012, leaving open the question of whether their fourth observation is true. The research results of many scholars demonstrate that when the work of individuals is linked well to a company's objectives, the firm does well; when it is fractured, the opposite is true.[36]

All three students of corporate culture come back to management as the key ingredient in shaping and managing culture. I do the same in this book. All four of us agree that management's role in creating and sustaining a culture is the direct result of their personal practices and is why chapter 4 is devoted to the recruitment and training of IBM's managers. In fact, Kotter and Heskett devote the last chapter of their book to describing the role of management in creating and sustaining corporate cultures.[37] While in hindsight, their observations seem obvious and are demonstrated in this book, such as the need to create a vision, implement practices that reinforce the vision, and so forth, for the historian, they become useful for studying the broader context of twentieth-century business history and, for management, for how to turn these insights into productive realities.[38]

In IBM's case, we see a century of changing technologies, but with considerable stability in that aspect of its world from the 1890s to the end of World War II, a period when IBM had time to develop a broad and sophisticated culture of success. The culture was so strong that in the subsequent nearly half century, one characterized by significant changes in technology (the emergence of the mainframe computer), it endured for both its employees and customers. This was so because management was willing to establish a point of view on how to use technology, deploy classic sales culture behavior of slapping a proposal (or perspective) on someone's desk, or plant an idea in an employee's mind (usually a male manager's). In the absence of credible options, this strategy worked.[39]

We have the example of Gerstner altering IBM's culture and behavior so directly that it should not be lost to the reader, buried in his memoirs. He was emphatic about what needed to be changed and committed to getting it done. In his words: "'There are no ifs in my vernacular,' I said. 'We are going to do it. We're going to do it together. This is going to be a group of change agents— people who are imbued with the feeling of empowerment and opportunity for our colleagues and us. Those readers uncomfortable with it should think about doing something else. Those of you who are excited about it, I welcome you to the team, because I sure can't do it alone.'"[40] The Cambridge professors would have understood, especially his list of what to change. It is worth quoting at length:[41]

FROM	TO
Product Out (I tell you)	Customer In (in the shoes of the customer)
Do It My Way	Do It the Customer's Way (provide real service)
Manage to Morale	Manage to Success
Decisions Based on Anecdotes & Myths	Decisions Based on Facts & Data
Relationship-Driven	Performance-Driven & Measured
Conformity (politically correct)	Diversity of Ideas & Opinions
Attack the People	Attack the Process (ask why *not* who)
Looking Good is Equal to or More Important Than Doing Good	Accountability (always move the rocks)
United States (Armonk) Dominance	Global Sharing
Rule-Driven	Principle-Driven
Value Me (the silo)	Value Us (the whole)
Analysis Paralysis (100+%)	Make Decisions & Move Forward with Urgency (80 percent/20 percent)
Not Invented Here	Learning Organization
Fund Everything	Prioritize

IBM employees then and now would argue that many of the things he wanted had long been part of their culture, and so he did not get it all "right." The case studies we present provide evidence that they were partially correct, but that is beside the point. The message he was delivering was to offer a perspective of how the enterprise should operate expressed in terms of behavior—culture—and then how this should be implemented. Gerstner recognized that the company he came into had a thick, well-established set of values, rituals, and behaviors that he had to work with, leverage, or change. The centrality of a CEO's work is managing culture. Almost every chapter in our book demonstrates this essential truth.

In recent years, a dialogue between those advocating relationship-oriented cultures and those advocating information-oriented cultures has developed. For example, IBM's employee, Hofstede, after leaving the firm wrote extensively about managerial styles manifested in the behavior of people of different nationalities. His ideas, and the ideas of others, such as anthropologist Edward

T. Hall, regarding the behavior of international businesses, suggested multiple styles exist.[42] Their thinking, and particularly Hofstede's, indicated that American managers operate without as much recourse as European managers, and thus, the latter are more individualistic. Managers raised in American and other Anglo-Saxon cultures (Dutch famously too) tend to be more direct in their language and gain efficiency through competitive actions. Their behaviors are characterized as information oriented, whereas European and Latin American managers generally rely on connections and high context and thus are described as relationship oriented. The latter achieve results by reducing transactions costs. American managers are examples of the first type, Japanese of the second.[43] IBM employed managers of both styles, but American approaches predominated.

Corporate language has embedded in it cultural styles. Multinational corporations require that the majority of their employees have a working knowledge of a universal language. In IBM's case, it was English; for centuries in the Catholic Church, it was Latin; at Phillips, it was Dutch, and so forth. Students of corporate managerial styles often look for the cultural baggage inherent in language and, to a lesser extent, associated national cultural features for insights about a company's style of operations. These approaches allow scholars to study use of language, what nonverbal behaviors to label as important, Schein's notions about values of course, and how companies and their managers think and make decisions.[44]

While these various issues were purposefully not selected for examination in our book for reasons explained later, they are emerging from what historians of business culture are able to learn. Already the cultural anthropological approach has established that "culture affects thinking and behavior."[45] This is important to corporations as they shape their hiring practices around the world. Diversity of styles is desirable but also, simultaneously, is conformity to a corporate monolith. Today, hiring locals by local national managers is seen as a crucial requirement. IBM had been doing that since at least the 1920s, as we discuss in the final chapter where we explain how IBM was able to create a high degree of monolithic behavior worldwide. Employees likened this achievement to what the Catholic Church accomplished centuries earlier.

A second finding is that boards of directors of U.S. companies tended to be overwhelmingly populated with Americans, with the result that they often omitted taking into account other contextual issues and styles prevalent in other countries. IBM was guilty of the same until the last quarter of the twentieth century when it began slowly to add board members of other nationalities. Historians will find that the adjective *slowly* accurately describes IBM's change in its board members' nationality.[46]

Students of innovation practices have long understood that corporate culture affects the ability of firms to compete regardless of the industry in which they operate. Michael L. Tushman, professor at the Harvard Business School, like his late colleague, Clayton Christensen, has spent decades exploring how to innovate to overcome the latter's conundrum about the innovator's dilemma, which has caused angst and is essential to understand by strategists.[47] Tushman identified practical, evidence-based managerial activities for companies to innovate in the face of constant changes, such as occur in the information technology industries, among others. His approaches are practical and work, and one of the reasons why they do is because management can use corporate culture "as a social control system."[48] Tushman argues that a well-functioning corporate culture "can be a source of competitive advantage," as he demonstrates through the experiences of Amazon, Netflix, and Nordstrom, or it can be a corporate killer, as in the cases of Sears Roebuck and Kodak. Second, he demonstrates that senior managers can change corporate culture, citing IBM and Microsoft as examples.[49] In our book, we go further to demonstrate how IBM did this long before the academics began exploring the role of corporate culture and, in the process, reaffirm his thinking. Like Tushman, management at IBM learned to create variant corporate subcultures when needed, such as when they wanted a part of the business to be entrepreneurial (e.g., in developing the PC outside the normal product development process) or more stable (e.g., in account management and products for the mainframe business).

Because he is as explicit as Schein, Tushman's key messages are listed, as they are relevant to historians and to today's management. He identifies five mechanisms—*levers* in his language—that are currently used by senior management in firms that have strong corporate cultures, cultures that are well aligned with a firm's strategies. His many steps can be summarized by listing the types deployed, all of which were in evidence in IBM by the 1920s and extended through the 1980s and then in modified form by the end of the 1990s. They are "Leader Actions," "Involvement in Social Activities and Ceremonies," "Clear Signals Through Stories, Specialized Language, and Symbols," "A Carefully Aligned Reward System," and "Aligned HR Systems."[50] If Tushman's ideas appear vaguely familiar it is because they align with Schein's, adding a layer of specificity on how one should use corporate culture and contributing to a growing collection of thinking that makes the notion of corporate culture less ambiguous or "fuzzy," the latter a descriptor often used but, thanks to Schein and Tushman, increasingly becoming an inaccurate adjective.

Business historians have paid attention to bits and pieces of corporate culture, which inform our book. Much of their work and that of economists up to the 1950s treated national economic and business cultures as homologous. Chance and contingency had little influence in such worldviews. Variations in local cultures and their influence on business practices remained absent.[51] Multinational corporations are now viewed as multifaceted communities held together by worldwide cultural norms shared by many. This book about IBM's behaviors focuses largely on those worldwide values and behaviors, knowing that local variants existed. As a small example, for nearly the entire twentieth century, it was IBM's policy that no alcoholic beverages could be served at company functions. If an American IBM employee had a martini for lunch with a customer, they were expected (instructed in many instances) to go home for the rest of the day. However, in Brazil, employees drank beer at company social events as early as the 1920s, and in IBM's cafeterias in France, one could buy wine with their lunch in any decade.

The IBM case suggests a timing complexity. At an aggregate level—say shared beliefs and values—the company appeared and was largely monolithic in its practices and behaviors. In what those were, change came very slowly. On the other hand, within parts of the organization, subcultures flourished; these changed far quicker because they responded more specifically to such realities as changing customer and market conditions, competition, and economic and regulatory forces. Thus, PhD computer scientists varied in their backgrounds and behaviors from, say, field engineers who installed and maintained hardware, with many having come into IBM from similar roles in the military. As the chapter on humor demonstrates, everyone thought salesmen lived in their own world. In this book, we focus on the macroculture, less so on the micro, drawing examples from the latter to explain the larger perspective.

For a long time, historians ignored culture, most notably one of their most respected business historians, Alfred D. Chandler, Jr., who essentially paid little attention to the topic per se. However, he needs to be defended. His central focus, endorsed by his generation of historians and just as important for someone working in a business school or business management, was strategy. Strategy was then—as now—central to the success of an enterprise. So, the topic was logical for his generation to study, particularly about how strategy was implemented. One of the findings about IBM's culture is how closely its creation and nurture were in support of the company's strategy. It grew out of what senior managers wished to accomplish and how they went about doing so. The facets of IBM's culture described here use language Chandler would have found familiar: vision, purpose, objectives, plans for implementation, steps taken and adjusted as need be, measures of progress, and processes for evolving them. The culture described here demonstrates that weak strategies caused negative alterations or atrophy of the company's culture. In short, strategy and culture were entwined. Strategy came first, culture second. So, we need Chandler's insights as a base in order to take the next step toward understanding how culture became part of the company's work. It is a matter of putting horses in front of carts. We can see the results of getting right the sequence of historical research. Schein blessed the value of historical perspective, too: "it always helps to think historically about the organizations you are observing."[52] He gave credit to a firm's founders for getting things started; we do too.

Historians after Schein increasingly studied corporate cultures, largely following his signposts for what to explore, such as values and rituals.[53] They joined consultants in discussing corporate cultures as either functional or dysfunctional.[54] Historian Kenneth Lipartito celebrated that in recent years historians have been learning from cultural theory to inform their work. Our book does too. He explained what is increasingly happening: "Rather than reducing culture to a function or effect of social structure, it starts from the position that all experience is mediated through some symbolic or linguistic system. Symbolic expression is necessary to social structure and action, because people can only coordinate behavior, gather information, make decisions, and react to their environment through some framework of meaning. Even when it is utilitarian and instrumental, action is also meaningful." Culture "constitutes . . . the social order."[55] Context and why people behaved in certain ways have become part of what historians are now exploring.[56] Symbols are important, as demonstrated when we use the methods of material culture studies. In that context, a coffee mug or a lapel pin has much to teach us.

We should add that the multiplicity of definitions and concepts pointed out by Peter Burke spills over into the objects studied here, such as coffee mugs and humorous cartoons. While I use the term *material* to categorize the several case studies, even here definitions vary. The very same Peter Burke calls these "cultural artifacts," a characterization with which I agree, but then he suggests historical study of these is more an exercise in "social" history, with which I would disagree slightly, as I think a more "cultural" form of study makes sense, at least with respect to IBM at this time.[57] Yes, we are splitting hairs, but that is what good scholars consider useful exercises, especially early in their understanding of a new issue to explore.

Business historians have carved out topics for their studies related to corporate cultures. David E. Nye wrote about General Electric's "Image Worlds," Stephen Harp explored the role of Michelin's anthropomorphic tire man in humanizing the tire business and giving the firm a French quality to its image, and Mark W. Fruin explored the philosophical dimensions of the Japanese firm Kikkoman that so relied on Confucianism.[58] The list is long. As historians dig deeper into corporate culture, the more a new subfield of historical research becomes important—the role of information. They are beginning to describe entire information ecosystems embedded in company cultures and the information infrastructures that support these. My own research on these twin issues—information ecosystems and information infrastructures— confirms the congruity of both ideas and their link to corporate cultures.[59] One is tempted to comment that information studies are finally beginning to move scholarship on business cultures sufficiently to overcome the long-lived problem that corporate culture has been a challenging, fuzzy notion. As with other aspects of history, historians strive for specificity, seek clarity of motives, and at a minimum identify a menu of topics to explore in order to understand a corporation's culture. For that matter, these aspirations apply to the identity and behaviors of entire industries, a subject in need of similar cultural historical research.[60]

Meanwhile, historians have been exploring the role of culture and consumption (e.g., advertising), material culture and design (I, too, in this book), and business in everyday life as part of a larger social order. This last topic is important because much has been written about the role of such famous business leaders as Henry Ford, Thomas J. Watson, Sr., and Alfred Sloan, among others, in promoting the new industrial order of the Western world since the 1870s.[61] In short, in recent decades, historians have moved to integrate business and cultural history across a number of dimensions, with new ones appearing more frequently in the past three decades. The history of information is one example. They are learning that cultural matters may take them to the core, to the center of the activities of modern companies and multinational corporations.[62]

What the Study of Material Cultures Can Teach Us About Corporate Culture

The study of "material cultures" is essentially about exploring what objects have to teach us about historical contingency, social conditions, and the behaviors, values, and practices of people. Historians of material cultures view items as "alternative sources" to the more widely studied documentary records.[63] Think of objects as three-dimensional historical records. One can conjure up images of archeologists in khaki shorts and pith helmets with tooth and paint brushes sweeping sand away from broken pots, bones, or Indian arrowheads. Other than the fact that today's sand brushers wear American-styled baseball caps, it is not an inaccurate mental metaphor for our purposes. Economic and social historians have long studied objects for insights about what their users did with them and how they affected such issues as trade, transportation of goods, forms of capitalism, and their role in various societies and social classes.[64] One might even add into the mix histories of automobiles, personal computers, and airplanes, although historians of technologies would claim these as their own.[65] There remains much debate on how to proceed in the study of these, even about the formulation of "thing theory."[66]

We will not engage with these issues here, but I do further discuss how historians treat the subject in chapter 7. Rather, we move to a new proposal: that the methods of material objects historians use can and should be applied to the study of corporate culture. That has barely started to be done. It lends itself to becoming an integral part of how one can help explain a corporation's culture because objects are tangible, visible evidence of the beliefs and behaviors of an enterprise. They have much to teach us about a company, information that is different than what documents can teach us alone. So, they are more than souvenirs, reminders of careers well lived. Leave aside products with a corporate brand, which have been studied for decades, and focus on objects used by employees, their families, and customers to learn about their various relationships.

We have many such items to draw upon, originating in the nineteenth and twentieth centuries when, for example, in the latter period "corporate clothing" went beyond being uniforms. Employees wearing baseball caps with the name of a tractor or truck manufacturer emblazoned on the front or similarly embossed T-shirts turned people into human billboards, while their owners were proudly identifying with an enterprise. Harley-Davidson's motorcycle culture comes to mind as a high art of social identity for riders and employees so central to the company's success. Nothing speaks more about reputation and commitment to a way of life than a tattoo of a Harley on one's arm. Corporate items were more than just souvenirs of a vacation. The connections with corporate objects tended to be more intimate and long lasting. For example, people did not normally wear IBM-logoed baseball caps unless they were or had been an employee of the company. Go to eBay and type in the name of any multinational corporation and one will be presented with an impressive array of corporate logoed items, from coffee mugs and postcards to clothing, pencils and pens, plaques with company sayings, every conceivable office paraphernalia, and even one-off commemorative plates, lapel pins, and cufflinks. These all have something to tell us about a company when studied the way an archeologist explores ancient Egyptian containers or Roman Empire wine mugs. Rummage through a retiree's personal collection of memorabilia and one will find mixed together in the same cardboard box photographs, letters, certificates, logoed medallions, lapel pins, a coffee mug or two, a few pencils, and plastic credenza dust collectors. Each item has a story attached to it of importance to the collector. Few archivists or even museums keep in one container such mixed items organized under the name of the owner.[67]

In this book, we test the value of studying material objects by looking at such items as coffee mugs, lapel pins, and postcards—items ignored by business historians and the archivists who build documentary collections for them to study. We extend the material culture analogy to a paper-based one that, too, is ignored largely by historians and archivists: the study of photocopied humor circulating in an organization that was never intended to be the official (or serious) representation of a firm or its archival record. Each has much to teach us about corporate culture, and each is intended to be an argument in favor of more studies about the beliefs and behaviors of a firm in ways Schein would understand. Studying postcards or coffee mugs does not need to be a trivial or eccentric exercise; these are multidimensional documents saturated with social and cultural meanings. In this book, we barely touch the subject of material culture even though we devote four chapters to it. An entire book about just one firm—IBM—and its three-dimensional remains could be written, as there is that much to study. There is too much of it to ignore any longer.

These material objects can be made out of anything, from plastic or metal to cloth and china, but so too, we propose, out of paper. In this book, we link examples of physical objects to paper-based ephemera that are normally ignored and to the more academic understanding of what constitutes the study of corporate culture. Put another way, relying just on traditional archival records is not good enough. Even the paper items upon which most of this book relies seem more like material culture evidence than the more seriously taken ephemera available in archives and libraries. That is so much the case that one would be challenged to find examples of these ephemera in a business archive: congratulatory letters welcoming someone to a company as a new IBMer, employee performance appraisals of actual workers, tickets or invitations to a company-hosted family event, or a photograph of a child sitting on Santa Clause's lap at a company country club in 1955. The list is endless. How is one to study these items and, more important, integrate them into other sources and academic theories regarding corporate behaviors to develop a fuller history of an enterprise? In search of an answer, we examine such objects with prior knowledge of the larger picture of how a company formed, grew, matured, and performed. It turns out it can be done. The message is that material culture studies should be applied as yet another tool for understanding business history.

The discussion about the role of objects raises yet another question that ties back to strategy, the role of corporations, and Chandler's work. Much that an enterprise does today to create value is the result of financial engineering, tax management, increasing the value of its stock, lobbying for regulatory advantages, or ideas, "intellectual ephemera." Thomas Piketty and Shoshana Zuboff have raised concerns about companies creating value out of bits and bytes, of coins and capital, yet in earlier times, enterprises largely made things.[68] As Mark Miodownik reminded us, "stuff matters."[69] Corporations, too, are objects of society, combinations of physical things like people, buildings, and products strapped together by a culture and a society's acceptance. As retirees on their websites do so often, they wax about their time in a corporation by illustrating an object, including a company's products and building interiors. If a customer, for example, one might see a programmer post a picture of themselves next to an IBM terminal or inside a data center. The point is, humans relate to products and societies have long valued physical products. But if Piketty and Zuboff are right, is the production of "material stuff" declining or, worse, evaporating? If so, what are the implications for management? Do they create more value, say for IBM, by hiring a brilliant CFO or an R&D genius who invents the next information processing device that sustains the company's revenue stream and profits for years to come? When does a corporation become so big and important in a society that its culture affects millions of people, while their role as a protector and nurturer of that society becomes essential for everyone's well-being? In other words, does, say, Facebook naming its driveway into its corporate headquarters Hacker Way reflect its current responsibility to everyone or is it an immature relic of the past? The study of material culture is not an abstract intellectual exercise; it speaks to the tangible realities facing management in any large institution and those that aspire to grow, regardless of the size of their revenue stream and number of employees.

Introducing *The* International Business Machines (IBM) Corporation

IBM was formed in 1911 out of several small American companies that sold mostly information processing equipment, including scales, time recorders for industrial uses, clocks, and punch-card tabulating equipment. In 1924, it adopted its current name, IBM. Its longest-serving leader, Thomas J. Watson, Sr. (1874–1956), thought the firm so unique that he caused every generation of employees to refer to IBM as "*The* IBM Company." It became so pervasive a practice that even today, over a half century after his death, employees speak that way without knowing it may be the only large company that informally attached *The* to its name. Over the course of its history, IBM employed approximately a million people in over 170 countries who generated in excess of a trillion dollars in revenue.[70] It leased tabulating equipment for its first half century to many of the world's largest enterprises and government agencies. By the end of the 1960s, it had become the world's largest supplier of digital computers, often commanding 70 to 80 percent of all computer sales in a nation.[71]

Before moving forward with our history of IBM, pause to consider the magnitude of its fundamental achievement—a long corporate life. As Tushman and others have reminded their readers, only a very small percentage of American firms even survive to the age of forty (0.1 percent). By 1976, only 10 percent even lasted ten years, and large enterprises might only last an additional six to fifteen years. Between 1962 and 1998, out of some 1,000 large enterprises, only 160 survived. In other words, companies do not even live as long as a human being. Conversely, well-run enterprises can go from one success to another for a very long time. As Tushman puts it, "companies have no obvious biological limitations to their continued success," even if they tend to "perish."[72] Now return to IBM's subsequent turbulent period in its history.

In the 1980s, IBM promoted use of personal computers in government and business. It became a major participant in cloud computing and artificial intelligence in the next century. It is the longest-surviving supplier of data processing equipment and software. One would be challenged to find any observer of the company's behavior, or employee memoirist, who did not think the company's corporate culture profoundly influenced its performance. Its culture was always at the center of any explanation of IBM's behavior.[73] Also remarkable is how consistent and resilient to change were many manifestations of this culture from the 1920s through the 1980s, before beginning to transform in dramatic fashion, but with many of its core beliefs and practices intact, if altered, into the next century. Just as remarkable, many of its rituals and artifacts remained essentially the same, even though the culture as a whole had sufficiently drifted away from its earlier effective alignment with market realities and now had to be adjusted to conform to the world of the late twentieth century.

IBM's culture is difficult to summarize briefly as it has been articulated, expanded upon, and transformed over the course of a century with many hands kneading the dough. But, in essence, it boiled down to several foundational concepts, referred to internally as its Basic Beliefs, whose descriptions evolved over the decades. These were routinely quoted on plaques that hung in thousands of offices, some carved in wood, others molded in metal, and yet many hundreds of thousands in plastic and paper. For decades, every new manager received one or more variations of these. They all said the same things: "Respect for the Individual," which meant "Respect for the dignity and the rights of each person in the organization"; "Customer Service," which translated as "To give the best customer service of any company in the world"; and "Excellence," which called up "The conviction that any organization should pursue all tasks with the objective of accomplishing them in a superior way."[74] A son of the first president of IBM, Thomas J. Watson, Jr. (1914–1993), codified these in speeches and writing during the 1950s and 1960s.[75] Generations of employees shaped their behavior, company practices, and decisions within the context of these Basic Beliefs. IBM's first CEO from outside the firm in nearly eighty years, Louis V. Gerstner, Jr., expressed surprised respect for how seriously employees embraced these three creeds.[76]

Executives and managers, in turn, instilled these in their employees. Employee opinion surveys documented the almost universal acceptance of these as the core operating principles of the company for decades, even though one could expect that their implementation varied from place to place and over time.[77] The Basic Beliefs composed a sales ethos, underpinned by a sense of optimism and confidence, the former reflecting faith that business and personal opportunities abounded and the latter that they knew how to seize upon these. A trillion dollars of revenue later, and after decades of often being seen as one of the best-managed companies, these beliefs seemed to ring true, even during periods of business downturns. The reality of success combined with these beliefs goes far to explain why rituals and other behaviors reinforced them over many decades. The culture called upon employees to behave in certain ways, abiding by both unwritten and later documented forms of ethical and legal standards, to Schein's point.[78]

The culture that emanated from these Basic Beliefs had sufficient flexibility baked into it to allow the firm to respond effectively to its markets for decades. Tushman refers to such flexibility as "ambidexterity," or the ability to tolerate multiple subcultures that made it possible, for example, to run a stable business while simultaneously nurturing future markets and products through the application of an entrepreneurial culture that, in practice, functions different than the more widespread "business as usual" one in the firm. That capability is challenging to implement, was evident in IBM in different ways over the past century, and proved sufficiently effective for Tushman to study how IBM did it.[79]

It is understandable that people who did not spend years at IBM might find it difficult to appreciate how central the Basic Beliefs were to the work of this company. The closest analogies from outside the firm one can point to might be to the theology of the Catholic Church or to the values expressed by Western military forces. In the Catholic Church, it would be the Trinity and such notions as the role of love, charity, and hope. In the military, it would be the centrality of patriotism, acceptance of personal responsibility to defend and care for fellow combatants, and dedication to "the mission."[80] As in these institutions, IBM's Basic Beliefs were articles of faith, guiding lights for how to make decisions and know what is valuable. Every business school student learns about the Tylenol crisis in 1982, when employees learned that some containers had been contaminated with poison, killing seven people, and about how nearly instantly, and before waiting for instructions from headquarters, employees all over the United States rushed to pull supplies of these products off drugstore shelves. It was the proudest moment in Johnson & Johnson's history. It was also its corporate culture in action.

Generations of IBM's customers relied upon that kind of predictable behavior motivated by an understood set of beliefs (values) in what was always a risky endeavor—use of complex data processing technologies—to such an extent that between the 1960s and the 1980s the quip was, "Nobody ever got fired for buying IBM." Customers became part of IBM's larger information and technology ecosystem. To be an IBM customer, or have a child working at IBM, was a proud distinction.[81] That was "Big Blue." To have an ex-IBM employee working as an employee of a customer was tantamount to having someone who practiced the Basic Beliefs in another part of the larger IBM ecosystem, and possibly drinking their coffee out of an IBM-logoed mug, while colleagues in the data center were using IBM publications with which to understand computers.

Senior management took seriously the image that IBM created for itself as a trusted member of the business community. Nowhere was this more evident than in curating and protecting IBM's logo. When Watson Sr. came to IBM, the company was called C-T-R, standing for the first letter of the three companies merged together in 1911. It was as unimaginative as, say, calling a firm the ABC Company, and all three failed to collaborate with each other. Watson Sr. fixed that problem and, in February 1924, changed the name of the firm to International Business Machines. At that time, IBM introduced its first global logo: a round image symbolic of the world with the company's name in the middle. In 1947, a simple IBM logo replaced it with a solid black **IBM**, and in 1956, it was modified again by the famed designer Paul Rand. The first of the pinstriped IBM logos appeared in 1972 and periodically underwent additional changes.[82] In each instance, development and use of the logo, a patent, and copyright permissions were controlled out of corporate headquarters in the United States.

Since the 1940s, a small staff has monitored and controlled its use, defining the technical printing details, color specifications, and where the logo could be positioned on a product, publication, or memento. They have carefully policed its use. To put the IBM logo on a memento required the staff's permission. When divisions sought to produce an item, its legal staff had to show corporate what they proposed. Normally that process worked for decades, with one partial exception: coffee mugs. However, since the violators of procedure produced perhaps hundreds of mugs (or fewer), they were able to avoid detection. Some logoed items had special status and protection; most notably, the THINK lettering in all capital letters was nearly the private preserve of Watson Sr. who brought it to C-T-R and promoted its use constantly for the rest of his life. The formal use of logos, even the design and "look and feel" of machines; all manner of publications, even stationery; and all communications with employees, customers, and the rest of the world were largely managed out of New York. Local country headquarters provided necessary foreign language versions of text but always conformed to the brand images IBM wanted worldwide.[83] We discuss each of these throughout the book because they are important cultural markers for scholars and today's management.

But why was so much attention paid to these details, such as on the company's three-letter logo? Like so many other corporations, when it was small before World War II and a giant afterward, management at both corporate and country levels paid close attention to the nurturing of an institutional image that Watson Sr. had drummed into their heads was essential to the success of IBM, in historian Roland Marchand's telling, "to cultivate a corporate personality." In this, Watson Sr. was not alone; every major American and European corporation was then, as now, fixated on its public image. That fixation drove advertising agendas for over a century, style designs of products, and the language used to communicate their offerings.[84] Watson and subsequent IBM managers borrowed ideas from other corporations, such as NCR, General Motors, Ford, and AT&T.[85]

More specifically at IBM, the company took extra steps following World War II to completely renovate its image to give it a more contemporary look.

The company had many fragmented images that needed addressing, from equipment with black Queen Anne legs to products made of stainless steel, to oriental carpets in executive offices, to machines looking more like furniture than technological marvels. As one of the architects of the new image, Eliot F. Noyce reported, "what IBM really does is to help man extend his control over his environment," and that was what all design work done in the post–World War II period centered on.[86] Shaping corporate culture and images was about management, a control function, which its historian described as its purpose, "to establish a material regime by, for, and of the logic of organization."[87] Watson Jr. reinforced Noyce's thoughts, using the language of design mixed with his concern for business results, and declared that "good design can materially help make a good product reach its full potential. In short, we think that good design is good business."[88] Every subsequent IBM CEO embraced similar beliefs and publicly said so to customers, employees, and the public.

Why Study IBM's Corporate Culture?

It is not enough that IBM is an iconic enterprise that has long attracted the attention of historians, business leaders, industry observers, or the media. Nor is it adequate to declare that since it was the largest corporation operating in the computer industry for decades it warrants continuing attention. While both those circumstances are true, for our purposes, they are insufficient justification. IBM was chosen for five reasons, which can be listed briefly, as the chapters make these more explicit.

First, this company survived long enough over multiple generations of management and employees during two world wars, various recessions, and the Great Depression such that one can see how it evolved over time in response to various circumstances. Few enterprises survive their founders' lifetimes, and if they do, they frequently become subsumed into another way of behaving and thus lose their identity and culture. Like Ford Motor Company and, to a lesser extent, Hewlett-Packard, IBM began as bits and pieces in the 1880s, merged those into one loosely configured company in 1911, and yet still operated over a century later. Its corporate culture accounts in part for its longevity. We need to dig into the details of its way of working to defend the case that corporate culture provided a strong assist. As in human life where DNA helps determine a person's longevity, corporate culture plays a similar role in a firm or society.

Second, IBM developed an information ecosystem in which employees, competitors, and customers operated, using IBM's products, but also embracing its views about technology and best ways to operate across all the normal functions of an enterprise. These include product development, sales, personnel practices, finance, and manufacturing, among other tasks. The firm was highly influential. CEO Louis V. Gerstner commented that if he changed the wallpaper in a restroom at corporate headquarters, the *Wall Street Journal* would publish about that action as news the next day because other firms would then want to review IBM's bathroom wallpaper practices to see if these should be adopted. Even in years when the company's fortunes were weak, it retained its influence due to its reputation for effective operations and the experience many people had in dealing with the firm's employees over the course of a century. We need to understand how trust, reputation, and corporate culture intermingled.

Third, it is an enterprise recognized by members of its information eco-system as having developed and sustained a strong corporate culture, but one poorly understood outside the company. It is routinely described in superficial ways without appreciating deeply why or how it formed as it did. Dealing with these concerns is a major focus of this book. IBM memoirists consider the company's culture the essential reason for its success, along with the quality of IBM's employees. There is mystery in the "IBM Way," of how "Big Blue" *really* operated, as if a secret, but it was not so. What our case studies demonstrate is that much of what shaped IBM's culture was open for all to see and can be explained using the historian's tools and methods. Other companies acted similarly, and today's companies can borrow a great deal while learning some mistakes to avoid.

Fourth, IBM's corporate culture endured for decades and, just as interesting, in a common form all over the world. For decades, one could walk into an IBM office anywhere on Earth and instantly see familiar behaviors, even how the space was laid out, just as one could walk into a Catholic church in Cairo, New York, or Hong Kong and recognize similarities to those in Western Europe or the Americas. IBM's Roman Catholic employees marveled at the global univer-sality of the firm, as did executives running other multinational corporations attempting to improve their operations through commonly used processes and corporate cultures.

Fifth, the quantity and diversity of objects and paper ephemera from this company are so great that, if not intimidated by those two realities, there was much to study. IBM has a corporate archive, as do universities (including mine, the University of Minnesota). There are computer museums with IBM prod-ucts. Over sixty books have been published on this company, and every divi-sion in the firm funded a newsletter of some sort. In the 1970s, employees were told that IBM was the world's largest publisher and they believed it because there were multiple manuals in a dozen languages published for each product, many thousands of publications about how individual companies were using IBM's technologies (called "application briefs" in IBM), and other publications explaining how IBM worked or about data processing and computing for the general public and for experts. IBM's employees published in all the techni-cal journals involving computing and in most business ones, too. Some one million people worked for IBM at one time or another, and it would be safe to say that the vast majority of them had at one time or another in their possession physical objects and IBM publications. It is a running joke at IBM that customer engineers—the people who install and fix hardware—keep parts and manuals in their basements and home garages, but for good reason, as they sometimes needed these for work faster than they could obtain them from their office or IBM's suppliers. Systems engineers—those who installed software and debugged software problems—were almost as fixated in hoarding everything from printouts of error-filled programs as their own library of user manuals. In short, there is a great deal of material to be studied.

In combination, these five reasons lead to a basic conclusion: that corporate culture is highly diverse, indeed vast, but management and scholars can profitably study it by examining much ephemera in new ways. In the last chapter, I list topics not discussed to suggest other fruitful areas of investigation, but also to reinforce the message that corporate culture is a broad field about which we know too little. While chosen topics are broad and in evidence in many countries, they represent the tip of the iceberg. But we must start somewhere, and so those selected for our attention were a few of the ones employees discussed the most on their websites and in their memoirs that would inform management in a most immediate way. Scholars have either completely ignored each of these or barely discussed them. Historians interested in IBM or other large corporations will find the majority of this book's content new to them. While historians always delight in presenting new content, the lesson is that the general historical topic of corporate culture has barely been explored to the extent we have come to expect for such others as strategy, biographies of CEOs, and technologies and markets. After reading this book, one should also be able to walk away puzzled, even frustrated, at not learning the boundaries of the general subject of corporate culture's history. That realization should cause us to explore other themes, hopefully not just to fill in more about IBM's business history, but also of some 80,000 other multinational enterprises. In short, corporate cultural history is more aptly *terra incognita* and full of lessons to learn. We turn to how to accomplish this task.

How We Explore IBM's Culture

The approach reflects both what archeologists and cultural historians have found useful and is one that can convey lessons to other scholars and to managers, particularly senior executives. Because most of IBM's corporate culture originated in the United States and was subsequently exported to other countries, the chapters concentrate on the American experience. The last chapter outlines how these behaviors and beliefs were transplanted to other countries.

The topics chosen were important to the company and to its employees over the longest period of time. We have substantive evidence upon which to base descriptions of the topics. I demonstrate how IBM's culture aligned with its strategies, and exploring these links is possible because IBM's business activities have been well documented. We are able to explore IBM's history from the ground up to where it meets the grand histories already written about from the perspective of the top down. An objective is to demonstrate how these histories are entwined. If we can do that for IBM, then we have a model of how it might be done for other company histories. The approach can inform senior management on how to create and sustain their own corporate cultures based on historical experiences.

I admit to a gap in our case study approach: what IBM employees and their families thought about IBM's culture. Outwardly they behaved as the company wanted, and to a large extent, what was required of them was far more consistent with what society expected of employees of large corporations living middle-class lifestyles. Memoirists and social media posters overwhelmingly endorsed the culture but also were not shy about describing its limits. Yet to what extent they disliked or liked the culture is difficult to document with, say, the hard certainty of statistics; however, opinion surveys of the work itself suggested that the vast majority were comfortable with the Grand Bargain of lifetime employment and economically comfortable lifestyles in exchange for doing the bidding of the corporation. Retirees who worked at IBM before the 1990s were generally very complimentary of the work environment at IBM in their comments on retiree websites. There are no extant records of complaints IBMers submitted during the years surveyed in this book, which would provide outstanding evidence of labor-management friction, although they existed. However, anecdotal evidence suggests that when tensions existed these were less about the culture and more about long hours, desires for more pay and career advancement, or some perceived individual mistreatment, for example, by a manager toward one of their charges. Labor historians might find such observations hard to accept, since in so many companies and industries employee-management relations were fraught with difficulties and confrontations. But, in the absence of even small amounts of evidence from the 1910s through at least the 1970s of friction, we have to argue that those seeking evidence of such tensions might have to turn to other manufacturing firms, such as those in the steel and automotive industries, or banks and insurance companies. Even our chapter-length exploration of unionizing activities at IBM demonstrates that turmoil only became serious in the 1980s and even labor's own leadership considered their responses to working conditions and family affairs as rather benign at that time.[89]

My long tenure at IBM suggested both a reason for employees accepting the Grand Bargain and later for being upset as the company began changing it in response to either negative financial results or changing circumstances in societies around the world. The key idea here is probably the values and priorities different generations brought to the firm. Those who came in the period before the 1930s had grown up in the rough-and-tumble world of bad working conditions, poor pay, and arbitrary personnel practices, including firings and hostility toward various minorities (varied by country). So, even a modicum of what today is considered minimum standards of personnel practices were welcomed, and companies like NCR, Ford, and IBM offered these.[90] The generation that lived through the Great Depression of the 1930s and World War II was a different breed. They absolutely and unconditionally insisted on job security; good salaries, benefits, and pensions; and a middle-class standard of living. They wanted to buy homes in the United States and rent spacious apartments in other countries. They wanted dignity and good education for their children.[91] They had served in military forces and government agencies that had prestige and so they wanted that too. IBM delivered on all of these requirements, as did corporations around the world in the three decades following World War II. My generation—the boomers—came into IBM with college degrees and greater interest in bringing in minorities and women into the world of business, and we wanted to have everything the prior generation had, but also more income. Our children's generation (born after roughly 1975) had the same level of education, wanted the same standard of living, but also reminded companies of their moral responsibilities to society and the environment. They also formed different families and so needed differing benefits: families with same-sex marriages, racially mixed families, families with only one parent, and families with both parents working. Before World War II, workers had to be taught the notion of being loyal and dedicated to IBM's overall success. The Greatest Generation understood loyalty and patriotism, so these values just needed nurturing as they were already defined, whereas later, younger employees felt less loyalty to a firm, especially after layoffs became widespread. Today, companies have to fight to keep their employees because they can leave literally by the thousands in days, as happened, for example, at Twitter in late 2022. We will have occasion to address the needs of all these various generations, compounded, too, by the fact that in a large company multiple generations were employed at the same time, almost always in the same buildings, and in every country.

Historians of corporate culture speak about the fundamentals of enduring beliefs, and IBM had its own situated largely around a code of ethics and an ethos of service, the subject of chapter 2. Chapter 3 explains the role of image and reputation and how they were shaped over the course of a century, as interest in sustaining them was an enduring feature of the company's behavior. The chapter extends that discussion to how the company created an image for itself that proved crucial in attracting and retaining employees and customers. The crew that most drove the shaping and implementation of IBM's culture were managers at all levels. This was no accident, as they were purposefully recruited, trained, mentored, and monitored for life. It is a story that has not been told before and so is the subject of chapter 4. Executives in many companies long marveled at how IBM was able to keep unions at bay in the United States, the subject of chapter 5. The topic is an important facet of IBM's history, which historians have not explored at all. Yet the company's culture unlocks the door to how this was done and for what reasons—lessons that many high-tech companies could learn from in the 2020s. IBM was considered a generous company for its benefits programs. In reality, its programs paralleled those of other large enterprises but with a twist, as chapter 6 explains. IBM borrowed practices from other firms but also motivated some customers to adopt practices. The company's broad entwined information ecosystem was designed to keep employees and customers inside the "blue tent." Chapter 7 concerns IBM families, because the company most purposefully integrated them into its ecosystem. Families remain an understudied and underappreciated part of a corporation's ecosystem, and they were a large stakeholder community that spilled out into communities where IBM had a presence.

We then shift to four chapters that demonstrate the kinds of insights one can glean about corporate behavior by studying its material culture. These chapters present evidence that things as seemingly trivial as lapel pins and postcards served as parts of the broader company strategy to create an effective corporate culture. Chapter 8 explores lapel pins and coffee cups, and a few pens for good measure. The company even used postcards to help create its image and culture, and as a consequence, historians can learn from these cards IBM's intentions for its reputation and image, explained in chapter 9. In chapter 10, humor serves as a window into the company's culture from a different perspective, exploring what some employees thought of it. While one could quote employee opinion surveys, if preserved (an unknown at this point), photocopied cartoons and other humor make evident some of the stress points, while suggesting that employees were not as serious as their image suggested. The last chapter in this section, chapter 11, discusses IBM's "gray literature," publications produced by the firm not generally available to the public the way journals and books normally are. The reader would be right to be shocked at how big an operation this was, but also how essential, too, in serving and controlling much larger stakeholder communities in the market, the industry, and science and government.

The final chapter, chapter 12, deals with issues of how the culture went global but, just as important, how it was created in general. There are lessons to be extracted from each chapter that transcend one to the other. These need to be called out, not inferred. There are specific lessons for management, too, that can be drawn from the totality of the case studies explored in this book that will be laid out for their consideration based on the historical record from the 1910s into the 1990s. Because the past is more than just prologue, it is continuation, and because many of the issues IBM and its customers engaged with over the past century are not gone, some are discussed in this chapter. IBM still wrestles with antitrust issues, retaining employees, engaging in innovation and entrepreneurship, and the role of companies in societies and in resolving environmental issues, in how governments and the public want to deal with them, among others.

I also include an introduction to briefly describe how the company's corporate culture has evolved in the past quarter century, as it is shaping up to be substantially different than in earlier decades. Because we are so close to current events and lack the normal evidentiary sources a historian insists on having, this introduction is briefer than a normal chapter but at least demonstrates that corporate cultures evolve and that management has no choice but to engage with these cultures.

Finally, because I am both a historian and a retired nearly forty-year employee of IBM, it is only fair to the readers that they know more about me. I am a student of IBM's culture, but also a reflection of it too, so I added a short précis about myself.

PART I

CASES FROM THE LARGER PICTURE OF IBM'S CORPORATE CULTURE

CHAPTER 2

ROLE OF ETHICS IN CORPORATE CULTURE

Enduring Beliefs at IBM

A sense of integrity, of responsibility, flows through the veins of IBM in a way I've never seen in any other company.

Louis V. Gerstner, Jr.[1]

Louis V. Gerstner, Jr., joined IBM in 1993 to return it to prosperity after several years of declining revenues and profits. By all accounts, and the revenue and profits that followed, he succeeded in quick and dramatic fashion. But it all came at a terrible cost: tens of thousands of employees dismissed or otherwise pushed out of the company and creation of reconstituted lines of business. Many corporate cultural norms discussed in this book transformed and new practices were introduced, while others that that had been discarded were revived.[2] While it all worked out in returning IBM to prosperity, it was a painful period for employees who had grown up in the world described elsewhere in our chapters. Yet, as the epigraph documents, through all the travail, one singular feature of the company was not fully dismantled or temporarily suspended: a core set of beliefs about how the firm should fundamentally operate. Often summed up as the Basic Beliefs—a reasonable bumper sticker codification of fundamental practices—these never quite captured the essence of IBM's core values because employees' views on ethics transcended the three Basic Beliefs—Respect for the Individual, Best

Customer Service, Excellence in All That Is Done—to such an extent that even Gerstner, as CEO with access to any information and authority he might have wanted, needed time, perhaps a number of years, to appreciate fully the role of ethics and their influence on the way employees went about their work. He even admitted so, as he looked back on his near decade-long tenure at IBM: "I was always an outsider."[3] It seemed to every insider at IBM, and eventually to Gerstner, that there was something baked into the culture that endured harm, prosperity, change, varying leadership styles, wars, economic downturns, changing workforces in the company, national variations in social and business norms, and massive technological transformations.

Our purpose, here, is to explain IBM's ethics as they evolved over time into a hardened set of behaviors that were both purposefully implemented through rules and processes and yet instinctive and unconsciously applied. Appreciating IBM's core understanding of the underlying principles even before one turns to any discussion of Basic Beliefs helps to expose much about IBM's corporate culture. This review even helps then to understand the mundane, such as a Quarter Century Club lapel pin, Endicott's IBM "School House," or why employees dared with great courage and moral turmoil to consider embracing unions in the United States.[4] This chapter begins by describing the origins of IBM's ethics, explains the special role of its Business Conduct Guidelines, and then summarizes their results on corporate behavior, before drawing conclusions about IBM's experience.

But there is a larger lesson to illustrate through IBM's behavior and the discussion in this chapter. Companies have embedded in them either unstated beliefs, such as those spun out by local national cultures, or beliefs that are stated explicitly by employees. IBM's experience demonstrates that an enterprise of any size can articulate a set of values that supports its mission and that these can apply over a long period of time. When its senior leaders began formulating their ethical framework for the firm, IBM had only some 3,000 employees, while at its peak with just over 400,000 workers in over 150 countries in the mid-1980s, the beliefs still existed. Why? How? What were their roles in good and bad times? We know they assist in helping employees make quick, wise decisions. So, one must get these right if they are to be embedded purposefully in a corporation because, once there, they become difficult to discard without much trauma and resistance. IBM's beliefs also are a reminder that the values embraced by the Business Roundtable in 2019 are not new. At IBM, they had been around in one form or another for a century; it seems the business community was catching up to an old model of management that had served this enterprise well. More immediate for today's management, IBM's Basic Beliefs had the particularly attractive feature that they could be applied to all of the company's stakeholders, a point made in the last chapter but one that warrants reinforcing as one works their way through the issues discussed in this chapter.

Origins of IBM's Ethics, 1910s–1950s

As with so many facets of IBM's culture, the company's ethics were shaped by Thomas J. Watson, Sr.'s, values and experiences on the one hand and, on the other, by his constancy of purpose and practice for over forty years at the helm (1914–1956). Over time, his beliefs evolved into policies and procedures codified and made evident in all corners of the company. Both his sons reinforced these during their time in senior leadership roles, Arthur K. Watson when running IBM's non-U.S. operations (1949–1970) and his older brother as CEO of all of IBM (1956–1971). Further codification continued as the company grew under the tutelage of Frank Cary (CEO, 1973–1981). The Watson sons and Cary spent their entire business careers at IBM and thus were shaped by the legacy of Watson Sr.'s values and practices. His sons served in the U.S. Army during World War II, where they were exposed to yet another institution with highly articulated values embraced largely up and down a chain of command that, too, endorsed a long existing set of ethics. It was not lost on the sons that such values had improved the performance of the military. As in other chapters, to understand IBM's beliefs and behaviors, we turn first to the work of Watson Sr.

Watson Sr. was no stranger to the brutish behavior of the robber barons of the late nineteenth century. His employer, NCR, even had him run an underground business to knock out competitors in violation of the Sherman Antitrust Act, of which a federal court jury found him and a number of senior executives guilty of violating in 1913. Watson's destiny seemed to be a jail cell. His leading biographer, Kevin Maney, explained the effect on him: "If there was a single moment when Tom Watson changed—when he decided that a squeaky-clean image and reputation were paramount in business and life—this was that moment."[5] Watson's friend Peter Drucker reflected back on Watson's reaction: "People underestimated how badly that trial hurt him" because it "portrayed him as a villain. I don't think he ever recovered from it."[6] Due to other circumstances, he never went to jail, but the scar remained. What he now wanted—felt *had*—to do was demonstrate that he was not dishonest, not a criminal. He chose a different path than some of his contemporaries, so when he came to C-T-R—less than a year and a half since his conviction, he charted an alternative course. From his earliest days at C-T-R, he espoused integrity with the evangelical enthusiasm that so characterized his explanations of IBM's behaviors and practices over the next four decades.[7] Watson Sr. proved so optimistic about the company's future that he did not believe unethical behavior was required to succeed.

As issues came up, he articulated his points of view, and these, too, evolved over time. In the 1930s, IBM confronted antitrust litigation launched by the U.S. Department of Justice concerning his dominance of the punch-card business. He pushed back against this criticism, arguing that IBM had not dominated its markets or acted in an improper manner but rather that it had been successful in selling his offerings. He proved stubborn, but in the end, IBM and the government worked out an agreement. Once again, Watson had faced the challenge of being personally criticized, along with his company. He had been forced to focus on the issue of ethical behavior as defined by antitrust law. It happened again in the 1950s at the end of his career with a similar reaction on his part, but that led to another settlement with the Justice Department, discussed further later.[8] In both instances, he confronted the problem of ethics from a legal point of view, while his company implemented the terms of the two settlements as part of its normal operating practices, always with his approval. He also saw these as personal attacks on him, both challenging his ethics and for running a successful business. For decades, he had preached to his employees that they *personally* take responsibility for their behaviors, not just because Watson Sr. told them to do so. So to be accused of violating his own beliefs in acting on one's values, in questioning the efficacy of what IBM was contributing to society (i.e., businesses and government agencies through modern data processing tools), and hence the quality of his employees' performance, grated on him.

Watson had an even more compelling reason for embracing ethical standards of behavior. He and others selling complex data processing equipment had learned it would be difficult, if not impossible, to do so without establishing trust between his employees and customers because the risk of business failure to a customer in misapplying IBM's expensive equipment was potentially enormous. Without that trust, his employees would fail to persuade anyone to use their products. So, almost from his earliest days at IBM, he imposed on his sales force, in particular, but essentially on everyone else in the company, the notion that there had to be honest recommendations to customers. That meant people really had to study what services were appropriate to ensure they got whatever they said or did right the first time, or they would run the risk of damaging a customer. Honesty proved essential to nurture the long-term relationships with customers needed to establish trust. Further, the "sell cycle" from start of conversations about a potential use of data processing methods to the finish resulting in the installation of a system of machines could take one or more years, while a customer's subsequent need to sustain those systems could last decades. So the mantra became "Service, Service, Service." Watson Sr. tied IBM's value proposition to the idea: "The only reason we have for being in business is to help people to conduct their own individual businesses better by means of the machines and appliances which we manufacture. That assistance is the thing in which business men are interested."[9] From that business requirement came truth, honesty, and a willingness to listen, to be open-minded, to adhere to local and national laws, and to mean what one says and say what one means.

These beliefs were less mandated than promoted. That should be of no surprise as IBM was simultaneously fostering a sales culture, which meant one
would argue for their point of view as a selling conversation. Employees came
to expect to be persuaded to do something; ordering never worked, and every
CEO to the present has made that point. IBM's beliefs were only codified incrementally into formal written practices over time as they demonstrated their
relevance and as IBM's business success continued. That is why Watson Sr.
personally preferred to persuade his employees how best to behave and then
to demonstrate his thinking through his personal behavior. Thus, the Basic
Beliefs that served as the foundation for so much of IBM's corporate culture
emerged in bits and pieces, although quickly, during the 1920s. These did not
become formally codified into a catechism until his son, Watson Jr., put these
down in a book, *A Business and Its Beliefs*, in 1963.[10] Like so many other cultural adaptations, Watson Sr. did not order people to do things a certain way
so much as to put people into management and other leadership roles who
shared his views. While it would be tempting to say his nineteenth-century
Protestant upbringing in central New York was influential, and possibly it had
a contextual effect on him and so many employees about "right" and "wrong"
behavior, he was not known for being a visibly religious practitioner. He had
more specific business reasons.

It is why, for example, he wore conservative suits and included customers among his friends, because he was like them. He never told his salesmen
to wear dark suits; they just emulated his dress code, and so in time, IBMers
were known for wearing blue suits and white shirts. The same can be said to
have occurred with the evolution of IBM's code of ethics. In other words, legal
and business considerations as affected by his experiences and those of other
employees shaped the evolution of the company's behavior and, hence, its ethics. That he remained at the helm for four decades with a worldview on many
matters settled in his mind early in his tenure goes far to explain how the habits
of many cultural features of IBM became the "IBM Way." Development of its
ethics proved to be no exception.

One important example drawn from IBM's Consent Decree of 1956 illustrates
how an action translated into company-wide behavior. Many historians have
described this antitrust episode, so we need only to briefly recall its main features. The U.S. Justice Department was concerned that IBM had monopolistic
control over the punch-card tabulating market and that IBM doing the same in
the computer market would follow this behavior. In 1952, it filed an antitrust suit
against IBM. Watson Sr. wanted to push back not just because the allegations
had a strong Sherman antitrust tone but also because he saw them as an assault
on him, all the while suggesting, too, that being a successful business was criminal. His son, Watson Jr., wanted to quickly resolve the case because tabulators
were the retiring technology, whereas computers represented IBM's future.

After bantering back and forth with his father, Watson Jr. won his consent to negotiate a settlement. Known as the 1956 Consent Decree, it required IBM to make available for sale, and not just for lease, its hardware, which would make it possible for computer dealers to also enter the market with IBM's products and parts. IBM would provide maintenance for dealers' copies of machines at competitive prices. IBM agreed to retire from part of its services business, known as the Service Bureau Corporation.[11] The agreement remained in force for decades, with specific clauses canceled over time. (Remaining ones were finally retired in 1996.) To Watson Sr.'s credit, he threw his support completely behind honoring the terms of the settlement, despite his personal grudge against it. His son had persuaded him to move on for the good of the business. In the process, the consent decree essentially closed the half-century tabulating business at IBM, committing the company's destiny to a new technology called computers. An older generation of employees must have held their collective breadth at this turn of events, but fortunately, they worked in a company that understood how to succeed in a high-tech environment.

This consent decree affected the entire company in the United States and increasingly, too, in other countries. Watson Sr. and his son, Tom, made sure product development plans did not violate the decree. In addition, all employees were personally enjoined by IBM management to adhere to its terms. To make sure that happened, all American employees were sent a copy of the consent decree and were asked to read it. Managers had to understand it, and IBM's lawyers were to make sure nobody violated its terms. When new employees went to Endicott, New York, or attended other initial American training programs, one of the documents they received in their welcome packets was a copy of the decree. They were told in class to read and understand it. Sales staffs, in particular, were pressed to make sure they knew its terms. Lawyers were often invited to speak to new employee classes and routinely at new manager schools about all manner of antitrust issues for decades. This kind of education increased across the entire company during the 1970s and early 1980s, when again IBM faced an antitrust suit filed (subsequently retired) by the U.S. Department of Justice.

For decades after the 1956 decree was signed, when a salesman wanted to negotiate a proposed offering to a customer that might either violate its terms or attack the communities protected by it (e.g., computer leasing companies), they were instructed to consult IBM lawyers or another group called Marketing Practices to see if they could proceed. If not, they and their management were rapidly told so. There was little or no tolerance for deviation from this position. As IBM did with benefits and unions, it relied on management to ensure compliance.

How does a consent decree fit with ethics? Watson Sr. and subsequent CEOs believed that part of a customer's trust in IBM is that it obeyed laws and regulations in a consistently impeccable manner. For international companies doing business with IBM in multiple countries, that was an equally important factor in determining from which firms to acquire high-technology products. Since the 1950s, different countries implemented increasing numbers of laws and regulations to control monopolistic behavior, bribes, and other forms of corruption, all of which IBM remained committed to obeying. To an overwhelming extent, it did. That was made possible by Watson Sr.'s abhorrence of any suspicion of bad behavior by any employee over such a long period of time that, after a few years in the 1920s and certainly by the 1940s, one could not remember a time when such expectations did not exist.

But a second consideration was the attitude of employees. Who wants to be told to do something illegal? Like Watson Sr., American and West European employees, and almost to the same extent Latin American and Asian ones, embraced honesty, truth, candor (often called "straight talk" at IBM), and compliance with clearly articulated company policies and practices. Having those and understanding them made it easier for staffs all over the company to make decisions without always having to run to a superior for guidance. For decades, employees repeatedly read and heard the mantra of reputation and integrity linked to service. These circumstances are what Gerstner was suggesting in the epigraph at the start of this chapter.

During his tenure as CEO, Watson Jr. explained that, "In the normal course of business we will do everything possible to maintain our reputation for service." He observed that, "In time, good service became almost a reflex in IBM."[12] The message to employees was not sugarcoated with polite corporate speak. In mid-century, the admonition was blunt: "IBM must be recognized as an organization with the highest ethical and moral standards in our business relations with customers, suppliers, competition and other businesses." As with all other aspects of IBM's business, company leaders turned to all managers to ensure this happened: "Managers bear primary responsibility for seeing that IBM policies are complied with and that violations are dealt with fairly and decisively."[13] More formally than his father, he delivered the same message to all employees in 1961 through the company-wide newspaper, *Business Machines*, messages that up to that time had been delivered in writing largely to salesmen and those involved in dealing with suppliers. After declaring that high ethical standards were good for business and society, he wrote, "each employee must observe the highest standards of business integrity and avoid any activity which might tend to embarrass IBM or him."[14] He then reprinted the memorandum that purchasers in IBM were already familiar with. Four years later, he reiterated the point to all managers, adding that all people should be treated fairly inside and outside the company to maintain IBM's "reputation for honesty and square dealing." To nail down his admonition, he proclaimed: "I hold every manager personally responsible for insuring that all of his people know our position on this subject."[15] The occasional violator was punished, usually dismissed from the firm, and such actions were not carefully hidden; IBM believed in the periodic public hanging to remind others how to behave.

Role of Business Conduct Guidelines

By the time Watson Jr. published his book-length codification of IBM's values in 1963, *A Business and Its Beliefs*, much of the company's thinking had been converted into policies and practices and articulated to employees at all levels. His explanations benefited from the development of practices emanating from the 1956 Consent Decree. That his articulation of IBM's rules of behavior remained relevant for decades, including during and after IBM's antitrust experiences between the 1960s and 1980s, was evident because new managers attending their initial management training during these years and through the 1980s were given copies of his book as part of their class materials. Even during the turbulent 1990s, when IBM's Basic Beliefs were under attack and even replaced by a set of principles personally written by Gerstner promulgated in September 1993, Watson's book still circulated. Long-term employees did not abandon the old beliefs, or even the language long used to articulate these.[16] Managers had been instructed for decades to personally "observe the highest standards of business integrity," which they took to mean support and practice the Basic Beliefs, the terms and conditions of the 1956 Consent Decree, and relevant business and labor laws in whatever country they worked.[17]

Central to implementation of these guidelines was a publication variously titled over the years that began life as a document but that quickly morphed into a pamphlet called *Guidelines for Business Conduct* and, by the end of the 1970s, *Business Conduct Guidelines*. It explained basic elements of what people could or could not do in the course of their work. Every employee since 1977 was required to read it every year, and many dealing with government officials, customers, and suppliers were required to read it as early as 1961. They were required to sign a form declaring they had done so and that they understood violations of any of its terms could result in punishment or dismissal.[18] It was one of the few sets of company rules that resulted in near certain dismissals, sometimes within days of an infraction, but more normally within several weeks. Its guidance was how IBM connected law and ethics to its operations. Let CEO Frank Cary explain, as he did to all managers in 1977: "Business conduct is not something that can be left to auditors and lawyers. It is the very cornerstone on which our business reputation is built, and is one of our most prized assets."[19] Historians should consider this publication one of the most important affecting behaviors and the shape of decisions in IBM, beginning in mid-century and still governing the work of employees as of this writing (2022). Figure 2.1 is the cover of the copy American IBMers received in the

2.1 IBM Guidelines for Business Conduct, circa 1960s, which formalized in writing the behavior expected of employees to customers, government officials, and suppliers.

(Courtesy, author's collection.)

mid-1960s; it was not the first edition. Foreign language versions were distributed, too. In 1965, IBM had 172,000 employees and, within a decade, 288,000. All had to be familiar with its contents.[20] By the early 2000s, over a half-million employees had read this document over the previous two decades.[21] The edition illustrated in figure 2.1 was a twenty-five-page humble affair but a forced "best seller" at IBM for over a half century.[22]

The major sections of the 1965 edition that were only slightly revised through the 1970s included, in the following sequence, "Antitrust Responsibilities and Guide," introduced by Watson Jr. with a policy statement regarding antitrust responsibilities; "Marketing Ethics: Responsibilities and Guide," which discussed relations with customers, competition, and other organizations; and a final section entitled "Conflicts of Interest and Ethical Conduct."[23] Managers were given a second pamphlet, *Doing Business with 20,000 Suppliers: A Guide for IBM Management*, because the majority of employees acquired or interacted with vendors, spending millions of dollars, activities that lent themselves to potential ethical conflicts.[24] Watson Jr. personally addressed the opacity of practices because he wanted no misunderstandings: "We want IBM always to be known as a good customer" to avoid "criticism in this area of supplier relations."[25]

Although IBM documented many ethical issues as training devices, such as whether an employee should accept a Christmas present from a vendor, even if trivial, or wanted to invest in stock in a competitor's company, the central issue with these sorts of situations was conflict of interest. Regarding some instances, the company stated the obvious, such as that an employee buying from a company "should not become a director or officer of such organizations."[26] Far more serious was the overt or accidental leaking of information to vendors or that could fall into the hands of a competitor. Such breaches could be seen as violations of law or antitrust restrictions or as a means of affecting markets and damaging (or helping) competitors. Employees received considerable training around this issue of information security and privacy, especially about the latter.[27] Managers were taken through a series of scenarios in which they role-played dealing with, for example, reporters in what might seem harmless conversations or with customers. IBM's strictures were stated in absolute terms: "We should never discuss highly confidential subjects, such as unannounced products, costs," and so forth; "we must assume that the press may be represented . . . wherever we go," and if not certain on how to deal with the press, "check with the people in your division whose job it is to handle this kind of problem and all clearance questions." Even better, "Do not deal with the press yourself." In addition, everyone inside IBM was reminded "that they are to discuss proprietary information only on the job" and that revealing "IBM secrets . . . is grounds for discharge."[28]

From these and other explanations involving such matters as privacy of personnel records, salary information, emerging products, and so forth emerged a concept of business ethics and behaviors that became embedded in the DNA of the company's behavior. "Ethical" to employees was about doing something "right," and for a company lawyer, "right" meant duties enforceable by law and hence not to be evaded. More obvious to management than to their employees was a corollary—knowledge that someone had violated a law or regulation, such as when someone "breached a contract" or agreement and they knew about it. The obligation then would be to bring it to the attention of those in IBM who could address the problem. Often a manager might be faced with a decision that bordered on a breach of marketing practices and that is when making the "right" decision was imperative.

Then there was the concept of the "assumed obligation," where one should personally embrace a practice, even though there might not be a law requiring it. For example, in dealing with competitors, employees had been admonished since the late 1910s not to disparage a rival, but rather to preach positive features of IBM's products in factual terms. That concept was a core principal in IBM's sales behaviors, and while difficult to practice, management rarely hesitated to fire salesmen for violating it, particularly if a rival complained. It was usually a competitor that brought to management's attention a pattern of disparagement, which the IBM manager could not ignore and so investigated with the help of a company lawyer, personnel manager, and their immediate superior. Managers were admonished that a salesperson who disparaged a rival "should seek a profession where he represents his own interests and not those of others" (i.e., IBM's or a rival's).[29]

Employees learned that while they had considerable leeway to spend and to commit company resources to a situation, they should do so without compromising the company or its stakeholders. What they and their long-term customers came to admire (many *expected*) was the practice that when an employee gave their word that something would be done or fixed, even if that individual's manager thought it a bone-headed gesture, the company routinely bent over backward to honor it. For example, suppose that a computer just kept malfunctioning and could not be repaired after moving heaven and earth to do so, and the salesman tells the customer, "I will get you a new machine." IBM would much rather have sent the inventor of the machine and a truckload of parts and people to fix the one already installed, rather than swap it out with a new one. But, having made that commitment, that salesman's managers would work quickly to replace it and then counsel the salesman on better options for solving the maintenance problem.[30] IBMers were proud of their word being their bond. It is how a famous saying floated through the computer world for decades that held, "Nobody was ever fired for recommending IBM." The personal bond and resulting trust reduced risk of failure on the part of a customer.

The bond was a core element of IBM's ethics, the basis of what Watson Sr. argued as early as 1915 was "sound judgment," which everyone valued.[31]

It all boiled down to the delicate balance of intangibles, what was "right" for IBM and for the other organizations and people in a situation. If a decision did not feel right, it probably was not right. Managers were told an "action that must be hidden and kept secret in order to avoid serious consequences for the corporation—any surreptitiousness—is in almost all cases unethical."[32] Silence should not be used to avoid an obligation. Truthfulness—"straight talk"—was a highly valued feature of IBM's ethics and behavior.

Tied into such conversations and training of several generations of employees was how to deal with antitrust issues. Employees participated in only minor ways in the United States in the company's issues with the U.S. Department of Justice in the 1930s, but the concerns of the 1960s to early 1980s were visible, broad, and a major threat to the company, requiring most employees to be aware of and to engage with these issues. An example of the latter comes from the 1970s. IBM was ordered by federal judges to save all correspondence relevant to one case or another; such orders included everyone in IBM writing or reading company text, hence millions of documents. Hundreds of people inside and outside IBM were deposed for cases. Meanwhile, it seemed everyone's neighbors periodically wanted to discuss the case with their IBM friends. So, everyone was counseled on what to do, say, or not, from the 1950s through the 1980s. They went to school on the subject in myriad training programs, read updates on the case in the company's *THINK* magazine, and were informed about circumstances by IBM lawyers, executives talking about it in meetings, and through formal notification, for example, by the chairman to all employees.[33]

The subject seemed behind them in the late 1950s and early 1960s, so one just needed to be aware of and adhere to the consent decree. But by the early 1970s, and extending until 1982, antitrust litigation was visceral, dangerous, and an always present existential threat to the company. It influenced almost every conceivable decision to such an extent that even long after the case had been resolved it still affected the behavior of employees. In the 1990s—a decade after the case closed—Gerstner still noticed its effects on the behavior of employees. While his interpretation that it caused employees to lose their "fighting spirit" is subject to debate (I agree this was one effect), that residual effects remained is not.[34]

Much of what IBM did after 1982 with respect to antitrust behavior was less a required obligation than a voluntary one. The company became more cautious and made decisions regarding product introductions in ways that would not cause antitrust issues for governments in the United States and around the world. Was such behavior a subconscious response to the realities of antitrust issues or the heavy hand of lawyers at work? Inside IBM, lawyers gained more voice to opine on increasing varieties of routine decisions, while every division acquired marketing practices staffs; think of them as thought and contract police, who had increasingly to sign off even on mundane standard contracts and other documents. It seemed every executive had been assigned a lawyer, a practice continued into the new century. Most managers had the name and telephone number of someone in "legal." IBM's brand of ethics had hardened into practices that slowed work. Marketing guidelines devoted increasing amounts of space to the subject of antitrust behaviors.[35]

A brief examination of one of the guides from the early 1990s—the first issued by the first new outside CEO to come to IBM since Watson Sr. and distributed some five months after his arrival—suggests enduring guidance to employees. Gerstner reaffirmed that "the basic honesty and integrity you and your IBM colleagues have lived by over the years has earned IBM a reputation for ethical behavior that contributes directly to the customer loyalty that is one of our greatest assets."[36] The sections were similar to those in earlier editions: personal conduct and protection of IBM's assets, obligations in conducting IBM's business, conflicts of interest and other considerations, and competition law. One's behavior rested "on the high measure of mutual trust and responsibility that exists between employees and the company" and that "comes down to honesty and fairness in dealing with other employees and with customers, suppliers, competitors, the government and the public." However, it warned that a violation not only could lead to dismissal but even to litigation, especially if intellectual property was stolen by an employee, ex-employee, or retiree. It read like earlier editions with a couple of exceptions. With spouses now working, too, some possibly in other firms deemed competitors to IBM, employees were cautioned to be careful about sharing confidential information. Missing was any direct mention of antitrust activity; rather, it included instructions on how competitors should be treated, guidance about which had not changed in decades.[37] So, much of the text remained essentially the same as that of the early 1960s.

Over the years, employees received copies of the Marketing Guidelines as pamphlets, and they continued to sign a form certifying they had read and understood it. By the late 1990s, these arrived through email. By the early 2000s, some divisions had an online tutorial on these guidelines with a test one had to pass. In the 2010s, the guidelines even floated around the Internet on IBM websites in various forms. For example, in 2019, it was entitled "Trust Comes First." It included seven principles of operation: "Trust means we commit to integrity and compliance; Trust means we protect IBM employees, IBM assets and the assets belonging to others; Trust means we respect intellectual property rights; Trust means we are honest, accurate and complete; Trust means we compete win business and treat others ethically; Trust means we meet our legal obligations; and Trust means we separate our personal interest from our business responsibilities."[38] Watson Sr. and Jr. would have recognized the text that underpinned each of these. Virginia (Ginni) Rometty, IBM's CEO in 2019, reminded employees that, "as times change, IBM's values endure" and then quoted Watson Jr. from his 1963 book: "If an organization is to meet the challenges of a changing world, it must be prepared to change everything about itself except its beliefs."[39] As IBM managers were told in the 1950s and 1960s, when they attended their training programs and in exactly the same language, she wrote, "IBMers must act ethically. Anyone doing otherwise doesn't belong at IBM."[40]

Over time, the guidelines evolved to take into account new concerns, such as environmental practices and human rights principles, but the fundamental strategy of hammering home basic ethical practices had not changed in over a half century: "IBM's Business Conduct Guidelines (BCGs) serve as our global code of conduct for IBM employees, and reflect our longstanding commitment to high ethical conduct and decision-making," and the guidelines were still communicated to every employee.[41] Notice in the phrase "our global code of conduct" specifically the word *global*. Since the 1920s, IBM executives had espoused global values, albeit American, which they imposed on dozens of nationalities working at the company.

Nonetheless, it was a common set woven into the fabric of its operations and values. That was purposeful as both a way to do business and also to facilitate running the firm in a globally integrated fashion. Employees behaved largely the same in Paris as in London, New York, Tokyo, or Mexico City. Historians have commented about that universality of the firm and its positive effects. Sociologists studying companies marveled at IBM's success in imposing and sustaining a global culture.[42] Nothing seemed to imbue and reinforce IBM's ethics as much as their actual relevance and articulation so that there would be no misunderstanding about what it all meant. One's behavior reinforced that of others, so too frequent communications about such corporate theology, and the inevitable normalization of such beliefs and practices.

Harvard business professor Michael L. Tushman and his colleagues, in discussing how companies could innovate, cited examples of values being implemented in other corporations, but apparently not as broadly or as methodically as at IBM, because they felt compelled to urge management to do so. Writing in 2021—over a century after IBM had started imposing a body of values—they first made the case for the power of such norms and then wrote that these "can be reinforced by leaders and the systems that those leaders put in place."[43] IBM shared its thinking on such issues over the twentieth century with customers when asked to do so, and it seemed any employee was also an expert to consult. When historians think of IBM's influence over the information technology (IT) ecosystem, there was more at play than technological standards and worldviews; IBM's behavior and values were also part of that environment.

Behavior of Sinners, Saints, and Congregants

If there is a whiff of religious metaphor floating through this text, it is because of the notion that ties back to the fundamental beliefs Watson Sr. was exposed to as a child that he shared with many thousands of American employees and that proved useable in most countries in which IBM operated. This last comment is a key finding of our discussion because many American corporations successfully transplanted their operating philosophies around the world in the twentieth century. So their social roots in American society are a factor influencing business behavior in one fashion or another.[44] As in other aspects of life, IBM employees' feet were made of clay, as they were mortal, but they exercised their ethics largely in the intended way. In some instances, they fell from grace, some to be redeemed, others not so.[45]

More importantly, IBM's ethics, while notable by both American religious and secular perspectives, were part of a larger historical process crucial to acknowledge. Historical context clarifies the notion of *notable*, while situating IBM's experience in the wider experience of peer companies. Academic explorations of ethics came into their own in the 1970s, and by the end of the 1980s, scholars had published extensively on the topic.[46] After paying deference to Aristotle, eighteenth- and nineteenth-century thinkers, and so forth, they saw formalized ethics in business flower in the post–World War II period, most specifically as if born in the 1960s and expanding in subsequent decades.[47] IBM's experience suggests this chronology is badly in need of correction, since the emergence of its body of corporate ethics dates to the 1910s to 1920s. IBM was not alone; Watson Sr. appropriated practices from NCR and others from the Johnson Shoe Company in Endicott, New York, both run by progressive executives. He would also have learned what *not* to do from the robber barons of his time and less effective managers, including perhaps some who served on his first board of directors at C-T-R (future IBM). Ancient Greek or English eighteenth- and nineteenth-century thinkers did not influence Watson Sr. He never went to college, and his calendars show that he did not spend time reading books. He was too busy working.[48] In 1937, the first textbook on business ethics appeared, signaling that the topic had circulated around long enough to generate sufficient material for a book. Much of its content paralleled issues still of concern to corporations in the 2020s.[49] The University of Wisconsin offered the first course on the subject in the United States in 1913–1914.[50]

Students of American business ethics think in terms of entwined branches of evolution. The first closely resembles IBM's experience of applying widely accepted ethical norms to business, which can be seen as a mixture of religious and secular beliefs and practices.[51] Those would have been the roots of Watson's thinking. A second line of development was the emergence of the subject as a field of academic research, a subject that lies outside the scope of this chapter, but nonetheless, it is important to acknowledge that its emergence has influenced discussions of business ethics since the 1970s.[52] A third involves adoption of practices, trappings, and corporate commitments to practices associated with ethics, most recently, for example, of policies related to corporate social responsibilities and to the care of the Earth's environment.[53] The first was about the application of beliefs, such as IBM's rules and guidance expressed in its various Business Conduct Guidelines, which predated those of most corporations whose own versions were introduced beginning in the 1970s.[54] It is within this context that more universally accepted ethics in life and society spread in the belief that these represented sound business practices. This discussion is not intended to say that IBM got there first, because it was an evolutionary process of development over decades, while other enterprises were able to build out quickly their own ethical guidelines based on the prior experiences of other companies, including IBM's.

Academic discussions, highly publicized scandals, and new regulatory and legal dictates in the United States and in other countries sped up awareness and implementation of business ethics practices in the last three decades of the twentieth century. IBM's practices benefited from the now current experience of others and were shaped, too, by new laws. Examples of the latter included passage of the U.S. Foreign Corrupt Practices Act (1977), which prohibited bribing foreign government officials in exchange for contracts; the Defense Industry Initiative (DII) on Business Ethics and Conduct (1986), which was an agreement among American corporations on how to conduct business, providing ethics training and creating monitoring systems; the U.S. Federal Sentencing Guidelines for Corporations (1991), which used the DII as a framework that motivated executives to make sure their firms did not violate laws, since penalties for doing so included incarceration of senior business leaders; and the U.S. Sarbanes-Oxley Act (2002) on corporate governance. The latter required CEOs, including IBM's, to personally sign off in writing on the veracity of the company's financial reports; falsification or misleading information was to be punished by imprisonment for the misbehaving senior executive. The law was a direct response to the scandals of the 1990s, most famously Enron's.[55] Around the world, similar practices were codified into corporate governance, laws, and regulations, but not in all countries.[56] The American government sent more corporate officials to jail for violating ethics laws than any other nation in the 1960s–1980s.

Surveys conducted in the 1980s suggest what other companies' practices strongly paralleled IBM's experience. Briefly summarized, these surveys often involved dozens then hundreds of small and large American and European firms. Addressing conflicts of interest in decision-making and work practices drew the most attention.[57] This should be of no surprise since the objective of ethical codes was to protect the company, less so the public. That was the case with IBM, even though by the end of the 1930s its practices also acknowledged the importance of how its behavior fit within society. All such studies documented that top management arbitrated and set the tone and terms of a company's beliefs and practices. Two generations of Watsons did that, too, at IBM. Everyone with an ethics code also implemented measures and oversight practices rather than rely solely on the integrity of employees.[58]

However, at IBM, there was the constantly repeated mantra that one had to take personal responsibility for their actions, not because Watson Sr. demanded it, but because it was part of a larger belief system that individuals had to take actions and make decisions on their own. Such behavior was needed because the company was too big to be run by the top of the house. This reality existed even though IBM had a history of strong top-down management that simultaneously sought to delegate authority and responsibility through the ranks, hence the need for a body of ethics essential to implement delegation. IBM's CEO in the early 2000s, Samuel Palmisano, may have provided the clearest explanation when he described how a highly professional workforce could not be managed: "The CEO can't say to them, 'Get in line and follow me.' Or, 'I've decided what your values are.' They're too smart for that. And as you know, smarter people tend to be, well, a little more challenging."[59] IBM's beliefs and practices were less about how to practice ethics as a new fad, even one apart from how a business was run, than an integral part of all that the company did. Like other codes of conduct, IBM's code included rule-based statements on what was or was not allowed with more commentary on shared values than in many other corporate ethics guidelines.

Role-playing exercises in management training programs demonstrated to participants how to link the two together. Looking at some of these scenarios points to common problems one encountered in all decades. Examples drawn from a sales training course in the 1960s, but that could just as easily have been from the 1930s or the 1980s, include:

> An executive from one of our biggest customers comes to you and states that he wants to offer one of your best salesmen an executive position in his company. What do you say?
>
> A customer with a new IBM installation contacts you, the IBM Branch Manager, to ask your opinion about a man, John Jones, that he is considering employing to be the Manager of his IBM Department. You know that John Jones and don't feel he is qualified for the position. In addition, he has had problems with the IBM salesman and customer engineer in a previous job. What do you say?
>
> You encounter a customer executive who asks about a product he has seen on a tour of an IBM Plant and Lab but which you know has not been announced. What do you say?[60]

Without guidance, these kinds of situations can be tricky, potentially illegal, unethical if handled incorrectly, damaging to intracompany relations, and hopefully always uncomfortable for the employee. But the individuals who put together these scenarios had experienced some of these before they were allowed to become instructors teaching others how to navigate these shoals. The issues were timeless. Pamela Losey, an IBM salesperson, opined in 1991 on the value of clarity on so many issues encountered outside of IBM and stated that the guidelines "separate the company from the sometimes down-and-dirty high-tech scrappers it competes with." IBM's guidelines "are very puritanical, a very well-defined set of ethics so that you know what to do or what not to do in your business dealings as a professional."[61]

By the mid-1980s, such codes in many companies had common features. These asked employees to do more than might otherwise have occurred; codes focused on those activities that could not be supervised sufficiently to ensure compliance. They were dictates that management believed served the interests of their company if employees applied them at least in circumstances where they could not be supervised.[62]

Surveys in the 1980s documented a near absence of discussions about broad-based corporate values in the business community.[63] This proved surprising, at least to IBM employees, because IBM had been building, shaping, and promoting its Basic Beliefs for decades and knew these were foundational principles of operation. When Watson Jr. published his book in 1963, it was considered partially a revolutionary text. The lack of similar expressions of corporate values goes far to explain why so much of his book was devoted to explaining why the Basic Beliefs were necessary and useful and less to describing their implementation. One could have concluded that his tone was that of a salesman, and like his father, who preferred to sell a point of view, as a salesman trying to close an order. The fact that surveys indicated that even in the 1980s many companies still did not have an articulated set of Basic Beliefs has to lead one to ponder how even more striking that circumstance must have been in the 1950s and 1960s when Watson Jr. was thinking through this issue and how different IBM must have felt to him and employees from their customers and suppliers. He knew he was on the right path because in the summer of 1961 the *Harvard Business Review* published the results of a survey of 1,700 executives and managers for a data-rich lengthy article entitled, "How Ethical Are Businessmen?" The results reported were mixed, but overwhelmingly, respondents wanted the sorts of things IBM had, such as documented clearly stated beliefs and rules of behavior.[64] Employees going through their initial management training were each given a copy of the article for years. IBM's possession of a written code helps to explain an important source of admiration for IBM as a company that for decades always placed it in the top rankings of corporations.

While the story of IBM's code of ethics turned out to be practical and lau-datory, no company is perfect. The fact that the number of scandals and other embarrassing episodes at IBM was very limited, however, speaks volumes about the practicality of the code. Nonetheless, occasionally they occurred, in addition to the rare but run-of-the mill cheating on one's expense reports or stealing ("losing") a laptop. On rare occasions, individuals violated a market-ing practice, such as when a handful of IBMers disparaged a competitor, with none knowing others had simultaneously done so, causing the vendor either to want to sue IBM for legal violations of one sort or another or to demand that the employees be fired. Ignorance of the rules was never an acceptable excuse, although managers worked mightily to make sure the facts supported the charges. On occasion, something spectacular would occur. For instance, in the 1990s in Argentina, the government accused several IBM managers of colluding with banks and of bribing officials. It turned out to be a highly public scandal in Latin America. It was made more onerous by the fact that there were U.S. laws against such behavior that potentially could have entrapped Ameri-can IBM executives in New York who probably had no idea of what was hap-pening.[65] The bigger point is that, because IBM had such an ethical reputation, when employees deviated from these standards their behavior became news. The Argentine case played out in the local press for years and resulted in at least three book-length exposés. In 2015, the media reported that the U.S. Securities and Exchange Commission (SEC) was investigating whether IBM had illegally reported financial transactions in the United States, United Kingdom, and Ire-land. The media was not kind.[66] No company was immune, but these incidents were infrequent at IBM.

Enduring Ethics, Changing Forms

The 1990s proved exhausting for IBM's employees. It seemed that their old Watsonian top-down support for the Basic Beliefs was being eroded by newly imported senior management; certainly, Gerstner challenged them with his eight principles that he attempted to impose upon the company. From the late 1980s, when it seemed the company was beginning to discard such old values as lifetime employment, to the early 2000s, much had changed. Many employ-ees were unhappy, indeed very nervous. The business was challenging. There seemed to be an ill sense that the company's markets, services, and sources of revenue were changing profoundly. How did the company's values—ethics—do in this period? CEO Samuel Palmisano—an IBM lifer—wanted to find out because he understood that values and ethics were crucial to the success of a firm, and nowhere more so it would seem than at IBM. He realized that these had to align with current business realities but that the top-down approach taken by his predecessor did not do the job. When Gerstner retired from IBM, old THINK signs came out of hiding; it would be difficult to believe Palmisano did not observe that behavior.[67]

Senior management launched a remarkable event. Rather than dictate what the values and ethics should be, they hosted two online open discussions with employees, allowing workers to express their views on these topics, with minimal participation by senior management. Called "Values Jams," in 2003, employees opined online in an open fashion for three days; over 3,700 employees participated in and upward of 65,000 viewed the conversation. A year later, IBM ran another called "World Jam," in which 13,000 employees participated with comments. These online conversations were freewheeling, passionate, and often included argumentative postings involving all levels of the firm from CEO to new hires.[68] Influenced by the first debate, senior management issued a new articulation of IBM's values. The exercise had been a bottom-up approach to test their assumptions of what IBM needed. Executives wanted an updated set of values expressing the idea of "a culture of collaboration and innovation," one involving more interactions with customers (although employees were sometimes confused by the change in terms in which customers were increasingly being called clients, even more so after the jams). Palmisano and his immediate circle wanted more collaboration across organizational boundaries and, perhaps wishfully thinking, wanted employees to accept the need to lay off colleagues and subcontract work.[69]

The first jam attracted many employee criticisms that the old Watsonian Basic Beliefs were under siege and complaints against senior management, some of which included charges that they had violated the company's Basic Beliefs, using blunt language.[70] Employee comments signaled to top management that the values needed (wanted) now were "trust and personal responsibility in all relationships," "dedication to every client's success," and "innovation that matters—for our company and for the world."[71] Leaving aside questions about wording, these echoed the Basic Beliefs and offered refinements of what Palmisano hoped would come out of the discussions, but in language that made sense to thousands of employees. In the second jam, much of the conversation had moved from complaints emanating out of the first debate to one where employees were working out how the new values statements should be viewed and exercised. Those advocating for essentially the old Basic Beliefs saw the Watsonian text relevant for returning IBM to greatness, whereas others saw the need for increasing collaboration with more nimbleness and responsiveness. It is not clear if the latter group had any sense of history, because what they advocated for was more in line with what the two generations of Watsons had promoted and, too, their successors.[72] Senior management considered the jams a success. Employees increasingly recognized the need for new framing of IBM's value statements, yet saw that they could vent too, while management better understood the realities of "the business."[73]

Behind the jams was a practical consideration. When the U.S. Department of Justice took IBM to court accusing it of monopolistic behavior, the firm organized itself into self-contained divisions, each with product development, manufacture, and sales divisions, in case the government broke up the firm. The antitrust suit went on for over a decade, time enough for the divisions—often pejoratively called silos by the press and IBMers—to begin operating with different behaviors and attitudes that Palmisano wanted to reverse in the early 2000s as a way of integrating—think teaming and collaboration—across the company, per the request of IBM's customers. Prior efforts to correct the inefficiencies of the silos model had proven inadequate, so the firm wanted to differentiate it from competitors by offering broad integrated goods and services. To assist in the effort, IBM needed to return to some of its enduring values and, to quote Palmisano reflecting on that experience in 2022, "we needed to at least recreate that value system."[74] Nick Donofrio, a senior executive in the early 2000s, reported that mandating values from the top down, as Gerstner did, would not work: "People were just too smart and too cynical. For the new set of values to stick and take hold, they had to come from the bottom up and from IBMers the world over."[75] In short, all the silos had to engage with a common set of beliefs. The results "were real."[76]

Academic observers saw the jams as constructive, if passionate, debates on how to move forward.[77] One can draw additional conclusions from these two jams. First, employees believed that a well-shaped set of corporate beliefs, values, and behaviors was essential for the health of the business. That fundamental idea was not widely understood in the 1910s or early 1920s but subsequently proved crucial at IBM for some eight decades.

Second, even during and after the jams, although the language changed, their core ideas remained largely the same, even though senior management touted the outputs as new and innovative. An example illustrates the point. Prior to the early 1980s, IBM only leased products to its customers, resulting in an ongoing relationship with them that lasted for decades, shaped by the necessary mutual collaboration required to find ways to use data processing equipment to benefit a customer's business. Sales personnel, indeed the entire company, were motivated to keep close to customers by how they were compensated and rewarded for maintaining those relationships. Then in the early 1980s, IBM decided to only sell—not rent or lease—equipment, and within several years, the old collaborative relationship had largely transformed into a transactional one, with the result that collaboration declined, price considerations increased in customer decisions to acquire IT products, and the distance between employees and their customers widened. Rather than understanding deeply a customer's business issues, employees became product specialists, knowing their set of goods and services to sell and less so about other ones, let alone about their customers' business realities.[78] By the time the jams were conducted, over two decades had passed, so the aspirations for collaboration in 2003–2004 were essentially a call to return to an earlier worldview, one that many employees in 2004 might not have known had once been a hallmark of IBM's behavior. The same story could be told about collaboration within the company across divisions, many of which had reduced collaboration across other parts of IBM. After the jams, when asked what he wanted IBMers to do differently, Palmisano seemed to channel Watson Sr.: "I want them to live the values; I want them to be obsessed with their clients; I want them to inno-vate. . . . Then there's this thing about trust."[79]

Academics looking at these events concluded nearly the opposite: that the Watsonian frames were partially delegitimized and marginalized as a result of honest and open debate about them. But the academics also acknowledged that their conclusions were "speculative and controversial" and "certainly require further research to confirm and develop."[80] That is where a healthy dose of historical perspective suggests the jams did not move the needle on values and ethics as much as they implied. However, what the observers did get right, based on behaviors before the 1980s, was that the jams contributed to engaging people in shaping their worldviews with senior management open to them, rather than driving them underground to protest.[81] Palmisano had watched the low tempo unionization efforts that had rumbled through the company's major manufacturing plants since the 1970s and so understood that not all was well at "Big Blue." The jams demonstrated that the old practice of "straight talk" was alive and well. What employees in the early 2000s realized, along with Palmisano and other senior executives (both veterans of IBM and newly arrived ones), could be summed up by quoting what Watson Jr. observed made the old Basic Beliefs work and that could be applied to what employees were trying to shape in 2003–2004: "Undoubtedly the principal reason these beliefs have worked well is that they fit together and support one another."[82] Nothing is more essential for understanding IBM's culture than what hundreds of thou-sands of employees believed and lived by for a century.

As IBM managers formulated their values and behaviors, they simultane-ously used these to shape the image and reputation they wanted to project for the company, as these represented early and sustained initiatives to bring them to life. How that was done is the subject that we turn to next in chapter 3.

But before proceeding, several lessons relevant for today's corporations need to be called out. The most important was the need for a company-wide set of explicitly stated operating principles drummed into everyone's head first by management and then constantly by peers over a long period of time. IBM's employees might say this should be done "forever." Second, value statements, training, and defined operating rules and practices need to link to a firm's basic beliefs. That requires considerable attention of the most senior executives but, increasingly, also of everyone else because we are talking about a way of life for a firm. Third, promotions and rewards, and possibly also compensation, should be linked to the beliefs of the enterprise. Fourth, all of these actions should be publicized, and at a minimum, the Basic Beliefs should be communicated to customers, regulators, legislators, media, and the public at large, again "forever." That requirement means, to use American slang, that everyone "walk the talk" and "practice what they preach." A CEO cannot delegate such a requirement. As IBM's CEOs demonstrated, that task remained on their short list of critical activities.

As large corporations come to realize that they are less enterprises and more economic and industrial ecosystems and pillars of modern society, they will need to reflect the values and expectations of all their stakeholders, who increasingly are demanding such behavior. That means corporations will need to have values and practices that are more than marketing pabulum; these must reflect the soul of the enterprise. Law professor William Magnuson cautions that history teaches a lesson when all that we discussed in this chapter is wrapped together: corporations "tend to bear an outsized role" in politics, the way business is conducted, and how its employees are treated, and "businesses should be cautious before seeking to craft society's values" because "their actions are magnified beyond what any individual could ever hope to achieve."[83] As we explain in chapter 11 about publications, management and their employees understood this maxim and concluded that to focus on dominating conversations about IT and international trade made sense over the course of more than a century.

CHAPTER 3

"THE IBM WAY"

Creating and Sustaining a Corporate Image and Reputation

IBM is a giant that does about everything right.

Time, 1983[1]

I t is a curious fact that if one scans the indices of business histories, or even just their table of contents, there are few mentions of corporate reputations. One has to turn to histories of advertising and public relations to find meaty discussions of the topic, and even then, those do not capture the full meaning of images and reputations.[2] In business memoirs one finds more discussions of the two topics, suggesting these were similar (if not the same) and important to employees and their employers. Is there possibly a gap in our general understanding of their roles? IBM's corporate culture demonstrates that to be the case and also that the subject is too important to ignore in any discussion of a corporation's history.

It is probably true that every retiree website and Facebook group for any long-lived company is populated with comments about how thirty-year veterans of the firm were proud to have worked for such a distinguished enterprise; IBM's retirees are no exception. On such sites, those with access can literally find thousands of such comments. Alumni know exactly what they are talking about. Those who disagree with such nostalgic postings probably worked at IBM in the 1990s or more likely in the 2000s, when the company had entered a long period of poor economic performance, when its dominance in the information technology (IT) world waned as a new generation of IT firms came to prominence and became respected and fashionable.[3] More than just a reminder that Facebook, Apple, Amazon, Microsoft, and others cannot maintain indefinitely their high status in the public's eyes, that does not mean their reputations are too ephemeral to be taken seriously.

To an employee or customer, reputations and positive images are important markers for job satisfaction, perceptions of product and service qualities, and trust in how one wants to interact with the other. *Trust* is the key, a theme that surfaces periodically in this book. When an IBM salesman asked a customer to invest millions of dollars to change how they did business, trust overwhelmingly trumped technology. Trust is built up over time through behavior and attitude that lead to perceptions of quality, of confidence. When the company commits to provide certain benefits and career opportunities, trust goes a long way in retaining effective employees. That is why image and reputation are so important in understanding the ebbs and flows of a company's history.

A personal example illustrates what happens. I became an employee of IBM on October 1, 1974. On that day, I joined what was universally thought to be one of the top five companies in the world, based on a decade's worth of surveys by trade and business magazines, all reinforced by decades of financial growth. The epigraph for this chapter is one of many that could have been reproduced here. Upon being offered—and accepting—a job that June, not only did I feel fortunate and optimistic about my future (trust), but relatives, friends, and even strangers that summer treated me with some awe (reputation), certainly with respect. They assumed I knew (or was smarter) about many things. But I had not changed since May, before I was associated with IBM. So, what was different between May and June, between June and October, or for whatever happened to me over the next thirty-eight years?

I was immediately clothed with the mantle of IBM's reputation even before I could say something wise, trustworthy, or ignorant. That is the power of image and reputation. It increases an employee's confidence in solving problems and accomplishing goals, their morale and sense that they are engaging with some of humanity's problems by doing good in the world, and the willingness of customers, politicians, regulators, and even competitors to respect (rivals to even fear) and listen to them. That experience bred more success and more confidence within a corporate culture that strived for excellence as a basic belief. IBM's reputation also put a burden on me to provide my customers with the best advice that one of the most influential corporations in the world could offer and to ensure when implemented that it all worked as anticipated by both customer and me. For years, a customer would look me in the eye and ask, "Do you really want me to do this?" The question would be asked after all the financial and technical analyses of proposals had been conducted, for it all boiled down to trust. I did not walk into IBM on that long ago day in 1974 with the knowledge to deserve anyone's trust. I had the right attitude, but I also had to be trained and to gain experience doing things the "IBM Way." In turn, hopefully, I could contribute to IBM's reputation and image; in other words, to live up to the epigraph's message.

The issue of trust has become far more complicated for corporations in recent years because the public in many countries has increasingly come to rely on business leaders to speak truth to power on issues involving racism, civil liberties, privacy, and environmental concerns, among others, and less so about the quality of their own products. Even more complicating, employees want their business leaders to take stands on these issues, which already divide customers, such as American Republicans and Democrats who eat McDonald's hamburgers, buy from Amazon, and want to use Facebook with their privacy protected. One global survey conducted in 2021 ranked businesses as the most trusted institutions, with a 61 percent approval rating, as compared to 57 percent for nongovernmental organizations (NGOs), 53 percent for governments, and 51 percent for media.[4] While none of these communities received high marks, senior executives are faced with the situation that they must trade on their firm's reputations because their stakeholders are demanding that they do so. These leaders turn to their management and public relations consultants for advice and are told to understand on what side of an issue their employees have staked out and where the firm's customers are, as they may also be split.

Pity the CEO who chooses the wrong side and then faces a boycott movement, which will damage all their good work to build trust. The other now growing stakeholder—the community in any nation or continent—wants the firm to take stands, and so one has to ask: How much reputational harm is at stake on an issue? IBM, other long-lived organizations (corporations and respected government agencies), and their consultants have been here before. As occurred at IBM, the most savvy in such matters align their positions with long-held values, resist taking a stand too early, look for support among their stakeholders (especially customers, employees, and peer companies), and avoid surprising any of them with sudden pronouncements. But to do any of these things and to worry about their reputation, they must have a positive reputation in the first place. Yet so many have not realized that their companies are so large and so powerful and influential that they must take a stand, they must stake their reputation on being positive players in a society. It is bad enough that law professor William Magnuson had to end his history of the development of corporations with a chapter devoted to prescribing what firms should do as pillars of modern societies.[5] Generations of IBMers would have reacted with incredulity that such obvious pointers had to be made. IBMers are reluctant to seem trite, or too obvious and simplistic, but there we are with Magnuson having to tell people not to break things, a swipe at Facebook's behavior, which he correctly called reckless.

The converse also occurs when too many errors in judgment or strategy are made. Reputations built up over decades can collapse in a matter of a few years, perhaps not completely, but severely nonetheless. That is what happened to a considerable extent to IBM, beginning by the late 1980s and more rapidly after 2012.[6] This chapter focuses on the creation and management of images and reputations from IBM's founding to the end of the 1980s. Many observers discussed its decline in subsequent decades, so we do not need to revisit these issues here. By the end of this chapter, however, it should be obvious what a massive break from the past that change proved to be for IBM. It was one that many employees, ex-employees, and retirees believe current management will have to reconstruct from the shards of their old corporate culture as they shape one more suited to current conditions in the decades to come.[7] Points made so far in this chapter enhance the Schein model in a complementary fashion, because, for example, trust facilitates the creation, operation, and change in corporate cultures.

This chapter proceeds by defining what the terms *image* and *reputation* mean, as used here. We next turn to the history of IBM's building an identity, image, and reputation, presented as a three-pronged strategy. Because of the design innovations introduced by Paul Rand at mid-century, we provide one of the first historical treatments of his work for IBM as a crucial element in the visual presentation of the company's image to the public. For some levity, but also as an important discussion of IBM's image, we discuss the role of blue suits and white shirts, because it has been of far greater discussion and banter than most other topics in this chapter. I conclude with findings that summarize what is known about IBM's experience but also suggest that similar explorations can be conducted of other companies, many of which mimicked IBM's behavior or, perhaps to put it from their perspective, that IBM copied.

Defining Image and Reputation

Like so many new forms of information and their attending professional supporters, images and reputations became contested terms, yet the concepts underpinning them are profoundly important to the success of large and small companies and to customers and employees. Advertising, public relations, media relations, corporate communications, and lobbying all entwined during the twentieth century to create "brand images" (e.g., what one thinks of when contemplating a McDonald's hamburger with, of course, French fries) or "brand reputations" (Enron as corrupt, Apple with wonderful products, or another as a good corporate citizen, such as a firm that donates portions of its profits to charities). These reputations change constantly, too, as events help or hurt.[8] Reputations emerge out of the unique historical experiences of a firm, which is one reason why the notion remains intangible but obvious to an observer knowledgeable of the company in question.[9] The preeminent historian of early twentieth-century corporate image making in America, Roland Marchand, pointed out that most large enterprises had come to realize these subjects warranted considerable attention by senior management by the late 1800s. He cited, among several, the example of NCR, where Thomas Watson, Sr., worked, who acknowledged that he brought his experiences in such matters to IBM.[10]

Most discussions about images and reputations center on brands and products, which is understandable, since everyone is concerned about selling and buying goods and services. It is the heart of marketing. Brand image is thought to be what customers think of a product based on their experience with it and its features, as compared to those of other suppliers. Reputation is what customers and the public think about the brand. An example of a product image is that "Microsoft operating systems are 'buggy' when they first appear"; an example of reputation is "Microsoft is a positive influence on the emerging cloud computing market." An image is what someone, usually a customer, creates by judging the quality, cost, and terms and conditions of a product. A reputation is the long-term opinion (impression) one develops over time—the value accorded to a brand or company.

A poorly performing product or ill-conceived advertising campaign can immediately hurt a product's image, but it would take more incidents over a period of time to damage a company's reputation. If a firm introduced a product with glitches, as IBM did with some of the software used to run its System/360 computers in the 1960s, these machines might suffer momentary image problems, but because IBM fixed these, its corporate reputation did not falter.[11] Images of products are affected by advertising, while images of companies are affected by public relations and the actions of a firm. Reputations are less affected by advertising, but enormously by the long-term behavior of the enterprise that is routinely touted through public relations but diminished by bad press. Students of the subject remain frustrated in their attempts to define reputations because, in its essence, it is an emotional response.[12] Students of corporate reputations, in particular, discuss it as largely a post–World War II corporate-level strategic issue.[13] But as Marchand and others documented, it is an older story, a socially constructed one developed over time.[14]

But to focus on brands and specific products is to miss a larger point about corporate culture. Yes, it was important to advertise the availability of good products—the three companies that eventually made up IBM did that to various degrees. But once the three were put together as C-T-R in 1911, and even more so after Watson Sr. joined the firm in 1914, the new enterprise developed a sales-oriented corporate culture that immediately began to create an image for the greater company that transcended any particular product. IBM's experience suggests that a key component of a corporate culture is what its various stakeholders thought collectively about the firm. Stakeholders included employees, stockholders, customers, regulators, industry analysts, the media, and one very large community: the public at large.

IBM's case was made more complicated in that its image—reputation—sustained with its constituents had to be mitigated through myriad social, political, and economic cultures of eventually 175 countries over many decades, not just in some North American ecosystem. IBM's own internal expert on cultural variations in the 1960s–1970s, Geert Hofstede, demonstrated that the firm was filled with employees who approached their work and views on all manner of business issues differently from each other—French versus Germans, Japanese versus Latin Americans, and so forth.[15] Yet, as other chapters in this book demonstrate, IBM evolved a reasonably coherent integrated operating culture that exuded a positive and effective image for its products and reputation for its employees, customers, and the firm as a whole for the majority of its history.

It helped that many of the tools for accomplishing this feat were developed in the United States, IBM's cultural home base. Advertising as a discipline developed first and quickest in the United States at exactly the same time that IBM was crafting its identity. Marketing as a new discipline was largely a post–World War II phenomenon, and again, it came at just the moment that IBM was becoming a behemoth.[16] Since IBM did not live in isolation, but rather learned from its customers, many of whom were also large, expanding, international enterprises, its staffs were able to apply new lessons in a timely fashion. Because creating an overall style of work and a reputation reinforced its activities, we do not discuss the narrower issue of advertising. It remains, however, important because it became a pathway for helping to educate publics around the world about what a computer did as much as it promoted specific products.[17]

Building and Sustaining IBM's Identity, Image, and Reputation

As with so much about IBM's history, everything seemed to start with Watson Sr.'s thinking and actions, and so it is with the development of IBM's culture and how one thought about it. Barely in the company six months, in January 1915, he spoke to factory workers in Endicott, New York, where they made time-recording equipment used by workers to clock in and out all over the world. He explained the importance of salesmen and how factory workers needed "to stand behind the salesman." He thanked the Endicott employees for doing so "by putting out the proper kind of goods, improving the product, getting the orders out promptly, and so on."[18] It helped salesmen to do their jobs. He said that all branches of the business—product development, manufacturing, and sales—"must all pull together and help each other."[19] Everyone in the firm was "standing together, shoulder to shoulder, all working for one common good; we have one common interest, and the good of each of us as individuals affects the greater good of the company."[20] He described how the company should work with "cooperation," "incentives," and "desires" for success, optimize and improve "ability," create personal "opportunity," and "capitalize opportunity," and all with "self-supervision" as the "most important factor" in any organization. Ultimately, "every man works for the same thing—success."[21] A couple of days later in a similar talk, he added that one should "combine enthusiasm with sound judgment."[22]

Watson Sr. realized early on that he had to create an objective for what he wanted his company to be known for that could be shortened to sound bites. "THINK" was his most spectacular one that endured for over a century. But there were others, most notably for decades, "IBM Means Service," and a variant, "Service, Service, Service." All three were in wide use by the 1930s. Three decades later, his son Thomas Watson, Jr., exclaimed that, "We want to give the best customer service of any company in the world."[23] From the 1920s to at least the early 2000s, the internal and externally proclaimed mantra was "customer first."[24] "Outstanding customer service" worked well as a shaping idea for IBM's image for a century. It was drilled into the heads of newly minted managers and reiterated by generations of IBM executives.[25] Lest the reader protest that customers played only a supporting role when IBM practiced excessive financial reengineering in the 2000s and beyond at their expense, let us acknowledge that the company's performance did not always match its mantra. Managerial fashions influenced managers with clay feet as in other firms, and there were always employees who would call out these deviations from beliefs.

But Watson Sr. was not a man working out his concepts over time; these came ready-made from his many years of experience at NCR.[26] To a twenty-first-century reader, these sound like simple, even too obvious, homilies, but to Watson and his employees in the 1910s, these were markers, objectives, and features of the company he wanted to shape. These were his messages for the next four decades and the focus of much of his attention. In hindsight, businesspeople and historians would say these were the foundation blocks for what someday would be called the "IBM Way." By the end of his life in 1956, Watson's company had a complex, multifaceted corporate culture that extended beyond his initial charges to his employees. The company fulfilled the more widely understood notion that corporate culture was nuanced and multilayered, but surprisingly less diverse than what historian David E. Nye wisely pointed out was normally the case. In Nye's anticipation, IBM became so in the 1990s.[27]

Be told for over four decades that such collaboration and personal initiative were important and observe that it resulted in success and you will have a committed employee. With IBM, a culture formed and a reputation was embraced by the majority of its stakeholders. It was not perfect, but it was cumulative. It is why, for example, just a few years before IBM entered an era of terrible business results, *Time* magazine in 1983 could quote a non-IBM software executive who stated that "IBM is simply the best run corporation in American history."[28] The magazine added, "At a time when American business sometimes seems to be slipping, IBM's triumphs have served as a reminder that U.S. industrial prowess and know-how can still be formidable."[29] Was this hyperbole? Perhaps, but exactly what Watson Sr. would have intended. An employee reading their copy of *Time* in 1983 had to have felt pride and confidence, IBM's customers too, while competitors seethed, envied such accolades, and had good reason to fear "Big Blue," even if the company was already challenged. IBM was facing negative conditions in its chosen markets; its internal expenses were too high; it was saddled with too many employees; and it lacked sufficient revenue to support the corporation's expense structure.

Much of how IBM's history has been documented centers on the way IBM progressed over its first eight decades. Historians and industry observers have doffed their hats to Watson Sr. and to subsequent generations of managers for building the firm. Simultaneous with the nuts-and-bolts work of creating and manufacturing products and selling and maintaining these were the expected promotion of these through advertising, participation at technical and industry conferences, and recruiting employees, suppliers, and later business partners. But not to be overlooked, the company always paid careful attention to make sure all stakeholders heard about what IBM was doing and broadcasted its successes. Historians have noted that IBM was also secretive, such as Apple's reputation today, about itself. But companies were secretive only about some issues, such as research and development concerning unannounced products or regarding marketing and sales actions intended to enhance business and constrain competitors. Occasionally, a personnel scandal would be tucked away, too, but IBM was rarely plagued by such incidents. For almost all other issues, the company methodically let the world know what it was doing. Over time, its activities shaped the images and reputation of IBM in essentially three ways, discussed later. Like so many other aspects of IBM's culture, its efforts were purposeful and viewed by several generations of managers as part of an integrated effort to achieve their business goals.

However, we return to Watson Sr. by examining figure 3.1, which readers may find vaguely familiar. Almost every historian who has written a book about the company has included it in their book. It has appeared in the print media for over a half century and in historical videos about the company. Yousuf Karsh took the photograph in 1948, late in the forty-two-year career of Watson Sr. The picture hung on the walls in many IBM offices around the world. If one had to select five photographs from the entire history of IBM, this one

3.1 Thomas J. Watson, Sr., was IBM's well-known face to the world by the time this photograph was taken in the 1940s. This image served as an iconic representation of the company for decades.

(Courtesy, IBM Corporate Archives.)

would make the short list. What does it convey? The eye would probably turn first to the THINK sign; IBM's bumper sticker logo Watson introduced in 1914 and that to this day remains the company's de facto logo. From the 1940s through the 1970s, THINK signs also appeared in customers' data centers. As I completed this chapter in 2023, I had one in my home office. They rarely varied: all capital letters black against a cream-colored background. THINK—it conjures up thoughtfulness, the complexity of issues that IBM worked on, the fact that employees and their customers worked in a cerebral environment.

Behind Watson are leather-bound books, suggesting education and scientific knowledge, all quite lawyerly too. IBM is a global company, hence the globe in the lower left-hand corner and the business periodicals on his desk suggesting that the company was still learning new things and living in the present. Then there is the "Old Man," as employees fondly referred to him. He is serious, wearing a dark business suit, regimental tie, and a white shirt with cufflinks. In short, to use American slang, he was "suited up to play," ready to go on a "sales call" to some customer or national leader. He is in serious repose. Step back and look at the whole picture as one composite image, and we have the epitome of what the company developed for itself, what it wanted people to think of IBM when it was on their minds. Customers were not being recruited to love IBM but to take it seriously when they had important things to do. There is no banter here, only earnestness. Of course, too, Watson epitomized IBM—he was IBM. After his death, no employee ever became such a symbol of the firm, even though photographs of all subsequent CEOs appeared frequently on the covers of business magazines.

There exist many other photographs of Watson as a younger man sitting at his desk, handsome, surrounded by other symbols of IBM's purpose—respected business magazines, notebooks with facts, and so forth—and, of course, him in a dark suit. These remind us that he was not always an old man, although even when Karsh photographed Watson, he still had a high level of energy and his mental acuity. By 1948, Watson had been a celebrity CEO for two decades; he had met "everyone" important in business and government. It would have been difficult to exaggerate what a giant in the business world he was at the time of the photograph. When he died in 1956, the *New York Times* obituary of him was the longest it had published to that time.[30] The photograph also reminds us that IBM's image, its reputation, and its brand were nurtured by the use of images, coffee mugs, and the most important: IBM's logo.[31]

The first approach in creating an identity or an image involved every CEO personally describing the one they wanted people to hold in their mind's eye inside and outside of IBM. They shared a common view over the next century. Throughout this book, there are quotes from Watson Sr. and his son, Tom Watson, Jr., speaking about IBM as a reliable, competent, serious, and honest firm. Watson Sr. attributed IBM's success to the "good will of others," while Watson

Jr. believed that this success could only be sustained by "the total impact of our personal and collective behavior." It was all about execution, what individuals did: "If we want to have an excellent reputation, we have to be excellent—in everything."[32] Watson Jr. reminded employees that little courtesies, not just big actions, sustained the company's reputation as professional and reliable.[33] Besides publishing his book about IBM's Basic Beliefs, he spoke frequently about IBM's reputation being built on those principles. He told employees and customers that the "IBM Way" was not about rules and bureaucracy, but rather, "it is whatever way is most efficient, no matter how it was done in the past."[34] Late in his tenure as CEO, Watson Jr. argued that the company's good reputation always had depended "upon the excellence of our own products, our own services, our own people. That's basic."[35]

In 1980, IBM's reputation became the subject of the next CEO's opining that he told all of IBM's managers. Frank T. Cary celebrated that the company was a "good corporate citizen," reminding them that giving to community initiatives was part of how that reputation was burnished. Giving involved more than money; it included personal participation in resolving local issues and providing leadership inside local organizations.[36] In the 2010s, CEO Virginia ("Ginni") Rometty put it simply, "I feel our purpose is to be essential to our clients," and when they believed IBM was achieving that, they embraced the company.[37] The downside of promoting such an image meant that when IBM stumbled customers and industry observers castigated the firm, as happened in the late 1980s and early 1990s and again after 2010. It seemed unfair to some employees that the company was held to a higher ethical and business standard than many of its rivals, but every CEO accepted that as the price for a competitive advantage that in the long run proved effective. So, the first strategy was to maintain a consistent profile of a company operating as an effective, efficient, ethical enterprise.

The second strategy applied to other facets of IBM's activities and involved the entire management team in promoting and defending the company's reputation. CEOs did not leave it to chance that they would do so. Rather, they made it part of their job, held managers accountable for results through the appraisal process, and trained them how to carry it out. For example, in 1980, Cary explained how management carried out this objective:

> In every city we do business, one branch manager has been designated as the focal point for community relations. Although this person is usually from the Data Processing Division, all branch managers in a particular city—no matter what division—share in the responsibility for community relations and should work as a team. When the designated manager, the team leader, needs help from other managers, they should give it promptly and in a spirit of cooperation.[38]

He clarified what he wanted and what earlier CEOs did too: "good community relations requires continuing management attention, and I am asking you to provide it."[39] He directed those instructions to all IBM managers around the world. In communities with IBM factories, the "site manager," always an executive guiding the work of thousands of employees, held that lead responsibility. They invested in staff to carry out such responsibilities. Cary knew whereof he spoke as he had spent the bulk of his career in the same part of the market as the Data Processing Division and had, too, been a branch manager. He had inherited a pattern of managerial behavior that for him dated to the 1940s and that he saw demonstrated in his various earlier managerial assignments by his managers, some of whom started their careers in the 1920s.

So, first was to set clear expectations for managers and then to train them on what to do. Their duties combined active participation in community affairs with how to deal with the news media, that is to say, with public relations. It was the latter—public relations—that normally most affected IBM's reputation in the media and in public, while personal behavior and dealings with customers in individual daily relations influenced the attitudes of customers' managers and IT decision-makers. By the 1960s, when the company had entered a period of significant growth in population and number of sales and field engineering offices worldwide, it increased training on public relations in a more formal manner than done earlier. As one set of classroom instructions articulated: "Basically we wish the community to know we are glad to be part of it and we are ready to share the responsibility for progress and improvement."[40] "As a manager, you represent IBM to the community."[41] They were encouraged to support local educational initiatives, an emphasis that continued into the next century.[42] Managers were admonished to participate in local politics as private citizens, not as IBMers; however, they could grant employees paid time off to do such things as work at polls, but they could not use IBM assets, such as stationery or telephones, for political purposes. Speaking in public should be politically neutral.

Management encouraged participation in local nonprofit organizations by all employees. In the United States, recommended organizations for managers, in particular, to engage with included United Fund, Red Cross, Heart Association, American Legion, Chamber of Commerce, and Jaycees, and such service clubs as Kiwanis, Rotary, and Lions, among others. With respect to education, the company encouraged managers and their employees to serve on school boards, teach, take leadership roles in parent-teacher associations, and participate in vocational guidance. Youth organizations attractive to IBM included scouting, Little League, both the YWCA and YMCA, and Junior Achievement.[43] Most of these organizations had existed for as long as (or longer than) IBM and had chapters in every city in the country where the company had a presence.

Second, public relations became the other half of the reputation story because, as managers were told, "IBM is news. We are a leading corporation among all corporations; we are a leader in our own field; we have a record of continuous growth and profitability; we are identified with automation. We need the good will of the general public or we may face the hostility of the mis-informed."[44] Beginning with Watson Sr., IBM cultivated press coverage since the early 1920s. From his earliest days at C-T-R/IBM, Watson Sr. assigned staff to deal with the media. For decades, everywhere he went the press was sure to follow, or at least his media staff and local management, to ensure coverage of his speeches and the events described in the previous chapter. Branch managers were expected to ensure continuous positive local press coverage. Professional media staff at regional, division, and corporate headquarters assisted them.[45] IBM's corporate archive preserves an extensive collection of newspaper articles, serving as a testimonial to the company's relentless focus on press coverage. As a result, we know that IBM was frequently mentioned in newspapers and mag-azines in the 1920s and 1930s and that probably no single day has passed when IBM was not discussed in the press somewhere in the world since at least 1950. That is a remarkable statement to make, but a perusal of those archives makes such a conclusion easy to reach.[46]

Watson Sr. had set the pace. His son, Watson Jr., explained in the 1960s that his "father realized 30 years ago what a great many of us in industry today are just beginning to understand. He believed that knowledge was power, and he believed that the power of a corporation could not fully bloom without public knowledge of what that corporation was trying to do. In other words, the cor-poration could not become successful and powerful without the approval of the public which it served."[47] Watson Jr. drew the essential lesson: "The reputation he built for himself and the company greatly exceeded the size of IBM at any given point in its growth."[48] In chapter 6, there is another example of this strat-egy at work—IBM's involvement in the 1939–1940 World's Fair in New York. Watson Sr. saw the wisdom of winning "a place for IBM in the estimation of people," but to do so, "we had to deserve it." When Watson Jr. went to work for the company in 1937, he was "amazed to find that the company was as well known as it was," since "it was really an insignificant part of the American industrial scene in 1937 . . . about 450th on the list of U.S. corporations."[49] The experience of dealing thoughtfully with the press was an early positive one, reinforced with such public relations actions as rebranding the company *The International Business Machines Corporation*, with Watson Sr. coming home one evening in 1923 to announce to his family that the company was not so big and so wanted to give it a boost by renaming it.[50]

That act reflected a growing consciousness of the power of public relations and media management. Not until IBM became large and was exposed to anti-trust litigation in the 1950s and 1970s did the company learn that there were risks, too, and hence the need to train managers (to a lesser extent all employees as well) concerning such issues and about the art of dealing with newspaper reporters. Managers faced numerous opportunities, as well as dangers. To protect IBM's reputation, they were instructed not to discuss rumors or hearsay "since they may be colorful but distort reality." Further, "at no time should we try to exaggerate the contributions computers are now making and will continue to make to society."[51] This large charge was challenging because, on occasion, salesmen either felt the need to commit that sin or accused IBM's advertising and marketing staffs in headquarter positions of doing just that.[52] They were forbidden to gossip, speculate, or discuss anticipated company financial performance (against U.S. and other laws in many countries anyway), activities of named IBMers, or unannounced products, services, or contractual terms and conditions. No discussions about activities or information about the internal operations of a supplier or customer were allowed without their express permission.

While managers were dealing with the media, IBM's own communications experts were sending out press releases about all manner of company activities, such as announcements of new products, changes in senior leadership (required by regulators), and financial results. Managers were counseled to coordinate their own public messaging with media staffs to be consistent in what they presented to the public. IBM always wanted to "be united toward the outside world," hence the need for a manager to prepare for any encounter with reporters. Middle managers, in particular, but even lower level ones, received "Meet the Press" coaching on how to handle questions, what to say or not say, and how to interact with the news media.[53] They were counseled on not being "smug" in how they presented themselves because even if they were not so, if people thought they were, it hurt the reputation of the company. By the late 1980s, middle managers being trained on media relations could view videos of their role-playing to improve their telegenic qualities and better control their body language and professional image.

Managers in mid-century were given a short document entitled "Meet the Press: How Professionals Tell the IBM Story."[54] They were told they could discuss subjects about which they were knowledgeable but were advised by media relations staff on how to do that. Managers received the advice one would normally expect: what questions to answer, the dangers of "off the record" comments, that reporters normally will not allow an employee to check a story's text before publication for accuracy, how to deal with perceived misquotes, and guidelines for press interviews. Topics did not change from one decade to another. Management in manufacturing received additional training with respect to plant operations and product features. They were required to go through a series of reviews prior to the release of any information, often as high as clearance by a division president. All managers were forbidden to discuss measurements, customer data, number of machines manufactured or sold, anticipated organizational changes, personnel matters, or anything about classified government projects or pending lawsuits. To add additional gravitas to these instructions, everyone had to adhere to the Marketing Practices Guidelines.

Because management was the primary channel through which the company communicated to employees and to the outside world and who executed policies and programs, the centrality and importance of their role were constantly emphasized. Every CEO did this repeatedly.[55] The message was nearly the same: "You are the Image." "Who you are, and what you do and say, tell more about the kind of company and division we are than all our advertising, publications and gleaming new offices." "Meet the press when the opportunity presents. . . . You will find it a stimulating and rewarding experience."[56] Managers proved cautious and, when they had to deal with the press, reached out to IBM's media staff for guidance and coaching. Too many managers and executives knew of cases where a faux pas had led to dismissal or a career-ending punishment.[57]

A third strategy shaping IBM's reputation involved image creation through integrated development of a "look and feel" across the company. This was largely a post–World War II initiative. From that effort came new images, such as "Big Blue" in the 1960s–1970s and introduction of humor to IBM's corporate persona in the 1980s through the use of Charlie Chaplin promoting IBM's PCs, "A Tool for Modern Times." Images representing IBM's products evolved in parallel with the company's personnel practices, training programs, and sales and marketing activities since 1911. They assumed tepid-coordinated impressions about what these should look like; management learned what these could do in the 1920s–1930s. These activities were disrupted by the design of so many new machines in the 1940s, soon called computers. IBM now ran the risk that the "old" impressions of IBM were just that, "old." The company needed an entirely new approach.

Before discussing the new strategy, examining several photographs explains a great deal. Figure 3.2 displays a photo of an office taken around 1950. Notice the equipment along the right-hand wall. Third up from the lower corner is a device that has Queen Anne–looking legs; a half decade earlier, they would have been black iron and more pronounced. The device next to it in the middle is a new model of a sorter with more contemporary-looking legs, and to the far right is an even more modern, circa 1950–style device. It appears as if multiple generations of IBM equipment were being used simultaneously, but most of it looks antiquated when compared to the new desks.

Now look at figure 3.3, which shows an IBM Card Programmed Calculator (CPC) from 1948. It looks more modern and coordinated in that at least the various devices appear to look like they belong with each other, signaling that we were now dealing with a *system*—items working in a coordinated fashion. One could think, "Ah, progress." But examine figure 3.4, which shows what

3.2 Circa 1950 office using tabulating equipment. At the time, data center rooms with air conditioning and raised floors were not the norm. This space might have been called the "IBM Department" or the "IBM Room."

(Courtesy, author's collection.)

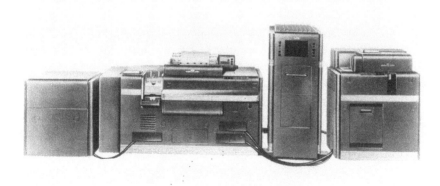

3.3 IBM Card Programmed Calculator (CPC), taken in 1948. Notice that the connecting cables were above the floor, suggesting that all the machines were part of a "system."

(Courtesy, IBM Corporate Archives.)

3.4 The Automatic Sequence Controlled Calculator was developed by IBM in collaboration with engineers at Harvard University during World War II.

(Courtesy, IBM Corporate Archives.)

appears to be an even more modern and integrated machine, except for the problem that this picture was taken earlier of a computer called the Automatic Sequence Controlled Calculator. Two years later, IBM produced a 603 Electronic Calculator, depicted in figure 3.5. It does not even appear to have come from the same decade, and it is clearly, well, ugly. Finally, glance at the 1949 IBM 407 (figure 3.6), a device that began to look like a post–World War II machine. Look at all the images as a group and two observations become obvious. First, little seems coordinated—there are different colors and shapes, but all machines come from the same company. Second, they had uncoordinated names and product numbers. Add in IBM sales and corporate offices furnished with a mixture of oriental carpets and wooden and metal chairs and tables from the 1930s and 1950s in the same facilities, and one quickly realizes IBM had an image problem. For a familiar image of what a coordinated look can say to a customer, imagine what you saw walking into an Apple store in the 2010s.

Senior management recognized the problem and went about addressing it in a coordinated manner in the 1950s and 1960s, laying down a set of design practices that shaped the look and feel of what customers saw from IBM for the

3.5 The IBM 603 Electronic Calculator became a widely used early computer in both commercial and government organizations.

(Courtesy, IBM Corporate Archives.)

3.6 In 1949, the IBM 407 began to reflect a significant change in the appearance of IBM's early computer machines.

(Courtesy, IBM Corporate Archives.)

3.7 The IBM 701 system demonstrates both a continuing move to a more contemporary image and also that these systems were becoming more sophisticated and larger.

(Courtesy, IBM Corporate Archives.)

next half century. That coordination involved the look and design of machines, sales and various headquarter offices, and product literature.

Before discussing this strategy, we examine several more images. Progress came with the "look," beginning with the introduction of the IBM 701 computer in the early 1950s. Figure 3.7 is a stock photo of an entire 701 system. Notice that every device is designed as an element of a coordinated presentation. Here IBM tells us there are more devices (input/output equipment) than in earlier systems. They appeared fashionable and contemporary in the early 1950s. That design style stayed essentially the same for several years. In the second half of the decade, the appearance of such machines changed, but again in a coordinated manner and with an integrated look—complex technology shown as sophisticated, modular, but synchronized. Veterans of World War II familiar with the interiors of navy ships and large aircraft would sense competence and sophistication.

Clean lines became part of the impression of what computers should look like. Figure 3.8 is a photograph of a large IBM 7090 taken in 1958, and figure 3.9, of an IBM 1401 from 1959. With these two images, we see what computers looked like into the mid-1960s. They are called "data processing systems," have a more contemporary look to them, were getting smaller (due to more modern

3.8 The very large IBM 7090 system represented the most complex computer of the time, circa 1958.

(Courtesy, IBM Corporate Archives.)

3.9 The IBM 1401 from a photograph taken in 1959 as marketing material. It became a popular system for use by mid-sized companies and agencies.

(Courtesy, IBM Corporate Archives.)

technologies), and displayed even cleaner lines. By then, various names had fallen by the wayside; IBM's processors were called computers. It took the company some time to stop calling their mainframes "calculators," fearful early on that the word "computer" might scare people into thinking these machines would automate away their jobs, as hinted at in the popular movie *Desk Set* (1957), staring Katharine Hepburn and Spencer Tracy.[58]

The evolution in the design of IBM's products culminated in the introduction in 1964 of the IBM System 360 family of mainframes and peripheral equipment, all representing a clean sweep to the dustbin of history of older lines of computers and input/output equipment to provide what the company wanted to sell—a comprehensive collection of compatible hardware and software encompassing a customer's 360 degrees of needs as they changed. That message was delivered with the image in figure 3.10. The fish-eye stock photograph speaks to the 360-degree message but also depicts an integrated "family" of machines that came in different colors, including IBM blue.

This line of computers did more to make ubiquitous computing in midsized to large enterprises and government agencies throughout the industrialized world. It was IBM's most successful product line, transforming IBM from a fast-growing computer company into a global behemoth to such an extent that everything discussed in this book was expanded more forcefully than in prior decades to integrate a large number of new employees coming rapidly into the firm. The challenge was to get them productive so they could perform the way prior generations of employees knew worked in the world of data processing. In 1964, worldwide, IBM employed slightly less than 150,000 people; in 1970, IBM employed over 269,000—adding over 100,000 new employees in six years. In 1964, IBM generated $3.2 billion in gross income; in 1970, $7.5 billion—more than double, along with comparable increases in profits.[59]

The "look" of IBM's systems settled down until the late 1970s. Figure 3.11 is a stock photo of the sequel to System 360 (System 370), which appears much like the prior one, illustrating the clean coordinated lines that were now seen as consistent with IBM's sense of modernity. One sees IBM offering a rational view of technology progressing in an evolutionary manner. The clutter of wires between machines or situated in offices was gone.[60] Systems were now in modern spaces dedicated to these products. 370s came in various colors, too, but if not specified, it came in one shade of blue used ubiquitously with all of IBM's products. The other colors were those in fashion in the 1970s evident, too, in clothing, furniture, and home appliances. An avocado-colored coffee pot would have seemed integrated into a data center's ambiance. This is not a trivial comment because coffee played an important role in the lives of data processing employees, a subject discussed in chapter 8.

For our discussion of computers, we only used stock IBM photographs because they could be guaranteed to present these products the way the

3.10 The System 360, introduced in the 1960s, reflects IBM's message of delivering a comprehensive computer with all necessary peripherals.

(Courtesy, IBM Corporate Archives.)

3.11 The IBM System 370 replaced the S/360 in the 1970s. The Model 158 shown here was one of the most widely used large computers. The image was aimed at experienced data processing organizations that expected the most modern up-to-date technology, as this image portrays.

(Courtesy, IBM Corporate Archives.)

company intended. We could have shown other photographs of, say, the IBM personal computer (PC) of the 1980s—small gray-colored systems—or laptops from the 1990s, which looked similar to the PCs but signaled the arrival of a new era where IBM's machines came in black, building on the look of an earlier new line of smaller computers (4300s) launched in the late 1970s. From then to the present, IBM's hardware came increasingly in black and were angular in look. Today's Z systems computers continue that angular black tradition launched in the late 1970s, four decades ago. Miniaturization of the relevant technologies made it easier to design equipment for ease of movement and to conserve space. Until the 1950s, machines were put together at a customer's data center from a plethora of parts, subassemblies, and individual machines, almost like one does Ikea furniture. Since then, the various devices (often referred to as *boxes*) could be wheeled through an office building, into a regular office elevator, and more quickly installed. It was not uncommon to bring in multiple copies (known as a *bank*) of tape or disk drives or a new computer itself and install them over a weekend. All machines acquired a fixed name and set of numbers with models representing variations. Thus, for example, one might have a System 370 Model 125; upgrade to a bigger computer in the family called a 135, 145, 155, and so forth; and yet continue to use the same peripheral equipment used by smaller models of the mainframe family.[61]

Rationalizing the look and feel of equipment, while giving these a contemporary image, helped to solve internal problems. IBM's world of technology following World War II can be conveniently summarized as two contending communities. Endicott, with its factory and research center, can be characterized as the Old School, Plant 1, home base for a half century of tabulating equipment now with its staff being forced into the world of computing. Then there was Poughkeepsie, which can be considered the New School, the emerging center for computers and software. Both sites competed for resources in the 1940s and 1950s; each produced lines of computers that were incompatible with each other's own products and across those of the other school. By the end of the 1950s, IBM had essentially a half dozen lines of computers, each with its own peripheral equipment and each requiring maintenance and development apart from the others. It was, to be blunt about it, a mess, driving up costs, while customers were complaining about the lack of technological compatibility with both hardware and software as their needs for computing grew rapidly. The warfare between the two camps need not detain us here, except to say Poughkeepsie won.[62] The R&D cultures of the two centers were different and have been described elsewhere, as they were unique unto themselves in addition to their sharing all the cultural norms described in this book.[63]

The Design Magic of Paul Rand

When turning outward to what the larger IBM population and the world saw, one might be excused for concluding that the view of the firm's image was spectacular in the post–World War II era, thanks to the genius of one person. When corporate management sought to modernize the company's image, a graphic designer came to their attention, Paul Rand (1914–1996). No other person in the history of the company contributed as much to shaping the public's ocular image of the company as he did. Watson Sr. used words to conjure impressions, while Rand used colors and designs. He would be remembered for designing logos for IBM, UPS, Westinghouse, and ABC, among others. He is considered one of the greats of his profession. Born and raised in Brooklyn, New York, as a young man, he designed magazine covers that garnered him acclaim in the 1930s. In the 1950s, he was busy designing corporate logos.[64] He had started to convince companies in the late 1940s that design was an important tool, coming to IBM at the moment senior managers had decided to do exactly that—to use design in combination with advertising and public relations to burnish IBM's image.

His most visible contribution came early in his relationship with IBM. In 1956, he completed his redesign of the IBM logo, which he continued to modify notably in 1960 and again in 1972. But it was his modification of 1972 that resulted in the striped logo that became almost as enduring an image as THINK. He subsequently developed variations of the striped logo, but no matter, they were slight.[65] From the 1950s until the mid-1990s, he designed images and covers for IBM publications. One of his most iconic was the "Eye-Bee-M" logo from 1981 that appeared on IBM posters, publications, coffee mugs, shirts, and baseball caps. Behind the scenes, however, he advised IBMers on how to integrate graphic designs into products, such as for the System 360 and 370, later laptops, and the colors, designs, and layouts of offices, indeed of buildings, in which products were exhibited. Figure 3.12 is an example where everything that one sees Rand designed: walls, floor, machine covers, even the layout of the hardware. In this case, it displays the IBM System 360 of the 1960s.

He went further to create images across multiple topics. One familiar to employees and customers in the 1980s was his signage for product centers: a gray circle with the stripped IBM logo and sign "Product Center," another in red.[66] His OS/2 Operating System logo from 1987 appeared on millions of PC manuals and diskettes. He designed entire issues of IBM's annual reports from 1957 through 1992. Rand prepared beautiful manuals to instruct product designers and media experts in IBM. These included *The IBM Look* (1973), *Product Center Guidelines* (1983), *IBM Logo Usage* (1985), *Guidelines for Using IBM Trademarks* (1986), *Sign Standards* (1986), *Use of the Logo, Abuse of the*

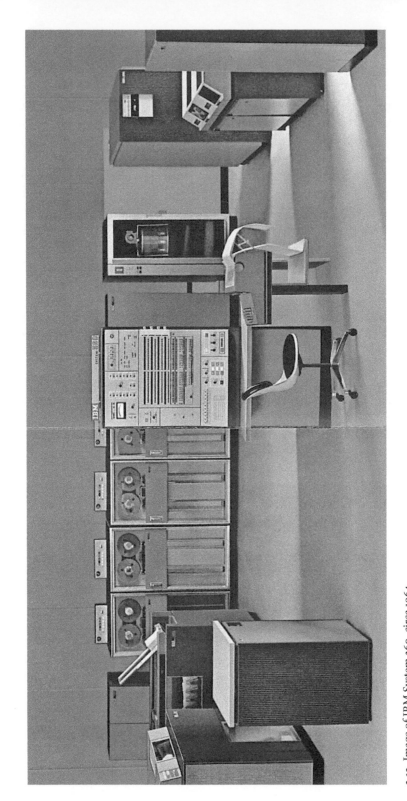

3.12 Image of IBM System 360, circa 1964.

(Courtesy, IBM Corporate Archives.)

Logo (1990), *The Logo Innovation* (1990), and *Advertising and Promotion Guide-lines for Remarketers of IBM Products* (1990).[67] He kept innovating his design. Figure 3.13 announced the arrival of yet another large mainframe late in his career, the System 390.

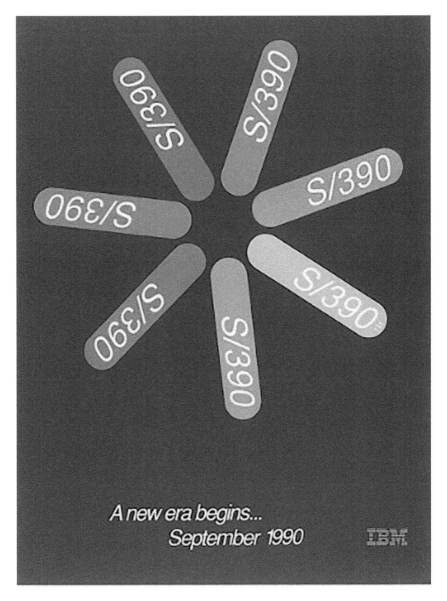

3.13 Cover design for IBM System 390 brochures and advertising, circa 1990.

(Courtesy, IBM Corporate Archives.)

IBM produced numerous posters, beginning in the 1950s, some of which Rand designed, such as for its customer support centers (1975); another to promote internal resource management (1980); for the Golden Circle of 1981, which were distributed to attendees; awards celebrating conferences in the early 1980s and IBM's seventy-fifth anniversary in 1989; and for various products, such as IBM's System 390 in 1989.[68]

Rand and his staff designed packaging for IBM's diskettes, ribbon and toner products, other miscellaneous product boxes, ink cartridges, and paper goods, and even for containers of IBM's printer ribbons, typewriter heads, and carbon paper. Even IBM batteries had logos on them, using a variant of the old black and white logo from the 1950s. Software and data cartridges from IBM in the 1980s and 1990s were packaged in his plastic and paper containers. He even designed the "look" of IBM pencils. His work appeared in almost every nook and cranny at IBM, including the cover of the *Business Conduct Guidelines* in the early 1980s (see figure 3.14), a telephone directory (1985), employee

3.14 Cover for IBM employee publication, *Business Conduct Guidelines*.

(Courtesy, IBM Corporate Archives.)

recruiting and product literature in the 1970s and 1980s, and materials for company-hosted events in the 1970s through the early 1990s. In short, he and his staff designed hundreds of publications, packages, facilities, corporate clothing, and parts for IBM. Most employees probably do not know that their calling cards were designed by his team, used since the 1960s, and also various versions of IBM stationery and business envelopes (including internal mail yellow large envelopes since the 1960s). Even the signs on buildings and at entrances to IBM properties came from Rand.[69]

The reason for going through this level of detail about what Rand did is to demonstrate how far IBM went to develop an integrated image for everything that touched a customer, employee, or the public. The fact that Rand was able to accomplish this over a long period of time meant that all of IBM's "touch points" with the world could be integrated—a key thought he brought to the process from his earliest encounters with IBM. He advocated that messages should be consistent, while color and design could be attractive and welcoming. IBM gave him the opportunity to embed his views across the company as it kept growing and increasing its needs for more and diverse messaging and image building.[70] He and his IBM clients were able to evolve over time, as happened with the most sacred of all images—the IBM logo, which for decades the company maintained a small staff to protect from even the slightest misuse or infringement. An example of control and protection illustrates the point. IBM's corporate archive is allowed to grant permission to an author to reproduce just about any image in its collection, such as the photographs used in this book. However, it is not allowed to grant use of the image of the IBM logo, even images that are no longer used and that have been retired for decades; for that, one must go to a designated corporate lawyer, and the company's guidelines are stringent.[71]

Ah! Those Blue Suits and White Shirts! Were They a Fourth Strategy?

It would be nearly impossible to discuss IBM's corporate culture, or at least the images held by employees, customers, information technology professionals, and even scholars, without discussing IBM's dress code. It has been the subject of much debate and many cartoons and jokes and is encased in more mythology than any other aspect of the company's culture. No material culture subject regarding IBM is more shrouded in misinformation and misunderstanding. While the subject of much joking and false facts, it remains an important feature of the company's image because the subject contributes positively to its reputation as a serious, responsible provider of information technologies and enlightened corporate practices.[72] It has since at least the late 1910s. The dress code was also a subject of some long-lived contention within the firm. To this day, the topic is discussed among employees and retirees even though the business world began going casual in the 1990s, first with "casual Fridays," then combination sports jackets and slacks (first with ties, then none), while women transitioned from dresses and high heels to pants suits and pumps in the 1990s. However, female executives kept wearing their bright red blazers, white blouses, and blue skirts deep into the next century but, for the most part, wisely gave up stiletto shoes.

From the dawn of the twentieth century, like every other profession, businesspeople had their own unofficial uniform—a suit with starched collars, silk ties, and polished leather shoes, especially in management and in all manner of office and technology work. Women wore dark dresses and white blouses, later dark skirts, and by the turn of the century, pants suits. Factory workers had their own uniforms—we conjure up the image of "blue collar/white collar" to explain. From the beginning, C-T-R/IBM personnel interacting with customers, the press, and government officials wore dark suits; they still do if, for example, calling on a senior government official, dealing with lawyers and courts, and in conservatively dressed industries, such as banking. In some countries, this generalization applied more broadly than in others. Watson Sr. set the pace when from his earliest days at C-T-R he wanted to professionalize his salesmen, and in part, that meant telling them they should dress like their customers.[73] As Walter A. Friedman, the preeminent historian of American salesmen observed, such a dress code was unusual for what otherwise was a highly unprofessional profession in the late 1800s.[74] Watson Sr. wore dark suits, often three-piece versions, starched collars, and dark ties. His son noted that the "Old Man" would come down to breakfast at home fully suited up for work.[75] In fact, when Watson Jr. took over the company after his father's death, he came to work one day wearing a blue shirt with a soft collar. The story goes that this was both a signal that there was a new boss in town and that the winds of change were blowing, while ambitious executives rushed out to buy new shirts.[76]

While the dress code is most often the subject of jokes and jabs, Watson Jr. did not think so lightly of the subject. In one of his last homilies to all of IBM's management written in the spring of 1971, he commented on the subject of personal appearances, one that he had studiously avoided discussing for decades. Appearances were important to him because a decline in standards "could eventually affect the performance of this corporation in a negative way," and so, he explained, "I am going to tell you candidly about my concerns and ask your help in getting back on the right track." He worried that too many people were exceeding "the bounds of good common sense in their business attire." He could have been channeling his father when he declared that "what we wear to work and how we look on the job does affect our business." Commenting on

customers, he stated that "the majority of the top executives across the country . . . still dress in a manner that would, on balance, be described as conservative." Further, "I do think it is safe to say that the midstream of executive
appearance is generally far behind the leading edge of fashion change." In short,
it is reality, and so, "a salesman who dresses in a similar conservative style will
offer little distraction from the main points of business discussion and will
be more in tune with the thinking of the executive." All IBMers should consider the possibility that, no matter their job, they might encounter a customer.
Watson Jr. went on to say, "In simple terms, this is why we have always had a
custom of conservative appearances in IBM. It made sense in the past and continues to make sense now, as a marketing tool," and he called on managers "to
set the proper example for your people." He refused to set guidelines, believing
it "impossible and inappropriate."[77] His comment is as close to an official IBM
mandate to wear dark suits as ever was issued.

In practice, it was another thing. Watson Jr. asked his managers "to apply
your individual judgment" as to what to do, and therein came the myths, the
confusion, and the relatively consistent practice of requiring people to dress
conservatively. It may not be an exaggeration to state that the vast majority
of employees who worked directly with customers had either experienced or
heard of some manager or colleague explain what the dress code was or that
someone had come to work wearing a blue shirt or a sports jacket and had been
sent home to change or was asked if they were taking a vacation day. New hires,
of course, were either counseled on how to dress or were astute enough to see
how they should dress by observing what everyone else was wearing. For the
better part of the twentieth century, sales office and field engineers always wore
suits and white shirts, even when they attended internal meetings or training.
We know because every class that an employee attended ended with a class
photograph; these documented the dress style for decades.

Let me make this simple. A thirty-year employee at IBM would have,
on average, attended several dozen one- to six-week classes and would
have kept a class photograph of many of these. Figure 3.15 is an example
from 1957; I have seen well over a thousand of these, dating from the 1920s
through the 2010s. All of those photographs looked exactly like this one until
about 2000. The people in this picture were customers and their instructors
(IBMers in the back row). The darkest-suited people would be the IBMers,
but note that the customers also wore suits. Figure 3.16 is an example from
1992; one hardly needed to take the picture in color.[78] The only difference
between the two is that the workforce had diversified by gender and ethnicity since the 1950s, beginning largely in the 1970s.

As amusing as it is to read the many comments made by employees and
retirees about the dress code—and there are many hundreds—a few extracted
from Facebook posted in the 2010s, when much of the old order of dark suits

3.15 Class photograph of an IBM class, this one for customers in 1957 in Endicott, New York. These photographs were given to attendees in all classes as a memento of their IBM experience.

(Courtesy, author's collection.)

3.16 Class photograph of an internal IBM class, taken in 1992, Palisades, New York.

(Courtesy, author's collection.)

had pretty much gone by the wayside, help situate the practices in IBM's culture. For example:

> I asked a branch manager why IBMers had to wear white shirts. He told me there was no mandatory rule or reason that we had to wear the white shirts but rather, it was just part of the company culture.
>
> 1974 I was refused entry into Houston Exxon Geo computer center because the folks there didn't think I was with IBM because I looked too young to be a CE for IBM . . . even though I had the required suit, white shirt, and Florsheim wingtips.
>
> When I joined a Baltimore Branch sub-office in 1965 I was handed a mimeographed "Dress Code" sheet. It specified: Dark gray, blue, black suit, no stripes, no patterns; white shirt and regimental tie.
>
> I was chastised for wearing a red wool suit [1980s] . . . if I really wanted to wear "those kind of clothes" I wasn't going anywhere.
>
> When Gerstner showed up in a blue shirt [1993–1994] you could not find one to buy two days later. I like white shirts because you could get dressed in the dark at 6 am. Just grab a tie, a dark suit and the 16 oz, wingtips and you were out the door.
>
> Every time I wore one [blue shirt, late 1980s], my Exec would stop by and say, "I see you are on vacation today." I gave in and went back to white shirts.
>
> In 1972 in a discussion with my manager, I said I wanted to be a manager one day, and he said, "You need to go shave your mustache, get a haircut, and go buy some long sleeve white shirts."
>
> When I first started, first day of orientation, a fellow newbie wore a pastel orange shirt, they sent him home to change.[79]

These quotes represent archetypical comments about the dress code. There were exceptions: "We were at the Motown Account in Detroit and I was introduced to an IBM Marketing Rep dressed like a Soul Train Rock Star." The humor was legendary, as an example from 1970–1971 suggests: "Watson Jr. on an executive call at a NY bank. He spotted someone in the back office area, dressed in bell-bottoms, dyed shirt, and long hair. He asked the bank CEO, 'Why do you let him work here, dressed that way?' The response, 'I'd fire him, but he works for IBM.'"[80] One employee reported that an employee walked in wearing loafers, and his manager sent him home because he was wearing slippers, requesting that he wear shoes.[81]

Nowhere was the unofficial uniform more prevalent than in divisional or corporate headquarters, where employees interacted mostly with other IBMers and where their superiors observed the behavior of these individuals. One recollection makes the point. In the late 1980s, Barbara Pinkston Barker, a technical staff member brought into corporate in Armonk, New York, to discuss patent infringement at one meeting recalled: "I remember my first trip to the IBM Armonk cafeteria. As I looked out over the room, all I saw were dark suits, white shirts, power ties and wingtip shoes."[82] Over the years, many employees made similar comments, including scientists at the research labs who kept a blue suit hung behind their office doors in case they had to run over to a meeting at a divisional or corporate office in the United States, or if senior executives came over to their facilities, such as to and from Zurich (Switzerland), Hursley (United Kingdom), Poughkeepsie, or Yorktown Heights.

Salesmen were always viewed as the elite in the company, in part because they dressed in expensive suits and were pleased with how they looked. Customer engineers (CEs)—those who installed and repaired equipment—felt slightly underclass, although customers highly respected them because of their work, yet they too wore dark suits, white shirts, and ties. The problem, of course, is that when installing or repairing machines, their clothing became dirty, ripped, and spotted with grease, oil, and printer toner. The casualty rate for their clothes was high, so they tended to buy less expensive suits and tried to wear short-sleeve white shirts too. They frequently related stories of damaged clothing, wishing they did not have to wear these.[83] The difference in suits between sales and CEs remained a cultural space for discussing differences between the two professions. Only in research laboratories could employees wear long hair, sweaters, and blue jeans in the post–World War II period, but not before.

Factory personnel operated in a different environment. Most workers, men and women, in most companies in most countries on either side of the Atlantic dressed the same way: men wore white shirts and dark wool or cotton pants and leather shoes, and women wore white blouses and dark skirts, normally cotton or wool. That was the uniform from the nineteenth century to World War II; little variety had ever been available for factory workers.[84] Men rolled up their sleeves, women did not. Blue jeans and colored shirts were a post–World War II phenomenon at IBM and elsewhere. It was also not uncommon for men before the 1920s to wear a tie of some sort while working on the shop floor. At IBM, as in most manufacturing companies, factory management wore black suits a cut above what their employees wore. From the dawn of the company's existence to the end of the twentieth century, if customers or senior or divisional management visited a factory, it was customary for local management to wear a suit and tie. By the end of the 1950s, women on the shop floor at IBM could wear "work pants," while by the early 1960s, men and women working in such high-tech areas as computer chip manufacturing were required to wear white jumpsuits and various head regalia because of the need to maintain "clean room" standards. The white jumpsuits were provided by IBM and had big blue IBM logos on them.

For a final point about the global practices of wearing suits and ties, we turn to a female salesperson from 1991, Pamela Losey. She told a reporter that she could spot an IBM employee in an airport from a distance. "It's a radar honing device, a sixth sense." With many years of experience and as a second-generation IBMer, she could say, "Long before the introductions are made, you know who the IBMers are."[85] The IBMer called IBM employees a "clan" and observed that "when dealing with the public, buttoned-up IBM employees take the job of representing their company serious . . . and that spit n' polish attitude stays with employees even after they leave the company. . . . IBM employees are well known for their professional touch. For the most part, they're conservatively dressed, generally unflappable, always polite—the IBM universe is clearly an orderly one."[86] This was the image the "dress code" was intended to facilitate.

When a new CEO came to IBM in the early 1990s, however, he noticed that some employees had departed from Watson Jr.'s admonishment that they dress like their customers. "Lou" Gerstner observed that while customers were dressing less often in dark suits and white shirts, some of his employees stuck to the old dress code. It was so obvious a behavior that in 1995 he actually had to "abolish" (his word) IBM's dress code, which he found everyone thought existed. What he did was to return to Watson Jr.'s advice that people dress like their customers for the same reason: "I simply returned to the wisdom of Mr. Watson and decided: Dress according to the circumstances of your day and recognize who you will be with."[87] During the 1990s and 2000s, how people dressed changed in the direction that both Watson men and Gerstner would have approved of, an affirmation of a century-long engagement less with clothing and more with customer relations.

Conclusions

Students of corporate cultures barely discuss a company's identity or its reputation, unless engaged in an exploration of the role of public relations or advertising.[88] They do this for good reason, because grand strategies, market and competitive issues, product development and innovation, and financial performance require priority attention. But as this chapter demonstrates, none of those issues can exist without the mundane day-to-day work of employees. Here we explain that issues of identity are deep, pervasive, and important. Pride in working for a highly regarded firm is an important motivator and marker for success, at least confidence (sometimes arrogance too). Reputation precedes performance. This needs to be nurtured because reputations are fragile flowers that can bloom, but even more quickly wither if not cared for. IBM demonstrated that process at work, indicating that the subject linked to all manner of work and perceptions. More than entwined in the work of an enterprise, it appears integral to a corporation's culture. This chapter barely exposed the evidence for that; much more study is warranted. It is a far larger, more nuanced subject than public relations, media management, or advertising, although these are components of a company's operational tool kit.

Creating and sustaining a corporate image involve a wide range of activities and, ultimately, all employees. In IBM's case, its first CEO led the charge, which probably consumed up to half of his time for many years. Increasingly over time, the other tools were added as large corporations learned how to use them, such as how best to manage relations with the press. But, as with other aspects of company operations engaging with its culture, all managers were expected to reinforce consistent messages and practices all over the world. By the end of the 1930s, Watson Sr. had fully engaged management in that task, one that became a permanent part of their job. By the end of the 1950s, it was clear that employees were involved, too, in protecting and promoting the company's values, practices, and reputation.

With the rapid and massive expansion of the 1960s, all had to reengage more, assume less, and educate over 100,000 new employees. One could not assume that everyone understood IBM's culture or reputation; IBM had to bring into its fold thousands of new customers, too. To preserve the company's reputation, new tools were needed, such as the Business Conduct Guidelines and the requirements that everyone read them and sign off that they had done so. In pre–World War II IBM, such practices were baked into how the business operated without the pseudo-contractual patina of a document having to be signed by employees to retain their employment. By the end of the 1960s, IBM had deployed staffs across all divisions, regional headquarters, and worldwide to handle media relations, marketing guidelines, lawyers to protect the firm and its reputation, and even advertising. In fact, one of the things the company had to do in the 1990s was to recentralize some of these activities to reduce expenditures, as for advertising, and to recalibrate practices in a consistent manner, as with marketing practices.

Although employee opinion surveys over the course of the second half of the twentieth century indicated they liked their company's values and reputation, there were some who criticized management for not living up to them.[89] With the fracture of IBM's lifetime employment practices in the late 1980s, criticisms of IBM's reputation became a permanent and substantial feature of the company's culture, damaging it in the eyes of many employees.[90] The employee jams held in 2003–2004 demonstrated that not all was well in Big Blue. Yet positive views outweighed the negatives even after 1990, suggesting how sticky corporate beliefs and behaviors could be.

But reputations could decline, so management and employees alike paid attention when such business publications as *Forbes*, *Fortune*, and others ranked companies by reputation and performance. CEO John R. Opel opined in a message to all managers in 1981 that reflected their collective interest: "As IBMers we take pride in the fact that we work for a quality company. . . . The very name

IBM, in fact, has always signified quality." He cited a recent survey regarding corporate reputations among twenty large firms and reported that 82 percent believed IBM provided high-quality goods and services, "seven percentage points higher than the second-ranking company." He drew the same conclusion as this chapter that "reputation is a fragile thing."[91] While he went on to discuss how the company would continue to focus on quality products—a widespread emphasis in the 1980s and 1990s across most large corporations because of successful Japanese incursions into American and European markets—he nonetheless linked it to a need to do more as a regular course of business.

Today, when management ponders what position to take with respect to some socially charged issue, such as data privacy considerations in Europe, access to voting in the United States, or to what degree to remain silent about Chinese human rights practices, reputation and image are always at stake. Does a company take what seemingly is a reasonable public stance on a "hot" issue today and risk the loss of a reputation built up over decades? Or does not doing so likewise tarnish a corporate image because it refused to be "on the right side of history"? These are the perils facing modern corporate management, and it does not help that these manifest themselves around the world in different forms. Watson Sr. faced these when he thought he could persuade Adolf Hitler to change his ways before World War II, and his son and Frank Cary encountered them with the growing hostility toward apartheid in South Africa in the 1970s, issues that IBM had to navigate through while simultaneously doing all the work to build out the reputation and image described in this chapter. Both sets of activities must occur, carefully calibrated. But if there is a lesson to be drawn, it is that reputation is more than just earned; it is created, and that task is complicated, extensive, serious, and never-ending.

Furthermore, it does not work out smoothly all the time because sometimes not all goes well in a company, and IBM was not immune to that reality. Nowhere was this most evident than in unionizing activities in the American side of the company, the issue discussed in chapter 5, and that is a story historians have not explored but represents an important chapter in the company's history. But before we can address that issue, one more set of actors in the development of IBM's culture must first be introduced: most specifically, how IBM recruited and developed this community—IBM's managers. We turn next to their role.

CHAPTER 4

DEVELOPING MANAGERS IN A MULTINATIONAL CORPORATION

... the continued success of our corporation clearly depends on how well managers bring out the energies and talents of their people.

Thomas J. Watson, Jr., 1968[1]

For over half of the twentieth century, corporate managers in large enterprises admired how IBM operated and thought them worthy of emulating. Business media routinely ranked IBM one of the best-run companies, and when it entered a period of sharp decline in the late 1980s, but then rapidly recovered in the 1990s, it continued to attract the attention of academics, media, and management teams.[2] Yet what is known about how IBM attained its iconic status remains surprisingly less understood than its reputation suggests is the case. The usual explanations of good management and the ability to control operations, develop and introduce relevant products at the right time, and use information technologies have been well articulated, but these explanations are insufficient, and exceptions always existed.

Increasingly, new lines of research offer clarifications built on earlier research regarding IBM's success that surfaced additional insights about how IBM did so well for so long. The first holds that IBM created an information ecosystem that enveloped its employees, customers, and even their collective industry into a closed-loop world of shared views and practices.[3] This closed loop included managerial philosophies and business values, operational practices and procedures, types of technologies, instructions on how to use these, and attitudes regarding politics and economic issues. The second was the notion that IBM, like many other international companies, created a corporate culture that aligned tightly with its strategic business and tactical operational objectives to explain its success—the central topic of this book.[4] This second concept has long been recognized as valid but not well understood outside the company. Yet employees considered it crucial in explaining IBM's success.[5] The many who have written about IBM over the decades additionally offered a third consideration: that the secret to their company's success was the quality of its workforce.[6]

As business historians and senior executives acknowledge, the truth lay within a combination of all these elements to explain IBM's stature and performance. Students of IBM and other corporations face the challenge of sorting out specific details, but, as two historians observed recently, "they entered the twenty-first century with a flourish," calling for multidisciplinary approaches, resulting in raising "novel questions, voiced and positioned beyond familiar queries."[7] Edgar Schein was one of the first students of corporate culture to do this effectively. I, perhaps more than other observers, emphasize the centrality of management's role in IBM's case, suggesting by implication that its activities are crucial to other companies. This emphasis is what makes Schein's list of processes a firm must nurture happen: having a compelling positive image, formal training for everyone, providing optional ways to learn and develop, having coaches (I use the word *mentors*), nurturing and celebrating positive role models, staffing support groups, and creating and funding systems and structures consistent with a company's beliefs, strategies, and desired changes.[8]

Embedded in the literature about corporate histories, including IBM's, is the notion that management enabled the firm's successes.[9] IBM employees who have written about the company have made the case that management's role proved crucial from the top of the house to a newly minted first-line manager in a sales branch office or factory floor.[10] All pointed to the continuous expansion of sales and number of customers, to the development of some of the most important technologies and products of the twentieth century, and to the high level of coordination and consistency of operations evident in this company around the world. Multinational corporations aspire to the qualities of being able to leverage their assets globally, of having all their offices look and act the same worldwide, and of sharing common values and predictable behaviors welcomed by employees, customers, and national governments. IBM accomplished these objectives, keeping them functional in both good and bad times and in the highly disruptive even chaotic periods of massive growth in its employee population, as occurred in the 1950s–1970s.[11]

Ask any employee how that was possible, and they will probably respond ambiguously that it was the "management system" that methodically accomplished this work. They less frequently use the word "bureaucracy," because that term was more narrowly—and pejoratively—ascribed to "paperwork" or "rules."[12] IBM's history illustrates, too, that managerial practices remained remarkably consistent and stable over the period from the 1930s to the mid-1990s around the world except where local law and government regulations dictated alternative procedures, before they began evolving into new forms that have yet to solidify into normative practices. Even then, some of the older behaviors remained, conditioned by government regulations; accounting rules; laws dictating personnel and unionizing activities; accepted "best practices" in strategy, marketing, R&D, production, and sales; and styles of management.[13] The commonly shared worldwide practices taught to generations of business and accounting graduates who worked in large corporations standardized how companies operated from one to another.[14] In such ways, IBM was no different, nor in the fact that approximately 5 to 7 percent of its workforce has been composed of managers and executives since the 1950s. So, one of the ways to understand how IBM succeeded (and stumbled occasionally) is by studying the character, personality, and behavior of its managers, and not simply by continuing to repeat what they accomplished.

Students of leadership and management concur that managerial activities are central to the creation and evolution of a company's culture and activities in many societies. Much of the literature on leadership announces that managers (leaders) are the key people who "make things happen." Historian Alfred D. Chandler, Jr., was not the first to demonstrate that reality with large corporations through his studies in the 1960s–1990s, bringing greater attention to the issue than earlier scholars. Today's experts repeat the lessons that Chandler had learned long ago.[15] But, in this chapter, we demonstrate that post-Chandlerian commentators can learn that many companies recognized the centrality of well-trained motivated managers over a century ago and that this kluge of firms included IBM.[16]

To get to the point, IBM senior management leveraged the firm's managers and executives to create the company's corporate culture to carry out its objectives and activities. A critical question, therefore, has to be: How were these people recruited, trained, and developed to do this work? Hiring smart people was part of the answer, but as employees will state, in any period, that act alone was not sufficient, nor was motivating everyone with properly aligned financial and career development programs. The company still needed its cheerleaders, or just leaders, equipped with shared values, common experiences, and skills to do this work. Managers had to be cultivated. To draw on this chapter's title, they had to be *developed*. Developing a manager involved a number of actions, ranging from hiring smart people to teaching them how to do specific jobs and how to work within the existing corporate culture of their day. They had to be *mentored* in various jobs to engrain in them both leadership skills and the shared aspirations of their divisions and of the corporation as a whole. Their careers also had to be *managed* to assure a constant supply of qualified managers—leaders—at all levels of the enterprise. That was never more necessary than for all senior positions in the firm. For our purposes, the term "senior positions" is defined as junior executives (e.g., directors and vice presidents) in a division right up through chairman of the board. But even in entry-level management positions, succession planning of all positions encompassed three requirements: development, mentoring, and career management. These responsibilities were shared up and down the organization and through the ranks, even involving those not in management. These activities were carried on during the entire time of a manager's employment, which for most employees, covered the span of two to four decades. In other words, everything discussed here remained part of what IBM managers did throughout their entire careers.

How did IBM's community of employees carry out these tasks? Our purpose is to begin answering this question. It focuses largely on the American experience, since it was in the United States that this culturally American corporation initiated and exported its managerial practices. Here, we use the word *manager* to include supervisors, managers, and executives because inside the firm their roles were essentially the same, regardless of level, and because IBM nurtured a culture in which meritocracy and ideas were more important in conversations than one's rank.

We proceed by first describing IBM's definition of the role of manager, because senior management wanted no ambiguity on the matter, followed by a discussion of how the company recruited managers. We then turn to how these managers were trained to fulfill their role, as it was a well-defined process, followed by an explanation of how they were mentored and managed over the course of their careers, again, because that too was not an accidental happenstance. As with everything else at IBM, managers were evaluated by the quality of their performance, a subject barely touched on by scholars and only by some IBM memoirists. We conclude with an evaluation of the effectiveness of the overall managerial development process and implications for scholars and other firms.

To clarify our objectives, let us state what is not discussed. I do not describe the specific actions managers took—that is largely what historians of IBM have done. That also means this chapter is not bulked up with war stories and case studies of "good" and "bad" managers, of which IBM had both—that is largely what the memoirists and historians, too, provide. Nor do I frequently point out individual managers as emblematic of managerial qualities and behaviors because every manager was expected to exercise their own way of doing things, within reason. All individuals were recognized as unique in their

personalities, experiences, and ways of behaving and speaking and had to integrate their roles into the specific realities on the ground. This last observation
is more than just obvious because, for the company to function in a cohesive
way around the world, it had to allow the existence of individual styles shaped
by local cultural behaviors.

IBM's Concept of the Role of a Manager

American business perspectives as defined inside IBM and by many peer firms
and customer enterprises largely shaped the concepts of management and the
position of manager. Early IBM executives were familiar with the work of Frederick W. Taylor from the dawn of the twentieth century, who is credited with
promoting the concept of management as a set of work practices.[17] Americans
and historians also thought of management as a profession, a new one certainly
by the early 1900s.[18] Such individuals worked for companies and government
agencies. Increasingly over time, their job as managers became socially and
professionally prestigious. From the 1870s to the 1920s, notions about what
managers did took shape across the American economy, engaging companies.
IBM—an American enterprise—was not immune to this shaping exercise and
to the influences of recently established academic business schools.[19] The latter
made it their purpose to define management as a profession with scientifically
based discipline-oriented practices.[20]

Inside the firm, many viewed IBM's management as seemingly monolithic
around the world. An IBM Dutch personnel manager in the 1960s and 1970s,
Geert Hofstede, was a student of the profession who argued, however, that the
role varied, affected by local cultural features. He acknowledged, too, that as a
general observation American firms placed greater emphasis on the centrality
of managers within the overall workforce than, say, Europeans. IBM's experience demonstrated his observation at work, at least during the 1960s–1980s,
the period he studied.[21] The reality at that time, as before and still evident
afterward, was that workers—nonmanagers—often made the many mundane
decisions about how work was to be done. Managers maintained networks,
coordinated accumulation and deployment of all manner of resources, took
direction from executive management on priorities, and responded to market
activities that so occupied the interest of managers and business management
scholars.[22] In short, there were basic notions about the role of management that
emerged from IBM's corporate culture that manifested themselves as the firm
desired with actions motivated by its shared values and culture.[23] So, definitions provided by IBM to its employees, while seemingly theoretical and high-
minded, where tempered by immediate realities filtered through the lens of the
company's Basic Beliefs of respect for the individual, excellence in all that one

did, and strong customer service.[24] Managers were expected to put into practice those beliefs and to instill them in all their employees. But first, we turn to more explicit definitions.

Watson Sr. established the company's culture and defined many of its work processes, while his son extended these in a much larger firm. The younger Watson did more to formalize the role of managers than prior executives. He periodically stated the obvious, such as about the role of managers: "Every member of management is expected and required, as an essential part of his responsibilities, to promote the interests of IBM as a whole, to conduct his activities within the framework of corporate policies, and to facilitate the work other IBM units which his actions affect."[25] That definition is broad, and he went on to clarify the role to include crafting business strategies, understanding and conforming to company guidelines, managing budgets, proposing necessary changes in the firm's operations, staffing these with appropriately skilled people, and communicating effectively with employees and others, among various actions—all fairly normal in any company. He mandated that managers had to "create an atmosphere conducive to management development by encouragement and praise for initiative, imagination and resourcefulness, and by advice and example in the exercise of judgment."[26] Watson Jr. made these statements in 1960, reflecting what had essentially been the expectations since he joined the company in the 1930s. They endured for decades after he was gone, remaining intact into the twenty-first century. One major effect on these over time, however, came when women became managers by the end of the 1970s, because many introduced new styles of carrying out the same managerial duties.

When an individual was promoted to the job of manager, they were required to attend "New Manager Training" or "Basic Management," cutely called "Charm School," beginning in the 1940s, although earlier ad hoc training programs began in the 1910s. In these classes that ran for one or sometimes two weeks, employees were taught all the usual things one might expect: recruiting, salary administration and performance evaluation methods, training of employees, assignment of work, strategy and planning, company policies, positions on issues (e.g., unionizing activities), legal matters, and so forth. Such training continued episodically for the duration of a manager's employment at IBM and at all levels through senior executive ranks. The definition of management given to new managers remained unchanged during the twentieth century. The new managers were immediately told that "management is primarily the task of getting things done through people." This was to be carried out through "the activity, which plans, organizes and controls the operations of the business, providing leadership and coordination to the human resources so as to achieve the desired objectives. An ability in working with people and in communications is essential in management success."[27]

Next, instructors—all experienced managers in their own right—explained the duties shared across all levels of management: "to employ; to teach; to supervise; to promote people who deserve it; and to discharge when necessary." More famously quoted for decades was a further explication: "To your employees, you represent IBM. It is your business to see that the company is represented fairly. To higher management, you represent your employees. Through you, management knows the needs and problems of the individual. Through you, management learns of the good and bad effects of its actions. To the public, you represent IBM—and you are judged by the impressions you make. To all groups, at all times, you represent yourself. You are judged by your actions."[28] Thus, managers were granted much authority—leeway—to do their work the way they thought appropriate, and they were encouraged to "use this authority."[29]

Every employee, regardless of title or position, received an annual performance plan, normally negotiated with their manager, but always documented on a standard form used across the second half of the twentieth century and that became the basis for judging one's performance at the end of the year. These plans took the lofty and generalized definitions of management and translated them into specifics relevant to an individual. Important to keep in mind, too, is that both employee and manager were required to agree to these.[30] An example of a performance plan adds specificity to the definition of an IBM manager. "Administrative manager" is a title used in most companies; it can mean anything. In our case, the definition, which was drawn from the 1960s and remained essentially unchanged for over a half century, stated that the objectives of this particular instance (in accounting) were to handle accounts receivables and aged items and to pass a satisfactory audit. These were given a relative importance of "one." Of relative importance of "two" were personnel matters: morale, training, and counseling. In third relative importance was general management, specifically demonstrating business judgment, initiative, and leadership. A second page described more specific tasks, such as, "Establish financial plan for Branch Office, initiate action and controls to insure attainment of plan. Perform regular analysis to measure actual vs. planned objectives. Direct administrative function to insure customer satisfaction and meet all objectives in this area." Regarding audits required one to "pass the audit with a Satisfactory rating in each functional area." The personnel tasks included: "Identify and train high potential employees for expanded responsibilities." There were three typed pages of descriptions of each of the manager's tasks and expectations. But one that appeared in many a manager's portfolio and that existed for our example, too, is the final one: "Conduct management development program for potential management personnel. Construct, review with me by May 1, and follow on a self-development program."[31]

Such shells of performance plans were tailored to each line of work. For example, "marketing managers" (a.k.a. sales managers with sales personnel reporting to them) would have similar language about developing personnel, customer relations (i.e., "Territory Management"), expense management, and the requirement to implement a personnel development plan for themselves and all their employees. They were responsible for sales, so, in the Territory Management section, they were directed to: "Establish well defined account marketing plans that include all IBM services. Makes plans work. For outstanding performance manage unit [all their sales staff] to exceed SRP 150 percent, IRP 110 percent, Services 110 percent, etc. Enhance our marketing posture with [name of customer company]." SRP and IRP were numeric sales targets in IBM language, but note in this plan, the marketing managers were expected to at least make their targets. Making "their numbers" and personnel management were ranked equally as a priority of "one," sound business decision-making and staffing a "two," and personal development a "three."[32] Even the chairman of the board had a performance plan negotiated with the board of directors, as required by U.S. laws and regulations.[33]

Several observations can be extracted from this brief discussion about the role of manager at IBM. At all levels of the company, managers shared common job definitions. They demonstrated through their actions that they shared IBM's worldviews and values and were prepared to enforce these. Thus, as individual managers moved from one job (or location) to another, they brought with them practices that they universally shared, familiar to their charges. As in other multinational corporations, there existed a belief that management was a ubiquitous skill set that could be applied anywhere in the firm. That was true, but only to a point, because while all managers had to exercise common personnel practices consistent with local national custom and law, develop strategies, control expenses, and so forth, in order to carry out these functions, they had to know the specific tasks and issues within an organization. For example, a competent marketing manager might work well in a sales division but would not do well in running, say, a microprocessor quality control team in a factory. However, our administrative manager might be able to function in a factory or sales office because such an individual understood the budgeting processes at IBM, which had similar features across the firm. In fact, some virtual fraternities emerged in support of these near-universal features, such as F&P (finance and budgeting) staff who created, distributed, and monitored budget matters; the community of lawyers who worked with common issues across all divisions; and most obvious, personnel. Those three informal fraternities (indeed social networks) provided vertical and horizontal matrices promoting standard practices across the corporation. That there was room for much subjective judgments (fair and unfair from an employee's perspective) cannot be denied, as no personnel process could be perfect, but what existed proved effective in shaping performance and supplying the corporations with managers.[34]

Managers also maintained relations with their peers in other multinational corporations, borrowing practices and learning from each other how to do their work. Personnel managers did this as a formal exercise, but managers dealing with other large enterprises learned too, if only by osmosis.[35] Such interactions help to explain why IBM was both like so many other corporations in its behaviors and also admired, because while IBM's managers were learning from other firms, those other enterprises were doing the same.

IBM's peer corporations and customers frequently marveled at the consistency of its organization and behavior, giving those who dealt with the company confidence in their understanding of how it functioned and how management would react to their requests, complaints, and expectations. One of the reasons global enterprises did so much business with IBM was that a customer executive in one country could hire IBM to build out a process or implement a computerized system worldwide for them, confident that IBM could coordinate internally what needed to be done, often better than the customer, and that the performance in, say, Indonesia, Canada, France, and the United States would be appropriately similar and synchronized.[36] That reflected IBM's ecosystem at work. Few of IBM's competitors could perform that consistently over the decades. By the end of the 1960s, IBM routinely did this. Its history remains almost anonymous.[37]

It is a feature of IBM's work normally overlooked by students of the company's activities, steering closer to a related but different point, that IBM could handle big, complex technical projects, such as helping the U.S. Social Security Administration launch its nationwide pension program in the 1930s or coordinating computing work related to the launch of the first humans to the Moon in the 1960s. The latter played to IBM's technical strengths and project management skills, the former to the construction and operation of a management system. Both shared one common requirement, of course: deployment of skilled, experienced managers and their employees across multiple divisions.

IBM had anywhere from five to ten layers of management over the course of its history; the number kept oscillating up and down. In the 1910s–1930s, three to five layers were more common, essentially for two reasons. Watson Sr. had a large number of "direct reports," to use an IBM term that almost echoed the management structure of a Catholic bishop if one accepted the analogy that priests were managers of their parishes. He also had a difficult time delegating authority, especially when the company was small.[38] By the time his son took over management of IBM in 1956, IBM was too big to be run that way any longer, and so within the year, Watson Jr. created a new organization that had divisions and similar substrata of management positions, mimicking structures emerging in other large American and European enterprises. He could now delegate vast amounts of authority, which would have been difficult for his father to acquiesce.

In addition, as the company grew in size, the number of physical locations and people to manage expanded. More specialized functions emerged, adding to the coordination of activities, normally described as bureaucracy needed to run the enterprise.[39] Yet to be studied by historians is the history of that bureaucracy, but to veteran employees, while they often perceived it as a nuisance, it proved essential in operating a company with several hundred thousand employees in over 170 countries.[40] It was all about coordination. But even the harshest critics of their company's bureaucracy had to admit that by the late 1960s the company's rapid growth made it inevitable that IBM would "become infested with bureaucracy," despite efforts to curb it as the company learned to operate as an enterprise now populated with hundreds of thousands of employees.[41] Having a shared vision of what managers did was not merely fodder for business professors; it was essential to the survival of "Big Blue."

Add in the practice of moving managers around from one location to another, reinforcing the old company joke that IBM stood for "I've Been Moved," because these employees carried from one site to another the corporate values and behaviors they learned and taught from one to another, thereby reinforcing common behaviors and formal practices (bureaucracy). As one critic—a manager—facetiously observed in the 1980s of management's behavior: "Bureaucracy does seem to be an equal-opportunity program. Anyone and everyone can play the game."[42]

Diverse participants in meetings and classes served the same purpose of creating shared views and practices. Attendees at management training classes came from all over the country or around the world and took back to their home organizations a commonly shared set of values, behaviors, and course content. One set of activities reinforced another in a virtuous circle across the life of all employees. For example, a Lebanese IBM manager in the 1970s and 1980s took the exact same courses as his peers in the United States, beginning with "Charm School" taught in Beirut, and then classes in Belgium, France, Kuwait, and Greece. These were on such subjects as communications, "IBM Business Practices," and "IBM Quality Management." Each class was populated with employees from various countries, including from around the Middle East for those held in Beirut and Europe.[43]

Where Did Managers Come From?

The answer to this question varied over time, with the result that how managers operated and their values varied as well, so it is an important question to explore. For the most part, the vast majority of managers were recruited from among IBM employees, a practice still widely evident. However, this is a general observation because there were exceptions. For example, Watson Sr., who shaped a loosely grouped collection of three firms into IBM, was an outside hire in 1914; Louis V. Gerstner, Jr., IBM's CEO from 1993 to 2002, was also an outside hire. Both had to lead significant transformations of the firm. To assist in that endeavor, each brought in from other companies managers to fill key senior positions. Besides having to demonstrate proven managerial capabilities to Watson in the 1910s and to Gerstner in the 1990s, managers newly hired into the firm had to bring with them perspectives unencumbered by experience in C-T-R's three companies or IBM, or of being a product of these two business cultures. The other general exception was the wholesale incorporation of managers from companies acquired by IBM. While acquisitions occurred over the decades, they were of small firms and few. This practice changed in the 1990s when the company acquired computing services enterprises and software houses and recruited experienced managers to rapidly increase its offerings in those areas (notably running data center outsourcing and, later, management consulting). Since 1990, IBM has acquired nearly two hundred firms. Some were large (e.g., Lotus, and PwC, the latter with 30,000 consultants and their management), which disrupted sharply the company-wide practice of hiring managers only from within many parts of the company.[44]

Future historians will have to assess the impact of such a change in recruiting practices—which I believe was significant—but here we explore the norm as it functioned from the 1920s to the mid-1990s. Even in those occasions of exceptions, the lower one went into the company, the more it was the case that managers were recruited from within the firm's ranks around the world. Despite the influx of many employees into IBM in the 2000s, including a great many senior executives, the firm still maintained long-serving employees in the highest ranks. For example, all three chairmen/CEOs who followed Gerstner's retirement in 2002 were career IBMers.[45]

By the early 1920s, Watson Sr. had a sufficient pool of long-serving employees from which to draw managers who knew how to get things done within IBM, which was essential given the nature of their activities. They understood the functions of the highly specialized work they had to manage because they had done the same themselves as a prerequisite to being considered for managerial positions. They supported the company's Basic Beliefs and ways of doing things. Those two last points—Basic Beliefs and ways of working—proved crucial by the late 1920s when IBM was beginning to operate in a relatively stable market environment that it dominated without severe changes or threats until the end of the 1970s, surviving even the Great Depression, World War II, and significantly different technological changes in data processing. That long half-century's relative operational and cultural stability remained intact during the transition from tabulating equipment to computers in the 1950s to early 1960s.

But the quality and commonality of management and their practices did not emerge in such an integrated fashion. The firm took decades to achieve what was just described. The quality of its management varied a great deal in the early decades. As long as sales were growing, as they did in the 1920s, variability was tolerable. During the early 1930s, at the height of the Great Depression, poorly performing managers were quietly taken out of their jobs (not necessarily fired), while it was understood by the sales force that poorly performing colleagues would, too, be removed from sales or more likely be dismissed from the firm.[46] During World War II, IBM found it difficult to develop or hire more managers and executives because so many individuals were pulled into military services around the world. With the end of the war and business expanding, the requirement for more executives and managers, not to mention employees for all manner of jobs, led to much discussion by senior leaders about how to address the need for training on practices and beliefs. These concerns were compounded by the arrival of the computer in the 1950s, which necessitated a company-wide education program and development of new business practices and procedures for dealing with this entirely new form of technology that proved complicated yet became quickly popular.

So, recruiting the "right" people proved essential. Because of the complexity of IBM's products, it was crucial that these people have several attributes. The first was a better-than-average intelligence. That proved so important that by the 1950s to even be taken seriously in an interview to work at IBM, prospective employees had to pass an intelligence test that could be administered in any IBM office.[47] It was mandatory. Managers did the actual recruiting and hiring, not someone from a personnel department, because another critical attribute one sought was fit. The person had to function well within IBM's world and culture, specifically in the office, factory, or laboratory in which they would work. Managers sought people with high physical energy and alertness, good communications skills, a willingness to learn, and skills that would make it possible for them to be productive early in their tenure. Many managers might add that they looked for people who could potentially rise in the company and had already demonstrated leadership appropriate for their age. With intelligence and fit, such people could be trained and mentored through what was expected to be a thirty- to forty-year career. So choosing well proved crucial; it was difficult to fire one's hiring mistakes. As one European IBM manager observed in the 1980s, "IBM is able to, and often does, employ as 'workers' people who would qualify as directors in many other organizations."[48]

All employees were led to believe they could rise in this corporation, an ethos expounded almost from the first day Watson Sr. came to work at the company in 1914. Regarding their recruiting responsibilities, managers were told for generations that they had to hire people "who may, one day, be guiding influences in the Corporation."[49] Managers had been given formal training on how to conduct recruiting interviews since the 1920s.[50] They were taught to look for features of character: loyalty, honesty, industry, perseverance, emotional stability, and initiative. They had to see mental capacity demonstrated, such as analytical and creative abilities, intellectual curiosity, and judgment. Physical appearances counted too, such as grooming, facial expressions, manners, and vigor. They needed social skills, such as the ability to "inspire confidence and admiration in others" and cooperativeness (today known as teaming); they had to have both professional and nonprofessional interests and be able to convey "ideas fluently, forcefully, and concisely."[51] Managers needed all these attributes to succeed in IBM, and most of these could not be taught; the employee had to have these coming into the company.

In periods of company growth when it needed many thousands of new hires, managers were still admonished not to hire just warm bodies but to adhere to the guidelines they were taught. The slang quip was "no breadth was better than bad breadth." But managers had to convince high-quality candidates that IBM was the place to be, especially in the 1950s through the 1970s. By the 1960s, IBM had its official position on the matter also communicated to all managers: "IBM's basic policy on employment is to hire the best qualified applicant for a particular job, regardless of race, color, creed, sex, national origin, or age. In this way, we will obtain the qualified people we need and at the same time provide equal opportunities for all applicants."[52] This was important because from these ranks came future managers. One additional comment, drawn from a manager's training course from the 1960s, is relevant: "It is the objective of IBM to employ: 1. The best qualified persons available in the various types of work carried on in IBM. 2. Technical competence on the level of initial placement. 3. People with a desire and potential for future advancement. 4. Persons who evidence good health, character, and citizenship." Further, a manager had to assess a potential hire not just "as he is, but also as he will be."[53]

Historians who have studied IBM tend to generalize about IBM's attitude toward women, minorities, Jews, and so forth, without much evidence as to what occurred and when. Admittedly, data on such matters are hard to come by, so they generalized about when, for example, women were "finally" allowed into the company and access to its mainstream career paths. However, such comments are based on the U.S. experience, and historians either assumed the experience was the same worldwide or enabled that impression through lack of qualification of their statements.[54] For most of the twentieth century, however, between a third and half of all employees worked outside the United States, so while general guidelines were universal (many described in this chapter more than in others), hiring practices also reflected local attitudes and behaviors. Historians have studied none of these. Employees could anecdotally speak of local practices, such as the propensity to hire male salesmen and to promote men into managerial positions in Asia or, in various European countries, to recruit nationals from the same socioeconomic classes as the hiring managers. The unique U.S. issue of African Americans for the American side of the business or the inability of Jews to come into IBM in Germany during the 1930s cannot be generalized across the entire scope of the company's practices. So, one has to be careful about such issues, especially those concerning gender, which is still a major lacuna in IBM's history.

On IBM retiree websites and Facebook groups, it has long been customary for members to tell their stories of how they came to work at IBM. After reading many hundreds of these accounts, several patterns became evident, based on these employee experiences from the 1950s to the early 2000s. Many mentioned the intelligence test; most also noted that several managers interviewed them before anyone made a hiring decision. Managers in these online groups wrote that they also went through the same exercise when they were being considered for managerial jobs. Rarely was one promoted without multiple people participating in the decision, even into the ranks of senior management. One interviewed for every position at IBM, managerial or not, worldwide. Many employees expressed surprise that they were offered their initial job at IBM, since in earlier decades few had college degrees, while many came from humble backgrounds or from what seemed unrelated experiences. Looking back, they saw their time at IBM as a "blessing," a "privilege," or a "fortunate" experience, even those who in the 1990s and 2000s were abruptly laid off during downsizing initiatives. My reading of their comments suggests that upon reflection, they viewed their experiences as a whole with IBM as a pleasant surprise, not an expectation, despite the long hours and frequent pressures to perform in complex operating circumstances.[55] We return to this issue of overall satisfaction with IBM in chapters 6 and 7 because these feelings were arrived at by accident.

In the 1990s, IBM began to hire managers from outside the firm who had little or no prior experience with the company, such as technical managers, consulting practice leaders, and herds of managers that came along with myriad software acquisitions. Such circumstances disrupted expectations of long-serving employees and created problems for newly hired managers who did not know how to navigate around IBM to accomplish their work or to adhere to company rules. Morale declined worldwide in affected parts of the firm, fueled by the fact that by 1990 IBM had discarded its eighty-year-old practice of full employment. To put such issues in perspective, today (2023), a twenty-five-year veteran of the company would have found the first part of this chapter alien to their quarter-century experience at IBM. How do we know? A new member of an IBM retiree Facebook account often posts questions such as, "When did IBM have a full employment practice?" "Did they really train you for a year?" "Who is Watson?" Language universally understood for decades inside IBM became the subject of such queries as, "What does *xxx* mean?" Someone would politely answer the question.[56]

So, for decades, managers came overwhelmingly from within the ranks. They were identified at various stages of their careers and given training and opportunities to gain the skills and exposure needed to move up. Employees were encouraged to aspire to be managers, managers to be even higher-level managers, and executives to become senior executives. At every level and across all organizations around the world, all managers were required to identify potential future managers and executives. It was a process engrained by the end of the 1940s, more informally since the 1930s. Managers had to submit forms that needed to be approved by one or two levels up in their chain of command entitled, "Promotability or Reassignment Recommendations," and for identifying potential executives (even among new hires) for "Executive Resource" lists. An employee's manager had to document annually what developmental needs the individual had (e.g., training, different job experiences), when they would be available for these, and how these linked to each individual's aspirations and to management's judgment. They were required to opine on the future potential (e.g., promotions) one could expect an employee to obtain in the next two to five years, without promising the individual would achieve those. Action plans for development were documented, along with results from prior developmental activities.[57]

The "Executive Resource" lists were kept secret from the person until they became an executive, in which case everyone at their level was being scrutinized for greater roles. These lists, like normal development plans, were routinely reviewed by one to three levels of management above the individual to ensure they were in agreement with the assessments and that they were being carried out. Rise high enough in the corporation, and IBM's board of directors would review one's potential. Most personnel and leadership literature only addresses the issue of "succession planning" as it applied to presidents, CEOs, and perhaps as low as senior executives.[58] Yet IBM did this from the ground up. Only when they reached mid-career (e.g., in a division) did such processes become a dominant influence in how employees were being shaped and managed. To clarify with a common example, say an individual was thirty years old in 1970 and was identified as a potential president of a division. They had to go through several positions to get there in time (e.g., age thirty-eight) so that they could go through that job in order to be a candidate to make it to the highest levels of the firm. Recall, IBM normally had up to ten levels of management; thus, to become chairman of the board, that divisional president, say, age thirty-eight, had several more hoops to jump through quickly. This is due to the fact that IBM's board of directors liked to appoint CEOs in their early fifties in order to get enough work out of them before the customary retirement at age sixty by executives. Since no company only wanted one candidate for president or CEO, IBM always needed a number of thirty-eight-year-old divisional presidents to ensure two to four of them made it to the top for the board of directors to choose from.[59] Some fell off the promotion track between division president and the short list presented to the board as a result of their inability to sustain their successes or due to the inevitable internal political rivalries inherent in the world of ambitious executives.

Training Employees to Manage and Lead

All employees underwent extensive training throughout their careers, regardless of whether managers, executives, or not, since the 1910s. Observers of America's technological and managerial prowess identified training of employees as a competitive practice not as evident in other nations. Christopher Layton, a highly regarded British observer of business practices, pointed out in the late 1960s that "for 40 years management has been taught systematically in the United States, while in Britain" those advocating for similar practices "were voices crying in the wilderness."[60] He distinguished this practice from those in Europe by calling it the "American model." The one difference is that IBM and other multinational corporations exported their penchant for training all employees to other countries, which in the last three to four decades of the century began implementing similar practices for both managerial and non-managerial employees, especially by firms that developed, sold, or used new technologies, such as computers.

Training came in several forms for managers. Besides initial "Charm School," mandatory by the 1950s, managers, like their employees, had to attend training classes for between one and two weeks per year; a similar requirement, but less enforced, held for newly minted executives. After an initial training class that lasted between one and two weeks (it varied over the years), normally about six months later, new managers attended a second class focused on leadership practices, with fewer discussions of processes and procedures. Training prior to the 1960s overwhelmingly concentrated on how to implement IBM's policies, less so later as more emphasis was placed on "people management" and leadership. Each division, region, plant, and laboratory annually held one- to two-day training sessions for managers specific to their mission, such as about technology, laboratory issues, selling against competitors, or how to deal with government contracts. IBM has run these more focused sessions since the 1910s. It was not uncommon for a manager to attend several each year in any decade. Also routine, educational presentations were given at myriad day-long meetings of managers on topics of a purely managerial nature or about their local economy, trends in unionizing activities, emerging employee benefits (including IBM's), and more effective strategic planning and communications. Such presentations should not be confused with normal public communications of new offerings, events in the company, or changes in practices.

All of these activities began with the arrival of Watson Sr. at IBM. He set the tone that *everyone* should be constantly learning. At an executive training program held in 1920, Watson Sr. said that the way to grow the business was "by studying, teaching and learning."[61] In this particular instance, teaching combined lectures, presentations by executives to each other, and conversations. This description could have fit any executive training program over the next century. In the 1920s, Watson Sr. established the practice of running what he called the "IBM Executive School," an event that ran from seven to ten days, with slight variants in Europe. That was quite an investment in training executives, not including educational staffs all over the world, particularly in that decade when profits were thin.[62]

In addition to making it possible for these employees to remain informed about the overall objectives and activities of the firm, they were tutored on personal attributes and about contemporary managerial practices. In 1924, Watson Sr. admonished his executives to "teach each other as well as our prospects." Watson Sr. declared that this training program was "a great thing in our business, because we are teaching each other."[63] Speaking to a two-day class of factory foreman in 1933, he was still preaching the same message, while these men learned about the philosophy he advocated for managing and carrying out the objectives of the firm. They learned about their role and how to improve it, such as how to increase the motivation of employees, which would end "service troubles," most notably the expense of "correcting mistakes, most of which never should be made."[64]

When one became a middle manager, that is to say had managers reporting to him (by the late 1980s, also to "her"), they attended a class often entitled "Middle Manager's School." These sessions focused on leadership, organizational transformations (a high-priority topic), trends in the marketplace and technology, how to lead through one's managers, and the importance of developing managerial talent. By the 1970s, increased interest in psychological topics caught the interest of business management professors and corporations. It was in this period, for instance, that personality profiles were measured through testing to help coach employees on how best to improve their work.[65] The most widely used assessment tool in IBM management training was the Myers-Briggs Type Indicator. It documented one's psychological preferences and was valued because it was intended to help people understand how they made decisions.[66] Employees began to listen to more lectures on such topics as "The Motivation to Work," "How Money Motivates Men," "The Managerial Grid" about people working in organizations, Theory X and Theory Y, and strategic planning. They received offprints of *Harvard Business Review* articles and others from *Business Horizons*. Instructors reinforced these subjects with talks about "Active Listening" and "Guidelines for Effective Meetings," while sitting in myriad other sessions on communications. All these various lectures were offered to first-line and middle managers and, increasingly by the end of the 1980s, to executive managers, largely to reinforce what they probably already knew.[67]

From the 1920s to the present, the most senior executives would gather for up to a week at a time, at least once a year by the 1990s, to discuss all manner of issues related to the welfare of "the business," as IBM's role was described.

By late in the century, these gatherings convened the company's three hundred highest-ranking executives. They discussed and learned, much as Watson Sr. wanted in the early 1920s, about world affairs and politics, industry and technological trends, and critical issues related to staffing, productivity, competition, and other issues important to the firm. By then, the company was so big that attendees used these occasions to meet colleagues for the first time to discuss issues of mutual concern. As new firms came into IBM through acquisitions, introducing their work to the rest of the executive staff became imperative, along with networking. Conversely, newly incorporated cadres of managers had to learn about the greater IBM, which for many presented a cultural shock of the first order.[68]

One final type of formal training involved use of business school week-long "executive seminars." These were taught by professors at prestigious business schools, such by those at Harvard University, MIT's Sloan School, University of Chicago, and University of Virginia in the United States and others in Europe and Asia. These events exposed managers to current managerial trends and issues, such as those explicated by Michael Porter at Harvard on strategy. These came in two forms: classes attended only by IBM employees and classes with attendees from multiple companies. Both types of seminars were similar to MBA classes, combining case studies (as at Harvard accompanied by lectures) or straight lectures (often Sloan's format). These were popular with IBM managers and executives and were hard to get into since so many people wanted to attend.[69] The business proved intellectually cerebral; thus, the higher one rose in the corporation, the more it proved useful to nurture a precocious intellect.

But as with most practices, training and development of managers were iterative processes. The creator of IBM's formal, regularly delivered education to executives and middle managers, beginning in the 1950s, was T. Elbert Clemmons, who had grown up on the sales side of the business since the late 1920s and had considerable middle-management experience. When tasked with developing managerial training programs, Watson Jr. called him into his office to explain the business issue. Paraphrasing Watson, Clemmons recalled Watson's conversation:

> We are faced with the opportunities of tremendous growth potential. Our finances are in good shape, we can secure any amount of money we need for expansion. The building of additional plants is no problem. We can hire all the architects and contractors necessary. The hiring and training of large numbers of employees may be a little more difficult, but constitutes no real problem. The bottleneck, if there is one, and the thing that will be a shortage of from capitalizing on this opportunity will be the shortage of competent executives. I want you to see what can be done to meet this need.[70]

Clemmons's first class for executives took place in 1957 and proved so popular that it immediately became a standard offering from then to the present, attended by employees from all over the world.[71] Its popularity led subsequently to a middle-management version of the course, an additional global source of training. This latter development came at the end of the 1950s, initially from American employees, and focused more narrowly on leadership skills, the overall state of the business, and operational procedures encountered by second- to fourth-line managers.

How Managers and Executives Were Mentored and Managed

Managers and executives were mentored for their entire careers. Their immediate managers were expected to teach and develop their skills for their current assignment and to prepare them for promotions and other managerial duties. Mentoring could be to improve personal skills (e.g., public speaking), to gain experience in community affairs (e.g., serving on nonprofit boards), to participate in company task forces (e.g., to expose them to more senior managers or to learn about a new function), to explore the possibility of working elsewhere (e.g., at a divisional headquarters), or to serve in a temporary assignment in another country (e.g., to learn about non-U.S. operations by working in, say, Paris or Tokyo). Mentoring could involve one- to two-year assignments in another country or division, which was part of managing a career. Managers were expected to "grow" all their people, including their young managers. It was a belief put into practice as part of the company's operating culture by the end of the 1930s that remained in full force until at least the end of the 1980s. In the 1990s, when IBM began shrinking its workforce, emphasis on mentoring declined, although formal succession planning for senior executives continued.

All managers were constantly tested to see their mettle. It bordered on a nearly combative constant test of wills—encounters as measures of a manager's qualities. One needed to prove themselves through the combat of thousands of conference room engagements, acquiring skills in the process needed to become more effective inside IBM and with customers. One observer from outside the company described the nearly daily ritual in the 1980s:

> An assistant controller at IBM is rehearsed for a stand-up presentation with flip charts—the principal means of formal communication. Each presentation gets "probed"—IBM's secret weapon for training and assessing young professionals. A manager states: "You're so accustomed to being probed you're almost unaware of it. IBM bosses have an uncanny way of pushing, poking, having a follow-up question, always looking for the hidden ball. It's a rigorous kind of self-discipline we impose on ourselves for getting to the heart of problems.

It's also management's way of assessing potential and grooming subordinates for the next job. Senior management spends most of its time 'probing.'"[72]

The same observer noted it was a "systemic means by which firms [not just IBM] bring new members into their culture."[73] IBM's managers and executives had long been concerned to make sure its members supported the firm's values until at least the early 2010s and that leaders at all levels carried out their duties consistent with corporate culture and beliefs. Just as relationships, fortitude, and solid performance landed an employee in a managerial job, these attributes were the same ones needed to keep that job and to advance to higher levels.

Watching the way higher-level managers worked became another crucial part of the mentoring process. This mentoring method was most widely used with managers destined soon to become executives and with junior executives slotted to move up executive ranks. It came into its own in the 1960s and remained widespread until at least the turn of the century. In 1956, senior management reorganized the company into groups and within those embedded divisions to facilitate delegating responsibilities and decision-making away from corporate headquarters, to improve focus and specialization, and to make it possible to expand the size of the business. It worked, but that reorganization created two problems. First, as divisions became more focused on either narrower markets (e.g., selling to large or smaller accounts) or products (e.g., mainframes vs. typewriters), more specialized knowledge increased about how those products were produced and worked and how individual divisions had to operate, each with a de facto business model often structured differently from others, for example, by cost structures and differing rates of gross profits. So, notions that a manager was an interchangeable part in the cog of a large enterprise, as argued by some business management professors and others, did not fully apply in an increasingly diverse business environment.[74] A vice president in the typewriter business had to know things that a vice president in mainframes did not; even though both had similar performance plans (e.g., manage organizations, appraise employees, develop strategic plans, manage budgets), they experienced different costs of doing business and profit margins.[75] The second issue was that the higher one rose in the company, the less they knew about what went on in the rest of the firm, especially by the early 1970s. Between 1960 and 1970, for example, the number of employees increased by well over 100 percent, and new divisions were created, each with thousands of workers.[76]

To address these issues, IBM launched such obvious initiatives as more worldwide education on the organization of the company aimed at all levels of the firm and published newsletters and other informative documents. Concurrently, people making presentations inside and outside of IBM fell into the habit of having a slide at the beginning of their talks identifying where they fit into the greater IBM. These were always organization charts.[77] Employees bemused that they could not talk without being armed with a fistful of slides, which usually contained an "org chart."[78]

To wrestle with such issues, which in mentoring parlance meant "developing" someone for future "opportunities," candidates were assigned to an executive as an "administrative assistant," or "AA," or if to the chairman's office or that of some other senior executive, as an "executive assistant," or "EA." These were not secretaries but expensive managers who shadowed an executive in the organization they were intended to serve in future capacities. They answered letters for their executives, wrote speeches and put together slide decks, took notes at meetings, did research for them, solved problems, spoke on their behalf, wielded influence, and so forth. They did not carry their executives' suitcases or get them coffee. The objective was to show a future executive what an executive did and how. This was mentoring and teaching by example.[79] Mentoring executives were expected to explain to their mentees why the mentor did certain things, how decisions were being made, and the rationale for "political" actions taken to move forward an agenda within the firm. In other words, they were to illustrate how actions were taken and not merely what were these activities. These assignments could last between six and eighteen months, followed by the promotion. Candidates for promotion highly prized these assignments as essential steps up, while giving them a much broader view of how their division (sometimes company) operated. These assignments increased their personal network of contacts useful for future promotions, in addition to teaching them how to accomplish tasks in their next role.

These assignments spun off two additional benefits. First, the individual was able to have a bird's-eye view of what else was going on within the division or group to which they were assigned, a not trivial result since some organizations employed tens of thousands of people scattered all over the world. Second, an AA perched high enough in the company's hierarchy was able to see a great deal more about what was going on across the entire company, divisions, and groups. That perspective proved useful as their span of control grew because increasingly they needed either to collaborate with other parts of the business to do their daily work or to accumulate political support for their own personal and organizational objectives. Watching their mentor executive at work demonstrated how transorganizational relationships worked. In the process, they developed personal networks and learned whom to call to solve a problem or gain an ally.

IBM was not alone in applying mentoring techniques to develop future leaders. As a student of the process evidenced in multiple firms observed, people on a fast track needed to emulate role models that the company's culture encouraged: "Far more can be taught by examples than can ever be conveyed in a classroom. The protégé watches the role model make presentations, handle conflict, write memos—and replicates as closely as possible the traits that seem to work most effectively."[80]

Another approach taken specifically to teach executives how to function within the company, that is to say, to socialize them within IBM senior management culture and to broaden their understanding of other activities of the firm, was for a mentor to arrange putting the fast-track junior executive through several jobs on their way up. These positions could include, for example, taking an American and embedding them inside IBM Japan or in Paris at its European headquarters for eighteen to twenty-four months to give them foreign experience. With roughly half of IBM's business originating outside of the United States since the 1960s, it was crucial that senior executives understand IBM's realities beyond their home country. The converse held too, that Europeans, Asians, and Latin Americans would do a "tour of duty" working in the United States, usually at a divisional headquarters, manufacturing site, or laboratory.[81]

Placing an individual in another part of the business to prove their worth became part of the career/mentoring process. For example, Samuel J. Palmisano, a fast-track executive in the 1990s, was put in charge of IBM's consulting practices (Global Services) in 1998 after successfully managing the hitherto unprofitable PC business (Personal Systems Group) in 1997. Earlier, he had done a tour of duty in Japan. These three experiences enhanced his internal resume, and in each instance, he proved to be a successful manager. In the case of the PC business, it had become the career graveyard of other potential senior executives to the point that some left IBM prior to his arrival there. Palmisano went on to become IBM's successor to Chairman Gerstner in 2002.[82]

During mentoring, the employee was not usually told that at the conclusion of their new assignment they were guaranteed a promotion. As with any job at IBM, at all levels and around the world, the candidate had expectations, because they knew that an AA's job with a particular executive was used as a short step to promotion and so would be wasted on someone not moving up. They "understood" that if they performed well, they could expect promotion. While our discussion focused on executives, the same mentoring methods were applied in preparing fast-track first-, second-, and third-line managers, even though their mentoring AA roles might last only ninety days or as long as a year.

The one exception to everything described in the past several pages is when an executive had an opening and knew exactly whom they wanted to fill it. They simply reached out to the employee's manager to say they wanted the individual and negotiated their release. But even in this instance, the employee would have already been identified as promotable through IBM's normal process and probably had already undergone mentoring activities. The desiring executive would probably have consulted peers and others about the viability of the candidate. Of course, the executive knew the individual through observing their work in some situation, in other words, through "exposure."

Evaluating Performance Against Expectations

Strict formality existed in the process of evaluating performance against expectations. Employees and management documented goals and assessed results annually. That process was well in place by the 1930s and, over the years, became regularized with standard forms and annual reviews and goal setting. The same process diffused up and down the organization, across divisions, and around the world. We mentioned many of components of the management process earlier—performance and development plans—but now describe how these were used. In a company that valued measurable performance within a meritocratic culture, one needed to be explicit at each level in the enterprise with each individual. The entrance intelligence test was only the start. To the extent possible, performance plans contained numerical targets, such as "achieve 100 percent of revenue quota," which at the end of the year, the reviewing manager could document on the performance review (another document): "John achieved 120 percent of his revenue quota," or "John attained 101.5 percent of his revenue target." Another numeric target might be: "John promoted 3 of his staff, exceeding his target by 1."[83] Even lab directors might have numeric objectives, such as how many patents their staff should submit (or obtain) or even the number of industry or professional awards they should garner. And so it went for every item in the performance plan, year after year. To become a sales manager, for example, for how many years in a row did the candidate achieve their targets? (The expectation was normally four years.) If a middle manager, for how many years did they achieve their budget targets (always a number), keep the number of workers at a specific population size, and also make their "sales revenue" targets? The objectives were often more varied as one moved up the organization, while the absolute numbers were larger (e.g., size of budgets, employee population, number of machines manufactured). In appraisals, everyone strived to describe numerical achievements (failures too) when possible, using such language as "Sara's organization increased its revenues by 10 percent year-over-year while managing a significant reorganization that resulted in a decrease of 5 percent of her headcount and 2 percent in expenditures."[84]

The next measurable activity concerned the employee's development plan and its execution. This tool played a crucial role in guiding the assessment of a candidate for future growth. Quoting from one of your author's development plans from the mid-1980s illustrates the exercise. "Jim wants to become a Branch Manager in the next 2–3 years. He would like to compete for an AA job in SWD HQ after he has worked in Financial Marketing Programs for 18 months in order to position him for his next move." This language was explicit. To execute this plan, both employee and manager had to agree on a plan of action, but first on what needed development: "Become familiar with all aspects of the ICC program; Build on his financial marketing expertise: Get exposure to SWD & ICC executives through special assignments, special projects for the Director and VP." Plans were specific and measurable: "Attend 1 week ICC seminar—February; ICC internship programs—April/May; Presentations to key executives—ongoing," and so forth.[85]

At the end of the year, the employee documented what they did, the reviewing manager obtained from administrative and personnel validating numbers, and then the two would meet to discuss progress toward objectives and what needed to be done next year. It was customary in most decades for managers to submit monthly or quarterly reports on what they did to carry out their plans. Modifications to the individual's entry in the Executive Resources lists occurred next to reflect that they should be taken off of it, that the individual was "on track" toward their career aspirations, or that the move to the next promotion or job should be advanced. The employee's manager reviewed each of these steps. Both employee and manager signed the document, and the manager's manager had to concur, and if the individual was on the Executives Resource list, personnel and executive management in the organization tracked progress. Management at all levels valued consensus in the assessment of an employee's performance and potential; indeed, it was expected if the assessment process was to succeed. The tone of reviews—in theory at least—was less to criticize an employee for failures and problems and more to encourage them to improve, to take charge of their personal destinies. It is difficult to assess to what extent this intent was practiced, but certainly, the mechanical details of the appraisal process and reviews of its effectiveness were strictly enforced since nearly the birth of IBM.[86]

Opinion surveys and other complaints demonstrate that the appraisal process was not always a satisfactory one from an employee's perspective because it was loose enough to allow one's manager to criticize an employee or rate them lower than an anticipated assessment, which had a direct bearing on future career prospects and salary increases. In other words, despite its process-centric approach, appraisals remained highly subjective. Let a manager of the 1970s–1980s explain: "management could . . . justify any appraisal rating they wanted to give you," using such criteria as attitude or appearance, for example.[87] Setting jointly agreed-to objectives by managers and their employees was, however, generally well accepted across the firm, especially after the appraisal process just described was diffused around the world by the early 1970s.

Since managers understood the personnel management process, other documents were prepared that both proved important to them and were made part of their record. The "thank you" letters sent either to the employee or to their manager with the employee copied became critical. These were not casual, quick "thank you" notes for a job well done. They were normally typed on stationery used exclusively by managers and executives that explained thoughtfully what was done. For example: "This is my personal thank you for an outstanding job at the April 16 Opportunity Workshop. My thanks are twofold: (1) for a quality presentation which was one of the highest rated of the session, and (2) for your willingness to help out. Both were essential in making the program a success." A divisional vice president signed the note.[88] Another from one manager to another, thanking him for his staff's support and how valuable it was in a meeting, included: "In particular, I would like to recognize the outstanding assistance the marketing team received from [named individual] who was effective in the strategy sessions and with locating distribution/retail expertise outside of IBM."[89] Note that each letter stated what was actually done (this could be tied back to performance and development specifics), the value these generated, and metrics that were measurable (presentations were subject to surveys with numeric results). Letters from people who were below and above a manager's rank were of near equal value. The more senior ones also affected an employee manager's perspective about future prospects. Having a raft of such letters proved necessary as one moved through their management careers.

How well did the overall measuring and evaluating process work? Most obviously, it was carried out for many decades as an integral task of management at all levels. One could not opt out unless they did not want to become a manager. Many employees did not want to be managers and, for the most part, felt comfortable informing their superiors of that fact; they were not punished for their attitude. They still had performance and development plans, just that in these instances development focused more on skills than on becoming managers. One could still be promoted in nonmanagerial ranks, gaining status and increased salaries. Engineers, technicians, programmers, scientists, administrative staff, and customer engineers often chose this path. Sales staffs seemed the most ambitious to rise in management, and certainly for a century, the most senior executives came out of sales with the general exceptions of the chief financial officer, head of legal services, and slightly less so research. Not until 2020 did IBM appoint a chairman of the board who had not come up through sales.[90]

But that was the least of it. Let a thoughtful IBM executive explain from his perch in the 1980s looking back two decades:

> Below Armonk [corporate HQ, ed. note], the management structure is probably weakest at the most junior level (but this is contained by the team leadership approach). As the level of management rises so does its quality (where the reverse is true in many companies); for IBM chooses its senior management very carefully indeed (measuring their track record by their subordinates' comments in the opinion survey just as much as by their performance against revenue or profit targets), and it trains them by moving them around almost as much as their Japanese counterparts.[91]

IBM embedded these people in a culture in which financial and operational controls and processes existed since the late 1910s. The process reinforced the implementation of "implicit understandings," in other words, "a common law to supplant its statuary laws," to use a business management scholar's language scripted by Richard Pascale.[92] A manager at IBM that he interviewed about the tools described earlier thought of these as part of the firm's socialization acts used "as a fine-tuning device; it helps us make sense out of the procedures and quantitative measures." He reported that these made it possible for managers to make better business judgments than otherwise, hence improving the quality of their achievements over time.[93] It also made clear through implicit and actual understanding how to develop and shape one's career, tamping down anxiety over the process, although never eliminating all of it, of course.

The Changing Landscape of Management Since the 1990s

Until the early 1990s, much of what is described in this chapter continued as normal, even routine practice that would have been recognizable inside the firm since at least the 1940s. Management existed in a stasis that reflected, too, the relative stability of how large firms in the computing industry and their customers functioned. But much began to change by the dawn of the 1990s as new technological innovations intruded, such as expanded distributed computing, thanks to PCs and their ability to communicate with each other and mainframes, and the Internet of course. In addition, many new startup hardware, software, and services firms began challenging IBM's hegemony in the IT industry, and by IBM increasing its acquisition of smaller enterprises, which it needed to integrate into the larger enterprise. A new CEO purposefully shook up the organization—its stable culture of old—and even in what businesses IBM functioned. It is a story observers of the company are taking up with much work yet to do.[94] Acquisitions increased in the new century, which meant accepting into IBM thousands of individuals and their managers in short order without their having grown up in the company.

These phenomena upended long-standing practices even though incumbent management, personnel, and other departments tried to retain these. Different divisions maintained prior standards for promotion of managers to one degree or another, largely because meritocratic values prevailed. Weak managers from outside the firm often did not survive long or left of their own volition. In the early 2000s, with the arrival of 30,000 employees from PwC, all of these new behaviors—erosion of prior practices, newcomers failing or leaving—accentuated the growing disconnect from the past. Churn in culture, expectations, internal politics, and changing marketing conditions disrupted much. For example, by the end of the first decade of the new century, not only did the number of opinion surveys conducted decline but also the old practice of reviewing results with employees. The period in IBM's history since about 1998 has yet to be seriously studied by historians. Only two senior executives have published their memoirs since 2003, and archival holdings on the modern period either do not exist or are closed to scholars.[95] Press reports about IBM's activities, however, documented enormous churn in the operation of the firm, supported by members-only Facebook employee and retiree pages, such that one can say with some confidence that how IBM managed its managers evolved in the 1990s and beyond.[96]

The year CEO Gerstner came to IBM, 1993, can conveniently be labeled the dawn of a new era in how managers functioned. Many managers lost confidence in their being able to work at IBM for life. They were already constantly being forced to dismiss employees, slash budgets, close buildings, seek new sets of customers, and develop products and services that diverted from earlier more stable practices and were pushed out of IBM before their expected time to retire.[97] Conditions worsened as the years came and went in the new century. Training budgets were severely slashed, and corporate headquarters intruded into mundane issues, such as by requiring multiple levels of permissions for travel unless directly involved in a customer transaction, even for buying office supplies. Much of what has been described in this chapter began eroding at different speeds and unevenly across the company worldwide.

Internal guerrilla wars ensued between legacy IBM managers and new entrants into the firm, fought largely within the services side of the company in the United States, where they competed for positions and endured prejudices of new managers toward the IBM "lifers" who they blamed for the firm's failures that now the new hires had to "save." Due to culture and labor laws, IBM Japan held on to older practices into the new century, and European national IBM organizations almost as long. Countries carved out of colonies with predominantly English cultural, political, and legal traditions churned nearly as much as the American side, specifically Canada, New Zealand, Australia, and both Irelands.

However, many newly arrived managers and executives brought with them different views and skills. For example, in the case of PwC in the early 2000s, they nudged IBM into taking a more industry-centered focus in how it developed and sold technology, addressing a long-called-for reform expressed by IBM's customers to have it sell them goods and services tailored to their specific industry, most notably insurance, finance, manufacturing, pharmaceutical, health care, and government. These new employees brought with them practices and expectations widespread in management and strategy consulting firms and a work ethic equal to any that one could find in IBM that injected new skills and energy into the company's affairs. Interspersed within their ranks were a few who had worked at IBM earlier in their careers; those individuals were priceless because they could bridge two cultures.[98]

As IBM entered a long period of weak business performance, beginning in 2012, basic managerial and personnel practices deteriorated in specific ways. For example, managers were now required to appraise their employees on a curve, much like a professor of students within a course, with certain percentages of top to low performers, even if a department was filled with "A" players. That was done so that the firm could select which of its "poor" performers to lay off. Additionally, to help in that process, ranking employees from best to worst had the unintended consequence of discouraging collaboration and cross-divisional teaming that senior management hoped for, while an increasing number of managers now harped that one should "swim in their own lane." These three actions—grading on a curve, ranking employees, and ordering them to focus on their immediate work—so destroyed the credibility of the appraisal process that it had to be replaced, and its sequel, if reports seeping out of the company were to be believed, was not taken as seriously by many up and down the ranks as it might have been in earlier decades.[99] Personnel career and development planning diminished, although we do not yet know by how much. Succession planning continued, particularly for top jobs in IBM, but the extent of that work remains completely unknown as of this writing, largely because we are too close in time to expect otherwise.

Implications and Lessons Learned

For over a century, historians, economists, regulators, politicians, and journalists have studied and commented on the role of large enterprises as dominant forces in the American economy. It seemed every major industry had six to eight oligarchic firms that shaped its form in the United States, and for many decades, IBM was one of those within the world of data processing and computing.[100] These were multinational firms operating all over the world, like IBM. Today over 80,000 large multinational companies exist, many learning from older ones, such as IBM. They, as in prior times in American business, want to learn how to expand and sustain their performance in various economies and in the context of national cultures. Given IBM's more than a century of existence, it has much to teach them.

A fundamental lesson is that developing a cadre of competent managers is crucial, if not central, to the process of corporate success. It is not enough to declare that the secret to IBM's accomplishments (or failures) was due to the qualities of its workforce (overwhelmingly highly respected), corporate culture (recognized as powerful and pervasive), or beliefs (admired for a century). Drop down one level of detail and one confronts the classic issue facing all managers—launching and then executing those three lofty notions. To do that, one needs to understand the role of management to provide an explanation for how that cadre developed and worked. Explaining how IBM did that was our purpose. This exploration occurred at a time when the historical fashion was more to explain discontent in firms, management/ employee friction, role of minorities, and so forth. But a lesson of history of large organizations remains what it has always been, a tale of leadership and execution.[101] In modern times, it began with management and only then seeped across successful enterprises through the ranks of labor, customers, and other affected individuals.

In particular, several insights from the company's experience with management prove useful. First and foremost, from its beginning, senior management recognized that it needed a cadre of highly skilled managerial teams from top to bottom, not just a small galaxy of stars surrounding the leader of the firm. Second, all managers needed to share, or be taught and convinced to embrace, a common set of values and ways of working applied consistently across the firm. The Roman and Chinese empires did this, so too the Catholic Church and long-lived corporations. That made possible shared responsibilities and diffusion of duties needed to coordinate the actions of the firm. This step received attention in this chapter but also has been the subject of memoirs and histories about IBM because that requirement of shared beliefs had to be diffused among the general workforce of the company. That was the single most important task of management, since not all decisions and actions could come directly out of the office of the chairman. To function in over 150 countries (eventually 175), employees on the ground learned the needed shared values and similar processes that they could adapt to local conditions in a timely fashion. Third, the firm had to "stick with the program" for decades. Every CEO reiterated the same values of the firm, decade after decade. It worked.[102]

One could argue that not everyone saluted these three points, since nearly a million people worked at IBM and because circumstances changed with respect to technological transformations and evolving markets, not to mention the influence of such existential events as two world wars, the recent rise of China as an economic force, the effects of the COVID-19 pandemic, and global inflation since 2021. No matter, these three realities shaped the formation and effectiveness of IBM's managers.

The bigger issue involves squaring our account of what arguably was an effective strategy for the development of a successful management team with the reality that, in the 1980s and early 1990s, they turned in disastrous results and then, to a slightly lesser degree, yet another string of poor business performances beginning in 2012. How are we to explain this seeming oxymoron? I have argued elsewhere that the answer lay largely with a small cadre of long-serving senior executives crafting a company-wide strategy in the 1980s that did not reflect the realities of their current markets. In other words, they made some bad decisions, compounded by a bureaucracy beholden to rival divisions run by these senior executives.[103] IBM's managers operated collectively in a blue fish tank, swimming in a culture insulated from their long-standing information ecosystem (market). They did this so effectively that IBM collectively could not figure out until almost too late how to repair the damage. It took the arrival of a new CEO in 1993 to harness the talent of a large pool of skilled managers and their employees to rescue the firm. Then in the 2010s, a combination of older problems—mainly bad strategy—coupled to a transforming corporate culture and a few poor choices of senior leaders not ideally suited to their roles resulted in another round of anemic business results. It is too early to conclude if members of the management community in the 2010s were of poorer quality than, say, those prior to the 1980s. We are too close to events and have insufficient data and perspective afforded by the passage of time with which to judge their performance. So for the moment, we must frustratingly suspend judgment.[104] In other words, we have to do a very IBM thing—wait for the facts before appraising the community.

IBM's experience teaches that companies and possibly civil service administrations should better understand how they nurture their management teams and what they can do to improve them, if that is what is needed, as a crucial feature of long-term success. When they do that, management will come to be seen as both a top-down and a horizontal wide collection of coordinated activities. IBM's case illustrates that one can learn once again a great deal about other corporations by exploring the demographics and activities of all manner of managers. For today's corporations, IBM's experience that the work of building an effective management team requires focus, extensive work, and a long-term commitment to a way of life and to a way of engaging ambitious, smart, and skilled armies of employees is essential.

There is an urgency in considering IBM's experiences because, just in the world of technology, it seems the stars are in crisis. That can begin to be examined through the lens of leadership, management, business, and socially responsible values and culture, not solely through strategic intent or actions at Facebook, Apple, H-P, Amazon, other social media firms, far less so Microsoft (finally), and Cisco, among others. IBM's experiences provide thoughtful "lessons of history," and historians prefer the idea of offering context to inform contemporary considerations. But the actions today's firms can take should be shaped in the specific by today's realities, such as the impact of COVID-19, supply chain fragilities, a renewed surge of government regulations, economic and industrial concentrations, and declining customer awe of technology-centric firms.

But, of course, when a company brings together hundreds of thousands of employees, unanimity and consensus are not always possible. At best, management can mitigate serious problems in the ways IBM did—the actions it took described in the rest of this book. A test of how IBM did that is the subject of the next chapter, which discusses employee unionizing efforts in the United States and the company's response. It is an important issue to explore because the firm spent so much time and effort over so many decades to make such activity unnecessary, indeed contrary to its values and practices. It was one of the most uncomfortable sensitive issues faced by senior management and the employee population in the United States with potentially fearful pitfalls for all involved.

CHAPTER 5

HOW IBM PREVENTED UNIONIZATION OF ITS AMERICAN WORKFORCE

Today, our frequent attitude surveys show that the importance we attach to job security is one of the principal reasons why people like to work for IBM.

Thomas J. Watson, Jr. (1963)[1]

Two realities are starkly evident regarding IBM's American workforce. First, it never unionized, despite efforts to do so by some employees and national unions, beginning largely in the 1980s. Second, historians studying the company have been silent on the subject for the late twentieth century and minimally for earlier decades. They have yet to offer insights on how the absence of unions was possible, given that so many other large manufacturing firms were extensively unionized, as in the steel and automotive industries.[2] IBM's circumstance is made more curious, indeed unique, by the fact that from the 1930s to the 1950s unions increased their membership and influence across multiple American industries. The post–World War II American economy experienced extraordinary prosperity that survived into the 1970s before slowing, so society could afford the growing costs of labor and their unions. IBM prospered, expanding by hundreds of thousands of workers in all manner of jobs from factory laborers to professional workers, scientists, managers, and executives. The absence of unions in the American IBM organization increasingly seemed an anomaly over the years. When employees commented on that circumstance, they spoke of unions as just not a good fit within "IBM's culture." That such a statement was true was beside the point because it did not explain the absence of unions. So, how are we to account for IBM avoiding unionization when so many other manufacturing firms could not? What does its experience teach us?

It is an important issue to understand because, when unions exist in a large firm, the organization's mode of operation, behaviors of its workforce, and corporate culture are profoundly changed from those of its pre-union days. IBM prospered in an uninterrupted fashion until the end of the 1980s, when its positive momentum was crippled by circumstances far more serious than whether or not its workforce was unionized.[3] Senior management could not blame unions for declining worker productivity and constraining work rules, charges typically leveled against unions, because IBM had no unions in the United States. The blame for failures lay at the feet of senior management that implemented faulty business strategies and mismanaged its workforce, while worldwide demand for computing products continued to increase. Management's failures help to explain why in the 1990s and 2000s there was an uptick in unionizing activities. Yet even then, such initiatives proved unable to introduce unions into IBM. Why? When IBM did poorly as an employer and business enterprise in the early 1990s and again after 2002, again, why did unions not form inside the company? When it laid off many tens of thousands of employees almost in a capricious manner, yet again, why no unionizing?

Senior IBM managers had concluded repeatedly since the 1920s that they did not want unions. Back in the immediate post–World War I period, timing proved auspicious because unionizing in the United States waned. The timing was good because IBM could not yet expand its salaries and benefits, such as other firms had to do, as its profits were still weak or borderline nonexistent. Management spent decades watchful for unionizing activities, always treating labor organizing activities as an existential threat to the company. It may well be one of the greatest concerns senior executives harbored, perhaps more than their business-as-usual regards concerning various forms of competition in the marketplace or repeated attacks on IBM by the U.S. Justice Department and competitors, who collectively accused IBM of various antitrust activities. Yet those two realities—competition and litigation—were routinely discussed within IBM across all divisions, jobs, and ranks with remarkable candor, whether in the 1930s, 1950s, 1960s, or 1970s, and also by historians. IBM's strategies for mitigating both were openly explained to employees, with detailed instructions and training for dealing with these at local and company-wide levels. That candor and broad collaboration worked, contributing to the business success of the firm over many decades.

Yet there was near silence about how to deal with perhaps an equally threat-ening worry—unionization. Over nearly forty years at IBM, during boom periods and challenging times, one rarely heard discussion at any level of the enterprise that was even remotely public about union activities. Let me repeat that statement another way: employees on the shop floor and in sales offices did not discuss unions, except those attempting to unionize. Employees who attempted to unionize were few in number and often needed to work in the shadows to get started. I spent thousands of hours in management meetings dealing with all manner of business issues but rarely, very rarely, were union issues discussed.[4] So, who did attempt to unionize, and how was that done if nobody was even discussing the subject? How did that opacity fit into IBM's corporate culture? While this chapter is not intended to be a fully developed history of IBM's relations with unions and of its labor policies, it offers a tenta-tive explanation for how unions were kept at bay. To a large extent, it was more than simply keeping everyone on heightened alert for signs of such activity, which could then be crushed by personnel staff and a small army of lawyers. Rather, it required educating generations of managers about the issues involved and how best to respond, all coupled to a collection of benefits competitive with what unions could win for their members. Timing and calibrating salaries and benefits to the larger unionizing activities across the nation was the quiet response by senior management. Thus, the story told in this chapter and the next should be seen as part of the larger answer to the question of why unions did not form.

The issue of unionizing in both American "high-tech" firms and such retai-lors as Walmart and Target or, recently, at an Amazon warehouse in Alabama in 2021, kept the subject before the public and corporate management. There is controversy about how to unionize or block such efforts. Labor historian Erik Loomis has argued, for example, that management has laws and regulations on its side, allowing it to take actions discouraging organizing by its employees or national unions working with these workers. He has called for new laws because the history of prior successful efforts by labor, say, in the 1930s to 1950s, "was nearly impossible without the government leveling the playing field."[5] How did IBM's experience square with that interpretation? The evidence only partially reinforces Loomis's interpretation. How IBM's management interacted with its employees—one of the company's key stakeholders—paralleled how they dealt with other members of their ecosystem. On the one hand, management wanted nothing to do with unions, yet on the other, IBM needed to address employee concerns if it was to make and sell products. In short, unionizing at IBM rep-resented another chapter in the company's history of stakeholder management.

The American experience was unique, which is why we will not look at Europe's history. European labor laws were different than American ones, espe-cially after World War II.[6] Even earlier, during the interwar years, European societies were building social and safety nets more inclusive than those of the Americans, which helps to explain the arc of Europe's postwar experience with management-labor relations and government regulatory practices. Where laws mandated unions, IBM's workforces joined. The history of that experience awaits its historians.[7]

To begin understanding the role of unions in IBM, I proceed with three discussions. First, we summarize the company's labor practices from the 1910s to the late 1980s, the period when the firm developed its antiunion views and strategies. The second discussion demonstrates how crucial managers and experts on labor laws and practices were, relying on training materials used for decades to inform and instruct IBMers. Third, a surge in unionizing activity in the 1980s continued for the next thirty years without success. We need to understand the contours of that activity because its failure was conditioned by what had occurred at IBM before the 1980s. This later period is also the one for which historians have the least amount of insight, but we must begin some-where. It is the experience between the 1980s and early 2000s that sheds light on how at least one large corporation addressed issues relevant to other enter-prises, not simply for those in the information technology (IT) world.

General Themes in IBM's Labor Practices, 1910s–1980s

American labor unions formed by the early decades of the twentieth century in response to objectionable management practices in large enterprises, such as with safety and working conditions in manufacturing across many indus-tries; these expanded during the 1930s and 1940s.[8] Corporations fought back their emergence, but many ultimately had to deal with them as large organized representatives of their workforces. General Motors, for example, accepted the existence of the United Auto Workers in 1937 and negotiated work contracts with it. Ford had to do the same, beginning in 1941.[9] AT&T became increas-ingly unionized, starting in the 1930s and extensively so after World War II. Salaries and work rules were increasingly negotiated between firms and unions, an activity that continued into the second half of the century.[10]

Such behavior stood in sharp contrast to what happened at IBM. From the beginning, IBM, too, resisted unionization. However, since it was so small before World War II, it was hardly a target for union organizers, let alone its employees. From its earliest days, the company provided working conditions, salaries, and benefits sufficient to recruit and retain workers in central New York State. In addition, management's philosophy was that (a) an individual worker should engage directly with his immediate manager to resolve work issues and (b) managers should treat workers as colleagues in a corporate culture that minimized emphasis on ranks and social or managerial hierarchies (although never completely avoiding these), all to discourage workers or unions to orga-nize IBM's workforce. But benefits alone would not be sufficient to stop union organizing or, even worse, strikes. In 1901, a strike at NCR, one of the most generous providers of benefits, was seen by workers, labor leaders, and other corporations as a lesson in the reality that benefits alone do not stop strikes. Thomas J. Watson, Sr., was working at NCR when the strike took place and, like his executive peers inside and outside the firm, drew lessons from the expe-rience. NCR's workers valued good salaries more than benefits and believed they were the best judges of how much they should be paid. They valued bet-ter working conditions and shorter hours. NCR targeted subsequent benefits more narrowly at such things as personal health benefits, benefits purchased by individuals, and fewer group benefits that had previously been favored as improving the quality of life of individuals in their private lives.[11] Many of the poststrike benefits at NCR eventually appeared at IBM. Watson Sr. also learned that he had to do more to block unions than offer generous benefits.

In the 1930s—a period of militant union organizing in the American economy—IBM prospered and thus could afford to increase salaries, for instance, what Watson Sr. called his own "New Deal" for employees, relying on his experiences at NCR. IBM had strong sales of leased equipment, which ensured long-term ongoing income from contracted revenue flows. These twin circumstances made it possible to increase salaries and provide longer-term benefits. These offerings combined became the economic and social contract with his employees. He wanted to enhance benefits for positive reasons but also wisely understood that these were needed to thwart the threat of unionization. It was, in the words of historian David L. Stebenne, Watson's "prudent response to concessions unions were winning at comparable firms."[12] His behavior was enhanced by making it a practice that individual salary increases would be the norm, rather than company-wide increases, thereby causing employees to interact with their managers who linked increases and promotions to perfor-mance, as described in the previous chapter. In other words, employees needed to communicate with their managers, rather than through some third party, such as a union representative. Table 5.1 lists other actions IBM took in the 1930s and 1940s. Watson's brand of welfare capitalism proved sufficient for the times. It allowed him to retain employees highly skilled in the manufacturing, sale, and maintenance of his complex products.[13]

This is a good spot to point out crucial distinctions in labor activism. Just because workers had disagreements with management did not automatically mean they wanted to form unions. In IBM's case, as in many earlier times in other companies, workers thought initially in terms of resolving grievances, many of them specific to one work site. When interviewing labor organizers in IBM active in the 1970s and 1980s, they often used the word "grievances" to characterize their concerns. They were motivated to fix problems, such as

TABLE 5.1 IBM's Salary and Benefits, 1930s–1945 in the United States

Early 1930s	IBM established first company welfare fund for employees in need
1934	Installed air conditioning in IBM's factory in Endicott, New York
1935	IBM ended piecework system; employees are paid hourly salary
1936	Initial "no layoff" policy introduced
1937	Paid vacations and holidays are introduced
Mid-1930s	Outdoor recreations at IBM country clubs became available; adult education programs also offered
Late 1930s	IBM introduced life, accident, and family hospitalization insurance and disability benefits

Source: David L. Stebenne, "IBM's 'New Deal': Employment Policies of the International Business Machines Corporation, 1933–1956," *Journal of the Historical Society* 5, no. 1 (Winter 2005): 56.

working conditions, hours of employment, salaries, and safety issues, not to form unions. When they concluded, first, that individual complaints were not being resolved and then, second, that they needed to become groups collectively lobbying for resolutions, they still thought in terms of solving problems and then getting back to their jobs.

They wanted to work at IBM and so did a very IBM thing: when they did not get the answer they wanted, they escalated. First, they did it within extant ways in the firm—largely up their managerial chain of command—and when that proved insufficient, they escalated by forming committees, later pushing for a union. To put a fine point on the matter, not until their group activities failed to satisfy their concerns to the extent that they wanted did they start thinking of unionizing in the 1990s. That is when they reached out to existing unions outside IBM for advice and were also approached by them. IBM employees underwent a transition in how they viewed unions over the course of several decades, while management assumed from the beginning that any worker-coordinated approach to managers regarding grievances was a unionizing initiative, one to be snuffed out. Yet right from the 1970s into the first decade of the twenty-first century, employees continued to talk more about grievances than organizing. Unionizing became an increasingly attractive option when their job security was endangered through layoffs beginning in the late 1980s and throughout the 1990s when the American side of IBM attempted to reduce retirement and medical benefits. Federal courts eventually ruled against the proposed significant changes in pension benefits, representing a high watermark in labor activism in the American IBM. The conversation about grievances and organizing

eventually extended over four decades. With this distinction between grievances and unionizing in mind, we return to our historical overview.

Prior to the 1940s, there was a third consideration, yet to be studied by historians, that differentiated IBM, namely, that few workers were concentrated
in large numbers. There was the plant in Endicott, New York, but also many
thousands of other employees clustered in small groups spread out all over the
United States in sales offices. Organizing, say, a dozen or even several dozen
employees proved impossible, if not pointless, whereas at Endicott, management experimented with and deployed its labor relations policies that, when
successful, were applied across the American side of the company.[14]

By the mid-1930s, both senior management and increasingly its workforces
in factories and sales offices came to accept what historian David L. Stebenne
described as "mutual obligations."[15] Thomas J. Watson, Sr., argued that employees deserved benefits "because they were earned."[16] Factory workers, in particular, were expected to turn in high-quality work, not unionize, and accept
that management needed the authority and leeway to manage work processes
and conditions. As Stebenne observed, employees "found such obligations less
objectionable than would workers at many other manufacturing firms, in part
because IBM gave its employees the higher wages and benefits unions were
winning elsewhere, and sometimes even surpassed them."[17] His assessment
held true to the late 1980s.

IBM management did not operate in isolation; its senior members understood what other corporations were doing to blunt the rise of unions, learning from them.[18] A combination of corporate, state, and IBM-specific actions
slowed the union movement in the United States, with both laws and government regulatory practices heightened in the 1940s and early 1950s. By the
mid-1950s, one could begin to document results, although to be realistic, that
is insight acquired by union organizers and then, years later, recognized by
scholars that, therefore, would not have been evident to most workers in the
1950s–1980s. In 1955, some 35 percent of the total U.S. workforce belonged to
a union, but at the turn of the next century, this number was only 15 percent.[19]
In the 1950s, when unions sought to represent workers in unionizing elections,
they won between 65 and 75 percent of those contests; in 2000, that number
was down to 50 percent.[20] They never won at any American IBM plant site in
the entire century.

Many reasons have been offered for why unions declined that blew wind to
IBM's back in its campaign to keep them out: use of welfare capitalist measures,
laws and government regulations permitting corporate practices that blocked
unions (e.g., in IBM's case what managers could do), strategic errors of unions
focusing too much on wages and working conditions and less on other concerns facing workers, and declining political influence of unions in general.[21]
In recent decades, observers noticed a shift from manufacturing to white collar

service employees, whose needs differed by the 1960s from those of earlier manufacturing workers and their attitudes toward labor unions.[22] American views concerning individualism, as opposed to group activities, reflected a constant theme evident in IBM over the past century.

One of the most important facilitative factors was the increasing worry that workers had of losing social status if they joined a union, an issue first identified in the 1930s.[23] Furthermore, as one labor historian concluded, "all these factors have no doubt contributed to union decline."[24] This historian, Lawrence G. Richards, Jr., could have been commenting about IBM when he argued that "in examining the methods management uses to fend off union organizing drives . . . its principal tool is a direct appeal to workers designed to heighten the opposition many employees already have towards organized labor. Likewise, welfare capitalist measures and human resource management techniques are geared to providing workers with many of the perceived benefits of unionism without the costs—both economic and psychological—of actually joining a union."[25] He reported that companies were assisted by a growing negative perception of unions that continued to the end of the century, which he described as "pervasive." It was driven by a combination of "suspicion and derision," even though Americans believed unions had done some good.[26] These views remained essentially consistent since the late 1930s. Not until the 1990s did IBMers at some plants reaffirm what one student of labor unions noted about unionizing activity in general: that the public saw this activity "as a strategy of last resort rather than as a natural or preferred means of improving job conditions."[27]

As IBM opened new factories and expanded plants and laboratories in post–World War II America, what worked at Endicott management applied in Poughkeepsie, East Fishkill, Boulder, Rochester, Santa Teresa, and elsewhere.[28] Meanwhile, American unions remained strong, but only until the mid-1950s, after which they began their slow decline for the rest of the century. In that period, IBM experienced a work environment less conducive to unionization, a circumstance that changed by the 1990s, discussed later.

IBM managers rarely spoke publicly about unions, focusing their comments regarding "labor relations" (IBM's preferred phrasing) on the importance of worker–manager interactions and using the elaborate collection of communications vehicles designed to bubble up issues before they became contentious, such as the Speak Up and Open Door processes. Watson Sr. spoke often of "man–manager relationships" for decades. His son and successor, Watson Jr., called that relationship as "essential to IBM as the family is to society." He explained: "We depended on this relationship to help safeguard respect for the individual no matter how highly structured the rest of the business became." He was clear on that relationship to unions: "As long as workers and supervisors understood each other, unions were superfluous at IBM, but if we let that bond erode, sooner or later the business was sure to become a battleground."[29] Watson Jr.'s concern is the scenario that played out in IBM beginning in the 1980s.

But earlier in the 1930s and 1940s, the introduction of various benefits blunted the need for unions, most notably the introduction of a retirement program for employees. Senior managers had learned through personal experience at NCR and later by observing what was occurring in other companies that benefits slowed unionization. However, they also realized that other circumstances helped, too, such as the rising salaries in the boom years of the 1920s, although working hours, factory conditions, and poor supervisory practices on the shop floor left room for improvements.[30] While the company implemented many reforms and enhancements to its labor practices, it was an iterative process that one might be tempted to say was slow but was informed by the experiences of other companies and what IBM could afford. Thus, it was not until 1958 that IBM finally abolished the last of the hourly wages and put all factory employees on straight salaries, affecting about 20,000 employees out of the total U.S. workforce of some 60,000; the other employees were already on salary (salesmen had bonuses as well).[31] All employees appeared now on an equal social standing in the firm. That extended even to earlier practices of executives, managers, and workers eating in the same cafeterias and to such other egalitarian practices as sharing the same parking lots and calling each other by first name. Even the Soviet Union's premier, Nikita Khrushchev, during his visit to an IBM plant in 1959 was impressed at the lack of hierarchy.[32] That same year, IBM made it possible for employees to conveniently buy IBM stock—possibly a "first" in corporate America. This offering gave employees the opportunity to accumulate capital and otherwise manage their own economic assets, further bonding them to the company.

As academic observers noted, all these behaviors were designed "to sustain the image of a collection of individuals all contributing to the overall company performance."[33] The same observers concluded in 1988 that as the result of IBM's various labor policies, workers did not need unions to get in the way of their own work and to communicate with the firm. They arrived at this conclusion before IBM's labor relations changed substantially from prior practice. Workers held the belief that "given their work environment and their perceptions of the *practice* of trade unions, they can see no advantage in joining one."[34]

Key to implementing benefits and nurturing dialogue with employees was the manager on the shop floor, in a remote sales office, in a laboratory, or in a headquarters office. That is a reason why understanding and discussing their role in some detail in the next section (and in the previous chapter) are crucial for appreciating the history of unions in the American side of IBM and, to an extent, even in countries where unions and other forms of worker councils were the norm.

IBM's Secret Weapon Against Unions—Its Vigilant Managers

With the enormous expansion of IBM's workforce in the 1950s, it should be no surprise that senior executives would have to implement formal, well-organized training for all managers and newly minted executives to reinforce IBM's values, to ensure they understood their policies, and to equip them to implement the company's processes. When extensive training programs for those purposes were launched in the last three years of the decade, recall our discussion in chapter 4 that instructors placed emphasis on how to carry out rules and procedures. Over the next few years, they learned how to balance three objectives for training—IBM's values (Basic Beliefs), policies, and procedures—incorporating these into the basic training all management underwent, better known as "Fundamentals of Management." Of all the modules (called *units*), the most detailed was entitled "Industrial Relations," which translated meant how to deal with the threat of unions at IBM. By the mid-1960s, it was a detailed training module that remained essentially unchanged over the next two decades. The objectives were to teach all managers to "know basic legal restrictions affecting relations between employer and employee" and to "understand IBM's position with regard to organized labor and that it is based on law."[35] Managers were instructed that it was their responsibility to manage the relationship of their charges with IBM, responding to an employee's problems and grievances fairly and promptly. At no time in the life of an IBM manager was more attention paid to the issue of unions than in management training classes. It was there one could learn what IBM intended.

IBM's admonition to managers was clearly documented in class notes: "Whenever this subject is mentioned as part of your management training, you will note that our company position is precisely in keeping with the law. As members of management, we shall never question an employee on this subject and we shall never voice any opinion or advice that might be interpreted as a threat to an individual's decision on this subject." Further, "we shall follow the law in giving an employee our views as to why we do not think that it is necessary for our employees to deal with us through an outside party."[36] One would be hard pressed to find a finer line being drawn between open discussions among managers and employees on any subject taught to them than about this subject.

Instructors distributed to each student a collection of publications they were expected to read; at least they had them in their binders and could consult them later when confronting a union issue. The basic legal foundation came from a thirty-one-page publication, *The Taft-Hartley Act as Amended in 1959: A Management Guide*, written by a professor and published by the California Institute of Technology, so by a third party, not IBM.[37] After describing the law's terms, history, and role of management and of employees, it included a list of fifteen actions managers were to avoid. Each was discussed in IBM's classes for newly minted and experienced managers and executives. These included taking part "in the formation of a union of employees," applying "pressure on workers to join or not join a union," digging for information about what employees were doing with respect to unions, joining a union, circulating antiunion literature or flyers, "collud[ing] with a union or its agents," or cooperating in strikes, picketing, and other similar activities.[38]

New managers received a copy of the Taft-Hartley Act because it was the current foundation "rules of the game" for engaging in union activities in the United States. The law, passed in 1947, was officially entitled the Labor Management Relations Act of 1947. It was intended to constrain the activities and power of unions. It prohibited unions from conducting wildcat strikes, strikes in solidarity with unions in other companies or industries, certain types of picketing, and myriad disruptive behaviors.[39] So, this was a tool available to IBM, and it was not necessary to tell managers that it was an important one. Instructors had merely to say that the law dictated how managers and labor should behave and that managers were simply to obey the law. It would have been obvious to anyone who read the law's language that the fundamental problem was to stop disruption of business operations due to strikes and interventions between management and employees resulting from union middlemen. The lectures about union issues were delivered by IBM's lawyers who were all deeply steeped in the terms and conditions of the legislation and how best to apply it. They chose their words carefully in classroom settings.

To assist managers in what was clearly seen as a complex fine line of behavior for them, IBM maintained an industrial relations staff that could be consulted on how to proceed should a situation arise. IBM's lawyers were taught how to interpret national and local laws related to such issues as wages and working conditions, equal opportunity in employment, and strikes and picketing and trained on court decisions and administrative rulings. A second arm within the industrial relations staff was Personnel, experts who defined and interpreted what managers needed to learn in classes, developed procedures to facilitate quick and appropriate communications on labor matters, and provided interpretations of IBM's personnel practices and policies.[40] Managers were encouraged to consult them.[41] In practice in the United States, managers were instructed by training, presentations made in their localities, and their own management to follow the "one breath" rule. Upon suspecting even the remotest hint of unionizing activities, such as a letter signed by more than one employee complaining about something, a manager could take one breath before picking up the telephone and calling personnel or a higher-ranking manager.[42] Probably every manager in the U.S. organization in the 1960s through the 1980s had heard the phrase "one breath"; it was that ubiquitous a focus on addressing possible unionizing activities.

Recommended readings for newly minted managers included a ten-page, single-spaced glossary of industrial relations and wage terms extracted from a publication of the U.S. Department of Labor on the history of labor in the United States from 1778 to 1964 and an addendum prepared by IBM that brought the chronology to the present.[43] These employees were also given a recent article from the *Monthly Labor Review*, a U.S. government journal, on current economic conditions as they affected labor in the mid-1960s.[44] Similar updated articles were distributed to attendees throughout the 1970s and 1980s.

As with other training modules, managers were asked to role-play situations to reinforce their knowledge of policies through practice. For example, a manager might be asked to determine the correct response to what constituted IBM policy toward unions, demonstrating that fine line between a plausible answer and the correct one:

1. IBM is not anti-union and is neutral regarding organization of our people by unions.
2. IBM is opposed to unions and their activities in the labor field.
3. IBM feels that labor unions have contributed to the nation, but do not feel that our employees need a third party to represent them in order to get good benefits and fair treatment.[45]

The correct answer was 3.

Because the company did not publicize its encounters with unionizing activities in these middle decades, one can only assume some activity must have taken place, at least unions reaching out to assess the appetite for organizing factory workforces. However, nothing came of these initiatives. One can conclude that the strategy worked to encourage employees individually to bring their concerns to their managers with the expectation that these would be addressed in some reasonable fashion, which is exactly what senior management wanted all to do. Opinion surveys from the 1960s and 1970s flagged few concerns about the responsiveness of managers to problems across the American part of the company as a whole. There were specific concerns, however, here and there, such as growing concerns about environmental pollution in Endicott, discussed later. Employees raised issues, largely through Open Door letters and other informal channels, with one or two levels of management.[46] Employees, however, were often concerned that individual managers might exact revenge on them, less so by the company as a policy, but by an individual's action. When retribution occurred, the victimized worker normally would turn in that manager, and if proven to have occurred, senior management sided with the employee. The vengeful manager could be expected either to receive a terrible annual review or be taken out of management, the latter an especially lethal blow to their career development, while the company rectified the aggrieved employee's issue.[47] These were also years in which salaries and benefits continued to increase, when the company prospered, and when the biggest complaints were related to long hours and great pressures to get new things done. It was IBM's Golden Age.[48]

Yet in a company as large as IBM, the entire workforce did not move in lockstep from one era to another. For example, Lee Conrad, who worked in Endicott and would largely be the IBM employee public face of unionizing in the United States, was already involved in organizing activities in the 1970s. That period saw the birth of early grievance activities, and then in the following decade, early unionizing efforts occurred at Endicott. Over the next fifteen years, a network of committees formed across the country. In 1984, IBM employee representatives from six countries met in Japan for the first IBM Workers International Solidarity. That was also the year Endicott's personnel made their first attempt to unionize.[49]

Birth of American Labor Organizing in IBM

Worker organizing originated in Endicott, New York, home to several thousand employees in the 1970s. Myriad products were manufactured there, including circuit boards, printers, and check sorting machines, among others. Many of these products were manufactured in the 1960s. But by the early 1970s, there were growing concerns about the negative effects of manufacturing these products on workers and their families.[50] Employees discussed their concerns with management but to no avail, from their perspective. As a new employee, Lee Conrad began to organize grievance conversations along the lines of a union leader in the mid-1970s. He worked in the factory and so understood the conditions. In time, he became the employee face to IBM and the media. At first, he found few people willing to formulate committees for fear of losing their jobs. Conrad himself remained "underground" (his term) in the 1970s out of the same fear, even adopting a pseudonym that he could use with local media, "Michael Maguire." It took management several years to conclude that he was the local agitator stirring up trouble for them. His manager attempted to fire him (he actually did once until overturned by Personnel). The issues he was concerned with involved long hours, breathing in and working with fumes and chemicals, and the desire of employees to be paid overtime. Management denied there were chemical problems, so he began writing and publishing an underground flyer distributed to cohorts in parking lots and on sidewalks entitled *IBM Speak Up*, beginning in 1976.[51]

Early issues of his two-page mimeographed flyers addressed health concerns. For example, from 1981—five years into the effort to solve local problems— he wrote, "WORK—it can be dangerous to your health," and "With the introduction of more and more chemicals into IBM Endicott, we should all be concerned with the question: what is this job doing to me?" He reminded workers of what they already knew to be true, that "Building 18 is Endicott's main sweatshop. Workers there are exposed to an assortment of toxic chemicals like trichloroethylene, methylchloroform and various acids; the noise level on 18–3 is too high; it smells and there is a constant haze around the copper line."[52] That flyer went on for two pages describing these conditions. The request of management at this time was limited: "post all department air quality, noise level tests and health and safety info on the department bulletin boards" and "explain state law to workers about what they are entitled to know about the health working conditions." He wanted to know what else was harmful and, finally, stated: "Our only hope is to ORGANIZE ourselves."[53] Participation remained low, sometimes with meetings attended by twelve to fifteen people operating "underground," and with between 500 and 1,500 flyers printed, even in the 1980s.[54] But, the media noticed them.[55]

In that second decade of labor activism, Conrad and others began to attend IBM stockholder annual meetings, now in solidarity with workers in many companies complaining about IBM's support of apartheid in South Africa, among other issues. The declarations were becoming more brazen, militant, and expressed in the vernacular of labor organizing.[56] In the early 1980s, employees had formed the IBM Workers United to provide an "organized voice of our own," thus ratcheting up activity.[57] Conrad went public and committees formed at other plant sites around the world. They began to sound and behave more like union-forming teams.

After an international gathering of IBM labor committees in 1984, American grievance activities became more open and aggressive. Labor was concerned about rising wages of executives and, by the end of the decade, IBM's slow but obvious reduction in benefits, forced and encouraged early retirements, and then layoffs in violation of the oft-stated promise of lifetime employment by generations of IBM executives. In the mid-1980s, Conrad renamed his news-letter *Resistor*, and he mailed about 500 copies to employee committees all over the United States, with the rest distributed locally.[58] Copies ended up in IBM management's hands, so all concerned knew what was happening. News of IBM's working conditions and grievances were reported, with publication occurring about every two months. Agitation for better pay was also on full display.[59] By 1990, American workers were complaining about IBM's layoffs.

Activity increased at other IBM locations, such as at Burlington, Vermont. IBM was the largest private sector employer in the state and so attracted the attention of both state officials and the U.S. congressional delegation, including Senator Bernie Sanders.[60] In the 1990s, Congress conducted hearings on what was going on in Burlington. The essential experience of the 1970s and 1980s is that a small group of employees continued to push for better working

conditions and later for improved benefits and saw quickly the impending crisis of layoffs. They did their work with few participants and on a shoestring
budget, learning what to do from one another around the world.

Union Activity Since the Late 1980s

IBM's corporate good times did not last. They changed so much that employees in 2019–2020, who had already been employees for twenty years or more,
commented on employee and retiree social media websites that they did not
know IBM once had a commitment to full employment, Family Dinners, and
company picnics or that IBMers had worked in a period without union activity,
in an era of general approval of how the company functioned. Many tens of
thousands of new employees had come into the firm in the 1990s to replace
earlier generations. To the new arrivals, the firm prior to the 1990s seemed a
different company. Retirees acknowledged the break with a past characterized
as a "magical time," as one put it.[61]

In 1994, the IBM Workers United discussed with the International Union of
Electrical Workers about trying another organizing effort in Endicott. Despite
official IBM guidelines and contrary to U.S. law, employees recalled IBM sending a letter to their homes discouraging such activity. "The Letter," as it became
known in Endicott, was seen as threatening. But just as obvious, it demonstrated
growing concern about the possibility that Conrad and others might succeed in
unionizing the workforce in Endicott, especially since he was now getting help
and advice from professional union organizers. In October 1996, Diana Bendz,
the senior location executive for Endicott, wrote to all local employees reminding them that they should treat organizers the way "you would treat anyone else
who solicits door to door" and that one did not "have to allow them into your
home." She added that "you should seriously consider the costs and obligations
of union membership," a subtle threat. The letter concluded with: "What can a
union do to make IBM a stronger company for all of us? In my opinion, nothing." The letter disturbed the organizers and employees; even the local press
reported the incident.[62] Local management coerced employees into a meeting
where they were discouraged from unionizing.

The tone set by IBM's adherence to the Taft-Hartley Act in earlier decades
seemed to be challenged right up to the "gray line" of the legislation. Clearly
IBM management was worried, at least senior leadership in the Endicott region.
But as Conrad observed, it might have been enough to scare employees from
joining the union, although he had witnessed little interest on the part of local
employees to do so for over a decade.[63]

Meanwhile, the professional organizers brought in from the International
Union of Electrical Workers ran into their own leadership problems and left the

IBM employees, in Conrad's words, "to flounder." Local employees gave up their efforts but reenergized in 1999 when IBM restructured its American pension plan, which they viewed as a significant "take back." Conrad and others stepped up their organizing efforts at multiple plants. Congressional committees held hearings on corporate pension plan changes (not just IBM's), employee meetings were held, and the original Endicott organization rebranded itself as the Alliance@IBM/Communications Workers of America. It now operated on a nationwide basis with other factory sites, while the IBM Workers International Solidarity became the IBM Global Union Alliance, chaired by Lee Conrad for several years.[64] Over the next half-dozen years, the Alliance@IBM published a newsletter, *Thinktwice!*, to keep employees informed about activities around the country. In an issue from 2006, it reminded them of why they needed a union: "To represent ourselves, to advocate pension protections, to build support for collective bargaining, and to gain professional assistance, because collection action works."[65]

After investigations, congressional hearings, and lawsuits, IBM was found to have altered its pension program to the detriment of younger employees in violation of national laws. The battle between employees and the company gained unwanted publicity for IBM. For example, the *Washington Post* ran a story, "IBM Workers Continue to Fight Pension Changes," in 2001. After reporting that some three hundred corporations had changed their pensions in the late 1990s, it noted that "employees at International Business Machines Corp. have been some of the most vocal opponents of this shift, which they say leaves older workers facing sharp pension cuts." The newspaper made clear that while IBM kept the pension plan for the older workers, "thousands of middle-aged employees faced sharp pension cuts." Then Bernard ("Bernie") Sanders introduced legislation to protect such workers, concerned that thousands of his state's IBM workers were being harmed.[66] IBM revised its offering to fix that problem such that it could continue on the path of shutting down the old defined benefits pension for new and some existing employees by shifting contributions to 401(k) accounts in a more equitable way. But up to this point, nothing had so attracted the attention of employees as their view that IBM was taking away their pensions.

Yet circumstances from prior times lingered. Managers were trained in a fashion similar to that of the earlier era, at least until the early 2000s, by when acquisitions of entire companies made such meticulous attention to training both nearly impossible and certainly no longer affordable.[67] However, IBM's stance on unions remained unchanged. With abandonment of the full employment practice and even the original language of the Basic Beliefs in the 1990s, Watson Jr.'s fear had come true. Union activity surfaced at almost all American IBM plant sites, while those in Europe that had been benign became more active as the company began discharging workers there as well. By the early

2000s, morale had declined all over the company. Tens of thousands of people had been dismissed or "sold off" as part of entire divisions. Increasing numbers of personnel practices had become shadows of their prior forms. Often these actions were taken in a swift and brutal manner with little sensitivity shown for the feelings of employees who had worked at IBM for decades.[68] A profoundly contrasting and, for employees who had been at IBM in mid-century, sad realization by them and current employees, news media revealed that IBM had engaged in a campaign of systematically dismissing older employees. Expelled employees had been complaining about this behavior for a half decade, and a few filed lawsuits against IBM, which were to virtually no avail, but it had all been quiet. No longer was this the case. Now the world knew about it, and while stock analysts approved of the cost cutting, it seemed "everyone" else below senior executive ranks saw problems with that practice and none more so than employees and ex-employees.[69] Just as bad as layoffs, IBM was shifting work to less expensive labor markets. In a flyer from 2000 soliciting employees to join the Endicott union (Local 1701), organizers posited: "IBM Corporate management is actively shifting US jobs to low cost countries. Is yours next? Join the fight back at www.allianceibm.org."[70]

A brief review of some of these changes offers context for understanding the experience IBM encountered with unions through its labor practices of nearly three-quarters of a century. Senior management knew that full employment was the key to keeping unions at bay. During the 1940s–1980s, the company changed so much that it often had too many employees in one part of the business or too many with skills no longer needed, yet not enough of both in another part. Various efforts were undertaken to shift people around and to retrain them as needed, while increasing or slowing hiring. These actions kept the full employment practice intact until the late 1980s.[71] Management continuously reassured employees that full employment remained rock-solid policy. As late as 1983, employees were assured of that in the company's magazine, *THINK*, quoting executives with the banner headline, "The Payoff: No Layoffs."[72] But that was not to last.

In the now familiar narrative, IBM overexpanded in the 1980s in the belief that mainframe computer sales would increase when, in fact, the world was moving rapidly to PCs and distributed network computing. Elsewhere, I have argued that management's failure to meet the challenges of changing markets led to IBM's severe decline in the late 1980s and early 1990s and that, as a by-product of their failure, the firm had no choice but to abandon its full employment practice.[73] Since the late 1980s and to the present (2023), IBM engaged in iterative waves of layoffs in a bid to lower operating costs and replace quickly no longer needed skills with those now in demand, with the result that job security for all vanished and morale dropped, along with motivation and devotion to the company. Revenue per capita shrank. Over half the employees on the payroll in the mid-1980s were gone in less than a decade. The employee population reaching retirement age in the 2010s who remembered a time of full employment now constituted a rapidly shrinking minority. The massive waves of departures of the early 1990s constituted what IBM's CEO in the 1990s, Louis V. Gerstner, Jr., called a "water torture" of continuous drops, which he tried to shut off, but continued exercising during his tenure, and which his two successors continued more aggressively.[74] The third successor, Arvind Krishna, continued the repeated drip of layoffs in his first eight months at the helm in 2020 until November of that year, when IBM publicly confirmed it would soon lay off 10,000 workers in advance of dividing the company into two parts in 2021.[75] Earlier, at Endicott, IBM's presence went from just over 10,000 employees to under 1,000 in less than fifteen years. Similar tales could be told about Poughkeepsie, East Fishkill, and other sites around the United States, and later in Western Europe, Canada, and Australia in the 2000s. Such losses negatively affected IBM company towns in visible ways.[76]

As Watson Jr. had predicted, union activity picked up at IBM. It took a while for employees to reach that point, but in the 1990s, they had. Activity popped up in Burlington, Vermont; Endicott and Poughkeepsie, New York; Austin, Texas; Raleigh, North Carolina; and California, among other places. The IBM Global Alliance formed, as did the Alliance@IBM. The Communications Workers of America had tried since the 1970s to penetrate IBM and quickly saw the Alliance@IBM as a way in and so supported its efforts. All the initiatives failed to unionize any location, but as a by-product, employees formed social media websites to stimulate such activity, share information about layoffs, and organize political pressure on IBM, especially in New England. Many thousands of employees all over the world read these postings, some of which have remained active to the present.

The key question is: Why, in the face of so much labor turmoil, were employees not able to organize? American law made it possible, and management at all levels was collectively becoming discredited and seen as impudent and ineffective. Their credibility shrank by the year. Employees were genuinely fearful of losing their jobs. Lee Conrad, reflecting back on his efforts, offered an answer to the question. He posited several reasons. First, IBM had conducted so many large reorganizations of divisions and sites from the 1980s through the 2010s that workforces remained fragmented and hence constrained in their ability to collaborate with each other on normal company business, let alone on unionizing initiatives. Some of those reorganizations included selling off chunks of the business along with their employees to other companies, such as the DASD (disk drives) and PC divisions. So, thousands of employees were cast outside the gates, no longer part of the unionizing conversation. Second, by laying off people in small numbers in a constant dribble around the country, IBM kept buzz about layoffs alive, but it became the "new normal," injecting a fatalism into the workforce. That new reality led many—if not most—employees to think this was not an immediate crisis to be solved.[77]

Third, Conrad observed that employees were too cautious, using the term "conservative," and fearful of calling attention to themselves. Visibility might make them targets for the next incremental layoff, should they agitate for unions. Equally important was the view—prejudice—against unions that had been so systemically ingrained in employees over many decades. Many employees who had joined IBM in the 1960s and 1970s embraced that perspective. Many at factory sites, such as in Burlington, Endicott, and Rochester, were older than those employed in sales offices and thus more shaped by these earlier views than other employees scattered in smaller field offices. Conrad believed workers were in denial that they would be let go. Their performance ratings were good, they had vast experience in getting things done successfully within IBM, and they wishfully held on to the old Basic Beliefs and the implied contract between IBM and themselves. Fundamentally, things remained so "topsy-turvy," in his words, that people were kept off guard.[78]

Recall that management had decades of experience dealing with factory labor issues, so their lines of defense held. By the 2020s, their experience with unionizing activities now had extended for over four decades, and they had been dealing with national labor issues for a century. Lawyers and personnel experts worked effectively to counter union activities, working normally out of the limelight for decades. It ultimately did not matter that employees complained about all manner of perceived bad managerial behavior: rich bonuses paid to executives, mistruths about how no more layoffs would occur, silence about the company's personnel plans, incremental withdrawal of employee pension and medical benefits, and simply bad business performance by the firm.[79]

By the early 2000s, the central topics of conversation among employees worldwide were the layoffs. The Alliance fueled their angst by reporting on these around the company since IBM management did not. Conrad and his fellow union organizers publicized that IBM had 230,000 employees in the United States in the mid-1980s, but in 2016, only 78,000.[80] The work had not all gone away; rather, it had been outsourced to contractors, such as those with H1b visas and to others in India, for example, using "us.bm.com" email addresses, implying they were resident in the United States when they were not. At that time (2014), IBM sold off yet another portion of its business to Lenovo, the Chinese manufacturer of laptop computers, pushing out additional employees from Raleigh and sales offices all over the United States. All of this happened as older workers—those who cost the most, some with less relevant skills, and who were most likely to be clinging to the old Basic Beliefs and notion of full employment—were being ousted by the thousands.[81]

Meanwhile, both Alliance@IBM and the Communications Workers of America kept stirring the fires of organizing while drawing the news media's attention to the plight of workers at IBM. Members of the IBM Global Union Alliance did the same, calling on management to stop cutting jobs. Speaking as if on behalf of IBM employees in 2015, it published bold headlines in large fonts declaring that "IBM workers worldwide want to see IBM succeed but IBM executives need to realize that employees are assets to business success and not liabilities. It is essential for IBM to urgently engage in open and constructive dialogue with the trade unions who represent IBM workers to explain what is happening and why. Stonewalling its workers is not an answer."[82]

But it did not happen. Website conversations failed to create sufficient community to organize. One analyst suggested that such sites satisfied employees with the kind of information they wanted about layoffs and company plans sufficient to reduce the uncertainty of their own circumstances during periods when layoffs were spiking at one site or another.[83] In 2016, the Alliance@IBM broke with the Communications Workers of America. It gave up the effort, "suspending" activities. In its press announcement, the Alliance stated that "years of job cuts and membership losses have taken their toll."[84] In 2016, there were only some two hundred members, and at its peak a few years earlier, there were four hundred.[85] Too many employees had left, been sold off, retired, or given up since the Alliance began its work in the 1990s. Management had won. In its heyday, the Alliance@IBM could reach some 140,000 employees through its website with immediate relevant information. Conrad reaffirmed his long-held observation that the ongoing restructuring and layoffs prevented the union from organizing. It needed a stable workforce to succeed. Management had prevented that from existing. Advocating for employees proved insufficient for the cause. Conrad retreated, having left IBM in 2000 to work full time for the Alliance and Communications Workers of America as the national coordinator for the IBM unionizing initiative. In 2016, he was done.[86]

Conclusions

We can conveniently divide the history of IBM's union activities into two chronological periods: 1910s to mid-1980s and then late 1980s to 2016. In the first era, IBM management made the decision not to welcome unions. It developed and implemented strategies and a corporate culture that made it either unnecessary or impossible for unions to form. The extant evidence suggests both circumstances prevailed. When the necessity for not having unions changed, it was management that exposed the company to union organizing. The tipping point for nearly a half century was always whether or not the company maintained its full employment policy. From 1921 to the late 1980s, no one had been laid off by IBM, and even in the 1980s, layoffs came through various ruses, such as voluntary early retirement programs. However, employees began to see these programs as a crack in the Grand Bargain of job security.[87] Early retirement programs became canaries in the mines.

When IBM wanted to shrink the size of a cohort of its American employees, law and effective practices in the 1980s called for the company to offer these employees early retirement programs. IBM did this by carefully defining who was eligible, such as only employees of a particular division, job classification, or age. They would be solicited as a group with a letter addressed, for example, as follows: "Dear IBMer: I am writing to tell you about a new—and temporary—retirement opportunity for which you are eligible." This letter just quoted was dated September 1986 and went out over the signature of the chairman of the board, John F. Akers, to thousands of employees. It is worth quoting further: "It is called the 1986 Retirement Incentive, and it is part of our continuing effort to make the IBM company as lean and vigorous as possible. . . . We have moved work to people and people to work." He spoke of "belt tightening" and asked that employees "take stock of [their] future plans" and "discuss it with [their] family." He urged them to take part in the plan as "it will help IBM remain competitive, and it also helps protect IBM's full employment tradition."[88]

IBM offered similar and increasingly less generous programs to employees over the next three decades. The early ones were so oversubscribed that first- and second-line managers began complaining that their best people were leaving because they were confident they could find employment with IBM's customers and competitors, while others retired or pursued other careers. To add salt to the wound, managers heard about the terms being offered at the same time as their employees. An eligible employee's manager received a small card entitled "TO: ALL MANAGERS" that read: "For your awareness, enclosed is a copy of the brochure, J. F. Akers' letter and the IBM Retirement Education Assistance Plan highlights being sent to all employees who are eligible to retire under the 1986 Retirement Incentive."[89] Until this card floated into a manager's mailbox, it had been customary to brief managers about changes in benefits and employment programs *before* their employees heard the news. They had little time to learn about the new terms or to determine how to distribute the work of retiring employees who had to leave by the end of the year, in other words, in 90 days.

Those who left in the 1980s survived their transitions to other careers and lifestyles reasonably well, while many subsequent waves of retirees fared less well. For most, it was an unwelcome jolt of reality, with many seeing the "handwriting on the wall." All other labor issues paled in comparison to full employment. Early retirement programs were precursors to layoffs that many employees saw coming, ushering in the events of the subsequent three decades.[90]

In each era, consequences flowed from the behavior of management and their employees that one could link to the history of union activity in IBM. In the first era—1910s–1980s—various grievance processes worked to address

labor's concerns, such as use of Speak Up, Open Door, and other communications vehicles, all discussed in subsequent chapters. In general, everyone was
civil to each other; one could stay calm, factual, and patient. In general, all
employees expected results when issues surfaced. Employees enjoyed adequate
to good salaries and a competitive portfolio of benefits, and management had
the flexibility to run the firm in ways that ensured decades of prosperity for
all. Unhappiness with the "IBM Way" proved minimal until the 1970s. Even
grousing in the 1960s remained limited to lengthy work weeks (due to the
launch of the System 360 products) and to the social conformism evident in
company towns.[91]

By the early 2000s, however, all that had changed. Massive cracks in the
larger IBM culture were obvious to employees, managers, the media outside
the firm, and historians and other IBM watchers. Less evident to the public
at large, however, was how the language and the tone of conversations about
grievances had altered. Members on IBM retiree and employee social media
websites posted harsh, even vitriolic criticisms of management in general, the
company, and even individual executives by name. Hate is not too strong a
word to use to describe some of the feelings expressed on these websites, while
many advocated and pled for their peers to organize. Such sentiments would
have been nearly impossible to find expressed inside IBM, let alone publicly,
before the 1970s.[92]

Local print and television media reported on picketing at various IBM plant
sites, while local U.S. congressional delegations were approached to investigate
and mitigate IBM's labor practices in Vermont, New York, Colorado, Minnesota, and Texas. IBM management's ability to defeat unionization did not lead
to a return to mutual collaboration of workers and managers; that employee
hostility remained steadfast. It was fueled by the continuous drip of layoffs and
curtailed benefits, notably the ever-extending stinginess of severance packages
in the 2000s, and by IBM's increased reliance on work outsourced to other
companies or exported to less expensive workforces in Asia and Latin America.
But eventually, even both workers and managers (and some junior executives)
experienced the same round of layoffs as IBM's financial performance continued its decline after 2012.[93]

Historians have identified practices similar to IBM's in all periods in many
industries. That should be of no surprise since lawyers, personnel managers,
and executives at many companies talked to each other, borrowing from each
other's experiences.[94] Historians documented the general decline of organized
labor's membership and influence since the 1960s, pointing to the fundamental
problems that unions had: largely their salary and benefit desires being met
regardless of union activities.[95] IBM's shift from large clusters of manufacturing employees to more dispersed services-oriented ones has yet to be studied,
but what little we know is that with the greater use of computing came more

synchronized work, often automating many activities and reducing the number of workers needed and hence diminishing their ability to dictate new working conditions.[96] Identities among workers became more "mixed," to use one historian's descriptor, as social status and job identities evolved.[97] To be blunt about it, information technology "architects" or consultants viewed themselves as white collar professionals, while factory workers were seen as lower status "blue collar" labor. The changing nature of work identities is a widely recognized shift that occurred since the 1960s across many industries and notably, too, in the IT sector where unions did not take root in the United States.[98] Labor historian Howard Gospel called out the need to better understand managerial practices regarding organized labor; this chapter contributes to that growing interest in the subject.[99]

While this is not the place to speculate about the arc of IBM's future labor relations issues or about broader trends across American industries, managers continue to be better armed than labor organizers. They can further automate work, thereby reducing the number of workers or the latter's ability to change working conditions. Management can quickly move work around the world to less expensive labor pools or to where unions are legally or economically discouraged. Work can be moved, too, within the internal labor markets inside a large company, a practice widely in evidence inside IBM since the 1980s at all of its densely populated sites.[100]

In the next chapter, we explore the benefits employees received, such as medical and life insurance, among others, which influenced IBM's culture more than its unionizing activities, providing context for many of the activities discussed throughout this book.

CHAPTER 6

CORPORATE BENEFITS IN BOOM PERIODS

IBM's American Experience

I wanted IBM to be recognized as one of the most generous employers in America.

Thomas J. Watson, Jr.[1]

P rosperous American corporations have a long history of providing their employees a broad array of benefits as part of their total compensation package. In addition to salaries, these ranged from pensions and health insurance to free country club memberships and family parties during holiday seasons. Benefits were collectively expensive yet continually offered one decade after another. Why? Historians studying such offerings argue that a combination of reasons offers an explanation: enlightened paternalistic management, competitive pressures for recruiting and retaining employees, habit (industry and professional custom) and culture (employee expectations), fear of unionization (or if unions were already established within a firm, curtailing further demands), or requirement by labor laws (as in Europe).[2] An IBM executive, Ted Child, offered another reason in 1991 for IBM's suite of benefits: "We're not in the charity business, we're in the productivity business."[3] One can find examples of each reason in many corporations, indeed across entire industries.[4] IBM's leader for nearly a half century, Thomas J. Watson, Sr., had learned what benefits attracted and retained employees, earlier at NCR, learning a great deal about how best to manage them, and later at IBM.[5] While he worked in the Office Appliance Industry, he was not alone in his views and practices. A mighty competitor, Burroughs Corporation, offered its employees collections of benefits.[6] There was good reason for why the lessons Watson learned at NCR were progenitors of his experience at IBM. As historian Andrea Tone put it, NCR "became the nation's leading example of welfare work."[7] NCR's management concluded sooner than many other firms that benefits improved the health, and hence productivity, of its workforce.[8] Many of these practices originated in the last quarter of the nineteenth century, so by the time IBM was creating its own collection of benefits, there were well-understood practices to draw upon.[9] The pace of their introduction proved less of an issue about the benefits of paternalism, or what to offer, than what it could afford. Not until the 1920s could Watson even start thinking of offering these to his employees, and even then, he had to wait until he could afford to do so.

Watson Sr. could build on his prior experiences as he shaped his successful company during the interwar years. Many of the most important long-term benefits enjoyed by employees were introduced in the 1930s, during the height of the Great Depression, while other companies cut back. His son, Tom Jr., explained his father's thinking: "From the minute IBM started making large profits in the 1930s, he kept the company in the vanguard of humane employers. IBM offered the best benefits money could buy, which in the early days meant good pay, steady employment, a chance to get promoted, educational opportunities, clean shops, and country clubs. The New Deal and the rise of labor unions changed the public's idea of what big institutions ought to provide, and Dad responded with a broad new plan."[10]

I describe in greater detail here than in the previous chapter many of these new offerings because the motives for their introduction exceeded concerns about labor organizing unions, as that issue did not surface at IBM until long after many of the benefits discussed here had become part of the overall fabric in the life of an employee. After the end of World War II, Watson Sr. continued to introduce new benefits. Watson Jr. reported: "When he announced the new IBM pension plan, Dad wrapped up his speech by saying that IBM's 'constant purpose' was to relieve its people of 'fear for the care of themselves and their families.'"[11] So much about benefits evident in the company in the 1950s and beyond built on a heritage that predated IBM's Golden Age of computer-driven prosperity. What IBM did with benefits reflected and shaped its corporate culture for over a half century. Its actions help explain further why unionizing became a nearly impossible project until the company began to take back some benefits, most notably job security, competitive salaries, pensions, and even medical insurance, in that order.

By the 1950s, when this chapter's account of IBM's benefits begins, the company had two decades of experience, and many senior members over twenty years of practice. In the post–World War II period, the American economy experienced a Golden Age of prosperity that extended into the 1970s and, for IBM, into the 1980s. All was, thus, affordable and generosity expected from a CEO to a newly hired employee. IBM's famed corporate culture included such expectations, summed up by the first of its Basic Beliefs: "Respect for the individual." For decades, senior management had spoken of the collection of employees as the "IBM Family." To make that a reality, this "family" required a standard of living that supported the aspirations of middle- and upper-class Americans and Western Europeans and increasingly, over time, all employees worldwide: health care, education for their children, home ownership, vacations, car ownership (maybe even a fishing boat), and at the end of a career, a good pension. The company delivered. Employees experienced a comfortable material quality of life. They were also welcomed members of their communities. Memoirs written by employees almost always spoke positively about the quality of life afforded by IBM's compensation, personnel practices, and benefits.[12]

Table 6.1 offers a brief chronology of when IBM introduced various benefits. It demonstrates that IBM implemented programs incrementally, but once unveiled, they remained. Each changed with improvements in response to new laws and competitive realities. Also notice that there were flurries of activities during the Great Depression, with military benefits during World War II, the Korean War, the Vietnam War, and the very prosperous 1960s. A similar table could be built to demonstrate the introduction of additional benefits during the 1980s, but a slowdown in their deployment began in the 1990s, with some pulled back in subsequent years, such as the pension provisions.

For some rounds of offerings, there are data on their costs.[13] For example, for the year 1971, the corporation said all benefits cost $585 million for U.S. employees or, on average, $5,043 for each employee by 1972. That expense was in the same year in which revenues exceeded $8.3 billion dollars and when it employed just over 149,000 American workers and a total worldwide staff of 265,000.[14] The expense just cited translated into slightly more than 14 percent of revenue. While we do not know fully what expenses were folded into the total cost of revenue, the percentage suggests it was a major line item in the budget. That came in a weak year, compared to the performance of the firm in the 1950s–1960s and again in the 1970s after the conclusion of an industry-wide recession at the start of the decade. As the employee population grew in the United States, so too did costs of benefits. For U.S. employees, these rose from $457 million in 1969 to $753 million in 1973. Medical expenses doubled between 1969 and 1972, while U.S. pensioners rose from 2,656 to 6,499 by January 1974, as did average monthly pensions, from $239 to $429.[15] Rising costs of medical coverage remained the fastest growing benefit line item from the 1970s to the 2010s. One can surmise that the patterns for American costs of benefits

TABLE 6.1 Chronology of When IBM Introduced Specific Benefit Programs and Number of Times Significant Revisions Were Made to Each, 1934–1973

Year	Program	When Modified/Frequency
1934	Life Insurance and Survivors Income Plan	Each year through 1938; 13 total
1937	Vacation Plan	6
1937	Holiday Plan	4
1940	Military Service Benefit Plan	Each year through 1947 and during each U.S. war; 10 total
1944	Sickness and Accident Plan	4
1945	Retirement Plan	18
1946	Hospitalization Plan	9
1948	Total and Permanent Disability Plan	13
1956	Family Major Medical Plan	6
1957	Thomas J. Watson Scholarship Plan	6
1959	Tuition Refund Plan	3
1966	Family Surgical Plan	3
1966	Medical Plans with Medicare (United States only)	5
1966	Special Care for Children Assistance Plan	2
1972	Adoption Assistance Plan	
1973	Family Dental Plan	

Source: Howard K. Janis, "IBM Benefits Move Dramatically Ahead," THINK 39, no. 1 (January/February 1973): 11.

were similar across Western Europe and Japan and in key IBM markets in Latin America, even though we do not have sufficient hard data to support that assertion; in addition, in some nations, those expenses were borne partially by government. However, it was IBM's general practice to offer similar benefits around the world, tempered by local laws and practices.

The company never publicly discussed why it had such a palate of benefits other than to routinely tell employees and the media that it was part of IBM's historic beneficence. Truth is that it had little choice. If it did not offer such benefits, potential employees could easily work for other firms, or even more disconcerting, its good people could be persuaded to join IBM's competitors. Since IBM had a policy of not permitting unions to form in IBM in the United States, it had to block any thought of employees considering such a possibility. Recall from the previous chapter that Watson Sr. to the present management believed that unions would reduce the company's flexibility in how it deployed its workforce and what it could request of them, not to mention running the risk of episodic work stoppages due to strikes, especially in the United States. In countries that required unions, such as in parts of Western Europe, IBM had no choice in the matter but worked to keep their activities benign. The big concern was in the United States, where entire industries were shaped by ubiquitous union activity, of which IBM wanted no part. So, whether it offered benefits and salaries through the pressure of union activities or voluntarily, it ended up at essentially the same spot: similar benefits as offered by unionized companies and, for those portions of its workforce that were not susceptible to unionization, by other competing firms.[16]

In exchange for good benefits and salaries competitive to its rivals, the company demanded absolute loyalty and commitment to its business objectives. While senior executives resorted to near-poetic language and homilies to espouse their commitment to employee welfare, and in practice normally believed their pronouncements because they, too, were beneficiaries of the same system, one did not need to be a manager for long before learning that there were cold practical reasons for such offerings.[17] The "Grand Bargain," as historians often called it, was acceptable to both IBM and its employees. In exchange for salaries, benefits, and job security, employees had to be loyal to the firm and be willing to change jobs and working conditions. All the evidence indicates they enthusiastically agreed to this arrangement.[18] Not until the deterioration of the company's business performance in the late 1980s did the Grand Bargain come under stress, and by the early 1990s, it had unraveled. That is essentially as far as business historians have gone in understanding the role of benefits in the post-1950s era.[19]

In this chapter, I dig deeper to identify what benefits IBM offered, how these were described, and what role management was expected to play in their implementation. This exercise provides additional access into the interior of IBM's corporate culture and indirectly into the behavior of other firms, since its culture was partially shared by and with other corporations. This point needs little defending, as business observers and historians noted that IBM was both a role model for other large multinational corporations and a student of the managerial and personnel practices of their customers—large enterprises—across the entire twentieth century.[20]

To understand how benefits were implemented and used in exchange for commitment to the firm through daily work performed to high standards, our discussion must take into account the role of all managers, particularly those ensconced within divisions. At IBM, however, personnel managers and staffs played an important, but secondary, role in explaining and implementing benefits. Those two tasks—explaining and implementing benefits—were the immediate and direct responsibility of any manager who had employees working for him or her at any level in the company, from CEO to the first-line manager (FLM). Personnel and education staffs prepared documentation and made presentations to groups of employees to explain the intricacies of a benefit, such as pensions and medical coverage. When a manager had a benefits or employee issue, it was customary to pick up the telephone and discuss with a personnel expert how best to deal with it, such as how to handle a mental health issue or an employee question on some arcane issue.[21] Delicate issues absolutely had to be run by "personnel" or, if even more serious, "legal" for coaching and to minimize operational and legal problems for the corporation. Examples of the latter included potential union organizing activity, someone's use of drugs, or falsification of requests for benefits or reimbursements for expenses.

Finally, benefits were not the only silver bullets used by management to focus the energies of its workforce, albeit they were important ones. These were already embedded in the work environment, like the air one breathed. In 1972, a senior executive explained additionally to his managers: "We must put people first, not by asking what more the company can do in terms of salary or fringe benefit programs, but by asking what more we can do in the sense of renewed management sensitivity, increased communications, unswerving fairness and integrity in decisions—all of which serve to tell our people where they stand, where the business is going, and what is required of them to help get it there."[22] In almost any decade, managers would have heard such messages. Benefits were just part of the total package of IBM's administrative and managerial processes.

Training materials used with new managers shed light on their roles, the breadth of the benefits, and their specific features. We also have access to public statements directed to employees explaining these, along with an assortment of publications doing the same. But first, in this chapter, we need to explain how the company developed and administered benefits programs because it was a carefully crafted managerial effort linked to other corporate strategies and intentions. Then the benefits themselves are described. Several communications tools were used to help calibrate and monitor the value of these benefits and other work circumstances, so to understand those, I explain the role of Open Doors and Speak Ups, before concluding with a discussion of lessons learned and implications for all involved. As in earlier chapters, the story told here is the continuing lesson on how one corporation nurtured and retained what it considered its most important community of stakeholders—IBM's employees.

The Centrality of Management in Administering Benefits

How does a large organization create and spread a consistent culture across its population of employees? It was the central question discussed in chapter 4 but needs repeating here. If the reader studied chapter 4, they can skip the several pages in this section if keen to get on with the discussion about benefits. Some repetition is necessary to provide a cohesive understanding of the benefits story. But back to our question here, the glib, largely accurate answer is by training and motivating those who are sandwiched between the mass of employees and the senior hierarchy responsible for defining and enforcing beliefs and behaviors of all.

In the Catholic Church, these people are the parish priests and their bishops; in Western militaries, noncommissioned officers, such as corporals and sergeants, and their immediate superiors (commissioned officers), such as lieutenants up through colonels; and in corporations, first-line managers and the two to four levels above them (called, e.g., second-, third-, and fourth-line managers) to executive ranks. One can think of divisional and business executives much like generals, archbishops, and cardinals. The Roman Empire ruled all sides of the Mediterranean Sea for centuries in an era without fast communications. That was possible in large part because of a shared culture and practices drilled into leaders at all levels of military and civilian government. As with the other institutions just cited, reinforced by experiences, many institutions are purposefully designed to equip leaders with necessary skills and perspectives. Thus, an up-and-coming priest might work for a bishop to teach him how a diocese is run, or a young colonel might work at a regimental or division headquarters to learn how a general operates. IBM had its executive assistants, who were mentored before moving up the corporate ladder. IBM applied the same approach, as did other large corporations and institutions.

IBM's official internal definition of the role of management explains what made up a manager's responsibility:

> Management is primarily the task of getting things done through people. No matter how well money, materials and other resources are worked in together, if the men who are working with them are not working effectively, the organization will fail. It is the activity, which plans, organizes and controls the operations of the business, providing leadership and coordination of the human resources so as to achieve the desired objectives. An ability in working with people and in communications is essential in management success.[23]

Every manager (in those decades, they were overwhelmingly men) was expected to carry responsibility for corporate success: "A manager still manages his department" and "must make these decisions."[24] These quotes came directly out of a training manual for managers, published in 1967. It did not proffer fresh thinking, as similar messages were delivered in earlier decades and continued circulating over the next quarter century.

To make sure this role was carried out by deliberate means, one became a manager after several years of experience as an employee. Additionally, managers were trained. With each promotion, one went through more formal training, including executives. The company paid special attention to newly minted managers in part because they were the individuals who spent the most time working with employees in understanding and using benefits. IBM dictated to middle management that the "minimum" training that a new manager had to receive included "completion of the *Fundamentals of IBM Management Course.* This study program is to be begun within two weeks following promotion, and the first four lessons completed within six months."[25] For the most part, the initial objective was achieved within six weeks. Additional training in their first year in management became normal practice on such matters as leadership, administrative and other technical topics relevant to their spheres of responsibility, product features, and issues of the day. Subsequent training could be about such topics as antitrust law or dealing with unions in more detail than initially introduced in new-manager school. A great deal of what these managers were taught continued to be about explaining and managing the company's benefits.

The strategy of relying on leaders at the lowest level, and not on middle management or staffs, to ensure implementation of the institutional culture and its practices proved effective at IBM. The key was nurturing a productive culture. An institutional culture had three features that can only be briefly cataloged here. First, the culture learned and applied by management was shaped by the needs of a firm in ways that made it possible for IBM to carry out its objectives. In corporations, that meant increasing revenues, maintaining profitability from those revenues, and meeting the needs of customers, all while performing effectively. Second, the culture managers and their employees learned evolved fast enough in sufficient collective fashion in response to changing business realities such that it was never static.[26] Third, training through schooling and exposure to relevant job experiences of culture spreaders (management) remained a constant unending priority in successful enterprises. These three features were evident at IBM from the mid-1930s to the end of the 1980s.[27]

A corporate culture emerged at IBM that historians largely acknowledged as effective and that remained strongly embedded in the enterprise through periods of positive and negative performance.[28] Corporations concurred in this assessment. One executive in the 1980s brashly, but largely correctly, referred to it simply as "The IBM Way."[29] The business philosophy underpinning how employees thought about their activities and the necessary core values, behaviors, and amenities of the workplace were IBM's "Basic Beliefs." Watson Jr.'s book, *A Business and Its Beliefs: The Ideas That Helped Build IBM*, was distributed for decades. A half century later, it remains in print.[30] It discussed benefits as a central building block of those beliefs and the culture that derived from these. While IBM's culture had its negative features, such as a growing inability to change quickly enough by the end of the 1980s, in prior decades, it aligned effectively with the needs of the business.

A crucial binding agent—think of it as a glue—that held the company together was, thus, its collection of benefits offered in exchange for an employee's performance. Benefits were explained, implemented, and changed by management. These actions became central components of their jobs, particularly the first two tasks, while continuously proselytizing the company's Basic Beliefs. The latter was a responsibility shared by all managers and executives and encouraged among employees and their families, much as one would expect from a "professional soldier," a "devoted parishioner," or a "loyal employee." The words in quotation are commonly used to call out appropriate behavior that combines acceptance of an institution's core values and their promotion and use with peers. So benefits are crucial for understanding a corporation's culture, but equally telling, in explaining the success or failure of an enterprise, including IBM.

In periods of prosperity and change, companies expand or transform benefits. IBM's management implemented increasing varieties of benefits to retain employees, while shaping their behavior to build, sell, and service tabulators (1910s–1940s), computers and software (1950s–1990s), and billable services (1980s–2020s). While historians debated the effectiveness of IBM's culture in each period, examining IBM's collection of benefits from the 1950s to 1990s is a useful exercise for two reasons. First, the company experienced enormous changes in the types of technologies it sold and the skills and hence training requirements needed for its employees, and all in the face of growing competition. Second, IBM expanded so fast in such a short period of time that management faced the fundamental problem of how to preserve its corporate culture—its proven "IBM Way"—while still growing. It did this through increased and repetitive training of all employees and by simultaneously offering them increased amounts of benefits as part of their total compensation.

Because managers were responsible for implementing these benefits, it is useful to see what they were specifically taught. Doing so allows one to understand more precisely what constituted these benefits valued by employees. There are two useful sources for information on benefits: "official" statements describing IBM's practices, known by various names, but usually as *About Your Company* booklets distributed to employees, and the *Manager's Manual*, or *Branch Office Manual*. The titles varied over the years, but there have always been anthologies documenting operating procedures one could consult locally. Additionally, training materials presented to managers provided explanations of policies and benefits and the rationale for these. Training programs summarized these in digestible bites. Our discussion relies on these materials to harvest insights into the subject much the way IBM's managers were exposed to these.

Lest one think this all too abstract a discussion, we need to understand the environment in which employees operated from the 1950s into the 1980s through the lens of their day-to-day work realities. These were turbulent times for them. Several data points make this clear, while many historians have described the underlying details that will not detain us here. IBM had increased in size during World War II from just over 11,000 employees in 1939 to more than 18,000 in 1945, with a temporary surge above 20,000 in 1943 and 1944. IBM kept growing. In 1950, it had a worldwide population of over 30,000, nearly 21,000 just in the United States. In 1980, IBM had over 340,000 employees, of whom 194,000 worked in the United States.[31] I call out the Americans because the benefits described below were tailored to U.S. law and practices. But just from looking at the demographics, one sees quickly that the challenge for management was how to integrate so many people so quickly into the "IBM Way" and then retain them. That was both the central personnel managerial challenge of the century for IBM and the purpose of benefits.

A second set of data points to revenue (gross income) and net earnings (profits) as an additional explanation of where the firm found the wherewithal to pay for these benefits, as these were expensive. While much of that story has yet to be unearthed by historians, the numbers themselves suggest IBM was able to add benefits over time with the result that the range of these proved impressive. In 1950, IBM collected $266 million in revenue, of which $37 million converted to profits. Benefits were paid out of revenue, which meant profits were the leftovers after paying for these, along with all the normal expenses of manufacturing and selling, and so forth. In 1980, IBM's gross income came in at $26.2 billion, which spun off nearly $4 billion in profits.[32] By any measure, those revenue numbers nearly take away one's breath. To achieve those remarkable results required IBM to run continuously at full throttle and, to extend the automotive metaphor, redesign the car, replace parts, and change flat tires while racing at top speed without pause. Employees of the 1960s swept away the world's first generation of computers with a new architecture and configurations called the System/360. They recalled seventy- to one-hundred-hour work weeks for years and thousands of competitors going after them in the 1970s worldwide, and yet they stumbled into the 1980s and into their retirements for over two decades speaking of these as great days, a period of personal prosperity, and possessing the wherewithal to take care of their families' health, educational needs, and desired housing—Watson Sr.'s wish for them.[33]

Compensation, challenging work, sense of success, and benefits played integral roles in this company's prosperity. Like the analogies cited earlier, however, the 1950s through to the end of the century were turbulent for others. The military had Asian wars (Korea, Vietnam), African civil wars, the Cold War, and Iraq. Priests had Vatican II to implement and respond to, and most of the world's largest business enterprises encountered globalization's profound effects on labor worldwide, inflation, and technological innovations. IBMers participated in many of these, whether as soldiers fighting in these wars or living in an increasingly secular society, while their children learned the "New Math," which many IBM parents could not help them with. As all of this was going on and as if that was not enough, the company asked thousands of employees and their families to uproot their personal lives to move to other parts of the United States or to other countries. It was also not uncommon for employees to report to new managers every year or two, sometimes even more frequently, and/or be required to work in different divisions. The concept of stability—or perhaps we should speak about instability—took on new meanings for IBMers from the 1950s to the end of the century. Benefits offered a promise of security, which, when linked to the promise of lifetime employment, made all their environmental churn bearable. With these contextual issues in mind, we turn to IBM's thinking about what benefits it made available to its employees.

Overview of IBM Benefits

The underlying organization of IBM's offerings emanated from a broad-based strategy for how benefits should help employees and IBM, while reinforcing each other and the corporation's approach to personnel management and compensation. All its elements were considered part of an integrated whole, labeled for decades as the "Employee Benefit Program." Note that the last word was not plural, rather one whole with components. Today one might think of these individual pieces much like Lego building blocks. But since the 1930s, management thought in terms of integrated wholes and company-wide strategies, so it was no surprise that such an approach would be applied to benefits. There were three parts to the program by the 1960s: income security, medical expense protection, and personal opportunity. The first was intended to provide income through the Sickness and Accident Income, Total and Permanent Disability Income, and several life insurance policies. Also included was the military supplemental income to make up for some of the partial loss of salary when an employee served in uniform. Medical programs were intended to assist employees to protect themselves from large medical expenses through Family Hospitalization, IBM Major Medical, and Family Surgical Plans. The personal opportunity plans were "for time-off for family, and personal leisure activities," and included paid holidays and vacations. The Watson tuition program helped with college education for employees' children and provided subsidies for employees attending college or graduate school on a part-time basis. Employees extensively used all of these benefits.

Employees were informed about these programs, not just managers. In the United States, for example, usually in the spring, the company mailed to each employee a booklet or binder entitled *About Your Company*, which described all the programs and how to use them. These were slick publications that read much like corporate annual reports with pictures, marketing-like text about IBM, and details of each program and benefit. By the end of the century, these were two-hundred-page publications, often accompanied with a companion booklet, *About Your Financial Future*, routinely more than a hundred pages in length. Other one-off publications and announcements appeared continuously, updating employees about changes to these benefits. Additionally, employees received annually a *Personal Benefits Statement*, which provided them with information on how they, by specific program, used their benefits and the payments received during the prior year. This was an important document because it personalized benefits. Normal contents included how long an employee had worked at IBM, referred to as "IBM service," amount of vacation earned and used, number of holidays on which company offices and factories were closed, the value of an employee's group life insurance as it increased over time and income, an estimate of what an employee would receive in both pension and, in the case of American employees, U.S. Social Security benefits at various ages, usually 55, 60, and 65 (rarely did anyone work full time at IBM after 65 in any decade), and other miscellaneous payments made in the prior year.

Over the years, these publications expanded in details provided to employees. A couple of examples from one American IBM employee drawn from these years illustrate their content. The one for 1970, which accounted for developments in 1969, was entitled *IBM Employee Benefit Plans 1970*. It was a modest three-page document that listed what that individual's life insurance plan was worth (in this case, $6,000) and travel accident insurance ($53,085). Should this individual retire in 2010, he would expect to receive a pension of $6,398, and it stated what it would be if he retired earlier, say at 55, 60, or 62, and also what his government pension (U.S. Social Security) would be. The last page listed how much various programs paid for this employee and his family during 1969. In this instance, someone in his family accumulated a payout of $270 under the Family Hospitalization Plan.[34] That same individual's statement for 1980, reflecting accumulated benefits from 1979, provided similar data. It also listed earned vacation time as it increased with longevity and the value of his various insurance policies, which had increased during the decade, such that the life insurance plan was now worth $42,000. In 1979, this family's hospitalization expenses paid by IBM amounted to $24, but the family now had a dental plan, which paid $158, so obviously a popular new addition to the benefits program. The pension, if started in 2010, would now be $19,576, and it listed early retirement amounts. Social Security had increased to $7,468. So it went each year for this employee into the new century. Because the pension plan changed substantially in the late 1990s, employees received descriptions of options and what these translated into in dollar amounts.[35] The benefits statement for 1975 dedicated one panel to declare, "The IBM Employee Benefit Plans Provide . . . Security, Protection, Opportunity . . . for you and your family."[36] IBM clearly wanted to impress employees by the breadth of the benefits programs. In the late 1980s, when the company was just entering what would evolve rapidly into a dark period in its history, it sent to employees a set of documents encased in a fancy, plastic box that waxed eloquently about benefits. Figure 6.1 is an example, with a hand calculator included to give the reader a sense of the quantity of this set of publications.

6.1 An example of IBM benefits explanations directed to employees and their families. The company published such explanations in local languages, as well, around the world.

(Courtesy, author's collection.)

Management at all levels was briefed on the rationale for these various benefits; some were mentioned earlier but bear repeating as these were taught to generations of managers as an integrated "philosophy of employee plans." There were four components:

- "Benefits are earned by employees" as part of their compensation.
- "All employees are eligible on an equal basis," for reasons stated earlier regarding financial security, protection, and opportunity.
- "Noncontributory feature gives employee maximum flexibility to plan," at no additional cost to them.
- "Plans are broad-based," so employees could create their own personal program.[37]

Table 6.2, summarized from the *Manager's Manual* and repeated in editions of *About Your Company*, provides a catalog of the various offerings as of the 1960s.

TABLE 6.2 IBM's U.S. Benefits, Circa 1950s–1970s

IBM Holiday Plan	Vacations
Educational Leaves of Absence	Benefits for Pregnant Women
Military Service Benefits	Employee Participation in Peace Corps or VISTA
Accrued Vacation Allowance (upon separation or leave of absence)	Employee Travel Accident Insurance
Group Life Insurance	Sickness and Accident Income
Family Hospitalization	Family Major Medical and Survivor Income Benefit
Total and Permanent Disability Family Income	Surgical Plan
Medical Plans with Medicare	Watson Memorial Scholarships
Retired IBMers Programs	Two-Generation Recognition
Emergency Aid Loans	Retirement Plan
Group Life Insurance for Retirees	Pre-Retirement Planning

Source: IBM, *Manager's Manual* (New York: IBM Corporation, 1967).

What employees thought about these programs remains a bit of a mystery, as the methodical understanding of their views was learned through formal opinion surveys, which were rarely preserved. When they were, paper reports of these remained as confidential as possible, even from company archivists, although results were reported to employees in meetings and occasionally in short reports. IBM began surveying employees in 1957 in Poughkeepsie, New York, and soon after began verbally sharing results with employees as a way of learning more about issues and problems to solve. It became a popular world-wide activity by the mid-1960s. Surveys soon covered all manner of IBM activities from the nature of one's work and job satisfaction to company policies and reputation, usually asking the same or similar questions for decades, and how they rated various activities of their managers. Opinion surveys became an important source of information about all manner of operational issues, comparable to the benefits obtained through customer satisfaction surveys.[38]

One early surviving American survey, circa 1959–1961, gives one a peek into what employees thought. Recall this was a period when the company was prospering and growing. IBM was moving successfully into the new field of computers. This survey had a question that appeared for decades in other surveys: "Compared with other companies that you know about, how would you rate the adequacy of each of these employee benefit plans at IBM?" Overall, employees rated these as "favorable," at between 60 and 93 percent, and almost the rest as "average," while "unsatisfactory" votes garnered only 1 to 3 percent. The most popular benefits with ratings above 88 percent favorable included all the medical and insurance programs, while the retirement plan was rated "favorable" by 82 percent. The least-approved benefits were paid vacations (60 percent) and number of paid holidays (72 percent); write-in comments called for more days off. Between 1 and 6 percent wanted additional information about various benefits, while for the pension program, 15 percent asked to learn more.[39] These results in general paralleled subsequent surveys conducted to the 1980s.[40] While it is too early to conclude that the collection of benefits met with employee approval before the late 1980s, this one example suggested employees did approve. Other anecdotal and survey data suggest approval ratings in the mid to high 80 percentiles from the 1960s to the late 1980s.[41]

Since learning about the firm was largely channeled through one's immediate manager, elsewhere in the survey quoted above, employees were asked how that was working as one of many sources of information available to them. Fifty-eight percent rated this channel as "favorable" and another 29 percent as "average," while "employee meetings with management" were rated by 65 percent as "favorable" and 23 percent as "average." In short, relying on management to educate and communicate with employees seemed to be working.[42] That was also good news for those executives worrying about potential unionizing activities.

Role of the Open Door Policy and Speak Up Program

There are two other programs never considered as formal "benefits" in management's thinking but that were so tied to the benefit of working at IBM that they should be included here: the ability of employees to express their concerns to management and expectation that these would be addressed. These became a core feature of IBM's corporate culture since the 1920s. They had a checkered history but remained a core element of how the firm operated into the next century. Without these two programs, which allowed employees to vent and to escalate issues, it is quite possible that the workforce might have unionized, that the number of lawsuits against IBM would have been greater, and that employees would not have given their all—the third of the Basic Beliefs—or simply would have left the company. These negative possibilities were the same that existed with respect to the benefits program. Benefits, the Open Door Policy, and the Speak Up Program combined were intended to keep employees loyal, productive, and happy within the context of the Basic Beliefs. That is why all these should be considered together. However, there is a problem for historians in that documentation about the results of these programs has never been revealed outside of a closed circle within IBM, largely kept within the personnel management community, divisional presidents, and more senior executives.

Dating to the 1920s, then as an informal method for shortening communications lines from all parts of the enterprise at all levels to senior management, the Open Door grievance process remained a highly visible practice for nearly a century. As of this writing (2023), it still existed, albeit changed over the years in its details and execution. If one had a complaint and could not get it resolved satisfactorily through their normal chain of command, they could appeal to the chairman's office or to lower-level management for redress, such as to division presidents. It was a process aimed at dealing with perceived injustices or grievances that an employee concluded needed to be fixed. For middle and senior management, it became another source of information about what was happening among employees and what they were thinking. Watson Jr. recalled that periodic reviews of "Open Doors" told him "an awful lot about the problems of the working man."[43] Watson's observation about the effectiveness of the program already existed, as the company was expanding rapidly when people were trying to shape new policies and define their work up and down the organization. Let him explain:

> Many employees did not want to take a complaint all the way to me, but the very existence of the Open Door was a morale builder. It made them feel free to approach a personnel manager or the man running the plant when they had a problem. As IBM grew, we tried to take care of more and more Open Door cases at the division-chief level, with only charges of serious mismanagement

that might reflect unfavorably on IBM coming to my office. But even so my office handled two or three hundred cases each year, with each case typically taking several days to resolve.[44]

What were managers told about the Open Door program? They were the people normally sandwiched between the concerned employee and senior management who took seriously escalations. Many managers assumed corporate or divisional investigators were too sympathetic to employees, while many employees thought managers were too often supported in how they had dealt earlier with the complainer's issues. New managers were told that IBM sought a "fair balance" between interests of employees and those of the company. As Watson Sr. and Jr. had learned, keeping a pulse on workers' concerns was crucial and no more so than in times of rapid change within an older IBM where nostalgia for earlier times and practices lingered, as happened between World War II and the 1980s. The program put "teeth" into the belief, "Respect for the individual." It was designed to give an employee a path to clear and definitive resolution of a grievance. "It is based on the principle that everyone has a right to appeal the actions of those who are immediately over him in authority."[45]

Employees were asked to resolve their issues first with their direct manager. Failing that or feeling it inappropriate to do so, they were urged to work their way up their organization's chain of command, jumping to the chairman's office only if those other efforts did not provide satisfactory resolution or might be inappropriate. An example of the latter could be a sexual harassment complaint against one's manager. An illustration of the former might be a denied request for a transfer. Normally, when a complaint came in, an investigator on behalf of the chairman (or whomever the Open Door went to) would reach out immediately (e.g., within twenty-four hours) if involving crime, sexual harassment, or some danger; if the complaint was less urgent, then perhaps they would reach out within two days, such as regarding a contested appraisal or denial of fair career development. The aggrieved employee would be contacted, giving them the opportunity to explain their situation, which the investigator would then explore, next hearing the other side's point of view. The investigator would make a recommendation that the recipient of the complaint normally accepted and order management that it be implemented. It was not uncommon for the entire cycle from start to finish to be completed within two to three weeks.[46]

A key point was speed of resolution. For decades, it was normal for an investigation to begin within twenty-four hours of receiving an Open Door. Employees would be summoned to a face-to-face meeting or contacted by telephone to hear the final decision, the reasons for the conclusions, and if actions were to be taken, what those would be. Managers sandwiched in the middle received similar communications. The entire process was explained to all employees, usually when they first came to work at IBM, but periodically during their careers. All heard the same message. The process was implemented worldwide and remained largely unchanged over the decades. All investigators came from divisions other than the one from which the Open Door submitter worked. Normally investigators were managers or executive assistants working for the executive receiving the grievance. They were pulled off their regular work to deal with the issue.[47]

That was the theory and largely the practice (at least on the investigator's side). By the 1960s, managers undergoing their initial training were exposed to findings regarding how it worked. Some employee complaints were about the lack of career advancement; managers were counseled to coach workers on how to prepare themselves for promotions, received advice to be candid with their charges regarding their strengths and weaknesses, and were encouraged to find opportunities for the ambitious ones, looking across the entire company. Managers were cautioned not to take too long to implement career development plans with employees lest those individuals become frustrated and "Open Door them."[48] Such situations often did not go well for the recalcitrant manager. Other problems included failures on the part of managers to recognize and reward a job well done, dealing with emotional or personal problems, or perceptions of favoritism within one's staff. New managers were told that "many Open Door cases develop out of a simple failure on the part of the manager to listen to the employee with both ears or to give him a straight answer or to give him enough information to do what he is expected to do."[49] More bluntly: "Your role is to manage people in such a way that they never need to invoke the policy—by settling issues before they reach that stage."[50] When a manager was found to have acted inappropriately and had a judgment made against them, the reason often came down to what they were told in Charm School: "The managers who get into trouble are the ones who do not face up to a crises when they see it coming."[51] Regarding the importance of the Open Door program, instructors and guest speakers summed it up as "the cornerstone of our relationship with our employees."[52] Nothing could destroy managers' careers faster than a collection of Open Doors filed against them, although an occasional one was normally not lethal, if it was about a more mundane issue, such as a disagreement about an appraisal, which managers routinely "won."[53]

While the number of Open Door submissions has never been made public, anecdotal evidence suggests strongly that it was well used by the 1950s. It served as a useful tool for releasing workplace tensions as the business underwent profound changes in midcentury, a time when many young employees were thrust into new circumstances as both workers and managers and when older ones wrestled with the ground shifting beneath their feet. It proved to be a successful program because, as one employee put it, management believed in its value and so "does everybody else."[54] Of course, some who found an investigator's conclusions not tilting their way thought otherwise. In 1982, the chairman of the board at IBM, John R. Opel, in a missive to all managers, reported the program was being used worldwide, largely to complain about an action taken by their managers. Some 70 percent of those were directed to their manager's manager or division, rather than to corporate headquarters, which he concluded meant employees were working out their issues across the enterprise. He also reported that about half of IBM's employees fully understood the program, so management had additional work to do to get the others briefed properly. About one in four employees (managers and nonmanagers) were cautious, fearful their management might exact retribution for filing an Open Door.[55]

A related program, known as the Speak Up Program, began in 1959 as an experiment at the San Jose, California, site and became a company-wide program in 1960 that was gradually implemented across the United States and then around the world. Less intimidating to management, it was yet another channel of communications for employees, one often used to communicate and complain about benefits or working conditions (e.g., dirty floors, smoking, malfunctioning vending machines) or to suggest improvements. In its first ten years, IBM workers wrote over 27,000 Speak Up letters. In 1966—a year characterized by the massive diffusion of S/360 computer systems and many long work weeks and, additionally, by new hires into IBM—6,454 questions were asked or opinions expressed through this program. By 1979, employees had written over 200,000.[56] They signed over 90 percent of their Speak Ups, although they were not required to do so. Since 1963, by when the program had been implemented globally, another 6,300 had been submitted in its first three years of deployment.[57]

What is a Speak Up? It is an employee writing a letter to management asking a question to clarify a company policy or program or to opine on one of these. This was a particularly useful channel of communication if one's manager or location proved unable to offer up a satisfactory answer. One can see the practice today often reflected on company, employee, and retiree websites when someone posts a question about how to use a company program, such as a medical insurance policy, or to obtain a discount on, say, rental cars or hotel rooms for their family vacation, or how to initiate some other benefit. That is essentially the idea behind a Speak Up, created decades before there was email or the internet.

It was also a means for employees to raise difficult questions uncomfortable for management, such as about disparities in promotional opportunities between men and women in the 1980s. Often employees wanted more explanations for why some practice existed beyond the glib answer of "It's company policy" or "The decision was made by Corporate." Employees were encouraged not to accept such superficial answers but rather to demand an explanation for the rationale, say, for specific terms of a benefit. New managers, when taught about Speak Ups, were told the story, possibly apocryphal but which experienced managers had encountered, of the employee who wrote: "The real injustice in this whole case is the double talk. . . . I do not want to be unreasonable in this matter, but I feel that I deserve an honest answer."[58] Such a comment could just as easily have been an Open Door. Evasive answers (*double talk* in American slang English) and noncommittal ones, too, could trigger either a Speak Up or Open Door, especially when it came to answering questions regarding how and when one could expect an increase in salary or a promotion. Without a clear answer, employees could feel victimized, instead of as a member of a team, and that managers were "passing the buck," and hence weak.[59] Hearsay policies and rumors could be quashed through Speak Ups.

Responses came in several forms. These could be direct answers addressed to an employee, such as why something was done at their location or why a particular benefit had a specific feature and what they could do about addressing their concern. Others were published in company (usually site) newsletters or posted on bulletin boards. Yet others would motivate those managing programs and policies up and down the organization to revisit, modify, or communicate better to a wider community of employees about an issue. There were no constraints on the topics one could raise. Managers were told in no uncertain terms what their duty was in the matter: "If an employee has a problem that is involved with a company policy, he is entitled to know the reasons for that policy. So is the customer with a special request and the vendor offering a new product," in other words, "answers, not alibis."[60] Further, "it is part of our job as managers to know and understand those reasons and to be able to explain them to others."[61] Ex-IBM employees who became customers did not hesitate to practice a form of Speak Up if their local sales team failed to sufficiently explain a situation or satisfy a need.

In the 1960s, newly minted managers were told that many Speak Ups dealt with issues not related to one's immediate manager, but that many of their questions should have been possible for local management to answer if they better understood, say, the details of a particular benefit program. Speak Ups informed managers and executives about issues on the minds of employees with the advantage that, if one so chose, they could be anonymous in their communications. Managers were reminded that they, too, could write Speak Ups if they did not feel they could access directly a source of information. They were told to take an interest in reading Speak Ups reproduced in company newsletters and publications as a way of staying informed about employee issues.[62]

As part of their training, managers were given actual Speak Up queries as test questions to see how well they understood company policies and their rationale. These give us a brief look at issues circulating in the 1960s. Examples include the following:

- "Why was IBM's liquor policy [drinking on the job or at any IBM-hosted event was not allowed] applied to social events hosted by IBM employee clubs?"
- "Does IBM's policy differ depending on what division you work in?" (Depends.)
- "Would such a person be condemned for refusing a promotional transfer?" (No.)
- "Can an employee read his manager's binder, 'Management Briefings'?" (Manager should discuss content, not share the binder.)
- "Employee insists IBM should order people to wear a 'business uniform.'" (Company response: there is no mandatory dress code at IBM.)
- "What is the company policy with regard to time off wherein an employee receives, either by election or appointment, a position in his community government?" (IBM had guidelines to facilitate time off, including local authorization for paid time off.)
- "I would like to know if an employee has the right to look at his personnel jacket?" (Yes.)
- "What [is] the company policy in giving a man time off when he gets married[?]" (Up to five days with salary.)
- One asked about moonlighting. (Allowed, but not if it interfered with IBM job performance or is competitive to the firm.)[63]

One question proved so relevant in the boom period of the 1960s that it should remind readers of why Speak Ups and Open Doors linked to everything IBM was involved with, including creation and deployment of its benefits in midcentury. "I am sincerely interested in knowing why IBM is in business, i.e., what are its goals, its reasons for being—aside from making a profit for its stockholders." At about that time (mid-1960s), CEO Watson Jr. was calling on managers to discuss the firm's Basic Beliefs and principles of operation with all employees:

> Those of us who have been with the company a long time have a tendency to assume that newer IBMers also know our traditional approaches to doing business and managing people. But our size and geographic spread today place a strain on conventional methods of education and communication, and unless we make a special effort, a lot of information that we want to get to our people never really gets through.
>
> Our domestic population is approaching 128,000 and in the United States alone about 12,000 new people join us each year. It's as important now as it ever

was that every IBMer have a firm grasp of what makes us tick and why we've chosen our particular direction.[64]

He concluded that while IBM's practices may not be unique, "they have worked well for us, and we're confident they'll help us in the future" to succeed.[65]

Was the program used? He reported in 1969, after one decade of it being promoted, that over 50,000 Speak Ups had been sent in and that, in the late 1960s, the company was responding to these at the rate of 10,000 per year. The majority revolved around the inability of one's manager to answer a question or to object to the answer they received. He acknowledged an unspoken truth, too: "Some of our managers, however, may think of the program as a threat."[66] But he reminded them that it was yet another channel of communication between management and employees, company, and everyone. In 1976, CEO Frank T. Cary wrote to all of IBM's managers that the program was "still working" but that its use had declined by a third since Watson Jr. had spoken about the program in 1969 and that a third of the comments coming in were unsigned. He urged managers to keep supporting this anonymous channel of communication for questions and comments.[67]

Lessons and Implications

Several lessons can be culled from exploring IBM's benefits programs that are useful for increasing our understanding of this company's corporate culture. Culture is the first concern here, but also corporate bureaucracy. Both topics— culture and bureaucracy—have long represented topics of interest to business historians and those studying the role of management. Alfred D. Chandler, Jr., is given much credit for introducing to generations of scholars and managers how to link strategy, purpose, and the role of bureaucracy.[68] Subsequent scholars and corporate employees developed an appetite for understanding how large enterprises functioned, reaching two conclusions in short order: that large ones were clusters of communities vying for attention and resources within their corporate tent and that the glue holding much of them inside it was their shared culture (values, practices, and rituals), the latter operationalized with tasks normally characterized as bureaucracy.[69]

IBM was both unique and typical of large manufacturing global enterprises. To attract and retain employees in ever-larger numbers as its business boomed, it had to compete against other successful firms. To succeed, its total compensation package—salaries, career opportunities, and benefits—had at least to be competitive with those offered by such enterprises as General Motors, Ford, U.S. Steel, and Boeing, among others in the United States, and with peer companies in Europe and Japan. Employees expected IBM to be at least on par with those others, or ahead.[70] The opinion survey reviewed earlier suggests IBM was able to do that, at least until the 1980s. But the total package kept evolving so new benefits, or changes to existing ones, remained a constant activity—the key finding exhibited in table 6.1. It was not a new issue; IBM's large factory in Endicott, New York, had to compete with a well-run paternalistic local shoe manufacturer for employees since the dawn of the twentieth century.[71] Not until the late 1980s and early 1990s did circumstances change sufficiently that IBM had to claw back benefits.

When IBM was a small company in the 1920s, an employee could sit down and talk to Watson Sr. to discuss issues, and almost in a nearly impromptu manner, the latter could make a decision, announce quickly a new benefit or policy, and somehow it would be implemented. That proved impossible to do when the company had many tens of thousands of employees and later hundreds of thousands. What this chapter demonstrates is that to implement a benefit or policy, it had to be thoroughly thought out, documented in detail, and methodically communicated to all concerned, and local experts (managers and legal and personnel staffs) had to be educated on its terms and conditions and about how to implement it. Historians have long noted how large enterprises used standard forms and reports as instruments for implementing these.[72] They should broaden their perspective to fill gaps in their understanding of how a company implemented its practices and beliefs. By looking at what enterprises taught their managers, one can see how the work was done at one firm, using an old IBM cliché, observing what goes on "where the rubber meets the road," or what the British call action taking place at the "coalface." Such a perspective makes it possible to identify links from intent and corporate values to policies and practices.

Documentation upon which this chapter was based demonstrates what large organizations do behind measuring activities. While monitoring and keeping score is often easily accounted for by laws, regulations, and managerial practices that result in such reports surviving useful to historians, there is a vast body of other required documentation that leads up to actions that can be tracked. IBM is famous for documenting "everything." What we learn here is that documentation is essential because there are too many people involved in doing work and managing and explaining. Much had to be formalized and communicated in massive ways. IBM product manuals ran into the tens of thousands of publications in innumerable editions (updates) and in many languages and are recognized because they seemed ubiquitous in corporations, IBM offices, archives, and libraries. Many thousands of old ones are even routinely for sale on eBay. These are so important for understanding a corporate culture in play that chapter 11 is devoted to the subject.

But similar publications covering other activities existed besides about products. How field engineers were to install or repair equipment and systems engineers software, how sales personnel were to sell and control their accounts, how one was to do accounting and various administrative work, what lawyers and media experts could say or not, or how employees were to respond and behave due to antitrust activities or marketplace laws and best practices were all documented in similar fashion. The fundamental difference between product manuals and these other publications is that the former were intended for wide circulation inside and outside of IBM, not these other documents, which were restricted to employees and, in some instances, to just a few of them. They had such markings on them as "For Internal Use Only," such as the training materials relied upon here, or "IBM Confidential." Thus, these documents were often ephemeral, tossed into a waste can the day a new edition appeared, and so they are not as well preserved in archives as product manuals, which needed to be consulted often for years. What we looked at here is the tip of a large iceberg of publications, suggestive of the subjects documented and the level of detail one could extract from them. Otherwise boring internal operational materials become interesting when they shed light on how a company operates. It is how one can begin to understand the role benefits played in IBM's history and in its culture.

An additional observation can be extracted that was part of the process IBM and other corporations used to diffuse information about products, internal procedures, and benefits coming from the training exercises themselves. In the 1950s–1970s, common teaching practice in Western societies involved an educator standing in front of rows of students delivering lectures and answering questions, with students taking notes and their instructors assigning reading materials, usually from a textbook. IBM's educators did not follow that approach, although classroom lectures remained. The normal routine was to give each student a binder, such as one for each lesson of the *IBM Fundamentals of Management* course, that the students used to follow along with the lectures or studied as prerequisites before attending a class. Each binder was numbered and dated, since management intended these only for internal use with the admonition of "Nothing is to be reproduced."

In addition to a table of contents, notes of the lectures were already typed and organized in these binders to make sure students had the precise language and details of the lecture. They were quizzed with copies of these in their binder (including their own personal responses) and then given the correct answers in detail, which they added to their binders. It was normal to include offprints of articles appearing in such journals as the *Harvard Business Review* and *THINK Magazine* or published by the American Management Association that the student-employees could read at their leisure. It was also common practice to include a short bibliography of a half- to one-dozen books related to the topic at hand. For *Lesson 1*, for example, the bibliography's header title was "Classics in Management," listing titles valued in the mid-1960s. These included a mixture of trade, academic, and IBM publications. Apparently, students read these because for decades they quoted popular managerial books of the day in their presentations or distributed copies to their staffs. Extant training materials from as early as the 1930s were organized in similar fashion, providing evidence of long-standing pedagogical practices at IBM.[73] With employees undergoing so much training over the course of their careers, a benefit in itself, the way it was done was de facto part of the company's culture, the way it went about engaging with new subjects. That experience was part of the "Grand Bargain" that in exchange for lifetime employment, one must be willing to learn new things, take on different responsibilities, and even relocate their families to new communities.

It is logical now to turn in the next chapter to how these benefits affected the most intended audience: IBM families. IBM did not ignore families or treat them as a side issue; rather, it saw them as an integral part of the company's wider ecosystem. It is a story often overlooked by those studying the history of IBM, and yet it is a crucial part of how the firm operated. For managers pondering how to satisfy all stakeholders, families represent a highly influential subset of an employee's world. Wise management teams recognize that reality and integrate them into their work. Here is how IBM did this.

CHAPTER 7

MANAGING A NEARLY INVISIBLE CORPORATE COMMUNITY

"IBM Families"

We're co-workers in IBM—all one big family.

The Songs of IBM, 1937[1]

As we left, the indefatigable quartet was playing Moon Over Miami, and half a dozen couples were doing a comfortable old two-step.

Peter Hillyer, 1974[2]

An IBM employee anywhere in the world would have frequently heard the term "IBM Family" in speeches made by their CEO, Thomas J. Watson, Sr., during his tenure as head of the company, occasionally by senior executives over the next thirty years, and probably not at all afterward. By the end of the 1980s, only those who had worked at the company for over twenty years would know it; probably none hired after 1985 would be familiar with it, unless they attended a family company-hosted event, such as a holiday party or, as the epigraph documented, a party with a mixture of active and retired employees with their spouses. If one went to an IBM employee or retiree website in, say, 2020, and discussed "Family Dinners," a well-known event for decades, or the term "IBM Families," many would question what was being discussed because they had not heard of such things.[3] So, it should be of no surprise that business historians have heard little about these, too, or have not discussed the families of IBM employees. Yet the company paid a great deal of attention to integrating families into its ecosystem. They were seen as agents in the environment that senior management expected, indeed needed (mostly wives before the 1980s), to nurture because of the long hours and career aspirations of their husbands. Many thousands of employees often were periodically required to uproot their families and move to other cities and, more normally, to work far more hours than the traditional forty or fifty. For decades, a joke inside the firm was, "What does IBM stand for?" Answer: "I've Been Moved."

A closer look at how IBM as a company interacted with families of employees demonstrates that families were critical enough in how IBM operated that the company could not ignore them, nor should historians or managers sorting through how to engage with all their stakeholders. Today's corporate managers are learning that these individuals help shape the values and levels of commitment to their firms by employees. Families participated in many aspects of the company's activities and yet still remain invisible. Their population was not small. An estimated one million people have worked at IBM, not including subcontractors or business partners who, from a practical point of view, were extensions of IBM's labor force and work activities. If one simply did the mathematics, based on what percentage of adults were married in any decade, you would quickly realize that these family members—wives and children and increasingly, over time, elderly relatives—comprised at least over two million souls; we really do not know how many, just that they comprised a large population.[4] At the height of IBM's size, they lived in over 170 countries scattered across several thousand communities, with less than half clustered in large groups of thousands in factory and laboratory towns or in cities housing regional, national, or corporate headquarters. The largest cluster of employees in the United States lived in the mid-Hudson Valley and central New York state in the twentieth century, while other large groups clustered in company towns in France and Germany and, to a lesser extent, in the United Kingdom, Sweden, Italy, Japan, China, Mexico, and Brazil.

To bring these family members of the IBM community out of the shadows, I identify who they were, the way senior management thought of how they should fit into IBM's ecosystem, and the actions taken to engage them. The company interacted constantly with them through various means and events that, when looked at in their totality, proved impressive. The strategy deployed was purposeful and consistent for decades. Indeed, generations of employees experienced the same touch points from one decade to another. For example, three generations of IBM families living in a factory town, such as Endicott, would have taken swimming lessons or played basketball or tennis at the same country club for the grand membership fee of $1.50 per year for decades. In childhood, they would have gone to the same building each Christmas season to receive presents, while their long-serving IBM parents would have attended Quarter Century Club lunches and holiday parties there as well. We sort through these and other touch points, both the positive and the negative. Not until the late 1980s did the composite apparatus of family relations with IBM begin to deteriorate, and it occurred so sharply during the 1990s that it is how we understand why social media comments made in 2020 by employees, some of whom had already worked at IBM for thirty years, would have considered these as unknown or strange elements of a bygone culture. Finally, note that the majority of the practices discussed here were deployed across IBM in other countries with modifications to accommodate local cultural practices.

I proceed through this chapter by, first, explaining how the company defined IBM families, as definitions changed over time, accompanied with historical context. Then comes a review of the overall corporate strategy for engaging with families. To illustrate activities implementing IBM's strategy requires that we understand the special roles of Family Dinners, other routine activities, and such corporate rituals as Quarter Century Clubs and their events. Because IBM communicated extensively with these families, how it did so is part of the story that needs to be told before drawing conclusions about the entire relationship between the corporation and families. IBM was not alone in how it interacted with families of its employees; other American corporations implemented similar strategies and activities. The difference here is that we are able to document a considerable number of these activities that are so universal and timeless that, as today's companies think about who their stakeholders are, they can go beyond Silicon Valley Friday afternoon beer parties to a more sophisticated approach for understanding and engaging a very large community present in their ecosystem. Here, we can move from generalities about corporate paternalism to the specifics of one company, offering markers of what to explore regarding what occurred in other large enterprises.

IBM Families: Two Definitions, One Community

Definitions are important because, as in all facets of life within IBM and outside in its markets, change remained a constant reality such that the notion of families and their relationship to IBM evolved, as occurred in American society as a whole. Senior management at IBM before World War II shaped their perceptions of what constituted their community of employees and families largely on the widely held views of their day or from practices and views acquired elsewhere. Watson Sr. brought over to C-T-R (future IBM) many perspectives from his previous employer, NCR, shaped in the 1890s and early 1910s. In those days, in the United States—the geographic focus of the discussion of this chapter—men went to work for a salary, and women raised children and took care of hearth and home. Social rank or profession mattered less because this model of the family was seen as normal and widespread. There were exceptions, of course, such as nurses, elementary school teachers, clerks, and secretaries. Most of these positions were filled by women, many young and unmarried, at least for a while.[5] The latter two groups—clerks and secretaries—often referred to as "office workers," expanded rapidly in number between 1890 and 1920.[6] But in corporate America, a woman was expected to leave IBM and other companies if she married and certainly when she became pregnant. Men were favored for jobs since they were seen as needing to support their families. That view of what constituted families remained remarkably unchanged into the 1950s.[7]

Underlying these perspectives in IBM's early decades was a corporate worldview inherited by companies in many industries that dated from the Victorian era of the late nineteenth century and the Progressive era of pre–World War I America. During those decades, senior management at C-T-R/IBM developed their concepts of gender roles and how best to deal with labor. A familial paradigm existed that lingered at IBM until the 1950s. According to Victorian tenets, women had certain roles to play in society, even if they worked. Women handled feminine, nurturing, supportive activities at work, such as the emerging human resources activities (known as "welfare work"), especially after 1900, and subservient ones, serving as clerks, nurses, and cleaning staffs, but certainly not as engineers or managers. Men designed and built products and went out into the world to sell and maintain them.[8] Amenities were introduced to promote social stability and assuage workers' demands in addition to salaries. Women often administered such programs in a company.

Families were still a collection of distant secondary issues, but the rhetoric of family was immediate and used widely.[9] Pre–World War I language in companies, and often at IBM in the 1930s, still used the language corporations had used for two or more decades: "family," instead of "company." One was part of the NCR "family." AT&T's rhetoric used "Bell Family." Other firms spoke of creating "family spirit," and so it went.[10] It was rhetoric Watson Sr. and his generation internalized. In Endicott, New York, near IBM's facilities, the Endicott Johnson Company competed for hiring employees, and its management maintained that "a business concern ought to be like a family as much as possible."[11] Local employees and managers of C-T-R/IBM would have been familiar with such thinking because their neighbors worked for that shoe company.

While this language was nonthreatening, tensions between management and labor in America existed in the early decades of the twentieth century. As one historian observed, "the Victorian family promised economic security to its members, the compassionate family promised emotional fulfillment."[12] However, between the 1890s and the 1920s, most American business executives proved reluctant to spend on corporate welfare that included clean bathrooms, cafeterias, medical facilities on campus, and lovely lawns and tree-lined walkways, let alone country clubs and family-oriented amenities, because it was not clear what the economic return would be on such expenditures. They did it when they had to in order to recruit and retain workers in an expanding economy. By the time IBM could afford to do any of these things, beginning in the second half of the 1920s, such amenities had become standard fare, minimal table stakes.[13] In chapter 9, we display images of beautiful corporate campuses that looked like Harvard University's. Postcards of NCR's facilities from the 1910s portrayed similar images, probably motivating Watson to order up similar ones for IBM. The young company had to catch up to more established enterprises, some of which were its competitors.

During the 1930s and 1940s, the American government and Western European societies forced corporate welfare systems to be codified into personnel practices, often required by government agencies to do business with them. New Deal laws and regulations in the United States in the 1930s reinforced such activities as providing clean water and bathrooms for employees and safer working environments to reduce injuries and sustain health. The American government was collectively IBM's largest customer across the twentieth century, and also of almost every large U.S. manufacturing corporation, at least during World War II. So, nothing seemed to promote common practices as much as government regulations.[14] These stimulated alternative strategies to the old Victorian familial model for dealing with employee complaints and demands for reforms.[15] More specifically, corporations now used personnel managers and dealt directly with unions in dealing with employees. Only through those two mediums did any consideration of families bubble up, except at IBM, as discussed below.

When the Boomer generation began entering the workforce in the 1960s, the definition of what constituted "the family" began to change, again. By the early 1980s, it had become so obvious that the definition of family was evolving that business operations were being affected negatively, requiring renewed attention. In a study of large corporations conducted for them by the Conference Board in 1985 to understand the changing definition, it stated that "today's businesses function in a volatile social and economic environment." Demographic changes were occurring too, albeit more gradually. The problem was the "diversity in family structures on personnel policies, employee benefits and services, and on the attitudes of management itself."[16] This is when a significant new phase began in how companies dealt with families, affecting what benefits they offered, how they sorted through work–life balance issues, and the role of women, who were becoming both breadwinners and eager to pursue careers (not just jobs) and were deciding when to have children (many after they were deeply immersed in their careers). While this is not the place to address those issues, as many others have, it is important to note that IBM was not immune to the impact of these changing demographics on its ability to operate.[17] Keep in mind the major categories of concern just listed because they had begun to emerge earlier, as when some women who had worked during World War II did not want to give up their jobs to get married and have children. Although a minority, they were the few canaries in the mine hinting of issues to come. For most of the post–World War II period, family issues centered on child and elder care, relocations when IBM transferred the breadwinner to a different part of the country, job pressures and long hours, and insufficient support to mitigate such issues by management and colleagues.[18]

Throughout the entire twentieth century, IBM management kept family issues firmly in mind as they shaped personnel practices. They did not ignore the structure of employee families and recognized that IBM needed policies and programs that facilitated the work and productivity of its workers. All managers had to understand and implement the company's personnel benefits programs and to deal with issues related to worker productivity, a topic discussed in the previous two chapters, and invariably, many issues concerned family issues. Echoing admonitions from earlier times still relevant in the early years of the 2000s, these issues seemed familiar, as messages delivered to managers demonstrated:

- "Work/family is a legitimate issue of the organization relevant to its mission
- Work/family efforts have the support of the President
- Different functional areas are considered together
- Work/family policies are assessed and reviewed regularly
- There is an emphasis on flexibility
- The organizational culture is recognized as central to work/family solutions
- Supportive policies are seen as essential in the recruitment and retention of employees."[19]

How to deal with each point was incorporated into management's training programs. Work for life stabilized IBM's operations, so including the family was a stabilizing force consistent with how many corporations operated. Layoffs would have been seen as a sign of failure by employee and employer, and also for the firing manager, while even the possibility (threat) of these occurring would have disrupted the company's overall objectives for how employees and families would respond to the needs of the corporation.[20] Newly minted managers were informed about such realities.

So, the initial definition of family is the professional, managerial, scientific one that became the stuff of personnel management. None of this came about by accident, as it was the by-product of new realities when large firms came into being and from the worldviews of the founders and subsequent generations of managers. Their perspectives were baked into IBM's culture through rhetoric and practice. It seemed the origin of so much of IBM's culture was the thinking of its nearly half-century leader. It centers on what Watson Sr. meant by "IBM Family," as it was not initially what personnel managers and social scientists had in mind decades later, although his thoughts made their work possible in the first place.

Watson Sr. and executives reporting to him were raised in the late nineteenth and early twentieth centuries. When he came to C-T-R (future IBM) in 1914, he was forty-two years old, married, and already a father. He had two sons and two daughters. His generation of managers and executives were largely married and enjoyed salaried jobs, their wives raised their children, and the little ones went to school. These generations lived comfortable lives with homes, health, good food, vacations, and interesting things to do. Watson Sr. became the highest paid executive in the United States during the 1930s, but he did not lead the ostentatious lifestyle of, say, some movie stars or equally wealthy businessmen of his day. But as a child, he had lived on a farm in a region of small towns in upstate New York. His father was of modest, if typical, means of a farm family. Watson Sr. lost his job at NCR after he was married and a father, and although he had accumulated financial reserves that carried him over until he began drawing a check and a share of his new employer's profits at C-T-R, he must have thought his financial circumstances precarious when compared to his previous circumstances. The early years at C-T-R were challenging for the firm, so there was no guarantee of employment security. He also had worked in a company considered in the late 1800s to early 1900s as generous in treating its employees *and* their families as part of a larger NCR community. These were notions and practices Watson Sr. brought over to his new employer.[21]

So, he and his generation of managers lived between two worlds. As a young man coming into NCR, where labor problems existed that sometimes overflowed in the main factory into unrest, the welfare capitalism practiced there incorporated the notion one historian called the "family-like intimacy of the small shop."[22] As he matured in the 1890s and through the first decade of the new century, he would have observed that this worldview was becoming less relevant as factories became larger with many hundreds and thousands of workers. He must have felt a loss of intimacy with employees on the floor as NCR grew, because when he arrived at C-T-R, he was back inside a small enterprise. The old rhetoric would work here, and he told employees many times that if they had a problem to let him know. Speak Up and Open Door processes were implemented when IBM became too big for people to sit down with him or to write him a letter about an issue. Yet after his generation at larger companies had shed their familial rhetoric, he clung to it, even as his IBM kept increasing in size. To put a fine point on this issue of connecting with the IBM Family, just on the American side of the business, in 1914, he had 1,217 employees in the United States, all quite accessible. Two decades later, IBM had 5,674 U.S. employees, still manageable since so many were not scattered in small offices. Fast forward yet another twenty years and there were 33,732 American employees, which meant even mid-sized cities had rooms full of IBM employees. All of these statistics leave out workers in many dozens of countries, compounding issues of executive–employee intimacy.[23]

IBM, similar to other large companies, developed personnel practices that incorporated much of the earlier concern for familial approaches into routines that managers and historians coldly referred to as "industrial relations" run out of "personnel departments" or by "human relations." However, Watson Sr. was able to maintain the fiction of a familial organization through his language and efforts, which led most employees to think of themselves as part of this special organization referred informally to as the "IBM Family." While seemingly anachronistic, and certainly not as evident in the language of executives who came after him, the seeming fiction of it stuck, reinforced by personnel practices that strengthened his enduring concept of the corporate family. Nowhere did that seem so much the case as with the company's way of dealing with families of employees. Historians will need to revisit their assumptions about the rhetoric and underlying assumptions of large enterprises in how large enterprises dealt with families beyond the normal collection of insurance, medical, and educational benefits because, as explained below, the notion of corporate family found a home in how the company dealt with spouses and children.

It is not clear when Watson Sr. first articulated in public his concept of the IBM Family, but the earliest documented instance came on November 10, 1926, at a company dinner held in Endicott, New York, at what otherwise was known as IBM Plant No. 1. On that occasion, he was addressing people who had worked for IBM and its predecessor companies for twenty-five or more years. We meet them later as members of the Quarter Century Club. This dinner included spouses. He thanked all for their many years of "loyalty" and "for the efforts [they] have put forth," which would have been heard by people used to working for one firm for their entire adult lives. It would be common for multiple generations to work for IBM in Endicott and, later, elsewhere in the firm. He spoke proudly of the "family spirit in IBM." Specifically, "We are one great big family. I have tried to develop a real family spirit in the business and I have received the full and hearty cooperation from our people all over the country. I feel that we have a real family spirit in the IBM. If you look upon me as the head of the family I want you to come to me as often as you feel that I can do anything for you."[24] That same week in another speech, he said, "IBM people are alike in all countries. . . . Wherever you go in the fifty-four countries in which we do business you will find the same IBM family spirit."[25] On June 4, 1927, at a dinner of employees and spouses, he recited statistics on how many children of IBM employees there were and the number of IBMers as "evidence that the older generation in the business thinks well enough of it to commend to the [sic] sons and daughters."[26] As the Great Depression began in 1929 and continued throughout the 1930s, he increasingly used the phrase "IBM Family" to motivate and calm anxious employees, linking their destinies to his optimistic vision of the future for IBM. His message remained essentially unchanged to the end of his life.

The original meaning of the phrase was very narrowly construed to focus on the relationship between IBM as a company and its employees, meaning, in the decades when Watson Sr. ran the company, largely his workers. There were occasions when he would speak to groups of employees with their spouses present, such as at 100 Percent Clubs, Quarter Century Club lunches and dinners, Family Dinners, and retirement events. Those organizations and events that are capitalized were formal company programs enveloped with ritual and expected speaking themes. Watson Sr. did more traveling to more locations where customers, employees, and government officials and other business executives met than did many of his peers. In fact, he was out of his office more than in it, operating very much like a CEO of a post-1960s corporation.[27]

As a result, he was able to hone his messages, delivering these over nearly a half century, sometimes repeatedly to the same employees and their spouses. As the company began implementing benefits after entering a period of profitability in the mid-1920s, his definition of "IBM Family" evolved to include families of employees. As described in the previous chapter about benefits, one could see this definition implemented through the establishment of programs aimed at the interests of children and spouses, such as the construction of country clubs at plant locations and events for them there beginning in the 1930s. By the time he died in 1956, the combination of "IBM Family" rhetoric and the company's benefits had fused, making speech and action a combined pattern of practice and habit and hence part of IBM's corporate culture. One might argue the motives for all this behavior were calculated to improve the business's success and less to do good in society, as observers have done for corporations in general.[28] Nonetheless, employees had come to expect that the idea of family, obligation, and loyalty were part of the Grand Bargain involved in being an IBMer. The idea of "IBM Family" had been incorporated into the firm's vernacular, much as had such other phrases and implied acceptance of beliefs, for instance, "IBM Basic Beliefs" and "THINK." As sociologist Robert Putnam phrased it, the collective perspective was one of "shared identity" and of "reciprocity," two ideas firmly embedded in corporate America by midcentury.[29]

Corporate Strategy for Engaging with Families

As with good corporate image-building practices, the notion of employees being members of an IBM Family needed to be instilled through repeated messaging and by implementing programs that reinforced such an idea to demonstrate that management really meant it. That is where ritual and communications became so important, as students of corporate culture almost universally have acknowledged.[30] It all began, as Watson Sr. did, by paying competitive salaries, creating healthy working environments, and convincing employees to embrace IBM's business strategy—what one today would call the company's "value proposition."

Not surprisingly, IBM management initially approached employees' families as a cohort, only differentiating between, say, those with children from others that were young or nearer retirement. In a sales-oriented company, one might think of families as a market needing to be persuaded to support the firm's business objectives. Without their endorsement, turnover in personnel would be higher and thus, too, training costs for replacements, even increasing the requirement for more employees than otherwise needed. The strategy for dealing with families involved providing employees, and by extension their families, a suite of salary, bonuses, and myriad benefits, which evolved over time. Overlaying these provisions was a second multifaceted strategy of hosting a collection of events aimed at adults, children, or a combination of adults and children—families—participating together. Examples of the first were Family Dinners (described below). Examples of the second were company-funded trips to interesting places for husband and wife to recognize outstanding performance by the employee and as a reward to the spouse for putting up with the long hours involved (e.g., Golden Circle trips). The third type included holiday parties with presents and games for the children and summer picnics held at county fairgrounds. There were other ad hoc activities, such as IBM-sponsored baseball teams or golf or bowling tournaments when there were large numbers of employees who worked at one location, who would play teams from other local companies, and the very unique trip made by 10,000 IBMers and their spouses to the World's Fair in New York in 1940, all paid for by IBM. Some of these activities are briefly described below. Yet other examples included Quarter Century Clubs and various retiree groups, with the activities of both partially funded by IBM. An additional prong was an extensive communications effort that reached both employees and spouses, reminding them of all that IBM was providing them.

This three-prong strategy—salaries and benefits, events and experiences, and a well-orchestrated communications campaign—had a remarkable consistency about it. Many were routinely deployed for decades such that they became annual rituals families looked forward to, for instance, the annual Christmas party for children in factory towns and field offices all over North America or annual golfing events at IBM country clubs. An additional feature of these three strategies is that they were implemented in almost the same forms in every country in which IBM had a presence.

But there was more. Upon the birth of a child, the family received an engraved silver baby spoon, a custom practiced for over a half century, as was that of giving an employee a gift on the occasion of having worked at IBM for twenty-five years and another upon retirement. The silver spoons were constantly remembered for decades, even occasionally mentioned on social media complete with photograph, although the custom of sending such a gift ended in the 1990s. A letter, usually from the CEO, accompanied these. The head of World Trade, Arthur K. Watson, for example, wrote one in 1969 to new parents in Beirut, Lebanon: "News of the little addition to your family has just reached me and I am delighted to extend congratulations and best wishes to you."[31] Christmas cards circulated all over the company as ritual, also for decades. Special events held every year, but that occurred for an employee only on rare occasions, were looked forward to as possible repeatable ones. An example was the opportunity to go on a Golden Circle trip to Hawaii, Mexico, or Italy; these trips were popular but hard to qualify to attend because these and similar other ones were aimed at the top 1 to 1.5 percent of performers as measured by quantifiable business results or other qualifications. So, who attended changed every year. For a family whose breadwinner was a lifelong employee, these events became part of life's rituals that served as markers of career successes. Disruptions to some of these, caused by economic downturns at IBM in the 1990s and after 2012, created concerns cited by employees and retirees as "take backs," evidence of the decline of IBM's successful culture.[32] In other words, once launched, the first two strategies had to continue, while the third one—communications—may seem mundane to the casual observer. However, this third strategy was impressive when one catalogs what kinds of communications literally came through the door into people's homes.

Managing IBM's benefits always involved maintaining staffs in each country capable of implementing these. Employees were annually informed about their benefits. Communications staffs always implemented the third strategy. But the second strategy was carried out locally without formal training. Normally, a group of local employees called the IBM Club would be responsible for organizing such events, tapping into local administrative funds to cover costs for food and presents.

However, for a formal, high-profile event, the senior location manager would personally be involved and assigned staff to work on it. What constituted a high-profile event? Usually it might be a large gathering of customers or the annual kick-off meeting for an organization held in January, but for family activities, it was always the Family Dinner. These dinners involved an IBM executive guest speaker, such as the chairman of the board or a division president, so certain rituals and expectations had to be met. Failure to flawlessly host a Family Dinner created serious problems for the local senior manager, including essentially slowing (or stopping) their future advancement. On the other hand, when well done, it enhanced it. For instance, Lloyd ("Buzz") Waterhouse, sales branch manager in Nashville, Tennessee, hosted a Family Dinner in 1984, combining it with a celebration of IBM's fiftieth anniversary of having an office in the city.[33] He so impressed the guest speaker, Sales Vice President Bud Cooke, that the latter soon after promoted Waterhouse into his initial executive position. Waterhouse had demonstrated he could put together and run a complicated event, proving that he had strong organizational and managerial skills.

Normally, one learned how to run one of these events by participating in local task forces that had hosted prior ones. With a senior executive attending, logistical practices for moving the guest about town and arranging customer visits and briefings would be added and be carefully choreographed. The host would have learned how to run one of these over many years. That is why a historian would find it hard to find any documentation explaining how these were run, knowing only that they had occurred.[34] So, let us explain how these unfolded.

Special Role of Family Dinners

Family Dinners were events held periodically for employees and their spouses in almost all, if not all, locations that had groups of IBMers around the world. Prior to the 1950s, such gatherings did not have a formal name; afterward, they were always called Family Dinners. They could be attended by small groups or groups of a thousand or more. In the early decades, these were often formal events with attendees dressed in tuxedos and evening gowns. Even in less formal future times, they were still suit and gown affairs. Normally, printed menus that included a schedule of speakers and entertainment and date and location of the dinner were at each place setting that people could take home as souvenirs. Family Dinners were normally held in the dining facilities of the largest or most prestigious hotel in a city. These events always included the senior location manager as host, welcoming everyone and thanking spouses for their support of their husbands and wives, and always, too, a senior IBM executive who made similar comments and then spoke about the greater IBM in glowing terms. In the early part of the twentieth century in the United States, it was not uncommon to display an American flag near the lectern and have a cleric lead attendees in a prayer of thanksgiving. These were celebratory events, even if some of the speeches were perceived as boring.[35] Until the late 1980s, IBM had a worldwide "no liquor policy" for any company-sponsored event, so wine or beer was rarely served at these dinners.[36] At large facilities, such as a plant site, if there was a local IBM band, other musical groups, or company choirs, they performed. Endicott set the pace for those kinds of activities.

Examine figure 7.1 because it tells us much about such events. Notice that it was a rather formal affair, although by the time this one took place (1947) in Seattle, Washington, not a tuxedo one. But all the elements were there. Watson

7.1 IBM Family Dinner, 1947. This picture is both a memento of the event and a press photograph that could be used by local media. Thomas J. Watson, Sr., is standing addressing
the audience, and his wife, Jeanette, is seated to his left.

(Courtesy, IBM Corporate Archives.)

Sr. is making a speech. He is seated at a head table, with a minister to his right
who would have delivered a prayer, IBM luminaries, and to his left his wife, Jeanette, reputedly the only person on the planet who dared signal to him that he
was talking too long. There is the IBM logo THINK but no alcohol. Husbands
and wives were in attendance. Lest the picture suggest these were small events,
see figure 7.2. This photo is of a luncheon in Poughkeepsie held at the IBM
Country Club and included employees and spouses. This particular event, held
in May 1952, was to present awards for various athletic contests hosted by the
club. Although not clear in the picture, in the back is a full orchestra providing
live music in what was the multipurpose gym and theater. Notice also, as with
family dinners, each guest has a program/menu.

In the 1910s and 1920s, Watson Sr. had encouraged IBMers to host such
events all over the world, and he spoke at a great many of them. After his death
in 1956, his son Thomas J. Watson, Jr., did the same, as did senior executives

7.2 This image shows a family event to celebrate winners of Watson trophies, held in 1952. It demonstrates, too, extensive planning for this large event, one that would have been anticipated for months in advance.

(Courtesy, author's collection.)

through the 1980s, after which these events were held less often. It was more normal for each location to host a Family Dinner about every three years, larger communities of employees more frequently. They were popular. In November 2020 on a retiree social media website, the topic came up and many who had been to such events waxed positively about them. A sampling of comments is worth quoting:

- "Great events when we were still a family company."
- "Family Dinners were the best way IBM could recognize their appreciation for the employees. As Branch Secretary it was a pleasure and an honor to be involved behind the scenes in their preparation. Plus it was a lot of fun."
- "What memories! Enjoyed the good times!"
- "Remember them well. It was done right."
- "It gave everyone a feeling that the company cared for us."
- "Everything was first class! IBM even paid for travel to the dinner and babysitting."[37]

One employee recollected that when Watson Jr. spoke at his dinner in the 1960s, it made the event "a big deal for a little branch office like ours."[38] Many of these engaged a professional photographer to document the event and to take pictures of every table of employees. It was a rare published IBM memoir that did not mention Family Dinners.

That senior executives spent so much time attending these events begs the question: What were their purposes? One American IBM executive who had experienced these events since probably the late 1920s, and certainly from the 1930s, until his retirement three decades later explained as clearly as any employee their intent:

> First, they enabled the home office executive to give the local people a better feeling for some of the things that were being done in New York and why, some of the plans that lay ahead and some of the directions the company was taking. Second, it permitted the local members and their wives to see some of our New York executives as actual human beings and, third, it forced the New York executive to get out of his ivory tower, see the situations as they were in the field, hear some of the complaints on the ground floor and to size up at first-hand some of the strengths and weaknesses of the field organization.[39]

Such experiences became shared cultural experiences. For example, in 1950, Watson Sr. visited Bogotá, Columbia, where the local senior IBM manager, Luis A. Lamassonne, presided. Let him explain: "We had already inspected the only hotel where we could hold the reception [he meant Family Dinner]. The Hotel Estacion! We found it in complete shambles, and had to arrange to renovate and paint the dining room, as well as change all the curtains.... We even had to buy the china that would be used."[40]

The sales branch manager in Madison, Wisconsin, in the late 1980s also hosted a Family Dinner. The event involved employees from three local IBM offices and their spouses at a large hotel. A team of administrative employees worked for several months to pull together the event, with careful coordination of logistics for visiting guest executives. Each of these guests was given an itinerary, provided a local IBM employee to drive them around, and taken on calls to senior local customers and public officials. The menu was carefully selected to account for dietary restrictions and to ensure that nothing was served that would be disliked by the guests. Menus were printed as elegant ephemera, photographs were taken, and subsequently, a round of appropriate thank you notes were mailed to all guests and to the team that pulled together the event. The guests paid their own travel expenses, but everything else came out of the senior location manager's budget. His experience was the same as that of literally thousands of other managers over the previous seven decades, including the manager in Bogotá.[41]

Other Family Bonding Activities

At large plant sites, IBM built country clubs that had all the amenities of any other country club: dining facilities, tennis courts, swimming pools, golf courses, and swimming and tennis lessons, all available to employees and their families, beginning in the 1930s until late in the century, by which time IBM had shuttered or otherwise disposed of these country clubs. These facilities were used to host Christmas parties for children and adults, family picnics, and other special events. As one retiree remembered, "The Christmas parties were great and the kids loved them. That's what they were for, IBM was a Family company back then."[42] Each child received a present paid for by IBM. Another recalled that "Christmas parties and summer picnics were terrific."[43] In company towns like Endicott and Poughkeepsie, events in the summer were so large that, on occasion, the local IBM Club would rent the county's fairgrounds, with all the operators running rides and carnival events for many thousands of employees and their families. More normally the routine, however, was the use of country clubs as part of people's daily lives. Figure 7.3 illustrates the country club in Endicott on a postcard published by IBM in the 1930s. Notice the two people playing golf, both genders represented in the foreground. Observe, too, the size of the clubhouse in the background. Even by twenty-first-century

7.3 This photo signals the "good life" at an IBM country club. Notice the golfers in the foreground enjoying a popular mid-century relaxing sport at an IBM country club.

(Courtesy, author's collection.)

standards, it was substantial. By those of the Great Depression–World War II era, it represented a large investment by IBM.

Because of all the construction underway and the hiring of many new employees in the Endicott area in the 1930s, the company published a thirty-two-page pamphlet distributed to prospective and new employees, customers visiting the various facilities, and families to explain what IBM did in Endicott. While it focused largely on the research and manufacturing activities under-way, it also included a two-page description of the IBM country club with pho-tographs of men and women relaxing or participating in various events. After describing its physical features and that some 4,000 employees belonged to it, this publication included information on various athletic activities, how many baseball games were played, and the number of employees using the golf, bowl-ing, and tennis facilities. Families could enjoy all of these and also learn about gun safety and how to shoot, use the swimming pool, and play indoor games such as shuffleboard, cards, and table tennis.[44] Of possible interest to spouses, one page described the "Medical Department," located on the company's cam-pus to handle injuries and routine illnesses, and ended with, "One of the male nurses is supplied with an automobile and visits all patients unable to report at the plant. He offers proper treatment and counsel and keeps a close record of their progress."[45]

On occasion, husbands and wives were treated to a special event, the most spectacular one, perhaps, in IBM's history was the invitation to over 10,000 from many parts of the world to visit the World's Fair in 1940 in New York at IBM's expense. The largest companies in the United States participated with pavilions and exhibits. Although IBM was not yet the size of AT&T, General Motors, or General Electric, it wanted to be seen as if so and thus participated to such an extent that this exercise cost just over 10 percent of the company's profits. The fair's organizers declared May 13, 1940, "IBM Day," for which Wat-son Sr. wanted a large crowd of employees, speakers, and entertainers. It must have been an exciting prospect for employees and their spouses who worked in remote offices around the country or in factory towns who did little or no trav-eling outside their regions. IBM scheduled twelve trains to bring the American contingents to the city. The adventure was promoted and described in internal company media and by newspapers.

Since the early 1920s, IBM plants and branch offices had honed ways of organizing events involving spouses and children. By the time 1940 came around, these were effective and had set levels of expectations for how these events should function. Each couple received a twenty-two-page booklet that described the logistics for the trip (e.g., what train to take, when and from where), transportation and hotels in the New York area, and help desks at each able to assist them, and included identification badges for everyone and their luggage, program of events, and so forth. An employee reading that booklet in any decade would have concluded that (a) it reflected, to use an IBM phrase, "completed staff work," as little was left to chance and (b) the details and plans would have been familiar to employees in the 1960s or the 2010s. These two observations are important to make because family events were intended to be fun, function with no tensions for the participants, and show off what a well-run company IBM looked like to the families. It would be difficult to exaggerate the amount of attention management and their staffs paid to ensure everything was thought through. In the instance of the 1940 World's Fair, even the size of the pamphlet (5" × 7") was an important decision—just the right size to fit into a woman's purse.[46]

However, this was also a tragic event because of a train wreck full of IBMers near Port Jervis, New York, resulting in some four hundred injuries and thirty-five hospitalizations but no deaths. It became a heroic moment for Watson, his family, and senior executives because as soon as they heard the news, they rushed to the location to assist. IBM headquarters in New York arranged quickly for doctors to come out to the town and acquired medical supplies. Watson and his New York–based executive team visited the hospitalized. Employees and their spouses retold the story of his personal involvement and of IBM's response in appreciative language for decades. As for Watson Sr., just as he demanded loyalty to IBM from his "IBM Family," he owed it to them to reciprocate in kind.[47]

IBM clubs all over the United States organized wives into groups serving their communities, such as in donating to food pantries and to addressing poverty. During World War II and the Korean Conflict, wives wrapped bandages for the American Cancer Society, as illustrated in figure 7.4, which shows IBM spouses in New Orleans, Louisiana, in 1959. This figure is interesting for yet another reason: the local IBM sales office had a photographer take the picture so that it could be used by the city's news media in its social columns and could be distributed to members of local IBM families. Since the 1960s in the United States, the company allowed families to apply through their employee spouses for donations of money or products in support of community projects that the families chose to help. This proved to be a popular program because it facilitated, for example, donations of small amounts of cash to local schools and, in the 1980s and 1990s, personal computers, which were just coming into vogue in classrooms. Such donations had the knock-on effect of exposing students to IBM's machines rather than to those of a competitor, making children and their parents favorably inclined to use what IBM's marketing called "A Tool for Modern Times." These community grants remained popular and available for over a half century into the next century.[48]

A long-serving employee or his or her spouse would find us remiss if the American Christmas parties did not receive additional discussion. Almost every IBM location in the United States and in various countries on both sides

7.4 IBM wives wrapped bandages for the American Cancer Society in mid-century, an activity organized by the local IBM Club collaborating with the local chapter of a community organization in New Orleans, Louisiana. This photo was intended as both a local press photograph and a memento for the ladies and the local IBM Club.

(Courtesy, author's collection.)

of the Atlantic hosted a Christmas party for employee children. It was a tradition that went on for decades but began to decline in the 1990s. These were popular. On a Facebook retiree website, one mother recalled the IBM Christmas party in 1962 held at the Waldorf Astoria Hotel attended by Watson Jr., then IBM's chairman of the board. He had his picture taken with individuals, while the children received presents from Santa Claus. "Life couldn't get better." Another recalled a party at the IBM country club in Poughkeepsie, New York: "The parties were awesome." An IBM child commented, "I recall getting a basketball one year and a skateboard another year . . . the NYC parties were the best." An employee announced that he had "played Santa for several years at the Detroit Christmas parties." Further, "as a second generation IBMer I also remember going to the parties in Baltimore with my Dad. Good memories." Yet another: "I remember my Dad taking me to an IBM Santa event in Hartford CT in the mid-1960s. Wonderful Memory!" Lest the reader think these were low-key events, one individual recalled a "3 ring circus" in Poughkeepsie, while another in Lexington, Kentucky, recalled that the IBM community had its party at the Rupp Arena with comedian Bill Cosby for entertainment.[49] Clearly these served the purpose that the corporation desired. How could one lose when they had Santa Claus in league with IBM?

Quarter Century Clubs

When Watson Sr. came to C-T-R in 1914, he found that its three firms rarely interacted with each other, even though they had been operating, in some instances, since the 1880s. Early in his tenure, he wanted to promote greater synergy and collaboration among the three parts of C-T-R, which had been created out of these firms in 1911. He intended to take steps that encouraged longevity of employment in the firm because their work was so specialized that he needed to retain staff. To do this, Watson needed to build their sense of loyalty to the new company. One of many steps he took to accomplish further integration was to recognize with praise as a group from all three firms those employees who had "served" in one of the predecessor firms and in C-T-R for twenty-five years or more. He lionized them in speeches, in company publications, and through social events. In 1924, he created the IBM Quarter Century Club (QCC) and celebrated its first members at a nationwide meeting of its members in Atlantic City, New Jersey, that June. They are depicted in figure 7.5 in a program/menu published on the occasion as a memento for its members. He called them "pioneers" and lauded their services.[50] At the second annual meeting in 1925, Watson repeated the same message: "It is the older men . . . who make our business what it is today."[51] He used these occasions to explain IBM's business to solicit their support for his plans and to arm them with

7.5 This image memorializes the first group meeting of the IBM Quarter Century Club in the United States, held at Atlantic City, New Jersey, in 1925. These individuals were treated as an elite community of IBM employees.

(Courtesy, IBM Corporate Archives.)

information they could use to describe to their colleagues, families, neighbors, and customers what IBM was all about.[52]

Watson used a similar technique to create a club for salesmen who achieved their business targets, called the 100 Percent Club. The concept of a club allowed IBM to annually add and withdraw people from exclusive recognition.

The QCC (Quarter Century Club), as it was often known, evolved from its original small group of less than four dozen members to many tens of thousands scattered across the world in local chapters. Just about anywhere where IBM had a long-operating office it had a chapter of the Quarter Century Club. The messages that Watson Sr. and subsequent generations of executives delivered to both groups (100 Percent Club and the QCC)—often with members in the audience who participated in each—remained the same: IBM is doing well, members contribute mightily to its success, you are role models for young employees, thank you for your service. Even during the Great Depression, Watson Sr. called upon both clubs to lead IBM forward, telling QCC members in 1931 that they "are going to make the IBM not only bigger, but better from every standpoint, every year."[53]

By the early 1930s, membership in the QCC was considered prestigious within the company, and nowhere more so than where many employees worked, such as in factory and laboratory towns and in headquarter offices. Members were both highly respected and confident they were never going to be demoted or fired. Put another way, the company would always find them a new role should their old one disappear. This is an important point because should a QCC member, say, be running an organization that no longer was needed, they could disband it, confident that in doing the "right thing" a new job of comparable importance (and salary and level) would be forthcoming. So when a senior executive stated in a speech that he needed the leadership and experience of such people, he meant it, because they knew how IBM functioned. Senior executives could not be part of this organization until they, too, had worked at IBM for twenty-five years, even if their last name was Watson. Membership was rank agnostic. Members were considered by themselves and by most of the company as elite true-Blue IBMers. Not until the 1990s did their status diminish when the number of members began to decline and, subsequently, entirely new organizations populated by professional hires came into the firm. By 2006, senior management had decided that the group was no longer relevant and thus cut ties with these chapters and their funding. QCC members protested but to no avail; afterward, some just kept meeting despite the lack of IBM approval.[54]

These clubs served as informal gatherings of a mixture of employees and retirees engaged in running IBM family events in collaboration with local IBM offices, fundraising for community activities, and communing quarterly or more frequently for lunches and parties. Where IBM had large facilities, club chapters had many hundreds of members, or thousands in places like Endicott and Poughkeepsie, and when they had a party, as one reminded in 1974, "each member gets to bring a spouse."[55] Membership involved a bit of a ceremony and a pin with a distinctive logo that one could also include on their IBM calling cards (see figure 7.6). Local IBM offices funded club events. When IBM no longer supported these chapters, it signaled to its members yet again that the old culture of respecting long-serving employees no longer held, nor job security or appreciation of their loyalty to the firm as a valued belief.[56] Many chapters

7.6 IBM Quarter Century Club pin. Employees were allowed to include this image on their official IBM calling cards, which was an additional badge of status inside the company. These were blue and white, circa 1970s–1990s.

(Courtesy, author's own pin.)

published newsletters providing biographical information about its members, announcements of upcoming events (trips, lunches, dinners), and obituaries. If there were multiple divisions or offices in a city, all participated in one local chapter, thereby extending their business relationships into personal ones as well—the idea of an IBM Family in yet another way.

Was IBM a Family Business?

Circulating through many of the chapters in this book is another underlying family theme warranting more attention that clearly ties to the topic of this one: the role of multiple generations of IBMers. For well over a half century, IBMers were encouraged to send their children to work at the firm when they grew up. Beyond the paternalistic practices documented here was another one rarely discussed in public: nepotism, as it is usually cast in negative terms. This is far more than Watson Sr. bringing into the business his two sons, Tom Watson, Jr., and Arthur (but not his daughters).[57] Ask any employee who worked in the company from the 1950s through the 1990s and they should be able to rattle off family names of high-profile executives and folk in their own offices who were multigenerational IBMers across most job classifications, but largely in factory towns and in sales. This was not an accidental circumstance. Watson Sr. promoted the practice, beginning in the 1920s. In fact, he even formed the IBM Father–Son Club, which did not take off, but as his son Tom explained, his father believed "that nepotism was good for business."[58] Children coming to work at IBM would have already known a great deal about the company's values, Basic Beliefs, and rituals and how it functioned; their parents could be counted upon to reinforce the benefits of working at IBM and answer many of their questions. If one thought that a sales manager could put pressure on one of his salesmen to "for sure" achieve his targets, and hence make the 100 Percent Club, imagine a salesman in a family of several salesmen daring to show up for a family Christmas reunion not having "made it."[59] Nearly impossible, the humiliation and the ribbing might have bordered on humorous domestic abuse.

One other variant of the IBM Family involved the many situations where both husband and wife were or had been employees. We do not know how many families consisted of two IBMers, but it would be difficult to find a sales office, for example, that did not have at least one such couple or one recently remembered by the staff, and of course at large company sites, these couples were numerous. These were truly IBM families. Your author's experience knowing many such couples suggests these were happy unions because each understood the work and issues of the other. Dinner table conversations would have been nearly impossible to understand by an outsider if they were engaged in "shop talk" because of the massive number of acronyms they used. "I like the way the BM complemented the new SE on solving the VTAM bug." "Yes, it was well deserved since it included an RPQ and the CU." Or, "I can't believe they RAed John!" "The Old Man would roll over in his grave if he heard that."[60]

Communicating with IBM's Extended Clan

Over the course of nearly a century, various parts of IBM communicated with members of an employee's family in five ways: executives and other IBMers in speeches at social events (e.g., Family Dinners, holiday parties), mailing of publications directly to one's home that spouses could see (e.g., *THINK* magazine, statements about company benefit programs), episodic mailings (e.g., photographic albums of a trip that husband and wife took, such as to a Golden Circle), a menu from the Family Dinner they just attended, and local IBM newsletters picked up at a meeting.

On the occasion of an employee's quarter century anniversary or retirement, the local IBM facility hosted a luncheon or dinner attended by the employee's spouse (sometimes children too) and some of their friends at which a book of letters would be presented to the guest of honor in the presence of his or her family. These binders routinely included a letter from the chairman of IBM congratulating the employee on reaching this milestone and thanking them for their "service" to IBM. Their binder included a certificate of achievement. Echoing the message delivered by Watson Sr. to the first Quarter Century Club meeting was a familiar theme. For instance, a 1999 QCC letter from Chairman Louis V. Gerstner read: "IBM is a company with a rich past, but I believe an even better future lies ahead. We have embarked on a new beginning and more than ever IBM will be depending on your wisdom and experience to help guide it."[61] The event and book of letters were a worldwide custom prized by employees. Spouses would have seen these, reading the letters collected from colleagues all over the company.[62] Such events were front-page news in local company newsletters, complete with a photograph of the new member or of the celebratory event.

Table 7.1 summarizes the more obvious communications documents mailed to an employee's home but is not a definitive list. It demonstrates a continuous flow of communications to an employee that his or her spouse would have seen. Some of these materials were intended as much for the spouse as for the employee, such as the various benefit statements and photographic albums from recognition trips. They collectively reinforced a family's awareness of what a positive thing it was that their relative worked at IBM, even the personal benefits to them, too (e.g., medical insurance, country club membership). Mementos reinforced that bond, such as gold charms of an event given

TABLE 7.1 IBM's Documents for Communicating with Employee Families

Document	Annual Frequency
THINK magazine	Every two months
IBM Annual Report	Once
IBM Employees Benefits Plan	Once
Summary of personal benefits (various titles)	Once
Company newsletters to those in military service	Episodic but continuously
Photographic album of 100 Percent Club	Once (for qualifying employees)
Photographic album for other recognition events	Once (for qualifying employees)
Salary receipts (sometimes to office address)	Every one or two weeks
Welcome to name of town or plant	Episodic
Quarter Century Club newsletters	Various
Notifications and invitations to Family Dinners, summer picnics, holiday parties, other social events	Various
Corporate Christmas card	Once

to wives, corporate clothing distributed on such occasions (e.g., logoed shirts, baseball caps), an expensive gift for members on their induction into the QCC selected from a catalog, with the chosen gift often for one's spouse. The same behavior applied at retirement. For decades, retiring executives were given old IBM wood and brass clocks from the 1920s and 1930s, which one could see operating in their homes, while about the only typewriter that would be used there was an IBM Selectric and later a PC, either of which could be purchased new at discounted prices.[63]

Physical items came into homes as well, most notably a silver baby spoon on the occasion of an employee becoming a parent, but also Christmas presents for children and twenty-fifth anniversary and retirement gifts.

Beginning during World War II, for American military forces, IBM mailed to employees in uniform company newspapers and magazines to sustain the latter's emotional ties to the company and as an implied reminder that, when back in civilian life, they were expected to return to the company. It was a practice continued into the next century. In addition, employees were sent a package of food and other items at holiday seasons, regardless of whether they were in war or simply serving overseas. It was not uncommon at their retirement parties when reminiscing about their careers to mention how meaningful those packages and company holiday cards were, often acknowledged tearfully. That experience was not lost on generations of personnel and communications staffs crafting their own work practices.

When all these bits and pieces of communications are looked at in aggregate, as partially attempted with table 7.1, that leaves out an even larger body of communications between the company and its employees done in their work settings. Yet it becomes evident that generations of executives and managers strived diligently to create an IBM ecosystem that included families. Their topics of communications, the way they went about it, and perhaps most interesting, the consistency of it all across at least three-quarters of a century qualify these activities as important components of IBM's corporate culture. Did other large enterprises behave similarly? Yes; however, they, too, await their historians to describe. The company's experience demonstrates that management believed families needed to be informed and committed to the firm's work, not just their IBM relatives, and that it was about far more than a gold watch presented at a retirement party.

How effective were all these communications? More specifically, how valuable did employees think these were? There is little extant evidence to measure results. One survey conducted with the Endicott community in 1963 reported that 83 percent of respondents thought the amount of communications they received were "exactly" or "approximately" the right amount about work, and so forth.[64] In a survey done with 17,000 retired employees in 1985, published in the company's magazine, *THINK*, 42 percent reported they thought communications between IBM and them was "very good," another 43 percent rated these "good," 12 percent "average," and 3 percent "poor." In the same survey, retirees were asked to rate their level of satisfaction with company activities, largely with Quarter Century Club events. Twenty percent rated these "very good," 32 percent "good," 43 percent "average," and 9 percent "poor." While one can only imagine what criteria composed each category and what retirees had in mind, the evidence seems to lean in the direction that contacts with the greater IBM Family were healthy.[65]

Yet this presentation of progress and satisfaction is not fully accurate. The survey data indicated a minority of unhappy employees and retirees, inevitable when looking at populations of hundreds of thousands, but not to be dismissed. Following the technique used in all chapters of looking at ephemera frequently overlooked by historians, we have the humble example of the IBM Christmas card. Figure 7.7 is an image of the card that went to employees in the 1950s–1960s from the chairman's office. One retiree provided a near-perfect example of how contacts with families changed—some might say languished or deteriorated—over the years, especially in the 1990s:

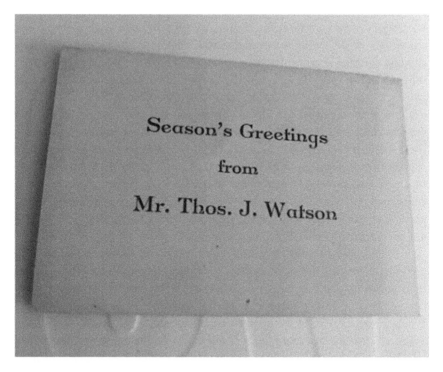

7.7 Prior to the 1970s, it was common for the chairman of IBM to send employees Christmas cards, in addition to senior executives and line management.

(Courtesy, author's collection.)

> In my early years it came to my house. Then it was in my mail at the office. Next it was reduced to a letter on official stationary in my office mail. That was replaced by a form letter copied in my office mail drawer. Then down to an email print out. And further down to a note on the office bulletin board. And lastly under Gerstner and York, nothing at all. Sadly, it kind of tracked the demise of the respect for the individual started by Thomas Watson.[66]

Another retiree reacted to the just-quoted comment: "I remember all of the above. The demise of caring hit us as IBMers so much because we were used to being reminded regularly about respect."[67] A retired salesperson recalled, "Down to a Happy Holidays email with a message to spend time with family, BUT, close out the quarter strong so there was no time for family."[68]

Did IBM benefit from the various measures intended to encourage loyalty and productivity? In today's language, one speaks of work–life balance; in

pre–World War II America, people spoke about families and, in other countries, usually less so within the context of work. While we do not yet know
empirically if IBM benefited from its family rhetoric and cultivation of family
support, for over seventy-five years, its senior executives and their employees
thought it (and they) did. That people spent their entire working lives at IBM
and then encouraged their children to do so, too, offers additional anecdotal
evidence that recruiting the support of families was smart strategy.[69] So, also,
was the combination of benefits that supported families and employees over
the twentieth century. In the 1990s, publicly available evidence from IBM
suggested that the answer to our question was yes. By then, both spouses
normally had careers, not just jobs, and they were still having babies, still
concerned about employment security, and still engaged in balancing family
needs and chores with work requiring travel and often unpredictable hours
and pressures.

Flextime was now more than just a concept in the air. Employees were having
difficulty balancing their private lives with work demands to a greater degree
than in the first half of the previous century when the "breadwinner" made
enough income to not require his spouse to also work outside their home.
Women with preschoolers experienced the greatest amount of stress in the
1990s, so flextime became more prevalent as a family-valued business practice, from which they and their IBM spouses benefited.[70] Although now more
obvious than in the 1990s, managers were nervous that they could not observe
their employees at work. Some questioned the value of the new approach, but
IBM implemented these. Evidence suggested that managers benefited the least,
workers the most. But more significant, work–life balance was now a major
issue for most employees, so much so that it could not be ignored.[71]

Conclusions

Exploring how IBM approached the role and influence of families in the United
States leads to several observations. First, families could never be ignored, as
they were too influential on the thinking and behavior of employees. So the
company had to assuage them and bring them along, which it did through
myriad combinations of salaries, bonuses, medical and life insurance, and such
other amenities as country clubs, college scholarships, and, later, assistance for
elderly relatives and special needs children. Second, IBM's actions mirrored
offerings that both unionized and nonunion workforces enjoyed, sometimes
offering these slightly ahead of other companies, sometimes a tad behind. From
the 1970s through the 1980s, the company was candid with employees, reporting what their workers said in surveys and what the firm learned about how
it compared to other corporations, communicating largely through *THINK*

magazine. That is one way how we know that IBM kept up with evolving times and circumstances and what the firm told its families.

But style and emphasis changed, too. In the first half of the twentieth century, the language of family permeated more intensely the rhetoric of senior leaders than later in the century. Take the example of the leading proponent of family rhetoric: Watson Sr. Language and thinking he learned as a child in rural agricultural America remained a part of his worldview for life, and nowhere did this appear so obvious as in Endicott. There, he built a training center, and rather than call it that, as IBM did such facilities by the end of the 1960s, he called it a "schoolhouse." One could see that as the building's identifier on postcards and in various IBM publications of the 1930s–1960s. Everyone would have conjured up an image of a small school that they had attended growing up where they learned many of life's essential skills and practices.

Then there was the hotel in Endicott for employees and customers who were in town for training or meetings. He called it the "Homestead" and used the same name for similar facilities elsewhere, most notably downstate in Poughkeepsie. As any American family raised on a farm will acknowledge, the word *homestead* referred to the farm from whence the family originated, typically a property occupied by the same family for generations. It is where the parents were raised, where grandparents and probably great grandparents lived, where the extended family would periodically reunite for family dinners at Thanksgiving or Christmas, where the interiors of the farmhouses remained essentially comfortable, familiar, and unchanged over time. Family reunions were held at the homestead farm. Postcard images of the IBM Homestead in Endicott depicted a house-like structure (not hotel-like), a large living room with sofas and overstuffed chairs (not hotel lobby–like furniture), and a dining room laid out much like that in a country club (another family-centric term instead of athletic facilities or gym), and for decades, it had no registration desk at the front door like the sort one would see at a hotel. While the terms used to describe this facility remained unchanged until sold off at the end of the century, such language seemed archaic, yet warm and inviting, to customers and newly hired employees in the 1970s–1980s. That would have pleased Watson Sr.

Exploring briefly the relations of IBM with its employee families suggests that this was a deep dive into an important, if little explored, facet of the company's corporate culture. Family issues were not just an ancillary collection of the company's issues, but rather a highly influential aggregation requiring the same serious consideration as any other aspect of employer–manager relations. Families affected almost everything: attitudes toward unions, salaries and benefits, where employees were willing to work and with what level of focus and dedication, how customers imagined a firm, employee morale and productivity, and what effects families and companies had in a community. For example, in company towns, it was possible to live in a neighborhood where over

95 percent of one's neighbors worked at IBM. How that circumstance affected everyone, including the broader community at large, remains poorly understood. Employees in such communities remark that social pressures to conform to the "respectable" behavior advocated by generations of IBM managers proved intense and essentially kept many in an insufferable company bubble all their waking hours.[72] If all this echoes some of the old Victorian paradigm, which characterized the thinking of IBM's founders, it should be of no surprise. While people work to feed and house themselves, they more fundamentally work to sustain the overall well-being of their families. IBMers were no exception to that reality.

IBM's family strategies had effects beyond programs and communications. On the one hand, employees gave their heart and souls to the firm with positive business results, and for most of them, the Grand Bargain was worth what they put into their work. On the other hand, as historians have pointed out but have yet to study thoroughly enough, one had to face the reality that the bargain limited employee freedom to behave as they wished. For example, they were discouraged from drinking alcohol, but there were employees who did so to excess requiring medical attention or counseling.[73] Employees were encouraged to attend religious services, be active in the social and charitable events in their communities, and otherwise not engage in activities in their private lives that could besmirch the company's reputation. In other words, they had to behave in their private lives as if "on the job." Marriage was strongly endorsed, divorces clearly not, and having children was ideal. Living a conventional middle-class life was the unstated preferred lifestyle. Stories of employees stepping outside these bounds leading to poor appraisals or outright dismissal circulated, more as mythology than fact, although Open Doors as a result of such incidents were not a rarity, especially at midcentury. One could reasonably conclude that in even earlier decades, when it was customary in American companies to display an almost evangelical attitude by managers toward their firms, such incidents would have been more frequent, especially in company towns like Endicott. But specifics still elude us, so generalizations by historians and business consultants who had not lived in such communities have to be read with caution.[74] Mental health problems and suicides remain poorly documented, although stories of these increased in the late 1980s and throughout the 1990s as layoffs and business decline increased.[75]

IBM had its beliefs, which some have characterized as near evangelical, pointing to the practice of IBMers singing songs from the 1920s to the 1970s, as our opening epigraph suggests. The songs, speeches, events, and publications made it clear for many decades that to work at IBM was not a job, it was a calling, working for a higher cause. Two music scholars studying IBM's signature practice of singing songs, in describing its role, provided a fitting concept of the IBM Family drawn from the lyrics of one song: "To follow the IBM calling was to be taken into the bosom of the IBM family, to be protected by this family, to receive succor and comfort and security in an insecure world."[76] It was an attractive message in the perilous times of the early twentieth century, a call to the strength of the collective.

But circle back to hard-core business practices. Underlying everything posited by this chapter was the notion that all employees should be paid—compensated—competitively and be provided with a comfortable standard of living. So, as compensation practices evolved in corporate America and around the world, so did IBM's. For example, in 1956, some executives were granted stock options for the first time, a pension, and other retirement benefits on which one executive reported he could "retire on a comfortable income" that did not change his standard of living from that which he had enjoyed while employed.[77] The same executive reported that "prior to this time Mr. Watson Sr. had maintained that all pensions should be the same to everyone, from janitor to president. The new plan was based on salary and years of service and actually was the first real pension and retirement plan that we ever had in IBM."[78] This design of the pension plan remained in force into the 1990s in the United States and in various local formulations in other countries into the next century.[79]

In the 2020s, large enterprises are required by law and market realities to provide numerous amenities to families. Companies grouse over that requirement, spending vast sums lobbying to keep in check increases in benefits to their employees. Recent unionizing activities, such as occurred in 2021 at an Amazon warehouse in the United States (although unsuccessful), were debated within the context of management control and costs. Undoubtedly, however, employees discussed the "pros" and "cons" of unionizing with members of their immediate families and friends. One could ask, did Amazon understand, let alone have a direct relationship with, those influencing voices in people's homes? For today's corporations with aspirations to be more inclusive of multiple stakeholders, how IBM engaged with families teaches more than to run out and build a country club and host Christmas parties for the children. Its experience speaks to the increased productivity of employees and, as uncomfortable as it obviously is to senior management, thinking through how, as pillars of society, their firms must act.

A running joke at IBM for decades was that employees were poorly paid because if one took the salary one was paid and divided it by the number of work hours they and their families tolerated, they were not being compensated even a minimum wage per hour. There is a hint of truth in that quip for some. But also entwined into the responsibilities of a large enterprise today are its social, ethical, and moral obligations to society. It is not only Facebook and Google being criticized around the world for not stepping up to assist societies and their national economies to remain ethical, inclusive, and stable, let alone distributing accurate information. It is a criticism of many enterprises, with demands for more socially conscious behavior increasingly lobbied for by their customers, regulators, politicians, employees, and various interest groups. Companies are especially being forced by employees to embrace a broader stakeholder relationship. Facebook's employees were not afraid to chastise CEO Mark Zuckerberg for not aggressively censoring purveyors of "misinformation" early enough.

IBM was not immune from employee activism. When President Donald J. Trump took office in 2017, he formed a business advisory council and appointed IBM chairman, Virginia (Ginni) Rometty, to it, and she accepted his invitation. Photographs all over the media for over a year showed her seated just two chairs down from him. Perhaps she was seated just so to show that he was inclusive by having a woman on the council, but employees (and more privately their families) circulated a petition calling on her to resign. Family members were surely encouraging their employee relatives to sign such a petition—a risky proposition in a company continuing to lay off workers. It was probably the first such petition to circulate inside IBM (and leaked to media) since the apartheid controversies of the 1970s, which in part led IBM to discard its operations in South Africa. IBM's experience suggests that the definition of relevant stakeholders is broader than corporations think.

The relevance of what IBM did in entwining employees and their families into its greater socio-business-economic ecosystem is made more urgent by the rapid decline in available employees to hire caused by the pandemic in 2020–2022. This was particularly the case in the United States, where the paucity of potential hires resulted in the unemployment rate of skilled IT candidates being half that for the nation at large; the latter was the lowest it had been in forty years. So, after recruiting someone—itself a real challenge—companies have to figure out how to retain them. The conventional wisdom is that people leave a firm today either for higher salaries or because they want to work from home—the work–life balance issue. IBM's lesson is different, to an extent. It did not always pay the highest salaries, but it long had the practice of having a broad, indeed rich, collection of benefits in combination with salaries, some components of which were inexpensive per capita but valued by those who needed them, such as college scholarships or paying adoption fees for children. IBM's lesson is that the combination of relevant, not trivial, benefits that enhanced both quality of life and employment security were important. So, too, was it to continuously remind employees of what they were getting in exchange for the Grand Bargain. While Amazon and other high-profile companies are again dealing with union organizing initiatives, IBM is not. While the firm never had perfectly clean hands, its history as explained in this and the previous six chapters suggests there are lessons to be learned here.

The next four chapters shift emphasis to IBM's material culture initially with a discussion of commonly used items, such as coffee mugs, because these illustrate many components of IBM's culture in action. These chapters do the same with postcards, office cartoons, and IBM's massive publishing practices. I employ similar methods used when earlier we discussed the image of IBM's machines in chapter 3, but with the difference that more people used coffee mugs, for example, in the computer industry and at IBM than they did computers. These chapters provide additional insights into the company's culture as displayed and played out over many decades, as much to suggest to students of multinational corporations how to view their operations more deeply as it is to remind management in all industries that there is more to how their enterprises function than what they think. What more routinely meets the eye is often a logoed coffee mug than a statement from personnel touting one's insurance benefits.

PART II

CASES FROM IBM'S
MATERIAL CULTURE

CHAPTER 8

FROM LAPEL PINS TO COFFEE CUPS

Links Between Corporate and Material Culture

IBM At Your Service.

IBM coffee mug, 1980s

A rcheologists have developed tools and practices for studying ancient objects, such as pots and swords; these techniques are also used to study today's societies by sociologists and cultural anthropologists. All have learned to analyze objects for insights on human behavior. Historians can use the same approach to study corporate cultures, even though students of that culture are largely sociologists, economists, business management professors, and consultants.[1] Their debates now focus on how best to leverage insights about corporate cultures to grow a business, make it more innovative, or fix problems. Historians have focused on how a corporation shapes its image, largely through advertising, pointing to new directions.[2] We can study a company's culture further by examining some of the many logoed artifacts distributed by modern corporations. Since IBM is a company whose employees, and sociologists, historians, and business management experts, agree long had a highly defined corporate culture, what can its artifacts teach today's corporations?[3]

I proceed first by defining briefly corporate and material cultures, to remind readers of what is generally understood about such concepts because objects matter; they influence one's identity with a company and their feelings toward its role. We then move to a description of a select group of material objects and discuss their role in IBM's activities. It is here that we study lapel pins and coffee cups, for example. To do that, we situate those objects into Edgar Schein's model of organizational culture. This chapter concludes with insights drawn from our discussion. As an archeologist does, I present numerous images as direct evidence of IBM's material culture.[4] This chapter links concepts of material culture to corporate culture, a connection that may appear to many readers as new, especially to senior management. At the end of our discussion, a logoed coffee cup should never look the same to most members of a corporation's stakeholders.

Introduction to Concepts of Corporate and Material Cultures

First, I will start with a reminder of what constitutes a corporate culture, introduced in the first chapter. Since the 1980s, the most widely accepted perspectives on the topic were those of Edgar Schein, then professor at MIT's Sloan School of Management. Over the course of several decades, he refined his definition. He argued that there were three aspects of these cultures: (1) artifacts and behaviors, such as furniture or dress codes and other visible elements and behaviors (rituals); (2) expressed values, which include stated and observed rules of behavior; and (3) assumptions shared by the majority of employees, such as taken-for-granted behaviors.[5] He introduced his model just as others were also exploring facets of corporate cultures. His proved useful for decades. John P. Kotter and James L. Heskett added insights on the role of management and the value of corporate cultures, arguing that culture influenced behavior from top to bottom in a firm because these cultural artifacts and concepts helped to solve problems and obtain results. They cautioned that "cultures can be very stable over time, but they are never static," a good characterization of IBM's culture.[6] For students of business behavior, their notion of artifacts was not the same physical ones as, say, meant by archeologists. Schein thought in terms of "dress codes, level of formality in authority relationships, working hours, meetings," how decisions were made, social events, uniforms, jargon, and rites and rituals, among others, while archeologists gleaned insights from objects.[7] We may take all this to mean there existed a sociological or cultural anthropological view of the enterprise.

Parallel to that perspective was another emanating from history, archeology, anthropology, and sociology, which steered closer to the study of physical artifacts and architectures, acquiring the name "material culture." By the 1980s, it had become a subfield of study in many disciplines in the social sciences and the humanities.[8] It is the study of objects—things—and how people used them and the context in which they were created and used. So, the study of material cultures is a variation of what Schein and his business school cohorts explored but typically done for societies and cultures of past history. It is interdisciplinary, by necessity. It accepts the idea that objects have identity, purpose, and value. It also is the obvious recognition that companies make things, like computers by IBM, shoes by Nike, or mobile phones by Apple. The existence of objects communicates expected behaviors and identities, while increasing bonds and understanding within groups.[9] Thus, an object in a museum has much to teach us about its users. Archeologists wax eloquently about ancient coins, but modern corporations have medallions and pins, too, and these look like coins. Anthropologists would agree with the comparison.[10] Some behaviors continue for centuries, even though they evolve.

Historians are weighing in on how to study corporate objects. Philip Scranton and Patrick Fridenson called attention to the fact that "artifacts are evidence," but quickly pivot to the point that historians still need to define what "constitutes the material culture of business" and "what artifacts capture an enterprise's cultural commitments or service."[11] In this chapter, we discuss several objects chosen purposefully, in some instances decades old, that represent IBM's values and behavior (e.g., THINK signs and 100 Percent Club pins), but also one other object that was both a more recent addition and unofficial, yet reflective of its culture: the coffee mug. Scranton and Fridenson point out that artifacts can be used in part to clarify behavior and values. They would have us study, for example, the history of the desk or of objects in an office (e.g., telephones, filing cabinets). They would like scholars to explore how buildings, for example, communicate cultural messages.[12]

I extend their suggestion to smaller, more mundane, yet ubiquitous items, such as to those discussed here. These meet one other criterion they recommend: they are "crucial to daily life." These small objects meet these criteria and so should be historicized as part of a corporation's description. The two historians wisely suggest, and we begin here, to think more "closely about artifacts that integrate business, technology, and consumption" as "an illuminating vector for business history."[13]

In addition to being a window into a company's culture—the main interest here—there is another aspect not to be ignored: the role of objects and their images in shaping people's views of a corporation. Normally this is a discussion about advertising and public relations. Historian Roland Marchand has shown that corporations strive for an image created by integrating messages, speeches, advertisements, and other publications. Large corporations have engaged in such activities since the late nineteenth century. NCR, General Motors, AT&T, and other firms led the way in the United States, and IBM often followed their lead, especially in the first half of the twentieth century.[14] As Marchand observed, it was about "the corporate quest for social and moral legitimacy," which describes much of the fundamental foundation of IBM's long-term adherence to its Basic Beliefs.[15] The many objects and images IBM introduced may not seem as grand as, say, its advertisements in major media outlets or in the design of its hardware, but these were ubiquitous and everywhere, a constant reminder of what IBM was about. That is why they are important to study.

We are thus presented with a problem that can be considered an opportunity for expanding our understanding of corporate culture. These questions and attending concepts and assumptions remain fuzzy and ill-defined and mean different things in different places and times. What are IBM's "values," and in what period? Employees would argue these were different in the 2020s than a century earlier.[16] We live in an age that demands more specificity than in preindustrial times. Archeologists and others working on material culture's history have developed techniques that add specificity, definition if you will, to concepts of corporate culture. One of their lessons is that every object has meaning, a story to tell, and a purpose to which it was put. One can study large corporations using their techniques to give substance and definition to their cultures, personalities, behaviors, values, and aspirations. Corporations create a great variety of artifacts that can be studied. IBM is an example of one that did that all before we even mention the most visible relics of its past: tabulators and computer systems.

By standards set by scholars of material culture, IBM is a sprawling example. Its artifacts include buildings, offices, equipment, documents, mementos, signs, logos, corporate logoed clothing, ashtrays, pens and pencils, lapel pins, coffee mugs, commemorative plates and Schein's list of events and rituals, proclamations and printed texts expounding on company values and practices, publications, and even humble postcards depicting factories and office buildings across many countries. Design of machines and discussions of architecture are important components of a company's material culture, and there is much that can be said of all these examples citing IBM's experiences.[17] This chapter is limited to a few items and thus can be viewed as emblematic of a much broader collection of IBM's artifacts, precisely because there are so many to explore, whether one applies Schein's model or takes the lead of Scranton and Fridenson, for example.

Since rituals and traditions played important roles at IBM, it should not be a surprise that material objectives are entwined with these. One brief example follows. When a salesperson achieved their annual targets, they were said to be a member of the 100 Percent Club, an internal prestigious recognition of their performance. From 1925 to the present, with a few interruptions here and there in the early 2000s, members of the 100 Percent Club were identified and given a lapel pin, which they wore proudly for a few weeks before the hard work of the current targets made the previous year's accomplishments seem ancient

8.1 The first image (a) is of a 1952 IBM 100 Percent Club pin displaying the design before the 1970s; the second image (b) is of the same pin (1982) used from the 1970s to the present.

(Courtesy, author's collection.)

history. The pins occasionally changed in design, but they were still pins, highly prized by their recipients for a century (see figure 8.1).

A salesperson's internal resume would always state how many 100 Percent Clubs they had "earned." In a sales office, employees knew in general how many clubs colleagues "had." Milestone achievements of, say, one earning their tenth or twentieth "club" would be an occasion for celebration and public presentation of the 100 Percent Club pin and accompanying certificate at a meeting of all employees in the building or at a widely attended social event. Regardless of how many clubs one earned, recipients always received a pin, a certificate with the number achieved as of that most recent year, and a small collection of congratulatory letters from various managers up and down the salesperson's chain of command.[18]

But there is a larger set of issues to contemplate. Increasingly today, corporations do not make things; they are "platforms" or trade in "big data" or create value through financial trades and accounting practices. They claim value as expressed in digital files, such as in financial assets, number of stocks and bonds, increases in stock prices, crypto currencies, and data sold to advertisers. A CFO is more important than a vice president of manufacturing. Facebook is a huge enterprise, but the only things it makes are coffee mugs and baseball caps. On occasion, it puts up a building. A software firm does the same. Have you ever seen a piece of software? Of course not, as it is both a figment of our imagination and the configuration of positive and negative electrons organized through the medium of magnetism. Yet as archeologists, sociologists, and even psychologists argue, things matter, "stuff counts." But corporations are none-theless making non-things that are increasingly viewed as valuable, at least by the business community. This discussion is not intended to be a criticism; we leave that to the Pikettys and Zuboffs to do. Rather, it is a reminder that, for the vast majority of time, humans valued things, be they manufactured, individu-ally crafted, or meant to serve as a memento of an experience or identity.

For a century, a debate has been underway about automation possibly reduc-ing jobs and about the negative effects of things, such as tabulating equipment, computers, and now robots, soon to be followed by a non-thing—artificial intelligence, or AI. We will not engage in debate on the last subject here, focus-ing instead on objects. Watson Sr. took a stand during the Great Depression that many in IBM embraced, for it spoke to the value of things: "Every industry which has installed improved machines and which has kept its machinery up to date has expanded and employed more people year after year."[19] We can haggle over the extent his statement is true, but there is the expression that things have value, purpose, and identity.

As corporations ponder their future and how to contribute to society's well-being or, more tactically, how to make a profit selling a non-thing (e.g., a digital service), these corporations should recognize how fundamental a shift in how they execute their purpose appears to have been underway now for a quarter of a century. Yet visit an employee or retiree Facebook group and one will see its members post pictures of products—things—with which they engaged as users, manufacturers, or people who repaired them. They anchor people to specific times, places, and cohorts. Even mundane objects, like a spe-cially designed tool or part, will generate nostalgic posts. A screw or mundane part is discussed and revered. This leads us back to one major point: things matter. As corporations shape their strategies for engaging with growing variet-ies of stakeholders, should they consider that fact?

So, IBM employees like their objects. Go to the home of a long-serving employee and you will probably see one or more IBM logoed coffee mugs in their kitchen, often a THINK sign in their home office, and all manner of pads of paper and notebooks with IBM printed on them. Go to a retiree's home, and even if they have been away from the company for two or more decades, they may have an oak and brass IBM clock from the 1920s or an avocado-colored Selectric typewriter that they do not use, while some may still wear a watch received on the occasion of their retirement. Employees may have more logoed objects at home than at work. But of course, like their cohorts at Apple, many have logoed baseball caps and T-shirts. They have become human billboards and have no objection to that because working for either company is probably a greater source of pride than embarrassment. What is an enterprise that does not make "stuff"? At the risk of overstating the case for integrating material culture into the work of corporations, this could be one of the most important chapters in our book for a senior manager to study. They should not, however, be fooled by the entertaining stories told below and in the subsequent two chapters on postcards and humor. They are as deadly serious as any academic discussion about strategy, Five Forces, or the role of the internet.

IBM's Logo, Lapel Pins, and Coffee Mugs

Hundreds of thousands of employees and millions of customer personnel acquired a large number of IBM corporate trinkets, baseball caps, coffee mugs, and other credenza dust collectors. These seemed ubiquitous in the computing world.

Students of such items point out that these were forms of three-dimensional advertising, items that kept IBM in front of a customer's mind every time they poured a cup of coffee; they also served as a form of propaganda for some, especially when the company was advocating for some technical standard to reinforce its market position, and increasingly also as part of the process of creating and sustaining its corporate culture.[20]

Exploring such a perspective departs from conventional inquiries of an object, for instance, histories of the potato or coffee, and broader observations about their role in society over long periods of time. Our intent is to look at a very narrow part of the story of, say, the history of coffee, focusing on the role of a necessary tool for its consumption (the mug) and what it teaches us about corporate uses, specifically in IBM's world.[21] It is a start, because we cannot yet link coffee mugs to the nature of shift work or social standing within a company, but we can begin defining its role in parts of IBM. These larger questions are aspirational intentions that future historians can explore. We are at a point, however, where one can establish the existence of specific mementos and provide a preliminary description of their features and uses.

There were many artifacts. Table 8.1 is an incomplete list of the types of IBM logoed trinkets and other promotional items commonly available from the 1950s through the 1990s. It is a diverse list, as printing technology made it possible to post both the company name and messages on almost anything. In some instances, literally millions of copies were made, such as monogrammed pencils and pens, but it seems that every division, headquarters, factory, office, and company organization produced these at one time or another.[22] One would be challenged to find many exceptions in most countries where IBM had a significant presence. These were embossed in every language widely used in the company. A check of IBM logoed items for sale on, say, eBay displays many hundreds of examples. Type "IBM," and the number jumps to over 175,000 items.[23]

TABLE 8.1 **Types of IBM Mementos and Decade Introduced, 1910s–1980s**

Class pictures, IBM education (1910s)	Quarter Century Club pins (1940s?)
100 Percent Club pins (1920s)	Employee clocks (1940s)
Postcards (1920s)	Photo albums (1940s)
Trophies (1920s)	THINK signs in multiple languages (1940s)
Brass medallions (1920s)	Posters on values, products, events (1950s)
Graduation certificates, IBM Education (1920s)	Paperweights (1960s)
Watches (1930s)	Ballpoint pens, pencils (1960s)
Golden Circle pins (1930s)	Coffee mugs (1960s)
IBM three-ring binders (1930s)	Leatherlike 8 × 11 notepads (1970s–1980s)
IBM leather THINK notepads (1930s)	Golf balls (1960s)
Baseball caps (1930s)	
**************************	
IBM Means Service Award pins (1970s)	T-shirts, golf shirts (1980s)
Drink coasters (1970s)	IBM Olympics pins, posters (1980s)
Staplers (1970s)	Quarter Century playing cards (1980s)
Key chains (1970s)	Commemorative plates (1980s)
Plaques for Means Service Awards (1970s)	Product pins (1980s)
Cross pen and pencil sets (1970s)	Ashtrays and crystal globes (1980s)
Sales School instructor desk sets (1970s)	Miniature plastic PCs (1980s)

Source: Items for sale on eBay, search under IBM or IBM Collectables, July 20, 2020; author's archives and collection.

The examples discussed here share several features of historical importance. First, they were widely diffused among those IBM populations that interacted with customers the most. These included sales personnel, customer engineers (who installed and maintained hardware), and systems engineers (who configured systems and repaired software). The vast majority worked out of many hundreds of branch offices and headquarter facilities. Second, some of these mementos were widely shared with customers, notably THINK signs and coffee mugs. These items were also diffused widely in other parts of IBM, such as at laboratories, manufacturing sites, and division, country, and headquarter offices. Third, the majority circulated around the world, with such items as THINK signs in multiple languages.[24]

Fourth, the three chosen for our discussion circulated concurrently in the firm for decades, providing yet another example of company practices that existed for decades, even though their physical attributes changed to conform to current styles. An example of the latter is a standard short military ceramic coffee mug design of the 1940s replaced with plastic versions in the 1980s and insulated metal ones in the early 2000s. THINK signs and 100 Percent Club pins predated all the post–World War II design initiatives of the company, endured almost untouched during that era of designing IBM's modern image, and still exist today. This suggests there are material features of a corporate culture that transcend design, advertising, and marketing activities of a particular era. If that is true at IBM—and the evidence demonstrates that is the case—then do other firms have similar ephemera that point one to a more precise description of their corporate values and cultures? In summary, however, is the most obvious reason for studying these objects: they communicate IBM's values, sales objectives, and culture. They shed light on how objects served as conduits for these ideas and, as in the case of sales mementos, enhanced the prestige of individuals within the sales force in the company.

We look at three objects in the chronological order in which they became a component of IBM's culture and image. THINK signs came into the firm in the 1910s, 100 Percent Club pins in the mid-1920s, and coffee mugs by the early 1970s. All three fit into a complex corporate culture and imprinted an image on employees and customers in a seemingly mutually reinforcing manner. But, as their chronology suggests, they overlaid other material objects, contributing to an almost cocoon-like environment in which IBM's employees and customers worked where much of their activities and tools had an IBM logo on it, as table 8.1 suggests. The first two material objects were designed, controlled, and distributed from the top of the business, while the third, coffee mugs, were often created and distributed at almost all levels of the firm. By the time this happened, these three had decades of a corporate culture endowed with material objects with a common look and feel to them that conformed to a set of beliefs and practices embraced by the majority of employees.[25]

THINK Signs

One of the most recognized corporate logos in the world is probably IBM's THINK sign. It permeated every nook and corner of IBM across all divisions and countries from the 1910s in most, if not all, IBM offices, laboratories, and factories, and in many of its customers' data centers around the world. It has its own history and mythology, but essentially, it meant two things: first, that IBM had a way of thinking about how the world should use data processing, and second, that employees should think the way Watson Sr. thought of business practices. IBMers came to view it more as applying thoughtfulness in creating solutions for customer needs. IBM's products were complicated and thus required cerebral horsepower. Figure 8.2 shows one of its first incarnations, as part of Watson Sr.'s many presentations; figure 8.3 shows an example

8.2 Thomas J. Watson, Sr., is talking to salesmen at IBM, 1929. Notice under the clock (an IBM product at the time) a small THINK sign, much like the one illustrated in figure 8.3.

(Courtesy, IBM Corporate Archives.)

8.3 The THINK sign distributed to employees and customers from the 1920s through the early 1960s.

(Courtesy, author's collection.)

8.4 The THINK sign displayed largely by IBM employees in their offices and at home since the 1960s. These were produced in over a dozen languages.

(Courtesy, author's collection.)

of a wooden version widely deployed from the 1930s through the 1960s, and figure 8.4 shows the plastic variation from the 1970s through the 1980s and that reappeared in 2002 after an anemic attempt to suppress or ignore it by some senior leaders of the company. It was not uncommon for ex-IBMers working for customers or for retirees to still display their THINK signs. The word was always spelled out in capital letters. It appeared on baseball caps, plastic baubles, coffee mugs, three-ring binders, covers of IBM publications, slide decks, and as decorations at corporate functions inside and outside the firm. Two IBM buildings at Plant No. 1 in Endicott, New York, had it emblazoned on their exteriors in the 1930s (and it is still there) (figure 8.5).

The slogan has a long history. Developed by Watson Sr. while at NCR for an employee training class in 1911, when he was the senior sales executive there, it spread quickly through the sales force and was picked up by advertising at headquarters at IBM once he joined the firm in 1914.[26] During its first few years of use at IBM, Watson stated: "The trouble with every one of us is that we don't think enough . . . we get paid for working with our heads."[27] He then summed up his message with THINK, which he would write in big capital letters on flip charts for years afterward. He explained, "By THINK I mean take everything into consideration"; further, "if a man just sees THINK, he'll find out what I mean."[28] He promoted it for the rest of his life. By the 1930s, the slogan was ubiquitous within the company. IBM used it in various branding activities, such as in naming the company's magazine *THINK* in 1935, later in trademarking the slogan, again in the 1990s to name its laptop computers as *ThinkPads*, and in naming its major information technology (IT) industry conferences "Think" since 2018.[29]

Watson's notion of THINK evolved. By the end of the 1920s, he meant the slogan to suggest that employees and customers think about how to run their businesses, how to use his technologies, and how to view data processing in the ways that IBM was promoting. That perspective was part of a larger effort by

8.5 IBM etched THINK on several of its buildings in Endicott, New York, in the 1930s. These buildings appeared on postcards. THINK is etched along the white trim on the left side of the IBM Engineering Laboratory and "School."

(Courtesy, author's collection.)

IBM to create an information ecosystem that sustained an "IBM Family" bonding within the firm extended to include its customers in a wide-ranging virtual community dominated by the firm.[30] That shared set of values represented by THINK and the Basic Beliefs became tools that supported the functioning of a highly disciplined organization and effective sales culture.[31] THINK signaled to employees and customers that use of data processing equipment was not a casual affair; rather, it required considerable attention to problem solving and determining how best to appropriate this technology. Those actions called for cerebral efforts, in other words, thinking. That perspective was deemed to separate IBM from its competitors.[32] It worked.

100 Percent Club Pins

A highly prized class of artifacts valued by IBM's sales force was the 100 Percent Club lapel pin and its attendant membership in this "club." Recall that to qualify to receive this pin, one had to generate at least as much revenue as their "quota" (business target) for the year. Approximately 80 percent of the sales force qualified for this distinction, one also necessary to achieve multiple times to be considered for promotion up the sales organization. Every salesperson knew how many they had qualified for over the years. To "miss a club" was more than a performance failure; it was a personal humiliation, no matter the reason. One normally needed to earn four "clubs" in a row to be promoted into sales management, while a successful salesperson who remained in their sales role for their entire careers might accumulate between twenty and thirty. The first annual gathering of its members occurred in 1925 in the United States and over the next century all over the world, involving many thousands of participants.

Figure 8.1 illustrates a 100 Percent Club pin from the 1950s and another from the 1980s. Figure 8.6 is an identity badge worn by an attendee at the 1937 annual meeting, held in the spring of 1938, the last one before the start of World War II interrupted such gatherings. Note the message on the ribbon: Watson had promised that next year's 100 Percent Club would be held in Europe, although the start of the war in 1939 aborted those plans. He honored that promise after World War II, and so that club took on a special identity for years. For a career salesman, it was not uncommon to have charm bracelets made for their spouses from these pins, signaling status for the employee and his wife that people would comment about in admiring terms at IBM gatherings.[33] The idea of the pin and the 100 Percent Club hardly changed over the past century. To have earned clubs created a bond among salespeople and to their company. Since many senior executives came out of sales, the club was an additional bonding force up and down the organization, while at the same time serving as a shorthand commentary on the competence of an individual.

This lapel pin was a symbolic memento of a great deal of hard work because quotas were routinely set just higher than a salesperson thought they would achieve, but then the majority did. The earning of a pin and the charm bracelets of these pins that spouses occasionally would assemble embodied a work ethic and a style of skilled salesmanship unique to IBM. The desire to "make the club" motivated sales personnel to improve their skills and to serve their customers well, even if it required the assistance of other IBMers, notably other salespeople and technical staff. The culture encouraged collaboration, leadership, a "failure is not an option" attitude, and a run for the numbers even as late as an afternoon on December 31.[34]

To differentiate the best of the best in sales, that is to say roughly the top 1.5 percent of achievers (meaning those who exceeded their targets by extraordinary amounts, such as by 125–150 percent), these individuals were also designated as members of the "Golden Circle," beginning in the 1930s. Their lapel pins literally had a gold circle around the otherwise normal pin all club members received. A career salesperson might achieve this several times in their

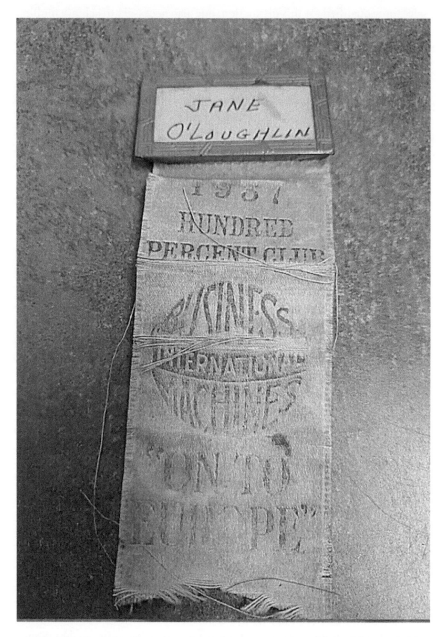

8.6 Identification badge for an attendee at the 1937 100 Percent Club celebration held in 1938.

(Courtesy, author's collection.)

career. These events entailed a half-week celebratory trip with one's spouse (later significant other) held in such places as Hawaii, Bermuda, Mexico, Rome, or the Mediterranean. In addition to their own pins, there were engraved invitations, photographic albums memorializing the trip, gold charms for the spouses commemorating the site of the event, famous speakers, great food, and popular entertainers of the day.

The two examples discussed so far—THINK and 100 Percent Club pins—reflect Schein's model of artifacts reinforcing espoused values and desired behaviors. These artifacts shared several characteristics. Both the signs and pins were deployed extensively for decades worldwide. They became iconic symbols of IBM's beliefs about customer service, the implied lifetime guaranteed employment, and respectful treatment in exchange for total emotional and professional commitment to the objectives of the company. Each was accompanied by rituals exercised repeatedly: THINK signs in evidence all over the firm, employees taking their own copy from one office or factory to another, and accumulating and participating in 100 Percent Club events as both a badge of success and a necessary inspiration for career development. Both survived the changes employees experienced as they lived through the life of the tabulator, the golden age of mainframe computing, and subsequent transformations into the next century.

A Brief Mention of Ink Pens

Had THINK signs and 100 Percent Club pins been the only mementos, the visible role they served in showcasing IBM's culture would still have proven impressive. But other material items played a role, too, as evidenced in table 8.1. These took the forms evident in many other companies, such as coffee mugs and ballpoint pens. But even here, IBM had its own distinctive style, notably its use of Cross pen and pencil sets (figure 8.7). The firm that produced these had operated since the 1840s and, a century later, still supplied expensive gold and silver pens, and later equivalent ballpoint and pencil products, to large corporations. Its gold pens were popular with American IBM salespeople, managers, and executives, and increasingly, with non-U.S. IBM management by the 1970s. Many had a tiny IBM logo attached to their clip. In that portion of IBM occupied by the sales organizations, these pens became as ubiquitous as THINK signs. So although marginal to IBM-created material objects, these pens have to at least be acknowledged as part of the sales mementos because the same people in the same space used them. One could never ask a customer to sign a contract, say, for machines valued at hundreds of thousands or millions of dollars, using an inexpensive plastic ballpoint pen. Ceremony was often required, and that meant use of an expensive signing instrument. Quite frequently, the

8.7 IBM logoed Cross pen, which were ubiquitous at IBM during the second half of the twentieth century.

(Courtesy, author's collection.)

customer manager signing such a contract also identified as an elite member of their organization and, by extension, IBM's ecosystem, and so too would have wanted to participate in the signing event with an appropriate pen.[35] Photographs taken of such signing ceremonies often displayed someone holding a Cross or otherwise elegant pen.

These pens were often given as gifts to recognize an achievement or career milestone. Pens used to sign an especially large contract might end up as gifts to customers with their names embossed on them. Desk pen and pencil sets in gold or silver could be found throughout the company. For example, on the occasion of a Sales School instructor being promoted to their first sales management position, they would receive such a desk set with a heavy medallion embossed with "IBM" and "Excellence."[36] For decades, it was customary to give similar sets to a sales rep to celebrate their first sale of a computer. Such gifts among staff or for customers were intended to reinforce bonds of shared experiences. Even in the new century, if an IBMer spotted someone at a conference using a Cross pen, they might assume that individual worked at IBM, even though other large corporations used these too.

IBM Coffee Mugs

Coffee mugs became one of the most widely distributed forms of inexpensive advertising and message-delivering mementos used primarily by American corporations. The modern ceramic thick-style mugs became available in the mid-1940s, thanks to its practical design promoted by the U.S. Navy. However, as a widespread material object for promoting corporate messages, these did not come into their own until the 1970s and, in the computer industry, not until the 1980s. Since then, it seemed no IT firm or division within a large firm in any industry failed to distribute vast quantities of these. They kept one's brand visible every day in front of whoever used them. Their return on investment (ROI) proved attractive. That is the business case for coffee mugs; when one turns to the cultural aspect, their presence seemed ubiquitous. How many mugs employees distributed to each other and to customers may never be determined because their manufacture and distribution were decentralized. But there is little doubt that almost every employee since the 1970s encountered IBM's and others' logoed coffee mugs.

In my over forty years of wandering into the offices of IBMers and their customers, I rarely saw an absence of some vendor's coffee mug somewhere present. Only in the offices of senior executives were such corporate ephemera absent, substituted with fine china. But from below the divisional VP level to the lowest parts of an organization, offices were filled with one or more of these objects. Some people collected these coffee mugs as souvenirs and had shelves or credenzas cluttered with them from IBM and its competitors, especially in the 1980s and 1990s. As workers became more mobile in the new century, such ephemera disappeared, perhaps relegated to home kitchen cabinets.[37]

Coffee mugs hold a special place in the hearts of members of the computer ecosystem. Theirs is an industry whose culture was characterized by a "roll up your sleeves and let's solve this problem now" egalitarian work environment. Its informality was punctuated by software and hardware crises and problems that urgently required immediate attention, whether in a small startup company or in IBM or Facebook-sized enterprises, when something did not work right or an opportunity beckoned. Many members of the industry experienced twenty-four-hour days, weekends that evaporated, or more normally, sixteen- to eighteen-hour days when developing new software or solving a technical problem. Enter the power of coffee to sustain energy. Since at least the 1950s, members of the industry had a reputation for consuming strong coffee in substantial amounts, male programmers liquor too. Their culture called for one to be able to consume vast quantities of coffee, mostly black, which may have been a leftover, perhaps, from military practice during World War II and Korea by so many veterans coming into the industry on both sides of the Atlantic.[38]

I tested for the significance of coffee at IBM in July 2020 by asking members of a closed IBM retiree Facebook group if they had any work-related coffee stories. Within twelve hours, some one hundred replied with caffeinated tales. Many recounted how gathering for a morning cup of coffee fostered teaming and allowed people to plan and coordinate that day's activities and solve problems. Drinking bad coffee was part of the culture, too, as one employee put it: "Our coffee machines in the Endicott factory were, OUTSTANDINGLY BAD COFFEE!" Another attending a preretirement briefing recalled that "one of the speakers said what we would miss most in retirement was socialization around the coffee machine. He was right." Another employee stated: "My mom and dad met at the IBM coffee machine in Endicott." In a lengthy discourse on the role of coffee, a field engineer opined, "Of course IBM was a coffee driven culture so I kept drinking it." Another, working in the Denver, Colorado, field engineering office, described the habit of everyone meeting for coffee first thing in the morning, nicknaming these sessions VTCs—"Verbal Technical Conferences," where "more problems were solved in that 10–15 minutes than was imagined." Yet another explained that "if you want an IBMer to come give them food and coffee!"[39]

Coffee mugs shared several features. They could be mass-produced and were inexpensive; almost any department in IBM could afford to acquire these. They were popular and practical, since most people could use these for coffee and other drinks or to hold their pens and pencils. They displayed a visible message, since so many of these cups remained in workspaces used every day. If celebrating an event, such as a conference, viewing the cup was a reminder of that occasion. They were also souvenirs of one's career. Often, one could find these cups and other ephemera in the homes of IT workers and IBMers, too. Monogrammed pens, pencils, staplers, three-ring binders, and pads of paper inevitably could also be found in their homes.[40]

As much as such cups were visible signs of IBM's culture at work, they were also carefully conceived. For decades, IBM corporate stood guard over the image of the word "IBM," ensuring that the logo was always presented in a highly prescribed way. Note that with the exception of figure 8.12 below, all uses of "IBM" were exactly the same, with the letters made up of horizontal stripes. Gold or white lettering was allowed within branding guidelines. Deviations from such displays of the lettering could be grounds for dismissal or "cease and desist" letters from lawyers to mug manufacturers. The IBM Consulting Group mug (figure 8.12) was purposefully allowed to be different, explained below.

Figure 8.8 displays a widely available common mug from the 1980s. These typically were dark blue with gold or white lettering. This example has along its rim in tiny letters, "Thank you for your business." Figure 8.9, also from that period, is an example of a localized version, this one from the Customer Center in Madison, Wisconsin. It also displays a phrase used within that sales

8.8 Many IBM coffee mugs of the 1970s–1990s were blue with gold or white lettering monogrammed with a message. This one was in wide circulation in the 1980s.

(Courtesy, author's collection.)

8.9 An example of a sales branch office mug, this one from Madison, Wisconsin, 1989.

(Courtesy, author's collection.)

8.10 An example of a division mug, this one from the computer financing part of IBM, circa 1980s.

(Courtesy, author's collection.)

organization about customer service: "Whatever It Takes." These were used to serve coffee to visitors at the center and as gifts to potential customers. Figure 8.10 is a stylistically designed example from a division, in this case, the IBM Credit Corporation, which provided financing for IBM hardware in the 1980s and 1990s. It, too, had a commercial tagline on the back, "See how simple financing can be." Smaller regional organizations distributed mugs that created local identity across multiple sales offices and to reinforce initiatives. In the example displayed in figure 8.11, the Sales Region of Wisconsin was launching its Total Quality Management campaign in 1991 as part of a company-wide initiative.

When IBM entered the management consulting business in the 1980s, it initially branded it as the "IBM Consulting Group," with its own gray and white logo to signal that it was apart, or "independent," from the hardware and software business, agnostic in its recommendations on what IT a customer (client) should use, even though the organization nested within the sales divisions. The logo was part of a settlement of an internal debate. When IBM entered the management consulting business, newly hired practice leaders from such

8.11 An example of a sales region's campaign mug, this one from Wisconsin, 1991.

(Courtesy, author's collection.)

firms as Booz Allen, PwC, and Ernst & Young, complained that IBM's customers would see them as lackeys of the sales divisions and that such an image compromised their professional ethics of being unbiased in their recommendations. To assuage them, IBM management agreed to use its branding and communications resources to blunt such concerns. The gray logo was part of that effort.[41] Figure 8.12 illustrates it. The logo was also applied to calling cards, pens, stationary, and other ephemera. This branding was coordinated and funded at the national level in various countries, unlike the image that appeared on other coffee mugs, which were normally implemented locally or by a division's headquarters in a country. The IBM Consulting Group continued appearing on coffee mugs until the early 2000s when the firm folded it into its own services organization.

To better understand the cultural role of mugs, recall that the company grew in size from just over 30,000 employees worldwide in 1950 to 341,000 in 1980.[42]

8.12 An example from the IBM Consulting Group, mid-1990s

(Courtesy, author's collection.)

IBM was essentially still divided into two halves—Domestic for U.S. operations and World Trade for everywhere else. Employee loyalties and customer identities with the firm continued aligning largely along national lines. Americans identified with the American side of the business, the French with IBM France, and so forth. Divisions within the firm fractured during World War II when German and Italian employees did not interact with American IBMers and IBM Japan was swallowed up by the Japanese national government. Senior management worked to reintegrate operations in the postwar period by such means as treating Western Europe as one integrated economy and establishing a worldwide network of research, development, and manufacturing facilities. Uniform practices and use of English as the official corporate language reinforced the sense of consistent practices and common purposes. Schein saw such activities evident in many large post–World War II enterprises, as did IBM's own expert on such matters, Geert Hofstede.[43]

By the 1970s, however, subidentities were in evidence, such as at the division level (e.g., salespeople in their divisions, employees in factories), then increasingly within divisions (e.g., one region versus another). These communities sported healthy rivalries and motivated pride in performance. On occasion, identities got out of hand, particularly if a region in the 1990s produced a region-wide poster that, say, used the IBM letters in an unapproved way.

Mugs provide insights into the internal changes underway at IBM during the years in which such mementos circulated. Figure 8.11, displaying messages from the sales region in Wisconsin (early 1990s), used the phrase "IBM Wisconsin," which landed the regional sales executive in trouble with corporate branding officials who ordered the cup and the logo retired. The regional sales executive's field staff of over five hundred employees was proud to be part of the "IBM Republic of Wisconsin," innovating various sales processes, some contrary to company practice. That mug was designed only for local internal consumption. This episode reflected a growing tension within the firm yet to be explored by historians as bits and pieces of IBM's organization challenged the prior harmony of structure and managerial control over the firm's operations at a time when the industry, the market, and technologies were undergoing profound changes. By contrast, mugs from the 1970s and 1980s conformed to corporate values and guidelines.

Loyalties and identities at either division or local levels were expressed in many forms of mementos, such as those listed in table 8.1; coffee mugs were part of such expressions of more narrowly defined identities. Field engineering and factory personnel had "site cups" that identified with the location they came from, such as Endicott and the Santa Teresa Labs in California.[44]

There were the more traditional customer-facing mugs that reflected normal branding, illustrated by the other images of IBM coffee mugs.[45] Yet even these were part of the process of self-identification. For example, an employee within the IBM Consulting Group would more likely have a gray logoed mug (figure 8.12) than a traditional blue IBM one; indeed, the employee might refuse to use the latter for fear of being associated with IBM's sales organization. On the other hand, being identified with a specific mission that had its own mug used with customers meant such a cup served both communities, as illustrated by figure 8.9 of the Customer Center mug.

Learning from Coffee Mugs and Other Material Objects

The IT industry is famous for hosting some of the largest industry conventions on the planet. From 1979 to 2003, Las Vegas, Nevada, served as the site for the Computer Dealers' Exhibition (COMDEX), and if one added events held by the same dealers, there were over 180 such conventions worldwide in the same period. COMDEX conventions in Las Vegas were mega-events; the last one in 2003 had over five hundred exhibitors and 40,000 visitors, while in 2000, some 200,000 people attended and 2,300 vendors set up exhibits. In 2000, COMDEX occupied one million square feet of exhibition space.[46] Vendors handed out trinkets: bags, calculators, mugs, flyers, pens, pencils, batteries, credit and calling card holders, luggage tags, and so many other items. A visitor could fill a shopping bag in less than an hour. Merchandising materials seemed to have no limits; their presence had been a signature feature of this event for years. COMDEX was emblematic of much of the industry's behavior: celebrity CEOs from major IT companies pontificating about the future, thousands of contracts negotiated in hotel rooms, managers recruiting employees away from one's rivals, and even "dancing girls" on tabletops. Everywhere huge screens blared out features of new software and services and old-fashion carnival barkers extolled their products.

So, discussing a few of IBM's rather humble, even restrained expressions of marketing and culturally rooted objects might seem small reflections of its values and behaviors that at first blush appear anemic. But that would be the wrong conclusion. IBM was only one of many thousands of vendors in its industry distributing massive quantities of mugs, key chains, and credenza ephemera. It was not the only firm that used monogrammed objects to communicate messages to its employees and customers. Stand by a luggage carousel at an airport and look at the banner advertisements—they are largely aimed at employees, many in IT companies.

IBM offers an early insight into the origins and value of monogramed use of material objects. As the 100 Percent Club images demonstrated, these predated the 1970s by a half century. Graduates from IBM's Sales Schools in the 1920s received a document mimicking a university degree, signed by Thomas J. Watson, Sr., "President of the International Business Machines Corporation," and the same size as an academic one. In the 1920s and more so during the 1930s, one could find in IBM's factories and other facilities a goodly supply of postcards displaying images of IBM's formidable and dignified grandeur. Revisit the image in figure 8.5, for example; it came from a postcard one could pick up in the lobby. Visitors took these home as souvenirs; others used them to communicate with friends and relatives. For the historian, they illustrated IBM's activities and projected images.[47] So, imagine what historians could learn about the corporate cultures of so many firms by looking at such items. The mementos began arriving in the 1920s, and they continue to do so a century later. Go back to eBay and query one's favorite IT firm and see what appears. Objects from Facebook, for example, a firm just established in 2004, are already offered, including coffee mugs with the firm's iconic "Thumbs Up" message and others embossed with "What Happens Tonight Goes on Facebook Tomorrow."[48]

The point is worth reiterating that there are many objects to examine that provide insight into the culture of a company. They offer insights not just available from paper ephemera in archives. Objects can be viewed as three-dimensional forms of documentation. Sociologists and cultural anthropologists have suggested methods for doing so, business school professors have already acknowledged the three-dimensional features of corporate culture, and historians can link these ephemera to more traditional sources of information.[49] Corporate information ecosystems and infrastructures were three-dimensional. Pins and coffee mugs have much to teach us as part of that world. One can follow the example of the archeologists and start digging for insights.[50]

But a more focused point is that these objects reflected three fundamental aspects of IBM's world. First, ownership of some of these objects reflected social capital accumulated within the firm, such as the 100 Percent Club pins and even Cross pens, since the latter were used largely by one of the culturally elite communities. Second, these were objects that reflected shared cognitive, attitudinal, and operational behaviors that transcended IBM by spilling into customer data centers—THINK signs are the ubiquitous examples. Third, objects can challenge widely held views about a corporation's culture. IBM was seen as enjoying a highly monolithic, disciplined global culture, yet the coffee mugs suggest that was not quite the case. Recall the gray Consulting Group or Wisconsin mugs. Our discussion also makes obvious that such mundane objects are important and so worthy of a large corporation's attention as they identify with new stakeholders about contemporary issues.

CHAPTER 9

THE ROLE OF AMERICAN POSTCARDS IN SUPPORTING IBM'S IMAGE, MARKETING, AND INFORMATION ECOSYSTEM

As a subset of photographs clearly made rather than "taken," as commodities to be sold, postcards are especially amenable to analysis as visual culture.

David Prochaska and Jordana Mendelson[1]

In the early twentieth century, postcards became a popular source of information about exotic vacation sites, visual testimonials to grand buildings, and local promotional efforts of towns and their main streets, historic homes, and companies. People collected postcards by the millions as souvenirs of interesting trips. Before the availability of small inexpensive cameras, these were often the only images one could acquire conveniently and inexpensively. On both sides of the Atlantic, collecting postcards became wildly fashionable in the decade prior to the start of World War I.[2] Companies realized the communications and advertising value of postcards in the first decade of the new century. Thousands of firms distributed these ephemera depicting their corporate headquarters, modern new factories, and scenes of hundreds of employees posing in front of industrial sites. These humble little cards became so convenient that they also served almost like paper-based text messages—"I'll be home by Saturday," or "The weather is great here." They were inexpensive to mail, too. They took up little room in albums or in trip files.

But few historians have studied postcards. Those who have acknowledge that overlooking this class of ephemera is a mistake.[3]

Business historians have all but ignored this class of ephemera. However, between the turn of the century and the 1980s, businesses did not. One would be hard-pressed to find a major European or American corporation that did not publish postcards. Even a casual glance at postcards for sale on, say, eBay demonstrates that even the most obscure and many long-gone companies published postcards as part of their advertising and branding initiatives. These include companies that had large buildings, such as automotive, shoe, and agricultural equipment manufacturers; electrical supply firms; and even companies that made women's underwear or linings for gloves. Large government agencies, too, participated, such as U.S. cabinet departments, and seemingly every state and national capitol were the subject of such ephemera. Yet because the academic literature on the history and use of postcards is limited, these cards remain a little-understood aspect of business history.[4] A great deal of extant literature consists more of price catalogs, much as long published for stamp collectors.[5]

Historians of industrial photography have studied their subject more thoroughly and have insights that can inform the study of corporate postcards. Briefly summed, these historians see images as informing about the history of institutions and the structure of power and influence within them.[6] That logic takes the historian beyond whatever the image portrays and, as normal for historical analysis, to the issue of context in which a photograph appears or, as in our case, about postcards. The discussion in this chapter is informed more by their methods of analysis than the sparser work of postcard historians. This can be justified because corporations were taking photographs and commissioning postcards at the same time for similar purposes. Photographs of IBM's products and events taken by individuals at the request of company personnel used throughout this book demonstrate that seemingly coordinated purpose of creating desired images.

What do postcards add to our understanding of a company's activities, its desired image, or its advertising initiatives? What role did postcards play in informing employees and customers about a company? With increasing interest in the history of business information ecosystems, there are questions to be asked of postcards as yet another type of documentation embedded into a larger montage of facts and images. To what extent did these postcards endow their users and recipients with some special status? Our purpose is to begin exploring the role of postcards in a business setting through IBM's experience. The historical record is thin, but approaches taken by postcard scholars are useful for extracting insights. This chapter is less intended to be a contribution to the history of postcards than to IBM's corporate culture, image, and messaging. These little ephemera were part of a much larger corporate branding initiative and sustained effort to remain tightly linked to employees and customers. These join a growing list of alternative sources of information about the firm that range from trinkets and monogrammed coffee mugs to pencils and pens and "corporate clothing."[7] Our exercise takes advantage of growing interest and new methods for the study of material culture history by exploring physical objects for insights that traditional archived documents may not provide.[8]

I rely on a cache of over 150 postcards from IBM, ten of which are from NCR, published between 1908 and the 1970s.[9] I first discuss the role of postcards in American corporations and then briefly discuss the power and types of images they projected. This chapter subsequently pivots to a history of IBM's postcards with specific focus on the experience of its facilities in Endicott, New York— Plant No. 1. A second genre of postcards that memorializes events is analyzed through IBM's participation in world fairs. I conclude with an assessment of the role that postcards played in IBM's large and diverse information ecosystem. To the extent postcards permit, this chapter follows cultural anthropological and ethnographic lines of study used by students of this medium.[10] They call for understanding the objects and their meanings, the context and purposes to which they were put, and their mobility and uses.

Postcards and American Corporations

Studies of postcards concentrate on their roles as part of a tourist's experience and as expressions of a community's culture and branding. Sometimes they reflected realistic images, which often were adjusted to project an underlying message or value. One student of the process described it as playing "on culturally held beliefs" to convince visitors to accept a point of view "since it addressed the fundamental question of how we endow visual images with meaning."[11] In other words, for example, a postcard of Hawaii showing coconut trees and hula dancers fit this requirement.[12] There are ramifications of such images that need to be explored. But first, a few basics are in order.

Postcards served as documentation, as evidence, of an experience, such as attending a seminar at an IBM factory or visiting an exotic country.[13] Since Western society privileged photographs as credible evidence, postcards were able to serve a similar purpose. However, as occurred within the tourist industry, one could expect that IBM and other corporations would develop marketing strategies for using attractive images of factories or corporate headquarters to demonstrate their financial success and modernity. Tourist postcards were developed a few years before corporate versions, so lessons about visual marketing were already being practiced immediately before the start of World War I. One of the lessons companies and tourist venues learned was to adjust photographs to create timeless images not specific to some historical reality, such as avoiding anchoring it to a specific date. A picture of a factory should work in 1910 and 1920. Some postcards from IBM's facilities in Endicott, New York, were in use for well over a decade. The adjustment of images (photoshopping to use a modern term) suggests these postcards should be viewed less as historically accurate images and more as expressions of an ideal prescribed condition. Students of postcard history emphasize the value of seeing these as "indicators of different aspects of culture."[14]

While the origins of the postcard date to the mid-nineteenth century, the modern version with a photograph on one side and, on the back, half the space set aside for a message and the other half for an address, and possibly even brief printed text identifying the image, came into wide use during the early decades of the new century.[15] To suggest their popularity, in 1909 alone, nearly one million postcards were mailed in the United States. That does not include the number collected and saved or the high volumes of cards circulating in Europe.[16] Postcards bestowed on their owners the status of being able to travel, while the format offered simple visual "statements packed with information."[17] The originator of a particular card would see it as "a form of self expression or boosterism."[18] Two students of these ephemera explained: "The appeal of postcards was that they, more than any other medium of the day, allowed people to see the world around them and to display their contributions to that world."[19] They make an important point because, as IBM's prestige rose in the 1920s, for someone in the data processing world to have an association with IBM as customer or employee became increasingly prestigious. In a small way, postcards contributed to that self-validation because to acquire these postcards required the owner to visit the IBM facility pictured in one's postcard, and not just anyone could walk into such a building without an important reason. IBM or whatever company one visited routinely gave these away inside the depicted facility. One could then boast about and be recognized for being within that exclusive community, even if ever so slightly.

By 1915, postcards competed for attention with a new generation of cameras used by journalists, professional photographers, and most importantly, individuals. To give postcards a competitive edge over photographs, postcard manufacturers added text describing the image.[20] That change worked deep into the 1930s to differentiate these images from other publications.[21] Technological improvements after World War II sustained interest in postcards, especially with the use of improved photochromic views and use of modern color 35-mm film.[22]

To understand how corporations used these cards, three aspects of the ephemera need to be examined. First, there is the image itself and what it tells the viewer—the key lesson learned from the tourist industry of creating a visual impression. Second, there is the backside text that helps either to reinforce and clarify the intended message from the picture on the other side of the card or to communicate specific information. IBM worked with both sides of the card to create an overall impression. Third, when used, that is to say, when a message was written by the sender and the card mailed, we can learn more about how people responded to the image or location and document the mobility of the card. The experience of IBM postcard users reflected the more widely evident patterns of use by tourists.[23] Looking at each of these dynamics contributes to our understanding of the role of postcards in a company's marketing or advertising strategies.

One can expand on those three aspects by looking at IBM's experience. As a group of scholars pointed out and reaffirmed by IBM's use of postcards and other marketing ephemera, "postcards are objects that circulate within networks of people who are distant and mobile."[24] They reflect widely shared practices of communications and uses. We use the term *information ecosystems*, whereas others use *mobilities*, but both are similar.[25] Each speaks to the movement of images, communication, physical transport of the card from sender to receiver, transport from a welcome desk in a company's lobby to one's briefcase, and transfer of cultural messages. Both concepts acknowledge the infrastructure needed, such as the financial capability to travel and acquire and use such cards, especially from corporations, as one normally needed to take possession of these inside those buildings, not necessarily at a local shop. People entering an IBM building were privileged because they had a relevant purpose for being there. They were managers, employees, or users of "high-tech" data processing equipment in a rapidly modernizing (industrializing) society. Postcards reflected the changing nature of communications from letters to quick notes that could be dashed off almost anywhere, much like a text message versus, say, an email or written paper letter.

Role of Images

Students of postcards begin their analysis with the largest attribute of these documents: the picture that takes up one full side of the card. One team of observers pointed out the following: "Credibility of information transmitted through postcards can be greater compared to specific commercial efforts of a destination. Postcards may reach more than a single individual, and thus they would hold a significant role in raising awareness about the destination not only of the recipient but also others within the social circle of the recipient."[26] This is exactly the central point of any marketing communication, one not lost on IBM. These images helped create a mental image of IBM as a modern high-tech organization, all containing promotional value in an inexpensive way. Image in the world of marketing—hence postcards—refers to the representation of beliefs and impressions over time from multiple sources. In the case of a corporation, impressions—messages—needed to be expressed through a variety of marketing materials in a consistent and constantly repeatable manner. These channels included advertisements, company publications (including newsletters and magazines), product brochures, and gray literature expounding similar messages and even behavior of employees with each other, customers, and other visitors.[27] The operating task was to *coordinate* messaging across all forms of media.

The topic of affective images (how people feel about the destination they visited) has not been well studied, but postcards are known to influence such views.[28] If exposed to positive images, visitors are expected to develop favorable views of the company they visited. Marketing moves a visitor from an unawareness of IBM to one of understanding. Generations of IBM employees brought customers to sales offices, factories, laboratories, and headquarters to do exactly that—to increase deep awareness of the firm. Invariably, visitors left with something of a souvenir to remind and reinforce that awareness. Postcards were one such vehicle, decades later coffee mugs, and, as always, thank-you notes, local meeting agendas, and other handouts.[29] As students of the process argued, "postcards can use the power of imagery to place the recipient figuratively in the picture," triggering memories of the experience of course, but also to "communicate attributes, characteristics, concepts, values, and ideas."[30] While students of postcards enthusiastically imply postcards have enormous influence and hence power of impression on their owners, it remains an unproven assumption. Yet American and European corporations recognized the positive influence of postcards when combined with other marketing activities.

From NCR to IBM: Early Appearance of Postcards

IBM's experience with postcards is a useful exercise to undertake for several reasons. Thomas J. Watson, Sr., leader of IBM from 1914 to 1956—a golden age in the company's use of postcards—came from the National Cash Register Company (NCR) with a fully developed sense of strategy and business practices. Remember, he was forty-two years old in 1914 and had over twenty years of experience. As a consequence, he wanted and was able to rapidly create a corporate culture and set of well-defined practices already learned. He honed his worldview and practices in one of the most admired, best-run companies in the United States—NCR. "The Cash," as it was often called, published postcards, as illustrated below, and Watson applied NCR's same methods at IBM. But why would he engage in such a mundane exercise as encouraging use of postcards? For decades at IBM, he micromanaged, engaging in an enormous number of the details of running all manner of activities there.[31] He fixated on major and minor issues related to the image of IBM. Watson had a distinct point of view on the subject and proved relentless in implementing it. As discussed in earlier chapters, he wanted IBM to be seen as a trusted business advisor to senior management in corporations and government, the producer of high-quality sophisticated office appliances, not the least of which were punch-card tabulators, the predecessors to computers. He wanted to be seen as running a well-operating enterprise known as a prosperous, effective global success—a business icon.[32]

Historians agree that he was successful in meeting each of his objectives.[33] But as a small testimonial to his achievements, consider that at the end of his first year at what eventually became known as IBM, in 1915, he had 1,672 employees worldwide who brought in $5 million in gross income, from which he extracted $1 million in net earnings. In 1935—when many IBM postcards existed—gross income reached $25 million, with $7 million of that converting to net earnings. That year, IBM had 6,268 employees in the United States—all potential consumers of his postcards—and another 2,400 employees in other countries. In 1956, Watson's last year at the helm of IBM, gross income came in at $892 million and net income at $87 million, with an American workforce of 51,192 and a total worldwide force of 72,504 souls, with postcards still being used.[34] Customers who were typical candidates to visit IBM localities numbered in the tens of thousands. His company had achieved iconic status despite its small size in the 1920s and 1930s and was already viewed as an up-and-coming corporation. Postal stamp cancellation marks on IBM postcards demonstrated they had been sent to many parts of the United States.

Did the postcards help achieve all that success? Of course not, but as part of IBM's overall image-creating tools, they assisted because they served as mementos of experiences for customers who spent so many millions of dollars on IBM products and services and had personally engaged with the firm in social and business circumstances.[35] It was no accident that factories and other IBM buildings these customers and especially their American IBM sales personnel visited would be subjects of postcards, flyers, class handouts, and product manuals.

Postcards and Endicott, New York—Plant No. 1

In the 1920s–1960s, much occurred in Endicott, New York, at Plant No. 1. It was here that IBM developed and manufactured its tabulators for decades and trained its American and many non-American equipment maintenance personnel, salesmen, other newly hired employees, and engineers for nearly a century. By the end of the 1930s in Endicott, IBM had manufacturing facilities, a building devoted to research and development, yet another for educating customers and IBM employees, the Homestead where these students and visitors could stay (and where Watson and his wife maintained a suite for their personal use), and the country club. Famous American and European social, military, and political figures routinely came to Endicott; many thousands of customers and employees did too—a practice that continued into the 1980s. More than any other site, Endicott was the preferred locality for IBM's myriad development, manufacturing, education, and customer sales activities for over a half century. So, it should be of no surprise that many types of postcards were published about Endicott over a long period.

Yet there was a problem with these: historians and media studies scholars have completely ignored Endicott's IBM postcard experience. Two experts on the role of image making and tourism may have explained why: "The domain of imagery has long been under 'house arrest' within the broad economy of signs. The rules of engagement with that economy are based on linguistics, so the semiotics of imagery has all too often been subsumed under 'text' and the power of visuality has been underappreciated as witnessings, observations, memory and experience," all of which "have been transformed into the written word."[36] They were not alone in their assessment.[37] Others observed that although images did not use words, they nonetheless had their own grammar and way of expressing messages.[38]

Buildings, nature, and culture entwine in images, each a human artifact in its own way. This circumstance suggests that more was going on than what appeared in an image. See a large factory building and one imagines (or remembers) the hundreds, if not thousands, of people busily at work inside, even conjuring up memories of sound, noise perhaps, smells, taste of food from the cafeteria, and conversations. Visualizations are always explained as cultural landscapes, but one can go further and argue that postcard images called up the activities and points of view in the minds of the postcard owners. So perhaps the admonition that "a picture is worth a thousand words" needs updating to include memories. Look at postcards of where you have been when you acquired these and see what floods into your mind. That is why IBM made so many postcards available to its employees and customers.

As we proceed through a series of postcards, be aware that various renditions of each appeared in every decade, some in black and white and others in brown then color-tinted editions and, by the 1950s, in the now more familiar photographic color. However, the composition of the images remained largely the same, suggesting that changes were more to keep up with evolving publishing technologies, while projecting consistent, even timeless, messages. That messaging remained consistent with the messages evident in IBM's marketing, advertising, and operational practices.

Figure 9.1 is an image of the factory complex of several buildings in Endicott. It portrays a large, imposing, indeed solid, modern-looking building as befits a major manufacturer. It is, of course, smaller than larger factories of the 1920s

INTERNATIONAL BUSINESS MACHINE CORPORATION, ENDICOTT, N. Y.   7A-H467

9.1 IBM's main factory in Endicott, New York, in the 1930s, where it produced tabulating equipment.

(Courtesy, author's collection.)

and 1930s in such industries as steel and automotive manufacturing, but nonetheless, it exudes stability and modernity. Notice that the picture is stylized, as if touched up, but even to this day, these structures look similar with their white exterior.[39] This image suggests it is a large facility with multiple floors dedicated to producing data processing equipment. This particular edition of the card had a long life. This specific copy was mailed from Buffalo, New York, in 1947 to let an unmarried woman know that her "love" would come to see her with a gray suit to wear at Easter. For her, the image made his absence less abstract; for him, it was a reminder that he was not necessarily where he wanted to be.

In the middle of the Great Depression, Watson built a research facility to accommodate his engineers who he touted as highly innovative. Figures 9.2 and 9.3 project images of their building, looking as if it was on a university campus. Its style mimicked buildings found at Harvard University with its cupola, pillars, and American flag. It looked solid, dignified, and imposing. The sepia version had a printed inscription on the back to ensure no doubt as to what it was: "THE IBM LABORATORY at Endicott, N.Y., houses research and development engineering activities of International Business Machines Corporation." IBM published this card; it was not a commercial product one could buy in downtown Endicott. Figure 9.3 shows the same building on a card produced

9.2 IBM engineering laboratory, Endicott, New York. This postcard was given to visitors and used by employees in the 1940s.

(Courtesy, author's collection.)

INTERNATIONAL BUSINESS MACHINE LABORATORY, ENDICOTT, N. Y.

9.3 This is the same building as in figure 9.2, but from the 1930s. Notice it has greater detail, with automobiles shown, and was published in color. "THINK" is etched on the right upper side of the building on the white stone.

(Courtesy, author's collection.)

9.4 IBM's "School" in Endicott, New York, circa 1930s to early 1940s. Barely legible over the main entrance is the word "THINK."

(Courtesy, author's collection.)

by a card manufacturing firm with a more imposing image, the postcard produced for IBM. Near the top as a white band of stone, IBM embossed "THINK" on the building, shown on the card to the front right; also on the right is the full name of the company. A visitor used this card, too, noting on the back that the facility was "monumental."

Figure 9.4 may well have memorialized Watson's favorite building at IBM Endicott, what he and many thousands of IBM employees called the "IBM School." Built despite objections of some members of his board of directors in the depths of the Great Depression, it was used for decades to train employees and customers.[40] This card informed that "THE IBM SCHOOL is the center of IBM Department of Education activities in Endicott, N.Y., where classes are conducted throughout the year for customers and employees of International Business Machines Corporation." For a postcard, that was a detailed marketing message. The image shows people coming and going, much as a similar image of a university building might, again an imposing structure, and the patriotic American flag. Figure 9.5 is a more stylized image of the same building with more context suggesting its scenic yet urban setting. Note that both cards were published in the same style as figures 9.2 and 9.3. It would not have been unusual for a visitor to have acquired a set of these IBM cards from Endicott.

International Business Machines School, Endicott, N. Y.   9A-H2287

9.5 This stylized print, circa 1930s, shows the building soon after it was opened and would have been distributed to all students and visitors there.

(Courtesy, author's collection.)

To quote the next card, "THE IBM HOMESTEAD, overlooking the Susquehanna Valley, is a residence for Endicott guests of International Business Machines Corporation" (figure 9.6). It did not feel like a hotel, but rather like a large home with dozens of bedrooms and a large dining room and a living room that were the settings for casual encounters among employees and customers.[41] Figure 9.7, from the 1950s, depicts the living room where Watson held court with newly hired employees. A portrait of him hangs over the fireplace. The printed text on the back of the card announces that this room is an "attractive lounge" that "provides a relaxed and homelike atmosphere for customers and guests of International Business Machines Corporation."[42] By the time this postcard was used, Watson had been an American business celebrity for over two decades. His portrait moved around IBM and eventually arrived at corporate headquarters. Guests at this facility would be given copies of this and earlier postcards and a sepia brochure describing the homestead illustrated with images of the grand staircase to the second floor, the game room, the lounge, the large dining facility, and a typical bedroom.

Finally, there is "THE IBM COUNTRY CLUB at Endicott, N.Y.," which the postcard announces with an implied pride "is a recreational center

9.6 The IBM Homestead, Endicott, New York, probably in the late 1930s or early 1940s. Notice that there appears to be a small garden party in the front, suggesting a more relaxed environment, as at one's home.

(Courtesy, author's collection.)

9.7 This is an image of the living room at the IBM Homestead in Endicott, New York, circa 1950s. It looked the same essentially into the 1990s, with just minor updates of the sofas. Thomas Watson, Sr., is the subject of the painting hanging over the fireplace.

(Courtesy, author's collection.)

9.8 This is an image of the IBM Country Club in Endicott, New York, 1930s–1940s. The message is clearly to suggest it is a large facility, with many activities, while displaying a golf course used by men and women in a relaxing environment.

(Courtesy, author's collection.)

for employees and guests of International Business Machines Corporation" (figure 9.8). It was located within a short walking distance to the Homestead. It shows the expanse of the setting and golf course, a popular sport among business leaders. Figure 9.9 is a close-up image of the clubhouse itself, also with golfing in the foreground, suggesting relaxation and yet another opportunity for customers and employees to mingle as peers. Over a half-dozen variations of these cards were published before the end of the 1970s. Figure 9.9 (circa 1930s–1940s) had a message directed largely to employees: "IBM COUNTRY Club—the social and recreational center for employees at Endicott. Beautifully located on a scenic tract of more than 700 acres, facilities are provided for 27 different kinds of indoor and outdoor sports." Similar postcards were published for IBM country clubs located at other factory sites, such as in Poughkeepsie, New York and later in California and Europe.

Figure 9.9 has more to teach us. IBM left no stone unturned when touting its paternalistic and, indeed, rich assortment of employee benefits. A country club where annual "membership" was $1 for decades was of enormous appeal to employees and their families in these company towns. These had tennis courts, swimming pools, eighteen-hole golf courses, outdoor spaces, indoor

IBM COUNTRY CLUB

INTERNATIONAL BUSINESS MACHINES CORPORATION, ENDICOTT, N. Y.

9.9 This is a much earlier image of the IBM Country Club in Endicott, New York, emphasizing, as did the prior image (figure 9.8), the size of the clubhouse and golfing. As was more the custom in the 1920s and 1930s, only men are shown golfing.

(Courtesy, author's collection.)

billiards, and classes on all manner of health, medical, political, and other self-help topics. One could take swimming or tennis lessons, children too. Parties were held there for children at Easter, Fourth of July, and Christmas. Families thought highly of these venues. Resident employees probably saw more country club postcards than they did of the other buildings in town.[43] Customers were given more cards of the other local IBM facilities. But in all cases, if a visitor used the cards, they could be left at any IBM building to be mailed at IBM's expense.

Earlier, I mentioned that IBM's use of postcards resembled practices evident at other corporations. A root source of inspiration for IBM's behavior can be gleaned from Watson's experience at NCR, a company whose practices he kept monitoring and borrowing from until at least World War II, by which time he had satisfied a secret desire of surpassing NCR as a great company. Lest there be any doubt about Watson's appreciation for postcards, he is in the middle of the back row in this picture of the "100 Point Club" (figure 9.10). All of these people worked for him in 1908. In addition to images of grand buildings, early-twentieth-century corporations published postcards of employees. Figure 9.11 of NCR's main plant in 1909 in Dayton, Ohio, is a typical example.

9.10 In addition to capturing an image of Thomas J. Watson, Sr., IBM's future leader, in the middle of the back row, this postcard shows other employees who came to work at IBM. This picture was taken while Watson Sr. still worked at NCR.

(Courtesy, author's collection.)

9.11 This is the NCR manufacturing plant in Dayton, Ohio, in 1909. A common practice of the day was to take such photographs with all employees in the picture. Here the women are wearing white blouses, with men behind them in suits. It is quite possible that NCR employees who came to work for IBM in key managerial positions are in the photograph.

(Courtesy, author's collection.)

It is quite possible that Watson is in that image, too. In the 1910s and 1920s, NCR published postcards of its buildings (and country club) and others celebrating events, exuding similar marketing and imaging messages as IBM's postcards.

Figure 9.12 depicts NCR's headquarter offices in 1910–1912. Also published while Watson was still at that company is another image of the main factory in Dayton (figure 9.13). This figure is an iconic image typical of what other manu-facturing companies published, including the Burroughs Corporation (also in the office appliance industry) and the Endicott-Johnson Factory in Endicott, Watson's largest rival for sourcing employees in the area and a firm he admired as a model of a well-run company. The NCR images broadcast size, solidity, respectability, reliability, and success. NCR was a larger company with bigger buildings than IBM in the 1920s and 1930s, but it would be difficult to realize that if one were in Endicott and had not visited Dayton, Ohio, so NCR's larger size would not have been a concern. Through the convenience of examining copies of postcards published just before or at the same time as those from various companies, it becomes obvious that IBM was duplicating their style and messaging as it was emerging, too, as a prosperous and growing company.[44]

9.12 This postcard depicts NCR's corporate headquarters and main office building. It is an imposing image of an eleven-story, three-part building. All other buildings are part of the NCR campus, circa 1910.

(Courtesy, author's collection.)

Plant of The National Cash Register Company, Dayton, Ohio

9.13 This image broadcasts three values IBM management wanted associated with their company: "big," "stable," and "modern." This stylized picture dates from 1910–1912 when Thomas Watson, Sr., was still working at NCR. Many companies at the time published similarly styled images for the same purpose.

(Courtesy, author's collection.)

Memorializing Special Events: The Case of World Fairs

World fairs were hugely popular in the nineteenth and first half of the twentieth centuries. They hosted exhibits about the future of society, new and wondrous technological innovations, and exotic cultures and served as showcases for companies and entire societies and nations. Tens of millions of visitors viewed the exhibits. IBM employees would have recalled the Columbian Exposition held in Chicago in 1893, which drew in 27.3 million people, and the Paris International in 1900 with nearly 51 million attendees.[45] So, when Chicago announced it would host the "Century of Progress" world's fair in 1933–1934, ambitious IBM seized the occasion as an opportunity to showcase its modern products and technological prowess. It proved to be a wise decision, because 48.6 million people came to the fair with countless visitors to IBM's pavilion. That massive exposure was replicated in 1939–1940 when IBM again exhibited, this time in New York, where some 45 million visitors came to the fair.[46] IBM's presence at both world fairs did much to increase the general public's awareness of what was still a small company in comparison to such giants as AT&T, General Electric, or General Motors, firms that also participated in these fairs.

Both events gave the company an opportunity to inform its employees and customers about IBM's products and values. Earned media was free and massive, too, because every major newspaper in the United States published glowing accounts of the optimistic presentations of new products and how they would improve society. IBM basked in that coverage even if it cost the company a fortune to fund its participation. As customary at such events, visitors to the various pavilions were given brochures and other handouts and, of course, postcards. The 1939–1940 fair went down in IBM history, however, for one other reason: the train accident carrying IBM employees and their spouses. Because Watson and his wife personally directed the relief efforts at the site of the accident, a generation of employees never forgot his actions that day. Memories of the event soon had to be pushed aside, however, as World War II had started in Europe and, a year later, would include the United States.

At the start of the 1930s, the world was already in the depths of the Great Depression. IBM was making decisions about its participation in the 1933 world's fair in 1929–1930 and spending money to design and build its pavilion in 1932–1933. In 1932, IBM generated $17 million in revenue and employed nearly 5,000 people in the United States.[47] In 1938, when it again had to spend for the next fair, its revenues amounted to $34 million with a handsome $9 million in net earnings on a base of 7,600 U.S. employees and 11,000 workers total worldwide.[48] In short, the company prospered in the run up to and following both world's fairs. For both events, IBM's marketing and advertising staffs produced the usual assortment of materials: 8 × 10 glossy photographs and press releases for the news media, brochures, advertisements for newspapers and magazines, and postcards for visitors to its exhibits. The exercise was repeated again for the 1964–1965 New York World's Fair—the largest so far in that century. It had over forty-five corporate exhibitors sprawled out over 646 acres. Fifty-one million people attended to see current and future cultural and technological progress underway.[49]

Figure 9.14 is a postcard from the 1933 event, portraying an IBM pavilion that signals that the company was a solid, classic institution. On the back of the card was IBM's message: "This beautiful building of Corinthian Architecture was specially designed and constructed as a display pavilion for International Business Machines. It typifies the leadership which IBM has achieved during the past forty-five years." IBM was declaring that it was victorious in its long march toward bigness, claiming a senior status among iconic corporations, and not going away or shrinking in the face of the Great Depression. It was succeeding. That was an important message to deliver at the height of the Great Depression. In 1933, unemployment in the United States hovered at 23 million people, or 25.6 percent of the workforce.[50]

THE EXHIBIT OF INTERNATIONAL BUSINESS MACHINES CORPORATION, GENERAL EXHIBITS GROUP, CENTURY OF PROGRESS, CHICAGO, 1933.

9.14 This postcard memorializes IBM's presence at Chicago's industrial fair in 1933. These were meant to be souvenirs of one's visit to IBM's exhibit but also meant to impress by showing the exhibit's stability and size, giving one a sense that the firm would be around for a long time.

(Courtesy, author's collection.)

The nation was still in the grips of the Great Depression in 1939. In that year, 9.5 million Americans were still without jobs, with unemployment having only shrunk by 900,000 from the previous year.[51] Watson Sr. had been optimistic that the depression would go away all through the 1930s and famously was criticized by employees, his board of directors, and CEOs of his competitors for investing too much in that optimism.[52] We saw that optimism about the future reflected in the postcards about Endicott published in the 1930s. In hindsight, Watson's optimism was well founded, as IBM's revenues grew from 1929 through 1939 with only a small dip in 1932 and 1933, while employment increased from 6,000 to over 11,000 in 1939.[53]

For the 1939–1940 fair, internal publications promoted the exhibition with what one today would refer to as a "full-court press." Watson Sr. played a direct role in the promotion of the fair. If we look at one postcard from the period, you can see signals of what was being communicated about IBM (figure 9.15). This is an interior image of its exhibit, displaying the wide variety of current "high-tech" products. Along the walls, IBM exhibited its rapidly growing collection of

GALLERY OF SCIENCE AND ART, WORLD'S FAIR OF 1940 IN NEW YORK

International Business Machines Corporation's Building

9.15 This postcard shows the interior of IBM's exhibit at the New York World's Fair in 1940. IBM went to great pains at this fair to introduce itself to the general public as a major corporation and to be compared to such other giants as General Electric and General Motors.

(Courtesy, author's collection.)

art from all of the American states and possessions. IBM's exhibit was situated in the Gallery of Science and Art, which helps to explain the thematic combination of art and machines.[54] On the back of the card, we see the explanation as "an unusual display of the talents of 53 painters—and 300 International Business Machines Corporation Research Engineers and their assistants." Thousands of employees received these cards, and many were these "engineers and their assistants" brought in from Endicott and many more thousands who had taken the train from that little town of 17,702 residents to New York City, the largest urban center in the United States of 7.5 million souls.[55] It was quite a difference for those employees and their spouses.

For the 1964 world's fair, IBM reverted back to its 1933 strategy of putting up a building. In this case, it became one of the iconic structures of the event. Recall that after World War II IBM had embarked on a complete makeover of the company's image from buildings to products, from marketing to advertising, all to make the firm appear more modern and to coordinate its activities more closely than possible during the frenetic years of World War II. Postwar economies represented a new era of growth and opportunity. By the time the

1964 fair came along, IBM had been reshaping its image for over a decade.[56] IBM's exhibit consumed 1.2 acres, and its large Ovoid Theater hovered almost one hundred feet above the ground. Well-known product and building designers Eero Saarinen and Charles Eames designed the building, exhibits, messaging, advertising, and ephemera distributed to the media, customers, employees, and visitors.[57]

Figure 9.16, produced by IBM, illustrates the company's unique building. It far exceeded IBM's physical presence of 1939–1940. By the 1960s, IBM was well on its way to becoming the dominant computer company of its day. To put a fine point on the matter, in 1963—the year before its pavilion opened but when expenses for it were required—IBM's revenues came in at $497 million, generating net earnings of $364 million by 46,000 employees. A mere five years later, in 1968, revenues reached $6.9 billion, with net earnings of $871 million, and IBM employed nearly 242,000 people.[58] IBM's senior management was optimistic about IBM's future at the start of the decade, and the firm was already large and well known. The public and IBM's customers recognized it as modern, reflecting the future of the nation's economy. Within that overarching context of IBM's environment, this postcard calmly explained that the exhibit was about "computers and other modern information-handling devices." There no

9.16 This watercolor postcard shows the outside of the building where IBM had its exhibit at the New York World's Fair in 1940. It was a dramatic image intended to make IBM look larger and more spectacular than its size warranted at the time.

(Courtesy, author's collection.)

longer was any need to hype the message; that was left to magazine advertisements, as was the practice of the day.[59] The postcard explained visitors would be raised up to the theater, "into the information machine." Perhaps IBM's importance was validated by another postcard, this one not produced by IBM but commercially available for sale at the fair, that displayed an image of the building with its iconic oval theater.

Other fair postcards appeared. For example, for a fair in Brussels in the 1950s, an image of a trendy modern building is accompanied by a message on the back declaring in English that this card was "for free distribution at the 1958 Brussels" fair and was available "exclusively" there. Ten years later at the 1968 World's Fair in San Antonio, Texas, the company distributed a postcard showing an interior image (figure 9.17). It projected a highly contemporary image of computer equipment (S/360 computers) and viewers in front of television screens. What were they viewing? The back of the card explains that Charles Eames, who designed the building and exhibit, had prepared "a light-hearted informative movie explaining the operation of modern computers." It was very

I.B.M. Durango Pavilion

9.17 This is an interior view of IBM's exhibit at the world's fair held in San Antonio, Texas, in 1968. Every detail of what one saw was coordinated with the design of IBM's publications and machines of the period, including the presence of its System/360 computer in the background and interactive screens in the front. It was all revolutionary and very advanced for its time.

(Courtesy, author's collection.)

much in the style of the 1960s, while a careful examination of its details shows integration of colors from machines to walls and lamp shades, classic Eames design. In short, even postcards did not escape his creative attention. These were that important, too.

What Can Recipients of Postcards Teach Us About IBM?

While it is not possible to answer this question with certainty, especially based on just 150 postcards, anecdotal and inferential evidence suggest possibilities. First, postcards were highly collectable throughout the twentieth century, so it would not have been uncommon for visitors to IBM locations to acquire these for their own personal collections or to give these to their children who, too, collected. That behavior would explain why so many were preserved that were not mailed or written on. In two instances, I acquired (a) a welcome packet for newly hired employees coming to Endicott in the early 1960s and (b) an education manual of the same period, both of which contained within them a postcard of the Homestead. So, might we conclude that many individuals acquired these cards and tucked them into their briefing materials obtained on their visits to IBM localities?

Second, about a third of the collection was used, often to announce when someone would be returning home after a trip to an IBM site or to comment about the weather. These cards were postmarked from the 1930s through the 1970s and mailed to all parts of the United States. It is not clear if the senders were employees or customers; however, what is obvious is that they came from across the nation. Other insights are evident as well. In 1945, one sales trainee commented that his "sales training at Endicott will be completed this week." But just as interesting, he announced that on Wednesday his class would be taken to Poughkeepsie to take a factory tour and then go to "World Headquarters building in New York City."[60] That same year, a postcard of the Endicott factory written by "Alice" declared that her trip there was "nice," but "enough is enough. I'm no traveler." In August 1941, an attendee at IBM's training let it be known to his father in New Jersey that "the food is fine and there are some 50 sports one can enjoy."

Other positive messages were the norm. Writing to a Miss Olga Badin of Holgate, Ohio, in 1939, "Harold" sent a postcard of the Homestead to announce that the countryside at Endicott was "beautiful" and that this is where he was staying. An undated postcard from the 1930s showing the factory building declared: "Everything is swell right now. I'm studying!" A postcard postmarked 1951 showing the laboratory building (similar to figures 9.2 and 9.3) has a message from "Bill" to a Miss Angela Justynski in Flint, Michigan, informing her that "the brains stay here all day" and that he was "doing OK so far and will try to keep it up." One card dated 1954 made it known that at Plant One there are 9,600 employees, "no unions," and "employee relations seem to be excellent. Utopia!!!" In a postcard (figure 9.4) postmarked in April 1956—a very late date for this card, which had been distributed since at least the early 1940s—"Dad" tells his family in Michigan, "This is where I go to school each day. It is all very interesting," and that the "snow is gone and the weather is nice." In 1962, a resident at the Endicott Homestead reported it "is certainly a most pleasant one." But even more telling, "Work (school) is not interfering too seriously with recreational facilities."

Postcards from other factory sites in the 1960s and 1970s carried similar messages. Technicolor images of factories were taken from aircraft, showing their sprawling buildings and large parking lots. Such facilities employed between 3,000 and 6,000 people and also had training facilities and customer demonstration centers. One postcard showing IBM's factory in Poughkeepsie, primary home for the company's computer development and manufacturing in the 1960s, sent to a lady in California, delivered a message from two other women that they "were having a wonderful time" but they also "had six weeks of snow." At the same time, Carl Busler wrote to family in Oregon from Poughkeepsie on a local IBM Homestead postcard that he had been there "for a week going to school. It is rather nice but have to be in class all day." IBM was still delivering messages to visitors. For example, a postcard of the IBM plant in Lexington, Kentucky, where the Office Products Division manufactured its popular Selectric typewriters, let the reader know that the factory was "dedicated in 1959," implying it was a very modern state-of-the-art facility of 28.8 acres of floor space. The themes of the 1920s and 1930s seemed alive: declarations of prosperity, modernity, growth, reliability, and stability.

Then there is the postcard of the IBM building in Dallas, Texas. Built in the 1970s in that colorful, boxy, multicolored industrial style of the period, the card had on the back, "Texas Headquarters for Sales, Service and Education Center of International Business Corporation at 2911 Cedar Springs Road." Field operations rarely warranted their own postcards, but then again, this was Texas. How could it not have a postcard? This one was available in the lobby, as was one in these same years at Endicott's School House building, the latter showing its refurbished contemporary interior foyer. The Texas one announced, as had many from other locations, "having a nice time." Since so much training was conducted here, largely for IBM sales, systems engineering, and some field engineering employees, a postcard was needed. Traffic soon diminished at the site when a few years later a training center was built closer to the local airport, which soon became known as the "Love Boat" because of its shape and due to the behavior of some newly hired employees. That facility apparently never published a postcard.

Role of Postcards in IBM's Information Ecosystem

As argued in this chapter, IBM's postcards were created as part of a larger mosaic of integrated messages directed to the public at large. That action was consistent with the public relations practices of other corporations keen to establish their legitimacy as worthy institutions in the industrializing economy.[61] How that was done evolved over time. For example, scenes of thousands of workers posing in front of a factory before World War I spoke to bigness, but not to a family culture. At IBM, where part of the internal mantra for decades blared "IBM Family," such images were rare, even in local factory newsletters at such sites as Endicott, Poughkeepsie, and Rochester, Minnesota. That same observation held for facilities in France and Germany, for example, in all periods. One saw images that contained only a few people, normally walking about as one might see in other settings, such as on a university campus. Most postcards did not include images of people, and rarely even a scene that could be dated. Figure 9.1 of the Endicott plant had an automobile parked in front of the building, a rare example. However, it was purposeful as one could identify the automobile as a modern technology rapidly being adopted across the nation, reinforcing the message that IBM was part of that modern world.

World fairs offered examples of large firms displaying their corporate images to employees, customers, and the general public, less so as an opportunity to sell products. One would not expect a visitor at an IBM pavilion to seek out a salesman to acquire an expensive tabulating machine, nor even a brass cash register at an NCR exhibit. Rather, as historian of advertising Roland Marchand explained, "American corporations . . . came to see the great expositions more as public relations projects than as an area for technical exchange and sales promotion."[62] IBM fit his description. As argued in this book, IBM wanted to be recognized as a large and progressive modern enterprise that was economically successful and good for society. Its postcards were expected to contribute to these objectives, as were all other marketing and advertising materials. When Watson brought thousands of employees to the world's fair of 1939–1940, he was not trying to sell them equipment, let alone teach them about these products—they designed, made, and sold these—rather he was reinforcing bonds among employees, their families, and the company. It was a lifelong objective of his, part of what became known as the "IBM Way." Postcards of country clubs and homesteads were intended to further entwine the "IBM Family." That objective hardly diminished until the late 1980s.

But in exchange for job security and benefits, the IBM Family had to tow a line: employees had to contribute to the betterment of society and to IBM. The images on postcards displayed in this chapter were largely produced in the 1920s through the 1940s, with the majority issued in the 1930s. These were challenging times when unemployment was high, so IBMers should be grateful

282 CASES FROM IBM'S MATERIAL CULTURE

that they were gainfully employed and that the economy was industrializing and becoming technologically more sophisticated. So there was IBM with tools to help tame and control what a 1936 Charlie Chaplin movie, *Modern Times*, conjured by the Little Tramp, depicted as a struggle to survive an age of machines and industrialization. That responsibility of the IBM community and the equally collective message of corporate America that technology and the modern enterprise held out hope for the betterment of the economy and way of life were on full display at world fairs and also, if less dramatically, in postcard images of factories and laboratories.[63]

Postcards published after World War II were available alongside older prewar ones. But postwar postcards differed, too. Those from Poughkeepsie, Rochester, Minnesota, and Europe displayed images of large newly constructed buildings, with the camera positioned almost an eighth of a mile or so away to make possible the wide shots required, or they were taken from aircraft flying over the massive rooftops and parking lots below. These were not as artistically elegant as earlier images, but they still conveyed messages of modernity, bigness, and permanence. No longer did corporations need to defend their legitimacy and positive contributions to society; they had arrived, they were permanent fixtures of modern economies. Country clubs were still subjects for postcards, but buildings were devoid of life, as there were no people to be seen. No apologies were required for emphasizing the humanity of such organizations. The war for acceptance had been won, largely through the efforts of these large enterprises in support of the nation's wartime efforts. In IBM's case, it had also bonded its employees to the firm in other ways, such as by mailing its company newsletters and other ephemera to those serving in the American military and paying them 25 percent of their salaries while in military service. We know little about how IBM in other countries communicated with their military employees in Europe. It was clear that post–World War II postcards were now playing a lesser role in corporate branding worldwide but still had not been completely retired because they retained their popularity as a genre of communications and image setting.

At a minimum, they continued to be corporate souvenirs of trips to IBM's facilities. From the 1920s to the end of the century, employees and visitors were routinely given a variety of paper items and trinkets to remind them of their encounters with the firm. Postcards were the fashionable mementos of the 1920s and 1930s. In the 1930s through the 1980s, those attending classes were also given monogrammed binders of teaching materials and information about the company's products. From the 1920s, too, photographs were taken of visiting groups, classes, and celebratory events with which to recall their IBM experience. These often included carefully annotated identification of each participant, much like a high school or college yearbook. By the 1970s, one might be given key chains with a computer chip embedded in a small clear plastic block, or a miniature plastic model of a personal computer in the following decade. Monogrammed coffee mugs were everywhere by the end of the 1980s.

We remain ignorant regarding much about corporate postcards. One cannot walk into IBM's corporate archives and ask to see records on the creation of these cards; so much of that dialogue is lost to history. Nor are we at a point to know how many various cards were produced. We still need to read thousands of cards mailed by visitors to IBM to see what they said about IBM and to where these postal messengers traveled, not a few dozen, as convenient as they were for writing this chapter. Our sample of such communications seems uncomfortably too small. The ones studied delivered positive messages, but we do not know if that was a common theme. Were visitors impressed and pleased by their encounters with IBM? Did the postcards achieve their objectives of promoting and informing about IBM and of incorporating visitors into IBM's information ecosystem? At this time, one can only guess and, in the process, surmise that they did. Their role was to deliver aspirational messages of success. We can reach such conclusions because they were part of the larger collection of marketing materials, which we know were effective in doing that for decades.[64]

Postcards provided one set of images of IBM, the impressions the corporation wanted the world to hold. Another perspective existed about the company presented in images by way of photocopied cartoons and other humor. These did more than affirm that employees had a funny bone; they shed light on the nature of the company's culture, as seen on the ground floor. That perspective is the subject of the next chapter, providing balance to the story told with postcards.

CHAPTER 10

HUMOR AND CORPORATE CULTURE

IBM, Cartoons, and the Good Laugh

If you can't dazzle them with brilliance, baffle them with bovine substance!

Anonymous, 1980s

For generations, customers, historians, government regulators, and competitors viewed IBM as a no-nonsense serious enterprise. Certainly its successes in shaping the role of information technologies around the world for over a century and the intensity with which it competed against rivals or defended itself in the courts confirmed that it was a disciplined enterprise.[1] Historians, industry observers, and IBM memoirists universally attribute the nature of IBM's behavior to its corporate culture, ubiquitous across the firm and finely tuned in most periods to support its business objectives.[2] While this book is about this company's culture, it bears reminding how serious everyone seemed to view it, especially since, with few exceptions, its culture was admired, especially by its customers, and envied or feared by its competitors. Other global enterprises developed their own cultures, which, too, were seen as keys to their successes with the result that, since the 1970s, the subject has been studied.[3] But, because what constitutes corporate culture and its features remains subject to debate, this chapter promises to add another twist to how one explores the topic.[4]

There has been some acknowledgement that one component of corporate culture is the role of humor; we elevate the topic's importance, largely because it seemed "everyone" in IBM's ecosystem had a hand in its creation and enjoyment.[5] But, almost every study of corporate humor conducted by students of humor begins with a near-obligatory lamentation at the lack of case studies and theoretical constructs, merely the existence of "frameworks" that could be used to understand the nature of humor and less so the role of humor in business behaviors.[6] Scholars who study business managerial and operational behaviors have yet to take up the study of humor as a method for gaining insights into corporate culture, which they too lament is not well understood.[7] This chapter demonstrates they can do better. Managers can learn that humor can play a profound role in shaping an organization's culture and image without having to fear it all going negative. If there is one truth about corporate humor, it is that it exists regardless of what corporate image makers think or want. As companies acknowledge that they have to pay more attention to a widening coterie of stakeholders, they should see humor as another lever to pull, another activity to pay attention to as "market signals." In other words, scholars and corporations should take humor seriously.

Describing the nature and role of humor in an enterprise can contribute useful insights about its culture, values, and behaviors, three elements widely embraced by those who study corporate cultures.[8] As serious as IBM has long been, it physically had within its buildings a vibrant humorous ethos that reflected many of the attitudes and behaviors of its employees and customers. Indeed, humor has linked together both communities—IBMers and their customers—for a century, not as their primary bond, but as a contributing glue holding together relations at the personal level. Although corporate management was building a no-nonsense image of IBM and its employees were serious when on the job, they also drank beer, held parties, performed skits, sang songs, and told jokes. For our study, about 25 percent of the ephemera examined was too risqué for even your prudish retired IBM author to reveal. So, there clearly is an underbelly to IBM's culture that may remain hidden to history. The purpose of this chapter is to begin describing the kinds of humor within IBM and to proffer insights about its use. It is currently not possible to describe the full scope of its role, but one can begin to identify bits and pieces based on extant ephemera from the 1970s through the 1990s.

The central qualifying criteria for consideration are paper ephemera such as cartoons, chain letters, and emails that circulated physically within the walls of IBM. Every document consulted was collected from employees within their buildings, with some coming from other firms circulating within those same structures. So, every document was acquired, seen, and distributed by employees, normally within the course of their workdays. That is an important observation: evidence of the physical existence of humor *within* IBM. To put a fine point on this observation, figure 10.1 is a photograph of the ephemera used in this chapter; every item was acquired onsite in IBM offices in the United States—New Jersey, New York, Tennessee, Georgia, Florida, Minnesota, and

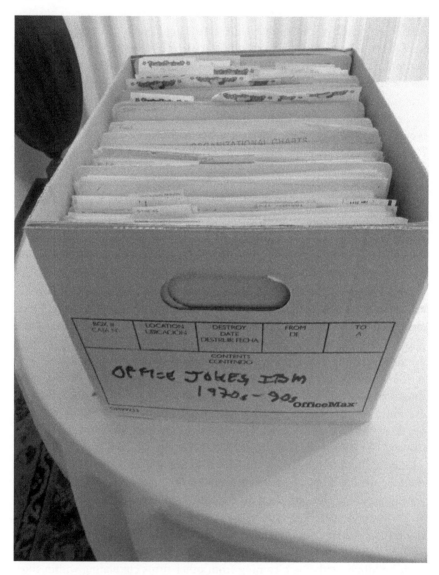

10.1 This collection of IBM humor is a testimonial to the kinds of jokes circulating within IBM in the 1970s–1990s in the United States.

(Courtesy, author's collection.)

Wisconsin—between the early 1970s and the late 1990s. It is not a comprehensive collection, just what was physically acquired in those localities. That sampling, however, reflects a broad range of topics that crowd under the umbrella of corporate humor.[9]

To contribute to the discussion of the role of humor in large corporations, I focus only on IBM's experience. I begin with a brief discussion of the links understood to exist between corporate culture and humor, but I focus less on the nature of humor, which is of central interest to students of humor and cultural anthropologists, and more on business operational issues in which humor plays a role. So, this is a business history essay, less a contribution to humor studies. Yet perspectives of humor scholars inform our work. I catalog types of humor evident in IBM, drawing upon the collection of ephemera that serves as the source evidence. Based on that material, we can explore the role of humor inside IBM, acknowledging that, at best, such an exercise is cursory, but a start within the study of IBM's corporate culture. This chapter concludes with a brief consideration of the implications about what humor can teach others studying corporate culture, aimed at addressing the needs of business historians. Managers learned in the 1980s and 1990s that humor was a positive activity and so have a growing body of practices they draw upon, which scholars have only just begun to understand. It is the business historian, however, who needs insights, so that is to whom I address this chapter. Not commented on is the massive body of computer humor that flowed through all industries since the 1950s, which others have studied.[10] That humor also flowed simultaneously through IBM and its customers' organizations.

Students of American humor point out a problem encountered, too, in this study of IBM humor. It is difficult to reproduce cartoons without often going through an enormous expense in time and money to obtain permissions from publishers and cartoonists to reproduce these materials, making it otherwise impractical to do so without violating American and European copyright laws. A related concern is that many of the cartoons circulating inside corporations were photocopies without attribution, and so it is difficult to establish their origins. For those reasons, you will not see as many illustrations as one might desire, nor the normal citations of sources, other than that these are copies of cartoons that circulated within IBM and were collected in what figure 10.1 illustrates.[11]

Links Between Corporate Culture and Humor

Let's begin with the most obvious link: ubiquitous availability of free photocopying anywhere within IBM and its customers' firms. Since at least the early 1970s, what came to be known as "photocopylore" and "faxlore" became widespread.[12] The technology made it possible to copy and distribute materials easily and, just as important (if not more so), anonymously. A "Xeroxed" sexually explicit or profanity-laced joke could have come from anyone. A cartoon critical of an employer could not be conclusively traced back to a disgruntled individual. One's prejudices could be put on display for pleasure: sexist materials, racially insensitive matter, and some outrageous pornography, for example. Materials that made lighthearted fun of a typical work condition were always popular and could draw a smile. Since management did not approve such uses of photocopying, these badly overcopied cartoons and jokes took on a mildly subversive quality, a form of gentle protest against the firm. In companies that had unionized workforces, such photocopying proved far more serious, as the technology could be used to upset the workforce, organize strikes, or worse. And of course, all these materials were in blatant violation of copyright laws, adding to the sense of naughtiness involved in their distribution. In the 1990s, telecommunications made it possible to begin downloading and transmitting remotely cartoons and jokes, adding to the humor milieu in a company.[13] To put a fine point on the use of this technology, one scholar concluded that "the photo-copy machine has been the most frequently used device for the unofficial circulation of humor, and accordingly had the dominant effect on that tradition."[14]

In the 1970s, the practice of photocopying expanded to such an extent that the U.S. Congress considered reforming copyright laws, while even Xerox Corporation executives wondered aloud if they had unleashed a Prometheus, with every person now a publisher of "nonsense." One historian pointed out that copying materials had become "an illicit thrill."[15] Workers could distribute off-color materials, fake memorandum, or even illustrations of their fannies. The examples paralleled exactly the materials uncovered at IBM, from pornographic *Peanuts* cartoons to fake project schedules to outrageous and often humorous memorandum from management on corporate letterhead. It was all part of an increased flow of information that companies and government agencies experienced. It is a useful point to make because one normally thinks of the flow of information in an enterprise as largely due to the arrival of distributed data processing, which occurred at the same time as photocopying began experiencing its own golden age. Photocopied humor became part of a much broader transformation in how information ecosystems expanded in the 1970s and 1980s.

Humor scholars focus more attention on the nature of verbal jokes than on cartoons, but those who do point out pictorial representations observe that pictures have two features: an image (i.e., "iconic character") and a symbolic nature. Both must be present to "get the joke," especially when one is highly specific to an organization.[16] In other words, understanding the context of the joke is essential. IBM's versions meet these two criteria and thus serve as added evidence of the relevance of understanding IBM's experience for the humor scholar. It is also why this chapter is offered up following earlier ones describing the world inside IBM. Studies of cartoons point out that content falls generally into several categories: gender and social stereotypes, political and social aspects, and sexual themes.[17] Students of the medium define cartoons "as a humor-carrying visual/visual-verbal picture, containing at least one incongruity that is playfully resolvable in order to understand their punch line." In other words, "cartoons are jokes told in a picture."[18] This is the definition used to categorize IBM humor documents as cartoons. These are not to be confused with comics; comics more often tell stories, and their artwork is normally more detailed and sophisticated. In contrast, a cartoon is normally one or few panels and usually crudely drawn. The majority of the IBM cartoon sources are one panel. Faces expressing emotions, such as anger, stupidity, shock, lust, and so forth, are common features of such artwork. Such documents exaggerate and simplify circumstances, and thus, those elements should be identified.[19] Exaggerated heights or physical features are common. It has been suggested that exaggerations with stronger contrasts to reality evoke heightened reactions.[20]

Humor scholars ask: What makes a cartoon funny? It is an important question because yet another boring document coming across one's desk or handed out to colleagues at IBM might not receive much attention beyond the mundane requirements of a job, let alone be memorable. In contrast, funny cartoons stimulate a response, such as a smile, laughter, or muffled giggles. Much of the language and observations used to describe cartoons are not yet sufficiently theory based for students of humor, so much remains speculative, such as about eye movement, juxtapositioned ideas and images, and cognitive responses.[21] Humor experts acknowledge that cartoons and other forms of humor are triggering mechanisms for procedural, social, and emotional responses and behavior. There is growing evidence, too, that humor patterns persist in circumstances of high and low job insecurity.[22] This is a crucial point because at IBM cartoon humor existed in times of low job insecurity (1950s–1980s) and in periods of high job insecurity (1990s–2000s). In the former situation, humor reinforces positive feelings toward quirky work circumstances (e.g., so many forms to fill out) and group bonding through shared identities, while in the latter instance, an individual has to govern more closely how they respond to humor and see it more as a criticism of their personal reality.

Types of Humor Evident in IBM

Humor existed inside of IBM, as in other enterprises and organizations, at all levels and around the world. However, IBM simultaneously spent a century cultivating a serious image of itself and vigorously paid attention to the details of its business. IBM did this to such an extent that it was able to dominate the tabulating business (1890s–1950s) with 90+ percent market shares and then the mainframe market (1960s–1980s) with 60–80+ percent market shares, depending on different national markets. The iconic image IBM marketing and advertising projected is captured in the iconic photograph of Thomas J. Watson, Sr. (figure 10.2), who, while paternalistic and admired, was not in the habit of displaying humor in public. However, figure 10.3 shows him in a different pose, a hint that, as was customary even in his era, employees displayed humor in their work lives. Until the 1980s, when it introduced the personal computer, the company did an excellent job of hiding from the public its internal penchant for humor. But at the individual level, humor abounded.

Materials flowing through IBM fall into several categories. One category can be described as cartoons. These show animals, people, and fictitious characters. They were routinely presented on 8 × 11–inch sheets of photocopier paper and had been copied so many times—Xeroxed to use a contemporary term—that they were often barely discernable. The poor quality of illustrations displayed below reflects that reality. Some cartoons had been published in national magazines or industry publications that were continuously reproduced and circulated among IBMers and their customers. A second category consists of letters or announcements about changed company policies. Like the cartoons, they were forms of fiction, sometimes reproduced on a company's letterhead or included in company logoed slide presentations, which for the latter is how we know they made it into formal speeches and other internal meeting discussions. Variations of these documents included typed poems and songs (e.g., *'Twas the Night Before Christmas*). Texts of standup jokes represented a third category of materials that one could incorporate in a speech or other presentation. The most benign of these materials were posted on bulletin boards in data centers and offices of technical staff and IBM field engineering workspaces. Field personnel often had one or more of these in their briefcases, and these certainly appeared in slide presentations for decades.

IBMers who were frequent public speakers collected these for their own use. Some are included in the collection used for this chapter. The tape marks from posting these to slides in the pre-PowerPoint era are in evidence on some of the ephemera. The collection includes cartoon slides, the famous 3M clear plastic versions known to generations of IBMers and customers as "foils." These latter ephemera have not stood the test of time well for chemical reasons and so are hard to find in corporate archives but were once so ubiquitous that when IBM's new chairman, Louis V. Gerstner, came into the company in 1993 he complained that executives could not conduct a conversation without using these. When he dismissed Robert J. ("Bob") LaBant as head of IBM's North American

10.2 Thomas J. Watson, Sr., of IBM in 1948. This is the image IBM wanted of itself and of its long-term leader. It stands in sharp contrast to the image presented in figure 10.3.

(Courtesy, IBM Corporate Archives.)

10.3 Thomas J. Watson, Sr., of IBM in the early 1950s. He is sporting a Dutch wooden shoe. It was common practice at IBM to display humor and present skits satirical of IBM. The company was famous for conservative attire, including leather shoes, except, perhaps, as in this photograph in the Netherlands.

(Courtesy, IBM Corporate Archives.)

business in 1995, 3M's stock coincidently dropped in value by several points that week; employees joked that it was because nobody replacing him would require such an extensive use of foils as he had allowed.

The subject matter of all these various ephemera fell into two categories; some were about life in general, and others were more specifically focused on IBM or some other vendor. Both were seen as comments about IBM's wider ecosystem of employees and customers. Table 10.1 lists general categories of these ephemera in no particular order. Note the diversity of topics.

They also reflect contemporary attitudes. For example, many were derogatory about women, ethnic groups, and classes of workers to an extent that would be impossible to present today in serious scholarly publications. Cartoons, for example, exaggerated female anatomy, while facial representations of ethnic men mimicked art in evidence in Nazi Germany in the 1930s characterizing Jews and Slavs, for instance. A variant of cartoons portrayed exaggerated illustrations of male sexual organs. Students of humor observe that such representations of groups and genders are a widespread genre of humor in all forms, so these IBM materials reflected similar behaviors.[23]

More shocking to our current sensibilities is how extensively foul language is used, again so frequently and extensively that one would prefer not to publish such materials in a scholarly publication. However, it is not difficult to explain the wide use of such language. Prior to the 1980s in the United States, IBM constituted a largely male culture in which use of foul language was more prevalent than after female employees populated all parts of the company and customer organizations. That observation applies to the sexist characterizations of women. In the 1980s, disparaging ethnic groups as a socially acceptable behavior also declined so sharply that every example in the collection predates the mid-1980s, whereas some of the sexist language and characterizations lingered to the end of the decade, albeit as a virtually underground flow of humor. The vast majority of the materials listed in table 10.1 were typed or drawn by individuals; few were extracted from published professional cartoonists or national publications.

TABLE 10.1 General Topics of Corporate Humor Ephemera, 1970s–1990s

Christmas	Ethnic—general	Stories
Feelings/emotions	Ethnic—Italian	Beliefs
Horoscopes	Ethnic—Polish	Quality
Recipes	People—types	Productivity
Language/words	Religious	Bureaucracy

Some served as shells for other commentary. Figure 10.4 is from a set of slide shells variously attributed to Xerox, 3M, IBM, and other companies, but because users did not provide attribution of sources, their origins cannot be identified definitively and are thus possibly lost to history. These images of cavemen, humorous to be sure, allowed one to add a message in the text bubble and so were widely used in IBM, particularly in the 1970s. A popular image that appeared frequently in presentations was of a duck above and below the water line with the advice, "The secret of success is to stay cool and calm on top and paddle like HELL underneath!" Above the water line, the duck is still, perhaps with a cigarette hanging out of its mouth, while underwater, its feet are moving furiously. The cartoon's advice resonated with employees in pressure-filled jobs, as in sales, maintenance, or product development. One that circulated for over two decades was of a canoe (figure 10.5) clearly not designed properly. It spoke to the problem that some IBM products were not as well conceived as employees wanted (e.g., 8100 or PC Jr.).

On occasion, characters from the popular *Peanuts* cartoons were recruited to help express emotions with home-drawn images, such as the one with characters sitting on the curb with one sadly declaring, "Doing a good job around here is like wetting your pants in a dark suit [what IBMers were famous for wearing]—it gives you a warm feeling, but nobody notices." Perhaps the most widely distributed joke has the dog from *Peanuts* on the commode declaring that, "No job is complete 'til the paperwork' is done!" At IBM, it seemed everyone complained about bureaucracy, expressed as "paperwork" from the chairman's office to the newly hired entry-level employee.

There were variations of the middle-finger salute as a statement of defiance and frustration with circumstances: the grandmother walking with a can of gas because her car ran out of fuel, Mickey Mouse smiling and saluting, or a mouse gesturing to a fearsome attacking bird with the tagline, "The last great act of DEFIANCE" or its optional text, "When faced with total disaster defiance is the only recourse." Many complexities confronted employees, not the least of which involved developing new products and installing or fixing them. Complaints of insufficient communications from management were rife from the founding days of the company. In the 1970s and 1980s, cartoons of mushroom-like people circulated with the lead line, "I think I am a mushroom, because they keep me in the dark and feed me Bull . . . !" A printout from the 1970s of Snoopy as a World War I pilot produced out of a series of Xs, asterisks, and dashes shows him yelling out, "Screw you Red Baron." The same software was often used to produce birthday and Christmas cards on eighty-column IBM cards years earlier.

Stories were often typed texts that circulated widely and, in some instances, were written-down jokes, the latter a topic not taken up in this chapter, but that can be defined as humor communicated orally, such as the standard jokes

MVS

DL/I   INTRODUCTION

2/20/75

10.4 This is one of a series of cartoons in which one would add in the stone above the man serious or humorous messages. These were widely infused into slide (foil) presentations of the 1970s and 1980s. MVS and DL/1 were early IBM database management software products.

(Courtesy, author's collection.)

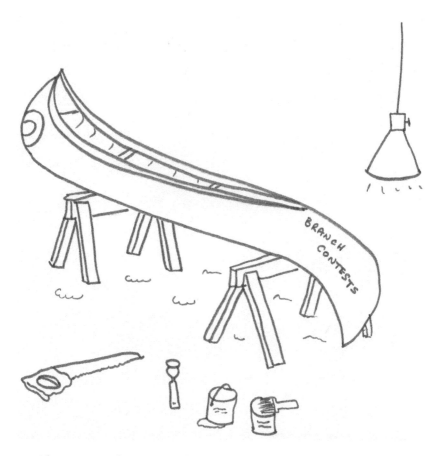

10.5 The message is that no matter how much planning one does, something is always going to go wrong. Branch contests refers to initiatives to stimulate sales increases, typically within the next ninety days.

(Courtesy, author's collection.)

that transcended industries and jobs (e.g., "How many IBMers does it take to change a light bulb?" or "Three guys walk into a bar: a salesman, a customer engineer, and a manager"). One copied so often that its text is barely discernable but can be quoted in polite society came from IBMers whose customers included many union staff (unions were not popular within IBM): "Four Union workers were discussing how smart their dogs were. The first was a United Auto Workers' member who said his dog could do math calculations . . . named T-Square, and he told him to go to the blackboard and draw a square, a circle and a triangle, which the dog did with no sweat." The United Steelworkers' dog, named Slide-rule, was instructed to "fetch a dozen cookies and bring them back and divide them into 4 piles of 3." The Teamsters' dog, named "Measure," was told to "get a quart of milk and pour 7 ounces into a ten-ounce glass." Again, there were no problems. Finally a longshoreman asked his dog, named "Coffee Break," to "Show the fellows what you can do!" "Coffee Break went over and ate the cookies, drank the milk, filed for Workmen's Compensation and left for home on sick leave."

Lists of excuses and definitions of words were popular; most involved use of profanity. Often such pronouncements were lists of numbers that one could use to mean a particular epithet in order to maintain professional decorum as opposed to relying on an actual expletive. The only one of this genre in the collection suitable for presentation here included thirteen excuses, entitled "Table of Excuses," offered "to save everyone's time" by simply uttering a number. A few included "1. That's the way we've always done it, 2. I didn't know you were in a hurry for it, 3. That's not in my department, 4. No one told me to go ahead, 5. I'm waiting for an O.K." All reflected experiences employees and their customers encountered in the course of their work.

The number of cartoons concerning beliefs is voluminous. These often reflected widely held ideas in IBM or fractured views of these, and there was always a tinge of cynicism laced through these. "You know it's going to be a bad day when . . ."; the list was endless and included:

> You wake up face down on the pavement
> You call Suicide Prevention and they put you on hold
> You see a 60 Minutes News Team waiting in your office
> You turn on the News and they're showing emergency routes out of the city and end with "Have a nice day!!!"

Also circulating is the declaration that, "We, the willing led by the unknowing are doing the impossible for the ungrateful. We have done so much for so long with so little we are now qualified to do anything with nothing." This one circulated at the end of the 1980s and early 1990s when IBM's business had entered a terrible period. Although one positive cartoon from the same time popular within the sales organization showed a king from the Middle Ages with sword in hand who says: "No! I can't be bothered to see any crazy salesmen . . . we've got a battle to fight!" To his right, just behind his tent, stands the "crazy salesman" with his product: a machine gun. Yet for others a certificate stating, "If you're going to be a phony, be sincere about it."

Humor About IBM

IBM-themed cartoons proliferated. In fact, since the mid-1950s, as IBM became a visible global corporation, professional cartoonists lampooned IBM's eccentricity, most notably its bumper sticker tagline, THINK. One could devote a lengthy chapter to THINK humor. There is IBM humor other than about THINK, but we begin with this most iconic saying. Remember, for a century, IBM advertising, communications, internal presentations, and the ubiquitous THINK signs in customer data centers and on employees' desks reflected two beliefs. First, it reflected that there was usually an IBM way of conducting work or using data processing equipment. And second, because products and services offered by IBM were so complex, these required much thinking and planning to use effectively, so IBMers had to think through how best a customer could appropriate their offerings. THINK captured these beliefs in one word.

THINK cartoons appeared across a wide range of American magazines without the need to even mention IBM. The company's diffusion of THINK signs and references to it had seeped extensively into the broad business and social fabric of the American public. THINK became familiar iconography in the popular culture of educated Americans, certainly by the end of the 1950s. Its luminance did not decline until the 1990s, when it retreated to the more closed world of IBM's employee/retiree world.

Humorists and cartoon artists had long played with THINK, such as Corey Ford (1902–1969) following World War I. In 1961, he published a collection of computer, IBM, and THINK cartoons as a way to explain to the general public what computers were and what they did. The text was straightforward but graced with some forty cartoons that had appeared in the 1950s from a diverse collection of cartoonists, including him.[24] Some are described later in more detail. The pure computer, non–IBM-specific ones spoke to the calculating capabilities of computers, including one counting on its fingers and toes just slightly out of sight of whirling tape drives and blinking lights.[25] Related themes included how people were still needed as backup, such as a nineteenth-century, green-shaded accountant using a quill pen with the tag line, "We just keep him on in case of emergency."[26] But the majority of cartoons focused on THINK.

Ford acknowledged the help of IBM in putting together this book, giving him access to its current line of computers and their operators, the IBM 704, 705, 7070, and RAMAC. This access is important for two reasons. At the time (late 1950s to early 1960s), IBM was increasing the public's awareness of what computers could do. Second, its marketing staff saw merit in leveraging humor, largely to diminish growing public concern about the "Big Brother is watching you" image of computers and fear that these machines would destroy lives. The project with Ford is an early example of IBM using humor to make computers more understandable, more approachable. Twenty years later, the company repeated the use of humor far more extensively with the introduction of its "personal computer."

Many cartoons showed the THINK sign hanging in an office or on a desk in various situations. There is one with a sign reading "SCHEME" in an office at night with a quasi-Martian-looking man contemplating something less than noble; another from the *Saturday Evening Post* shows two men moving a desk into a building with the first one carrying the furniture and the second one smiling and only carrying a desk version of the THINK sign; yet a third one from 1967 shows a THINK sign in the trash can and a new one on the desk: RATIONALIZE.[27]

One cartoon created inside IBM, probably in the 1970s, but unidentified, declares, "Tom Watson said 'Think,' " showing a group of slightly overweight middle-aged men contemplating, most holding pencils to suggest intellectual work (figure 10.6). One image pointing out the lack of thinking shows a man mindlessly printing copies of THIN with the K reversed and appeared in the

10.6 Many hundreds of jokes and cartoons have appeared since the 1930s about THINK, often making their way into presentations and handouts.

(Courtesy, author's collection.)

Saturday Review. The *American Legion Magazine* published a cartoon by Dave Hirsch showing the delivery of a computer while an employee is busily throwing away multiple copies of THINK signs, since machines would now carry out that cognitive work. One that circulated for decades inside IBM shows a man at his desk with a THINK sign on the wall and just behind him his boss sitting in his office with the door open. The boss is smoking a cigar and on his wall is a sign, "THINK BIG."

Look magazine published a four-panel cartoon of a man at his desk and a THINK sign on the wall; the man gets up and leaves his office, goes to presumably his manager's office and obviously proposes an idea to him, but over the manager's wall hangs a sign reading "THINK AGAIN," suggesting that just because one thinks and comes up with an idea does not mean it will be accepted. A variation of that idea appeared in the *Saturday Evening Post* with the sign over the company president's desk saying "NO." So much for IBM's long-promoted suggestion program!

An earlier cartoon from 1948 published in the *New Yorker Magazine* shows a roomful of desks with most men leaning back in their chairs with their arms clasped behind their heads or in other contemplative postures with THINK signs on the walls. In the doorway stands the president of the company who just walked in looking disappointed that a dozen people were only thinking, not working.[28] Academic journals participated, too. The *Journal of the American Medical Association* published a cartoon with a patient lying down on a psychologist's sofa. Over the head of the psychologist with his pen and pad in hand is a THINK sign, but over the head of the patient, there is a sign reading "THINK BACK."[29] An unidentified cartoon from the 1950s shows two men at their desks talking and a THINK sign on the wall. They are discussing what they think about, and one turns to the other and says, "Mostly about women— what do you?" In 1956, *Esquire* (in those days an edgy men's magazine) carried a salacious cartoon of a man trying to seduce a woman who is standing on the other side of a desk with lamp and trash can turned over and she is holding a THINK sign in her hand.[30] *Sports Illustrated* published a lineup of football players with one team sporting THINK on their helmets at a time when football players were not always considered cerebral (i.e., "dumb").[31] The *Wall Street Journal*, always supportive of IBM, published a cartoon from probably the 1950s or 1960s showing a man walking into a typing pool of women and on the wall is a sign: "THIMK."[32]

Then there is the name itself—IBM—which has been the butt of many jokes over the years and the subject of many photocopied lists of definitions. IBMers created most of these definitions, and there are now well over a hundred definitions. What they speak to, however, is more than humor; they offer insights about the company's culture. The listings began probably in the early 1950s and had moved to private retiree and employee websites by the early

2000s. These lists are, by definition, properly referred to as acronyms. It may be more insightful to think of these as definitions with socially laden meanings. Table 10.2 provides a sampling.[33] There is much to comment on here. The oldest and most widely known within IBM is "I've Been Moved," because so many employees were transferred from one state or another during their careers from the 1920s through the 1980s, less so later, but still they moved to various cities or countries. Others refer to competitors, such as Memorex in the 1970s competing against IBM's tape and disk drives, Microsoft and its products in the 1980s competing against IBM's PC software, and Dell afterward. Mainframe references date to the 1960s and 1970s (e.g., "Incompatible Business Machines," which was an enormous problem for the firm prior to 1965). References to beards and mustaches originated in the 1970s and were intended to describe unacceptable appearances in customer-facing jobs, such as in field engineering and sales during a period when long hair and facial hair were fashionable in American and European societies. Criticizing bureaucracy and management was always a perennial favorite. Managers even occupied space in definitions

TABLE 10.2 Definitions of IBM

I've Been Moved	I Believe in Memorex
I Buy Mainframes	Idiots Built Me
I Blame Microsoft	It's Better Manually
Identical Blue Men	I've Been Mugged
Idiots Become Managers	Idiotic Bit Masher
Incompatible Business Machines	Incredibly Boring Machine
Inferior But Marketable	Infernal Bloody Monopoly
Internal Bureaucratic Mess	Institute of Black Magic
Intolerant of Bears and Mustaches	It's Backward Man
It Barely Moves	Industry's Bulging Monolith
It'll Be Messy	Itty Bitty Machines
It's Being Mended	It Barely Moves
It's Better than Macintosh	Itty Bitty Morons
I'm By Myself	I've Been Misled
Increasingly Bad Manufacturing	Incredibly Belligerent Marketing

of IBM (e.g., "Impeccably Blue-dressed Managers"). Many of these definitions have a lightly cynical theme but were seen as amusing observations about the company's eccentricities. These definitions were routinely circulated as typed lists, all undated, but continuously updated and added to over the decades.

A third category of cartoons and other humorous commentaries concerned the roles of various groups within IBM. While collaboration and teaming were more ubiquitous the lower one went into the organization, seen as crucial for the success of any part of the firm and that of individuals, nonetheless, good-spirited jesting rivalries existed. The two groups that routinely were the subject of cartoons and jokes were managers and salespeople. THINK cartoons and IBM definitions about management abounded but need not be discussed further. Rather, salespeople should be because, in IBM, the elite were the sales-force. It was from their ranks that came so many executives and almost all of IBM's most senior executives from the 1910s to the present. IBM's culture was a sales-oriented one. So it was inevitable that these people would come in for ribbing. Cartoons portrayed salespeople as being considered of low intelligence by systems engineers (the technologically skilled software troubleshooters for customers) or as people carrying a large "bag of tricks" when entering a cus-tomer's office. Customer engineers who installed and repaired equipment were authors of many of these characterizations, while across divisions, sales man-agers were portrayed as thinking they could manipulate sales staffs by writing "sales plans" (compensation plans) that would cause sales representatives to do whatever management wanted. Saleswomen in the 1980s were routinely pictured by chauvinists as seductive creatures trading allure in exchange for business. Headquarters managers who thought salespeople were paid too much portrayed them as walking around with big bags of money (commissions, bonuses). Salespeople were portrayed as being viewed by their wives as con-stantly cavorting with other women, drinking, and just having a party of a time.

Salespeople were always portrayed as wearing blue suits, regimental silk ties, and wingtip leather shoes. In all divisions, there were employees who consid-ered IBM salespeople the best-dressed IBMers, driving the best automobiles, and arrogant. There were four types, according to cartoons of the 1970s and 1980s: the "academician," shown smoking a pipe; the "looks good in a suit," who is Hollywood handsome; the "tavern marketeer," who is overweight, slightly fleshy, and IQ challenged; and the "dirtball," with a cigarette hanging out of his mouth. A cartoon that circulated since at least the early 1970s depicts a hand-some salesman on the phone with golf clubs, scuba equipment, skis, darts, and baseballs and bat cluttered around his desk. Figures 10.7 and 10.8 appeared in numerous slide decks in the 1970s and 1980s. They also occupied lists of IBM definitions (e.g., "Incredibly Belligerent Marketeers").[34] The humor worked because salespeople were respected for the complexity of their roles and for the fact that they were responsible for bringing in the revenue that made possible

10.7 IBM's salesmen were often presented as living the "good life," taking customers out to lunch and to play golf or going on lavish company-sponsored trips that frequently included afternoon sports and other adventures.

(Courtesy, author's collection.)

everyone else's job at IBM. But employees' IBM culture did not approve of elitism or classes, even if they existed mildly in unspoken ways.

In their own defense, salespeople argued that their work was challenging, often having to sell products that were 20 percent more expensive than those of their rivals from the 1920s through the 1970s. A leading computer publication, *Datamation*, published a cartoon that seemed to appear all over the industry depicting a salesman with his flipchart presentation on a page stating " . . . and the cost of the system is only $122,000,000" and, further, "We resuscitate free of charge." The customer is seen as having fallen behind his desk with his feet up in the air and his eyeglasses aside on the floor.[35]

Since at least the 1970s, cartoons appeared pilfered from science magazines that had shown how mankind had evolved in a series of figures in profile walking in a perpendicular line from a knuckle-dragging ape to one walking upright, to a Cro-Magnon person, and finally, to modern man, all naked. However, in the IBM world, the knuckle-dragger is seen holding computer cards,

10.8 The epitome of an IBM salesman as depicted in humor: arrogant, dressed in expensive clothing, and confident; image circa 1980s.

(Courtesy, author's collection.)

next computer printouts, then as a Cro-Magnon a disk pack, and finally walk-ing upright as modern man with a briefcase and tennis racket. Sometimes the reverse of the "Evolution of the Marketing Rep" appeared, with the modern man presented with tennis racket on the left side of the panel, reverting from left to right backward to a Cro-Magnon, and so forth to the knuckle-dragger dropping cards as he moved along. These cartoons spoke to the evolution of the salesperson's self-image as important and advanced, ending up solving mun-dane problems such as billing issues, querying factories and administrative per-sonnel about delivery schedules, and so forth, either by depicting him evolving to the "good life," represented by the tennis racket, or grubbing as he moves from a high-profile position to mundane tasks. Such characterizations also reflected IBM's gender realities: they were overwhelmingly men until the 1970s when women began to occupy more important roles at IBM, initially in sys-tem engineering, next sales, and last customer engineering. In the laboratories, diversification began, too, in the 1970s.

Generations of IBMers spoke about the complexity of their work in memoirs and websites and made jokes about this situation. Perhaps the most repeated, even cynically believed insight that attracted them was Murphy's Law, which held that "Anything that can go wrong will." While its antecedents have a long history, the current variant was the product of post–World War II United States and most likely from a combined ecosystem of the U.S. Air Force, the aero-space industry, defense contractors, and the emerging computer industry of the 1950s. While it is referred to either as an adage or epigram, and not taken seri-ously as a scientific law, or more specifically physics, it was believed to be more than anecdotally true in communities that engaged with complex technologies, such as at IBM.[36] The reason can be explained by the fact that packages of technologies, such as airplanes, submarines, or computer systems, have many thousands of components dependent on each other to work with com-puters that included hardware, parts, software, and layers upon layers of pro-grams. The amount of complexity involved tends to create an environment in which the failure of one small component can bring down an entire system, such as a faulty computer chip preventing a million-dollar computer system from functioning. An O-ring (a circular gasket) failed causing the NASA shuttle *Challenger* to explode, killing its crew of seven on January 28, 1986. These were realities, if more often mundane, that challenged anyone working with computers in the mid- to late-twentieth century.

To capture that notion, IBMers and the entire computer industry collectively referred to the phenomenon of risk and danger as Murphy's Law. Everyone had personally experienced Murphy's Law at work. The idea was even dignified by a leading management consultant of the time, Peter Drucker, who applied it to the profession of management: "If one thing goes wrong, everything else will, and at the same time."[37]

One could find Murphy's Law expressed in cartoons embedded in presentations, in the 1990s at the bottom of emails, and in anthologies of underground collections of IBM jokes. A variant holds that "An object will fail so as to do the most damage," while the Clare Boothe Luce's Law postulated that "No good deed goes unpunished." Cheops's Law (Egyptian pharaoh who built a pyramid) states: "Nothing ever gets built on schedule or within budget," a truism for project managers. A related aphorism that began circulating in the 1950s put it this way: "My objective is . . . to thoroughly analyze all situations; anticipate problems prior to their occurring; have answers for these problems ready, and move swiftly when called on,"—so far normal and reasonable expectations of an IBM employee—"however. . . . When you are up to your (expletive) in alligators, it is difficult to remind yourself that your initial objective was to drain the swamp." Literally dozens of other variations of laws about how things do not work out well circulated, such as Miller's Corollary: "Objects are lost because people look where they are not instead of where they are," and, "No matter how trivial the assignment, it is always possible to build it up to a major issue." A favorite from the 1960s and 1970s is Herman's Rule: "If it works right the first time, you've obviously done something wrong."

Since the central issue of Murphy's Law concerned development, manufacture, installation, and resolution of problems and product issues, much attention was paid to training and managing projects by IBM organizations, most of which were, indeed, complex and subject to problems. More specifically aimed at IBM was Murphy's Credo:

> Be humble—You can't know it all.
> Think—It isn't what you know that counts; it's what you think of in time.
> Be wary of free lunches—You pay and pay. . . .

For decades, there were the Six Phases of System Development:

- Wild Enthusiasm
- Disillusionment
- Total Confusion
- Search for the Guilty
- Punishment of the Innocents
- Promotion of Nonparticipants

There were variations of these six statements, such as:

- No major project is ever installed on time, within budgets, with the same staff that started it. Yours will not be the first.
- Projects progress quickly until they become 90 percent complete, then they remain at 90 percent complete forever.
- When things are going well, something will go wrong.

- No system is ever completely debugged; attempts to debug a system inevitably introduce new bugs that are even harder to find.
- A carelessly planned project will take three times longer to complete than expected; a carefully planned project will take twice as long.

It sometimes became worse: "If there is a possibility of several things going wrong—the one that will go wrong is the one that will do the most damage," and "Nature always sides with the hidden flaw." And then there was the ever-popular pearl of wisdom: "No amount of planning will ever replace dumb luck." A poem circulated in the 1980s, possibly earlier, called *The Nothing Machine*:

> Ah, what a stroke of genius!
> A miracle of the mind!
> Brilliant in conception,
> Flawless in design.
> But this fantastic new idea
> Has one annoying quirk—
> Each time you throw the switch on
> It never seems to work.

A cartoon of some fictional nineteenth-century-looking machine usually accompanied the poem with an "Out of Order" sign pinned to it.

If one detects a whiff of cynicism permeating the environment of problem solving as expressed by Murphy's Law, there also were signs of optimism laced with humor and creativity. However, good project management was serious business, and failures to do this well could be expensive for all involved. IBM training courses on project management sought to make this point, albeit in a positive manner. Figure 10.9 did this in the 1980s and is extracted from training materials.

Another expression of optimism harkened back to earlier decades when employees sang songs about the company, a practice that all histories of the company and many memoirists declared ended in the early 1970s. But they were wrong, because in an ad hoc manner and always locally, popular songs or stories were rewritten for special occasions, just as employees had done before World War II. In the United States, it was always a popular practice in all walks of life to rewrite the poem *'Twas the Night Before Christmas*. A salesperson in Nashville, Tennessee, penned this variant in 1985 that became a slide and a handout at that December's meeting of the local sales office:

> 'Twas the night before Christmas, when all through the land
> Not a creature was stirring, not even Jim Spann
> The points were all booked through Bethesda with care
> In hopes that our Clubs soon would be there.

10.9 Used in training programs and often as part of initial planning exercises, this cartoon reminded IBM employees that careful planning was essential and that, without it, serious and expensive problems are probable; image circa 1970s–1980s.

(Courtesy, author's collection.)

The managers were nestled all snug in their beds
While visions of careers danced in their heads.

And Roger with Biddle and Dave with NTI
Had just ended '85 on another great high.

Away to the window squeak flew like a flash
Caught an SE spending money, gave his manager a bash.

Opportunity, on the crest of a new-fallen snow,
Gave the luster of blue birds to the branch below.
When, what to my wondering mind would hit it,
But a new Area and Atlanta to visit.

We end a great year on a note of good cheer
Knowing the sounds of success always ring in our ear.

Utz was dressed all in fur, from his head to his foot,
And his pink ties all tarnished with soot,
A bundle of tasks he had flung on his back,
And he looked like a peddler just opening his pack,
His eyes—how they twinkled as he thought of next year,
And the prospects of more quota to clear.

After this poem, I need to blow out of sight
But before I do, let me say with no fear,
Happy Christmas to all, and to all a good year!

This version mentions local salesmen (Jim, Roger, and Dave) and local customers (Biddle and NTI), uses internal language (points and sales plan), mentions an administrative headquarters (Bethesda, Maryland), uses sales language (blue birds), and mentions the branch manager (Charlie Utz) who was famous for wearing pink ties and had a disarming, warm sense of humor.

Christmas carols were constantly rewritten to reflect stereotypical behaviors. Systems engineers (SEs) were the technical specialists in sales offices who solved the software problems of IBM's customers. One song—*SE Wonderland*—began as follows: "SEs sing! Are you listening?/Up at Hoechst [a customer] Hurley's whistling/With FE [field engineering] on site we're happy tonight/Selling proven code across the land." Three more verses addressed the challenges of fixing broken software. For a salesperson, there was *It Came Upon a Quota Year*: "It came upon a quota year/That glorious song of old/We've raised the number of clubs you need/To make the circle of gold," and another, *I'm Dreaming of a Low Quota*.

Since managers appraised employees in all decades at all levels of the firm, it was inevitable that handouts providing guidance on performance criteria would circulate. This one, dated July 1991, was in evidence at least two decades earlier:

Performance Factor	Quality
Far exceeds job requirements	Leaps tall buildings with a single bound
Exceeds job requirements	Must take running start to leap over tall buildings
Meets job requirements	Can only leap over short or medium buildings with a running start
Needs some improvement	Crashes into buildings when attempting to jump over them
Does not meet minimum requirements	Cannot recognize buildings much less jump over them

Until 2013, the language used to describe degrees of performance achieved used the verbiage on the left (e.g., "Far exceeds," "Meets job requirements"). Each was numbered, with a "1 Performer" far exceeding requirements, whereas a "5 Performer" ("Does not meet minimum requirements") was scheduled to be dismissed unless they could improve their performance, usually within ninety days.

Because the company was large, one could make fun of some of its operations. Figure 10.10 circulated between 1988 and 1992 when there were an extraordinary number of corporate-wide reorganizations disruptive to the sales and manufacturing parts of the company. Figure 10.11 spoke to the requirement that employees participate in various ad hoc activities not directly seen as part of their immediate performance-measured jobs, in this case, the IBM Club (local task forces that put on Christmas parties for employee children, hosted parties, and so forth). Figure 10.11 dates from the 1970s and, as can be seen by its quality, had been copied many times over the years.

Perhaps the most widely known humorous piece to circulate throughout the company across all divisions and countries on paper and as email in the

10.10 IBM was a large company with multiple divisions competing against each other for resources and markets. The division on the left just developed a telecommunications product, whereas the one on the right just outsourced telecommunications to AT&T, circa 1970s.

10.11 More often than one was willing to acknowledge, employees were recruited to serve in their local time-consuming IBM Club, which was responsible for hosting family and office events, with members not recognized for their extracurricular activities in their appraisals.

(Courtesy, author's collection.)

1980s was a product announcement that must be presented in full, with inappropriate language; otherwise, it makes no sense. Periodically, the availability of a product or part would be announced through a formal system that circulated through PROFS (IBM's earliest email system). This actually went through that system in the late 1980s, after IBM had been in the PC business for nearly eight years. After declaring its date of availability and some other normal technical data:

Abstract: MOUSE BALLS NOW AVAILABLE AS FRU
(Field Replaceable Unit)

If a mouse fails to operate, or should perform erratically, it may be in need of ball replacement. Because of the delicate nature of this procedure, replacement of mouse balls should be attempted by trained personnel only. Before ordering, determine type of mouse balls required by examining the underside of each mouse. Domestic balls will be larger and harder than foreign balls. Ball removal procedures differ, depending upon manufacturer of the mouse. Foreign balls can be replaced using the pop-off method, and domestic balls can be replaced using the twist-off method. Mouse balls are not usually static sensitive, however, excessive handling can result in sudden discharge. Upon completion of ball replacement, the mouse may be used immediately.

It continues, but one gets the idea.[38] People used an IBM PC trackball mouse in the 1980s to move curser arrows on a screen. It sat on top of a small gray ball that allowed people to move it about on a pad next to their keyboards (figure 10.12).

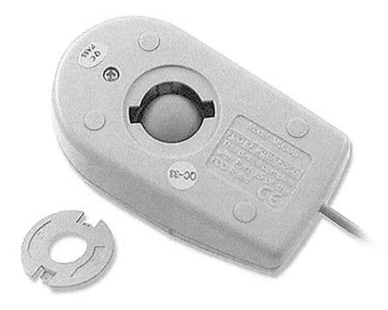

10.12 The famous PC track, known as a "mouse," that made it possible for a user to move as it was situated above a round ball.

(Courtesy, author's collection.)

Role of Humor in IBM

Materials discussed in this chapter beg the larger question of what role humor played inside IBM. These circulated among individuals and occasionally as content in slide presentations made to customers and in internal speeches and training. They were relatively ubiquitous within at least the American side of the company. The nature of these cartoons and other handouts reflects patterns identified by humor experts: a tinge of cynicism, a slightly ajar description of reality that humorists call incongruities, reliance on insider knowledge and language, and social prejudices and concerns of the day. Some of these circulated for decades, reappearing repeatedly either redrawn or retyped, such as those concerning project management and work realities. Yet others disappeared, such as the sexist and ethnic cartoons. Product-specific materials had a short shelf life, being funny only when a particular device or software was in wide use. For example, one document talked humorously about the features of the System 370 Model 135—a computer of the 1970s— that disappeared after that model was no longer sold in the 1980s, while a bibliography of made-up names of books also dropped from circulation when the topics were no longer relevant to a technical community. As a general observation, humor flowed through the company. Jokes about IBM did, too, in all periods since at least the 1930s.

What was the company's general policy regarding humor? Company archival sources are silent on the matter; however, in the early 1980s, it was clear that humor was embraced as a marketing tool. The challenge that the serious IBM Corporation had when it introduced its personal PC in August 1981 was how to make the technology less intimidating to a public used to IBM selling large, fearfully complex systems. To make the new technology more approachable, IBM's marketing and advertising communities settled on the tagline, "A Tool for Modern Times," and used the Tramp that comedian Charlie Chaplin had created decades earlier as its spokesperson. Television spots and magazine and newspaper advertisements used the comedic character to promote the PC for several years.[39] It worked. It also made IBM appear less serious and more human and, crucially, its technology more approachable and less complicated than one might otherwise have thought. These developments came at a time when companies were beginning to understand the power of humor.[40]

In the 1990s, it seemed most large enterprises were methodically applying humor in their training of employees and customers, in presentations by executives and other corporate speakers, and in advertising. For instance, IBM's customer training organization, the Advanced Business Institute, used humor in the early 2000s as part of its management practices presentations.[41] "Humor consultants" became a near subindustry hired by corporations.[42] Meanwhile, employees and customers stopped photocopying their humorous materials, having moved them to email or to posting these on the internet. Employees did not, however, post much of these ephemera on official IBM websites, as these were strictly monitored to keep spurious materials off of them.

While the ephemera reflected the practices, work ethics, and social values of employees and customers, there is no evidence that they commented directly about IBM's Basic Beliefs, the company's secular theology.[43] These beliefs were so sacred and embraced by generations of employees that one never saw a cartoon mocking or commenting in a negative manner on them until mass layoffs of employees in the early 2000s, and even then, only the first of the Basic Beliefs ("Respect for the Individual") was targeted, since employees thought it included an unstated managerial commitment to lifetime employment. These three beliefs were the single, most off-limits topics one could find. Employees might complain that management was not adhering to these beliefs in one situation or another, but those criticisms were normally posed seriously, not humorously, even in closed employee and retiree websites and Facebook pages in the 2000s.

Individuals by name might be criticized or jokes made about them, such as a senior executive, but these were not the subject of cartoons or other paper ephemera, only verbal communications until employee websites in the early 2000s made it possible to vent. Venting then was not humorous, especially when criticizing the performance of CEO Virginia ("Ginni") Rometty, whose tenure as IBM's leader was fraught with poor business results. So, there were boundaries around what employees considered humorous.

Implications of Humor Research for Corporate Cultures

Humor in IBM reflected many of the topics and issues normally considered part of a corporation's culture. Humor is another source of information about corporate culture, one that business historians routinely overlook. This case study about IBM unearthed a cache of documentary evidence of humorous activities and commentary about the company's affairs. These represent a topic at the tip of an iceberg of information about a company for two reasons: first, because the documents are only a small sampling, and second, because as humor experts point out, most humor is expressed orally. Spoken jokes represent an additional genre of humor but are often not written down. However, the cache of materials used in this chapter included some jokes written down and passed around much the way cartoons and other paper ephemera circulated.

Humor scholars have long asserted that approaching a serious subject in a lighthearted manner takes the sting out of fear and complaints, making such subjects less threatening and more amenable to discussion and resolution. It is probably a long overdue exercise that business historians begin to apply their lessons by listening to the cartoonists. Let us return again to cartoonist Corey Ford to see how he dealt with serious computer issues sixty years ago. He told the story of a man teaching his computer to play chess, and of course, the machine never lost a match. His patience gone, the man barked out: "Can't you ever lose?" The story continues:

> He even tried pressing the wrong button a couple of times, but its electronic brain was too quick for him . . . [and the] computer proceeded to clobber him three games in a row, whereupon he lost his temper and kicked it. This proved to be a mistake, not only because the computer was encased in a solid steel cabinet and he was only wearing carpet slippers . . . but also because the machine was so shaken up by the harsh treatment that it suffered a complete nervous breakdown, and from then on would give out nothing but a googol of ooooooooooooo's, to the nth power. He finally had to send it away to be analyzed.

The lesson: "The owner of a new data-processing system must remember that his machine is only inhuman, after all. All it can do is repeat the facts, and it has no capacity for feeling."[44] In our current age when extensive conversations are taking place about the future role of artificial intelligence and Big Brother social media, one can learn that such weighty issues can be approached with humor and have been by humorists and cartoonists for a long time. We can learn from them.

IBM's use of humor to advertise PCs in the 1980s sends a signal to management that one can use humor to make their products and their corporate images friendlier, more approachable, and understandable. But, one can reach out further. As large enterprises become subject to increased public scrutiny, allowing internal humor to leak out can make otherwise inscrutable cold enterprises more sympathetic. Apple is considered too secretive, Facebook too loose in its protection of information, Amazon a draconian retailer, and Wells Fargo unethical and criminal in its treatment of its customers. Police departments shoot too many people. Fox News is a purveyor of dangerous misinformation. Boris Johnson is an incompetent British prime minister, and so forth. The list is endless, but as the IBM experience suggests, a little humor humanizes organizations and people. Humor can be used to blunt some of these images. As the number of stakeholders increases, corporations may want to take a page out of business history. They are just as capable as IBM of letting humor about them seep into the ecosystem they live in, some that they manage well. Purposeful and accidental diffusion of a good joke or cartoon works well. Studies of human cognition are altering how companies deal with their constituents.[45] Humor is part of that construct.

We now move to a very serious body of other publications: IBM's technical, marketing, and business literature, because unlike humorous photocopies, these materials went to many millions of people. These publications made it possible to use computers and shaped how people thought of the technology. This is the topic of our discussion in the next chapter.

CHAPTER 11

GRAY LITERATURE IN IBM'S INFORMATION ECOSYSTEM

As a programmer, I had perhaps 20 pounds of manuals at my desk to be able to do my job. It was a very paper intensive time.

Dana Marks[1]

It was said within IBM in the 1970s and 1980s that the company was the world's second-largest publisher after the U.S. Government Printing Office (GPO), as measured by the number of pages printed. It might have been an urban myth because there are no extant statistics to document how much IBM published, but a look at a KWIC (Key Word in Context) index of its publications from that period reveals it occupied four to five linear feet. Each page in it had two columns of brief citations printed in font sizes normally reserved for endnotes in academic publications.[2] Another, published in 1990, listed 108,566 individual publications still available from IBM.[3] It was not uncommon for documentation accompanying a new computer system to take up at least thirty linear feet in a data center library. Nor was it uncommon for any of nearly 1,000 sales offices to spend tens of thousands of dollars each year on sales and technical literature their staffs distributed to customers; that expenditure did not include the cost of some publications charged to customers after 1969.

No large organization could function in the twentieth century without an information ecosystem that allowed all its parts to coordinate their activities.[4] As the number of stakeholders increased in the 2010s for most large enterprises, this reality became even more the case. Historians know such an information ecosystem involved all members, such as employees and those they served, and was not merely to inform management of what was happening.[5] It is becoming clear that this information ecosystem included participants in the welfare of an organization that resided outside its legal walls, such as suppliers, customers, regulators, and the media.[6] Large corporations and government agencies became significant publishers of content relevant to their scope of interests. Dan Schiller, who spent decades exploring the diffusion of information, characterized such corporate publishing as "ubiquitous" and that it extended to "*every* economic sector."[7]

It is within this larger context of an information ecosystem that one can search for facts participants needed in order to do their work. A major source of that information consisted of publications issued by their employer. Called by librarians in a slightly pejorative manner "gray literature," it is a body of publications that has barely been studied by scholars in any discipline, and nowhere more so is that the case than as part of corporate history.[8] Yet corporations, along with national governments, were the largest creators of such material.

There is much to learn, but we move quickly to IBM as a case study, because not only did it publish a great deal, and about which no historical research has been conducted, but also because its materials led to millions of users of computers to view all manner of computing issues through this company's lens. Its information worldviews and technologies were even co-opted in Soviet countries where local manufacturers copied IBM's technologies at similarly high rates (or more) and translated IBM publications into local languages. IBM held a near dominant position on how people in the world of computing thought about data processing and, to a large extent, what they read about it from the 1950s until at least the end of the 1970s. The major exceptions to this sweeping generalization are the publications of computer scientists and others working at rival computing firms. But collectively, even those communities represented smaller constituencies and distributors of such materials. They often interacted with IBM employees at conferences and shared space in proceedings and other publications. Such broad statements can further be made despite thousands of commercial books and hundreds of journals published outside of IBM, many of whose authors were IBM employees. Our purpose here is to begin to explain how IBM became such a dominant force through the distribution of its gray literature and the effects its availability had on the work of employees and their customers.

I begin by describing why IBM published gray literature, followed by a brief discussion of how scholars and others defined this class of publications.

I pivot to an historical account of IBM's publications prior to 1950 and then explore the massive increase in such materials produced when IBM entered the world of computers. Because production of corporate gray literature remains so unknown, I examine how IBM did this with an emphasis on process steps and the numbers of people and volumes of publications involved. The chapter concludes with observations and recommendations with respect to the study of corporate gray literature and its diffusion by corporations.

Overview of the Purpose of IBM Publications, 1920s–1990s

IBM operated as a highly developed corporate ecosystem that had, as one of its central features, a well-developed body of information supporting its world and culture. Important features of its ecosystem included extensively informed and thoroughly trained employees, versed in both the business and technical aspects of IBM's products and services. Its workforce was also highly diverse in its skills and expertise, with specialists in the technologies of developing and servicing products, managers able to synchronize ever-growing diverse parts of the company around the world, bureaucrats operating procedures and administrative systems to optimize work and strategy, and sales personnel able to explain why customers should use their products. Beliefs of the firm reinforced these features by valuing meritocratic judgments and behaviors, respect for the work and ideas of employees, high-quality customer service, and an integrity largely respected by customers with the result that they maintained high levels of trust in what the company had to say and do.[9] But notice, each facet of its beliefs systems and activities required an underpinning of organized information relevant to the tasks at hand.

Like employees at IBM, customers (users) had to work with complex technologies from the company and later with those of other firms. So, they, too, faced complex technical and managerial challenges that required informed and trusted collaboration with vendors, industry associations, internal experts, and academics. A symbiotic relationship developed among participants in the data processing world from the dawn of the twentieth century that grew in diversity, complexity, and numbers engaged. Their environment became fertile ground for growing an information ecosystem. Today, one would be hard-pressed to define the boundaries of any large corporation. It was easier to do in the 1920s and 1930s, but a century later perhaps nearly impossible. But as in the 1930s, self-identified stakeholders and interested parties could reach into a company for information, imposing a greater pressure on such enterprises to populate their ecosystems with a body of gray literature in service to the enterprise.

Management at IBM concluded that in order to sell their products and to increase sales employees and customers had to function within a shared information ecosystem. Both parties needed to use much of the same information, just as they had to do with mutually understandable vocabulary and appreciation of business issues. They recognized these two realities from the earliest days of the company, building on lessons learned initially at another data processing company, NCR, prior to 1914, but also from that sector of the business that used punch-card tabulating equipment. IBM's information ecosystem was constructed by having salesmen educate customers about the possibilities of these technologies and how best to use them and by IBM training customer personnel on the same issues and how to operate equipment. IBM delivered education through various company schools with staff located at plant and research laboratory sites around the world; at conferences that IBM employees attended and made presentations at or were sponsored by professional and industry associations; through sponsorship of user groups, such as SHARE and GUIDE; and by others located in sales branch offices.

Their activities were supported by the distribution of massive quantities of documentation, always kept up to date and tailored to the needs and interests of specific audiences. An IBM manager responsible for shipping publications on the installation and use of software in the United States in the late 1960s, Rich Rarco, recalled that over two hundred employees ran an operation seven days a week almost around the clock just to meet the demand. Their work did not include a separate function at various manufacturing sites doing the same for many thousands of machines.[10] Large volumes of shipments of literature also took place in Europe, Asia, and most of South America.

It was their diversity that accounted for the enormous variety of gray publications, while the sheer volume of people, machines, and software involved explains the number of copies. For example, with every computer shipped to a customer came a set of publications—user manuals—to explain in great detail the use and maintenance of the software and equipment. If IBM shipped a million personal computers (PCs), a million copies of a user manual went out with these devices. If IBM installed 12,000 copies of a specific type of computer, then 12,000 sets of manuals went to customers, too. These publications did not consist of a single ten- to twenty-page booklet. Some for individual devices occupied a foot of linear shelf space, not to mention operations manuals that lay next to so many of these that a user needed to consult regularly, which often ran into hundreds of pages.

The context in which data processing functioned compelled increasing focus on nontechnical issues over time. Thomas J. Watson, Jr., explained the need to managers: "There is a close relationship between all parts of our product line. Any major decision in one part of the business inevitably affects many other parts of the business. We are not a group of unrelated businesses tied together by a corporate structure. We are one business."[11] Customers and the industry at large faced the similar requirement to coordinate various information handling activities. In the process, they turned to IBM because they were dependent on its products and because the company had become a respected model to emulate when running their own operations. In other words, customers and other users of IBM's products were exposed to more than user manuals. They attended briefings on how to apply the technologies in running organizations and about how to emulate IBM's administrative practices with respect to such issues as human relations, benefits, and business strategy.[12]

The other contextual consideration is that use of tabulators and, later, mainframe computers required considerable cognitive capabilities. Let us be blunt: one had to be smart and able to absorb and deal with technological, scientific, and mathematical issues beyond what perhaps the average "person on the street" might require. Increasingly over the course of the twentieth century, participants in data processing were more extensively educated, were proficient mathematically, often had advanced university degrees, and had increased amounts of training than one might find in many other professions.[13] Recall that by the end of the 1950s, as an example of those requirements, to be even considered for employment at IBM, individuals had to score well on an aptitude test.[14] That single act alone reduced the possibility of managers who were recruiting from making idiosyncratic hiring decisions.

As reported in chapter 4, once inside the company, employees were extensively trained and retrained throughout their careers. The combination of good intelligence, training, and well-described job expectations made it possible to give them considerable authority and responsibility for their area of work. They needed that freedom of action to tailor IBM's offerings to specific customer needs and to guide (or push) IBM into adapting their products to the needs of the market. IBM made publications available to them in support of each of these activities. Employees shared such inclinations for leading with documented facts and insights with their customers and other industry, technical/scientific, and business cohorts. It would be difficult to explain the breadth of IBM's gray literature without taking into account the high value placed on such publications inside and outside the firm.

It was a dependency and process of production built up over time. In the 1920s and 1930s, the company was expanding, although its product lines concentrated on typewriters and tabulators. The firm concurrently built up its reputation for being a modern, well-run operation, enjoying growth in a transforming part of business and public sector management. After World War II, its authority expanded with the arrival of the computer as the centerpiece of IBM's business. The paper trail of gray literature makes that obvious. Not until the end of the 1970s, when new competitors began to crack IBM's solid control over most data processing, did its de facto intellectual near monopoly begin to shrink. With the arrival of PCs and their competitors in the 1980s, it fractured sufficiently that in the 1990s many of the information ecosystem's thoughts came from outside of IBM. It was also from the late 1960s to the end of the 1980s that many consumers of computing shifted from solely centralized main-frame computing to centralized and/or vast networks of distributed comput-ing, a presage to computing practices in the internet era.[15]

While IBM continued to publish extensively, most notably its Redbooks (technical manuals for use with its products), beginning in the 1990s, and its business publications from the IBM Institute for Business Value (IBV) in the 2000s, and continued its marketing and training practices honed over decades, its intellectual hegemony waned. Simultaneously, beginning in the late 1980s and definitively during the 1990s, its gray literature morphed into databases, digital copies of publications, blogs, and online meetings. Gray literature increasingly transformed books to bits, from traditional publications to hyper-text. Clearly, the notion of corporate gray literature awaits its historian.

But First, the Idea of Gray Literature

The term "gray literature" remains ill-defined, made even more evident by the fact that even the term is spelled in multiple ways. Americans use *gray*; it appears that everyone else spells it *grey*. It may seem a trivial point, but it sug-gests that thinking about the topic evolved along multiple paths, a history we will not digress to discuss here.[16] Much of the discussion about gray literature has been conducted within the library community. Our description of IBM's use of this genre of publication is focused on business concerns. Forty years ago, librarians posited a definition that such publications were "material pub-lished non-commercially, e.g. government reports."[17] At the time of that defini-tion's publication, in 1983, IBM employees involved with gray literature would have been comfortable in concluding that their company published more titles in greater quantities and formats than any commercial publisher and that the former did not know what gray literature meant. They spoke in terms of "IBM pubs." Librarians thought to push business literature into the contexts of com-mercial and academic formats and categories. Corporate publishers did not; IBM's instance is a case in point.

In business, gray literature is different than much of commercially available publications, such as those in bookstores or on Amazon. Differences include the greater speed with which these can be produced than by traditional pub-lishers, often in days or weeks rather than in many months or longer; greater flexibility in how to present content without conforming to someone else's for-mats; ability to delve in greater detail than a trade or academic publisher would tolerate, such as the technical literature on what might seem obscure topics running close to many hundreds of pages; and protection of the security and privacy of information that cannot otherwise be so ensured and, hence, who

could read the material. Companies can budget far more for such publications than traditional publishers. Their publications can be targeted to specific
audiences, such as repair manuals for customer engineers at IBM who had to
fix broken machines or publications about computing in banking for banking executives. In these two examples of focused audiences, IBM could reach
almost every potential reader for decades, knowing almost all of them by name
and their location. As a result of all these features, large multinational corporations became massive publishers dwarfing traditional publishing practices.
In that capability, IBM was quite normal in how it approached gray literature.[18]

Librarians point out that gray literature comes in many formats, as does
IBM's. These include books, conference proceedings, preprints, offprints, pamphlets, longer booklets, multivolume anthologies, scholarly journals, trade and
thematic magazines, technical newsletters, photocopied or mimeographed
reports and flyers, and white papers, among others. Today, the list additionally
includes videos, websites, podcasts, and databases. British librarians get the
credit for inventing the phrase "grey literature."

Much gray literature follows publishing traditions evident in other publications. For example, some technical reports (IBM has published thousands of
these since the 1930s) had named authors; most others just had IBM as author,
but in all cases, IBM's identity was associated with these documents. Some
were reports of progress on projects, while others justified internal budget
requests or were proposals addressed to customers produced in very limited
editions, but they were published nonetheless, and not simply a letter with a
computer-printed list of products, prices, and contract terms.[19] It was customary throughout the period for final reports about a project to be printed, ranging from a few pages of text or a PowerPoint narrative to book-length accounts.
Others were reports by committees or state-of-the-art types of documents,
again in various formats.[20]

Librarians tend to think of business gray literature largely as research and
development reports, working white papers, market research, financial documentation, or reports about scientific and technological issues directly related
to the economic interests of the firm publishing these.[21] Such a list is too restric-
tive, perhaps even displaying insufficient understanding of what happens inside
a corporation, let alone in a large multinational one. At IBM, the scope of gray
literature proved far broader. Put another way, the features of most IBM publications meet the criteria of what constitutes gray literature.

However, librarians have also sometimes divided what they consider to be
gray literature into another category of publications they call *trade literature*.
Leaving aside a possible debate splitting hairs on definitions, the category of
trade literature informs what constitutes IBM's information ecosystem's publications. Trade and gray literature are largely the same. The fundamental difference a librarian attributes to trade literature is that its primary purpose is

to promote the sale of a product or service. In this category of publications one might include product descriptions and catalogs, price lists, flyers, and even company annual reports. These publications tend to be more widely available to the public at large and are considered ephemeral, that is to say, of only momentary use, like today's newspaper discarded tomorrow.[22] One could argue that because many of IBM's publications were used far longer than trade/marketing materials, and hence are not the same, even the most substantive publications ended their shelf life. The point is that IBM treated all of its various publications as part of a cohesive whole.

Today, the analogy of ephemera can be extended because a company's information websites may update content multiple times in a day; thus, instead of throwing out yesterday's newspaper, one might refresh, say, a news website and see articles different than those posted by the publisher in the middle of the night. Companies do that frequently, too, particularly with respect to their posting of news stories, product announcements, and updates to these, such as warnings regarding security breaches in software. Microsoft is an example of a company that frequently updates the status of its products. That is today's digital gray literature in play.

Thus we turn back to the librarian's definitions because there are two problems with their characterizations of trade literature. The most obvious from a business perspective is that a majority of gray literature published by a company is intended to promote its products and services and to burnish the firm's image. With highly technological issues, promoting simultaneously commercial offerings and a complementary image of the vendor is essential to the success of the company. IBM's management subscribed to that notion since the earliest days of the firm, or at least since Watson Sr. came to it in 1914, when he brought over a fully developed concept of how a high-tech firm had to operate and, soon after, colleagues from NCR who joined him.[23]

The second problem with the librarian's view is that IBM integrated messages across *all* its publications from its earliest days, while, say, an academic or trade publisher did (does) not, nor as much commercially published magazines, for example. IBM was able to do that in the 1910s–1930s because it was a small firm with most of the key influencers of its culture, operations, and messages able to fit into a small auditorium. Dozens, then hundreds, not thousands, participated in shaping the purpose of gray literature in that one company over the course of more than two decades. So by the time IBM became a rapidly growing behemoth in the 1960s, its style of publishing and the policies and practices related to the creation of its publications had been sufficiently set to make it possible to scale its gray literature by types across multiple markets and languages. For example, before World War II, IBM publications originated largely in only three types of localities: within a division responsible for developing and selling products with their attendant operational and marketing materials; corporate and divisional (later groups, too) headquarters that published about the company at large or delegated specific messaging to a division, such as sales organizations to discuss business topics and uses not necessarily tied to a specific product; and national company headquarters that published local-language translations of select American IBM publications, such as user manuals. When the private sector, government research laboratories, and universities began hiring computer scientists and engineers, a fourth source emerged: scholarly and academic research, scientific presentations, papers, and books. It was common in the 1950s through the 1980s to find book-length technical and business discussions published by trade houses authored by IBM employees, obfuscating the boundaries of what librarians and business management considered gray literature.[24] We turn next to examples and typologies of IBM's gray literature to more fully describe many of these myriad publications.

Early Publications from IBM, 1910s–1950s

All corporations need to communicate information to at least five stakeholders: employees, customers, media, regulators and other public officials, and industry influencers (e.g., think tanks, experts, stockbrokers). In industries where technological or scientific changes occur rapidly (or constantly), there is the academic and engineering world, too, that needs to hear from corporations, as was the case beginning in the 1930s. IBM's constituencies were the same as those of other enterprises. That is the theory, but in practice, IBM learned additionally that it should reach out to other audiences as well. Since the 1920s, management sought to communicate with families of employees, the subject of chapter 7.[25] In communities that employed hundreds, then thousands of employees, relations with local leaders and other citizens also proved essential. Occasionally the company reached out to the public at large, such as in 1933 and 1939–1940 at world's fairs and in the 1980s when it introduced the personal computer. But in the years prior to the 1950s, the communities it needed to reach were fewer and smaller. Yet, from its earliest days, the company determined the kinds of information to communicate through its gray literature, publications that reinforced the exchange of information delivered through speeches and one-on-one meetings.

In the years between 1911 and roughly 1950–1952, some standard publications appeared, while others were ad hoc but subsequently became standard fare. Examples of the latter were booklets that described the functions of a specific type of product for customers or repair manuals for such equipment in a format proven to be useful for those employees installing or repairing products. The first were not simply one-page advertisements that appeared in magazines and newspapers but rather documents with more descriptive content. For multiple audiences, there was, of course, the annual report, which appeared every year in the same format from 1911 through 1954, after which these were converted into the style one is familiar with today in a typically 8 × 12–inch format with color photographs and text complimenting achievements of the firm and providing the financial data required by regulators. That specific example of gray literature will not take up our time, as these are widely familiar.[26]

IBM's gray literature from the 1910s to the early 1950s reflected several features. These were intended for multiple audiences when reasonable to do so. Catalogs describing IBM's products were for customers and IBMers (as employees were known by the 1930s). A catalog from 1926, simply entitled *International Business Machines* and sporting its logo, carried descriptions and photographs of all its products and included information about when these goods should be used and often how long the product had been available. This publication included information about the company and a bit about how innovative it has been: "The INTERNATIONAL BUSINESS MACHINES CORPORATION is the pioneer in the manufacture and sale of the most comprehensive line of business machines of any single company in the world."[27] Product descriptions explained their features and uses. This catalog did not yet have the common look and feel that IBM's future publications would have within a decade. It was a humble forty-page affair, but it made clear that IBM aspired to be a force to be reckoned with in the data processing world.[28]

A second type of dual-purpose publications were training manuals used to educate employees and customers on the use of its products. For example, salesmen being trained about the products in the 1920s and 1930s often studied one- to four-page flyers about the features of an IBM machine but, like their customers, were also informed about the nature of its uses, often through a combination of lectures at Sales School and mimeographed texts they could share with their users. An example from 1938 discussed IBM's scales (yes, IBM sold industrial scales) authored by a foreman involved in their manufacture. As customary for nearly a century, product descriptions included the business case for their use, rather than solely information about their technical features. Here he began with, "The product of scales is 'Figures.' With this in mind, the person most interested in the figures supplied by the scales, next to the management itself, is, of course, the accountant. In the balancing of his inventory, he is absolutely dependent upon the information furnished from the scale."[29] He went on for six single-spaced typed pages to describe their features and how to acquire these machines, their sizes and purposes, and their guarantee "for one year from date of purchase."[30]

By then, such documents were being included in three-ring binders of uniform design, with an olive-green cover, blue lettering, and company logo. The binders were labeled "Manual of Instruction." Many factory walls at IBM in

TABLE 11.1 IBM Publications Intended for Internal Use Only, 1920s–Early 1950s

Sales manuals
Customer engineering reference manuals
Manual of Instruction Customer Engineering on installation and repair of products
Anthologies of speeches by T. J. Watson, Sr. (1924, 1927, 1934)
Various internal procedures instructions
IBM Business Machines (newspaper)
THINK magazine (after 1970–the early 1990s)
Souvenir yearbooks for 100 Percent Clubs
Training materials, such as about the theory of electronics or salesmanship
Pamphlets describing the role of a specific factory, such as at Endicott, New York
Book-size publications memorializing IBMers who died in World War II

the 1930s were also painted in the same drab green, a fashionable color in the United States at that time. These binders began to hint of purpose and branding because other training materials from the period used the same binder. Their contents were mimeographed, with texts sometimes running into hundreds of pages.[31] From IBM's earliest days, such publications were copyrighted and with the publisher listed as located at IBM's headquarters in New York City, occasionally at Endicott, New York. European-language editions came out of such cities as London, Milan, and Paris.

IBM's early gray literature, like that in subsequent decades, can be bifurcated into "pubs" (IBM slang), meant solely for use by employees and others intended primarily for customer use, but with the understanding that employees would be familiar with both. Table 11.1 lists types of publications—gray literature— intended for use by employees, whereas table 11.2 lists those intended for use by customers. The list is not definitive because the typology is the result of only examining extant materials. Thus, for example, user manuals for punch-card equipment from the 1890s have apparently not survived, so we do not know what they were like. But the list is sufficient enough to suggest the breadth of materials IBM published. IBM's Corporate Archives is a monument to these publications, occupying many linear feet hiding in boxes.

The phrase "Internal Use Only" was printed on many IBM publications throughout the century, although some of the publications listed above did not have that level of security, such as *THINK* magazine, which was distributed to

TABLE 11.2 IBM Publications Intended for Customers and the Public, 1920s–1950s

Annual reports
THINK magazine (1935–end of 1970)
Art exhibit catalogs
Brief flyers and pamphlets of specific products
Customer product operating instruction manuals
Sales catalogs
Publications explaining the theory and practice of data processing
Postcards of IBM facilities
Technical seminar proceedings
General information (GI) manuals

employees and the public. Many publications were also translated into French, German, and Spanish, for example.

The most detailed publications of the period were the one- and two-volume customer engineering manuals used by those who installed and maintained equipment. That genre of publications required a great deal of work to put together. Every "CE," as customer engineers were known, received their manual as part of their training that they used on the job, in most instances, every day. They were thoughtfully designed to be maintained as current and useful. They had a trim size of 9 × 6 inches and were bound in black leather. A quick glance at any would suggest they looked like a Bible, and indeed, they were the CEs' technical bible. Often a CE would write their name in it to identify whose copy it was, while others were embossed with the name and address of their owners. They were loose-leaf affairs. When new pages were published, these were mailed to the CEs who would then swap out old ones or add the new ones. In that way, their bibles remained current. Their contents were organized by machine type. Each section included engineering drawings of all components and directions on use and replacement and how to adjust and replace parts. Illustrations complemented instructions that neatly folded to fit the contours of the manual. These often included photographs, all with instructions such as, "Adjust stud for .010–0.12 clearance when clutch engaging arm is against stop."[32] A quick glance at the endnote for this quote illustrates that there was a structured cataloging system of numbers to track the release (edition) of the document being consulted. Other pages in a manual were published on other dates.

CEs recorded all their work on eighty-column cards to account for their time and materials expended and by type of activity. These were reflected in a collection of numbers called "codes." The manuals had a list of these codes, usually in the first several pages. Everyone working on machines was admonished to take "extreme care . . . in selecting the proper code for each Customer Engineering Report that is prepared."[33] Salesmen did the same for the kinds of sales calls and activities in which they engaged. Their sales manuals listed the codes and contained similar admonitions to be accurate. Figures 11.1 and 11.2 illustrate the ubiquitous CE handbooks of the 1920s–1950s.

11.1 IBM, *Manual of Instruction, Customer Engineering*, circa 1932–1933.

(Courtesy, author's collection.)

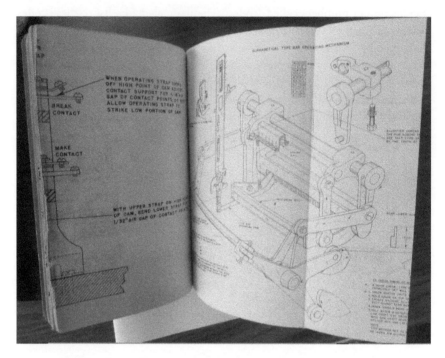

11.2 Same handbook as in figure 11.1, displaying interior pages.

(Courtesy, author's collection.)

Some versions included a brief history of the division from which a machine came or about the purpose of the device. In the 1920s and 1930s, it was often already necessary to have specialized CEs, that is to say, those who only worked on tabulators or others who only worked on time-recording devices or type-writers, because there was that much to know. But the formats and content of the handbooks were similar. Like cookbooks, they were used and so had torn pages, smudges, and oil stains. One would be challenged to find one in mint condition.[34] Some editions provided blank pages for CEs to add comments. A typical printed page included the name of the device or component to be worked with; sometimes the name of the IBM division whence came the machine or part; always a date of the current edition of the page, such as March 15, 1938; a form number; and if multipage, a page number within that section. These manuals included copies of instructions issued to customers on how to use the devices. All operating literature presented to a user had a similar size and format as the CE's manual, only printed on better-quality paper.

A parallel set of publications described specific tools, for example, about meters and test devices essential for maintaining electronic products. IBM produced lightweight tools for CEs to carry from one customer to another in the trunks of their cars, such as volt-ohm meters, dynamic timers, and oscilloscopes. The publications for these tools had the same format and design; some were well over one hundred pages in length. They constituted another class—series—of publications entitled "Customer Engineering Reference Manual." These, too, provided brief historical perspectives along with detailed descriptions of the tools, their purposes, and how and when to use them.[35]

Portions of these various publications were repurposed for use in educating customers about IBM's products and about the firm itself and to train IBM's salesmen on the same topics. These publications, published by topic, such as about a particular machine, or uses, better known in the industry for decades as "applications," were presented in an attractive 8 × 11 format, complete with detailed photographs. Training included how the world was changing because of data processing and IBM's historic involvement in that evolution.[36] Admittedly intended as marketing material, these also informed new employees about IBM's breadth of products and activities. Publications were updated as products changed, a practice continued to the present.

A writing staff in Endicott, New York, in collaboration with the engineers who developed the machines, prepared these manuals. Some production was done through a publishing department in Endicott; in other instances, this work was outsourced. All these publications shipped from the factory site responsible for the production of the machines or the training of CEs, customers, and IBM salesmen. The same was done in Europe and South America, but not routinely until after World War II in Asia. One-off editions of some of these materials were prepared as well, most notably foreign-language versions. While few have survived from before the 1950s, extant copies demonstrate how these were produced. A bilingual staff member of IBM Spain, Luis A. Lamassonne, translated the CE's handbook, completing the task in 1941. It ran to hundreds of pages. It was distributed in Spain and in those Latin American countries that had IBM offices, at the time largely Argentina, Mexico, and Peru.[37]

In February 1924, the three companies that were progenitors of IBM, called C-T-R, changed names to International Business Machines Corporation, better known as IBM. IBM immediately changed its signs, introduced a new logo, and rebranded its publications.

The anthologies just described were a gesture in that direction, but so too a new publication launched at the time, *IBM Business Machines*. It was a newspaper designed to look and report on company-wide news much like an American city or town newspaper. It had reporters, photographs, and common themes. It reported on new products, employee events, and family gatherings; celebrated achievements of its salesmen; summarized speeches by IBM executives; and ran feature stories about what was happening in branch offices and factories. IBM published this newspaper until 1963. Variations of the same type of publication also appeared in some countries in local languages. This publication went far to present a company-wide image to its employees. Beginning distribution in the United States, at its birth, that would have meant shipping it to nearly 2,500 people, a modest print run, but by 1941, this number increased to over 10,000. By 1963, there were 81,500 American employees. While it is unclear how many copies went outside the United States, in 1963, the total population of the firm hovered at 137,600 souls, so even if only a few copies were sent to non-U.S. employees, it was not an inconsiderable print run.[38]

This publication was distributed at work or mailed to one's home, so even spouses had access to the newspaper. It also played another role in IBM: to bond and keep connected to the firm employees who were away at war. During World War II and the Korean Conflict, the company mailed these to American IBMers in uniform wherever they were. Copies showed up on the front lines in combat zones. During the 1950s, employees drafted into the U.S. military serving in Europe and elsewhere received copies of the newspaper. Sending IBM publications to employees in uniform continued past the Vietnam War. At retirement parties for employees in the 1970s–1990s, one could hear stories about how ex-soldiers valued these touches of home, along with packages containing food from IBM with an enclosed newspaper. When they came back from military duty, they were normally run through refresher courses on IBM's products and activities, but they had read the newspaper. So they knew what new products had been introduced, changes in management from the top down to third- and sometimes second- and first-line management, and other changes at the factories. In the post–World War II period, every factory, research site, and division published a newspaper or newsletter. They had learned lessons from *IBM Business Machines*. One reason for discontinuing it was because there now were so many other publications aimed at IBMers to keep them informed about their corner of the firm.

In 1927, most IBM employees in the United States and many in other countries received an anthology of speeches made by President Thomas J. Watson, Sr. Two expanded editions appeared in 1931 and 1934. Referencing the 1934 edition, one could see that *Men-Minutes-Money* was long, 886 pages to be exact, and included illustrations and a few photographs. It was a substantive volume that clearly took time to organize and was expensive to produce. Like its earlier editions, it was intended to explain the operating philosophy of the company and its attitudes toward good work habits and to encourage and celebrate the company's achievements and prospects. It contained most of Watson's speeches delivered to internal IBM groups and others in public forums.[39] So, one can assume copies seeped outside of IBM. Watson spent considerable time personally promoting IBM; this publication was a by-product of that effort. A French edition of the same anthology was published duplicating exactly the same trim size, cover, title, and page layout as the original English 1934 edition.[40] Watson soon after launched a magazine called *THINK*, which he intended for both employees and the public at large, much along the lines of, say, *The Atlantic*. He personally wrote a short editorial for each issue until his death in 1956, espousing many of the values of the anthologies.

For special occasions, IBM published booklets for narrowly focused audiences. Four examples illustrate this genre of publications from the United States. On September 19, 1942, the mayor of Endicott, New York, home of IBM's largest manufacturing site, hosted a "War Rally and IBM Day," which involved a parade and other ceremonies. IBM published a 125-page, large-format booklet that included color photographs, speeches, and other information of a celebratory nature.[41] In 1947, a monument was dedicated in Endicott at the IBM Country Club to memorialize the fifty-seven local IBM employees who died in World War II. IBM sent copies of this beautiful publication to families of these deceased IBMers and made it available to all employees and citizens in the area.[42] One could also acquire a postcard of the monument. In the postwar years, and only for several years, IBM published a hardback book modeled on college yearbooks to celebrate events held at the annual 100 Percent Club gatherings. Each attendee received a copy. These commemorative publications included group photographs from each sales office and coverage of the ceremonies and speakers and of the physical site.[43] In other countries, IBM also published books and pamphlets relevant to their localities, largely in Germany, the United Kingdom, and France, such as for commemorating the opening of a new plant. Decades later, country organizations published (or commissioned) similar pamphlets and books celebrating their fiftieth anniversary of being in that country.[44]

Our survey of IBM's internally directed gray literature would be incomplete without mentioning, briefly, *Songs of the I.B.M.* Until the 1970s, but beginning by the 1920s, employees sang songs about the company and its leaders set to popular tunes of the day. If the reader knew only two things about IBM's culture it would probably be the THINK logo and that employees sang these songs. They were collected into booklets and published informally either by IBM or employees using local printers. They have been discussed by others so will not be discussed here.[45] Editions of these appeared every several years, such as in 1931, 1934, and 1937, and again after World War II.[46] The company commissioned its own anthem in the 1930s for full orchestra presentation entitled *Ever Onward*, as an IBM rally song. The corporation in numerous editions published the music score for it, and it was played at IBM events, largely between the 1930s and the 1960s.[47] It would be difficult to imagine any employee not having sung its words in that period.

In the years between World War I and the end of the 1940s, IBM had created writing and publishing operations in New York City and Endicott in the United States and smaller staffs in major European countries. Standard types of publications appeared that, over time, became the same references employees used around the world. A CE manual from 1932 makes clear that the owner was trained in Endicott, where he received the publication, while his working location was in China.[48] Publications were stocked in sales offices for local staff to consult and distribute to customers. In large data processing installations (often called the "IBM Department," or "IBM Room"), CEs had an office, which would also have contained copies of such publications. By the 1930s, "pubs" had a common look and feel consistent with the publishing styles of the day. The amount of information in each was impressive and understandably so, given the complexity of the machinery and their technology. But that attention to detail also spilled over into other nontechnical publications.

Because customers and the public at large were objects of IBM's publishing intentions, the firm wanted to project an image of being concerned about the welfare of society and to be seen as sophisticated. The Watson family collected art from all the countries in which IBM had a business presence, exhibiting these at its headquarters in New York and at the 1939 World's Fair. IBM periodically published catalogs of the collection in support of its image.[49] Meanwhile, the company began publishing proceedings of technical conferences, as it broadened its participation in events involving computing and other advanced electronics, beginning in 1948. Annually for years, it published these under various titles. For example, the proceedings for the technical conference it hosted in November 1949 was entitled *Seminar on Scientific Computing*. It was held in Endicott, New York, and organized by IBM's Department of Education, the same organization that produced many of the training materials mentioned earlier and that collaborated with the publishing department at that site. Presenters included academics and IBM engineers.[50] The format remained essentially unchanged throughout the 1950s as it published proceedings of subsequent gatherings.

But the centerpiece of IBM's outreach gray literature of the period was *THINK* magazine. IBM began publication of *THINK* in June 1935 and did not cease until the early 1990s. Until the end of 1970, the magazine was aimed at customers and the public at large. IBM distributed it at no charge to readers. Subsequently, it became an internal magazine for employees, replacing older company-wide newspapers. External distribution ended while employees continued to receive copies mailed to their homes. But although a public-facing magazine, it rarely carried any articles about IBM; rather, it published essays by individuals with ideas, such as book and magazine authors, artists, educators, business leaders, and others with national reputations. Watson Sr. wrote 252 editorials for this magazine, presenting the only company content. In his first editorial, he said the magazine's purpose was "to help to develop in its readers a more conscious and active impulse to *think*."[51] While designed as a slick publication comparable to high-end general trade magazines of its day, in its early years, it went out only to thousands of people. As an internal publication, tens, then hundreds, of thousands of employees had access to it.

When IBM Publications Became Massively Available, 1950s–1980s

IBM's world changed so much in the 1950s, along with its gray literature, that it may seem difficult to link prior practices to those that came initially in the 1950s. But lessons learned from prior experiences carried over into the next era. These included what kinds of publications were needed by employees, customers, and the public; how to blend technical details with messages about IBM as a technical powerhouse and good corporate citizen; and how best to write, produce, print, and distribute these. In the 1950s, IBM moved from electromechanical products—tabulators—to computers, which incorporated hardware, software, and computer science. All were new fields of knowledge, products, and markets for IBM and everybody else. This new information had to be represented in its literature. That reality alone resulted in IBM becoming one of the world's largest publishers by the mid-1960s. The volume of publications it distributed dwarfed the efforts of most, if not all, commercial publishers of its day. That volume combined more text, because the products and services required were more varied and complicated than earlier ones, and more copies, because instead of having a few thousand customers, IBM now serviced tens of thousands of them, with the largest having multiple data centers each in need of IBM's publications. If one acquired, for example, six tape drives, they received six sets of operating manuals; every time a new release of a software package arrived at a data center, so too a new set of updated installation and operating manuals or pages. Customers frequently wanted multiple copies of publications, particularly user manuals.

A few statistics set the scene for the massive changes. In 1950, IBM employed just over 30,000 people worldwide; in 1985, over 400,000. In 1950, IBM's revenue totaled $266 million; in 1985, it had increased to $50.7 billion.[52] To put those revenue numbers in perspective, the revenues from 1950, if expressed in 1985's purchasing power, would have been $1.19 billion. Instead of shipping hundreds of computers and a few thousand peripheral machines for those mainframes by the mid- to late-1950s, IBM was shipping thousands by the mid-1960s, and in the 1980s, millions of PCs, all accompanied by gray literature. For example, in the mid-1960s, IBM had 2,500 software programs; manuals accompanied each product. In 1965, IBM shipped to customers 30 million pages of documentation for its products.[53] IBM's popular 1400 computer system, shipped between the late 1950s and early 1960s, opened a new market to thousands of additional customers. IBM produced several dozen publications for each computer model and its peripheral equipment. The same was done for software. By 1963, IBM had published over 300,000 copies of manuals and the product had yet to be retired.[54]

The introduction of the System/360 family of computers and related hardware and software products in 1964 totaled 150 products, and that stimulated the massive growth of the firm in the 1960s. That transformation represented nothing less than a publishing tsunami such as the business world had never seen before. David Larkin, a writer in Poughkeepsie—ground zero for the System/360—worked sixty- to seventy-hour weeks in the late 1960s as part of a staff comprised of young technical writers. "We did not complain," even if they had tight deadlines, which when they met them led to "a great sense of celebration."[55] Not even such widely diffused products as the automobile or television approached their volumes because these two consumer products did not require as much documentation with which to install, use, and repair them. It becomes understandable why employees in the 1970s believed that, after the U.S. government, IBM was the world's largest publisher. Their customers and IBM offices were swamped with publications.[56] Larkin recalled customers complaining about the number of "librarians" they needed to employ to keep manuals updated with new inserts or to replace older editions. But they needed these in order to use IBM's products.[57]

At the start of the 1950s, the challenge before IBM, every customer (known soon after as users of data processing equipment), regulators, vendors, and academics is that they knew too little or nothing about computers, as there were only dozens installed at the start of the decade and software was just beginning to be created. It would be later in the decade that even such terms as "software," "programming languages," and "computer science" appeared. IBM made and sold proto-computers in the late 1940s, portending of things to come, but avoided the word computer, rather applying the term "calculator."[58]

Three challenges confronted IBM and its rivals: teaching people about what computers were, teaching them about what they could be used for and why ("applications"), and training them on how to use these systems (operations, installation, programming). These problems were compounded by the fact that, in the beginning, vendors and government agencies needed to learn a great deal about electronics themselves and had to invest enormous sums in developing the base technologies before converting them into marketable products. All of these activities had to be dealt with while the technology and products continued to change every year, decade after decade. Everything had to be documented in user manuals and in all manner of training. These activities were in the service of tens of thousands of people in dozens of countries by the mid-1950s and in over 150 nations by the end of the 1980s. Central to the transmission of information about computing was IBM's library of gray literature. The first step toward understanding this massive literature from this period is to identify the types that appeared between the 1950s and the end of the 1980s. Later, we discuss how these were created at IBM.

Beginning with educating "everyone" about the nature of computing led to publication of many pamphlets, books, and articles, some by the same title in various iterations, such as those describing the concept of data processing. For both employees and customers, early on, IBM focused on electronics because, as one publication from the early 1950s reported, "many people are genuinely interested in learning about the fascinating science of electronics," but most non-IBM publications on the subject were "not easy to understand" and "fail[ed] to meet the needs of those looking for general information applicable to their particular problem."[59] That quote essentially expressed the message of many generalized publications issued over the next four decades. Besides concepts, these included examples (applications) of using computers and bibliographies of IBM and other publications.[60] In the years 1959–1963, the need for more of these kinds of publications surged as IBM became fully committed to selling computers.[61] The Data Processing Division (DPD), housing the employees who sold large mainframes to large customers, published a set of seven pamphlets in 1960 and 1961 as a self-study program entitled *Punched Card Data Processing Principles*. Clearly written and illustrated, each was thirty to fifty pages in length. Topics included *The IBM Card and Its Preparation*, *The IBM Sorter*, and so forth for all the major components of a computer system.[62] They focused on hardware. A companion series entitled *Principles of Programming* consisted of a dozen pamphlets with software-centric topics. These included *The Nature of Programming*, *Introduction to Computing Equipment*, *Coding Fundamentals*, *Symbolic Programming*, *Magnetic Tape Operations*, *Random Access File Storage*, and *Planning and Installing a Computer Application*.[63] These topics represented a major break from those of the late 1940s to early 1950s. They were largely directed to IBMers.

For customers, IBM created a series in the 1960s called general information manuals, or in IBM and customer slang term, "GI manuals." These were widely consulted as initial, yet sufficiently detailed introductions to concepts of data processing and to specific topics. GI manuals were produced for decades and had their own look. One could spot these from across a room. Figure 11.3 illustrates their style in the 1960s and 1970s. These had a slightly more marketing edge to them. For example, *Introduction to IBM Data Processing Systems*, published at the same time as the two self-study pamphlets, was boiled down to a single ninety-three-page volume in the now standard 8 × 11–inch format. Chapters included such topics as data representation, storage devices, central processing unit (mainframe), input-output devices, stored program concepts, programming systems, procedure controls, and business practices.[64]

GI manuals were produced for specific systems, such as for the 1400 Data Processing System (updated annually), which introduced all facets of the product with illustrations in forty-three pages.[65] Other booklets were subsequently issued doing the same for every computer and piece of peripheral equipment coming from IBM and, similarly, for every software product. By 1980, sales manuals (consulted by sales representatives and systems engineers in branch offices) had to keep up with some 3,000 products. If undergoing training, both

General Information Manual

Introduction to IBM Data Processing Systems

11.3 Sample IBM General Information (GI) manual, 1960.

(Courtesy, author's collection.)

customers and employees would read similar materials but with less marketing sizzle and more factual descriptions of components and how they worked.[66]

GI publications informed the reader about a subject's scope, largely to teach "basic knowledge of computers," not necessarily about specific hardware or software. They usually added additional text such as "because of the dynamic nature of data processing, where changes and improvements are being made at a very rapid pace, the reader is advised to refer to the IBM Systems Reference Library and other IBM publications for the most current information."[67] Reference Library publications did not have fancy covers, and their first page was made of the same paper stock as the rest of the booklet, which was simply stapled together. They often ran into hundreds of pages, shared similar internal two-column formats, and contained many black and white photographs and largely technical details. They were written in collaboration with engineers most familiar with the subject. IBM CEs and systems engineers used these, rarely sales staff, while systems analysts, computer operators, and programmers in customer installations constantly consulted these. Like well-used cookbooks, it is rare to find one in pristine condition.

These were frequently updated so their publication history often included a short paragraph to explain that history; these were always posted on the copyright page. With a widely installed product, such as the thousands of System/360s in the 1960s and early 1970s and for their accompanying software, it would not have been uncommon for several copies to exist in a data center, and of course, the IBM CEs would have additional ones as well.[68] Such publications existed for every product, features of machines, and software. These, too, appeared in multiple editions. The one just cited was in its eleventh edition, yet more appeared until this product was retired.

Within the Reference Library were other publications in their own series entitled Reference Manuals. These came in different formats but served the same purpose, to guide a user of a product on how to use it. These combined overviews of a device and also, in effect, how to push the buttons. As IBM moved away from tabulating to calculators to digital computers, some of the manuals from an earlier period were updated, which one could understand by reading the edition histories on the backside of the title page. For entirely new products, a fresh publication was needed. Often these were small spiral affairs that could literally be placed next to a machine that an operator could consult frequently. The one for the System/370, which replaced the System/360 computers, was first issued in July 1974 and would have been delivered along with the shiny new computer at the same time. As with any operating manual, it provided instructions on all the codes an operator might use to command a computer system; in this case, it also provided instructions for all peripheral equipment and additional specific instructions for the operating software used by the mainframe.[69] Because even an experienced computer operator could not run a computer system without this publication, it was not uncommon to have multiple copies circulating in the data center with backup copies in a tape library. IBM CEs used these when installing, testing, or repairing systems and so also had their own and others at branch offices. When new editions appeared, older ones were discarded or new pages inserted after struggling with the industrial-grade staples that caused many a bloodied finger to wrestle off the updates.

For customer engineers working in the Field Engineering Division by the 1960s, the next level of detail must seem excruciating to an historian. Training on the System/360 was ongoing and consumed months with a combination of pre-school self-study, in-person classroom sessions, and hands-on instruction in Poughkeepsie, New York, where the majority of the 360s were made, and subsequently on the use of the product handbooks needed in order to repair equipment. Figure 11.4 illustrates one of these handbooks, and as becomes quickly obvious, it continues the useful tradition of the CE handbooks of earlier decades. A CE who obviously consulted it a great deal owned this particular copy. He added handwritten tabs to differentiate models of the System/360.

11.4 An IBM System/360 *Field Engineering Handbook*, circa 1965.

(Courtesy, author's collection.)

IBM engaged with one other stream of publications beginning in 1981 and continuing unabated until the early 2000s—publications in support of the IBM personal computer (PC). This product was integral to shifting computing from being mainframe centered (or distributed) to minicomputers and desktop computing. While IBM continued publishing materials in support of its traditional lines of business and its worldviews regarding computing in general, the PC caused the birth of a different paradigm. For one thing, people scattered in buildings and offices all over Earth now had an IBM product on their desk, and the vast majority of these users were not computer experts. IBM could not support all of these people with CEs and classes to the extent that it had customers in the past. These machines had to come out of a box, be plugged into an electrical wall socket, and run. In reality, of course, that proved difficult to do. However, with every machine came a fat manual mimicking the traditional product guides of old. Soon, much of this kind of material was included additionally on diskettes, later on CDs, and finally accessible over the internet. More than earlier products of the 1970s and increasingly evident in the 1980s, gray literature became mixed media and even later was embedded in the installation diskettes and CDs for software. DOS manuals for the operating system came from Microsoft; commercial publishers stepped in as well, such as with the Idiot Guides.[70]

Binders with text published by IBM included both paper and digitized materials. Figure 11.5 is an example. Its physical appearance represented a step into a new dimension of IBM literature, although still formatted to sit in a bookcase. With the PC, many commercial software products became available that were not sold by IBM, and these items came with their combination paper binders and media cluttering shelves alongside IBM's publications. By the 1990s, large bookstore chains in the United States, Europe, Japan, and South Korea, such as Borders and Barnes & Noble in North America, had sections devoted to PC guides and contemporary programming languages and database software. Because mainframes did not go away, and still have not, publications in support of these continued to appear, increasingly in electronic media formats, as text embedded in products, or in paper book-like formats.

One final set of publications that proved useful were called "Application Briefs." Published since the 1930s, but in a standard format by the end of the 1960s, these were two- to eight-page slick documents that described how a named customer institution was using a set of specific products. These were positive but factual testimonials (case studies) with quotes from named customer managers about how they used IBM products and the benefits derived from these. The vast majority were industry specific, meaning that they were tailored to those industries IBM had targeted to market computers. Thus, banking uses of IBM products, others about computing in the automotive industry, and so forth were published for decades. Many thousands of pages of these

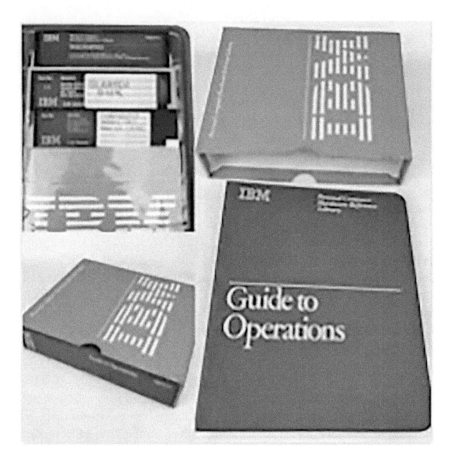

11.5 IBM *PC Guide to Operations*, 1982.

(Courtesy, author's collection.)

marketing aids were produced. A salesperson who thought their account had a good story to tell would reach out to the appropriate IBM product division or work through their own sales division's communications staff to arrange an interview with a customer. Photographs of the installation or customer personnel using the application were taken; a draft was written and then approved by the sales representative, the customer (often by their communications and legal staff, too), and communications and legal in IBM; and finally, the brief was published. IBMers would distribute these to other customers and at conferences, while their customers would do the same with their management to demonstrate how progressive and successful their data centers were—so good that even the "Great IBM Company" was so impressed that it sent people to interview the staff. Historians wanting to document how computers were used by specific companies and across entire industries can consult this large body of materials as a major historical source.[71]

A significant gap in our knowledge of these publications is what customers used—were required to use—often simultaneously. Knowing that would go beyond the obvious documents we have discussed. We do not have good insight to create a topology, even though we know what "pubs" they needed for every piece of software and equipment they used. However, once in a while, we can count on a little luck. The GI manual for CICS (Customer Information Control System) provides a bit. CICS was probably installed on 99 percent of all IBM mainframe computers (not PCs) since the early 1970s because it was the software that made it possible to move data from one computer to another, anywhere. But, like all software, it must operate within a larger collection of software, including an operating system and with the assist of utilities and other database management code. In the back of its GI manual of the 1970s, there was a list of publications needed to be consulted. These were listed by software required to use CICS. These included literature on CICS itself (providing an example of what normally was available for any software), publications for the operating system in which CICS would operate (but only those actually needed to make CICS work), and database manuals. Under each were listed between ten and twelve publications and, for each, a use key. Use keys indicated if they were generally available (i.e., free with no charge in reasonable quantities), sold for a fee through IBM's sales offices, or "licensed materials, Property of IBM," which is the software itself, licensed to customers per terms of a contract. Notice that IBM treated software as a publication. Every publication had an ordering number, and the first letter in that number communicated if it was free ("Generally Available"), S ("Sold" like one buys a book at a store or IBM branch office), or L ("Licensed Material"), demonstrating the precise hand of the legal folks on full display.[72] IBM's culture was always influenced by the thinking of its lawyers.

IBM also published various manuals for use by employees in their private lives to inform their relations with the company. The central publication of this type, which was updated every year from the 1950s, generally retained its title over the decades: *About Your Company*. Like reference publications, these often were in spiral binders so that one could add and change pages and consult the work about everything from pensions to medical benefits. These were normally sent to each employee's home. Over the decades, they became elegant publications. Figure 11.6, for example, included various pamphlets published between the mid-1980s and the early 1990s on subjects similar to earlier editions. From having no illustrations to having fancy multicolored ones, IBM used these to promote the firm and its benefits to both employees and their families. The set of manuals illustrated in figure 11.6 was encased in a plastic box embossed

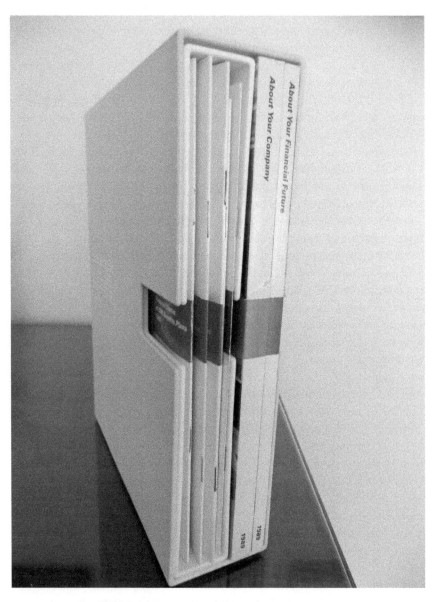

11.6 IBM, *About Your Company*, 1988–1992. Box set of benefits booklets for U.S. employees.

(Courtesy, author's collection.)

with the IBM logo. Its pamphlets were tailored to individual IBMers by name to show them, for example, specifically what *their* pension would be when they retired at different ages, complete with charts and graphs. Earlier editions from the 1960s often ran to over one hundred pages. At the time, IBM employed some 400,000 individuals, so many copies were produced.[73]

Structuring the Content and Format of Publications, 1950s–1980s

How did IBM put together so many publications? How extensive was that operation? The history of gray literature in large multinational corporations remains largely unknown, so too about the scope of the activities required to support it. Since IBM routinely adopted and shared practices from other companies, most of whom were its customers, answers to these questions regarding IBM's experience suggest how other enterprises created their own publications. The process for producing publications had stabilized into long-lasting practices by the 1950s. Over time, these were modified to account for the emergence of new writing and publishing software tools and in response to reorganizations, largely concerning where publishing, warehousing, and distribution took place.

From the 1940s to the present, organizations that developed and manufactured products were also responsible for producing for each a set of publications as part of their "deliverables" to the rest of the company and to customers. One writer, Cathy Sheffler, explained what was required for each product and, if necessary, for each new version of one (e.g., software), requirements that also applied to hardware. These included "an announcement letter," known as a Blue Letter because these two- to four-page documents were printed on blue paper, and "general information manual, installation and operation manual, reference manual (commands and messages), and a user's guide or two, depending on how many types of users the product had." Years later, writers produced text to embed in software for end users to access while in a program (e.g., "How to" text). Writers were instructed by the *IBM Style Guide* in use for decades that "followed the *Chicago Manual of Style*." Writers "always used the Oxford comma."[74] One writer noted: "Writers were expected to produce material written to an eighth-grade reading level (a difficult task when writing about a complex technical topic) in straightforward active voice. Internally, people in the community might have known who wrote a specific manual, but the manuals were always anonymous. The only way in which a writer could insert an 'Easter egg' into a manual was in an example, by using a friend's name or a hometown street name."[75]

By the 1940s, and extending to the end of the century, the process for writing and producing publications remained essentially unchanged. A product division staffed a small coterie devoted to the task. Several technical writers, known as information developers by the1960s, would review the technical specifications developed for the new or updated product and then work with product developers and engineers to understand the topic by interviewing them. They would create an outline of the publication to be written or changes to be made, confirm with the technicians that this made sense, and then after numerous discussions would write a first draft. The technicians would critique the text for accuracy and completeness. A draft would be written by hand or typed. Once a draft had settled, then the manuscript was passed to an editor to polish, followed by an art department and photographers contributing illustrations. Then, all was entered into a software system designed to lay out pages. These were reviewed again and, if needed, updated or corrected and then signed off by appropriate product managers and the legal department, before typically being shipped to the Program Information Department (PID) located in the DPD sales division for printing and stocking in a warehouse (in the United States in the middle decades in Hawthorne, New York, or at Mechanicsburg, Pennsylvania). From there, publications would be distributed to customers and the rest of IBM, as needed.

The writers' biggest challenge was often to translate what the technologists were saying into "understandable language," because as one, George DeSalvo, recalled, engineering notes and language had "too much jargon for sales and customers." He considered the task one of "translation."[76] Given the range of publications associated with each product, the task required considerable flexibility to be able to prepare a general press release announcement all the way to CE manuals of excruciating detail. DeSalvo became a manager of the writing department located near Poughkeepsie. In the 1970s and 1980s, his department had four to five writers and up to forty to fifty additional staff associated with it to do art work, layout, and so forth. Often outside editors were engaged to polish texts. His organization had a broad scope of publications, because in addition to the normal suite of publications, he had to produce pocket foldouts and templates. In one two-year period in the 1970s, he published fifty to sixty manuals.[77]

A great deal of work involved revising earlier editions of a publication. One writer explained the process as of the 1970s (but that dated to much earlier times) as follows:

> We revised manuals on paper. To make revisions, you'd copy the pages from the existing manual, marked them up with changes, copy the marked-up pages, and then send them to the reviewers by interoffice mail. In a few days to a week, we would hold a scheduled inspection, where the writer typically brought treats to bribe the inspectors to show up and give feedback. When the process was completed, the updated or new pages went to an Editorial Assistants group that updated the computer files with the new material and performed indexing. The

manuals were then released to a Controlling Party, who arranged to have them printed and stocked in PID, where they could be ordered by IBMers or customers based on unique manual numbers.[78]

One writer recalled that "by the mid-1980s, though, most if not all Information Developers were doing their own formatting while writing and editing using ISIL, a publishing tool based on Generalized Markup Language (GML), which later became a product called BookMaster."[79]

All product groups used the same process, style manuals, and Mechanicsburg. Prior to the 1960s, one wrote to a technical publications department at a factory site for copies, or a customer simply reached out to their salesman to deal with procurement, as publications were free until 1970, when IBM began charging for some of these.[80]

For many decades, there existed books and articles from book and magazine publishers about how to write press releases and perform technical writing and, of course, concerning writing styles and grammar. While these were readily available to IBM's writers in all periods, it became clear by the early 1950s that management had to establish common practices that transcended the increasing variety of publications emanating from the company. At first, writing guidelines were few, but by the end of the 1960s, these were being issued as publications to a growing community of writers. None of this ephemera from that decade seems to have survived, but samples from subsequent years prove they existed and had gone through multiple editions. Some were presented as guides and suggestions, while others mandated standards. One from the 1970s–1980s presented advice by topic, not chapters, such as on the use of grammar (e.g., capitalization, dashes), on copyediting (e.g., figure numbering, type fonts), and on policy (e.g., indexing, notices, references to other manuals).[81] The writer's bible was *IBM Editorial Guidelines*, variants of which were published for over a half century.[82] It was nearly two hundred pages in length and had chapters on the role of IBM's publications, how to organize content for different audiences (e.g., management, employees, customers, technicians, editorials for the general public), writing styles and editing, design and layout of publications, techniques (e.g., interviewing and taping, bylines and credits), writing bulletin board notices and their purposes, and surveys; it ended with sample documents and forms. Because consistency was desired, the company even published a one-hundred-page manual that explained why and how to maintain consistency.[83] In the late 1980s, quality management had become a widespread interest across the corporate world, and so the technical community received quality control publications and presentations.[84]

To ensure that publications were not overlooked, IBM's formal, rigorous product development processes from the 1950s onward included the requirement for the development of a publications plan. It had to be checked off before a product developer could move on to the next step. Larkin recalled that engineering "hated that step." In his case, at least he knew a great deal about software because he had undergone training in programming early in his writing career at IBM.[85] The process applied to hardware and software.

Writers and related staff came from all walks of life. Some were secretaries who were promoted to these jobs, others drifted in from part-time writing and graphics art gigs to permanent positions, still others began as technical or programming college majors. Most were not what one might think of, say English majors or journalists, but Larkin was an Ohio State University graduate with majors in English and journalism. Those who wrote press releases for a division or corporate office were by the 1980s professional media writers separate from those producing manuals and other product-related literature.

Occasionally, one division or corporate headquarters would host a seminar on technical writing for the writers. Many were sent off to technical schools to learn about the products they were writing about. Some periodically participated in internal meetings attended by large numbers of CEs, salesmen, and customers, where they obtained feedback about publications. Colleagues and their direct managers taught them in an ad hoc way, while on-the-job experiences provided the rest of their education. They reported to similarly named organizations within a division, such as the Information Development Department. These included writers, editorial and artwork staffs, and others responsible for preliminary production of page-ready materials.

In Rochester, Minnesota, for example, the combined total hovered at about one hundred in the early 1970s: dozens in production, twelve in editorial, twenty graphic designers, the rest writers, and six managers. The large number can be accounted for by the fact that Rochester produced a wide range of minicomputer systems, including the S/32, S/34, S/36, S/38, and beginning in the late 1980s, the AS/400. Each required its own collection of publications and frequent revisions, all destined to many thousands of locations.[86] Rochester faced a unique challenge also faced by the writers attached to PC products in that most users were not as technically savvy as those in large mainframe "glass houses," although large corporations acquired these midrange systems, too. As Glen Douglas recalled about the early 1980s, he wrote manuals intended for CEs and other technical staffs, also for the less technologically initiated: "I interacted heavily with Market Planning and Programming Development on the System/36 Release 1 project as one of the primary objectives for System/36 was an ease-of-use installation."[87]

Moving from creation of a publishable document to a deliverable in the hands of a customer or IBMer for decades before the 1950s had been handled by major plant sites, where publishing departments made arrangements with print shops to produce documentation. But two new circumstances in the 1950s made that long-standing approach woefully inadequate: the move to computers and software as IBM products and the vast increase in the number and type of publications that needed to be distributed.

It was in the 1950s, too, that the company concluded software was a type of publication, a type of information. That conclusion, a by-product of the evolution of technology from just cards and metal machines, was both profound and logical. It was profound because historians of gray and other literature think in terms of paper ephemera, such as books, pamphlets, journals, and newspapers. But here, we see an industry, not just IBM, adding to that list paper tape and more expansively magnetized media as publications. That represented new thinking, different, say, from a librarian's or traditional publisher's perspective, but also a continuation of an older idea at IBM. The older concept from which magnetic tape libraries and deliverables emerged was the notion that decks of computer cards and paper tape had long been viewed as information, as publications, as deliverables that needed to accompany machines in the 1910s–1950s. So millions of punch cards, for instance, were shipped monthly out of Endicott, New York. IBMers and their customers used librarians' language to describe first cards, next tape, and by the end of the 1980s, diskettes as "publications," "literature," and "libraries."

Beginning in the 1950s, IBM had to ship a combination of cards, paper tape, reels of tape, and machines in whatever combination a customer or IBMer required. Even if only shipping out software on cards or tape, paper ephemera accompanied these *at the same time*. As volumes of everything increased, often even at exponential rates from the 1950s through the 1980s, IBM had to constantly revise the older approaches for distribution to keep up with demand. Since most of the initial documentation—including software—originated in the United States, much of the innovation in distribution did too.

Each of the product divisions kept reorganizing its publishing operations, tending to create centralized sites (warehouses and distribution departments) where cards, paper tapes, magnetic tapes, and manuals were stored and then packaged to send out to customers and other IBM localities. In the case of magnetic tapes, data centers were established around the world to make copies of software, which then were combined with paper ephemera. For example, in 1958, IBM opened such a facility in Hawthorne, New York. Its tagline was a "Library without books." Known as the Program Information Department (PID), it reported to DPD and was responsible for materials for computers and all their peripheral equipment and software. In 1965, it moved into a 74,000-square-foot facility solely devoted to the production of copies of software and their distribution and shipment, too, of paper ephemera. Its data center had three System/360 computer systems, and three 1401 systems, along with specialized tape reproduction equipment (IBM 7299). Just regarding software, PID had to manage deliverables for some 3,000 programs. Orders came in and were met, and boxes were filled per order and shipped out by the truckload every day.[88] By the mid-1960s, PID was annually shipping out over 400,000 computer programs, often doubling volumes year-over-year in the 1960s. It also delivered to other facilities master copies of everything for distribution elsewhere, with centers located in Paris, Toronto, Rio de Janeiro, Tokyo, and Sydney. These additional facilities were collectively distributing 300,000 programs in the mid-1960s. Since IBM did not charge fees for software or publications until 1970, the company paid for all these shipments as part of the cost of doing business.[89]

To add to the complexity, IBM required that publications distributed in other countries be translated into many local languages. The local country usually outsourced that work. One writer in Poughkeepsie recalled that even software manuals were translated into Icelandic even though there were only two banks there in the 1960s that needed these and the customer staff spoke English![90]

In the second half of the 1960s, facilities such as Hawthorne's proved essential, due to the great popularity of the IBM System/360 family of computers, peripherals, and software. IBM management anticipated in mid-decade that Hawthorne alone would have to be able to ship "more than 300 million punched cards and more than 100,000 reels of magnetic tape, accompanied by 60 million pages of documentation."[91]

An IBM manager responsible for shipping publications about the installation and use of software in the United States in the late 1960s, Rich Arco, recalled that employees ran an operation seven days a week almost around the clock to meet demand and that effort did not include a separate function at various manufacturing sites doing the same thing for many thousands of machines. To be even more specific, Arco was one of the computer center managers at PID (Program Information Department) in Hawthorne, New York, responsible for also creating machine-readable materials (tapes, disks, cards). This material was paired with necessary documentation that was drop shipped from Mechanicsburg, Pennsylvania, to be sent to customers. PID's overall population to support this operation in the 1970s exceeded two hundred employees. At that time, they had to work weekends to keep up with demand. His organization required between 200 and 225 employees to support media distribution. His staff comprised over sixty programmers, between twenty and thirty systems analysts, and others, and everyone seemed to be working constantly under pressure to meet tight deadlines. Arco recalled volumes being "huge," with over 40,000 customers to satisfy and, for example, shipping out "15 to 20 million cards per week," and later diskettes. He was also the manager who had to rebuild the data center after a devastating fire completely destroyed it in 1972.[92] His recollection of having many emergency "rush jobs" to ship that often had to be packaged overnight and on weekends was confirmed by a press release of the period that reported a weekly average of three hundred of these:

"Customers on tight deadlines have sent helicopters, private airplanes and couriers to pick up programs. The U.S. Navy has delivered a program at sea by destroyer."[93] The same infrastructure that supported publications of software and their attendant manuals existed for hardware as well, particularly for writing and preparing manuals for printing.

Expansion of various delivery facilities punctuated the story of IBM's distribution activities from the 1950s through the 1980s. Each product division eventually established a distribution system apart from its writing departments. Online orders were received worldwide from field sales offices through the sales order processing application (AAS). That application sent orders to the appropriate division that combined ephemera with products. For example, Poughkeepsie, home to the development and manufacture of many of IBM's early computers in the late 1950s, felt the pinch of growth. In 1960, local management announced the consolidation of various publishing and distribution operations. Additionally, they declared that consolidation into one organization named Product Publications "will reduce costs by eliminating duplication and improving planning, and will also result in standardized uniform publication formats." To give a sense of the work to be done, several units were created in this new organization: Customer Engineering Reference Manuals, Customer Manuals, Customer Engineering Instruction Manuals, Customer Engineering Installation Publications, Publications, Publishing, and Administrative Services, each led by a manager. Collectively, they were responsible for producing and supplying "manuals, catalogues and other printed material to IBM customers and IBM's sales and service organization."[94] Several years later, there were usually five to six writers and one editor just for software manuals, another fifteen or so administrative, data entry, and text-formatting personnel, and even a publication planning team of four to five people. Production work on manuals required up to fifty people, all at the height of the S/360 days.[95]

A quarter of a century later, the Boulder, Colorado, site, which was responsible for development and manufacture of mid-range systems in the mid-1980s, had a distribution center that included publications. IBM's publications warehouse in Mechanicsburg, Pennsylvania, transferred some of its responsibilities to Boulder. Boulder's mission expanded in the 1980s to include production of printers, copiers, and miscellaneous plastic parts. Additional responsibilities fell to it to also produce more documentation.[96]

The Research Division published two journals, while corporate had *THINK* magazine and annual reports.[97] All were printed outside of the internal publishing operation; however, they were distributed by the same infrastructure used to ship manuals and software to customers. Their order numbers, and hence identifiers, were consistent with IBM's broader publishing numerating system developed decades earlier. Curiously, all publication numbers referred to these pubs as "forms."

Insights from One Multinational Corporation's Experience

What limited conversations occurred among academics about gray literature frame issues largely within the context of either the book as their key lens or as a librarian's cataloging paradigm. The IBM case demonstrates that gray literature is a vast topic far exceeding the breadth of a librarian's perspective. IBM's experience suggests that the volume of its activities parallels or exceeds those of the trade and academic publishing industries. However, there is much yet to compare and contrast with commercial publishers of books, regarding both processes and topics, but this can be productively done with respect to other large corporations and government agencies. To be caddish about it, the role and nature of gray literature need to be taken out of the hands of book historians and librarians because the subject on the business side of the topic is so different than what has been available to consult, so far. It fits squarely into such topical areas as business history, especially of multinational or large corporations; organizational and public administration; the sociology of enterprises; and understanding aspects of one's corporate culture. The IBM case suggests that corporate literature is a different creature than what extant research has explained so far.

There are several lessons to be drawn from IBM's experience. First, as incomplete as the data are because we are missing, for example, data on the cost to IBM of publishing or the exact number of copies of particular publications, we do know this company was prepared to spend far more on publications for a century than, say, a handful of large universities. When millions of publications are distributed (with most if not all costs borne by IBM), one is talking about many tens of millions of dollars to do that and millions of people who used such materials. These proved so useful that the firm was willing to spend the money. It recognized the need to do so from its founding, even in the early years when profits were thin and cash flows carefully managed. There was essentially no choice if employees were to sell, install, and maintain its thousands of products and to shape world views about computing and IBM.

Second, topics chosen for writing and publishing were substantially different than what most commercial and academic publishers produced. IBM did not publish novels or biographies and only rarely published what one might charitably call history. Publish a reference guide about virtual memory (VM) architecture and programming? No problem. Need a guide to IBM 1400 compatibility and error stops? Absolutely. Produce proceedings of learned papers on computer science topics? Just as good. The company printed tens of thousands of copies of publications on many topics that an outsider might consider arcane.[98] IBM had its best sellers, too, such as the many editions of the CEs' bibles, *Manual of Instruction* or *Field Engineering Handbook*, which every CE probably consulted almost every day. Every salesperson had their copy of the

Sales Manual, too. Topics of publications tacked far closer to the day-to-day activities of IBMers and their customers than most "how-to" books from trade publishers. Not until the late 1980s did a few commercial publications achieve similar volumes and then largely for just the operating systems of IBM PCs and their clones and a few popular games and application software, enjoying sales that exceeded a million copies of some publications. Welcome to IBM's experience with publications. Corporations were not frivolous with their budgets, so when one published something, it was because the information it contained had proven vital to the successful operation of the firm.

Third, understanding both the topics and creation process serves as a window into a company's activities and culture. David Larkin, writer in Poughkeepsie in the 1960s, made it clear that the entire formal process imposed by senior management on all divisions for designing and manufacturing new products had to be rigorous. The design process had to come to a hard stop if a publishing plan had not been developed and integrated into the written production development master plan. It was not that senior managers were intellectual in some abstract way or "book people"; it is because the success of large investments in new products would fail without an appropriate suite of publications supporting these. In Larkin's day, the issue was System/360, on which IBM spent approximately $5 billion to develop in 1960's dollars ($38 billion in today's). It was in its day the largest product development investment ever made in American history up to that point. Tough hard-nosed executives insisted on rigor in product development, which they had learned through experiences in prior decades, and even then, they faced nearly insurmountable challenges.[99]

Larkin and his colleagues may not have known it at the time, but their collective publishing output assisted IBM to double in size in a few years and essentially convince advanced economies that it now was time to make computing ubiquitous. Without their publications, none of that could have been accomplished. While it may seem an exaggeration to give publications so much credit, as this chapter suggests, exploring the creation of documents and their diffusion opens windows into aspects of a company's activities that otherwise might not be possible to uncover, let alone understand.

Fourth, and not meant as a criticism of librarians or academic scholars, to understand the role of gray literature in a corporation calls for being knowledgeable about what companies do, how they go about their work, and the technical specifics of their products and services. Without such an appreciation of business activities, much of, say, IBM's publications would make little or no sense to the uninitiated. Librarians and academics need to understand business functions and the specifics of individual industries and technologies to work with this literature. Otherwise, they will remain stuck having conversations about how to catalog and organize such collections and parsing such issues as trade publications versus advertisements versus gray literature.

Fifth, leave aside more classical literary investigations, such as possibly comparing CE manuals produced by other corporations with those from IBM. We are in a situation where we do not know sufficiently what other enterprises have produced, so comparisons of one to another is an example of attempting to put carts before horses. Much basic historical work has yet to be done before one can engage in more comparative discussions about corporate literature. This chapter feels very much like an initial statement announcing that this literature even exists.

Sixth, corporate archivists ponder what to collect. They are constrained like their cohorts in academic settings and government by struggles for space, budget, and attention. IBM has an excellent, well-stocked corporate archive, but as that staff and I discovered when conducting research for this chapter, the paucity of material about IBM's gray literature was borderline embarrassing. It has many publications—our gray literature—but we do not know how complete a set it has, nor if it should have copies of everything. The archive has site and division newsletters, annual reports, various other magazines (such as *THINK*), and company newsletters but is hard-pressed to know how substantive is its collection of more product-centered support materials. Yet the company has a complete set of all its hardware introduced since the 1880s. Creating topologies and literature surveys offers corporate archivists potential shopping lists for what to acquire to improve the company's own understanding of its literature, not to mention assisting, too, historians and other media experts.[100]

IBM's long history with gray literature was fluid. It began with ad hoc publishing as needed in the 1910s–1920s. The types of publications quickly increased from press releases, annual reports, and product manuals to complex maintenance publications in the 1930s, to a variety of descriptions about how to use the technology in business terms, and to celebratory marketing pieces for world's fairs and art exhibits. With the arrival of the computer in the 1950s, the variety, length, and quality of publications grew nearly exponentially, which led to the rapid response to establish publishing guidelines for series, formats, writing styles, and publication practices. By the 1960s, many writing teams were called information developers. They worked throughout all the divisions, a practice maintained since the founding of the company. In the 1950s, they needed to know how to document and have good writing and editing skills; in the 1970s, they had to also be able to work with graphics and to test for accuracy of content; in the subsequent decade, they added word processing and online publishing to their skill set, requirements continued into the next century. Their outputs evolved too, which they referred to as "ID products": "books" (their term for manuals) in the 1950s–1960s, "libraries" in the 1970s, "information" in the 1980s, and "user interfaces" in the 1990s. Their goals changed too, from just product descriptions in the 1950s and 1960s to functional descriptions in the 1970s, then "task-oriented use descriptions" in the 1980s, and in the next decade, a mix of all these goals into software and the machines themselves.

From the 1910s through the 1950s, product literature was normally written after a product was developed. Subsequently, this literature was written as these were being developed and, by the mid-1980s, as an integral part of these efforts. By the 1990s, publications were developed as actual enhancements to a product. Measures of quality and effectiveness evolved as a result. In the first half century, one only had to be complete in their descriptions of products, but by the 1970s, they had to be technically accurate too. Customers and IBMers let the writers know if this was not so.[101] In the 1980s, management became more concerned about improving how easy such publications were to use by the user community and the cost of all "pubs." In the next decade, they also began to study how publications added competitive value to products.[102]

IBM's experience with gray literature as recounted here seems cursory, even though this is the longest chapter in our book, mainly because the subject is vast and central to understanding many of the activities of the firm and how its employees and customers viewed uses of its products and technologies. Publications were central ephemera of the company's culture, but we can see that the daily activities of its employees and customers were influenced by these publications, too. The history of gray literature in large corporations remains a little-understood topic both as an individual subject and as part of understanding a firm's culture in daily practice. It is long overdue to pay more attention to this topic.

Implications for Large Enterprises

This has been a long chapter on purpose. It was important to demonstrate the extent to which a company went—has to go—to construct the information basis for a firm's ecosystem of stakeholders. If this chapter teaches management anything, it is that publishing is a large effort inextricably entwined in both its business strategy and in its execution and in the daily activities within its corporate culture. Publishing is not a sidebar activity. As demonstrated here, it penetrated the lives of employees and customers far more than could advertisements. Those are still needed to call attention to one about a company's offerings, but that scholars and managers have paid so much attention to it does not mean that a firm gets a pass on producing gray literature. It is irrelevant if publications are just 100 percent digital, served up as Google searches, podcasts, or downloadable manuals. That's management's choice, providing, however, it has wisely consulted *all* its stakeholders to understand what they want and have used their own insights to offer what they should want (the Steve Jobs approach to marketing and product development). Facebook groups have taught the world that communities form around information and shared communications. IBM's historical experience demonstrates that Facebook was not the first to learn this lesson. Management does not need a lecture on how to execute a well-thought-out plan for producing publications. More to the point, they need to recognize that this should not be done superficially. Links count.

During the COVID-19 pandemic in 2020–2022, the vacation cruise liner business came to an immediate halt. Viking Cruises, one of the premier participants in its industry, learned lessons IBM had discovered decades earlier. Viking refunded travelers with minimal resistance. But, the company also made sure that everyone in its customer database received frequent, beautifully prepared publications announcing future trips with richly informed content. These felt very much like what employees' families received on a regular and frequent basis from IBM. In addition, Viking published short videos of all the places that were normally visited by their cruises. These were target marketed on television and even through the online news media consulted by previous travelers. Torstein Hagen, the gray-haired leader of the firm, spoke to his audiences about viewing these videos "until we can again travel." He conjured up an information ecosystem comprising people who, as a community, travel on his ships. His gray literature was on paper, digital, and verbal. Databases, phone banks, and his image were all designed not to let potential customers slip away to other pursuits, such as to land-based travel tours to national parks. Watson Sr. would have approved. Everything was purposeful and integrated.

The Viking story reminds us of two glues that make dealing with a company a successful one regardless of who are its stakeholders. First and most obvious is that information, and hence a stakeholder's familiarity with one's products, gives it a preferred status. Second, drawing from notions of material culture, "stuff matters"; in Hagen's case, videos that one can download and not just view, lengthy well-written booklets not just sales flyers, and ships, real ones that previous travelers had spent days on, are powerful adhesives to Viking.

The detailed description of IBM's publishing activities teaches us yet another lesson by raising the question about what else IBM had to do to sustain its corporate culture. We could have written a similarly long chapter to unveil the large number of employees and budgets expended to provide such benefits as insurance, medical coverage, employee investment advice, management of salaries and pensions, employee training, and, of course, all those country clubs. But the lesson would have been the same: it takes enormous quantities of staff and budgets and managerial attention to sustain the basic pillars of a corporation's culture and supporting publishing programs.

Three additional insights from IBM's experience inform what today's corporate management needs to confront. Briefly put, first, many if not most corporations do not communicate as comprehensively as they need to with all their constituencies. Put another way, they need to have a communications strategy for each constituency, including such broad ones as a society's adult population, not just niche occupants, such as lobbyists, regulators, and news media. So, one could ask of their own efforts, are they adequate and comprehensive enough for today's needs?

Second, are corporations producing sufficient amounts of point-of-view publications concerning broad issues of interest to society at large, such as about environmental concerns, role of social media, and effects on children's development that tie back to the firm's priorities and roles? There are many press releases, speeches, and product announcements and propaganda, but not enough empirically funded honest research on issues relevant to a firm and its industry. IBM's history demonstrated that a company needed a broad publication program if it was to shape how the public—and its customers—viewed an issue, in its case, the need for computing and how this technology could assist the evolution of the modern world.

Third, publication programs have to be continuous, voluminous enough, and linked to the concerns of each constituency, forever. Advertisements were never enough, while having employees meet with each constituency, while effective, is never enough either. So much is published and broadcast today that, as marketing experts tell us, to be heard and be paid attention to, one needs to be loud, noisy, and commenting in the right places. How visible in the right corners of a society are the messages a company wants to impart? To what extent are they effective? Sadly, the known cases involve negative ones, such as the tobacco industry's multidecade campaign to persuade consumers that cigarettes did not cause lung cancer and, today, the petroleum industry questioning the reality of environmental degradation. IBM's history demonstrates that the conversations can be broader and less negative too.

These three messages may seem like harsh criticism, but just because a company is doing well today does not mean it will do well tomorrow or, more to the point, win the hearts and minds of the societies in which it operates. Companies are exposed to regulatory and societal backlashes of far greater danger to their business success than competitive assaults or leapfrogging technologies or disgruntled employees whose values are not moored to those of their employers; low salaries mean less in affluent societies, fueling a new wave of ethical considerations. IBM's move from tabulating to computing sales in the 1950s and 1960s was accomplished to an important extent by it persuading entire societies that the new technology was a good move, not a threat to, say, employment or to the advent of a 1984 "big brother" government.

In addition to presenting a summary of key findings, the next chapter discusses the broader implications for studying the role of corporate and material culture. What are firms to take from this exercise as they consider their future? A great conundrum for senior managers is what to propagate that worked in the past and how to do that in a future that we are told will be so different, so digital, so disrupted by the same kinds of issues historians have long studied. That is the task to which the last chapter is assigned.

PART III

HOW IBM'S CULTURE WENT GLOBAL AND ENDURED

CHAPTER 12

THE ESSENTIAL STRATEGY FOR CORPORATE SUCCESS

They say a man is known by the company he keeps. We say in our business that a company is known by the men it keeps. You are the picked men and women of our company and the outstanding men and women of the communities in which you live.

Thomas J. Watson, Sr., 1926[1]

When asked what is the essential strategy for corporate success, IBM employees overwhelmingly answer the same way, regardless of whether in 1926 or in any subsequent decade: the superior caliber of the company's workforce. Every published memoir makes the same point. Two professors at the University of Wisconsin, writing in the 1930s, reporting on their research on the nature of business ethics that flirted with our question observed, "There is no substitute for character. And only in a society where there exists a very high level of character can there be any near approach to adequate standards of production whether in quantity or quality, faithful and loyal service, genuine satisfaction in work, and an equitable distribution of wealth."[2] From good people and an aspiration to operate a fair business for *all* their stakeholders sum up what generations of IBM employees thought they were about. From those core thoughts flowed the company's Basic Beliefs, values, and actions that ultimately shaped IBM's corporate culture.

Everyone knew that inside the firm; they did not need to read this book to learn that fact. Thomas J. Watson, Sr., their early guiding force, solidified these aspirations, recruited high-quality employees, and motivated them to exercise their work ethic.

It took another outsider, Louis V. Gerstner, in the 1990s to tell the rest of the world that what IBM employees believed about their values was truly so. Generations of customers knew that, too; it was why for decades one would hear the quip, "Nobody was ever fired for recommending IBM." Choosing IBM was the safe bet, the low risk, based on the quality of its people and their culture of commitment to service, success, and the betterment of society, and less about the quality of its products. It is why even decades after their retirement, employees on social media speak reverently about their experience at IBM. As a test, I randomly went into one of those websites when initially writing this paragraph, looking for a pithy supporting quote, and there it was in the first entry, posted minutes before I logged onto it in December 2020: "I spent 33 years at IBM from 1972 to 2005. There were some ups and downs but overall it was a wonderful experience. Great people to work with and great products and services to sell." This retiree posted a picture of the book cover of Thomas J. Watson, Jr.'s, *A Business and Its Beliefs*, published in 1963. He added, its "principles are sound."[3] Dozens of respondents reacted to his posting saying that they, too, still had their copy, with one opining that "today's executives should read this book. Learn from it." Another stated that "there was always a feeling of honor to have worked for IBM back then."[4] Nearly a half century later, the book remains in print.

Add to these sentiments and beliefs IBM's increasing prosperity, beginning in the 1920s and extending to the end of the 1980s and for a while again in the second half of the 1990s, and one can see how beliefs could be applied through affordable processes, rituals, training, and investments in buildings. We could end this chapter with this paragraph, but if we dig further, it becomes more evident how pervasive the twin issues of quality employees and corporate culture defined IBM more than could a history of its products or biographies of its leaders.

From the epigraph to the social media quotes, one sees little space between the top of the house of IBM's CEOs and individuals drawn from the ranks. On the same day as the quotes were posted on Facebook, a recent chairman, Virginia (Ginni) Rometty, who is widely credited with having done a poorer job running the company in the 2010s than earlier CEOs, wrote a farewell letter, as she slipped into retirement that week. Forty years at IBM had left their mark on her, too, regardless of what one thought of her performance: "I'm so thankful to have worked for a company with enduring values and a strong sense of purpose. As IBMers, we internalize these values," and as so many other IBMers have said on the occasion of their own retirement, "It has been the honor and privilege of a lifetime to work with all of you."[5] As earlier chapters demonstrated, her comments were not just corporate rhetoric; her phrasing makes that clear. The chapters in this book were infused with a mixture of idealism, values, and pragmatic actions. That combination goes far to explain the nature of corporate culture at IBM. Culture guru Edgar H. Schein got it right.

There was a dark side to all of this, of course, because an underlying theme pervasive in IBM's culture was the requirement to conform to it or leave. In this book, we quoted Gerstner telling his senior management to support his plans or go find something else to do. There were stories of people violating the nonexistent dress code being sent home to change shirts and shoes. If one lived in a company town where the majority of one's nearby neighbors were employees, as many tens of thousands experienced in Endicott and Poughkeepsie, New York, it seemed risky to be seen drinking alcoholic beverages or not going to church, while beards and mustaches were unacceptable if in a "customer-facing" role. Only computer scientists ensconced in laboratories could get away with blue jeans and ponytails. Sales executives accused the latter of hoarding technologies that could be converted into products, while the scientists complained that product executives acted like feudal lords protecting their technologies from perceived threats posed by potentially new ones.[6] While there was much talk by executives declaring that a successful career required managers to make their own people successful and not to worry about pleasing their own superiors and prioritizing their own careers, the opposite was often the case, as in other companies.

On balance, if one could fit into IBM's always evolving culture, it was good for them and comfortable; if not, they either were pushed out or left voluntarily. It seemed every employee knew of someone who left in either way. Fit was defined by one's ability to thrive in IBM's world. Often, evidence of the dark side surfaced: the African American who experienced racial prejudice, employees who were pushed out and talked about, and protests against the break against IBM's Basic Beliefs in the 1980s and 1990s that motivated unionizing activities.[7]

While employees overwhelmingly attributed IBM's success to the quality of its workforce, historians and business professors emphasized strategy, market conditions, and economic externalities. The employees understood those, too, but got it right when they concluded people responded to those circumstances, not buildings, cash in the bank, or strategies. The halfway point between the two extremes were the observers of IBM's corporate culture, such as Edgar H. Schein, whose observations about corporate cultures aligned neatly with IBM's experiences. Writing over thirty years after his initial introduction of the framework used in our book, he affirmed what we learned here: "The essence of culture is then the jointly learned values and beliefs that worked so well at that time that they have become taken for granted and nonnegotiable even as times change" as they make it possible to "'weather' good times as well as bad, and therefore must be 'right.' "[8] But our conclusions are similar to his version of the "bottom line": "Culture is deep," "Culture is broad," and "Culture is stable." On the last point, it is stable up to a certain point (e.g., values, beliefs, many rituals), but largely, IBMers, like employees in other institutions, held "on to their cultural assumptions because culture provides meaning and makes life predictable."[9]

This chapter, as do the others, focuses discussion about IBM's culture from a "push" perspective, that is to say, as the creation by senior managers imposed on the workforce as part of their strategies for implementing business plans but, simultaneously, what it looked like from the ground up. With the exception of union organizers, there is little evidence of *sansculottes* at IBM rising against management the way their French counterparts of the eighteenth century did against their superiors, or later workers who Karl Marx anticipated would shape a new economic order, or more recently, workers at Amazon distribution centers and at corporate headquarters of Alphabet (Google) and Facebook. Management developed and nurtured a culture that worked for most employees and for other IBM stakeholders.

To wrap up our study of IBM's corporate culture, we proceed, first, by identifying insights about the culture that transcend the subjects of earlier chapters but were present in each. Because the company's culture was strongly uniform around the world, how that happened warrants at least a brief discussion, provided next. This chapter concludes with observations concerning what other aspects of corporate culture can be studied, based on the lessons from this book about IBM, but also about other multinational corporations. My message is that IBM's experience has much to teach today's corporate management in multiple industries. IBM's culture has universal qualities relevant today and even more so for companies serious about cultivating multiple stakeholders in a way that benefits all of them. We are talking about balance and trade-offs, and for that, one should draw from a set of values and behaviors shared across an enterprise. That is why corporate culture attracts the attention of so many business leaders and academics. It is also why implementing these is hard work; corporate rhetoric was—and is—woefully insufficient.

Insights Drawn from IBM's Corporate Culture

Only some aspects of IBM's culture were explored in this book by following the tried-and-tested historian's method of preparing case studies. The ones selected would have been obvious to the largest number of employees because they all experienced these touch points. The cases shared at least four features. First, they all left a paper trail one could follow of two types: publications, such as newsletters, books, and publications, distributed widely and, additionally, a more hidden paper trail of training materials, notifications, and other communications directed to individual employees at their homes and offices. Second, the subjects were discussed in published memoirs and in open and closed employee social media groups. Those commentators acknowledged the existence of a belief or ritual, for example, and explained its effects on them and their families. Third, all the topics could be linked directly back to publicly stated objectives and behaviors of the corporation at large, primarily through public pronouncements and actions of its senior leaders. In this third endeavor, it proved useful to have so many books and articles published about IBM. Finally, they had a three-dimensional quality to them—the material culture conversation—that reminded employees and other stakeholders about all that IBM was and how employees should behave and identify and that stimulated memories spilling out into communities carried by stakeholders who shifted roles from, say, employees to customers, community leaders, and stockholders.

These cases collectively flushed out several insights. The most obvious is that, internally combined, all these activities and features of IBM's culture were seen as effective, accepted, and aligned tightly with what normally were successful corporate business strategies. In addition to their alignment with strategy is that they were compatible with each other as part of a larger mosaic of cultural features that management constantly tinkered with to keep them connected to the overall objectives and values of the firm. For example, no benefit was introduced out of beneficence but rather because it would help IBM be more productive. Country clubs and Family Dinners had purpose, as business management professor Edgar Schein argued, as part of rituals and bonding.[10] When they were deemed no longer beneficial by senior management in the new century, they abandoned these quickly with no apologies. They did the same with IBM's support of the Quarter Century Clubs, just as management did not hesitate to sell off the hard drive and personal computer (PC) lines of business when these no longer served the corporation's business objectives.[11]

Because senior leadership remained essentially intact for decades, the time needed to make behaviors permanent features of the firm existed. Watson Sr. stuck to his "talking points" for over forty years. His successor, son Tom Watson, Jr., did too, with the same purposes and actions for an additional sixteen years, by which time the next three CEOs could look back and remember working at IBM only either under Watson Sr. or Jr. Right behind them were thousands of managers and hundreds of thousands of employees worldwide living within that shared cultural heritage. The hard break with that past did not occur until the 1990s, when Louis V. Gerstner became CEO; he had never worked at IBM before taking charge of the firm, although he had a brother who had for decades. So, good choices as to what the culture should comprise and longevity of application and fine-tuning of these had long contributed to the company's business success. In an effective feedback loop, circumstances reinforced what worked and created knowledgeable insights about what needed to be periodically modified.

Bringing in a new CEO from outside a long-lived firm is a strategy fraught with mixed results and always is seen as potentially disruptive, in either a good or bad way. One has only to think of the experiences of General Electric and, most famously, Kodak to be careful rushing to judgment that it is bad strategy because the outsider does not understand the culture of the enterprise. In Kodak's case, one could argue that its last CEOs did not understand the technology underlying its products and technologies. Fair enough. However, Gerstner understood the power of corporate culture, and while he found fault with IBM's, he knew enough to learn about it, respect its power, and then to take on the task of leveraging and changing it to go about running the company. IBM's board of directors, populated with CEOs from other long-lived firms with their own corporate cultures, concluded what many observers may not have fully appreciated: that the good of a company's culture could be preserved while infusing it with renewed energy reminiscent of a prior time and/or with new elements to meet contemporary needs. IBM collectively kept many elements of prior times and refurbished its culture.

All of this made sense because it was consistent with what historians of culture find elsewhere. For example, one of the leading lights of the subject, Peter Burke, points out that traditions within a culture survive either openly or in hiding even as the organization or society evolves. The beliefs embodied in the THINK sign or Basic Beliefs affirm his observation. A problem for management, employees, and scholars is that, in his words, "apparent innovation may mask the persistence of tradition," the problem confronting Gerstner in the 1990s. Traditions affect behavior and attitudes. But, on the other hand, we face the converse as Burke describes it: "outward signs of tradition may mask innovation," a challenge I faced when writing this book.[12] For a management team, what they pass on to the next generation of employees changes, if for no other reason than the next wave comes in with different experiences and hence attitudes toward many practices and beliefs that may be at odds or only partially in conformance. Watson Sr. must have seen this, just as professors do when, every year, their students seem to be the same age but, of course, are different than earlier ones.

Michael L. Tushman, who teaches today's business students and senior corporate leaders how to lead, explained the essence of what happened at IBM and at other firms that succeed or overcome problems. He and his colleague, Charles A. O'Reilly III, are worth quoting: "Execution of a strategy is all about aligning the organization—making sure we have the right people, are structured in a way that decision makers have the right information, measuring and rewarding the right things, and having a culture that promotes the behaviors we need to accomplish the key success factors." Doing all of that "is the hard work of management."[13] This book suggests how hard that is to accomplish, especially since at the center of it all is one's corporate culture, as Gerstner learned. Gerstner concluded that IBM's failing performance was due less to weak strategy and more to its values and culture, which were designed for an earlier different time and no longer fully aligned with the reality of the 1990s. Without changing those, it would not have been possible to turn the company around. It was all about culture. Let him explain: "It took me to age 55 to figure that out. Culture is everything."[14] So even Gerstner seemed to have learned Peter Drucker's admonition that "culture eats strategy for breakfast." Today's corporate executives ignore these insights at their peril. IBM's experience suggests multiple actions they can take to improve their firm's relevance when a healthy profit and loss statement is no longer good enough.

Did everyone like what happened? Absolutely not. But did IBM's various stakeholders survive and, indeed, prosper? They did. That the company stumbled again in the 2010s was perhaps less a criticism of the culture than of poor decisions and some weak managers, but it involved allowing elements of the culture to deteriorate, such as occurred with the employee appraisal process and increased layoffs in what many employees thought were disrespectful ways of being treated. IBM's senior leaders periodically had made bad decisions before, but, as in the 1990s and again in the 2010s, the company endured. The culture had built into it enough elasticity that its employees could craft and embrace changes in markets, technologies, products, skills, and stakeholders. That is why Gerstner and his board could change course and why IBM's stakeholders welcomed the results. Customers voted by opening their wallets, people were willing to come to work at IBM, regulators left the firm sufficiently alone, and only Wall Street analysts groused about quarter-to-quarter performance. Gerstner did what the two Watsons had done: he ignored them. Unfortunately, his successors did not. Rarely was IBM's business strategy designed for a quarter-to-quarter way of operating, and when its operations were bent to that behavior, it did poorly.

Longevity itself was not just due to the senior managers at the helm for decades but also to the stability of the markets IBM served. That may seem an odd comment given the churn in the firm's underlying technologies over the past century. However, in IBM's case, tabulating technology lasted from the 1890s to the 1960s with IBM controlling its evolution. The firm played a similar role with large computers from the mid-1950s to the end of the 1980s.[15] In fact, mainframes (now called servers) continued to play an important role long after the arrival of the PC and, later, the internet. Not until distributed computing finally made its breakthrough in the 1980s, and which one could argue affected IBM's bottom line until the early 1990s, did IBM's world change dramatically.

For over a century, IBM had a highly defined set of customers—essentially the same ones and types that it has today—large corporations and government agencies. It is not uncommon to know of customers that had been doing business with IBM for a century or more, and many thousands with seventy-five years of customer experience. This collection of stakeholders provided stability, regardless of periodic battles with competitors. The same held for two other stakeholders: stockholders and employees. Both of these communities had been part of IBM's ecosystem for a very long time, providing more stability than churn.[16] One could thus ask: Does such stability encourage development and success of a culture? The answer would seem in the affirmative. But more research needs to be done to confirm what otherwise might seem an obvious conclusion, especially since stability, too, facilitated the growth of cultural atrophy, one of Gerstner's complaints about IBM.

Senior management created a culture on purpose, by design, more than by accident. They left little to chance. They used their managers to promote and reinforce the culture. These were the shock troops sent in to persuade employees to behave in certain ways and to reinforce the culture by personal example and authority. When changes were required, managers became responsible for finding out from their charges what was needed and sending those thoughts up the line, even if it meant contesting resistors in middle and upper management. Since the culture valued facts and "completed staff work," and IBM had staffs dedicated to nurturing every major topic discussed in this book, the company could modify its culture in an informed manner. Management knew what Speak Ups, Open Doors, and the suggestion process did for the firm, so too how important it was to discourage in legally allowed ways unionization in the United States. Linked to management's activism was their tactic of training employees on all manner of subjects, including how to read faster; how to sell, install, and repair equipment; how best to plan for retirement; how to leverage insurance and medical benefits; and even how to play tennis and golf. It was routine for employees to be required to attend business-specific training for a minimum of two weeks per year; often, new employees were trained for as long as eighteen months before they were let loose on customers.

Did it all work? A retired employee, Peter E. Greulich, did what IBMers always valued, he "crunched the numbers" and was able to go beyond discussions about revenue and profit growth that one finds in most books about IBM.[17] Greulich calculated the revenue and profits per employee across the entire history of IBM. Growth in both proved spectacular during Watson Sr.'s time (1914–1956).[18] Both continued to increase during Watson Jr.'s tenure and in the 1970s under Frank T. Cary's leadership.[19] While IBM's success was due more than just to an effective corporate culture, it bears repeating that IBM memoirists attribute the company's successes to twin features: its culture and the quality of its people. A student of the company's history would be hard-pressed to challenge their conclusions. Greulich's analysis documented the recent decline in IBM's various measures of performance that surfaced in the early 1990s and again in 2012 unabated through 2020, opining that the explanation lay in poor management but also in departure from the company's culture.

Those two recent periods came when many features of IBM's long-term corporate culture changed, deteriorated, or were removed. Breaking with the Quarter Century Clubs in the early 2000s is a telling example of IBM walking away from a nearly century-long tradition of celebrating long-term employment. Now it was focused on removing those folks and replacing them with a workforce that could be turned over quickly as "needs of the business" required. The most sacred component of IBM's grand bargain—commitment to lifetime employment in exchange for lifetime commitment to serve the company—fractured in the late 1980s and was never reinstated. That caused morale to deteriorate to such an extent that the entire edifice of IBM's corporate culture began transforming from top to bottom. Knowledgeable experts, such as business school professors, laid out the case for our argument.[20]

Gerstner suggested that the old culture had perhaps been too successful, slowing the company's ability to change fast enough going forward. He was undoubtedly correct, given what had occurred inside the firm in the decade before his arrival. However, as I demonstrated elsewhere, it was more than about an ossifying culture; it also involved bad strategy implemented by two CEOs (John Opel and John F. Akers) and their direct reports running the business.[21] Many of the previous features of IBM's culture remained intact: deployment of managers to enforce and preserve IBM practices, beliefs and rituals, and use of a suggestion process and Speak Ups, although the latter declined as employees became nervous about putting their jobs at risk using this channel of communications. Employees had been comfortable in their pre-1990 world, almost like fish in a tank in a restaurant's lobby, not knowing that there were dangers poised outside their watery world, they had little way to address these.

How the Culture Went Global

IBM's culture went global in phases, beginning with creating one in the United States, actually moving major components of it out of the mind of Watson Sr. sitting in his office at 50 Broad Street in New York City into the operations of three unrelated businesses composing the firm, while refining it to align with his emerging business plans. So, development and diffusion of IBM's culture began in the United States. In 1911, C-T-R was formed out of three companies, each operating in different markets: one for time-recording equipment, another for scales and other business measurement products and paraphernalia, and what would eventually be the core of IBM: a third selling punch-card tabulating equipment. They had continued operating relatively independently with uneven performance, so Watson Sr. was hired to improve operations in June 1914. By the end of that summer, Europe had plunged into the First World War, with millions of people thinking it might last ninety days only to have it become one of the bloodiest wars in human history. The United States entered it in 1917, and it was not until 1919 that C-T-R could even dare think globally. Understandably, in the interim, Watson focused on the healthy American economy and its business opportunities from his first days at the firm, while shipping products to the three parts of C-T-R still operating in Europe to sell in any way they could.[22]

It was just as well because slightly over 90 percent of his employees were located in the United States during the war years. Watson Sr. would have done what a modern historian or business professor would do: add up the total number of employees and then calculate percentages based on the numbers brought to his desk by staff. Watson would have known, therefore, that the number of employees outside the country was low and scattered across capital and industrial cities and thus were small communities in any locality. He would also have understood that American exports to Europe rose sharply all through the Great War, including products manufactured in Endicott. So clearly Europe was a market to exploit, but not realized in 1914, only known in hindsight by 1918. Worldwide, C-T-R had 129 employees outside the United States in 1914 (most in war-torn Europe), in the following year 155, then 206 in 1916, 212 in 1917, and 279 in 1918—all tiny numbers. However, in 1919, the number jumped to 479, whereas the U.S. pool of employees dropped by some 200 to just over 2,400 the following year. The non-U.S. workforce increased in 1921 to 514, and from then on, it kept growing for decades.[23] Management in New York City would have translated those numbers into sales per capita to realize the obvious: that the world's economy was beginning to recover from the war and the worldwide Spanish Flu pandemic, so the firm needed to seize the moment on both sides of the Atlantic.

Watson Sr. spent a great deal of time visiting American IBM employees to personally communicate his ideas while forcing the three little businesses to collaborate or drop products from their offerings. He cultivated other stakeholders by calling on senior government officials, customers, and others who were influential in government and commercial spheres. No country in which C-T-R had a presence was overlooked.[24] That attention to multiple stakeholders remained a hallmark of his managerial behavior for nearly a half century. To this day, his successors have followed that path. But what we can see here is that IBM early on, while still C-T-R, led its evolution through a combination of familiar strategies and operational behaviors on the one hand and, on the other, by creating an integrated company-wide culture that reinforced behaviors in support of the firm's objectives.

Speaking to an audience of Italian employees in Florence in 1930, Watson Sr. explained how the company as a whole operated and needed to continue growing: "Our policies must be shaped so that they will apply to every country in the world. They are simple: Cooperate with one another, give the best possible service to the users of our products, continue to study and learn more about all business in general and our business in particular; be loyal to your customers and yourself as well as your company. It has been our policy to cooperate at all times."[25] Lest there be any doubt about what he was doing, Watson Sr. made perfectly clear to an audience of German employees where the pollinating originated: "IBM policies—which are formulated in the United States—are enforced in all seventy-seven countries in which our products are used."[26] After predicting that the day would soon come when the American side of the business would not be the majority contributor to the firm, Watson Sr. said the reason the Americans dominated is because "we enforce the same policies in every one of the forty-eight states. In every one of our branch offices over there, identical policies are maintained. That is what we are doing all over the world, and we want you to realize that this is the only successful way to run a business." If someone in the audience had a problem with that strategy, he advised them: "you ought to work for some other concern."[27] Gerstner delivered the same message in the 1990s, while similar messages were delivered to IBM employees over the century in less blunt language.

Watson's initial strategy for diffusing a new culture was to go out to various locations and explain what he wanted, imposing his will by a combination of requests and mandates. Another approach, demonstrated in earlier chapters, was his use of training worldwide that was centered in Endicott.[28] A third was to host what must have been expensive meetings for C-T-R/IBM that brought together employees from various parts of the country for 100 Percent Club rallies, national Quarter Century Club gatherings, and additional meetings for his executives. His published speeches from 1915 to 1934 documented use of all three approaches.[29]

He implemented two additional strategies. First, early on it became his practice to send managers and executives from New York to investigate, inspect, learn from, and advise field staff and factory employees. In other words, senior managers did not rely on just routine sales and manufacturing reports to understand what was occurring inside IBM.[30] This practice allowed for interactions and dialogue where ideas and processes could be understood and implemented, reinforcing and rewarding effective ones. There was always the hunt for knowing the unknown, for measuring activities, and for seeking new ways to work. A related approach, one that has been the subject of many jokes, quips, and some complaints, involved transferring people from one location to another. Anecdotal evidence suggests that until the 1990s, when the expense of moving people no longer proved affordable or so necessary (thanks to conference calling), in many years, up to roughly 5 percent of the workforce may have been transferred.

Relocating people facilitated cultural pollination. Here is how it worked from the dawn of IBM to at least the end of the 1980s. As the company grew, it created new positions that needed to be filled with staff and IBM-experienced managers. Given that the company had a full employment practice, it preferred to fill new positions with existing staff, which meant workers often received a promotion and an increase in salary and had their moving expenses absorbed by IBM. Some of those new jobs, therefore, required someone to be brought in from another location, rather than, say, hire a sales manager from outside the firm or immediate location.[31] Promoting a salesperson to that position meant that the next day they already knew how sales operated in the company and so could continue immediately carrying on successful company practices. Often filling such a position required bringing in someone from another part of the company who already knew IBM's practices and would thus reinforce what they had learned in an earlier position elsewhere in the firm in their new job.[32] That is exactly what senior management wanted to happen.

For someone to advance their career, being willing to move from one office to another as they progressed through their promotions helped many of them along and even sped their climb up the corporate ladder. By the end of the 1930s, career paths had essentially been defined; although not written down in a manual, they were understood. People needed to acquire specific experiences in order to progress. For example, a salesman in Nashville might need to go to a regional headquarters staff in Washington, DC, to learn how a regional headquarters operated because he would have to rely on such an organization when next a sales manager, say, in Memphis. He had to (a) have personal relations to gain attention, help, and later exposure at promotion time; (b) know how such an organization and specific individuals could help in a particular situation; and (c) demonstrate acceptance of IBM's values and social and business priorities. After Memphis, his management might suggest that the sales manager now needed divisional headquarters experience and so would ship him off to Atlanta or White Plains, New York. Two years later, that individual might become a branch manager and be assigned, say, to Minneapolis. This would usually go on so long as the employee was moving up the corporate ladder.[33]

At a large site, such as a research laboratory or factory, progression might involve fewer physical moves, just switches in offices on the same campus. On occasion, even those individuals would be moved to impose practices learned at one place on another. This was famously done in the 1950s and 1960s when senior management wanted to promulgate Poughkeepsie's views about computing on management at Endicott.[34]

Watson Sr. explained that moving employees around to populate new positions required people to be flexible in assuming new responsibilities and, by implication, in different communities: "We are all IBM men. We may call upon any one of you to do something outside of the particular division in which you are most interested," and his punch line, "We want those of you who are ambitious to get ahead to make up your minds now that you are IBM men and that you are going to study every division."[35]

During the 1960s when the company grew rapidly, Watson Jr. thought use of transfers for career advancement was getting out of hand and so, in one of his management briefings, reiterated an old principle at IBM: "make only those relocations that are essential to a person's career growth and the health of the business."[36] He reminded management that all moves were disruptive to the employee and to their families.[37] He encouraged management to look first from within their ranks for qualified people to fill jobs in their locality. By then, the expense of moving people and the risk of overlooking local candidates for a position were being felt. CEO Frank T. Cary raised the same points in 1974, but, too, stated: "There are times when a move is essential—for instance, when a certain skill is urgently needed or when organization or workload changes make a move necessary."[38] Every time someone moved, they brought with them what they knew, which, if they had spent their prior work years at IBM, was the company's culture.

In the 1980s, when IBM began reducing expenses, the greatest to squash were salaries and benefits, and so to preserve its full employment practice, a division or corporate headquarters would periodically offer to move people (or cajole people into moving) to existing openings. The most widespread of these programs, known as "Back to the Field," was the reduction of thousands of staff jobs, transferring people into sales offices. This form of movement did not always pair well people and positions but allowed some to remain on the payroll before being dismissed either for performance issues or due to outright layoffs. Many successfully made the transition to what was known as a new "career path." When IBM retired from the typewriter business, disbanding the Office Products Division (OPD) in 1981, it sent many of its members to sales offices to sell personal computers and, new to them, computer "systems." Some made the transition, others did not, but sales skills famously honed in OPD transferred to young sales staff selling computers.[39] Again, corporate culture moved with each transferee.

When World War I ended, Watson Sr. went immediately to Europe to expand business and, in the process, began assigning American managers to facilitate growing it. For the next half century, American executives were often put in charge of IBM's non-U.S. operations, which in 1949 were organized into the World Trade Corporation. Its first leader was Arthur K. Watson, his second son. An examination of Arthur's correspondence demonstrates that one of his purposes was to impose on all countries the American "IBM Way" of doing things: selling the same products, organizing sales offices in a similar fashion and doing the same with factories and regional and national headquarters, and carrying out long-standing rituals. He moved people about within a country for the same reasons as in the United States, even bringing some into the New York area to learn how headquarters worked.[40]

But Arthur Watson did not invent this approach for transferring corporate culture; his father had. Watson Sr. went to Europe several times in the 1920s–1930s, and on each trip, he brought together employees from multiple countries into one meeting for the express purposes of encouraging them, learning about their needs and issues, and exchanging information with them and they among themselves about how best to run the business. He was candid about the matter of how to transfer IBM's way of working. In August 1929, he addressed IBM employees in Vienna with others in attendance from parts of Central Europe:

> Our representatives in England, Germany, and France have made great progress during recent years, and I want you, our representatives in Southeastern Europe, to do likewise—to *learn* how to make more money for yourselves [my italics].
>
> One way that this can be accomplished is by learning as much as possible at this convention. We are all here in order to exchange ideas, and after we have exchanged them we must profit by applying them to the best advantage.
>
> We are here to help you, to assist you in your work of building a greater IBM business in this territory, and in so doing we are helping you to build a big future for all of you.[41]

Two weeks later at a gathering of German employees in Stuttgart with a larger audience, he continued his explanation of diffusion: "I believe conventions do more to build up a business than anything else we can do. We must distribute our knowledge through conventions to the men in other countries. We will have representatives from New York come over to give whatever help they can."[42] A week later in Paris to an IBM and customer audience from nine European countries, he repeated his message, also complimenting the French for their successes and speaking to customers in the audience about his interest in expanding collaboration among nations.[43]

To make sure things were done the IBM way in Europe, in 1930, Watson Sr. appointed Walter Dickson Jones, an American who had started at what would become IBM in 1912 and a close and trusted colleague of his, European general manager. Watson explained in detail all the various jobs Jones held prior to this appointment in sales and manufacturing, in all three divisions, and as a branch manager and executive. Watson went on to state that Jones "is now in charge of every branch and every department of our European business," a position he held for four years.[44] The company was concerned about the growing problems posed by the global Great Depression, so its leaders were doubling down on practices and their mode of doing business as a way of responding to their growing concerns. In other words, they relied on their culture to get through the crisis. Watson Sr. had a successful strategy working, which is how he arrived at the idea of appointing his American son, Arthur, to his role years later for running World Trade.[45]

In recent years, it has become, dare one use the word—fashionable—to speak about American business as "capital colonialism" or "capital imperialism." Such notions would have been alien to Watson Sr. and his American executives. No apologies would have come from them; they had a way of doing business that they, and others in so many large American firms, were convinced worked. Watson's paternalism, often described in positive terms, also had a hard deter-mined side to it. A student of business cultures, Mark Casson, argued that in addition to using American practices to create monopolistic markets, Ameri-can executives favored "a strongly paternalistic culture which emphasizes the national authority of the founder of the firm."[46] It is a cautionary statement, suggesting that while discourses about capital imperialism are interesting, they may be less important when studying the bowels of a firm led by successful, confident leaders.

The American or "IBM Way" persisted. Figure 12.1 shows the anthology of Watson Sr.'s speeches, quoted above, but notice the volume next to it: it is an exact replica, but in French.[47] There is no mistaking the conclusion one

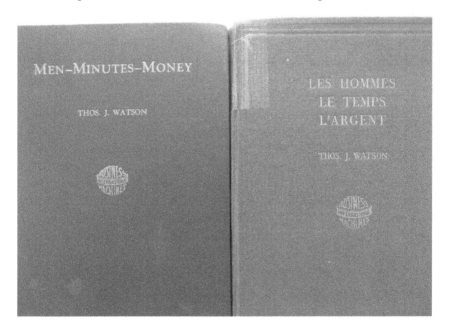

12.1 Thomas Watson's anthology of speeches in English and French that circulated widely inside IBM in the 1930s.

(Courtesy, author's collection.)

can draw from this image. Other IBM publications appeared in multiple languages. For example, in 2011, on the occasion of IBM celebrating its hundredth anniversary, it published a combination history and marketing story about the company that it distributed to most of its employees. That book appeared simultaneously in ten languages.[48] No content was tailored (i.e., rewritten) to accommodate other national cultures; even the covers were the same. Recall that IBM had been translating publications for decades to inform but also to reinforce IBM's ways of doing things.

As "the business" (IBM speak for IBM) expanded over the years, multinational meetings continued to be held with their cross-pollinating aftereffects. But, the key to spreading the IBM Way came with the natural development of larger populations of local employees around the world learning on the job under the guidance of IBM-experienced managers. The expanding population of employees in time made it possible for countries in Europe and in Latin America, for example, to staff from within their own ranks. This was particularly the case in large national markets in Great Britain (but also in other parts of the United Kingdom), Germany, France, Italy, Spain, Mexico, Brazil, Argentina, Peru, South Korea, and Japan. The IBM Way was in evidence in each, albeit conducted in local languages until the Americans would show up for, say, an inspection, which would (of course) be conducted in English. But the messages, practices, and rituals were similar.[49]

Two circumstances facilitated IBM's global diffusion of its culture. The first was the economic expansion that occurred across the twentieth century that, despite the Great Depression and a string of recessions, raised most boats in most industries.[50] IBM rode that wave, providing the global economy the wherewithal to support its own successes. Put another way, fostering a corporate culture with all its features, such as employee benefits and travel for employees, was expensive, but given the economic prosperity in that century, affordable for IBM. The second was the acceptance by Americans and Europeans in the 1920s–1950s that large American businesses were now part of the norm, the source of necessary bureaucracy. Those ideas were based on the realization reached in the 1920s that big enterprises could claim many achievements. Historian Louis Galambos observed that this development drew together enterprises and the public "around a culture tailored to the needs of a highly organized society."[51] Against those two backdrops, IBM expanded its global footprint in ways that it chose to, with little pushback until the last two decades of the century.

What Can Be Learned from IBM's Experience

Our case studies, while informative, were never intended to serve as a comprehensive history of IBM's corporate culture or as a specific blueprint for other corporations to follow to succeed and to serve all its stakeholders. Their purpose was to drill for samples for what the larger story could be and to shed light on other issues that, in hindsight, might prove even more significant that offer context for all interested parties from academia to the conference rooms of multinational corporations. Several broad, hard-to-define issues surfaced that became obvious or, to employees, a reminder of the obvious.

From its earliest days with Watson Sr., the company became fixated on control over everything, it would seem. Accounting, sales strategies, product development, market analysis, image building, monitoring reputations, and so forth were subject to control. Allowing events to occur by accident was unacceptable. Watson Sr. famously criticized managers who just turned in a great year in revenue, wanting to know why, if they could do that, they didn't have better control over the demand for IBM's goods. Would that not have led to even better financial results? From his day to the present, control remained a feature—one could argue fixation—of IBM's behavior evident in every corner and level of the firm.

Linked to control were myriad rules, procedures, and guidelines. To senior managers down to the newest employee, those translated into bureaucracy, a term derided in the West, which early Iraqi rulers and Chinese emperors invented to facilitate the work of their empires even before the Roman Empire created even better "best practices" in public administration. It worked for them. As historians such as Alfred D. Chandler, Jr., and others observed, with development of the modern corporation, bureaucracy became essential as the operational tool needed to coordinate the work of organizations that, too, were dispersed around the globe.[52] Yet a pervasive Western perspective was that it encumbered workers. In IBM, every CEO and many managers complained about it, usually objecting to too many layers of management, multiple reviews, and required "signoffs," that at times seemed ridiculous or counterproductive. For an extreme example, in the 2010s, to travel by air to a customer meeting momentarily required prior approval of a division president. That was laughable and often simply ignored. CEOs tried to "flatten" the corporation to reduce levels of management; it remained an ongoing crusade that always failed. Layers were needed to measure, manage, control, and communicate. Six layers became ten, then seesawed between seven or eight and ten again, and so forth over the decades. It was the same issue faced by other multinational corporations. There were good reasons for bureaucracy and control, so these features of IBM's culture warrant further research to gain a more nuanced understanding of their role.

In addition to control and bureaucracy, IBM's obsession with measuring was linked to all it did. It is a quip at IBM that anything that can be measured will be. One would have found that to be as true by 1915–1916 as much as today. Watson Sr. had learned at NCR the power of measures in improving sales operations. He even had used C-T-R's tabulating equipment to do this before joining the firm.[53] Every department and individual were measured numerically and qualitatively. One can challenge any historian to find an exception; it is that pervasive a feature of IBM's culture.

Measures, in turn, help shape features of an organization's culture, an environment of information, or what I have referred to elsewhere as an information ecosystem buttressed with an information infrastructure.[54] That interest in the mixture of qualitative facts and quantitative data was evident in IBM from its earliest days. In this book, I quoted executives regarding their use of metrics and facts as a basis for making decisions. Very few decisions and actions were taken before someone had studied the pros and cons of an issue. Staffs would have read the academic and business literature, conducted surveys, conversed with customers and experts, and then paid substantial sums to consultants to conduct further research to translate their findings into recommended actions. IBM managers and their staffs mimicked behaviors of other Western multinational corporations, most of whom were customers.[55]

If we pull together these various features of IBM's behavior, one can begin to create a composite view of what constituted pillars of the company's culture. Specifically, control, bureaucracy, measures, and information combined were at the heart of the "IBM Way." It is possible that these four features will eventually serve as the basis for a realistic framework with which to understand the activities described in earlier chapters and that can add relevance to so many other obvious ones. These other topics include the role of lawyers and government regulators and antitrust litigators. The practice of frequent and detailed communications with employees, communities, and customers that IBMers considered good, too much, or simply massive has a hidden history that needs to be flushed out. We saw examples of the latter in each chapter. Historians can seek out these pillars in other companies as topics for discussion by corporate management. Today's senior management can do some of the same.

IBM's documentation supported much of how the culture worked. Its publishing initiatives predated websites and the internet, supported printing shops within the company all over the world, produced publications in multiple languages at great expense and detail, and required over a dozen libraries at IBM laboratories and factories, some of which were the size of small American public libraries. When the System/360 was introduced to the world on April 7, 1964, so too were supporting manuals. Within two years, a data center with a S/360 would routinely have a librarian to maintain a large collection of magnetic tapes full of data, but also over fifty linear feet of IBM paper manuals, most of which received frequent updates to replace earlier pages. Stakeholders were subsumed in other literature, allowing IBM to extend its behavior into its customers' organizations.

Additionally, while much has been written about IBM's management, still too little is known about their practices. I was an IBM manager for thirty-three of my thirty-eight years at IBM and so can confidently state that the wider world outside the company knows little about how we operated. In the case studies in this book, I pulled back the curtain to partially show IBMers at work, much like the man behind the curtain in the movie *The Wizard of Oz*. We managers turned the cranks to make the machinery work, to bellow out smoke from the Green Wizard or, in our case, blue. But, I offered only a peek. So we still have to ask: Who were IBMers, what were their behaviors, how did they run the company, what were their values and aspirations, and how did they live in communities in up to 175 countries? Why did they bring their sons and daughters into the firm, jostling to do the same as so many nonmanagerial parents? How did they interact with customers and government officials? What was their status in IBM? What did they do after they left IBM? That last question will surprise as they became presidents of other companies, cabinet officials, civic leaders by the tens of thousands, authors, and professors. How did they treat women, minorities, and people with different religious values? We need sociological, ethnographic, and anthropological assistance to understand this large demographic, if for no other reason than they became stakeholders in new roles.[56]

When discussing managers, one should consider yet another feature of IBM's culture: the command and control obsession that coalesced at the highest levels of IBM. To be sure, having a hands-on micromanaging general manager with a mature vision of what to do with the company was key in enabling IBM's early successes. But every subsequent CEO consolidated power in their hands at the same time that they were trying to distribute it to an ever-growing, ever-improving community of experienced managers and executives. The most famous example was of Watson Jr. completely reorganizing the company in 1956 to break up the concentration of reporting that came directly into his father's office. Having over two hundred people report to you is impossible, and Watson Jr. knew that.[57] But even in the 2010s, while CEO Virginia (Ginni) Rometty complained about centralization, she micromanaged. In that behavior, she worked like many a typical IBM executive, providing they, like her, grew up in the company. We need to understand why that behavior persisted in every decade, regardless of IBM's business circumstances.

In our case studies, some of IBM's cultural norms were originally conceived by the CEO and then staffed out to fill in the details. The 100 Percent Club and its lapel pins can be credited to Watson Sr. The same held for the Quarter Century Club and possibly for the Speak Up and suggestion programs, too. CEOs would periodically read selections of Speak Ups and personally draw conclusions about actions to be taken, directing staff to pursue them and to return with specific recommendations on actions. They made decisions regarding these at the highest levels, often in collaboration with other senior executives. Watson Sr. sometimes traveled by automobile with regional sales managers to identify locations for future sales offices in the years immediately following World War II. Such behavior was normal for twentieth-century CEOs in most companies entwined with their centralization of authority. Was there more of that behavior at IBM than elsewhere? The subject is worth exploring. One cannot assume that at a certain size such behavior was automatically delegated. IBM's CEOs demonstrate that they could, indeed should, have delegated more than they usually did. Why?

Much has been made of managers in this book, and rightly so because they played such an important role. But what of nonmanagers? What about their roles? One finding worth exploring further is the authority and freedom of action that nonmanagers had in various periods. As the practice of meritocracy took hold in the firm, and as educational levels increased too, experts often gained a great deal of authority, power, and influence. They may not have directly controlled budgets, hiring, and people management, but they often did everything else. It was empowerment but done the IBM way. That feature of IBM's culture peeks out from inside dozens of privately published memoirs but needs further investigation. Our discussion about unionizing also pointed out that nonmanagers were willing to provide leadership. That definitely characterized the behavior of sales personnel who, unless held back, charged forward as if bred to the role. A detailed study of how scientists and other researchers worked within IBM's research and development (R&D) facilities, too, begs for attention.[58] For decades, IBM had designations for its best R&D members—Distinguished Engineer and IBM Fellow—that in the company's world were highly prestigious designations. But IBM put muscle behind it, because once designated a Distinguished Engineer, one was often promoted, even to executive status with all the perks that come with that; more so with IBM Fellows. Most Fellows were given five years to work on any R&D project they wanted relevant to the business, and they were in high demand for consultation inside and outside the firm. Some received Nobel Prizes.

Finally, and related to all the other topics, is the language used in IBM. It has been called "corporate speak," which is essentially the idiom of euphemisms. Instead of saying, "we have a *problem*," one would say, "we have a *challenge* before us." Circumstances dictate language. Gerstner discovered the absence of normally used words in business, only to find out that the company's lawyers had ruled out these to avoid any insinuation of antitrust behavior by employees.[59] There was an entire vocabulary for use outside of IBM with customers. Noted in the earlier discussion about IBM's dress code was the notion of having on one's "game face" or being "suited up to play," as a way to talk. Some of that behavior bubbled up in cartoons and other humor. Any list of definitions of "IBM" suggests more that an imaginative gene existed in the company's cultural DNA: "I've Been Moved," "I Blame Microsoft," and "Idiots Become Managers" are a few of the most obvious.[60] Each is obviously saturated with cultural meaning. Edgar Schein and others have noted the presence of an internal language in organizations. In his words, language was used as a vehicle to "establish a system of communication and a language that permits interpretation of what is going on."[61]

Then there is the vocabulary itself. It is not to be minimized or underestimated. The technologies underpinning the company's products for 130 years led to development of a vast vocabulary, one that exploded in volume with the arrival of the computer no matter the manufacturer. IBM published over a dozen dictionaries of these words that became standard reference books across the data processing world.[62] It published dictionaries that translated technical terms from one human language to another, such as from English (where most such vocabulary originated) into French, German, Italian, Portuguese, Spanish, Korean, Japanese, and Mandarin, among others.[63] It would help to have literature and linguistics experts study these. Some of this work has already begun, but not in linking these to the fabric of the spoken and written manifestations of IBM's culture.[64] IBM was not alone in compiling vocabularies, but it clearly dominated the genre.[65]

As if not enough, employees were notorious for butchering the "king's language." We do not understand why, as most employees were well educated.[66] "We will solution the problem" is my favorite egregious use of English. Statements had to be action oriented, so nouns became verbs until a lawyer or media expert fixed the problem on a slide deck. Employees had a notorious reputation for being unable to discuss a business issue with anyone inside or outside the firm without using slides. Their behavior can be characterized as a chronic condition; Gerstner famously ordered his executives to sit down, look at him, and verbalize *sans* slides what they wanted to talk about.[67]

One can spot an ex-IBMer even a decade after they have left the firm still using overcrowded PowerPoint slide decks. The condition has existed since at least the 1950s with Kodak's slide deck format, although perhaps even to a predecessor—the flip chart—which dates probably from the first day Watson walked into C-T-R in June 1914, as he was a notorious advocate of their use. One cannot pick up a history of his period at IBM, an illustrated biography, or even anthologies of his speeches without seeing his ubiquitous flip charts.[68] Even in the 1980s, a newly arrived sales trainee was still expected to master the art and diction of a flip chart presentation. In hindsight, we could have justified adding a chapter just on flip charts and slide decks as additional examples of material culture in use because they were that ubiquitous, visible in every office in IBM anywhere in the world in any period, and available in almost every collection of IBM ephemera that I have looked at in nearly fifty years. That circumstance clearly fits into the rituals and practices of IBM's corporate culture. The narrative typed reports that paralleled use of slides were more commonly evident in business until World War II; afterward, a slow shift occurred away from that previous style of reporting to the sound bites of bulleted lists and more graphical representations. IBM behaved the same way.[69]

The list of topics to chase could be extended. However, the ones listed earlier are more difficult to document than the cases presented in this book. What we did, here, was to flush out the more substantial research agenda by examining such issues as Christmas parties and postcards, medical benefits, and unionizing activities. They often hinted at much more, such as the debate about suits between sales personnel and customer engineers and other social status issues not discussed ensconced in the attire conversation. The postcard case study calls for a more detailed examination of IBM's buildings; indeed, for decades, the company even had a real estate division to build factories, laboratories, skyscrapers, and sales offices; to buy large tracts of land for potential future use for factories; and to rent offices. If the reader found the discussions in prior chapters novel, imagine what they might discover if those listed above were properly flushed out. Historians would probably then conclude that they finally had penetrated into the heart of what constituted IBM.

This book has made it a point to demonstrate how studies of material culture can be integrated into the more sociological studies of corporate culture. I also linked both of those topics directly to the more traditional business history interest in strategy, business models, and the implementation of each. These topics are entwined, and so scholars could accept that. Two scholars articulating the benefits of studying the history of material cultures provided an example of what they meant that could have been drawn from our chapter 8 on 100 Percent Club pins: "A pin, for instance, can convey social status or aspiration as a matter of communication, yet it can simultaneously, and equally important, hold two pieces of fabric together."[70] As scientists learn more about human cognition, the more it becomes necessary to broaden one's understanding of how large institutions function, such as multinational corporations.[71]

As archeologists and others have come to see "biographies of a thing" as relevant topics, one could ponder the degree to which objects in IBM changed in identity and role from one period to another and their effects on behavior of the firm. For convenience, we have presented objects as static manifestations of IBM's culture, but should we simply rely on that shorthand? For example, back to our pin, sales executives did not earn 100 Percent Club pins, although they were required to achieve their revenue targets. Why? We do not know the answer. It is an important question, however, because the company's culture discouraged too much focus on the differences in levels, even though a general manager was going to be treated differently than a first-line manager on a shop floor. We would not have even conceived of this question if we had not explored the little 100 Percent Club pin. Since we have much to learn, exploring material culture in a corporation helps.

Experiences in one company can be transferred, modified, and applied from one to another. Edgar H. Schein demonstrated that could be done. He described how founders shape a culture—we did a great deal of that in this book—and companies transmit it.[72] His work encouraged leaders to believe that cultures could be built and changed.[73] For most of IBM's history, transference took place through one-on-one conversations between interested individuals and presentations made at conferences and other meetings. In the second half of the twentieth century, consulting firms acted as additional transfer agents using staffs expert in specific business issues, who kept up with what others were doing in their specialty and applied methodologies for determining how best to proceed.

Academic experts from such other fields as business strategy and economics contributed insights, too, on how to transfer cultural features of one firm to another. Recently, Michael E. Porter, Harvard University's most famous expert on business strategy, collaborating with a business executive, Katherine M. Gehl, demonstrated that methods used in, say, one industry could be applied in another, for example using his Five Forces framework, which probably almost every MBA student has studied and that has certainly been applied at IBM. Many of the questions in his methodology speak to the behavior—culture—of corporations. He demonstrated how both soft and hard issues related to the behavior of institutions could be applied to transforming American governments, which for most readers resonate as a different form of culture than what one finds in corporations.[74] Although they used the language of the strategist and sociologist/economist (e.g., "political-industrial complex," "politics industry"), much that they discuss parallels discussions about IBM's behavior. In their words, "the politics industry is driven by the same five forces that shape competition in any industry" and then demonstrates that method at work.[75]

I am not recommending that IBM's culture be packaged the way a professor or consultant would advise and simply carried over to Facebook, General Motors, or a large bank. But what they advise and what the story about IBM's culture makes clear is that there are lessons to be learned, which can inform the values, behaviors, and processes of other firms. What IBM created worked for it but would not necessarily apply exactly the same to, say, a media or insurance company today. But IBM's experience teaches that a company, by just existing, will have a culture, so it is up to management to decide what shape it should take, treating the issue like a strategic imperative. Second, whatever management decides to do, they must stick with it for years, tuning it as the years pass, of course. Third, their efforts must be diffused to the far corners of a corporation's empire and then out to *all* the stakeholders in its ecosystem. Computing and online communications make the process of diffusion easier and less expensive every year, so too constant focus. Watson Sr. might have added "with obsession."

Diffusion is not just to people, but also to algorithms and robots. Those latter two constituencies are just becoming influential components of a company's collection of stakeholders. So, these technologies will be subject to regulatory interest, not to mention lawyers, customers, legislators, military services, and corporate rivals. In the United States in 2019–2022, for instance, Facebook and Google came increasingly under scrutiny over how their algorithms targeted advertising to minorities and genders, with much suspicion floating through social media and in political circles. Concerns came less from customers and employees and more from public officials and businesses and general media on both sides of the Atlantic. These are constituencies that played less significant roles in IBM's history, while algorithms were hardly an issue for IBM's stakeholders.[76] In other words, corporate cultures change because they are dynamic, while some features may remain permanent features, such as the way companies treat their employees regarding individual respect, types of benefits and job security they offer, and the challenge and fun of the work. It is an old lesson. A writer in *The Economist* noted one should understand "history's chariot," thundering "at a furious pace."[77] While he accused historians of being too narrowly focused in their research about big issues, he suggested that the rest of us should not. A collective IBM would agree.

With this last sentence, our history of aspects of IBM's corporate culture as it evolved in its first century ends. This study has been largely a combination of looking at how IBM as a whole implemented its corporate culture and what functioned on the ground of importance to hundreds of thousands of employees. That approach departs from others that address more often grand strategy and such traditional business results as sales and competitive actions. These refer to corporate culture as a cause of success and failures and, when it comes to failures, as the primary culprit. Certainly CEO Lou Gerstner did, but that assessment discounts other factors, some of which deserve more credit for the successes and failures of a company's performance. Addressing some of these issues may be problematic because many are sufficiently current that the normal archival evidence historians normally would rely upon are not yet available. However, there is enough evidence that I can comment on recent circumstances at IBM and also introduce other considerations that created greater problems for IBM than corporate culture or its legions of trained, motivated, and knowledgeable workers, especially in the past quarter century. To do that, we have included an introduction that is as much aimed at senior business and public leaders as it is at scholars and especially historians.

AUTHOR'S NOTE: IN THE SPIRIT OF TRANSPARENCY

While the research methods employed to study IBM's culture were those of the historian, the topics and their context were informed by my personal experience, which is why I am writing this Author's Note. I was trained in history and have a PhD in the subject, but I spent nearly four decades working at IBM as salesman, consultant, manager, and researcher. During my career, I continued to practice the historian's craft and investigated IBM's history and the industry of which it was a part, publishing books and articles. As a participant in the industry as an IBM employee, I also studied and implemented contemporary business practices of my time there (1974–2012) and wrote books and articles about management and computing technology, too. Thus, I brought to this project the two disciplines reflected in this book, in addition to my having experienced the cultural experiences discussed.

My family and I moved five times during my IBM career. We have lived in a company town—Poughkeepsie, New York—and in cities in which I worked in five sales branch offices. I worked in a regional sales office, in two division headquarters, in one independent business unit, and in one of IBM's research centers (IBM Institute for Business Value). Half of my career focused on U.S. operations, and in my last decade, I had staff scattered around the world. My family and I attended Family Dinners, and two employees "Opened Doored" me (both found to be without merit by investigators). I redesigned IBM's worldwide Suggestion Process and how all of the company's tens of thousands of consultants were certified so that they could be put in front of clients. I taught salesmen their profession for two years at "Sales School" and spent eight years conducting research on modern businesses practices. My children attended company holiday parties, and I organized and hosted two Family Dinners. I also used IBM postcards to communicate with my family written from Endicott, New York, before home email was available and the arrival of the internet.

In addition to collecting books and articles about IBM since 1974, in mid-career, I recognized that the ephemera of IBM's history and culture should be preserved (such as employee benefit statements and Family Dinner menus), especially since some of it was not being collected by the otherwise outstanding company archive, although I relied on much from that source. The materials I collected and my experiences helped shape the agenda for this book. Historical records provided evidence I needed with which to do that, and my roles as writer and historian prepared me for how to present my findings. I avoided turning this book into an account of my own encounters with IBM's corporate culture to the extent possible, parking the majority of my few personal comments in endnotes, while keeping in the main text less than a handful of personal opinions.

But perhaps the key point to make about my experience at IBM is that I entered the firm while the old long-standing Watsonian paternalism characterized its behavior and values. It impressed me in positive ways. I then experienced the decay of that culture in the face of new market and managerial realities that influenced the behavior of the firm and that shaped changes in its culture in the 1990s–2010s. Finally, from roughly 2000 to the present, I experienced and observed additional changes in IBM's corporate culture and practices that made what I first experienced in the 1970s and 1980s alien. An employee at IBM today would not recognize the IBM of the 1970s. What I can say, therefore, is that the evolution of the company and its culture was massive, profound, and so dramatic that it may be one of the most interesting subjects for historians and scholars in other disciplines to study regarding large organizations.

This book was driven by what most employees encountered with the culture and also by what I learned from having earlier written about IBM's history. I am not done discussing it, so let us continue the conversation. I can be reached at jcortada@umn.edu.

NOTES

Introduction

1. Daniel Renjifo, "Inventor of the World Wide Web Wants Us to Reclaim Our Data from Tech Giants," *CNN*, December 16, 2022, https://www.cnn.com/2022/12/16/tech/tim-berners-lee-inrupt-spc-intl, accessed December 16, 2022.
2. Kevin Roose, "Elon Musk, Management Guru," *New York Times*, December 16, 2022, https://www.nytimes.com/2022/12/16/technology/elon-musk-management-style.html?action=click&pgtype=Article&state=default&module=styln-elon-musk&variant=show&region=MAIN_CONTENT_1&block=storyline_top_links_recirc; John Ganz, "The Emerging Tech-Lash," *Unpopular Front*, https://johnganz.substack.com/p/the-emerging-tech-lash, accessed December 16, 2022.
3. Roz Brewer, "It's Time to 'Rephrase' How Companies Work," in *The World Ahead 2023* (London: Economist, 2022), 120.
4. James W. Cortada, *IBM: The Rise and Fall and Reinvention of a Global Icon* (Cambridge, MA: MIT Press, 2019).
5. In addition to Cortada, *IBM*, a convenient table of such statistics is available in Emerson W. Pugh, *Building IBM: Shaping an Industry and Its Technology* (Cambridge, MA: MIT Press, 1995), 323–324. Pugh was an IBMer working in research and is the author of four books about the firm, three of them on the history of its technologies.
6. For a brilliant and thorough analysis of the economic performance by IBM, Peter E. Greulich, *THINK Again! The Rometty Edition* (Austin, TX: MBI Concepts, 2020), and for the statistics cited here, 195.
7. For her defense, Ginni Rometty, *Good Power: Leading Positive Change in Our Lives, Work, and World* (Boston: Harvard Business Review Press, 2023), 148–149.
8. Daniel Quinn Mills and G. Bruce Friesen, *Broken Promises: An Unconventional View of What Went Wrong at IBM* (Boston: Harvard Business Review Press, 1996).

9. Thomas Claburn, "IBM Ordered to Hand Over Ex-CEO Emails Plotting Cuts in Older Workers," *Register*, June 13, 2022, https://www.theregister.com/2022/06/13/ibm_discrimination_email/, accessed December 15, 2022.

10. Mary Anne Pazanowski, "IBM to Face 'Piggybacked' Age Discrimination Claims, for Now," *Bloomberg Law*, July 5, 2022, https://news.bloomberglaw.com/litigation/ibm-to-face-piggybacked-age-discrimination-claims-for-now, accessed December 15, 2022.

11. Peter Gosselin and Ariana Tobin, "Cutting 'Old Heads' at IBM," *ProPublica*, March 22, 2018, https://features.propublica.org/ibm/ibm-age-discrimination-american-workers/, accessed December 15, 2022.

12. Posted on IBM's newsroom site, https://newsroom.ibm.com/Obed-Louissaint, accessed December 15, 2022.

13. IBM equipment was also used by Germany during World War II largely for the same business management purposes as did American companies. Controversy over possible uses of this equipment in labor camps erupted in the 1990s, but the evidence demonstrates equipment was used largely to manage labor scheduling, beginning in 1944, Cortada, *IBM*, 121–145.

14. Melissa S. Fisher, *Wall Street Women* (Durham, NC: Duke University Press, 2012), 17–19. Also useful for exploring the history of early American companies, many of which became multinationals, see Nikki Mandell, *The Corporation as Family: The Gendering of Corporate Welfare, 1890–1930* (Raleigh, NC: University of North Carolina Press, 2002). Both have rich bibliographies.

15. GlobalData, "IBM: Racial Diversity in the Leadership in 2021," https://www.globaldata.com/data-insights/technology—media-and-telecom/ibm-racial-diversity-in-the-leadership-2091451/#:~:text=In%20leadership%20roles%20(executive%20and,the%20US%20workforce%20in%202021, accessed December 16, 2022.

16. Ruth Leach Amonette wrote her memoirs, *Among Equals: The Rise of IBM's First Woman Corporate Vice President* (Creative Arts Book Co., 2000).

17. The American experience regarding female workers has been studied extensively, but not as much regarding that experience in multinational corporations. To understand the complexity of gender issues, see studies by Claudia Goldin, *Understanding the Gender Gap: An Economic History of American Women* (New York: Oxford University Press, 1990) and *Career & Family: Women's Century-Long Journey Toward Equality* (Princeton, NJ: Princeton University Press, 2021); J. Bradford DeLong, *Slouching Towards Utopia: An Economic History of the Twentieth Century* (New York: Basic Books, 2022), 373–394.

18. Clyde W. Ford, *Think Black: A Memoir* (New York: HarperCollins, 2019).

19. Like other American corporations, personnel tracked employees by self-identified ethnicity. When I joined IBM, I listed myself as white, not Hispanic, since I was concerned about possible prejudice, an experience my father saw in the U.S. Foreign Service as a young diplomat in the 1940s and early 1950s, but thereafter not at all. I never changed my identification, so I assume people probably thought I was of Italian descent!

20. William Lazonick, *Sustainable Prosperity in the New Economy? Business Organization and High-Tech Employment in the United States* (Kalamazoo, MI: W.E. Upjohn Institute for Employment Research, 2009), for data on IBM, 272.

21. Lazonick, *Sustainable Prosperity in the New Economy?*, 272.

22. William Lazonick and Jang-Sup Shin, *Predatory Value Extraction: How the Looting of the Business Corporation Became the U.S. Norm and How Sustainable Prosperity Can Be Restored* (New York: Oxford University Press, 2020), 1.

23. Cortada, *IBM*, 582–587.

24. Lazonick and Shin, *Predatory Value Extraction*, 70.
25. Lazonick and Shin, *Predatory Value Extraction*, 78.
26. Lazonick and Shin, *Predatory Value Extraction*, 81.
27. I explain how this happened in Asia; James W. Cortada, *The Digital Flood: The Diffusion of Information Technology Across the U.S., Europe, and Asia* (New York: Oxford University Press, 2012), 307–570.
28. William Magnuson, *For Profit: A History of Corporations* (New York: Basic Books, 2022), 301.
29. Magnuson, *For Profit*, 301.
30. On the decline of IBM worker productivity, see Greulich, *THINK Again!*, 146, 167–168, 174, 190–191, 288–289.
31. Julie Froud, Sukhdev Johal, Adam Leaver, and Karel Williams, *Financialization and Strategy: Narrative and Numbers* (London: Routledge, 2006), 36–64.
32. Froud, Johal, Leaver, and Williams, *Financialization and Strategy*, 63.
33. "Multinational Corporations," *Espace Mondial Atlas*, September 28, 2018, https://espace-mondial-atlas.sciencespo.fr/en/topic-strategies-of-transnational-actors/article-3A11-EN-multinational-corporations.html, accessed December 16, 2022.
34. Andrea Murphy and Isabel Contreras, "The Global 2000," *Forbes*, May 12, 2022, https://www.forbes.com/lists/global2000/?sh=34ce10895ac0, accessed December 16, 2022.
35. Data from International Monetary Fund (IMF), December 17, 2022, https://www.imf.org/en/Publications/WEO#:~:text=Global%20growth%20is%20forecast%20to%20,and%202.7%20percent%20in%202023, accessed December 17, 2022.
36. Data from U.S. Bureau of Economic Activity, November 12, 2021, https://www.bea.gov/news/2021/activities-us-multinational-enterprises-2019, accessed December 16, 2022.
37. Magnuson, *For Profit*, 304–323.
38. Thomas J. Watson, Sr., *Men-Minutes-Money* (New York: International Business Machines Corporation, 1934), 82–83.

1. From Theories of Corporate Cultures to the Realities of Life Inside a Global Enterprise

1. Louis V. Gerstner, Jr., *Who Says Elephants Can't Dance? Inside IBM's Historic Turnaround* (New York: HarperBusiness, 2002), 182.
2. It was routine for employees at IBM to work fifty-five hours per week, which would translate to some 2,500 per year, with occasional spikes to seventy or more per week during periods of crises or product development and installation. Anecdotal observation based on the author's thirty-eight years of experience as an IBM employee.
3. For a wide-ranging discussion of cultures in general, see Peter Burke, *What Is Cultural History?* (Cambridge, UK: Polity, 2019).
4. The most prolific sources of evidence of that resistance can be found in social media postings by employees, laid off ones too, and retirees, largely on Facebook and blogs. This resistance was early identified by Daniel Quinn Mills and G. Bruce Friesen, *Broken Promises: An Unconventional View of What Went Wrong at IBM* (Boston: Harvard Business Review Press, 1996).
5. Such as effects on productivity and financial results, Peter E. Greulich, *THINK Again! The Rometty Edition* (Austin, TX: MBI Concepts, 2020).
6. Nick Donofrio with Michael DeMarco, *If Nothing Changes, Nothing Changes: The Nick Donofrio Story* (Houndstooth, 2022), 159.

7. On the canonization idea, Burke, *What Is Cultural History?*, 143.
8. Philippe D'Iribarne, Sylvie Chevrier, Alain Henry, Jean-Pierre Segal, and Geneviève Tréguer-Felten, *Cross-Cultural Management Revisited* (Oxford: Oxford University Press, 2020), 2.
9. For example, one well-regarded text on the subject appeared in 1990 and is now in its eighth edition and includes a detailed useful bibliography on the subject, Gary P. Ferraro and Elizabeth K. Briody, *The Cultural Dimension of Global Business*, 8th ed. (London: Routledge, 2017).
10. The most relevant for the discussion, James W. Cortada, *IBM: The Rise and Fall and Reinvention of a Global Icon* (Cambridge, MA: MIT Press, 2019).
11. For an excellent recent example that uses IBM, among others, as a case study, see Charles A. O'Reilly III and Michael L. Tushman, *Lead and Disrupt: How to Solve the Innovator's Dilemma* (Stanford, CA: Stanford Business Books, 2021).
12. Edgar H. Schein and Peter A. Schein, *The Corporate Culture Survival Guide*, 3rd ed. (Hoboken, NJ: Wiley & Sons, 2019), 88.
13. Edgar H. Schein, *Organizational Culture and Leadership* (San Francisco: Jossey-Bass, 1989, originally ed. 1985), 6.
14. Schein, *Organizational Culture and Leadership*, 6.
15. Schein, *Organizational Culture and Leadership*, 9.
16. Schein, *Organizational Culture and Leadership*, 14.
17. See, for example, Schein and Schein, *The Corporate Culture Survival Guide*, which includes a bibliography of the author's publications and of other culture experts.
18. Geert Hofstede, *Cultures and Organizations: Software of the Mind* (London: McGraw Hill, 1991).
19. Mikael Søndergaard, "Research Note: Hofstede's Consequences: A Study of Reviews, Citations and Replications," *Organization Studies* 15, no. 3 (1994): 447–456.
20. Schein, *Organizational Culture and Leadership*, 14–16.
21. Katherine M. Erdman, *An Analysis of Geert Hofstede's Culture's Consequences: Comparing Values, Behaviors, Institutions and Organizations Across Nations* (London: Macat International, 2017), 65–71.
22. Daniel R. Denison, *Corporate Culture and Organizational Effectiveness*, 2nd ed. (www.denisonculture.com, 1997), 175.
23. Edith T. Penrose, "Growth of the Firm and Networking," in *International Encyclopedia of Business and Management* (London: Routledge, 1996), 1722. Corporate boundaries are a critical idea to understand within the context of corporate culture. For a brief introduction, see Mark Casson, "Institutional Economics and Business History: A Way Forward?," in *Institutions and the Evolution of Modern Business*, eds. Mark Casson and Mary B. Rose (London: Frank Cass, 1998), 151–171.
24. Edith T. Penrose, *The Theory of the Growth of the Firm*, 4th ed. (New York: Oxford University Press, 2009), 132.
25. Penrose, *The Theory of the Growth of the Firm*, xxxiv.
26. Peter Burke, *History and Social Theory* (Ithaca, NY: Cornell University Press, 1992), 118; see also his brief discussion of definitions from an historical perspective, 118–126.
27. For a useful discussion of his ideas and how other students of the issue see it, see Denison, *Corporate Culture and Organizational Effectiveness*, 22–38; this discussion reaffirms the similarity of Schein's ideas as well.
28. Schein and Schein, *The Corporate Culture Survival Guide*, x.
29. Schein and Schein, *The Corporate Culture Survival Guide*, 4, 18.

30. I discuss these issues more thoroughly in James W. Cortada, "Change and Continuity at IBM: Key Themes in Histories of IBM," *Business History Review* 92, no. 1 (2018): 117–148.

31. The literature is extensive; however, two suggest the approaches: Daniel R. Denison, *Corporate Culture and Organizational Effectiveness* (Hoboken, NJ: John Wiley & Sons, 1990); Schein and Schein, *The Corporate Culture Survival Guide*. Schein's book is intended for a business audience but is a useful summary of his long-held views about the nature of corporate culture.

32. Gerstner, *Who Says Elephants Can't Dance?*, 181–213.

33. John P. Kotter and James L. Heskett, *Corporate Culture and Performance* (New York: Free Press, 1992). See their bibliography for other related sources, 199–208.

34. The favorite method applied by historians is that of the case study approach. For those interested in understanding how case studies are developed and used, see M. Q. Patton, *Qualitative Research & Evaluation Methods: Integrating Theory and Practice*, 4th ed. (Thousand Oaks, CA: SAGE, 2015); Harmeet Sawhney and Hamid R. Ekbia, *Universal Access and Its Asymmetries: The Untold Story of the Last 200 Years* (Cambridge, MA: MIT Press, 2022), 10–17.

35. Kotter and Heskett, *Corporate Culture and Performance*, 11–12.

36. Especially those from Denison, *Corporate Culture and Organizational Effectiveness*, 65–85.

37. Kotter and Heskett, *Corporate Culture and Performance*, 141–151.

38. For a brief but excellent summary of other typologies and frameworks, see Schein and Schein, *The Corporate Culture Survival Guide*, 71–92.

39. IBM purposefully created an information ecosystem that enveloped employees and their customers. I have commented further on this enveloping ecosystem; James W. Cortada, *Building Blocks of Society: History, Information Ecosystems, and Infrastructures* (Lanham, MD: Roman & Littlefield, 2021), 181–223; and James W. Cortada, "Viewing Corporations as Information Ecosystems: The Case of IBM, 1914–1980s," *Enterprise & Society* 23, no. 1 (March 2022): 99–132.

40. Gerstner, *Who Says Elephants Can't Dance?*, 205–206.

41. Gerstner, *Who Says Elephants Can't Dance?*, 206.

42. Geert Hofstede, *Culture's Consequences: International Differences in Work-Related Values* (Beverly Hills, CA: SAGE, 1980, 1984) is his key study; Edward T. Hall, *The Silent Language* (New York: Anchor, 1959), but see also Edward T. Hall, "The Silent Language in Overseas Business," *Harvard Business Review* 38, no. 3 (1960): 87–96; John L. Graham, "Culture and Human Resources Management," in *The Oxford Handbook of International Business*, 2nd ed., ed. Alan M. Rugman (New York: Oxford University Press, 2009), 511–512.

43. Graham, "Culture and Human Resources Management," 511–512.

44. Christopher W. Allinson and John Hayes, "Cross-National Differences in Cognitive Style: Implications for Management," *International Journal of Human Resource Management* 11, no. 1 (2000): 161–170; John L. Graham, "Culture Influence on Business Negotiations: An Application of Hofstede's and Rokeach's Ideas," in *Cooperative Strategies and Alliances: What We Know 15 Years Later*, eds. Forak L. Contractor and Peter Lorange (Amsterdam: Pergamon, 2002), 461–492; Lawrence E. Harrison and Samuel P. Huntington, eds., *Culture Matters* (New York: Basic Books, 2000); Bradley L. Kirkman, Kevin Lowe, and Cristina B. Gibson, "A Quarter Century of Culture's Consequences: A Review of Empirical Research, Incorporating Hofstede's Cultural Values Framework," *Journal of Internal Business Studies* 37 (2006): 285–320; Joel West and John L. Graham,

"A Linguistic-Based Measure of Cultural Distance and Its Relationship to Managerial Values," *Management International Review* 44, no. 3 (2004): 315–343.

45. Graham, "Culture and Human Resources Management," 533.

46. Graham, "Culture and Human Resources Management," 533. The solution is to form global management teams with diverse backgrounds because there is realistically no such thing as an international manager, or at least not enough of them to make a difference, Nick Forster, "The Myth of the 'International Manager,'" *International Journal of Human Resource Management* 11, no. 1 (2000): 126–142.

47. It is the idea that a well-run firm can do everything "right" and still lose the leadership in a market and even go out of business because they were not able to adapt to new technologies and circumstances. Clayton Christensen explained the idea in his book, *The Innovator's Dilemma: When New Technologies Cause Great Firms to Fail* (Boston: Harvard Business Review Press, 1997). Management in many industries paid attention to this problem, not just those in high-tech ones.

48. O'Reilly III and Tushman, *Lead and Disrupt*, 19.

49. O'Reilly III and Tushman, *Lead and Disrupt*, 88–89.

50. O'Reilly III and Tushman, *Lead and Disrupt*, 98–101.

51. Kenneth Lipartito, "Business Culture," in *The Oxford Handbook of Business History*, eds. Geoffrey Jones and Jonathan Zeitlin (New York: Oxford University Press, 2007), 603.

52. Schein and Schein, *The Corporate Culture Survival Guide*, 49.

53. Burke, *What Is Cultural History?*; Rob Goffer and Garth Jones, *The Character of a Corporation: How Your Company's Culture Can Make or Break Your Business* (New York: HarperCollins, 1998); Kenneth Lipartito, "Culture and the Practice of Business History," *Business and Economic History* 24, no. 2 (1995): 1–42. I made these issues central in my history of IBM, Cortada, *IBM*.

54. The most widely known example is Thomas Peters and Robert Waterman, *In Search of Excellence: Lessons from America's Best-Run Companies* (New York: Harper & Row, 1982). However, their study was flawed because some of their case study corporations soon after entered periods of business decline, including IBM, which, I have argued, was just starting to falter as their book was being written, Cortada, *IBM*, 421–470.

55. Lipartito, "Business Culture," 604.

56. For example, Victoria Bonnell, Lynn Hunt, and Richard Biernacki, eds., *Beyond the Cultural Turn: New Directions in the Study of Society and Culture* (Berkeley: University of California Press, 1999).

57. Burke, *What Is Cultural History?*, 117–120.

58. David E. Nye, *Image Worlds: Corporate Identities at General Electric, 1890–1930* (Cambridge, MA: MIT Press, 1985); Stephen Harp, *Marketing Michelin: Advertising and Cultural Identity in Twentieth-Century France* (Baltimore, MD: Johns Hopkins University Press, 2001); Mark W. Fruin, *Kikkoman: Company, Clan and Community* (Cambridge, MA: Harvard University Press, 1983); see Lipartito, "Business Culture," for an extensive bibliography, 621–628.

59. I have pulled together my work on this topic, Cortada, *Building Blocks of Society*.

60. James W. Cortada, "A Framework for Understanding Information Ecosystems in Firms and Industries," *Information & Culture* 51, no. 2 (2016): 133–163; and for an applied example, David B. Gracy II, "A Cowman's Eye View of the Information Ecology of the Texas Cattle Industry from the Civil War to World War I," *Information & Culture* 51, no. 2 (2016): 164–191.

61. David F. Nye, *Henry Ford, Ignorant Idealist* (Port Washington, NY: Kennikat, 1979); Judith A. Merkle, *Management and Ideology: The Legacy of the International Scientific Management Movement* (Berkeley: University of California Press, 1980); and by a journalist, Kevin Maney, *The Maverick and His Machine: Thomas Watson, Sr. and the Making of IBM* (Hoboken, NJ: John Wiley & Sons, 2003).

62. As often is the case with a new topic, historians notice a subject when there is activity on the part of participants and then become interested. This happened with me as I first turned my attention as a business manager to the topic, before exploring its history, James W. Cortada, *Information and the Modern Corporation* (Cambridge, MA: MIT Press, 2011).

63. Fernand Braudel, *Capitalism and Material Life, 1400–1800* (London: Weidenfeld and Nicolson, 1973); Asa Briggs, *Victorian Things* (London: Batsford, 1988); K. Harvey, ed., *History and Material Culture: A Student's Guide to Approaching Alternative Sources* (London: Routledge, 2009).

64. Dan Hicks and Mary C. Beaudry, "Material Culture Studies: A Reactionary View," in *The Oxford Handbook of Material Culture Studies*, eds. Dan Hicks and Mary C. Beaudry (New York: Oxford University Press, 2010), 1–21.

65. Eric Schatzberg, *Technology: Critical History of a Concept* (Chicago: University of Chicago Press, 2018).

66. B. Brown, "Thing Theory," *Critical Inquiry* 28, no. 1 (2001): 1–22.

67. I have begun to do this for IBM retirees and collected over a dozen sets of materials; all included objects with paper ephemera.

68. Thomas Piketty, *Capital in the Twenty-First Century* (Cambridge, MA: Harvard University Press, 2014); Shoshana Zuboff, *The Age of Surveillance Capitalism: The Fight for a Human Future at the New Frontier of Power* (New York: Hachette, 2019).

69. Mark Miodownik, *Stuff Matters: Exploring the Marvelous Materials That Shape Our Man-Made World* (New York: Houghton Mifflin Harcourt, 2013).

70. Cortada, *IBM*.

71. Routinely reported by IBM country managers each year to corporate headquarters, Country Files, IBM Corporate Archives, Poughkeepsie, NY. These reports were so detailed and comprehensive that one can build a rough account of computer uses in many countries from the 1950s through the 1970s just from these records.

72. For citations of the various longevity statistics, O'Reilly III and Tushman, *Lead and Disrupt*, 3–4, quote, 4.

73. I discuss these issues in more detail in James W. Cortada, "Longevity and Corporate Ecosystems: How Did IBM Exist for Over a Century?," *Entreprises et Histoire* 94 (April 2019): 104–127.

74. The version that hung in my various offices at IBM between the 1980s and the 2010s.

75. Thomas J. Watson, Jr., *A Business and Its Beliefs: The Ideas That Help Build IBM* (New York: McGraw-Hill, 1963).

76. Louis V. Gerstner, Jr., *Who Says Elephants Can't Dance?: Inside IBM's Historic Turnaround* (New York: HarperCollins, 2003).

77. As a manager for three decades, I read these opinion surveys every year; I also have a few copies in my private files. These documents were never made public, and few exist in IBM's corporate archives in Poughkeepsie, New York. Those that do exist there are closed to the public. Rarely did an employee publicly deride these values and, when doing so, complained about the quality of their execution, not the merits of these beliefs. For such a rare account about life in the firm during the 1950s through the mid-1980s in the United States, see Jack D. Martin, *Inside Big Blue: Will the Real IBM Please Stand Up?* (New York: Vantage, 1988).

78. All managers were trained in how to implement, promote, and enforce these beliefs, IBM, *GSD Atlanta Management Seminar*, training materials (1980s) and IBM, *Fundamentals of Management Course* (1967) in three three-ring binders, author's files.
79. O'Reilly III and Tushman, *Lead and Disrupt*, 146–164.
80. In nearly four decades at IBM, I have had the occasion to discuss these analogies with IBM employees who were Catholics and military veterans from multiple countries. They often raised the analogies themselves, and when I did, I never encountered a disagreement about the validity of the comparison.
81. Customer–IBM ecosystems became a key focal point of discussion in Cortada, *IBM*.
82. For images of each and their chronology, see IBM Archives, "IBM Logo Exhibit," https://www.ibm.com/ibm/history/exhibits/logo/logo_4.html, accessed October 6, 2020.
83. John Harwood discusses some of these behaviors, although he focuses largely on the design of IBM's image and its manifestations, John Harwood, *The Interface: IBM and the Transformation of Corporate Design* (Minneapolis: University of Minnesota Press, 2011), 1945–1976.
84. Roland Marchand, *Creating the Corporate Soul: The Rise of Public Relations and Corporate Imagery in American Big Business* (Berkeley: University of California Press, 2001), 26–41, quote, 26.
85. Marchand, *Creating the Corporate Soul*, 26–41.
86. Harwood, *The Interface*, 5.
87. Harwood, *The Interface*, 4.
88. Thomas J. Watson, Jr., "Good Design Is Good Business," in *The Art of Design Management* (New York: Tiffany & Co., 1975), 79.
89. A point made by Lee Conrad to the author in a series of discussions from 2017 to 2021. Conrad was one of the principal leaders of unionizing initiatives inside of IBM from the 1980s into the early 2000s. It was slow going in the 1980s, when he had to remain underground in his initiatives, not able to generate much interest on the part of IBMers until essentially the next decade, and even then, he and his colleagues around the company encountered insufficient support to be successful. Was that due to fear of corporate retribution, or more due to employees being comfortable with the Grand Bargain? The answer was probably a combination of both or, as many retirees noted in Facebook posts in the 2000s, an inability of employees to recognize how seriously the company had started to change by the end of the 1980s.
90. Explained by Gerald Zahavi, *Workers, Managers, and Welfare Capitalism: The Shoeworkers and Tanners of Endicott Johnson, 1890–1950* (Urbana: University of Illinois Press, 1988), 1–62.
91. Zahavi, *Workers, Managers, and Welfare Capitalism*, 126–149.

2. Role of Ethics in Corporate Culture: Enduring Beliefs at IBM

1. Louis V. Gerstner, Jr., *Who Says Elephants Can't Dance? Inside IBM's Historic Turnaround* (New York: HarperBusiness, 2002), 183.
2. James W. Cortada, *IBM: The Rise and Fall and Reinvention of a Global Icon* (Cambridge, MA: MIT Press, 2019), 421–502.
3. Gerstner, *Who Says Elephants Can't Dance*, 282.
4. As a nearly forty-year employee of IBM who had worked in the pre- and post-Gerstner eras, and so saw the contrast between two profoundly different periods in the company's history, I approach this topic with the profound trepidation that a Catholic priest

must have experienced when challenging the practices of the Vatican at the dawn of the Protestant Revolution. On the one hand, the ethics and Basic Beliefs that so character-ized the behavior of generations of IBMers are part of who I am, yet another feature of IBM behavior is the ability to recognize the need for change and to confront weaknesses in the company's performance, which affected how I worked. Navigating through those two features of IBM's culture is, I believe, a greater challenge for an IBM veteran than it might be for a scholar who may only come close to understanding how important this subject is for the history of the firm and how difficult it is to describe.

5. Kevin Maney, *The Maverick and His Machine: Thomas Watson, Sr. and the Making of IBM* (Hoboken, NJ: John Wiley & Sons, 2003), 25.

6. Quoted in Maney, *The Maverick and His Machine*, 25.

7. Thomas J. Watson, Sr., *Men-Minutes-Money* (New York: International Business Machines Corporation, 1934).

8. For a summary of the case, which has been discussed by many historians, see Cortada, *IBM*, 185–189; Emerson W. Pugh, *Building IBM: Shaping an Industry and Its Technology* (Cambridge, MA: MIT Press, 1995), 250–256; both authors were career IBM employees.

9. Watson, *Men-Minutes-Money*, 755.

10. Thomas J. Watson, Jr., *A Business and Its Beliefs: The Ideas That Helped Build IBM* (New York: McGraw-Hill, 1963).

11. Watson Jr. provided an account of the settlement: Thomas J. Watson, Jr., and Peter Petre, *Father Son & Co.: My Life at IBM and Beyond* (New York: Bantam, 1990), 215–220.

12. Watson, Jr., *A Business and Its Beliefs*, 32.

13. IBM, *Fundamentals of Management Course, Lesson 3* (New York: IBM, 1967), 4-1.

14. Reprinted in IBM, *Thirty Years of Management Briefings, 1958 to 1988* (Armonk, NY: IBM Corporation, 1988), 37.

15. IBM, *Thirty Years of Management Briefings*, 79.

16. See Gerstner, *Who Says Elephants Can't Dance?*, 200–203 for the eight principles. Because he attempted to displace the Basic Beliefs with these, when he retired, employ-ees dismissed his principles, which, on their face, made sense to embrace. He made a critical mistake when he labeled the Basic Beliefs "now homilies," when he should have given these more respect. In fairness to him, he had only been in the company barely five months.

17. IBM, *Fundamentals of Management Course, Lesson 3*, 4-1.

18. IBM, *Thirty Years of Management Briefings*, 197.

19. IBM, *Thirty Years of Management Briefings*, 197.

20. Pugh, *Building IBM*, 324.

21. Half million is a larger number than the size of IBM's workforce in any year because employees came and went. As long as someone was working at IBM, however brief, they were subject to its guidelines. IBM's business partners too learned of IBM's prac-tices, although they had more freedom of action to exercise their own value systems if they differed only mildly from IBM's.

22. Subsequent editions reflected more fashionable designs, such as with illustrated covers. They were reprinted in slightly revised editions every year over the next half century. The publication was printed in the shade of green consistent with other IBM publi-cations and fashion of the day; it appeared before it had become practice at IBM of publishing many of its internal booklets in shades of blue.

23. IBM, *Guidelines for Business Conduct* (Armonk, NY: IBM Corporation, August 1965).

24. IBM, *Doing Business with 20,000 Suppliers: A Guide for IBM Management* (Armonk, NY: International Business Machines Corporation, September 1965). It was a better-designed

document because it was distributed to suppliers as well as to IBMers to make clear company policies regarding purchases and dealing with suppliers.

25. IBM, *Doing Business with 20,000 Suppliers*, 1.
26. IBM, *Fundamentals of Management Course, Lesson 3*, 4-3.
27. Written guidelines were published periodically across the century, such as, for example, IBM, *IBM Confidential Information Handbook* (Armonk, NY: IBM, 1972, 1976), and IBM, *Information Classification and Control* (New York: IBM, multiple editions, 1950s–1990s).
28. IBM, *Fundamentals of Management Course, Lesson 3*, 4-4-4-6.
29. IBM, *Fundamentals of Management Course, Lesson 3*, 4-11. As a side note, your author, in his over thirty years in IBM management, encountered such situations rarely, perhaps three to five times, but when he did, they were thoroughly investigated and decisions to dismiss an employee were not taken lightly. This was particularly the case before the early 2000s when layoffs and such dismissals were entwined, such that it would be difficult to generalize on managerial practices.
30. Your author as manager is guilty as charged. While the new machine's cost might not be charged to the manager's budget, transporting it and other experts to the customer would be, and pulling a new machine off the production line meant that another customer anticipating its momentary delivery might have to be told it would be delayed. So now IBM had two concerned customers. In critical situations, we might not have been allowed to obtain a replacement machine if, for example, the target product about to come off the production line was headed to a national security installation or a military base.
31. Watson, *Men-Minutes-Money*, 29.
32. IBM, *Fundamentals of Management Course, Lesson 3*, 4-12.
33. Cortada, *IBM*, 325–352.
34. Gerstner, *Who Says Elephants Can't Dance?*, 118.
35. Based on editions in the possession of the author from the 1980s and 1990s.
36. IBM, *IBM Corporate Business Conduct Guidelines* (Armonk, NY: IBM Corporation, September 1993), 1, http://www.oocities.org/~keithgibby/business_conduct_guidelines.htm, accessed December 8, 2020.
37. IBM, *IBM Corporate Business Conduct Guidelines*.
38. IBM, "Business Conduct Guidelines," 2019, https://www.ibm.com/investor/att/pdf/BCG_accessible_2019.pdf, accessed December 8, 2020.
39. IBM, "Business Conduct Guidelines," 4.
40. IBM, "Business Conduct Guidelines," 5.
41. IBM, "IBM Policies & Principles," updates vary from 2018–2020, https://www.ibm.org/responsibility/policies, accessed December 8, 2020.
42. James W. Cortada, "Change and Continuity at IBM: Key Themes in Histories of IBM," *Business History Review* 92, no. 1 (2018): 117–148; Edgar H. Schein, *Organizational Culture and Leadership* (San Francisco: Jossey-Bass, 1989), 23–84, 209–222; and by an IBMer who surveyed nearly 70,000 IBM colleagues on all manner of issues, Geert Hofstede, *Culture's Consequences* (Beverly Hills, CA: SAGE, 1980).
43. Charles A. O'Reilly III and Michael L. Tushman, *Lead and Disrupt: How to Solve the Innovator's Dilemma*, 2nd ed. (Stanford, CA: Stanford Business Books, 2021), 91.
44. On the historiography, Franco Amatori and Geoffrey Jones, eds., *Business History Around the World* (Cambridge, UK: Cambridge University Press, 2003); see the first six essays in Alan M. Rugman, ed., *The Oxford Handbook of International Business*, 2nd ed. (New York: Oxford University Press, 2009), 3–180.

45. For a collection of examples where execution did not meet up to expectations from the 1950s into the 1980s in the United States, see Jack D. Martin, *Inside Big Blue: Will the Real IBM Please Stand Up?* (New York: Vantage, 1988).

46. Vincent Barry, ed., *Moral Issues in Business* (Belmont, CA: Wadsworth, 1979); Richard T. De George, *Business Ethics* (New York: Macmillan, 1982); Linda K. Treviño, G. R. Weaver, and S. J. Reynolds, "Behavioral Ethics in Organizations: A Review," *Journal of Management* 32, no. 6 (2006): 951–990; M. G. Velasquez, *Business Ethics: Concepts and Cases* (Englewood Cliffs, NJ: Prentice Hall, 1982); Brian J. Farrell, Deirdre M. Cobbin, and Helen M. Farrell, "Codes of Ethics: Their Evolution, Development and Other Controversies," *Journal of Management Development* 21, no. 2 (2002): 152–163.

47. Richard T. de George, "A History of Business Ethics," paper presented at the Third Biennial Global Business Ethics Conference, Markkula Center for Applied Ethics, Santa Clara, CA, February 2005.

48. His son, Watson Jr., spent considerable time in his memoirs describing how his father spent his time, *Father Son & Co.*

49. Frank Chapman Sharp and Phillip G. Fox, *Business Ethics* (New York: D. Appleton-Century, 1937).

50. *The University of Wisconsin Catalogue 1913–1914* (Madison: University of Wisconsin, 1913), 12, 243.

51. George, "A History of Business Ethics."

52. Jane Collier, "*FOCUS: Research in Business Ethics* Business Ethics Research: Shaping the Agenda," *Business Ethics* 4, no. 1 (January 1995): 6–12; Stephen Brigley, "*FOCUS:* Business Ethics Research: A Cultural Perspective," *Business Ethics* 4, no. 1 (January 1995): 17–22.

53. See, for instance, the Caux Principles, formulated in 1995, http://hrlibrary.umn.edu /instree/cauxrndtbl.htm, accessed December 8, 2020.

54. Farrell, Cobbin, and Farrell, "Codes of Ethics," 152–156.

55. Kirk O. Hanson and Marc J. Epstein, *Rotten: Why Corporate Misconduct Continues and What to Do About It* (Lanark Press, 2020); Thomas K. McCraw, *Prophets of Regulation: Charles Francis Adams; Louis D. Brandeis, James M. Landis; Alfred D. Kahn* (Cambridge, MA: Harvard University Press, 1984), 300–310; Thomas Philippon, *The Great Reversal: How America Gave Up on Free Markets* (Cambridge, MA: Harvard University Press, 2019), 259–286; Edward J. Balleisen, *Fraud: An American History from Barnum to Madoff* (Princeton, NJ: Princeton University Press, 2017), 245–350.

56. For examples, B. Kaye, "Codes of Ethics in Australian Business Corporations," *Journal of Business Ethics* 11, no. 11 (November 1992): 857–862; R. Rowan and D. Campbell, "The Attempt to Regulate Industrial Relations Through International Codes of Conduct," *Columbia Journal of World Business* 18, no. 2 (Summer 1983): 64–72; B. Schlegelmilch and J. Houston, "Corporate Codes of Ethics in Large UK Companies: An Empirical Investigation of Use, Content and Attitudes," *European Journal of Marketing* 23, no. 6 (1989): 7–24; Farrell, Cobbin, and Farrell, "Code of Ethics," 156–159.

57. Farrell, Cobbin, and Farrell, "Code of Ethics," 152–163.

58. Farrell, Cobbin, and Farrell, "Code of Ethics," 152–163.

59. Samuel Palmisano, "Leading Change When Business Is Good," *Harvard Business Review* 82, no. 12 (2004): 63, but see the entire article, 60–70, where he discusses also how a global organization has to be run in a decentralized manner and that requires common views.

60. IBM, *Fundamentals of Management Course, Lesson 3*, 6-8-6-13. As an IBM manager, your author encountered each of these situations more than once, including others

involving potential bribes, documenting customer embezzlement of their own resources, a few sexual harassment instances both inside of IBM and within customer organizations, questionable company-to-company collusion, and possible contract violations, among others.

61. Jenny C. McCune, "Who Are Those People in the Blue Suits?," *Management Review* (September 1991): 17. The head of IBM in the United Kingdom made the same point a few years later and in the process described the specifics of the Business Conduct Guidelines using the same language as in the original editions of the publication produced over thirty years earlier; A. B. Cleaver, "Business Ethics in IBM," *Business Ethics* 1, no. 1 (January 1997): 4–8.

62. M. Davis, "Working with Your Company's Code of Ethics," *Management Solutions* 33, no. 6 (June 1988): 4–10.

63. D. Robin, M. Giallourakis, F. David, and T. Morotz, "A Different Look at Codes of Ethics," *Business Horizons* 32, no. 1 (January/February 1989): 66–73.

64. Raymond C. Baumhart, "How Ethical Are Businessmen?," *Harvard Business Review* 39, no. 4 (July–August 1961): 6–31.

65. Santiago Pinetta, *La nacion robada* (Buenos Aires: Editorial Azur, 1994); Gustavo Soriani, *La Corporacion: El escándelo IBM-Banco Nación contado desde adentro* (Buenos Aires: Planeta, 1996); Jesús Rodríguez, *Fuera de la ley: La relación entre IBM y los funcionarios públicos en los contratos informáticas del Estado* (Buenos Aires: Planeta, 1998).

66. See, for example, Arne Alsin, "The IBM Hall of Shame: (Semi) Complete List of Bribes, Blunders and Fraud," *Worm Capital*, November 26, 2016, https://medium.com/worm-capital/the-ibm-hall-of-shame-a-semi-complete-list-of-bribes-blunders-and-fraud-19e674a5b986, accessed December 10, 2020.

67. Academics studying the jams and interviewing employees observed that "employees [who] were interviewed could not recall Gerstner's eight kitchen-table principles, even though they were widely posted on walls around the company; when reminded, they interpreted them very differently; and they generally saw little actual effect on their own work"; Charles Heckscher, Clark Bernier, Hao Gong, and Paul DiMaggio, "'Driving Change by Consensus': Dialogue and Culture Change at IBM," March 2018, https://smlr.rutgers.edu/sites/default/files/documents/ResearchDocs/heckscher_culture_change_at_ibm_-_draft_march_2018.pdf, 2, accessed December 8, 2020.

68. For the most complete account of the jams, see Heckscher, Bernier, Gong, and DiMaggio, "'Driving Change by Consensus.'"

69. Heckscher, Bernier, Gong, and DiMaggio, "'Driving Change by Consensus'"; David Yaun, "Driving Cultural Change by Consensus at IBM," *Strategic Communication Management* 10, no. 3 (2006): 14–17; Lynda M. Applegate, Charles Heckscher, Boniface Michael, and Elizabeth Collins, "IBM's Decade of Transformation: Uniting Vision and Values," 9-807-030, Harvard Business School (2006).

70. While there is a rich literature on the methodologies used to identify corporate cultures, we do not need to engage with it. For useful examples, see J. R. Barker, "Tightening the Iron Cage: Concertive Control in Self-Managing Teams," *Administrative Science Quarterly* 38, no. 3 (1993): 408–437; Michael Beer and Russell Eisenstat, "How to Have an Honest Conversation About Your Business Strategy," *Harvard Business Review* (February 2004), https://hbr.org/2004/02/how-to-have-an-honest-conversation-about-your-business-strategy, accessed December 9, 2020; Michael Beer, Russell Eisenstat, and B. Spector, *The Critical Path to Corporate Renewal* (Boston: Harvard Business Press, 1990); R. Charan, "Conquering a Culture of Indecision," *Harvard Business Review* 84, no. 1 (2006): 108; T. E. Deal and A. A. Kennedy, *Corporate Culture: The Rites and*

Rituals of Corporate Life, vol. 2 (Reading, PA: Addison-Wesley, 1982); Jurgen Habermas, *Legitimation Crisis* (Boston: Beacon, 1975); G. Hamel, "Waking Up IBM: How a Gang of Unlikely Rebels Transformed Big Blue," *Harvard Business Review* 78, no. 4 (2000): 137–146; Talcott Parsons, "On the Concept of Value-Commitments," *Sociological Inquiry* 38, no. 2 (1994): 169–189; R. Simmons, "How New Top Managers Use Control Systems as Levers of Strategic Renewal," *Strategic Management Journal* 15, no. 3 (1994): 169–189.

71. Applegate, Heckscher, Michael, and Collins, "IBM's Decade of Transformation."
72. IBM, *Thirty Years of Management Briefings*.
73. The phrase "the business" has long been used inside the firm to mean IBM.
74. Nick Donofrio and Michael DeMarco, *If Nothing Changes, Nothing Changes: The Nick Donofrio Story* (Houndstooth, 2022), 114.
75. Donofrio and DeMarco, *If Nothing Changes, Nothing Changes*, 115.
76. Donofrio and DeMarco, *If Nothing Changes, Nothing Changes*, 116.
77. Heckscher, Bernier, Gong, and DiMaggio, "'Driving Change by Consensus,'" 14; Paul DiMaggio, Clark Bernier, Charles Heckscher, and David Mimmno, *Interaction Ritual Threads: Does IRC Theory Apply Online?*, Working Paper No. 16, Center for the Study of Social Organization (April 2017).
78. Cortada, *IBM*, 85–86.
79. Heckscher, Bernier, Gong, and DiMaggio, "'Driving Change by Consensus,'" 15.
80. Heckscher, Bernier, Gong, and DiMaggio, "'Driving Change by Consensus,'" 18.
81. Heckscher, Bernier, Gong, and DiMaggio, "'Driving Change by Consensus,'" 19.
82. Watson, Jr., *A Business and Its Beliefs*, 39.
83. William Magnuson, *For Profit: A History of Corporations* (New York: Basic Books, 2022), 299.

3. "The IBM Way": Creating and Sustaining a Corporate Image and Reputation

1. John A. Meyers, "A Letter from the Publisher," *Time*, July 11, 1983, 3.
2. Yet much work has been done on aspects of the story. See, for example, Pamela Walker, *Advertising Progress: American Business and the Rise of Consumer Marketing* (Baltimore: Johns Hopkins University Press, 1998); Roland Marchand, *Creating the Corporate Soul: The Rise of Public Relations and Corporate Imagery in American Big Business* (Berkeley: University of California Press, 1998).
3. Facebook includes "IBM Retirees," "IBM Atlanta Area Retirees," "IBMretiree," and "Watching IBM."
4. Edelman, "Edelman Trust Barometer 2021," https://www.edelman.com/trust/2021-trust-barometer, accessed April 21, 2021.
5. William Magnuson, *For Profit: A History of Corporations* (New York: Basic Books, 2022), 297–326.
6. James W. Cortada, *IBM: The Rise and Fall and Reinvention of a Global Icon* (Cambridge, MA: MIT Press, 2019), 421–438, 547–577.
7. Peter E. Greulich, *THINK Again! The Rometty Edition* (Austin, TX: MBI Concepts, 2020), 213–239.
8. Gregorio Martín de Castro, José Emilio Navas López, and Pedro López Sáez, "Business and Social Reputation: Exploring the Concept and Main Dimensions of Corporate Reputation," *Journal of Business Ethics* 63 (2006): 361–370; P. Roberts and G. Dowling,

"Corporate Reputation and Sustained Superior Financial Performance," *Strategic Management Journal* 23 (2002): 1077–1093.

9. I. Diericks and K. Cool, "Asset Stock Accumulation and Sustainability of Competitive Advantage," *Management Science* 35, no. 2 (1989): 1504–1513.

10. Marchand, *Creating the Corporate Soul*, 21.

11. While Emerson W. Pugh and colleagues at IBM wrote extensively about the S/360, he summarizes some of the issues in *Building IBM: Shaping an Industry and Its Technology* (Cambridge, MA: MIT Press, 1995), 292–296.

12. Castro, López, and Sáez, "Business and Social Reputation," 362.

13. O. Shenkar and E. Yuchmann-Yaar, "Reputation, Image, Prestige, and Goodwill: An Interdisciplinary Approach to Organizational Standing," *Human Relations* 50, no. 11 (1997): 1361–1381.

14. D. Deephouse, "Media Reputation as a Strategic Resource: An Integration of Mass Communication and Resource-Based Theories," *Journal of Management* 26, no. 6 (2000): 1091–1112; J. D. Norris, *Advertising and the Transformation of American Society, 1865–1920* (New York: Greenwood, 1990).

15. Geert Hofstede, *Culture's Consequences: International Differences in Work-Related Values* (Beverly Hills, CA: SAGE, 1980).

16. Robert Fitzgerald, "Marketing and Distribution," in *The Oxford Handbook of Business History*, eds. Geoffrey Jones and Jonathan Zeitlin (New York: Oxford University Press, 2007), 408–410; D. Pope, *The Making of Modern Advertising* (New York: Basic Books, 1983); P. Shuwer, *History of Advertising* (Geneva: Edito-Service, 1966); J. Sivulka, *Soap, Sex and Cigarettes: A Cultural History of American Advertising* (Belmont, CA: Wadsworth, 1998); R. Tedlow, *New and Improved: The Story of Mass Marketing in America* (Oxford, UK: Heinemann Professional, 1990).

17. William Aspray and Donald deB. Beaver, "Marketing the Monster: Advertising Computer Technology," *Annals of the History of Computing* 8, no. 2 (April 1986): 127–143.

18. Thomas J. Watson, Sr., *Men-Minutes-Money* (New York: International Business Machines Corporation, 1934), 15.

19. Watson, *Men-Minutes-Money*, 16.

20. Watson, *Men-Minutes-Money*, 16.

21. Watson, *Men-Minutes-Money*, 20–23.

22. Watson, *Men-Minutes-Money*, 29.

23. Thomas J. Watson, Jr., *A Business and Its Beliefs: The Ideas That Helped Build IBM* (New York: McGraw-Hill, 1963), 15.

24. After 2000, some would argue even earlier, corporate management became more mute about customers and growing revenues, shifting to financial engineering practices to sustain profits and stock prices, described in some detail by Cortada, *IBM*, 561–563; Greulich, *THINK Again!*

25. IBM, *Fundamentals of Management Course, Lesson 3* (New York: IBM Corporation, 1967), 6-1–6-4.

26. Marchand, *Creating the Corporate Soul*, 21.

27. David E. Nye, *Image World: Corporate Identities at General Electric, 1890–1930* (Cambridge, MA: MIT Press, 1985).

28. "The Colossus That Works," *Time*, July 11, 1983, 45.

29. "The Colossus That Works," 45.

30. "Thomas J. Watson Sr. Is Dead; I.B.M. Board Chairman Was 82," *New York Times*, June 30, 1956, https://archive.nytimes.com/www.nytimes.com/learning/general/onthisday/bday/0217.html, accessed December 20, 2021.

31. "IBM Logo," IBM Archives, https://www.ibm.com/ibm/history/exhibits/logo/logo_1 .html, accessed December 20, 2021.

32. Thomas Watson Jr. to management, March 16, 1961, IBM, *Thirty Years of Management Briefings, 1958–1988* (Armonk, NY: IBM Corporation, 1988), 25.

33. Even decades after he left IBM, employees were being taught good manners. For examples, IBM, *101 'Plus' Ways to Say Thank You; A Manager's Guide* (Bethesda, MD: IBM Federal Systems Division, 1987); IBM, *How to Win Telephone Friends and Influence Callers* (New York: IBM Corporation, circa late 1980s).

34. Watson to management, June 14, 1962, IBM, *Thirty Years of Management Briefings*, 47. Like all CEOs at IBM, he railed against the evils of bureaucracy; for an example, Watson to management, September 29, 1967, IBM, *Thirty Years of Management Briefings*, 104–105.

35. Watson to management, December 30, 1968, IBM, *Thirty Years of Management Briefings*, 124.

36. Frank T. Cary to management, April 11, 1980, IBM, *Thirty Years of Management Briefings*, 206–207.

37. Quoted in Cortada, *IBM*, 579.

38. Cary to management, April 11, 1980, IBM, *Thirty Years of Management Briefings*, 206.

39. IBM, *Thirty Years of Management Briefings*, 207.

40. IBM, *Fundamentals of Management Course, Lesson 3*, 5-1.

41. IBM, *Fundamentals of Management Course, Lesson 3*, 5-2.

42. One CEO even coauthored a book on education, Louis V. Gerstner, Jr., with Roger D. Semerad, Dennis Philip Doyle, and William B. Johnston, *Reinventing Education: Entrepreneurship in America's Public Schools* (New York: Plume, 1995). He also hosted conferences on education at IBM's facilities at Palisades, New York, where much education was conducted for customers and employees.

43. IBM, *Fundamentals of Management Course, Lesson 3*, 5-3–5-4.

44. IBM, *Fundamentals of Management Course, Lesson 3*, 5-4.

45. The newspaper clipping file for the IBM sales office in Nashville, Tennessee, for the 1950s–1970s, for example, contained several for almost every year, including notices of promotions, changes in branch managers, opening of a new office, and major computer installations in the area, in the author's IBM files.

46. I have looked at many of these files over the decades. They include discussions about products, local company events, national IBM activities (e.g., the search for Louis Gerstner as CEO in 1993), local customer installations of IBM products, announcements of promotions, and so forth. I have collected selective articles about IBM for over two decades, and each annual cache takes up approximately one banker box. A complete collection would require many more boxes per year, and it may be impossible to calculate how many articles were published.

47. Speech made by Thomas J. Watson, Jr., before the Twelfth Annual Convention of the Public Relations Society of America (undated, circa early 1960s), copy included in IBM, *Fundamentals of Management Course, Lesson 3*, within tab marked "Community & Public Relations." This was also a point made by Marchand in his study of several other major corporations, *Creating the Corporate Soul*.

48. Watson speech at Public Relations Society of America.

49. Watson speech at Public Relations Society of America.

50. Watson speech at Public Relations Society of America.

51. IBM, *Fundamentals of Management Course, Lesson 3*, 5-4.

52. Your author encountered both forms of exaggeration from the 1970s through the 2010s in small but irritating amounts, so we can conclude that the instructions to management

had two effects: to dampen exaggerations (since to exaggerate could lead to dismissal or some other punishment) and to minimize the frequency of such violations.

53. IBM, *Fundamentals of Management Course, Lesson 3*, 5-5.

54. Reprinted in IBM, *Fundamentals of Management Course, Lesson 3*, 5-8–5-15.

55. The anthology of CEO letters to all management on corporate policies and practices is an example, IBM, *Thirty Years of Management Briefings*, and before 1958, for two decades through *Management Briefings*. CEO communications to management as a community were largely replaced after 1993 with letters to all employees, beginning with CEO Louis V. Gerstner, Jr.

56. IBM, *Fundamentals of Management Course, Lesson 3*, 5-15.

57. Not to overstate the risk of dismissal, the largest number of such cases involved preannouncing earnings and other financial data before corporate headquarters had released such information. Such premature releases could be as benign as saying, "We are going to be reporting a solid performance this quarter."

58. Amy Sue Bix, *Inventing Ourselves out of Jobs? America's Debate Over Technological Unemployment, 1929–1981* (Baltimore, MD: Johns Hopkins University Press, 2000).

59. Pugh, *Building IBM*, 324.

60. All the cabling was placed under the specially designed raised floors of a data center, while the room itself was temperature and humidity controlled to an extent never applied to normal office spaces.

61. Carliss Y. Baldwin and Kim B. Clark, *Design Rules: The Power of Modularity* (Cambridge, MA: MIT Press, 2000), 169–194.

62. Cortada, *IBM*, 149–232.

63. Emerson W. Pugh, Lyle R. Johnson, and John H. Palmer, *IBM's 360 and Early 370 Systems* (Cambridge, MA: MIT Press, 1991); Pugh, *Building IBM*, 131–182.

64. Steven Heller, "Thoughts on Rand," *Print* (May–June 1997): 106–109+. He published on his thinking and work, Paul Rand, *Design, Form, and Chaos* (New Haven, CT: Yale University Press, 1994), but see also his earlier book, *Paul Rand: A Designer's Art* (New Haven, CT: Yale University Press, reprinted New York: Princeton Architectural Press, 2016).

65. For a nearly complete exhibit of his IBM work, see the website where his organization presents his work, "IBM," https://www.paulrand.design/work/IBM.html, accessed December 22, 2021. For his account of developing the IBM logo, Paul Rand, *Design, Form, and Chaos*, illustrated ed. (New Haven, CT: Yale University Press, 2017), 113–150, but see also for his account of relations with IBM more broadly, 179–188.

66. Mark Favermann, "Two Twentieth-Century Icons," *Art New England* (May 1997): 15.

67. All displayed at "IBM," https://www.paulrand.design/work/IBM.html, accessed December 22, 2021.

68. For images of each, see "IBM," https://www.paulrand.design/work/IBM.html.

69. "IBM," https://www.paulrand.design/work/IBM.html.

70. His working records include documentation on his relations with IBM, "Paul Rand Papers," Box 1 and 2, Archives at Yale, https://archives.yale.edu/repositories/5/resources/322/collection_organization#scroll::/repositories/5/archival_objects/123288, accessed December 22, 2021.

71. When I was publishing my history of IBM with MIT Press in 2019 and we were designing the cover, we went to IBM to gain permission to use the current IBM logo. The book was not seen as an attack on IBM, and MIT Press had decades of positive relations with IBM. The production department at MIT Press finally gave up trying to get permission

and so developed its own design, although it used the exact shade of blue that Paul Rand had selected for IBM in the 1950s.

72. The general subject of clothing in the workplace also draws serious academic study, for example, see Erynn Masi de Casanova, *Buttoned Up: Clothing, Conformity, and White-Collar Masculinity* (Ithaca, NY: Cornell University Press, 2015), 7–30.

73. He commented frequently on how companies were judged by their people and each other by the company they kept, Watson, *Men-Minutes-Money*.

74. Walter A. Friedman, *Birth of a Salesman: The Transformation of Selling in America* (Cambridge, MA: Harvard University Press, 2004), 117–150.

75. Thomas J. Watson, Jr., and Peter Petre, *Father Son & Co.: My Life at IBM and Beyond* (New York: Bantam, 1990).

76. This is not an exaggeration. This happened again when Louis V. Gerstner came to IBM in 1993 wearing the then popular white collar/blue shirt combination, while newly hired executives purposefully wanted to signal that they were different. One wore red suspenders—probably a first in IBM history—while many of the new executives would take off their suit jackets while on stage making a speech. That was just never, ever done at IBM, especially in front of customers. Some even wore loafers.

77. Watson Jr. to managers, March 26, 1971, IBM, *Thirty Years of Management Briefings*, 150–151.

78. Your author is the fourth in from the left on the back row with a striped tie.

79. "IBM Retirees," Facebook, July 2018, author's files.

80. "IBM Retirees."

81. "IBM Retirees," undated, circa 2020, author's files.

82. Barbara P. Barker's posting to IBM Retiree Group, Facebook, November 22, 2021.

83. Discussed repeatedly in the memoirs of a customer engineer of the 1950s, Jack D. Martin, *Inside Big Blue: Will the Real IBM Please Stand Up?* (New York: Vantage, 1988).

84. Daniel Dells Hill, *American Menswear: From the Civil War to the Twenty-First Century* (Lubbock, TX: Texas Tech University Press, 2011).

85. Jenny C. McCune, "Who Are Those People in the Blue Suits?," *Management Review* (September 1991): 17.

86. McCune, "Who Are Those People in the Blue Suits?," 18.

87. Louis V. Gerstner, Jr., *Who Says Elephants Can't Dance? Inside IBM's Historic Turnaround* (New York: HarperBusiness, 2002), 184–185.

88. John P. Kotter and James L. Heskett, *Corporate Culture and Performance* (New York: Free Press, 1992), and for an excellent example of modern business history, Robert Fitzgerald, *The Rise of the Global Company: Multinationals and the Making of the Modern World* (Cambridge, UK: Cambridge University Press, 2015); but see the massive historical discussions, too, including about corporate culture, in Jones and Zeitlin, *The Oxford Handbook of Business History*.

89. Published complaints were few, but for three examples, see Milton Drandell, *IBM: The Other Side, 101 Former Employees Look Back* (San Luis Obispo, CA: Quail, 1984); Clyde W. Ford, *Think Black: A Memoir* (Pittsburgh, PA: Amistad, 2019); Martin, *Inside Big Blue*.

90. D. Quinn Mills and G. Bruce Friesen, *Broken Promises: An Unconventional View of What Went Wrong at IBM* (Boston: Harvard Business Review Press, 1996); Greulich, *THINK Again!*

91. John R. Opel to management, December 1, 1981, IBM, *Thirty Years of Management Briefings*, 215.

4. Developing Managers in a Multinational Corporation

1. Thomas J. Watson, Jr., to management, August 9, 1968, reprinted in IBM, *Thirty Years of Management Briefings, 1958–1988* (Armonk, NY: International Business Machines Corporation, 1988), 117.
2. C. E. Makin, "Ranking Corporate Reputations," *Fortune*, January 10, 1983, 33–44; James W. Cortada, "Change and Continuity at IBM: Key Themes in Histories of IBM," *Business History Review* 92, no. 1 (2018): 117–148.
3. James W. Cortada, "Viewing Corporations as Information Ecosystems: The Case of IBM, 1914–1980s," *Enterprise and Society* 23, no. 1 (March 2022): 99–132; James W. Cortada, *Building Blocks of Society: History, Information Ecosystems, and Infrastructures* (Lanham, MD: Rowman & Littlefield, 2021), 181–223.
4. The notion is also referred to often as bureaucracy or organizational capabilities, Steven W. Usselman, "IBM and Its Imitators: Organizational Capabilities and the Emergence of the International Computer Industry," *Business and Economic History* 22, no. 2, papers presented at the Thirty-Ninth Annual Meeting of the Business History Conference (Winter 1993): 1–35.
5. Cortada, "Change and Continuity at IBM," 117–148.
6. For examples, Luis A. Lamassonne, *My Life with IBM* (Atlanta, GA: Brotea, 2000); Omar Harvey, *My Life at IBM* (self-published, 2012); Don Waldecker, *One Career at IBM* (self-published, 2016); John C. Sak, *The Computer Guy Is Here! Mainframe Mechanic* (Middletown, DE: self-published, 2018); and by an IBM CEO, Thomas J. Watson, Jr., and Peter Petre, *Father Son & Co.: My Life at IBM and Beyond* (New York: Bantam, 1990).
7. Philip Scranton and Patrick Fridenson, *Reimagining Business History* (Baltimore, MD: Johns Hopkins University Press, 2013), 1, 9.
8. Edgar H. Schein and Peter A. Schein, *The Corporate Culture Survival Guide*, 3rd ed. (Hoboken, NJ: Wiley & Sons, 2019), 118–120.
9. D. L. Stebenne, "IBM's 'New Deal': Employment Policies of the International Business Machines Corporation, 1933–1956," *Journal of the Historical Society* 5, no. 1 (Winter 2005): 47–77.
10. It began with comments by Thomas J. Watson, Sr., *Men-Minutes-Money* (New York: International Business Machines Corporation, 1927, 1931, 1934) to most recently by another IBM CEO, Louis V. Gerstner, Jr., *Who Says Elephants Can't Dance? Inside IBM's Historic Turnaround* (New York: HarperCollins, 2003).
11. In 1950, IBM had just over 30,000 employees and a gross income of $335 million; in 1989, it employed 383,000 people who generated over $62.6 billion in gross income; Emerson W. Pugh, *Building IBM: Shaping an Industry and Its Technology* (Cambridge, MA: MIT Press, 1995), 324.
12. Quoted phrases signal that these were words used by IBM employees in normal discourse within the firm; see also, Jack D. Martin, *Inside Big Blue: Will the Real IBM Please Stand Up?* (New York: Vantage, 1988), 91–99.
13. The latter point—styles of management—has received remarkably little attention despite constant mention of management practices in general. For an example of what could be done, with specific references to managerial practices at IBM in the 1990s to early 2000s, see Scott W. Spreier, Mary H. Fontaine, and Ruth L. Malloy, "Leadership Run Amok: The Destructive Potential of Overachievers," *Harvard Business Review* 84, no. 6 (June 2006): 72–82.

14. For an introduction to how companies behaved similarly over the second half of the twentieth century, see Brian R. Cheffins, *The Public Company Transformed* (Oxford, UK: Oxford University Press, 2019).

15. Most famously in Alfred D. Chandler, Jr., *The Visible Hand: The Managerial Revolution in American Business* (Cambridge, MA: Harvard University Press, 1977) and with comments about IBM, Alfred D. Chandler, Jr., *Inventing the Electronic Century: The Epic Story of Consumer Electronics and Computer Industries* (Cambridge, MA: Harvard University Press, 2009).

16. For a recent example by thoughtful scholars, Philippe D'Iribarne, Sylvie Chevrier, Alain Henry, Jean-Pierre Segal, and Geneviè Tréguer-Felten, *Cross-Cultural Management Revisited: A Qualitative Approach* (Oxford, UK: Oxford University Press, 2020), 74–87.

17. Frederick W. Taylor, *Shop Management* (New York: Harper & Brothers, 1903); Frederick W. Taylor, *The Principles of Scientific Management* (New York: Harper & Brothers, 1911).

18. While many have written on the subject, the iconic study that shaped a generation of analysis on it was written by Chandler, *The Visible Hand*.

19. It was American because for almost its entire history its most senior executives were U.S. citizens, over half its revenues came from the American market for over half of its history, and almost all of its products and practices originated largely in the United States.

20. Alfred D. Chandler, Jr., *Strategy and Structure: Chapters in the History of the American Industrial Enterprise* (Cambridge, MA: MIT Press, 1962); Chandler, *The Visible Hand*.

21. Geert Hofstede, *Culture's Consequences: International Differences in Work-Related Values* (Beverly Hills, CA: SAGE, 1980).

22. For example, J. Bruce Harreld, Charles A. O'Reilly III, and Michael L. Tushman, "Dynamic Capabilities at IBM: Driving Strategy Into Action," *California Management Review* 49, no. 4 (Summer 2007): 21–28, and perhaps the most thorough and insightful study of IBM's managerial practices written by an IBM manager, David Mercer, *The Global IBM: Leadership in Multinational Management* (New York: Dodd, Mead, 1988).

23. It was a process developed in the 1920s and refined over the next several decades, James W. Cortada, *IBM: The Rise and Fall and Reinvention of a Global Icon* (Cambridge, MA: MIT Press, 2019), 61–90.

24. Famously codified by Thomas J. Watson, Jr., in a book-length discourse that was given to every manager at IBM from the 1960s through the 1980s and that still remains in print, *A Business and Its Beliefs: The Ideas That Helped Build IBM* (New York: McGraw Hill, 1963, 2003).

25. Thomas J. Watson, Jr., to management, July 29, 1960, reprinted in IBM, *Thirty Years of Management Briefings*, 19.

26. IBM, *Thirty Years of Management Briefings*, 20.

27. IBM, *Fundamentals of Management Course, Lesson 1* (New York: IBM Corporation, 1967), 1-1.

28. IBM, *Fundamentals of Management Course*, 1-2.

29. IBM, *Fundamentals of Management Course*, 1-2.

30. For a description of the process by an IBM manager, Martin, *Inside Big Blue*, 40–51.

31. IBM, *Management Development: Performance Planning . . . Examples and Analysis* (Southeast Region, Data Processing Division, IBM Corporation, undated [circa 1970s]), "Performance Planning: Administration Manager," unpaginated, author's collection.

32. IBM, *Management Development*, "Performance Planning: Marketing Manager." Your author was a marketing manager in 1983–1985 and had almost the exact same performance plan and, in subsequent years, issued similar ones to his sales managers.

33. For chairman's compensation/performance plan, always reported to the U.S. Securities and Exchange Commission in what is referred to as the "Form 10-K," example for IBM, 2017, https://www.sec.gov/Archives/edgar/data/51143/000104746918001117/a2233835z10 -k.htm, accessed April 15, 2021.

34. On the limitations of these processes, Martin, *Inside Big Blue*, 43.

35. For a history of how human resources staffs did this across multiple American firms, see Frank Dobbin, *Inventing Equal Opportunity* (Princeton, NJ: Princeton University Press, 2009).

36. Buck Rodgers with Robert L. Shook, *The IBM Way: Insights Into the World's Most Successful Marketing Organization* (New York: HarperCollins, 1986).

37. Your author ran two of these in sales in the 1970s and 1980s and also as a remote member of the SNA organization. Organized as Selected National Accounts (SNA), a formal management and compensation program, I had authority to coordinate sales and support across the world for a specific account and was measured against global targets and compensated accordingly. All SNA customers also had a senior IBM executive assigned to them who they could call for assistance if the SNA managers needed help or were not performing as they wanted. They often used such calls to suggest what new services and products IBM should consider introducing.

38. Kevin Maney, *The Maverick and His Machine: Thomas Watson, Sr. and the Making of IBM* (Hoboken, NJ: John Wiley & Sons, 2003).

39. Mercer, *The Global IBM*, 59–73.

40. In this book, the number of countries cited in which IBM operated varies because IBM's presence expanded, so depending on which decade we are discussing, the number of nations it served will vary.

41. Martin, *Inside Big Blue*, 91.

42. Martin, *Inside Big Blue*, 91.

43. H. Soubra (IBM Human Resource Manager) to Whom It May Concern, July 31, 1990, regarding an employee's training record, copy in the author's IBM files.

44. Prior to these wholesale acquisitions of new employees, occasionally IBM brought in a manager from outside the firm with highly specialized skills, such as in corporate law to manage IBM's responses, say, to American antitrust litigation in the 1970s, and occasionally others to run specific R&D projects.

45. Cortada, *IBM*, on Samuel Palmisano, 524–525, on Virginia M. Rometty, 554–556; "Arvind Krishna," *Wikipedia*, https://en.wikipedia.org/wiki/Arvind_Krishna, accessed April 14, 2021.

46. A sales branch manager of that period provided examples of this process at work, R. Elbert Clemmons, *A Great Time to Be Alive: An Autobiography* (Stuart, FL: privately published, 1968), 107–108, 173–180.

47. In the United States, this was a DPAT test, which tests for personality, pattern recognition, and algebra, among other factors.

48. Mercer, *The Global IBM*, 124.

49. IBM Midwest Region, *Management Development: Interview Techniques* (Chicago: IBM Corporation, June 1960), unpaginated.

50. IBM, "Employment, Transfer, Promotion and Separation of Employees," *Fundamentals of Management Course*, 3-1.

51. IBM, *Fundamentals of Management Course*, 3-1.

52. IBM, *Manager's Manual* (New York: International Business Machines Corporation, circa 1960s), 1-01.

53. IBM, "Employment, Transfer, Promotion and Separation of Employees," *Fundamentals of Management Course*, 3-1.

54. For an example of this overgeneralization about IBM, see David L. Stebenne, "IBM's 'New Deal': Employment Policies of the International Business Machines Corporation, 1933–1956," *Journal of the Historical Society* 5, no. 1 (Winter 2005): 47–77. The same applied to comments about the social expectations of employees (e.g., about alcohol consumption, attending church). Stebenne was not alone; most historians looking at IBM relied either on the U.S. experience or simply did not explore behaviors in other countries.

55. For example, "IBM Retirees," Facebook with over 12,000 subscribers, accessed April 15, 2021; even those highly critical of IBM reached similar conclusions, Martin, *Inside Big Blue*, 121.

56. "IBM Retirees," Facebook.

57. Copies of these forms can be found in IBM, *Fundamentals of Management* (New York: New Manager School, 1974), unpaginated.

58. IBM, *Fundamentals of Management*.

59. This process did not always work well. In the case of Virginia Rometty, she became CEO and chairman because she was the "last man standing" when the board of directors had to pick a new leader. For details, Cortada, *IBM*, 554–555.

60. Christopher Layton, *European Advanced Technology: A Programme for Integration* (London: George Allen & Unwin, 1969), 27.

61. Thomas J. Watson, Sr., *Men-Minutes-Money* (New York: International Business Machines Company, 1934), 51.

62. Historians have yet to study IBM's extensive investment in training and its training centers. Management training centers, in particular, even had their own staffs and buildings, including one on the campus of corporate headquarters within walking distance.

63. Watson, *Men-Minutes-Money*, 68.

64. Watson, *Men-Minutes-Money*, 776.

65. By the 1980s, nearly 40 percent of large American firms used such tools; S. Blinkhorn, C. Johnson, and R. Wood, "Spuriouser and Spuriouser: The Use of Ipsative Personality Tests," *Journal of Occupational Psychology* 61, no. 2 (1988): 153–162.

66. Charles Krauskopf and David R. Saunders, *Personality and Ability: The Personality Assessment System* (Lanham, MD: University Press of America, 1994); Isabel Briggs Myers, Mary H. McCaulley, Naomi Quenk, and Allan Hammer, *MBTI Handbook: A Guide to the Development and Use of the Myers-Briggs Type Indicator*, 3rd ed. (Palo Alto, CA: Consulting Psychologists, 1998).

67. For copies of these lectures and handouts, see IBM, *IBM Management Development, New Manager School* (New York: International Business Machines Corporation, 1974).

68. When 30,000 people from PwC consulting came into IBM in the early 2000s, emails and comments flew around in that community about how different IBM was. Your author was tasked with mentoring eight PwC practice leaders who were, to be blunt, shocked at the way the firm operated, its rules about expenditures, and so forth. Hundreds of PwC employees left IBM within a year, and after three years, many of their executives after their employment contracts made it possible for them to depart.

69. Your author attended four to five at Harvard, one at Sloan, and two at Virginia over the course of three decades. They were interesting, relevant, and challenging.

70. Clemmons, *A Great Time to Be Alive*, 257.

71. For a detailed account of its development, Clemmons, *A Great Time to Be Alive*, 157–279. When your author attended this class in 2000, it was structured essentially as

originally conceived: business professors, company executives, and permanent teaching staff instructing small classes; case studies; team-based exercises; outside speakers; lectures on the economy; IBM's business conditions and finances; and mixed classes with executives from all parts of the company.

72. Richard Pascale, "The Paradox of 'Corporate Culture': Reconciling Ourselves to Socialization," *California Management Review* 27, no. 2 (Winter 1985): 26.

73. Pascale, "The Paradox of 'Corporate Culture,'" 26.

74. For an introduction to some of the issues, R. Barker, "No, Management Is Not a Profession," *Harvard Business Review* 88, nos. 7–8 (June 2010): 52–60, 169; Rakesh Khurana, *From Higher Aims to Hired Hands: The Social Transformation of American Business Schools and the Unfulfilled Promise of Management as a Profession* (Princeton, NJ: Princeton University Press, 2007); Dilek Cetindamar, Robert Phaal, and David R. Probert, "Technology Management as a Profession and the Challenges Ahead," *Journal of Engineering and Technology Management* 41 (July–September 2016): 1–13.

75. The most high-profile example of not making a manager serve as an interchangeable tool, Watson Jr. appointed his brother Arthur, who had grown up in sales and served as general manager of IBM's non-U.S. operations, to head up the final development of the S/360 computers in the early 1960s. It did not work, and Arthur had to be replaced, essentially destroying Arthur's career. His brother thought that the manufacturing assignment would buff his brother's resume for further advancement in IBM, classic development of a future leader. Taking him out of his job was the right thing to do, but as Watson Jr. confessed in his memoirs, "whenever I look back on it, I think about the brother I injured"; Watson, *Father Son & Co.*, 360.

76. Pugh, *Building IBM*, 324.

77. In my nearly forty years at IBM listening to thousands of presentations, the vast majority began with an introduction about where either someone else or the presenters themselves fit in the company, often accompanied by a slide showing their organization chain of command. I have over one hundred such presentations in my personal files demonstrating this feature.

78. In his memoirs, outsider CEO Louis V. Gerstner, Jr., commented about how his senior executives could not discuss their business without using a stack of slides. He ordered them to set them aside and just discuss their activities, *Who Says Elephants Can't Dance*, 43.

79. When your author went through this experience, he saw a vast landscape of IBM activities, politics, and leaders. AAs and EAs in the process enjoyed considerable influencer authority, too.

80. Pascale, "The Paradox of 'Corporate Culture,'" 33.

81. Jacques Maisonrouge, *Manager international: 36 ans au Coeur d'une multinationale de l'informatique* (Paris: R. Laffont, 1985); Luis A. Lamassonne, *My Life with IBM* (Atlanta, GA: Protea, 2000).

82. Palmisano served as an executive assistant to CEO John F. Akers for one year (1989–1990) and lunched monthly with an earlier, now retired CEO, Thomas J. Watson, Jr., as part of his mentoring.

83. Quotes drawn from two appraisals from the 1970s.

84. Quotes drawn from two appraisals from the 1970s.

85. Quoted from one of the author's own personal development plans from the 1980s. In case the reader is curious, all of that played out as planned.

86. However, complaints about specific reviews by employees provided management with an indication of how it was all going. Records of these complaints have not survived for historians to study.

87. Martin, *Inside Big Blue*, 40, and for a detailed explanation of the process, 40–51.

88. A 1986 note in the author's files.

89. A 1987 note in the author's files.

90. Gerstner technically grew up through consulting—a profession with many of the attributes of sales—before entering the ranks of general management prior to his arrival at IBM.

91. Mercer, *The Global IBM*, 123.

92. Pascale, "The Paradox of 'Corporate Culture,'" 34. IBM began conducting opinion surveys in the United States in 1959 and expanded these around the world in the 1960s, usually conducted approximately every year to eighteen months. The results were reviewed with employees and their managers. Few examples have survived for historians to study. Mercer is correct in that, if someone's employees rated a manager poorly, that often ended the rise in management by that individual. It also represented an opportunity for a succeeding manager, as happened in your author's case when he took over a sales office with one of the lowest morale ratings in the United States.

93. Pascale, "The Paradox of 'Corporate Culture,'" 34.

94. Gerstner, *Who Says Elephants Can't Dance*; Doug Gaar, *IBM Redux: Lou Gerstner and the Business Turnaround of the Decade* (New York: HarperBusiness, 1999); Robert Slater, *Saving Big Blue: Leadership Lessons and Turnaround Tactics of IBM's Lou Gerstner* (New York: McGraw-Hill, 1999).

95. Nick Donofrio and Michael DeMarco, *If Nothing Changes, Nothing Changes: The Nick Donofrio Story* (Houndstooth, 2022); Ginni Rometty, *Good Power: Leading Positive Change in Our Lives, Work and World* (Boston: Harvard Business Review Press, 2023).

96. Cortada, *IBM*, 501–618.

97. Daniel Quinn Mills and G. Bruce Friesen, *Broken Promises: An Unconventional View of What Went Wrong at IBM* (Boston: Harvard Business Review Press, 1996), 80–81, 126–131, 157–158; Peter E. Greulich, *THINK Again! The Rometty Edition* (Austin, TX: MBI Concepts, 2020), 140–146.

98. A dramatic example was Michael Albrecht, who worked at IBM in the 1970s, rising to a first-level manager in sales at IBM before leaving to work for a utility company, followed by years of consulting, then returning to IBM in the 1990s to serve in various capacities, the last one as general manager of IBM's consulting operations for all of North America. It was during his time, for example, that PwC had to be integrated into IBM's operations. As he once explained, one of his duties was to "translate" for the newly arrived practice leaders.

99. Based on dozens of Facebook postings to IBM retiree sites to which the author, as a retiree himself, had access and personal conversations with friends within the firm between 2014 and 2020.

100. For a masterful brief introduction to this community of firms, see Walter A. Friedman, *American Business History: A Very Short Introduction* (New York: Oxford University Press, 2020); for a more detailed analysis, Brian R. Cheffins, *The Public Company Transformed* (Oxford, UK: Oxford University Press, 2019).

101. Echoes of Chandler, *The Visible Hand*.

102. Retired employees who had been out of the company for a decade or more reported on Facebook of still having in their home offices plaques stating IBM's Basic Beliefs and affirmed in their posts that they still adhered to these after thirty to forty years of applying them at work.

103. Cortada, *IBM*.

104. A major argument and attention in Cortada, *IBM*.

5. How IBM Prevented Unionization of Its American Workforce

1. Thomas J. Watson, Jr., *A Business and Its Beliefs: The Ideas That Help Build IBM* (New York: McGraw-Hill, 1963), 16–17.
2. For one who mentioned them briefly, David L. Stebenne, "IBM's 'New Deal': Employment Policies of the International Business Machines Corporation, 1933–1956," *Journal of the Historical Society* 5, no. 1 (Winter 2005): 47–77.
3. James W. Cortada, *IBM: The Rise and Fall and Reinvention of a Global Icon* (Cambridge, MA: MIT Press, 2019).
4. I kept meticulous notes of almost every meeting I attended from 1974 through 2012 and recently went through these to identify themes and topics and found only four discussions of union activities and, even then, ever so briefly.
5. Erik Loomis, "Why the Amazon Workers Never Stood a Chance," *New York Times*, April 15, 2021, https://www.nytimes.com/2021/04/15/opinion/amazon-union-alabama.html, accessed April 20, 2021.
6. C. Schlombs, "The 'IBM Family': American Welfare Capitalism, Labor and Gender in Postwar Germany," *IEEE Annals of the History of Computing* 39, no. 4 (October–December 2017): 12–26.
7. That work is just starting, C. Schlombs, "The 'IBM Family'"; on Scotland, T. Dickson, H. V. McLachlan, P. Prior, and K. Swales, "Big Blue and the Unions: IBM, Individualism and Trade Union Strategy," *Work, Employment and Society* 2, no. 4 (December 1988): 506–520; Alice Le Flanchec and Jacques Rojot, "The 'Open Door' Policy at IBM France: An Old-Established Voice Procedure That Is Still in Use," *Journal of Comparative Labor Law and Industrial Relations* 25, no. 4 (2009): 411–429.
8. Howard Gospel, "The Management of Labor and Human Resources," in *The Oxford Handbook of Business History*, eds. Geoffrey Jones and Jonathan Zeitlin (New York: Oxford University Press, 2007), 420–446, for both a summary and extensive historiographical discussion.
9. Steven Tolliday and Jonathan Zeitln, eds., *The Automobile Industry and Its Workers: Between Fordism and Flexibility* (Cambridge, UK: Polity, 1986); Sumner H. Slichter, James J. Healy, and Robert E. Livernash, *The Impact of Collective Bargaining on Management* (Washington, DC: Brookings Institute, 1960).
10. Howell Harris, *The Right to Manage: Industrial Relations Policies of American Business in the 1940s* (Madison: University of Wisconsin Press, 1985), but see also David Brody, *Workers in Industrial America: Essays on the Twentieth Century Struggle* (New York: Oxford University Press, 1993).
11. Andrea Tone, *The Business of Benevolence: Industrial Paternalism in Progressive America* (Ithaca, NY: Cornell University Press, 1997), 223–225.
12. Stebenne, "IBM's 'New Deal,'" 55.
13. Thomas Graham Belden and Marva Robins Belden, *The Lengthening Shadow: The Life of Thomas J. Watson* (Boston: Little Brown, 1962), 151.
14. I deal with these issues in more detail for every decade in Cortada, *IBM*.
15. Stebenne, "IBM's 'New Deal,'" 60.
16. Belden and Belden, *The Lengthening Shadow*, 153; William Rodgers, *Think: A Biography of the Watsons and IBM* (New York: Stein & Day, 1969), 95.
17. Stebenne, "IBM's 'New Deal,'" 60.
18. Sanford Jacoby, *Modern Manors: Welfare Capitalism Since the New Deal* (Princeton, NJ: Princeton University Press, 1997); Gerard Zahavi, *Workers, Managers, and Welfare Capitalism: The Shoeworkers and Tanners of Endicott Johnson, 1890–1950* (Urbana:

University of Illinois Press, 1988). IBM competed for workers with this company, both of which had plants nearly within walking distance of each other. See also, William Forbath, *Law and the Shaping of the American Labor Movement* (Cambridge, MA: Harvard University Press, 1961); Daniel Ernst, *Lawyers Against Labor: From Individual Rights to Corporate Liberalism* (Urbana: University of Illinois Press, 1995), because IBM paid close attention to the legal aspects, which were also taught to its managers in the 1950s through the 1980s.

19. Seymour Martin Lipset, "The Future of Private Sector Unions in the U.S.," in *The Future of Private Sector Unionism in the United States*, ed. James Bennet and Bruce Kaufman (Armonk, NY: M. E. Sharpe, 2002), 10. On NCR's experience that so informed Thomas J. Watson, Sr.'s, views on unions and benefits, Nikki Mandell, *The Corporation as Family: The Gendering of Corporate Welfare, 1890–1930* (Chapel Hill: University of North Carolina Press, 2002), 1–10, 128–129.

20. Lipset, "The Future of Private Sector Unions in the U.S.," 10.

21. For a discussion of these various perspectives and its literature, Lawrence G. Richards, Jr., "'Union Free and Proud': America's Anti-Union Culture and the Decline of Organized Labor" (unpublished PhD diss., University of Virginia, 2004), 5–9.

22. Richards, "'Union Free and Proud,'" 5–9.

23. Seymour Martin Lipset, ed., "North American Labor Movements: A Comparative Perspective," in *Unions in Transition: Entering the Second Century* (San Francisco: ICA Press, 1986); Charles Craver, *Can Unions Survive? The Rejuvenation of the American Labor Movement* (New York: New York University Press, 1993), 51–55.

24. Richards, "'Union Free and Proud,'" 9.

25. Richards, "'Union Free and Proud,'" 9.

26. Richards, "'Union Free and Proud,'" 11.

27. Thomas Kochan, "How American Workers View Labor Unions," *Monthly Labor Review* (April 1979): 30.

28. T. Dickson, H. V. McLachlan, P. Prior, and K. Swates, "Big Blue and the Unions: IBM, Individualism and Trade Union Strategy," *Work, Employment & Society* 2, no. 2 (December 1988): 510–512. This article is about IBM's experience in Scotland, demonstrating that its human resource practices were relatively similar outside of the United States as well.

29. Thomas J. Watson, Jr., and Peter Petre, *Father Son & Co.: My Life at IBM and Beyond* (New York: Bantam, 1990), 302.

30. Mandell, *The Corporation as Family*, 128–129.

31. Mandell, *The Corporation as Family*, 310.

32. Mandell, *The Corporation as Family*, 326–331; Cortada, *IBM*, 354–355.

33. Dickson, Prior, and Swates, "Big Blue and the Unions," 509.

34. Dickson, Prior, and Swates, "Big Blue and the Unions," 520.

35. IBM, *Fundamentals of Management Course, Lesson 3* (New York: IBM Corporation, 1967), 3-1.

36. IBM, *Fundamentals of Management Course, Lesson 3*, 3-2.

37. Waldo E. Fisher, *The Taft-Hartley Act as Amended in 1959: A Management Guide*, Bulletin Number 31 (Pasadena, CA: California Institute of Technology, 1960). Why this document was chosen above all other possible ones to distribute is lost to history. However, it was an effectively written explanation, and IBM instructors in all manner of classes distributed non-IBM publications they thought useful, such as Harvard Business School case studies and articles and official court judgements.

38. Fisher, *The Taft-Hartley Act as Amended in 1959*, 30.

39. Harry A. Millis and Emily Clark Brown, *From the Wagner Act to Taft-Hartley: A Study of National Labor Policy and Labor Relations* (Chicago: University of Chicago Press, 1950); Mevyn Dubofsky and Joseph A. McCartin, *Labor in America: A History* (Hoboken, NJ: John Wiley & Sons, 2017), 305–311; Nelson Litchtenstein, *State of the Union: A Century of American Labor* (Princeton, NJ: Princeton University Press, 2002), 141–177.

40. IBM's human resource (HR) staff was largely professionally trained by the 1970s and maintained close ties to other HR staffs in American multinational companies, sharing information and learning from each other. For details, Frank Dobbin, *Inventing Equal Opportunity* (Princeton, NJ: Princeton University Press, 2009), 101–132.

41. IBM, *Fundamentals of Management Course, Lesson 3*, 3-4. In fact, generations of managers routinely consulted these experts on all manner of personnel issues, not just about labor organizing.

42. Martin, *Inside Big Blue*, 54.

43. U.S. Department of Labor, *Important Events in American Labor History, 1778–1964* (Washington, DC: U.S. Government Printing Office, 1965).

44. Offprint, Hyman L. Lewis, "The Economy in 1966," *Monthly Labor Review* (February 1967): 1–11.

45. IBM, *Fundamentals of Management Course, Lesson 3*, 3-8–3-9.

46. A few years before grievance and unionizing activities began in Endicott, about 75 percent of employees reported in a confidential opinion survey that they had no hesitancy to speak up about negative working conditions or the behavior of their managers if they felt aggrieved; IBM, *Employee Opinion Survey, Endicott, New York 1963* (New York: International Business Machines Corporation, 1963), unpaginated.

47. As a manager between the 1980s and 2012, I personally read annual opinion survey results for the entire American workforce, and not just of my division or region, and it is on the basis of that experience that I made these general observations. Opinion surveys have never been made accessible to scholars by any part of IBM.

48. Cortada, *IBM*, 147–352.

49. Email from Lee Conrad to James W. Cortada, December 1, 2020.

50. Studied by Peter C. Little, *Toxic Town: IBM, Pollution, and Industrial Risks* (New York: New York University Press, 2014), 118–147.

51. Interview with Lee Conrad by James W. Cortada, February 24, 2021.

52. "IBM: A Danger to the Worker," *IBM Speak Up*, no. 10 (April 1981): 1.

53. "IBM: A Danger to the Worker," 2.

54. Interview with Lee Conrad.

55. Increasingly over time, Lois Fecteau, "IBM Workers Question Chemical Safety," *Binghamton Sun Bulletin*, February 10, 1981, and Paul Shukovsky, "IBM Worker: Watchdog Needed," *Binghamton Sun Bulletin*, February 10, 1981; Hank Gilman, "IBM Dissidents Hope for Increased Support as Work Force Is Cut," *Wall Street Journal*, January 13, 1987, 1.

56. Reported on each year in the *Resistor*. In one undated flyer distributed at the annual stockholders meeting in the early 1980s addressed to Chairman Frank Cary from the IBM Workers United, he declared that this organization "will no longer passively accept the dictates of a management whose overwhelming concern is with profits and the IBM image, and who are increasingly becoming unconcerned with the day to day needs of the people who work at IBM." Flyer in author's possession.

57. Ibid.

58. He explained why the name changed to *Resistor*: "First, *Resistor* (as in the component), signifies the electronics industry. Second, that things are changing in IBM for the worse.

As workers we might be forced to resist management's attempts to push us backwards. In short, we will have to become resistors." *Resistor*, no. 14 (undated, circa 1978–1988), 1.

59. *Resistor*, no. 20 (March 1986), 2.

60. The organizing leader at IBM's Burlington plant was an experienced political organizer, Ralph J. Montefusco. He followed Conrad's lead and worked with the same issues, leveraging the state's political community. Interview with Montefusco by James W. Cortada, February 23, 2021.

61. While such sites are closed to non-IBMers, they are active with much discussion about current and prior conditions at the firm. The largest of these had over 11,000 participants from all over the world, "IBM Retirees," Facebook, https://www.facebook.com /groups/62822320855/members, accessed November 26, 2021.

62. "The Letter," *Resistor*, October 1996; "Bendz Letter to IBM Employees," *Press and Sun-Bulletin*, October 25, 1996, 24; interview with Lee Conrad.

63. Interview with Lee Conrad.

64. Email from Lee Conrad to James W. Cortada, December 1, 2020.

65. *Thinktwice!*, 2006, copy in author's files.

66. Kathleen Day, "IBM Workers Continue to Fight Pension Changes," *Washington Post*, April 18, 2001, E01.

67. Training budgets for all manner of subjects were repeatedly slashed (but not completely eliminated) from 2006 through the 2010s across the entire company.

68. For the most complete account of this changing approach to personnel management at IBM, Daniel Quinn Mills and G. Bruce Friesen, *Broken Promises: An Unconventional View of What Went Wrong at IBM* (Boston: Harvard Business Review Press, 1996), 65–84, 117–134. My own work parallels their analyses, Cortada, *IBM*, 539–543.

69. Peter Gosselin and Ariana Tobin, "Cutting 'Old Heads' at IBM," *ProPublica*, March 22, 2018, https://features.propublica.org/ibm/ibm-age-discrimination-american-workers, accessed November 28, 2020; Sheila Callaham, "EEOC Finding of Age Discrimination Against IBM Signals New Requisite for Diversity, Equity and Inclusion," *Forbes*, September 20, 2020, https://www.forbes.com/sites/sheilacallaham/2020/09/20/eeoc-finding -of-age-discrimination-against-ibm-signals-new-requisite-for-diversity-equity-and -inclusion/?fbclid=IwAR3mZXVWvGFUHlDJ72E7t1B5CNZ4BoobBh1QaT7zyZAc8Cr _aJyZ5V52S9s&sh=1f7ff8d73793, accessed November 28, 2021.

70. "Where Is Your Job Going?" hand flyer, author's collection.

71. Cortada, *IBM*, 254–255.

72. "The Payoff: No Layoffs," *THINK* 49, no. 3 (May–June 1983): 3.

73. Cortada, *IBM*, 421–470, but see also, Mills and Friesen, *Broken Promises*.

74. Cortada, *IBM*, 494–495, 539–577.

75. Helene Fouquet, Daniele Lepido, and Olivia Carville, "IBM Planning 10,000 Job Cuts Ahead of Unit Sale," *Bloomberg Technology*, November 25, 2020, https://www.bloomberg .com/news/articles/2020-11-25/ibm-planning-about-10-000-job-cuts-in-europe -ahead-of-unit-sale, accessed November 26, 2021.

76. As the initial draft of this chapter was being written in November 2020, a local news media in Endicott, WNBF, and local print media carried a story about how IBM's factory there was to be dismantled, posting photographs of the deteriorating building site, still in effect calling attention to the company's decline in the area, even though the buildings had been sold off two years earlier; Bob Joseph, "Old IBM Endicott Buildings Could Be Removed for Battery Factory," *WNBF New Radio 1290*, November 23, 2020, https://www.google.com/search?q=Bob+Guy,+%22Old+IBM+Endicott +buildings%22&rlz=1C5CHFA_enUS851US856&tbm=isch&source=iu&ictx=

1&fir=jgQm4BXJlsEq7M%252CCylWUrWNwT4oyM%252C_&vet=1&usg
=AI4_-kSKvMg5eEV7bOrYfrwnDB6AVPqkFw&sa=X&ved=2ahUKEwiA8IGwo
KHtAhUrSjABHVBPB-sQ9QF6BAgEEAw#imgrc=tykfsJ9iE5AlaM, accessed November 28, 2021.

77. Interview with Lee Conrad by James W. Cortada, November 18, 2016; email from Lee Conrad to James W. Cortada, November 14, 2016.

78. Email from Lee Conrad to James W. Cortada, November 14, 2016.

79. Peter E. Greulich, *A View from Beneath the Dancing Elephant: Rediscovering IBM's Corporate Constitution* (Austin, TX: MBI Concepts, 2014), 161–162.

80. Email from Lee Conrad to James W. Cortada, November 14, 2016.

81. Cortada, *IBM*, 537–544.

82. "IBM Workers' Unions Call for Halt to Job Cuts," *industriall*, February 20, 2015, http://www.industriall-union.org/ibm-workers-unions-call-for-halt-to-job-cuts, accessed November 28, 2021.

83. Roxana D. Maiorescu, "Using Online Platforms to Engage Employees in Unionism: The Case of IBM," *Public Relations Review* 43, no. 5 (December 2017): 963–968.

84. Patrick Thibodeau, "IBM Union Calls It Quits," *Computerworld*, January 5, 2016, https://www.computerworld.com/article/3019552/ibm-union-calls-it-quits.html, accessed November 28, 2021.

85. Interview with Lee Conrad.

86. Interview with Lee Conrad. The end of unionizing at IBM was reported on by the media; Jeff Kiger, "Alliance@IBM Dissolved After 17 Years," *Post Bulletin*, January 6, 2016.

87. Of course, individual employees were dismissed from IBM for poor performance, illegal activities (e.g., stealing), or egregious violations of company practices (e.g., revealing IBM confidential information). In all three circumstances, IBM was no different than any other American firm.

88. John F. Akers to "Dear IBMer," September 19, 1986, copy in the possession of the author (who, at the time, did *not* qualify for this program as he was too young).

89. Copy of card in author's possession.

90. These early programs were attractive. This one added five years of eligibility to one's current retirement qualification, which included medical coverage that all fully qualified retirees could enjoy. Qualifiers included individuals who were within five years of full retirement anyway, including spouses; IBM, *1986 Retirement Incentive* (Armonk, NY: International Business Machines Corporation, 1986).

91. Yet to be investigated are issues concerning race and socioeconomic relations and complaints in any of the IBM national companies, especially for the decades prior to the 1980s.

92. This statement does not mean all employees were docile and happy. Work pressures were high in all decades, resulting in some grousing, mental health issues, strained marriages, and some alcoholism, but these conditions did not lead to calls for changes in the work bargain.

93. Cortada, *IBM*, 547–578.

94. James W. Cortada, *The Digital Hand: How Computers Changed the Work of American Manufacturing, Transportation, and Retail Industries* (New York: Oxford University Press, 2004); Sanford Jacoby, *Employing Bureaucracy: Managers, Unions and the Transformation of Work in American Industry, 1900–1945* (New York: Columbia University Press, 1985); and *Modern Manors: Welfare Capitalism Since the New Deal* (Princeton, NJ: Princeton University Press, 1997); Dobbin, *Inventing Equal Opportunity*.

95. Gospel, "The Management of Labor and Human Resources," 432–436.
96. A point made by labor historians; Gospel, "The Management of Labor and Human Resources," 433–435.
97. Gospel, "The Management of Labor and Human Resources," 435.
98. Richard Hyman and Robert Price, eds., *The New Working Class? White Collar Workers and Their Organizations* (London: Macmillan, 1983); Jürgen Kocha, *White-Collar Workers in America, 1900–1940* (London: SAGE, 1977); Gospel, "The Management of Labor and Human Resources," 437–438.
99. Gospel, "The Management of Labor and Human Resources," 438; he was not alone in making such a plea.
100. For a well-documented example of changing missions at plant sites, there is a history of the Rochester facility; Arthur L. Norberg and Jeffrey R. Yost, *IBM Rochester: A Half Century of Innovation* (Rochester, MN: IBM Corporation, 2006).

6. Corporate Benefits in Boom Periods: IBM's American Experience

1. Thomas J. Watson, Jr., and Peter Petre, *Father Son & Co.: My Life at IBM and Beyond* (New York: Bantam, 1990), 313.
2. Howard Gospel, "The Management of Labor and Human Resources," in *The Oxford Handbook of Business History*, ed. Geoffrey Jones and Jonathan Zeitlin (New York: Oxford University Press, 2007), 420–446; Fred K. Foulkes, *Personnel Policies in Large Nonunion Companies* (Englewood Cliffs, NJ: Prentice Hall, 1980).
3. Quoted in Julie Cohen Mason, "IBM at the Crossroads," *Management Review* (September 1991): 10. His comment came in one of the worst years in IBM's history. Your author knew Ted Child and can affirm that he was a hard-nosed personnel executive with an eye always cast on the bottom line. It was a lesson understood at IBM since the 1910s, when Thomas J. Watson, Sr., came over from NCR where management knew that benefits increased employee productivity; Andrea Tone, *The Business of Benevolence: Industrial Paternalism in Progressive America* (Ithaca, NY: Cornell University Press, 1997), 66–98.
4. Frank Dobbin, *Inventing Equal Opportunity* (Princeton, NJ: Princeton University Press, 2009).
5. Kevin Maney, *The Maverick and His Machine: Thomas J. Watson, Sr. and the Making of IBM* (Hoboken, NJ: John Wiley & Sons, 2003), 3–6, 173.
6. James W. Cortada, *Before the Computer: IBM, NCR, Burroughs, and Remington Rand and the Industry They Created, 1865–1956* (Princeton, NJ: Princeton University Press, 1993), 31–37, 174–77.
7. Tone, *The Business of Benevolence*, 66–67.
8. Tone, *The Business of Benevolence*, 66–70.
9. I discuss these in James W. Cortada, *IBM: The Rise and Fall and Reinvention of a Corporate Icon* (Cambridge, MA: MIT Press, 2019), 61–89.
10. Watson, *Father Son & Co.*, 150.
11. Watson, *Father Son & Co.*, 151.
12. For discussion of these publications and what historians also said about IBM, see James W. Cortada, "Change and Continuity at IBM: Key Themes in Histories of IBM," *Business History Review* 92, no. 1 (2018): 117–148.
13. Some additional data are available deep in the pages of the financial reports IBM was obligated to provide American, European, and Japanese regulators, although they largely describe costs, with fewer descriptions of the benefits themselves.

14. "$5,043 That's What It Costs IBM for Benefits, on the Average, Per U.S. Employee," *THINK* 40 (October/November 1974): 46–47; Emerson W. Pugh, *Building IBM: Shaping an Industry and Its Technology* (Cambridge, MA: MIT Press, 1995), 324.
15. "$5,043 That's What It Costs IBM for Benefits," 48.
16. In my thirty-eight years at IBM, I saw that nothing caught the immediate and intense attention of IBM's management, lawyers, and personnel directors faster than the whiff of union activity. Every manager I ever talked to about this issue agreed.
17. While this chapter relies on the usual historical records one would expect, your author was also an IBM manager from the early 1980s to the end of 2012, and so I rely on that experience for insights too.
18. Opinion surveys documented this agreement from the late 1950s to the end of the 1980s, and IBM retiree websites and Facebook groups carried many positive endorsements of the bargain.
19. Cortada, *IBM*, 233–438.
20. Cortada, "Change and Continuity at IBM," 117–148; but see also by an IBM executive, Buck Rodgers with Robert L. Shook, *The IBM Way: Insights Into the World's Most Successful Marketing Organization* (New York: HarperCollins, 1986).
21. In those days, IBM published a telephone directory organized by location and subject that everyone had.
22. C. B. Rogers, Jr., to GSD Management, April 1972, *GSD Management Focus* no. 8, copy in author's possession.
23. IBM, *Fundamentals of Management Course, Lesson 3* (New York: IBM Corporation, 1967), 1-1. This "IBM Internal Use Only" document was in its third edition in 1967.
24. IBM, *Fundamentals of Management Course, Lesson 3*, 1-2.
25. IBM, *Fundamentals of Management Course, Lesson 3*, 1-2. The term "lessons" is the same as today's usage of "modules."
26. The classic model used by historians and business experts on this subject is by Edgar H. Schein and Peter A. Schein, *Organizational Culture and Leadership* (San Francisco: Jossey-Bass, 2017). His work on this subject dates to his original research in the 1970s.
27. A major theme in Cortada, *IBM*.
28. Cortada, "Change and Continuity at IBM," 117–148.
29. Rodgers, *The IBM Way*. This Rodgers is not to be confused with C. B. Rogers quoted earlier.
30. Thomas J. Watson, Jr., *A Business and Its Beliefs: The Ideas That Helped Build IBM* (New York: McGraw-Hill, 1963, 2003).
31. Pugh, *Building IBM*, 324.
32. Pugh, *Building IBM*, 324.
33. These comments are based on reading thousands of comments made by retirees in closed Facebook IBM retiree sites between 2010 and 2020.
34. The employee who donated his benefits records to my files asked that he remain anonymous. He worked largely in a sales office in Ohio during his years at IBM from 1967 to June 2000. The data are from IBM, *IBM Employee Benefit Plans 1970* (New York: IBM Corporation, 1970). The first such personalized statement was mailed to employees in 1956, demonstrating in the process what could now be done using computers to prepare such tailored reports.
35. The same individual received *Some Information That Is Just Yours* (1980), which included earlier types of information and a statement about how much IBM had paid into the Social Security fund for IBMers, and a pamphlet, *Current IBM Retirement*

Plan or New IBM Personal Pension Account in 1999, with detailed examples with dollar amounts on optional plans that had to be selected by July of that year.

36. IBM, *1975 Employee Benefits Statement* (New York: IBM Corporation, 1976).

37. IBM, *Fundamentals of Management Course, Lesson 3*, 1-5–1-6.

38. Personal observation: I must have filled out over thirty of these and presented results to my staffs at least once in thirty years, and I used consolidated summaries of trends from such reports in at least three to four positions at IBM. My use of these surveys was normal, widely practiced at all levels of the firm. Speaking as an historian, if available, these would collectively represent a source of information about IBM far more valuable than board minutes, corporate management committee records, or the private papers of a handful of executives.

39. IBM, *Field Opinion Survey Results IBM* (New York: IBM, circa 1959–1961), 10.

40. Observation is based on author's personal experience as both employee and manager hosting opinion feedback meetings.

41. Comment based on the author's small collection of American opinion surveys and reading of retiree comments regarding benefits in those years posted to closed IBM retiree Facebook groups.

42. IBM, *Field Opinion Survey Results IBM*, 9.

43. Watson, *Father Son & Co.*, 309.

44. Watson, *Father Son & Co.*, 309.

45. IBM, *Fundamentals of Management Course, Lesson 1* (New York: IBM Corporation, 1967), 2-10.

46. For a fairly lengthy description of the process written by a retired employee, see Earl Ronneberg, *Work—A Memoir* (self-published, 2010), 87–105.

47. I know, because this is what happened to me when ordered to resolve an Open Door.

48. Open Door was used as both a verb and noun by employees, as in "I am going to Open Door my manager."

49. IBM, *Fundamentals of Management Course, Lesson 1*, 2-13.

50. IBM, *Fundamentals of Management Course, Lesson 1*, 2-14.

51. IBM, *Fundamentals of Management Course, Lesson 1*, 2-14.

52. IBM, *Fundamentals of Management Course, Lesson 1*, 2-14.

53. In over thirty years in management, I was subject to two Open Doors with the judgment going my way, while I investigated four on behalf of senior management. By far, the largest number of Open Doors concerned disagreements over appraisal ratings.

54. Rodgers, *The IBM Way*, 90.

55. IBM, *Thirty Years of Management Briefings, 1958 to 1988* (Armonk, NY: IBM Corporation, 1988), 218.

56. Harrison Kenney, "Speak Up Comes of Age," *THINK* 45, no. 6 (November–December 1979): 45.

57. IBM, *Fundamentals of Management Course, Lesson 1*, 2-15.

58. IBM, *Fundamentals of Management Course, Lesson 1*, 2-6.

59. "Passing the buck" is American slang for shifting one's own responsibility for addressing an issue to some other person or organization, e.g., "It is not part of my job," "I don't know," or "It's company policy." Besides being considered morally reprehensible by employees, it was considered across the company as a failure in both managerial and leadership skills.

60. IBM, *Fundamentals of Management Course, Lesson 1*, 2-8.

61. IBM, *Fundamentals of Management Course, Lesson 1*, 2-8.

62. IBM, *Fundamentals of Management Course, Lesson 1*, 2-15–2-16.

63. IBM, *Fundamentals of Management Course, Lesson 1*, 2-26–2-31. "Moonlighting" is American slang for holding a second full or part-time job simultaneously with regular employment at IBM. This rarely occurred at IBM in the United States due to lack of time to do so and because salaries were high enough to obviate that need.

64. IBM, *Fundamentals of Management Course, Lesson 1*, 2-29–2-30.

65. IBM, *Fundamentals of Management Course, Lesson 1*, 2-30.

66. IBM, *Thirty Years of Management Briefings*, 126.

67. IBM, *Thirty Years of Management Briefings*, 189.

68. Most notably through two books, Alfred D. Chandler, Jr., *Strategy and Structure: Chapters in the History of Industrial Enterprise* (Cambridge, MA: MIT Press, 1962) and Alfred D. Chandler, Jr., *The Visible Hand: The Managerial Revolution in American Business* (Cambridge, MA: Harvard University Press, 1977).

69. Kenneth Lipartito, "Business Culture," in *The Oxford Handbook of Business History*, ed. Geoffrey Jones and Jonathan Zeitlin (New York: Oxford University Press, 2007), 603–628.

70. Geert Hofstede, *Culture's Consequences: International Differences in Work-Related Values* (Thousand Oaks, CA: SAGE, 1984).

71. Endicott-Johnson Shoe Company, Maney, *The Maverick and His Machine*, 103–109; David L. Stebenne, "IBM's 'New Deal': Employment Policies of the International Business Machines Corporation, 1933–1956," *Journal of the Historical Society* 5, no. 1 (2005): 47–77.

72. The key work among many, JoAnne Yates, *Control Through Communication: The Rise of Systems in American Management* (Baltimore, MD: Johns Hopkins University Press, 1989).

73. For example, *Manual of Instruction* of various IBM products, dated May 3, 1938, copy number 6568, and the name of the student to which it was given, Leo Haruk, copy in author's possession.

7. Managing a Nearly Invisible Corporate Community: "IBM Families"

1. Song 67, "The IBM Family," in *The Songs of IBM* (New York: IBM Corporation, 1931, 1937).

2. Peter Hillyer, "Reunion at Princeton," *THINK* 40, no. 5 (June 1974): 34. The writer had been assigned to prepare a history of the Quarter Century Club (QCC) and was describing one meeting of the QCC in Princeton, New Jersey, in the spring of 1974. The accompanying photographs of active and retired employees included spouses; it was an IBM family event.

3. Your author did exactly this with two IBM closed groups in November 2020. However, results were uneven. Some retirees remembered attending Family Dinners, while others reported they never had, although the latter group knew what they were. Both cohorts had worked at IBM between the 1960s and the 1980s.

4. Two studies, however, provide a sense of scope and some hard data for IBM in the 1980s–2000s, Helen Axel, *Corporations and Families: Changing Practices and Perspectives. A Research Report from the Conference Board* (New York: Conference Board, 1985); E. Jeffrey Hill and Andre D. Jackson, "Twenty Years of Work and Family at International Business Machines Corporation," *American Behavioral Scientist* 49, no. 9 (May 2006): 1165–1183.

5. As in many other American and European firms before the 1950s and 1960s, women who married were expected to resign from IBM to take up their domestic responsibilities as wives and mothers. It was not uncommon in the 1920s–1930s for managers to insist on this practice, changing their attitudes during World War II as staffing needs could not be met with male employees as so many had joined military units. The wartime experience contributed to many companies increasingly allowing married women to work and develop careers.

6. Margaret W. Davies, *Women's Place Is at the Typewriter: Office Work and Office Workers, 1870–1930* (Philadelphia, PA: Temple University Press, 1983); Dana Goldstein, *The Teacher Wars: A History of America's Most Embattled Profession* (New York: Anchor, 2015), 13–46; Steven Mintz, *Domestic Revolutions: A Social History of American Family Life* (New York: Collier Macmillan, 1988), 83–132.

7. Stephen Meyer, *Manhood on the Line: Working-Class Masculinities in the American Heartland* (Urbana: University of Illinois Press, 2016); William H. Whyte, Jr., *The Organization Man* (New York: Simon & Schuster, 1956).

8. However, there were exceptions, such as women becoming field engineers in the 1930s and a handful of women in sales in the 1940s, most of whom had entered that profession at the start of World War II.

9. Nikki Mandell, *The Corporation as Family: The Gendering of Corporate Welfare, 1890–1930* (Chapel Hill: University of North Carolina Press, 2002), 32; Thomas Bender, *Community and Social Change in America* (New Brunswick, NJ: Rutgers University Press, 1978), 7–9.

10. Mandell, *The Corporation as Family*, 33.

11. Quoted in Mandell, *The Corporation as Family*, 27.

12. Mandell, *The Corporation as Family*, 133.

13. Mandell reviews results of government surveys defining what amenities and percentages of firms with them were already implemented in the 1920s; Mandell, *The Corporation as Family*, 144 for details.

14. For an example of how government regulations affected companies, in this instance, equal opportunities for jobs and civil rights, see Frank Dobbin, *Inventing Equal Opportunity* (Princeton, NJ: Princeton University Press, 2009).

15. Dobbin, *Inventing Equal Opportunity*, 132.

16. Axel, *Corporations and Families*, vii.

17. Hill and Jackson, "Twenty Years of Work and Family," 1165–1183.

18. Ellen Galinsky and Peter J. Stein, "The Impact of Human Resource Policies on Employees: Balancing Work/Family Life," *Journal of Family Issues* 11, no. 4 (December 1980): 368–383. This article cites various IBM programs; J. Pleck, G. Staines, and L. Lang, "Conflicts Between Work and Family Life," *Monthly Labor Review* 103 (March 1980): 29–32.

19. Galinsky and Stein, "The Impact of Human Resource Policies on Employees," 380–382.

20. Louis Echitelle, *The Disposable American: Layoffs and Their Consequences* (New York: Random House, 2007), 24–49, and on layoffs, 124–150.

21. Kevin Maney, *The Maverick and His Machine: Thomas Watson, Sr. and the Making of IBM* (Hoboken, NJ: John Wiley & Sons, 2003), 1–36; on NCR's programs, Samuel Crowther, *John H. Patterson, Pioneer in Industrial Welfare* (New York: Doubleday, Page, 1923).

22. Mandell, *The Corporation as Family*, 132.

23. Emerson W. Pugh, *Building IBM: Shaping an Industry and Its Technology* (Cambridge, MA: MIT Press, 1995), 323–324.

24. Thomas J. Watson, Sr., *Men-Minutes-Money* (New York: International Business Machines Corporation, 1934), 102.
25. Watson, *Men-Minutes-Money*, 106.
26. Watson, *Men-Minutes-Money*, 121–122.
27. Maney, *The Maverick and His Machine*.
28. See, for an early example, Lewis A. Coser, *Greedy Institutions: Patterns of Undivided Commitment* (New York: Free Press, 1974).
29. Robert Putnam, *Bowling Alone: The Collapse and Revival of American Community* (New York: Simon & Schuster, 2020), 31–48, 183–215.
30. For decades drawing on the thinking of Edgar H. Schein, *Organizational Culture and Leadership* (San Francisco: Jossey-Bass, 1985), 148–243, but kept in print in revised editions for decades; John P. Kotter and James L. Heskett, *Corporate Culture and Performance* (New York: Free Press, 1992), 15–67.
31. Arthur K. Watson to Mr. and Mrs. Bassill Mardelli, June 26, 1969, copy in author's files.
32. There were over a dozen private Facebook employee and retiree social media sites where comments about the decline of these events were periodically made, beginning largely in 2005–2006 and continuing over the next fifteen years. These included "Watching IBM" and "IBM Retirees," both of which had thousands of "hits" or members.
33. The combination Family Dinner and celebration of fifty years in Nashville drew three hundred IBMers and spouses to the event, which included a country music band and an opulent but regional dinner at the Opryland Hotel; the event attracted local media coverage, "IBM Celebrates 50th Year Here," *Nashville Tennessean*, June 27, 1984.
34. IBM newspapers, site newsletters and magazines, and occasionally social pages of the local newspaper reported on events, including Family Dinners and large summer picnic events and, rarely, celebration of an executive's twenty-fifth anniversary of being with IBM or an executive's retirement. Formal reviews of local business activities made to upper levels of management normally included a line item acknowledging the occurrence of such events, because the senior manager at a location was expected to host such events as part of their job.
35. Watson Sr. was considered a boring speaker at some of these events because of the length of his speeches. However, his wife could be counted upon to signal to him that it was time to close his talks.
36. The liquor ban was enforced the most in the United States where a heritage of disapproval of drinking was strong, but not in Europe or Latin America, where local cultural norms dictated its availability, but of course, per IBM cultural standards, it was to be consumed in moderate amounts.
37. IBM Retiree Facebook group, November 2020.
38. IBM Retiree Facebook group, November 2020.
39. T. Elbert Clemmons, *A Great Time to Be Alive: An Autobiography* (Stuart, FL: self-published, 1968), 219–220.
40. Luis A. Lamassonne, *My Life with IBM* (Athens, GA: PROTEA, 2001), 79.
41. Your author was the senior location manager at the same time as the branch manager of the local sales office. There were 187 employees in the Madison area, and most were married. The Latin American host also went on to have a further successful career as an executive.
42. "IBM Retiree Group," Facebook, accessed November 26, 2020.
43. "IBM Retiree Group," Facebook.
44. IBM, *A Visit to the Endicott Plant of the International Business Machines Corporation* (Endicott, NY: International Business Machines Corporation, 1936), 28–29.

45. IBM, *A Visit to the Endicott Plant of the International Business Machines Corporation*, 30. It also reported that some 1,500 such visits were made annually.

46. IBM, *General Information: Guests of International Business Machines Corporation* (Endicott, NY: International Business Machines Corporation, 1940), copy in author's collection. Your author planned family affairs several times in his career and thus saw the level of detail, planning, and managerial scrutiny involved, and also attended several dozen family or corporate events that included similar briefing documents as the 1940 publication.

47. James W. Cortada, *IBM: The Rise and Fall and Reinvention of a Global Icon* (Cambridge, MA: MIT Press, 2019), 107–109.

48. The program was an example of a "take back," when in 2020 the company discontinued the program in the United States.

49. All quotes drawn from IBM Retiree Facebook group, accessed December 22, 2020.

50. Watson, *Men-Minutes-Money*, 64–66.

51. Watson, *Men-Minutes-Money*, 74.

52. Watson, *Men-Minutes-Money*, 74, 96, 98, 103, 164, 234, 236, 538, 539.

53. Watson, *Men-Minutes-Money*, 539.

54. Interview with Joe Lucchesi by James W. Cortada, December 3, 2020. Lucchesi joined IBM in 1964 and became a member of the QCC in San Jose, California, in 1989. He worked in product development and sales, and as president of the San Jose chapter of the QCC in the early 2000s, when IBM dropped support for these clubs.

55. Peter Hillyer, "50th Anniversary of the Quarter Century Club," *THINK* 40, no. 5 (June 1974): 30–35, quote 32.

56. The San Jose chapter was not happy with that and posted on its website its displeasure: "We are a proud group of IBMers who achieved the distinction of 25 years or more of service to IBM." Adding, "Since IBM no longer values long term commitment this distinction is no longer given. Regardless we earned it and are proud we did and will support our fellow IBMers who also did," IBM San Jose Quarter Century Club, https://qccsj.org/, accessed December 2, 2020. IBM's CEO at the time, Samuel J. Palmisano, had been a member of the QCC since 1998, by which time the QCC was declining in importance at corporate headquarters, where the then-current CEO had not grown up in the company nor many of his direct reports.

57. Paul Carroll, *The Big Blues: The Unmaking of IBM* (New York: Crown, 1993); Cortada, *IBM*, 184, 195, 200.

58. Thomas J. Watson, Jr., and Peter Petre, *Father Son & Co.: My Life at IBM and Beyond* (New York: Bantam, 1990), 75.

59. Your author knew of four salesmen in one family in Pennsylvania, in the 1970s and 1980s, where family pressure to perform well at IBM far exceeded any that could be exerted by a mere sales or branch manager.

60. Translation: "I like the way the Branch Manager complemented the new Systems Engineer on solving the telecommunications software problem." "Yes, it was well deserved since it included a made-to-order piece of software installed in the 1705 telecommunications unit." "I can't believe they laid off John." RAed = slang term used after 2000 meaning Resource Action as a verb to mean lay off. Employees had the bad habit of turning nouns and adjectives into verbs, such as "solution the problem," as in "I will solution the problem," a 1980s–1990s headquarters language.

61. Louis V. Gerstner to James W. Cortada, October 1, 1999.

62. In addition to his own, your author has in his files examples from other IBMers in the United States and Latin America from the 1950s to the 2010s. He had heard of similar binders of letters being put together since the 1930s.

63. Physical reminders of IBM in an employee's home periodically are discussed on employee and retiree social media websites. Anecdotal evidence suggests that the most widely evident objects included IBM logoed staplers and pencils and, among field engineers (they installed and repaired machines), tools designed for use with IBM hardware and odd parts stored in their homes. Retirees frequently posted images of these with comments such as "Look what I found in my garage today"; other comments asked if anyone remembered for what a particular item was used.

64. IBM Corporation, *Employee Opinion Survey, Endicott, New York 1963* (Endicott, NY: International Business Machines Corporation, 1963), unpaginated.

65. Chuck Boyer, "On Their Own Time, All the Time," *THINK* 51, no. 4 (1985): 47.

66. "IBM Retiree Group," Facebook, November 27, 2020, accessed November 28, 2020.

67. "IBM Retiree Group," Facebook, November 27, 2020, accessed November 28, 2020.

68. "IBM Retiree Group," Facebook, November 27, 2020, accessed November 28, 2020.

69. That practice of sometimes as many as four generations working at IBM was not nepotism, although critics could assume that, because the company's culture was meritocratic so an aspiring employee still had to qualify for a job in the company, even again as their career evolved over time. But, they had the advantage of knowing a great deal about IBM and how it worked by having been raised in an "IBM family."

70. E. Jeffrey Hill, Alan J. Hawkins, Vjollca Märtinson, and Maria Ferris, "Studying 'Working Fathers': Comparing Fathers' and Mothers' Work-Family Conflict, Fit, and Adaptive Strategies in a Global High-Tech Company," *Faculty Publications* (Brigham Young University, 2003) 4046, https://scholarsarchive.byu.edu/facpub/4046/, accessed December 3, 2020.

71. E. Jeffrey Hill, Alan J. Hawkins, Maria Ferris, and Michelle Weitzman, "Finding an Extra Day a Week: The Positive Influence of Perceived Job Flexibility on Work and Family Life Balance," *Family Relations* 50, no. 1 (January 2001): 49–58.

72. Your author and his family lived in one such neighborhood in Poughkeepsie, New York (Pleasant Valley), in 1981–1983. It was there that he learned about what engineers and computer scientists, technical writers, and even building maintenance managers did at IBM. To cash a check at a grocery store, one did not need to show a driver's license to verify their identity; the cashier would simply lean forward and stare at an employee's IBM ID badge hanging from their neck.

73. Anecdotal evidence and experience of the author, 1970s–2010s, but see also William Rodgers, *Think: A Biography of the Watsons and IBM* (New York: Stein & Day, 1969), 157–164, 265–266 for the pre-1970s.

74. In what otherwise is an informed study of IBM's personnel practices, one historian incorrectly reported that failure to conform to social conventions "constituted grounds for dismissal," David L. Stebenne, "IBM's 'New Deal': Employment Policies of the International Business Machines Corporation, 1933–1956," *Journal of the Historical Society* 5, no. 1 (Winter 2005): 63. In fact, that was not true, and when managers attempted to do so, the practice was routinely overturned by personnel and line management.

75. As early as the 1980s, layoffs were having negative psychological and emotional effects on employees and their families. For a well-written description of those dating from the mid-1980s that remained a similar experience for those detached from the company as late as the 2010s, see Jack D. Martin, *Inside Big Blue: Will the Real IBM Please Stand Up?* (New York: Vantage, 1988), 77–78.

76. Amal El-Sawad and Marek Korczynski, "Management and Music: The Exceptional Case of the IBM Songbook," *Group & Organization Management* 32, no. 1 (February 2007): 97.

77. Clemmons, *A Great Time to Be Alive*, 255.
78. Clemmons, *A Great Time to Be Alive*, 255.
79. The history and explanation of IBM's pension programs could consume an entire chapter, as it did for an excellent discussion of the benefit as it was in the 1960s–1980s in the United States written by an experienced manager, Martin, *Inside Big Blue*, 128–130.

8. From Lapel Pins to Coffee Cups: Links Between Corporate and Material Culture

1. Examples, Daniel R. Denison, *Corporate Culture and Organizational Effectiveness* (New York: John Wiley & Sons, 1990); Judith M. Bardwick, *Danger in the Comfort Zone* (New York: American Management Association, 1991).
2. Roland Marchand, *Creating the Corporate Soul: The Rise of Public Relations and Corporate Imagery in American Big Business* (Berkeley: University of California Press, 1998).
3. I have discussed this issue extensively, including the ideas of other students of IBM, James W. Cortada, *IBM: The Rise and Fall and Reinvention of a Global Icon* (Cambridge, MA: MIT Press, 2019), and in James W. Cortada, "Change and Continuity at IBM: Key Themes in Histories of IBM," *Business History Review* 92, no. 1 (2018): 117–148.
4. Edgar H. Schein, *Organizational Culture and Leadership* (San Francisco: Jossey-Bass, 1985).
5. Schein, *Organizational Culture and Leadership*, and for his later thinking, Edgar H. Schein, *The Corporate Culture Survival Guide* (San Francisco: Jossey-Bass, 2009).
6. John P. Kotter and James L. Heskett, *Corporate Culture and Performance* (New York: Free Press, 1992), 7.
7. Schein, *The Corporate Culture Survival Guide*, 84.
8. For an overview of the entire new field with many hundreds of citations, see Dan Hicks and Mary C. Beaudry, eds., *The Oxford Handbook of Material Culture Studies* (Oxford, UK: Oxford University Press, 2010).
9. Daniel Miller, *Stuff* (Oxford, UK: Polity, 2010); Victor Buchli, *Material Culture: Critical Concepts in the Social Sciences* (London: Routledge, 2004); Helen Sheumaker and Shirley Wajda, *Material Culture in America: Understanding Everyday Life* (Santa Barbara, CA: ABC-CLIO, 2008); Arthur Asa Berger, *What Objects Mean: An Introduction of Material Culture* (Walnut Creek, CA: Left Coast, 2009).
10. Claude Lévi-Strauss did for cultural anthropology what Schein did for corporate culture studies, *Myth and Meaning: Cracking the Code of Culture* (Toronto, Canada: University of Toronto Press, 1978), and his earlier, *Structural Anthropology* (New York: Basic Books, 1974). The most useful source is Hicks and Beaudry, *The Oxford Handbook of Material Culture Studies*.
11. Philip Scranton and Patrick Fridenson, *Reimagining Business History* (Baltimore, MD: Johns Hopkins University Press, 2013), 57.
12. Scranton and Fridenson, *Reimagining Business History*, 59.
13. Scranton and Fridenson, *Reimagining Business History*, 60. Lessons can be learned from the study of products, too; see Kerry Seagrave, *Vending Machines: An American Social History* (Jefferson, NC: MacFarland, 2002).
14. The singular excellent study on IBM's role from the 1940s to the 1980s is John Harwood, *The Interface: IBM and the Transformation of Corporate Design, 1945–1976* (Minneapolis: University of Minnesota Press, 2011).
15. Marchand, *Creating the Corporate Soul*, 3.

16. This is a subject of extensive discussion by retired and laid-off employees on Facebook. Unfortunately, these sites are closed to the general public and historians; however, as a retired IBMer, I have access to many, which I monitor on a regular basis.

17. Harwood's contention and considerable evidence, *The Interface*.

18. While tens of thousands of these various 100 Percent Club mementos were distributed between the 1920s and the end of the 1980s, they were so highly prized that the only ones that would come up for sale on, say, eBay, were less than a handful, often from the estate of a deceased salesperson.

19. Thomas J. Watson, Sr., *Men-Minutes-Money* (New York: International Business Machines Corporation, 1934), 663.

20. "More Than Trash and Trinkets: 7 Reasons to Include Promo Items in Marketing Campaigns," *ImageMark*, May 13, 2019, https://www.imagemarkonline.com/2019/05/13/more-than-trash-and-trinkets-7-reasons-to-include-promo-items-in-marketing-campaigns/, accessed August 1, 2021.

21. Coffee itself and its producers are being studied, see Augustine Sedgewick, *Coffeeland: One Man's Dark Empire and the Making of Our Favorite Drug* (New York: Penguin, 2020); Jonathan Morris, *Coffee: A Global History* (London: Reaktion, 2019).

22. Inexplicably, it seemed most American IBMers possessed a black stapler embossed with a white pinstriped "IBM" logo. The ACCO 30 Model 1 was supplied to IBM as part of a nationwide procurement arrangement. In retiree Facebook comments made in the 2000s, these were mentioned as part of the IBM scene.

23. eBay, "IBM" search, https://www.ebay.com/sch/i.html?_from=R40&_trksid=p2334524.m570.l1313.TR10.TRC2.A0.H0.XIBM+.TRS2&_nkw=IBM+&_sacat=0&LH_TitleDesc=0&_osacat=0&_odkw=IBM+logo, accessed August 1, 2021.

24. Images of a dozen foreign-language versions, author's collection.

25. It was common, for example, at 100 Percent Club conventions for the president of the 100 Percent Club that year—always a high-achieving salesperson—to make speeches reaffirming the company's beliefs that were then communicated to all IBMers through various internal corporate and division newsletters. This remained a practice late into the century.

26. NCR histories do not mention THINK as originating there, but early histories of IBM do; see especially Robert Sobel, *IBM, Colossus in Transition* (New York: Times Books, 1981), and the excellent biography of Watson Sr. by Kevin Maney, *The Maverick and His Machine: Thomas Watson, Sr. and the Making of IBM* (Hoboken, NJ: John Wiley & Sons, 2003), and anthologies of speeches by Watson Sr., *Men-Minutes-Money: A Collection of Excerpts from Talks and Messages Delivered and Written at Various Times* (New York: IBM Corporation, 1930, 1934) and *"As a Man Thinks . . .": Thomas J. Watson, the Man and His Philosophy of Life as Expressed in His Editorials* (New York: IBM Corporation, 1954). Other corporate histories do document Watson's learning from NCR almost all of his early managerial skills; see Isaac F. Marcosson, *Wherever Men Trade: The Romance of the Cash Register* (New York: Arno, 1948), 127–129; Samuel Crowther, *John H. Patterson: Pioneer in Industrial Welfare* (Garden City, NY: Doubleday, 1923), 231–132; and Roy W. Johnson and Russell W. Lynch, *The Sales Strategy of John H. Patterson* (New York: Dartnell, 1932).

27. For a recording of Watson Sr. speaking about THINK, circa 1930s, see https://upload.wikimedia.org/wikipedia/commons/4/49/Think_Thomas_J_Watson_Sr.ogg, accessed October 7, 2021; see also Thomas Belden and Marva Belden, *The Lengthening Shadow: The Life of Thomas J. Watson* (Boston: Little, Brown and Company, 1962), 157–158.

28. Belden and Belden, *The Lengthening Shadow*, 158.

29. Watson wrote every editorial that introduced each issue of *THINK*, many of which were gathered up in Robert Cousins, ed., *The Will to THINK: A Treasury of Ideas and Ideals from the Pages of THINK* (New York: Farrar, Straus and Cudahy, 1957).
30. James W. Cortada, "Viewing Corporations as Information Ecosystems: The Case of IBM, 1914–1980s," *Enterprise and Society* 23, no. 1 (March 2022): 99–132.
31. The multidecade strategy was explained by a senior sales executive, Buck Rodgers, *The IBM Way: Insights Into the World's Most Successful Marketing Organization* (New York: HarperCollins, 1988).
32. In my nearly forty years at IBM, all in sales and management, I personally found dealing with all manner of data processing and operational issues to be intellectually challenging, with obvious answers to problems rarely in sight, calling instead for creativity and the ability to negotiate and communicate. THINK was a relevant concept in that environment, even a half century after Watson's death in 1956.
33. Until the 1980s, the overwhelming majority of salespeople were men.
34. The fear of achieving only 99 percent of one's target was palpable to such an extent that salespeople were known to remain in their sales offices into the evening of December 31, to make sure no order for which they had been given credit was cancelled at the last minute by a customer trying to close out their year. Coming in just shy of 100 percent indicated that the salesperson was unable to manage their customers and would be the subject of snickers behind their back and receive a terrible performance appraisal by their manager.
35. For large contracts, either IBM or the customer arranged for photographs to be taken, similar to what national leaders do when they sign diplomatic treaties.
36. For a Sales School image, James W. Cortada, "'There Is No Saturation Point in Education': Inside IBM's Sales School, 1970s–1980s," *IEEE Annals of the History of Computing* 37, no. 1 (January–March 2015): 56–66.
37. Perhaps I am wrong because IBM retiree websites and Facebook accounts routinely show images of various IBM logoed items in their homes: tools, machine parts, publications, personal correspondence, photographs and logoed IBM staplers, pencils, pens, stationary, envelops, and coffee mugs. These are usually closed Facebook sites, so regrettably, they are not accessible to many readers. The Computer History Museum in Mountain View, California, has a collection of these mugs from many vendors.
38. Coffee was a prominent drink during World War II within Allied military; Mark Pendergrast, *Uncommon Grounds: The History of Coffee and How It Transformed the World* (New York: Basic Books, 1999), 199–212.
39. A dozen respondents also commented on the power of donuts and pizza as central to work, particularly when engaged in long hours of problem solving or installing hardware and software. Customers set up office and coffee space for their IBMers in large data centers, stocked with coffee, mugs, and other food. The comments offered about coffee came from the United States, Latin America, and Europe.
40. Occasionally I receive from an individual in California who cleans out homes of deceased or elderly individuals such ephemera, if from a retired IBMer. Some items came from this person when an IBMer had been retired for over twenty years and yet still had old pens, pencils, and coffee mugs in their home.
41. I was privy to some of those debates as representative of the Consulting Group's North American General Manager's Office.
42. Emerson W. Pugh, *Building IBM: Shaping an Industry and Its Technology* (Cambridge, MA: MIT Press, 1995), 323–324.
43. Geert Hofstede, *Culture's Consequences* (Beverly Hills, CA: Sage, 1980).

44. As early as the 1930s, IBM's guest house for customers and IBMers in Endicott, New York, known as the "Homestead," had Endicott monogrammed IBM fine china, which, of course, included coffee cups. So the tradition of branding coffee experiences has a long history.

45. By "normal branding," I mean the use of IBM's corporate guidelines on such matters as image of the company's logo, where it could or could not be used, gaining permission from marketing and legal departments within a division or corporate, and often linked and timed to such other branding activities as product introductions and advertising campaigns.

46. "COMDEX," *Wikipedia*, https://en.wikipedia.org/wiki/COMDEX#:~:text=COMDEX%20 (an%20abbreviation%20of%20Computer,November%20from%201979%20to%202003, accessed August 1, 2021.

47. I accumulated nearly a hundred of these, some of which describe training at IBM and other local activities. There are about forty different postcards of IBM's facilities. I seriously considered adding a section to this chapter on the role of postcards but decided they deserve their own treatment as a window into IBM's culture.

48. eBay, https://www.ebay.com/itm/Facebook-Coffee-Cup-Mug-Bachelorette-Birthday-Funny -Gift-White-Elephant/254648692846?hash=item3b4a3eb06e:g:6IEAAOSwi7RfBoKe :sc:USPSPriority!53713!US!-1, accessed August 1, 2021.

49. I am currently studying three roles in IBM of postcards, gray literature, and humor. Posters await their historian, although work on that material object is beginning; see Robert Finkel and Shea Tillman, *The IBM Poster Program: Visual Memoranda* (London: Lund Humphries, 2021).

50. Coincidentally, the study of ceramics by archeologists has a long history worth learning from for exploring corporate mementos; Carl Knappett, Lambros Malafouris, and Peter Tomkins, "Ceramics (as Container)," in *The Oxford Handbook of Material Culture Studies*, ed. Hicks and Beaudry, 588–612.

9. The Role of American Postcards in Supporting IBM's Image, Marketing, and Information Ecosystem

1. David Prochaska and Jordana Mendelson, *Postcards: Ephemeral History of Modernity* (University Park: Pennsylvania State University Press, 2010), xii.

2. Steven Dotterer and Galen Cranz, "The Picture Postcard: Its Development and Role in American Urbanization," *Journal of American Culture* 5, no. 1 (Spring 1982): 44–50.

3. Christin J. Mamiya, "Greetings from Paradise: The Representation of Hawaiian Culture in Postcards," *Journal of Communication Inquiry* 16, no. 2 (Summer 1992): 86–101; Atila Yüksel and Olcay Akgül, "Postcards as Affective Image Makers: An Idle Agent in Destination Marketing," *Tourism Management* 28 (2007): 714–725; K. Andriotis and M. Mavrič, "Postcard Mobility: Going Beyond Image and Text," *Annals of Tourism Research* 40 (2013): 18–39; David Prochaska, "Thinking Postcards," *Visual Resources* 17 (2001): 383–399.

4. Thousands of varieties were pictured on eBay, "Business Postcards," https://www.ebay .com/sch/i.html?_from=R40&_trksid=p2380057.m570.l1313&_nkw=business+post cards&_sacat=0, accessed September 29, 2021. On the other hand, the manufacture of these cards has been partially studied, Dotterer and Cranz, "The Picture Postcard," 44–45.

5. For example, Robert Bogdan and Todd Weseloh, *Real Photo: Postcard Guide: The People's Photography* (Syracuse, NY: Syracuse University Press, 2006); Daniel Friedman,

The Birth and Development of American Postcards: A History, Catalog, and Price Guide to U.S. Pioneer Postcards (Classic Postcards, 2003); J. L. Mashburn, *The Postcard Price Guide*, 4th ed., *A Comprehensive Reference* (Winter Garden, FL: Colonial House, 2001).

6. Elspeth H. Brown, *The Corporate Eye: Photography and the Rationalization of American Commercial Culture, 1884–1929* (Baltimore, MD: Johns Hopkins University Press, 2005), 14–16; John Tagg, *The Burden of Representation: Essays on Photographies and Histories* (Amherst: University of Massachusetts Press, 1988), 4; Geoffrey Batchen, *Burning with Desire: The Conception of Photography* (Cambridge, MA: MIT Press, 1997), and not to be overlooked, Alan Trachtenberg, *Reading American Photographs: Images as History, Mathew Brady to Walker Evans* (New York: Hill and Wang, 1989).

7. An ongoing research initiative of the author, James W. Cortada, *Building Blocks of Modern Society: History, Information Ecosystems, and Infrastructures* (Lanham, MD: Rowman & Littlefield, 2021).

8. Dan Hicks and May C. Beaudry, eds., *The Oxford Handbook of Material Culture Studies* (Oxford, UK: Oxford University Press, 2010), 25–190.

9. The author assembled this collection, largely from postcard vendors.

10. R. Appadurai, *The Social Life of Things: Commodities in Cultural Perspectives* (Cambridge, UK: Cambridge University Press, 1986); S. Lury and S. Lash, *Global Cultural Industry: The Mediation of Things* (Cambridge, UK: Cambridge University Press, 2007); G. E. Marcus, "Ethnography in/of the World System: The Emergence of Multi-Sited Ethnography," *Annual Review of Anthropology* 25 (1995): 95–117.

11. Mamiya, "Greetings from Paradise," 88.

12. For cases of such studies, see David Crouch and Nina Lübbren, eds., *Visual Culture and Tourism* (Oxford, UK: Berg, 2003).

13. Susan Sontag, *On Photography* (New York: Dell, 1977).

14. Dotterrer and Cranz, "The Picture Postcard," 44.

15. George Miller and Dorothy Miller, *Picture Postcards in the United States, 1893–1918* (New York: Crown, 1975).

16. Miller and Miller, *Picture Postcards in the United States*, 22.

17. Dotterrer and Cranz, "The Picture Postcard," 45.

18. Dotterrer and Cranz, "The Picture Postcard," 45.

19. Dotterrer and Cranz, "The Picture Postcard," 45.

20. The absence of such text is how one can date postcards to an earlier period.

21. IBM mandated restrictions on photographing the interiors of its buildings for security and competitive reasons once cameras became massively available after World War II. Employees and visitors took photographs of buildings at a distance and often of data center interiors housed in customer buildings that apparently did not have such restrictions.

22. One technological improvement was the process of creating colorized images from black-and-white images using lithographic methods. Many new postcards were simply rephotographed pictures reflecting the use of modern color film, and their subjects were buildings put up post World War II.

23. Andriotis and Mavrič, "Postcard Mobility," 18–20; C. K. Corkery and A. J. Bailey, "Lobster Is Big in Boston: Postcards, Place Commodification, and Tourism," *GeoJournal* 34, no. 4 (1994): 491–498; M. Marwick, "Postcards from Malta: Image, Consumption, Context," *Annals of Tourism Research* 28 (2001): 117–138; K. Spennemann, "The Imagery of Postcards Sold in Micronesia During the German Colonial Period," *Micronesian Journal of the Humanities and Social Sciences* 5, nos. 1/2 (2006): 345–374; P. Albers and W. James, "Tourism and the Changing Photographic Image of the Great Lakes Indians,"

Annals of Tourism Research 10 (1983): 123–148; K. A. Schulle, "Reading the Aesthetics of Picture Postcards: An Argument for Their Use in Historical Study," *Nanzan Review of American Studies* 2 (1998): 79–86. On written messages, see T. Phillips, *The Postcard Century* (London: Thames and Hudson, 2000).

24. Andriotis and Mavrič, "Postcard Mobility," 19.

25. See, for example, Andriotis and Mavrič, "Postcard Mobility," 19.

26. Yüksel and Akgül, "Postcards as Affective Image Makers," 715.

27. J. L. Crompton, "An Assessment of the Image of Mexico as a Vacation Destination and the Influence of Geographical Location Upon That Image," *Journal of Travel Literature* 17, no. 4 (1979): 18–24l, and the bible of marketing based on the work of Philip T. Kotler, Gary Armstrong, and Prafulla Agnihotri, *Principles of Marketing*, 17th ed. (Upper Saddle River, NJ: Pearson, 2018); J. Day, S. Skidmore, and T. Koller, "Image Selection in Destination Positioning: A New Approach," *Journal of Vacation Marketing* 8, no. 2 (2002): 177–186; C. M. Echtner and J. R. B. Ritchie, "The Measurement of Destination Image: An Empirical Assessment," *Journal of Travel Research* 31, no. 4 (1993): 3–13.

28. S. Kim and Y. Yoon, "The Hierarchical Effects of Affective and Cognitive Components on Tourism Destination Image," *Journal of Travel and Tourism Marketing* 14, no. 2 (2003): 1–22.

29. V. Winiwarter, "Buying a Dream Come True," *Rethinking History* 5, no. 3 (2001): 451–454; Adrienne Baker, "Uses of Postcards," *Primary Research*, https://primaryresearch.org/uses-of-postcards/, accessed September 30, 2020.

30. Yüksel and Akgül, "Postcards as Affective Image Makers," 717.

31. A behavior demonstrated in considerable detail by his leading biography, Kevin Maney, *The Maverick and His Machine: Thomas Watson, Sr. and the Making of IBM* (Hoboken, NJ: John Wiley & Sons, 2003).

32. For examples of his thinking, Peter E. Greulich, *The World's Greatest Salesman: An IBM Caretaker's Perspective: Looking Back* (Austin, TX: MBI Concepts, 2011).

33. On their assessments of his performance, James W. Cortada, "Change and Continuity at IBM: Key Themes in Histories of IBM," *Business History Review* 92 (Spring 2018): 117–148.

34. Emerson W. Pugh, *Building IBM: Shaping an Industry and Its Technology* (Cambridge, MA: MIT Press, 1995), 323–324.

35. I explore these issues more thoroughly in Cortada, *Building Blocks of Modern Society*, 181–223.

36. Roger Balm and Briaval Holcomb, "Unlosing Lost Places: Image Making, Tourism and the Return to Terra Cognita," in Crouch and Lübbren, *Visual Culture and Tourism*, 157.

37. M. S. Ball and G. W. H. Smith, *Analyzing Visual Data* (Newbury Park, CA: Sage, 1992); Jessica Evans, "Introduction," in *Visual Culture: The Reader*, ed. Jessica Evans and Stuart Hall (London: SAGE, 1999); see also Nicholas Mirzoeff, ed., *The Visual Culture Reader*, 3rd ed. (New York: Routledge, 2012), various essays but especially 3–26, 60–73.

38. E. Sironen, "Reading My Landscape," in *Strangers in Sport: Reading Classics of Social Thought*, ed. S. Veijola, J. Bale, and E. Sironen, Department of Social Policy, University of Jyväskylä, working papers 91, 25.

39. In 2022, these buildings began to be knocked down to be replaced with others; IBM had sold off the property a few years earlier. Retired IBMers rescued fragments of the buildings as souvenirs; Vince Briga, "Endicott Prepares for Resurgence: Here's How We Got Here," *Spectrum News 1*, September 26, 2022, https://spectrumlocalnews.com/nys/central-ny/news/2022/09/25/endicott-prepares-for-resurgence—here-s-how-they-got-here?cid=id-app15_m-share_s-web_cmp-app_launch_august2020_c-producer

_posts_po-organic&fbclid=IwAR02s-2ceMrOZsEHbDdMsJGcmknqVWCC4
Aq3rVXKwzNSnnJrHMm04FQ2egs, accessed December 12, 2022, and IBM retiree
closed group comments, December 2022.

40. Your author's first class at IBM was held in this building in October 1974. I was impressed
with the size and quality of the entire Endicott campus.

41. Your author stayed at this facility in 1974, 1975, and again in the 1980s, each time for a
week.

42. Your author stayed at the Homestead three times between 1974 and 1999, and it felt
more like a home or bed and breakfast than a hotel with a relaxed informality that
encouraged conversations among employees and customers. In nearly four decades,
I never heard a criticism of the building, only effusive complements and fond memories.

43. Your author attended classes and stayed at the local homesteads in both Endicott and
Poughkeepsie. As a two-year resident in Poughkeepsie, he also witnessed the flow and
use of postcards by employees and customers.

44. Examples in author's private collection that included a dozen images of NCR, several
from Burroughs, and one from the shoe company.

45. For the standard history of these events, Robert W. Rydell, *World of Fairs: The Century-
of-Progress Expositions* (Chicago: University of Chicago Press, 1993).

46. James W. Cortada, *IBM: The Rise and Fall and Reinvention of a Global Icon* (Cambridge,
MA: MIT Press, 2019), 107–109.

47. Pugh, *Building IBM*, 323.

48. Pugh, *Building IBM*, 323.

49. Lawrence R. Samuel, *The End of Innocence: The 1964–1965 New York World's Fair* (Syracuse, NY: Syracuse University Press, 2007).

50. U.S. Bureau of Labor Statistics, "Labor Force Employment and Unemployment 1929–
1939," https://www.bls.gov/opub/mlr/1948/article/pdf/labor-force-employment-and
-unemployment-1929-39-estimating-methods.pdf, accessed November 1, 2020.

51. U.S. Bureau of Labor Statistics, "Labor Force Employment and Unemployment
1929–1939."

52. Cortada, *IBM*, 97–98.

53. Pugh, *Building IBM*, 323.

54. For a short film of the event that mentions IBM three minutes into it, see YouTube,
"History Brief: 1939 World's Fair," https://www.youtube.com/watch?v=jIlhPFasI38,
accessed November 1, 2021.

55. U.S. Census Bureau.

56. The makeover has been well documented by John Harwood, *The Interface: IBM and the
Transformation of Corporate Design, 1945–1976* (Minneapolis: University of Minnesota
Press, 2011).

57. For a brief film of IBM's exhibit prepared by Eames, see YouTube, "IBM at the Fair
(1964)," https://www.youtube.com/watch?v=2UZYG33D2B4, accessed November 1, 2021,
and another that appears to be a home movie showing the building, YouTube, "1965
NYWF 2 IBM Pavilion et al," https://www.youtube.com/watch?v=p51aj56doIc, accessed
November 1, 2021.

58. Pugh, *Building IBM*, 324.

59. On its origins that so influenced the generation of advertisers and marketing professions working in the 1960s, see Roland Marchand, *Creating the Corporate Soul: The
Rise of Public Relations and Corporate Imagery in American Business* (Berkeley: University of California Press, 1998); Jim Heimann, *The Golden Age of Advertising—The 60s*
(Cologne, Germany: TASCHEN, 2005).

60. This documents a practice still conducted in the 1980s, when your author, a Sales School instructor, bused sales trainees to corporate headquarters, then located in Armonk, New York, where executives spoke to them about various sales and company issues.

61. Marchand, *Creating the Corporate Soul*, 107.

62. Marchand, *Creating the Corporate Soul*, 250.

63. Marchand, *Creating the Corporate Soul*, 202–311.

64. Harwood, *The Interface*.

10. Humor and Corporate Culture: IBM, Cartoons, and the Good Laugh

1. William Rodgers, *THINK: A Biography of the Watsons and IBM* (New York: Stein & Day, 1972); David Mercer, *IBM: How the World's Most Successful Corporation Is Managed* (London: Kogan Page, 1987); Thomas J. Watson, Jr., and Peter Petre, *Father Son and Co.: My Life at IBM and Beyond* (New York: Bantam, 1990); Kevin Maney, *The Maverick and His Machine: Thomas Watson, Sr. and the Making of IBM* (Hoboken, NJ: John Wiley & Sons, 2003).

2. James W. Cortada, "Change and Continuity at IBM: Key Themes in the Histories of IBM," *Business History Review* 92, no. 1 (Spring 2018): 117–148.

3. Kenneth Lipartito, "Business Culture," in *The Oxford Handbook of Business History*, ed. Geoffrey Jones and Jonathan Zeitlin (New York: Oxford University Press, 2007), 603–628.

4. I wrote a history of IBM that focused largely on explaining its culture and the problems of studying the topic in general; James W. Cortada, *IBM: The Rise and Fall and Reinvention of a Global Icon* (Cambridge, MA: MIT Press, 2019).

5. Robert I. Westwood and Allanah Johnston, "Humor in Organizations: From Function to Resistance," *Humor* 26, no. 2 (2013): 219–247; Bruno Lussier, Yany Gregoire, and Marc-Antoine Vachon, "The Role of Humor Usage on Creativity, Trust and Performance in Business Relationships: An Analysis of the Salesperson-Customer Dyad," *Industrial Marketing Management* 65 (August 2017): 168–181.

6. Explained by Barbara L. Gunning, "The Role That Humor Plays in Shaping Organizational Culture," Unpublished PhD diss., University of Toledo, 2001.

7. Gunning, "The Role That Humor Plays in Shaping Organizational Culture."

8. The standard guidance on this topic is by Edgar H. Schein and Peter A. Schein, *Organizational Culture and Leadership*, 5th ed. (Hoboken, NJ: John Wiley & Sons, 2017).

9. John Morreall, *Humor Works* (Amherst, MA: HRD Press, 1997).

10. Linda Weiser Friedman and Hershey H. Friedman, "A Framework for the Study of Computer-Oriented Humor (COHUM)," *CIS Working Paper Series*, #CIS-2003-1 (New York: Zicklin School of Business, August 2003). For an example, S. Harris, *What's So Funny About Computers?* (Los Altos, CA: William Kauffman, 1982).

11. As a partial workaround, the author's collection of cartoons will be donated to an archive as part of his collection of IBM ephemera, which will allow others to examine more fully the documentation of IBM's humor.

12. In the United States, it was largely customary to only charge fees for pages copied in higher education libraries and buildings and in public libraries from the 1950s through the 1990s; afterward, package delivery firms also provided photocopying for a fee, too.

13. Mary Jo Hatch and Michael Owen Jones, "Photocopylore at Work: Aesthetics, Collective Creativity and the Social Construction of Organizations," *Culture and Organization*

3, no. 2 (July 1997): 263–287; Michael J. Preston, "Traditional Humor from the Fax Machine: 'All of a Kind,'" *Western Folklore* 53, no. 2 (April 1994): 147–169.

14. Preston, "Traditional Humor from the Fax Machine," 147.

15. Clive Thompson, "How the Photocopier Changed the Way We Worked—and Played," *Smithsonian Magazine*, March 2015, https://www.smithsonianmag.com/history/duplication-nation-3D-printing-rise-180954332/?page=2, accessed September 8, 2021.

16. Christian F. Hempelmann and Andrea C. Samson, "Cartoons: Drawn Jokes?," in *The Primer of Humor Research*, ed. Victor Raskin (Berlin: Mouton de Gruyter, 2008), 609–640; see also their extensive bibliography on humor.

17. Ann Marie Love and Lampert H. Deckers, "Humor Appreciation as a Function of Sexual, Aggressive, and Sexist Content," *Sex Roles* 20 (1989): 649–654; Teresa L. Thompson and Eugenia Zerbinos, "Gender Roles in Animated Cartoons: Has the Picture Changed in 20 Years?," *Sex Roles* 32 (1995): 651–673; Ronald E. Anderson and Elaine Jolly, "Stereotypical Traits and Sex Roles in Humorous Drawings," *Communication Research* 4 (1977): 453–579.

18. Hempelmann and Samson, "Cartoons: Drawn Jokes?," 614.

19. Hempelmann and Samson, "Cartoons: Drawn Jokes?," 625.

20. Hempelmann and Samson, "Cartoons: Drawn Jokes?," 625.

21. Ray Morris, "Visual Rhetoric in Political Cartoons: A Structuralist Approach," *Metaphor and Symbolic Activity* 8 (1993): 195–210; Patrick J. Carroll, Jason R. Young, and Michael S. Guertin, "Visual Analysis of Cartoons: A View from the Far Side," in *Eye Movements and Visual Vognition: Scene Perception and Readings*, ed. Keith Rayner (New York: Springer, 1992), 444–461.

22. Nale Lehmann-Willenbrock and Joseph A. Allen, "How Fun Are Your Meetings? Investigating the Relationship Between Humor Patterns in Team Interactions and Team Performance," *Journal of Applied Psychology* 99, no. 6 (2014): 1278–1287.

23. W. H. Decker, "Sex Conflict and Impressions of Managers' Aggressive Humor," *Psychological Record* 36 (1986): 483–490; P. Derks and S. Arora, "Sex and Salience in the Appreciation of Cartoon Humor," *Humor: International Journal of Humor Research* 6, no. 1 (1993): 57–69; L. La Favre and R. Mannell, "Does Ethnic Humor Serve Prejudice?," *Journal of Communication* (Summer 1976): 116–123.

24. Corey Ford, *Corey Ford's Guide to Thimking: A Handbook for the Home Cybernetician* (Garden City, NY: Doubleday, 1961).

25. Ford, *Corey Ford's Guide to Thimking*, 52.

26. Ford, *Corey Ford's Guide to Thimking*, 61.

27. For example, Ford, *Corey Ford's Guide to Thimking*, 25.

28. Reprinted in Ford, *Corey Ford's Guide to Thimking*, 15.

29. Ford, *Corey Ford's Guide to Thimking*, 16.

30. Ford, *Corey Ford's Guide to Thimking*, 13.

31. Ford, *Corey Ford's Guide to Thimking*, 23.

32. Ford, *Corey Ford's Guide to Thimking*, 11.

33. Some of these lists are now available on the internet at Ahajokes.com, "Possible IBM Acronyms," ahajokes.com/com028.html, accessed August 25, 2019.

34. The term *Marketeers* may have been inspired by the popular Mickey Mouse TV programs of the 1950s and 1960s where fans were called Mouseketeers.

35. *Datamation*, October 1975, 58.

36. Nick T. Spark, *A History of Murphy's Law* (Periscope Film, 2006); "Murphy's Law," *Wikipedia*, https://en.wikipedia.org/wiki/Murphy%27s_law, accessed September 7, 2021.

37. Peter F. Drucker, *Management, Tasks, Responsibilities, and Practices* (New York: Harper & Row, 1974), 681. There was a corollary called "Mrs. Murphy's Law," which stated that

things will go wrong when Mr. Murphy is away, humorously postulated by, among others, Ann Landers in her column in the *Washington Post*, May 9, 1978.

38. Charles R. Stephens to James W. Cortada, December 1, 1989, author's archives.

39. Stephen Papson, *Jump Cut: A Review of Contemporary Media* no. 35 (April 1990): 66–72.

40. C. M. Consalvo, "Humor in Management: No Laughing Matter," *Humor: International Journal of Humor Research* 2 (1989): 285–297; W. J. Duncan and J. P. Feisal, "No Laughing Matter: Patterns of Humor in the Workplace," *Organizational Dynamics* 17 (1989): 18–30; W. J. Duncan, L. R. Smeltzer, and T. L. Leap, "Humor and Work: Applications of Joking Behavior to Management," *Journal of Management* 16, no. 2 (1990): 255–278.

41. John Morreall, "Applications of Humor: Health, the Workplace, and Education," in *The Primer of Humor Research*, ed. Raskin, 449.

42. The industry also produced "how-to" books on the subject. For examples, Sandra Meggert, *Creative Humor at Work: Living the Humor Perspective* (Lanham, MD: University Press of America, 2008); Andrew Tarvin, *Humor That Works: The Missing Skill for Success and Happiness at Work* (self-published, 2019); and the foundational manual, Morreall, *Humor Works*, which first appeared in 1997.

43. Cortada, *IBM*; articulated by IBM CEO Thomas J. Watson, Jr., *A Business and Its Beliefs: The Ideas That Helped Build IBM* (New York: McGraw-Hill, 1963).

44. Ford, *Corey Ford's Guide to Thinking*, 93–94.

45. Andy Clark, *Being There: Putting Brain, Body and World Together Again* (Cambridge, MA: MIT Press, 1997), and Andy Clark, *Supersizing the Mind: Embodiment, Action, and Cognitive Extension* (New York: Oxford University Press, 2008); Richard Menary, ed., *The Extended Mind* (Cambridge, MA: MIT Press, 2010).

11. Gray Literature in IBM's Information Ecosystem

1. Dana Marks worked in publications production and was also on and off a programmer at IBM in the 1970s, IBM Retirees Facebook posting, February 25, 2021. He also reported that IBM was the second most prolific publisher if one counted pages published.

2. As a small note of history, the modern form of the index was developed by an IBM computer scientist, Hans Peter Luhn (1896–1964), in the 1950s.

3. IBM, *Publications KWIC Index* (Mechanicsburg, PA: IBM Corporation, December 1990). These indices, published several times per year had appeared for decades. They also explained the numbering and code abbreviations that would be useful for historians of IBM's products and publications.

4. The point was made earliest by Alfred D. Chandler, Jr., *The Visible Hand: The Managerial Revolution in American Business* (Cambridge, MA: Harvard University Press, 1977); more explicitly by JoAnne Yates, *Control Through Communications: The Rise of System in American Management* (Baltimore, MD: Johns Hopkins University Press, 1989).

5. James W. Cortada, *All the Facts: A History of Information in the United States Since 1870* (New York: Oxford University Press, 2016), 98–105, 287–304.

6. While the subject is just beginning to be studied regarding many organizations, we have some research about IBM's experience; James W. Cortada, "Viewing Corporations as Information Ecosystems: The Case of IBM, 1914–1980s," *Enterprise and Society* 23, no. 1 (March 2022): 99–132.

7. His italicized word; Dan Schiller, *How to Think About Information* (Urbana and Chicago: University of Illinois Press, 2007), 39.

8. C. P. Auger, *Information Sources in Grey Literature* (London: Bowker Saur, 1998), 111–120.

9. Explained in considerable detail in James W. Cortada, *IBM: The Rise and Fall and Reinvention of a Global Icon* (Cambridge, MA: MIT Press, 2019).

10. Interview with Rich Rarco by James W. Cortada, March 11, 2021.

11. Thomas J. Watson, Jr., "Briefing," Number 3–62, June 26, 1962. IBM, *Thirty Years of Management Briefings, 1958 to 1988* (New York: IBM Corporation, 1988), 48.

12. One of the most useful explanations of these circumstances, written at the height of IBM's information ecosystem, is by an IBM manager of the 1970s and 1980s; David Mercer, *The Global IBM: Leadership in Multinational Management* (New York: Dodd, Mead & Company, 1988).

13. When IBM moved from selling tabulating equipment to computers, management had to replace many salesmen who had sold the earlier technology with a new generation who had college education and had to add a new class of workers to assist customers on all manner of software and application technical matters, called systems engineers, beginning in 1962. These were often university graduates in engineering, mathematics, and computer science. From the 1950s through the 2010s, most employees had a university-level education; not until after 2015 was that guideline for hiring eased.

14. Mercer, *The Global IBM*, 124–125.

15. All of this happened in less than the length of one business career; James L. Pelkeu, Andrew L. Russell, and Loring Robbins, *Circuits, Packets, and Protocols: Entrepreneurs and Computer Communications* (New York: ACM Books, 2022).

16. But for brief summaries, Auger, *Information Sources in Grey Literature*, 3–16; Pratibha Gokhale, "Grey Literature Varieties—Definitional Problems," *Third International Conference on Grey Literature: Perspectives on the Design and Transfer of Scientific and Technical Information, 13–14 November 1997*.

17. Auger, *Information Sources in Grey Literature*, quote ix, also 3–7.

18. A personal example illustrates the point. If your author published an article in an academic journal, it might be read by dozens or maybe a few hundred people, while a trade book on a business topic might be read by anywhere from 1,500 to 10,000 people. A "best-selling" business book might go out to 30,000 purchasers. When working at IBM's Institute for Business Value in the 2000s, article-length studies routinely went out worldwide to 10,000 people or more within days of publication, and books often to over 30,000 either for free or a fee.

19. Examples of each can be found in the James W. Cortada Papers (CBI 185), Charles Babbage Institute, University of Minnesota, https://archives.lib.umn.edu/repositories/3/resources/289/collection_organization, accessed March 15, 2021.

20. For examples and sources, Auger, *Information Sources in Grey Literature*, 10.

21. Auger, *Information Sources in Grey Literature*, 111–119; identified early by K. D. C. Vernon, ed., *Use of Management and Business Literature* (London: Butterworth-Heinemann, 1975) and with *Information Sources in Management and Business* (London: Butterworths, 1984); John Eric Juricek, "Access to Grey Literature in Business: An Exploration of Commercial White Papers," *Journal of Business and Financial Librarianship* 14, no. 4 (2009): 318–332.

22. Auger, *Information Sources in Grey Literature*, 165–168.

23. He was able to do this because he worked for nearly two decades at NCR, which was considered a sophisticated, well-run, high-tech firm in its day; Kevin Maney, *The Maverick and His Machine: Thomas J. Watson, Sr. and the Making of IBM* (Hoboken, NJ: John Wiley & Sons, 2003), 37–126.

24. Your author was one of those individuals; James W. Cortada, *EDP Costs and Charges: Finance, Budgets, and Cost Control in Data Processing* (Englewood Cliffs, NJ: Prentice-Hall, 1980), *Managing DP Hardware: Capacity Planning, Cost Justification, Availability, and Energy Management* (Englewood Cliffs, NJ: Prentice-Hall, 1983), and *Best Practices in Information Technology: How Corporations Get the Most Value from Exploiting Their Digital Investments* (Upper Saddle River, NJ: Prentice Hall PTR, 1997).

25. James W. Cortada, "Managing a Nearly Invisible Corporate Community: 'IBM Families,'" forthcoming.

26. As a side note, newly hired salesmen were taught how to read a corporate annual report as another way of showing them how to glean information about a customer useful in selling expensive equipment. That required sales personnel to understand the basic features of an annual report, why they were part of such a document, and how to interpret their language.

27. International Business Machines Corporation, *International Business Machines* (New York: International Business Machines Corporation, 1926), 4.

28. I describe IBM's image- and culture-building activities in Cortada, *IBM*.

29. A. W. Hanson, "International Scales," May 3, 1938, 1, author's collection.

30. Hanson, "International Scales," 6.

31. For example from 1940, "Elementary Electricity," produced by the International Business Machines Corporation, Educational Department in Endicott, New York, site of most of IBM's worldwide education before World War II and for all employees in North America, author's collection.

32. "Alphabetic Accounting Machine Type 405," in *Customer Engineering Reference Manual EAM Section 405* (New York: IBM Corporation, 1942), unpaginated, Form 82-3075-0-1500-JCP-2.51.

33. IBM, *Manual of Instruction, Customer Engineering* (New York: IBM Corporation, n.d.).

34. It was not uncommon for CEs to go into retirement with both these handbooks and their personal tool bag. Both become available on occasion when their estates are dismantled. Your author acquired his half-dozen copies through eBay.

35. IBM, *Meters—Test Devices* (New York: International Business Machines Corporation, 1952).

36. In training materials from the mid-1930s for a class entitled "Machine Methods of Accounting," the course binder began with a publication, "Development of International Business Machines Corporation," author's collection.

37. *Manual tecnico mecanicto. Maquinas commerciales Watson S.A.E.* (Madrid: Watson S.A.E., 1941). At the time, not all subsidiaries of the company were called IBM. This was one of them. Portuguese editions were available in Brazil, while Spanish ones were available wherever IBM did business in Latin America.

38. For employee statistics, Emerson W. Pugh, *Building IBM: Shaping an Industry and Its Technology* (Cambridge, MA: MIT Press, 1995), 323–324.

39. Thomas J. Watson, Sr., *Men-Minutes-Money: A Collection of Excerpts from Talks and Messages Delivered and Written at Various Times* (New York: International Business Machines Corporation, 1934).

40. Thomas J. Watson, Sr., *Les Hommes-Le Temps-L'Argent: Les trois facteurs de success dans la vie et dans les affairs* (Paris: no publisher listed, but clearly IBM, 1935). This edition consisted of 1,324 pages.

41. IBM, *Dedicated to Victory* (New York: International Business Machines Corporation, undated, circa early 1943).

42. IBM, *Memorial to the War Veterans Who Gave Their Lives in World War II, 1941–1946* (New York: International Business Machines Corporation, 1948). A similar volume was published to celebrate IBM's activities in Poughkeepsie, New York, in conjunction with city leaders, IBM, *Dedicated to Progress* (New York: International Business Machines Corporation, 1948).

43. Entitled, for example, IBM, *1950 Hundred Percent Club Meetings*, examples from the author's collection. Every participant was photographed and identified, which gives historians insights into the composition and approximate ages of the sales force at that time.

44. For examples, Jacques Vernay, *Chroniques de la Compagnie IBM France, 1914–1987* (Paris: IBM Corporation, 1988); IBM, *Chronik de IBM Deutschland, 1910–1985* (Stuttgart, Germany: IBM Deutschland GmbH, 1985); IBM, *IBM: 50 anos em Portugal* (IBM Portuguesa, 1988). Others appeared from IBM in Ireland, the Netherlands, Norway, and Australia.

45. A. El-Sawad and M. Korczynski, "Management and Music: The Exceptional Case of the IBM Songbook," *Group and Organization Management* 32, no. 1 (February 2007): 79–108.

46. The employee most credited with writing the lyrics for many songs was Harry S. Evans, and it was he who pulled together all the material into various editions of the music. It appears that the 1931 edition was published by the company, IBM, *Fellowship Songs of the International Business Machines Corporation* (New York: International Business Machines Company, 1931). Author's collection.

47. For a recording of employees singing this song, see IMB, "IBM Archives," https://www.ibm.com/ibm/history/multimedia/wav/everonward.wav, accessed March 17, 2021.

48. How that publication made it back to the United States, where your author acquired it, remains a mystery. However, the owner was an American who may have been sent to China to support equipment there and then, upon the occasion of war breaking out with Japan in 1937, came back to the United States.

49. For examples, for the 1939 World's Fair, IBM, *Contemporary Art of 79 Countries* (New York: International Business Machines Corporation, 1939); IBM, *Contemporary Art of the United States* (New York: International Business Machines Corporation, 1940); IBM, *Arte Grafico del Hemisferio Occidental: Coleccion Permanente International Business Machines Corporation* (New York: International Business Machines Corporation, 1941); John Taylor Arms, *Seventy-Five Latin American Prints* (New York: International Business Machines Corporation, 1946); *Twenty Contemporary Sculptors* (New York: Grand Central Art Galleries, 1946). On occasion, IBM published one-off publications, such as IBM, *Dr. Edvard Benes President of Czechoslovakia: The Czechoslovak Stateman's Official Wartime Visit to the U.S. and Canada in 1943* (New York: International Business Machines Corporation, 1943), a 156-page publication.

50. Cuthbert C. Hurd and the IBM Applied Science Department, eds., *Proceedings Seminar on Scientific Computation, November, 1949* (New York: International Business Machines Corporation, 1950). It was an elegant hardback volume printed on cream-colored paper and ran to some one hundred pages in length.

51. *THINK* 1, no. 1 (June 1935): 1.

52. Pugh, *IBM*, 324.

53. Press release, "Hub of World-Wide System: World's Largest Computer Library," November 30, 1965, IBM Corporate Archives.

54. "Product Publications Back Up New GP Systems with Printed Manuals, Catalogs," *IBM Endicott News* 11, no. 11 (June 21, 1963): 4.

55. Interview with David Larkin by James W. Cortada, March 22, 2021.
56. In the 1970s, your author frequently found that data centers had "libraries" (their term) attached to their computer rooms or down the hall, with floor-to-ceiling bookcases with manuals and tapes (considered literature in the industry), many in stacks maintained by "librarians" (their job title). Technical support staff often worked in rooms with wall-to-wall floor-to-ceiling bookcases crammed with IBM publications.
57. Interview with David Larkin.
58. Senior management was concerned that the word "computer" would conjure up thoughts that people would lose their jobs due to automation because, prior to the development of computers, that word meant people who computed manually mathematics and accounting using pencil and paper or desktop calculators.
59. IBM, *Electronics in IBM* (New York: International Business Machines Corporation, 1952), 3.
60. IBM, *General Information Manual: Introduction to IBM Data Processing Systems* (White Plains, NY: Data Processing Division, International Business Machines Corporation, 1960); IBM, "Data Processing Bibliography," *Data Processing Systems Bulletin*, 1959, 1961.
61. For examples, IBM, *IBM Data-Processing: Machine Functions* (White Plains, NY: Data Processing Division, International Business Machines Corporation, 1950, 1954, 1957); IBM, *General Information Manual: An Introduction to IBM Punched Card Data Processing* (White Plains, NY: Data Processing Division, International Business Machines Corporation, undated, circa 1960).
62. IBM, *Punched Card Data Processing Principles*, 7 vols. (White Plains, NY: Data Processing Division, International Business Machines Corporation, 1961).
63. IBM, *Principles of Programming*, 12 vols. (White Plains, NY: Data Processing Division, International Business Machines Corporation, 1961).
64. IBM, *General Information Manual: An Introduction to IBM Punched Card Data Processing.*
65. IBM, *General Information Manual: 1401 Data Processing System* (White Plains, NY: Data Processing Division, International Business Machines Corporation, 1959, 1960). On the copyright page, we see a typical annotation regarding editions found in most IBM manuals: "Major Revision (September, 1960) This edition, D24-1401-2, is a major revision of the preceding edition, and obsoletes D24-1401-1." The numbers translate into division number 24 (DPD), product number (1401), and edition.
66. Widely circulated examples include, IBM, *Introduction to Computer Systems*, 4th ed. (Atlanta: Technical Publications Department 796, International Business Machines Corporation, 1978); IBM, *Introduction to IBM Data Processing Systems, Student Text*, 4th ed. (White Plains, NY: Data Processing Division, International Business Machines Corporation, 1972); IBM, *Introduction to Teleprocessing, Student Text* (White Plains, NY: Data Processing Division, International Business Machines Corporation, 1970) and co-published with IBM World Trade Corporation in New York for global distribution.
67. IBM, *Introduction to IBM Data Processing Systems*, unpaginated on copyright page.
68. For example, IBM, *IBM System/360 System Summary*, 11th ed. (New York: Data Processing Division and IBM World Trade Corporation, International Business Machines Corporation, August 1969). For feedback to the authors, readers were instructed to contact the Customer Manuals Department 898 at IBM's research and manufacturing center where these machines were designed and built, in Poughkeepsie, New York. The author's copy was typical in that it had someone's name handwritten on the first page, clear signs of coffee stains, and curled and torn pages.

69. IBM, *System/370 Operator's Reference Guide* (Poughkeepsie, NY: DPD Education Department, Publication Services, Education Center, July 1974).

70. *Complete Idiot's Guides*, https://www.penguinrandomhouse.com/series/IDU/idiots-guides, accessed March 13, 2021.

71. Your author relied on the large collection of these housed at the IBM Corporate Archives in Poughkeepsie, New York, as the primary source underpinning a three-volume history of how computers changed the nature of work in American corporations and government agencies, James W. Cortada, *The Digital Hand: How Computers Changed the Work of American Manufacturing, Transportation, and Retail Industries* (New York: Oxford University Press, 2004); *The Digital Hand: How Computers Changed the Work of American Financial, Telecommunications, Media, and Entertainment Industries* (New York: Oxford University Press, 2006), and *The Digital Hand: How Computers Changed the Work of American Public Sector Industries* (New York: Oxford University Press, 2008). Copies of the application briefs used for these volumes can be found at the Charles Babbage Institute, University of Minnesota–Twin Cities.

72. IBM, *Program Product: Customer Information Control System/Virtual Storage (CICS) General Information Manual* (Palo Alto, CA: IBM Corporation, 1975), 157–158.

73. Few have survived. Old editions were discarded, and after the death of a retiree, the remaining one might be too. By the end of the 1990s, much of this content was available on company websites and later through retiree websites in various countries.

74. Cathy Sheffler to James W. Cortada, email, February 25, 2021. She worked in Poughkeepsie, New York, home to mainframes and attendant software in the 1980s.

75. Cathy Sheffler to James W. Cortada, email, March 26, 2021.

76. Interview with George DeSalvo by James W. Cortada, March 14, 2021.

77. Interview with George DeSalvo.

78. Cathy Sheffler to James W. Cortada, email, February 25, 2021.

79. Cathy Sheffler to James W. Cortada, email, March 26, 2021.

80. The same process was described by the publications product manager located at a factory in California in the early 1970s; interview with Dana Marks by James W. Cortada, March 2, 2021. In the early 1970s, this manager had, in addition to several writers, four typists and one artist, one editor, and several employees devoted to production, and confirmed by another from the Rochester, Minnesota, site; interview with Glen Douglas by James W. Cortada, March 16, 2021.

81. IBM, *Writer's and Editor's Handbook* (Boca Raton, FL: Boca Raton Information Development, IBM Corporation, 1987). At the time, this facility was home to the development of IBM's PC products.

82. IBM, *IBM Editorial Guidelines* (Armonk, NY: International Business Machines Corporation, 1986). Extant copies are torn and ruffled, suggesting these, like favorite cookbooks, were consulted frequently.

83. Brad Kramer, *A Practical Guide to Consistent Books*, 2nd ed. (Research Triangle Park, NC: International Business Machines Corporation, 1988).

84. Written by staff in the Information Development Department at the IBM Santa Teresa Laboratory, IBM, *Producing Technical Information Producing Quality Technical Information*, 2nd ed. (Santa Teresa, CA: Information Development, IBM Corporation, 1986); PowerPoint presentation, "Producing Quality Technical Information," IBM Santa Teresa Laboratory System Information, 1983, author's collection.

85. Interview with David Larkin.

86. Interview with David Larkin. IBM sold over 500,000 AS400s between 1988 and the dawn of the next century.

87. Glen Douglas to James W. Cortada, email, March 14, 2021.
88. "Bookless Library Keeps Customers on Program of Satisfaction," *IBM News* 5, no. 5 (March 11, 1968): 4–5.
89. "World's Largest Computer Library Opens New and Unique Headquarters," Press release, November 30, 1975, IBM Corporate Archives.
90. Interview with David Larkin. Iceland had one city and a U.S. Air Force base in Reykjavik.
91. Interview with David Larkin.
92. Interview with Rich Arco by James W. Cortada, March 11, 2021.
93. "World's Largest Computer Library Opens New and Unique Headquarters."
94. "Division Centralizes Product Publications; Smyrski Promoted," *IBM Poughkeepsie News* 8, no. 3 (June 8, 1960): 1–2.
95. Interview with David Larkin.
96. "Mission Change Announced for IBM Boulder," *Corporate News Bulletin*, April 22, 1986. *Corporate New Bulletin* was IBM's internal communication vehicle that listed all manner of announcements, such as promotion of executives, organizational changes, and other news relevant to employees.
97. The two research journals were *IBM Journal of Research and Development* (established 1957) and *IBM Systems Journal* (established 1962). The first was aimed at computer scientists, and the second at IBM employees, later at customers; George C. Stierhoff and Alfred G. Davis, "A History of the *IBM Systems Journal*," *IEEE Annals of the History of Computing* 20, no. 1 (January–March 1999): 29–35.
98. Often kept throughout their careers at IBM even if their work roles changed.
99. Cortada, *IBM*, 203–231.
100. These issues have long been recognized by some archivists as a problem and some have attempted to address it; Bruce H. Bruemmer and Sheldon Hochheiser, *The High-Technology Company: A Historical Research and Archival Guide* (Minneapolis: Charles Babbage Institute, University of Minnesota, 1989). They also cite other conversations held around these issues by historians and archivists.
101. Since the 1930s, publications used by customers and IBMers have included a postcard-like sheet in the back encouraging feedback and including a mailing address, with IBM usually paying for postage. A manual's author normally was responsible for correcting errors and responding back to whoever wrote about a publication.
102. Material for the last two paragraphs drawn from a PowerPoint presentation, IBM, "Information Development Strategy for the 90s," copy in author's collection.

12. The Essential Strategy for Corporate Success

1. Thomas J. Watson, Sr., *Men-Minutes-Money* (New York: International Business Machines Corporation, 1934), 97.
2. Frank Chapman Sharp and Philip G. Fox, *Business Ethics* (New York: D. Appleton-Century, 1937), 291.
3. "IBM Retirees," Facebook, December 29, 2020; Thomas J. Watson, Jr., *A Business and Its Beliefs* (New York: McGraw Hill, 1963).
4. "IBM Retirees."
5. Ginni Rometty to IBMers, December 28, 2020, LinkedIn, https://www.linkedin.com/pulse/ever-onward-my-farewell-ibmers-ginni-rometty/?trackingId=i9oGKaZ5ThGd%2B3ZUlowsZA%3D%3D, accessed December 28, 2020.

6. Most famously were the rivalries between Endicott and Poughkeepsie in the 1950s and 1960s over whose worldviews of computing should predominate; James W. Cortada, *IBM: The Rise and Fall and Reinvention of a Global Icon* (Cambridge, MA: MIT Press, 2019), 208, 210.

7. Clyde W. Ford, *Think Black: A Memoir* (New York: HarperCollins, 2019); Milton Drandell, *IBM: The Other Side, 101 Former Employees Look Back* (San Luis Obispo, CA: Quail, 1984); Daniel Quinn Mills and G. Bruce Friesen, *Broken Promises: An Unconventional View of What Went Wrong at IBM* (Cambridge, MA: Harvard Business Review Press, 1996).

8. Edgar H. Schein and Peter A. Schein, *The Corporate Culture Survival Guide*, 3rd ed. (Hoboken, NJ: Wiley & Sons, 2019), 51.

9. Schein and Schein, *The Corporate Culture Survival Guide*, 53–54.

10. Edgar H. Schein, *Organizational Culture and Leadership* (San Francisco: Jossey-Bass, 1989), 49–83.

11. IBM engineers had invented hard drives, an achievement of enormous pride to IBMers for decades; a similar statement could be made about the PC, the product that caused the business world to take seriously desktop computing, yet another source of enormous pride. So selling off these two businesses was emotionally difficult but the right action to take. I discuss these decisions more fully in James W. Cortada, *IBM*.

12. Peter Burke, *What Is Cultural History?* (Cambridge, UK: Polity, 2019), 27.

13. Charles A. O'Reilly III and Michael L. Tushman, *Lead and Disrupt: How to Solve the Innovator's Dilemma*, 2nd ed. (Stanford, CA: Stanford Business Books, 2021), both quotes, 47.

14. Spoken at the Harvard Business School in 2012, quoted in O'Reilly and Tushman, *Lead and Disrupt*, 87.

15. Elsewhere I made the case that the underlying technological basis supporting IBM changed slower than historians of technology normally would acknowledge; Cortada, *IBM*, 594–601.

16. Multiyear lease contracts with customers from the 1880s to the 1980s are often cited as why customers remained with IBM, but that argument makes little sense. Customers did not have to sign them in the first place or renew them, especially since there usually were options for products from other vendors. As to employees, the company cultivated them for a lifetime, as this book has shown. Thus, for both constituencies, they required more deep-seated reasons to offer IBM stability. In exchange, customers wanted quality service and value, and employees wanted relevant compensation, job security, and interesting work.

17. Emerson W. Pugh, *Building IBM: Shaping an Industry and Its Technology* (Cambridge, MA: MIT Press, 1995), 323–324.

18. Peter E. Greulich, *Think Again!* (Austin, TX: MBI Concepts Corporation, 2020), 258–259.

19. Greulich, *Think Again!*, 262–263, 266–267.

20. Mills and Friesen, *Broken Promises*.

21. Cortada, *IBM*, 421–470.

22. Kevin Maney, *The Maverick and His Machine: Thomas Watson, Sr. and the Making of IBM* (Hoboken, NJ: John Wiley & Sons, 2003), 59–90.

23. Calculated based on data in Pugh, *Building IBM*, 323.

24. Cortada, *IBM*, 27–90.

25. Watson, *Men-Minutes-Money*, 373.

26. Watson, *Men-Minutes-Money*, 389–390.

27. Watson, *Men-Minutes-Money*, 390.

28. I have a field engineer's installation and repair manual for tabulators given to each person trained on IBM's hardware, dated 1932. It indicated that (a) the training took place in Endicott, New York, and (b) the student was given a monographed copy of the manual (as was the custom) with their name and address. This engineer's address was in China. Europeans routinely came to New York State for training as well.

29. Watson, *Men-Minutes-Money*, the entire 886-page volume.

30. James W. Cortada, "Viewing Corporations as Information Ecosystems: The Case of IBM, 1914–1980s," *Enterprise and Society* 23, no. 1 (March 2022): 99–132; "Longevity and Corporate Ecosystems: How Did IBM Exist for Over a Century?" *Entreprises et Histoire* 94 (April 2019): 104–127; "IBM Branch Offices: What They Were, How They Worked, 1920s–1980s," *IEEE Annals of the History of Computing* 39, no. 3 (July–September 2017): 9–23.

31. Beginning in the 1990s and massively so after 2000, the company did just that: hired staff and management from outside the firm who had no familiarity with IBM's culture. The confusion and other operational problems await its historian.

32. It was not uncommon in sales management, for example, to make critical decisions within one hour of being on the job, such as how to deal with a personnel crisis, solve a billing issue with a customer, or advise someone about a sales problem. I personally cannot recall that *not* happening to me in at least my first three managerial positions, but in every one, certainly within a couple of days.

33. If they no longer could be kept in a particular position, the company might move that individual to a lateral or slightly lower position.

34. This was a major event in the history of IBM's move into computing, which I explore in detail in Cortada, *IBM*, 149–232.

35. Watson, *Men-Minutes-Money*, 115.

36. Thomas J. Watson, Jr., to management, May 24, 1968; IBM, *Thirty Years of Management Briefings, 1958–1988* (Armonk, NY: International Business Machines Corporation, 1988), 112.

37. He would have been familiar with the problem that many spouses and children would have protested moving, disrupting their family lives, schooling, and other affairs. It is not known how many employees turned down transfer (promotions) because of family resistance, but it was a few.

38. Frank T. Cary to management, November 20, 1974; IBM, *Thirty Years of Management Briefings, 1958–1988*.

39. Cornelius E. Deloca and Samuel J. Kalow, *The Romance Division: A Different Side of IBM* (New York: Vantage, 1991).

40. A memoir from a long-serving employee and executive in Latin America sheds light on the practice and culture associated with it; Luis A. Lamassonne, *My Life with IBM* (Atlanta: Protea, 2001).

41. Watson, *Men-Minutes-Money*, 250.

42. Watson, *Men-Minutes-Money*, 264.

43. Watson, *Men-Minutes-Money*, 271–274.

44. Watson, *Men-Minutes-Money*, 433; and for his memoirs, W. D. Jones, "Watson and Me: A Life at IBM," *IEEE Annals of the History of Computing* 25, no. 3 (August 2003): 4–18.

45. Historians and other observers have suggested that this was an act of nepotism, as he had to find a job for his son. While I am sure that might have been a factor—more finding a job for him rather than this job—his son was a faithful and trustworthy son and employee, spoke several languages, and had already held managerial positions at IBM. Given Watson Sr.'s passion for IBM, it is difficult to imagine he would give that much responsibility to anyone that he doubted could do well, even if it were one of his sons.

46. Mark Casson, *The Economics of Business Culture: Game Theory, Transaction Costs, and Economic Performance* (Oxford, UK: Clarendon, 1991), 237.

47. Thomas J. Watson, Sr., *Les Hommes-Le Temps-L'Argent* (Paris: International Business Machines Corporation, 1935). It included statistics and other data about IBM France, 1320–1324. Even the two books' covers were exactly the same.

48. Kevin Maney, Steve Hamm, and Jeffrey M. Obrien, *Making the World Work Better: The Ideas That Shaped a Century and a Country* (Upper Saddle River, NJ: IBM Press—Pearson, 2011). Other versions from the same publisher included, among others, *Au Service D'Un Monde Meilleur, Im Dienst der Welt, Trabajando Por Un Mundo Mejor*, and *Costruire un Mondo Migliore*.

49. For accounts of life in IBM's World Trade, Nancy Foy, *The Sun Never Sets on IBM* (New York: William Morrow, 1975); David Mercer, *IBM: How the World's Most Successful Corporation Is Managed* (London: K. Page, 1987); Jacques Maisonrouge, *Inside IBM: A Personal Story* (New York: McGraw-Hill, 1989).

50. Robert J. Gordon, *The Rise and Fall of American Growth: The U.S. Standard of Living Since the Civil War* (Princeton, NJ: Princeton University Press, 2016), 172–205, 441–460, 535–565.

51. Louis Galambos, *The Public Image of Big Business in America, 1880–1940: A Quantitative Study in Social Change* (Baltimore, MD: Johns Hopkins University Press, 1975), 221.

52. The modern conversation about control in business accelerated with Alfred D. Chandler, Jr., *The Visible Hand: The Managerial Revolution in American Business* (Cambridge, MA: Harvard University Press, 1977), particularly with his discussion about railroads, 122–187; but was extended to other industries with the use of information processing by James R. Beniger, *The Control Revolution: Technological and Economic Origins of the Information Society* (Cambridge, MA: Harvard University Press, 1986).

53. Maney, *The Maverick and His Machine*, 12–13. To be precise, he used this equipment from the "T" part of what became C-T-R before the tri-part firm became one.

54. James W. Cortada, *Building Blocks of Society: History, Information Ecosystems, and Infrastructures* (Lanham, MD: Rowman & Littlefield, 2021).

55. Christopher D. McKenna, *The World's Newest Profession: Management Consulting in the Twentieth Century* (Cambridge, UK: Cambridge University Press, 2006); but see also about managers themselves in Rakesh Khurana, *From Higher Aims to Hired Hands: The Social Transformation of American Business Schools and the Unfulfilled Promise of Management as a Profession* (Princeton, NJ: Princeton University Press, 2007).

56. For example, news reporters periodically interview your author about events at IBM, and so I have an opportunity to affect how thousands of people view the company. Occasionally I am consulted by academics studying IBM and by government regulators. This is the situation in every large company.

57. Historians mention this event but have not yet learned its significance. Some of the most useful insights came from the communications coming out of it to employees, Thomas J. Watson, Jr., "A New Pattern for Progress," *IBM Business Machines* 39, no. 19 (December 28, 1956): 1–15.

58. A major step forward came with the publication of the memoirs of a senior IBM R&D executive in which he described many of the technological innovations and research culture of the firm from the 1960s to 2008; Nick Donofrio with Michael DeMarco, *If Nothing Changes, Nothing Changes: The Nick Donofrio Story* (Houndstooth, 2022).

59. Louis V. Gerstner, *Who Says Elephants Can't Dance? Inside IBM's Historic Turnaround* (New York: HarperBusiness, 2002), 196–198.

60. "Possible IBM Acronyms," *AHAJOKES.com*, http://www.ahajokes.com/com028.html, accessed December 31, 2021.

61. Schein, *Organizational Culture and Leadership*, 65, but see his wider discussion of the subject, 65–82.

62. One widely distributed example is George McDaniel, *IBM Dictionary of Computing* (New York: McGraw-Hill, 1994), which was the tenth edition of this publication with 18,000 terms, and IBM, *IBM Vocabulary for Data Processing, Telecommunications and Office Systems* (White Plains, NY: International Business Machines Corporation, Data Processing Division, 1981), which was already by then in its seventh edition and ran 478 pages in length.

63. I collected over two dozen of these; most run into many hundreds of pages and were published by IBM or locally commissioned firms.

64. For example, Stuart M. Shieber, "The Design of a Computer Language for Linguistic Information," *Proceedings of the Tenth International Conference on Computational Linguistics*, 362–366, Stanford University, Stanford, California, July 2–6, 1984, https://dash .harvard.edu/handle/1/2309659, accessed December 30, 2021, although most studies are about how to use computers in the study of linguistics.

65. Charles Babbage Institute at the University of Minnesota and the Hagley Museum and Library have collections of these dictionaries.

66. Since its earliest days, most employees were at least high school graduates, and by the end of the 1950s, it was nearly impossible to obtain a job in sales, technology, or many factory jobs without some college (or more) education. Secretaries (now called assistants) could still enter IBM as late as the 1980s with only a high school degree, but by then, the company was eliminating that role for almost any department except for executives.

67. Gerstner, *Who Says Elephants Can't Dance?*, 43.

68. He even published one of his most famous charts, used initially at Endicott, New York, in January 1915, Watson, *Men-Minutes-Money*, 18.

69. Edward R. Tufte, of Yale University, became a well-known critic of people using slide decks but also a master teacher on how best to use visually present information; see Edward R. Tufte, *The Cognitive Style of PowerPoint: Pitching Out Corrupts Within* (Cheshire, CT: Graphics Press, 2006) for his critique of the medium; he cites IBM as a notorious example, 4.

70. Ivan Gaskell and Sarah Anne Carter, "Why History and Material Culture?," in *The Oxford Handbook of History and Material Culture*, ed. Ivan Gaskell and Sarah Anne Carter (Oxford: Oxford University Press, 2020), 11.

71. Richard Menary, ed., *The Extended Mind* (Cambridge, MA: MIT Press, 2010).

72. Schein, *Organizational Culture and Leadership*, 209–243.

73. Schein, *Organizational Culture and Leadership*, 297–310.

74. Katherine M. Gehl and Michael E. Porter, *The Politics Industry: How Political Innovation Can Break Partisan Gridlock and Save Our Democracy* (Boston: Harvard Business Review Press, 2020).

75. Gehl and Porter, *The Politics Industry*, 8.

76. That circumstance may change for IBM, too, because it increasingly is encouraging customers to use its artificial intelligence tools in combination with its hybrid cloud computing offerings. IBM's customers and the users of IBM's offerings will want observed standards and opacity that will call on the company to find ways to engage computers and new people through a corporate culture for the future.

77. "The End of History," *The Economist*, July 20, 2019, 49.

INDEX

management training for, 131–34; work
week of, 389n2. *See also specific topics*
Endicott, New York, 17; benefits at, 192;
coffee at, 248; corporate success at,
363; global diffusion and, 271, 372; gray
literature from, 331, 333–34; in Great
Depression, 264–65; IBM Country Club
at, 207, *210*, 210–11; IBM Families at, 196–
97, 202, 210; job security in, 17; layoffs
at, 164; in New Deal, *152*; postcards
from, 258, 259, 262–72, *264–73*, 279, 281;
punch-cards tabulators from, 349; QCC
at, 216; THINK at, 241, *242*, *265*, *266*;
toxic chemicals at, 160; unionization
at, 152, 154, 159–60, 161, 163, 164, 165,
412n46; War Rally and IBM Day in, 333
Enron, 72, 83
Equal Employment Opportunity
Commission, 10–11
Erst & Young, 251
ethics, 46, 57–79, 394n4; BCGs and, 58,
64–70, 72; behavior of sinners, saints,
and congregations and, 71–75; changing
forms of, 75–79; corporate success and,
361–62; at C-T-R, 59; origins of, 59–64;
trust and, 67–70. *See also* antitrust suit;
Basic Beliefs
European Union, privacy in, 21, 115
Evans, Harry S., 435n46
Ever Onward, 333
Excellence in All That Is Done, 58, 120–21
executive assistant (EA), 136
Executive Resource lists, 130, 139
executives: compensation of, 18, 20;
language of, 381; mentors for, 134–37;
seminars for, 133; training for, 131–32,
133–34; T. Watson, Jr., and, 133
ExxonMobile, buybacks at, 18

Facebook, 2, 409n102, 430n32; coffee mugs
of, 235, 254; corporate culture at, 43, 383;
corporate success on, 362; dress code on,
110–12; IBM groups on, 129, 142; image
of, 81, 83; information ecosystem of,
356; management at, 145, 364; material
culture of, 235; public scrutiny of, 315,
384; pursuit of profit at, 19

facial hair, 301, 363
factory employees: coffee mugs of, 253;
competitive salaries for, 155; dress code
for, 112
Family Dinners, 161, 195, 197, 203, 204,
205–9, *208*, 385, 386, 418n3; at Nashville,
205–6, 420, n33; as rituals, 365; THINK
and, 207; T. Watson, Jr., at, 207–9; T.
Watson, Sr., at, 206–7, *207*
Family Hospitalization Plan, 180, 181
Family Surgical Plan, 180
faxlore, 287–88
Federal Sentencing Guidelines for
Corporations, 72
field engineering: cartoons of, 290; in
Christmas carols, 309; coffee cups for,
253; employee diversity of, 14; gray
literature for, 340, *340*; humor of, 301;
IBM Way for, 91; postcards for, 280;
VTCs of, 248
Field Engineering Handbook, 352
finance & budgeting (F&P), 123
financialization: at IBM, 16–20; layoffs
and, 16; at multinational corporations,
16, 18
first-line manager (FLM), 175
Fisher, Melissa S., 13
Fisher, Waldo E., 411n37
flextime, 222
FLM. *See* first-line manager
Forbes, 114
Ford, Corey, 298, 315
Ford, Henry, 41
Ford Motor Company, 23, 48, 52; benefits at,
191; image and reputation of, 47
Foreign Corrupt Practices Act of 1977, 72
For Internal Use Only, 193
Fortune, 114
407 Accounting Machine, 97
1400 Data Processing System, GI manual
for, 337
F&P. *See* finance & budgeting
Freidman, Walter A., 108
Fridenson, Patrick, 233
Frieden, 234
Friesen, G. Bruce, 8
Fruin, Mark W., 40

Roman Empire: management at, 144, 176; material culture of, 42

Rometty, Virginia (Ginni), 8, 14; age discrimination under, 10–11; on ethics, 70; farewell letter of, 362; humor and, 314; layoffs under, 9; micromanaging and, 379; on Trump advisory council, 226

Roosevelt, Teddy, 10

Rotary Club, 91

Russian invasion of Ukraine, 12, 20; rebuilding Ukraine after, 23; sanctions in, 23

sales: annual reports for, 434n26; Back to the Field for, 373; cartoons on, 294; CEs and, 382; coffee mugs in, 248–53, 249, 252; culture of, 27, 35, 61, 242; dress code for, 112–13; employee diversity of, 14; GI manual for, 337; in global diffusion, 372; gray literature for, 319–20, 334, 348, 352–53; humor of, 301, 302–3, 303, 304, 307–9; IBM Way for, 91; image and, 86; information ecosystem for, 48; ink pens for, 246; in Nashville, 372; performance plans for, 122–23; postcards for, 260–61, 280; of punch-cards tabulators, 433n13; SNA and, 406n37; THINK and, 242; women in, 302. See also Golden Circle; 100 Percent Club

Sales Manual, 353

sales order processing application (AAS), 351

Sales School, 386, 430n60; certificate from, 254; gray literature for, 326; ink pens at, 246; material culture of, 238

San Antonio, Texas, 278, 278

Sanders, Bernard ("Bernie"), 162

Sarbanes-Oxley Act of 2002, 72

Schein, Edgar H., 31–34, 38, 40, 42, 46, 117, 245, 383; corporate success and, 363; on language, 381; on material culture, 232–34; on rituals, 365

Schiller, Dan, 318

"School House," 58

science, technology, engineering, and mathematics (STEM), 12–13, 15

Scranton, Philip, 233, 234

SE. See systems engineers

Securities and Exchange Commission (SEC), 75

securities fraud, 11

Selected National Accounts (SNA), 406n37

sell cycle, 60

Seminar on Scientific Computing, 334

Service, Service, Service, 86

701 Electronic Data Processing Machine, 98, 98

sexism, in humor, 288, 293, 313

sexual harassment, 397n60; Open Door Policy for, 186

SHARE, 320

Sheffler, Cathy, 345

Sickness and Accident Income, 180

Sign Standards, 103

silos, 77

603 Electronic Calculator, 96, 97

Sloan, Alfred, 41

SNA. See Selected National Accounts

social media, 22, 315; on corporate success, 362; on IBM Families, 197. See also Facebook; Twitter

Social Security Administration, pensions of, 124, 181

software: GI manual for, 337; gray literature for, 335, 337, 345, 349–50; PID for, 349–50; Reference Manuals for, 339; security, 7

Songs of the I.B.M., 333

South Africa, apartheid in, 115, 160, 226

Speak Up Program, 154, 168, 175; benefits and, 188–91; corporate success and, 368, 369; management and, 189–90

Stebenne, David L., 151, 153

STEM. See science, technology, engineering, and mathematics

stock-based compensation packages, 18

straight talk, 63, 68

strategy: benefits and, 191; best practices in, 118; in corporate culture, 39, 365; for corporate success, 361–84; for IBM Families, 203–6; for management, 145; management training on, 131

strikes, 151, 157